Product Recall, Liability and Insurance

A Global Guide

Consulting Editors **Mark Kendall** and **Jason McNerlin**

Consulting editor
Mark Kendall, Jason McNerlin

Publisher
Sian O'Neill

Commissioning editor
Katherine Cowdrey

Editor
Carolyn Boyle

Production
Russell Anderson

Publishing directors
Guy Davis, Tony Harriss, Mark Lamb

Product Recall, Liability and Insurance: A Global Guide
is published by
Globe Law and Business
Globe Business Publishing Ltd
New Hibernia House
Winchester Walk
London SE1 9AG
United Kingdom
Tel +44 20 7234 0606
Fax +44 20 7234 0808
Web www.globelawandbusiness.com

Printed and bound by CPI Group (UK) Ltd, Croydon, CR0 4YY

ISBN 9781905783670

Table of contents

Preface

Mark Kendall
Jason McNerlin
Sedgwick, Detert, Moran & Arnold LLP (London)

When this book was first conceived over two years ago, our objective was to provide risk managers and insurance professionals with an accessible guide to the regulatory regimes governing the recall of unsafe products, as well as the law relating to the liability of companies that fail to adhere to their obligations or whose products cause injury or damage. It was also important to summarise the insurance products available to transfer this risk (which are becoming ever more sophisticated and sector specific).

Given the global nature of product distribution, to be useful, it was essential that this book dealt with obligations and possible liabilities in many jurisdictions.

Achieving this objective has been challenging. There has been a significant volume of new legislation and regulation in recent years, as the responsibilities of those in the product supply chain become more developed. This is, of course, a moving picture. As we neared completion, a number of chapters had to be revised to reflect very recent changes to the regulatory framework of their jurisdictions. This book is therefore necessarily a snapshot of the current framework as at September 2012.

A significant number of recalls involve multi or cross-jurisdictional issues. I hope that this book will be a useful tool in assessing how different jurisdictions might approach the same problem, and assist in strategic decision making when liaising with the enforcement authorities in different territories.

The profile of product safety issues has increased significantly in recent years, and the speed with which images and opinions can spread online has played a large part in that. This, in turn, has increased the focus of those in the supply chain and the enforcement authorities on safety and recall issues.

With the obligations and penalties being enshrined in legislation more clearly than ever before, the perceived increase in risk has led to increased demand for insurance. In London, the insurance market has responded by increasing capacity (there have been a number of new entrants to the product recall market in the last two to three years, and capacity has almost doubled in that time).

Insurance offerings have become more tailored to specific sectors, be it food, automotive, consumer goods or pharmaceuticals. Cover has, generally speaking, broadened, and continues to evolve. We anticipate that this will continue over the next few years.

Each of the chapters in this book has been written by an expert in the field. We have sought to adopt a similar format for each jurisdiction, to make cross referencing easier. We would like to extend our thanks to each of the contributors, whose expertise, commitment and diligence have made this an easier project than it might have been.

We would also like to thank our firm, Sedgwick, Detert, Moran & Arnold LLP (London) and Sedgwick LLP (US), for supporting this project and our involvement in it. In particular, we would like to thank Chris Novak and Chris Celentano (New York) and Steve Di Saia and James Holmes (California) for their excellent contributions.

Finally, a big thank you to Katherine Cowdrey at Globe Law and Business for keeping the project on track, despite a number of challenges along the way.

Mark Kendall is an equity partner of the international law firm Sedgwick, Detert, Moran & Arnold LLP. He has been practising in the field of product recall and liability for over 15 years, and acts for both insurer and corporate clients. He is experienced in advising on recalls in the automotive, food, consumer goods and pharmaceutical sectors. He also regularly advises insurers on their wordings (both from a coverage perspective and on the product development side). Mr Kendall routinely advises in relation to multi-jurisdictional issues arising from defective products and lectures widely on the subject.

Jason McNerlin's practice is focused on product recall, product liability and all types of product insurance. He advises manufacturers and insurers on regulations, compliance and crisis management, and acts on their behalf in commercial disputes relating to products. He has drafted numerous insurance policies for products insurers.

Argentina

Luis D Barry
Luis Ignacio Porthé
Pérez Alati, Grondona, Benites, Arntsen & Martínez de Hoz

1. Product safety regulation

The Civil Code includes a number of regulations on product safety.[1] However, few cases were taken under the Civil Code for damages caused by defective products until after Argentina enacted a specific Consumer Protection Act in 1993.[2]

Consumers in general also enjoy in principle protection under Argentina's constitution, as follows.[3]

Consumers and users of goods and services have the right to expect:

- protection of their health, safety and economic interests;
- adequate and accurate information;
- freedom of choice; and
- equitable and reliable treatment.

The Consumer Protection Act, as amended, reflects most of these principles, having pre-empted amends made to the Constitution (in 1994).[4]

In addition, and prior to the enactment of the Consumer Protection Act, regulators in specific sectors issued sets of rules regarding safety requirements for their products[5] and in some cases have set individual recall procedures as well as regulations.

Finally, some regulations in the Criminal Code punishing wilful misconduct could affect third parties, but case precedents on this are thin on the ground. There is no specific regulation or obligation in the Criminal Code mandating the recall of products.

What follows focuses on the Consumer Protection Act provisions on product safety, always bearing in mind the overarching principles of the national constitution.

2. Obligations of producers and distributors

2.1 Sources of duties

Safety liabilities and obligations in Argentina have their source in:

1 Sections 505, 520, 521, 2104, 2164, 2166 and 2176 of the Civil Code.
2 Law 24,240.
3 These principles were included in the constitutional amendment of 1994.
4 The Consumer Protection Act was amended by Law 24,999, Decree 1798/94 and Law 26,361.
5 Food, pharmaceuticals products, personal care products, cosmetics and perfumes.

- general regulations (eg, the Civil Code);
- specific legislation (eg, the Consumer Protection Act); and
- contractual agreements among the parties.[6]

2.2 Pre-market obligations

Prior to the sale of any product, producers and distributors are subject to the following general requirements.

(a) *Supplier's duty to inform*

Section 4 of the Consumer Protection Act states that "suppliers are obliged to provide to consumers in a clear, detailed and accurate manner, everything relating to the essential characteristics of the goods or services provided, and any marketing conditions. The information must always be free to consumers and clearly expressed to enable it to be readily understood".[7]

This general principle, commonly known as the 'consumer right to information', governs each and every relationship between suppliers and consumers.

Detail on the manner in which relevant or mandatory information should be communicated and displayed is also legally regulated. Since July 6 1999, wording included in documents delivered by suppliers which are binding on them or on third parties (ie, obligations) must be presented in the Spanish language and in a font above a specified size (not smaller than 1.8mm). We interpret this as applying to, among other things, price information, offers, discounts and promotions, as well as all mandatory information provided in writing by suppliers to consumers, including warranties and operating instructions.

All information which must appear by law must in addition appear in a prominent, conspicuous position and must be in bold print with characters equivalent to at least one-and-a-half times the size of the characters used for the body or general text.

Suppliers and producers are not obliged to keep records so that a product can be traced if there is any problem.

(b) *Consumer protection duty*

Section 5 states that goods and services must be supplied or rendered in such a way that used under predictable conditions or normal use will not imply any danger to the health and physical integrity of consumers.

It states that: "Products and services must be delivered in a way that, in the regular and predictable course of its use, and under normal conditions, they will not represent any risk to the health and personal safety of consumers or users" (Section 5 of the Consumer Protection Act). There is no specific definition of 'any risk', however: the Consumer Protection Act only provides a broad formula referring to unreasonable or unexpected risk in normal and predictable conditions of use.

So, the Consumer Protection Act provides a general formula, but not specifics on

---

6 Section 1197 of the Civil Code.

7 For high risk goods, Section 6 of the Consumer Protection Act states that the supplier is obliged to provide a manual in Spanish, including warnings about safety and conditions of use.

consumer protection duties, leaving the courts to decide on a case-by-case basis, whether a product or service meets the required safety conditions – or not.

Section 40 imposes responsibility on each link in the distribution chain, including the owner of any trade marks (who may not be the same as the producer, supplier, distributor or seller).

For the compensation and sanction regime please refer to Product liability; but note here that in a recent case, a court ordered a beer producer to pay Ps2 million (€400,000 approximately) to a consumer who found a pack of intimate gel inside a bottle of beer.[8]

2.3 High-risk products and services

The Consumer Protection Act does not prohibit the selling or supply of high-risk goods or services, but it does apply conditions to their marketing.

Goods and services (including utilities services rendered in the consumer's home) which may present a high risk to the consumer's health or physical integrity must be marketed in compliance with established rules under Section 6 of the Consumer Protection Act, which also states that instructions related to the use, installation or maintenance of those products or services, and all warning notices, must be provided in Spanish.

Warnings and instructions must be 'adequate' (not defined) to situations where the product or service is used under ordinary conditions.

Some sectors have specific additional standards.

(a) Foods

Argentina's Alimentary Code contains the national system of rules relevant to the production and marketing of different categories of food and beverages. It also covers production and distribution processes and labelling conditions.

Penalties for infringing the Alimentary Code are as follows:

- fines from Ps5,000 (€1,000) to Ps1 million (€200,000);
- seizure and attachment of goods;
- closure of facilities;
- suspension of licences to produce, distribute and sell; and
- publication of the decision to impose any sanction (Section 9, Law 18,284).

At national level the administrative authority empowered to enforce the Alimentary Code is the National Drug, Food and Medical Technology Administration (ANMAT). ANMAT governs the registration of foods and can issue seizure orders where products do not meet with the standards contained in the Code.

Food producers must comply with rules at both national and provincial level: since Argentina is a federal country,[9] each province has also its own health and safety authority which will apply the Alimentary Code as well as any applicable local regulations.

---

8 *Juzgado de 1a Instancia en lo Civil y Comercial de 5a Nominación de Córdoba*, 23/03/2011, *"Teijeiro ó Teigeiro, Luis Mariano v Cervecería y Maltería Quilmes SAICA y G."* AR/JUR/12898/2011.

9 Section 1 of the National Constitution.

(b) ***Medicines***

Argentina has had general legislation regulating the production of medicines since 1964,[10] which has been supplemented by a vast body of resolutions issued by ANMAT.

ANMAT is the enforcing body and has powers to impose fines for violations, to seize medicines and close establishments that do not fulfil the regulatory requirements or standards.

ANMAT can impose the following penalties:

- fines from Ps2,000 to Ps5 million;
- seizure and attachment of medicines; and
- suspension of the authorisation to produce, distribute and sell the medicines (Section 20, Law 16,463).

The regulations cover labelling and marketing conditions for medicines, and are enforced actively by ANMAT and less actively by the provincial authorities, which also monitor compliance in the provinces.

The regulations also provide for the sale and marketing of generic products, encouraging their local production and their substitution for imported branded products.

(c) ***Electrical equipment***

The Secretariat of Interior Trade issued Resolution 92/98 (implementing EU Directive 73/23) to establish electric product safety standards seeking to reach world-standard levels of safety.

Resolution 92/98 changed the rules on how most everyday electric products should be presented for sale and established a registration and qualification process for manufacturers.

It has now been supplemented by 71 resolutions making electrical device safety an extremely complex and regulated area: eg, Resolution 197/2004 of the Secretariat of Technical Coordination rules that electric products should carry an icon in their packaging to show that they comply with applicable safety standards.

A significant number of products which fail to bear such marks have been seized by the Secretariat of Interior Trade, which has imposed fines on the companies involved.

Recently, the Secretariat of Interior Trade imposed a fine of Ps50,000 (€10,000 approximately) on Walmart for selling electrical equipment without the safety icons required by Resolution 197/2004.[11] Two years earlier, the Secretariat of Interior Trade fined Carrefour for the same reason for Ps100,000 (€20,000).[12] In both cases, the Court of Appeals rejected the appeals of the retailers and confirmed the fines.

---

10 Law 16,463.

11 Expte 10596/2010 – *"Walmart Argentina SRL c/DNCI-Disp.142-10 (expte SO1 171892/07)"* – CNACAF – SALA V – 203/08/2011.

12 Expte 1896/06 – *"Carrefour Argentina SA y otro c/DNCI-Disp 812/08 (expte S01:115829/06)"* – CNACAF – SALA II – 04/05/2010.

(d) *Toys*

Argentina has incorporated several resolutions issued at MERCOSUR[13] level on toy safety regulation.[14] Argentinian manufacturers can therefore refer to a complete list of permissible materials for toys, and must adhere to a registration process and quality assurance regime.

The Secretariat of Interior Trade is the enforcing authority at national level which imposes fines and seizes products that do not comply with toy safety regulations. In a high-profile recent case, the SIC fined McDonald's Ps123,000 (approximately €24,600) for selling toys with its meals without a toy safety certificate as required by Resolution 851/98 (supplementing the Fair Trade Law 22,802). The Court of Appeals rejected McDonald's appeal and confirmed the fines.[15]

(e) *Cosmetics*

ANMAT is also the regulator for the production, marketing and distribution of cosmetic products. Manufacturers can refer to an ANMAT list of permissible ingredients; and must register their products and facilities with ANMAT.

ANMAT has powers to fine companies in breach of the regulations and to seize products. Recently, it banned the importation of an electronic cigarette.[16] In addition, it is quite common that ANMAT issues orders to stop selling products which have either misleading or incomplete information on their labelling or packaging.[17]

The ANMAT regulation has incorporated several MERCOSUR resolutions and therefore applies the same standards agreed on by the MERCOSUR member states. One of the most important of those is MERCOSUR Resolution 35/05[18] dictating standards for the manufacture and marketing of cosmetic products.

2.4 Post-market obligations

(a) *Recall regulation*

Section 5 of the Consumer Protection Act does not contain any express recall obligation, it simply states how products and services must be sold and supplied.

Section 4 of Regulatory Decree 1798/94, implementing the Consumer Protection Act, goes a step further in imposing on suppliers of goods or services an obligation to immediately inform the relevant authorities and consumers on receiving notice that goods or services may pose a risk to consumers after introducing them onto the market. That information must be sufficiently advertised by suppliers.

---

13 The MERCOSUR is an economic and political agreement among Argentina, Brazil, Paraguay and Uruguay. Founded in 1991 by the Treaty of Asunción, which was later amended and updated by the 1994 Treaty of Ouro Preto. Its purpose is to promote free trade and the fluid movement of goods, people, and currency. The regulations issued at MERCOSUR are important in facilitating fluency of traffic among the Union.

14 Resolutions 54/92 and 23/2004.

15 C. 54.220 "*INTERPACK SA – ARCOS DORADOS SA y ZOTT PRODUCCIONES SRL S/ LEY 22.802*" – CNPE – Sala A – 28/02/2006.

16 Expte 17.683/2011 – "*Winged SA c/ EN -ANMAT DISP 3226/11 s/ amparo ley 16.986*" – CNACAF – SALA III – 30/09/2011

17 Disposition 7153/20 prohibited the marketing of "*Coniglio perfumador Clásico*"; Disposition 5195/10 prohibited the sale of several cosmetics products.

18 Incorporated by Disposition ANMAT 799/07.

However, it should be noted that such an obligation might be considered null and void under the National Constitution, for this reason the obligation of reporting the existence of a defective product on the market effectively involves the supplier admitting that it has failed in its legal obligation to provide harmless products; and that could be self-incrimination, which is expressly forbidden by Section 18 of the National Constitution.[19]

In conclusion there is no express general regulation imposing on suppliers the obligation of recalling products in the Consumer Protection Act. Suppliers are obliged only to:

- provide goods and services that will cause no harm to consumers;
- for high-risk goods and services, provide full information to consumers and meet safety standards;
- where a supplier is aware of any serious risk (even once the product is on the market), it must report this to the authorities and to consumers.

That said, academic opinion is that an obligation to recall might be construed and is to some extent implied in the obligation to report to consumers the existence of a high risk product. In addition, there may also be a good faith obligation to recall and take preventative actions under the Civil Code.[20] It would be safest therefore (following that academic view) for suppliers to take all necessary actions to deal with risks and potential risks, including taking actions after the product has reached the market.

In the authors' view however, the regime established by the Consumer Protection Act does not oblige suppliers to recall products or take actions to prevent further damages. Suppliers' obligations are limited to reporting incidents to the authorities in order to allow them to take relevant action. Section 45 of the Consumer Protection Act allows the authority to take preventive actions in order to cease any action violating the Consumer Protection Act, which is interpreted by some as meaning the authorities can require product recalls. So, where suppliers violate the general rule that suppliers must supply harmless products, the authorities may issue a cease order (Section 45(m) of the Consumer Protection Act) stopping the sale of the products and take preventative actions including recall of products.

And suppliers must also keep consumers fully informed of any risks or defects.

There are not many case precedents in Argentina on this but the following cases have arisen:

- *De Blasi de Musmeci, Claudia v Sevel Argentina Sociedad Anónima*[21] (2001): – the Court ordered Sevel Argentina SA to compensate Mrs Blasi and her family in the amount of Ps600,000 (€120,000) for damages suffered in a car crash and notified the Secretariat of Interior Trade of the fact that all "Fiat Dunas" launched on the Argentine market in 1994 had a defect in one part of their steering system and urged Fiat to take all corrective measures necessary.
- *Yectafer (r)* (2004) – by Resolution 7.917 issued on December 23 2004, ANMAT

---

19 Section 18 of the National Constitution rules that: "... Nobody may be compelled to testify against himself ...".

20 Section 1198 of the Civil Code.

21 CNCOM – SALA C – 05/10/2001 File 82003/94 -.

banned the distribution and sale of such medicine nationwide;

- *Aguas Danone Argentina SA* (2005) – in November 2005, the company detected some alterations in the colour and flavour of their juices. The company decided, voluntarily, to recall the products from the market. Shortly after, ANMAT prohibited the sale and distribution of the juices by Resolution 1/2005.
- *Pepsico de Argentina SRL* – the director of fair trade banned the distribution and sale of the drinks "Pepsi with lemon juice" and "Mirinda" based on Section 998 of the Argentine Alimentary Code on the basis that the language of the packaging may confuse consumers. The Court of Appeals suspended the injunction.[22]

So far, Section 45 of the Consumer Protection Act has not been actively used by the authorities to instigate product recalls. As a legal construct, Section 45 appears to be weak and ambiguous. An express provision about the recall of products based on the general provision of Section 42 of the National Constitution (consumers' right to protection of their health, safety and economic interests) would have been preferable.

However, it would clearly be wise for businesses to minimise their exposure to risks and product recall may therefore be necessary as a practical step even if it is not a clearly, positively and expressly stated statutory obligation.[23]

(b) *Special regimes*

Despite this lack of any general positive obligation at national level mandating recall of products, ANMAT has enacted some express recall procedures which apply to products falling under its jurisdiction.[24]

The following procedures apply to both voluntary recalls and recalls required by ANMAT or another local authority.[25] ANMAT can order suppliers to remove a product from the market if it is dangerous or if it has not been manufactured in accordance with applicable "good practice" rules.

(c) *Foods*

Based on ANMAT's rules and guidelines,[26] manufacturers, packers, distributors and importers (grouped as a shorthand as 'the supplier') must arrange a recall plan in the form of a Recall Handbook. Argentine legislation does not dictate any detail on how to implement a recall procedure, but suppliers must take into consideration: the Argentine Food Code (Law 18,284, Decree 2126/71, Annex I, Annex II and MERCOSUR Resolutions); Decree 815/99; and other ANMAT regulations.

The Recall Handbook must cover the following:

- detection of the incident or problem;

---

22 CNPE, Sala B, 26/6/2003.
23 MERCOSUR regulations also do not impose a general recall obligation for exports.
24 Food, pharmaceuticals products, personal care products, cosmetics and perfumes.
25 That is, provincial or municipal authority.
26 Joint Resolution SPRel 200/2008 and SAGPyA 567/2008.

- description and identification of the infringing products;
- notice to the authority;
- identification and separation of any infringing products still at the company's premises;
- drafting of press releases (if necessary);
- keeping records about product marketing;
- drafting and distributing recall notices;
- review of the recall's effectiveness;
- management and registration of recalled products;
- other corrective measures to be taken.

Suppliers must keep records of complaints which must be reviewed by qualified personnel in order to ensure necessary measures are taken.

When a local authority detects unsafe products which may have been manufactured or marketed infringing the law, it may initiate an investigation to decide if a recall is needed. Accordingly, it must notify ANMAT within 48 hours to coordinate the recall procedure. Within the 48-hour period, the supplier may propose a recall strategy. ANMAT will evaluate the proposal and recommend a strategy.

Likewise, if a supplier decides to recall a product, it must notify the local authority and ANMAT, if applicable, within 24 hours.

ANMAT will then be able to decide whether consumers need to be notified about the recall.

The mechanism for the recall and its scope will vary depending on the risk. Risks are categorised in this way:

- Class I – the use of the product may result in serious health impairment or cause death; the product may not be used anymore and should be removed from the market.
- Class II – the use of the product may reasonably and probably result in temporary and/or reversible health impairment.
- Class III – the chances of health impairment are low, but the product infringes a law or regulation.

Suppliers are responsible for notifying everyone in their distribution channel and/or consumers as appropriate and for providing all necessary information about the product. It will also be responsible of carrying out the recall procedure.

The local health authorities and ANMAT will audit the process and may inspect suppliers' premises. Generally, audits will be initiated 10 days after the supplier has been notified about a recall decision.

Where the recalled products should be stored will be determined by the local health authority or ANMAT, depending on the case. The local health authority will decide when the recall is completed at the local level and ANMAT will make this decision for the national operation.

(d) ***Pharmaceuticals, personal care products, cosmetics and perfumes***

The recall process regulated by ANMAT[27] aims to remove products that infringe the law or where infringement is suspected.

The mechanism for the recall and its scope will vary depending on the perceived risk, which will fall into one of three categories:

- Class I – the use of the product may result in serious health impairment or cause death. The product may not be used anymore and should be removed from the market.
- Class II – the use of the product may reasonably and probably result in temporary and/or reversible health impairment or when the probability of serious health impairment is remote. The product may not be used anymore and should be removed from the market.
- Class III – the use of or exposure to the product will not cause health impairment, but the product infringes a law or regulation.

The recall strategy will be decided on a case-by-case basis. If the recall is found necessary, the supplier can propose a recall strategy to ANMAT which will evaluate the proposal and make a recommendation. The supplier implements measures mandated by the authority.

The supplier will always be responsible for the recall follow-up as well as for determining necessary measures for its implementation. In addition, the supplier will be responsible for ensuring that everyone in the distribution chain is notified and taking necessary measures to comply with the agreed recall procedure. The manufacturer may request the assistance of ANMAT, which will be entitled to audit the process.

In urgent and extreme situations (Class I and occasionally Class II recalls), consumers will be informed that the product which is being recalled represents a serious threat to health. In other cases, they will only be warned that a product may be inadequate. ANMAT will decide whether this communication must be made by the company or if information on ANMAT's website is enough.

ANMAT will decide when the recall can be considered to be complete and when products should be destroyed.

3. Enforcement

In most cases, recall will have a worldwide dimension. Companies therefore need a recall policy for each jurisdiction and must coordinate processes internationally.

Because of the self-incrimination point made above, companies are left with the choice of either:

- launching a campaign to remedy the situation without fulfilling the requirements of Section 4 of Decree 1798/94; or
- reporting to the authorities that a recall is going to take place in compliance with Section 4 of Decree 1798/94.

27 Disposition 1402/2008.

Most companies prefer the second route and choose to report to the authorities that a recall campaign is going to be launched. This pre-empts and avoids the need for any subsequent involvement of the authorities.

However, in other cases companies may report to the authorities, but may not invoke Section 4 in order to avoid admitting that a harmful product has been released. Thus, some companies do not acknowledge that the defective product may cause harm or damage, to avoid being subject to further investigations or to hinder the progress of damages claims.

The authorities can request further information from the company, but in most cases they do not investigate too deeply, and the authorities do not generally encourage consumers to initiate claims. In very rare cases aggravated fines might attach to companies, but most recall campaigns are successfully completed.

3.1 Appeals

Since there is no general rule regarding the powers of authorities to issue recall orders (except in relation to food, pharmaceutical products, personal care products, cosmetics and perfumes) there is no specific regulation for appeals to such orders either.

Product recall may be specified in a cease order, which has the same legal effect as an injunction. Any appeal of a cease order has no suspensive effect; compliance is thus required while the appeal is ongoing. A manufacturer seeking to avoid a product recall required under the order must thus first obtain a suspending resolution from the court.

In practice, therefore, where a recall order is issued by the authorities, it will be difficult to avoid executing it, since any appeal will not suspend the effects of the resolution.

However, if the manufacturer obtains a reversal order from the court, it may be entitled to claim damages from the administrative authorities.

3.2 Sanctions and compensation

No specific sanctions are mandated by the Consumer Protection Act, which consequently applies general fines and sanctions.

Third parties affected by the product may claim for damages (see below).

4. Product liability

4.1 Potential defendants

Producers, importers, distributors and sellers of products are jointly responsible for granting and enforcing legal warranties ruled by Section 11 of the Consumer Protection Act, as well as for any harm suffered by consumers (Section 40, Consumer Protection Act).

However, under the Civil Code regime responsibility falls mainly on the person who causes the damage (except in cases of objective responsibility or strict liability).[28]

---

28 Section 1113 of the Civil Code.

4.2 Sources of liability

(a) Statute

Section 11 of the Consumer Protection Act provides that consumers and subsequent purchasers of movable goods enjoy a legal warranty for defects or faults of any kind, even if they were visible or apparent at the time of purchase, if the defects affect the nature of the product or its proper functioning. The warranty is valid for three months in the case of movable products, and six months in other cases from the date of delivery of the product. The parties can also agree to an extended warranty.

Under the Civil Code[29] any breach (unless in circumstances of *force majeure*) empowers the consumer to:

- require enforcement of the obligation, wherever possible;
- accept a replacement product or equivalent service; and
- terminate the contract and be reimbursed.

Under the Consumer Protection Act consumers can:[30]

- require replacement of the product or service by a similar one (in which case the warranty term starts again from the date of delivery of the new product);
- return with price paid reimbursed; or
- obtain a rebate on the price paid.

These remedies are all without prejudice to any further actions for damages by the consumer.

Litigation and administrative sanctions under the Consumer Protection Act are barred by a three-year statute of limitations.[31] When other general or special laws provide for different time limits, those most favourable to the consumer or user will apply. The statutory limitation period will be interrupted by a consumer claim, the commitment of a new offence or on the instigation of administrative or judicial proceedings. The legal warranties provided in Section 11 of Consumer Protection Act and in the Civil Code starts to run from the time of delivery of the product.

The plaintiff bears the burden of proof of the defect, of the harm sustained, and causation between defect and harm. The parties may reduce, waive or extend their responsibility for hidden defects, as long as there is no wilful misconduct on the part of the seller.[32]

Under the Consumer Protection Act, suppliers cannot limit their responsibility to restrict customers' rights.[33] Regarding the legal warranty of six months, the parties may agree a longer period.[34]

The Consumer Protection Act defines 'direct damage' as any injury or detriment that the consumer suffers to property or person, suffered as a result of the unlawful

---

29 Sections 505 and 1204, among other things.
30 Section 17.
31 Section 50 of the Consumer Protection Act.
32 Section 2166 of the Civil Code.
33 Section 37.
34 Section 11 of the Consumer Protection Act.

actions of the supplier. Producers, importers, distributors and sellers of the products are jointly liable for the damages caused by the product.[35]

The Secretariat of Interior Trade, and the provincial authorities, can determinate the existence of direct damage and require the supplier to pay the consumer up to the amount equivalent of five household baskets, level 3, according to the Argentine National Institute of Statistics (INDEC; nowadays approximately €1,000). That sum of money will be deductible from other compensation the consumer may obtain from other judicial claims (eg, actions commenced under the Civil Code are not excluded and may be taken in addition).[36] The Secretariat of Commerce is also entitled to impose on producers and distributors of products and services in violation of the Consumer Protection Act, fines from Ps100 (€20) up to Ps5 million (€1 million approximately; Section 47, Consumer Protection Act).

(b) Tort

Duty of care: Two provisions in the Civil Code define the standard of care: Section 512, as a general objective standard of the ordinary reasonable man; and Section 902, a higher standard for those in the production chain who have a level of skill.

It is important to point out that producers, suppliers, retailers and sellers owe a duty of care not only to consumers who buy the product, but also to those who freely use it or are in any way exposed to the product (Section 1, Consumer Protection Act).

Breach of duty: There is a breach of duty towards consumers if the conduct of those in the supply chain falls short of the standard expected in the circumstances and if the product fails to perform its function or causes injury to consumers or damage to their property.

Injury and damage, impairment; consequential loss: If such a duty of care is breached, and as a consequence an injury or damage takes place, consumers are entitled to take any of the following actions.

The injury or damage does not have to be foreseeable to the supplier or seller. Any injury or damage is recoverable.

Contractual provisions which purport to release suppliers and sellers from their duty of care are void and have no effect (Section 37, LDC).

However, producers or sellers can show that consumers were negligent because they did not use the product in such conditions as would be considered regular and predictable. In such cases, producers or sellers bear the burden of proof.

(c) Contract

The Consumer Protection Act applies not only to end customers who acquire goods or services for their final use under contract, but also to consumers who acquire such goods or services free of charge.

---

35 Section 40.

36 Sections 10*bis* and 17(c) of the Consumer Protection Act.

In addition, under Sections 7 and 8 of the Consumer Protection Act, offers made through advertisements will constitute a contract and fully bind the seller.

The contract governs the relationship between the parties, and may therefore[37] contemplate specific levels of compensation for defective products. However, clauses which purport to limit consumers' rights are usually considered abusive, unreasonable and therefore null and void.

4.3 Claimants

Claimants in product liability cases can be:

- persons or consumers who are directly affected by a product; and
- consumer rights organisations (authorised and recognised by the Secretariat of Interior Trade) where collective interests are involved (Sections 52 and 55 of the Consumer Protection Act).

4.4 Causation

There must be a casual connection between the product defect and the injury or damage caused. It is therefore necessary to examine whether the damage would have occurred in absence of the defect.

Causation in product liability is often problematic because of the inherent difficulty in proving that an omission, such as a failure to warn, actually caused the harm. Courts will consider the grounds on which such a warning might be necessary, either to reduce the risk involved or to promote individual responsibility.

4.5 Remedies for injury/damage and consequential loss

Claimants can choose between two remedies:

- report the defect to the authorities or the Secretariat of Interior Trade; or
- go to court.[38]

If the applicant choose to report the defect to the Secretariat of Interior Trade – or provincial authorities – that authority can determine the existence of direct damage and require the supplier to pay the consumer up to an amount equivalent to five household baskets, level 3, according to the Argentine National Institute of Statistics (INDEC) and impose fines as stated above. Those sums are deductible from any other compensation payment amounts that the consumer may obtain from other judicial claims.[39]

Under the Civil Code, the measure of damages differs and the full compensation principle applies.[40] Actions taken under the Civil Code can be in addition to reparations ordered by the Secretariat of Interior Trade.

In tort law, levels of damages are determined by reference to the proximate

37 Section 1197, Civil Code.
38 Sections 17, 43, 48 and 52 of the Consumer Protection Act.
39 Sections 10bis and 17(c) of the Consumer Protection Act.
40 Supreme Court, 05.08.1986, *"Santa Coloma, Luis F. y otros v Empresa Ferrocarriles Argentinos"*, Fallos Corte: 308:1160 and Section 21(2) of the American Convention of Human Rights –Pacto de San José de Costa Rica.

causation test. Damages for pure economic losses are not generally awarded. In contract law, there are some further hurdles for the plaintiff to overcome: the duty to mitigate, foreseeability and proof of negligence of breach (as opposed to deliberate and wilful breach).

The duty to mitigate damages, although not expressly embodied by statute, is widely recognised in case law as a consequence of the general rule of good faith. All kinds of damages and, particularly, consequential damages will be limited by the principle of good faith.

If a breach was negligent as opposed to deliberate and wilful, the defendant should be held liable only for foreseeable consequential damages, including those disclosed by the non-breaching party at the time of the contract.

Conversely, if the breach was deliberate and wilful, the defendant should be held liable for all consequential damages (Sections 520 and 521, Civil Code). Actions for damages in contractual cases shall be extinguished on the expiry of a period of 10 years, unless special provisions provide otherwise.[41]

The Consumer Protection Act applies punitive damages to wrongful conduct of the supplier even if the conduct does not cause material damage, moral, psychological or otherwise.

The level of punitive damages will depend on the seriousness of the conduct and other circumstances, but will be capped at approximately €1,000,000. Under the Civil Code regime parties must expressly agree the level of punitive damages.

Consumers and suppliers/contractors can choose to waive or modify by common agreement the consequential damages or the exemplary damages regime established by the law. Argentine regulations disallow the waiving of liability only in cases of deliberate and wilful breach. However, care needs to be taken that such a waiver clause is not considered abusive such that the supplier is seen to be trying to escape paying damages to the consumer (in which case the abusive clause will be void).[42]

4.6 Procedure, limitations, funding and costs

Both administrative and judicial proceedings are free to consumers who are exempt for paying court fees.

However, if claimants lose the case against a supplier or seller, attorneys' fees will be awarded against them, even though they are consumers.[43]

4.7 Trends

The following trends can be identified in Argentina's legal system, based on the last modification to the Consumer Protection Act by Law 26,361:

- The law covers not only consumers who have entered into a sales contract, but every person who enters into a consumer relationship, even free of charge.
- The Secretariat of Interior Trade has the greatest powers to prevent risks and

41 Section 4023, Civil Code.
42 Section 37, Consumer Protection Act.
43 Consumers can freely agree a fee with their lawyers. But no regulation obliges consumers to pay their lawyer in advance. If successful, the lawyer is entitled to require his fee be paid by the defeated defendant. But legal costs are not recoverable from the losing party in litigation.

award damages for product liability, and can impose the highest fines for infringing the Consumer Protection Act.

- Punitive damages were established by Section 52 of the Consumer Protection Act and are awarded by judges.
- Administrative authorities can order sellers and suppliers to compensate consumers in the form of direct damages.

5. Insurance

Insurance policies will generally be are interpreted in favour of the insured (Section 3, Consumer Protection Act). So where the policy wording is unclear, there is a presumption in favour of the insured.

The insured has three days to notify the loss (Section 46, Law 17,418). If the insured notifies the loss late, the insurer can deny liability. After notification, the insurer has 30 days to raise any coverage issues but if the insurer is silent in that period, Section 56 of Law 17,418 presumes the insurer has accepted the coverage.

5.1 Product recall

(a) *Cost of recall*

Product recall insurance is not compulsory in Argentina and indeed is not commonly held by local companies, even large ones exposed to enormous risks. In practice suppliers and companies are self-insured, assuming to themselves risks associated with the possibility of recall expenses. However, many foreign companies with business in Argentina have product recall insurance with worldwide coverage.

Few local companies are even aware of the need for some type of product recall insurance coverage, perhaps because there have been few instances where the Secretariat of Interior Trade has forced companies to perform a recall. Moreover, apart from cases involving medical and food products (ANMAT-regulated), no specific legal proceedings attach to the recall of defective products. Finally, there are no case precedents for large-scale product recalls involving well-known companies – or at least, they have not been documented in the media.

The few known examples of such recalls include:

- Mattel's voluntary product recall of a toxic product (a Barbie toy accessory sold in Argentina between July and August 2007); and
- the Toyota Prius recall in 2009 – although Toyota voluntarily instigated the recall after selling only six units.

In both cases, the recalls had no major legal consequences for the companies involved.

(b) *Insuring provisions*

Since this kind of insurance is still a speciality in Argentina, customers may not be aware that many of the costs of a product recall are excluded by standard policies.

The costs of a recall can be incurred anywhere in the distribution chain: by the manufacturer or importer, wholesaler, distributor, exporter or retailer (since Section

40 of the Consumer Protection Act states that producers, importers, distributors and sellers of the products are jointly responsible for granting and enforcing a legal warranty of the product, including its recall if necessary).

Insured's decision to recall: The event triggering the product recall insurance cover must be an actual or imminent threat of danger, injury or harm associated with the product's use. Not any event triggers the recall and the insured's decision must be well grounded.

The insured will need to pay close attention to the notification provisions in the policy and consider these carefully whenever a product safety situation arises.The notification requirements under a product recall policy written on a 'claims made' basis will invariably include provisions relating to notification of claims and of circumstances which may or are likely to give rise to a claim. The requirement for notification of circumstances will usually also include a 'deeming' provision under which claims which arise after the expiry of the policy period but out of circumstances previously notified to insurers are deemed to attach to the policy under which notification of the circumstances was given.

The insured assumes the burden of notifying strictly in accordance with the policy notification provisions and in a timely manner.

Pre-recall expenses: The policy should cover the pre-recall costs and expenses incurred by the insured which are associated with the costs associated with deciding whether a recall is necessary, including testing costs and consultancy costs. The latter include advisers' fees for assisting as required with all aspects of the incident. Unlimited cost coverage in this regard is advisable.

First party recall expenses: The policy should include:

- the costs of advertising the recall throughout the media;
- costs to recover the products from customers/retailers;
- the cost of hiring additional warehousing or storage space;
- the cost of disposing of or destroying recalled products;
- salary costs to hire additional personnel;
- overtime paid to regular employees;
- refunds given to purchasers;
- costs associated with repairing insured products;
- cost of repairing the insured's unsold finished stock;
- replacement costs;
- cost of unsold finished stock if it cannot be replaced; and
- gross earnings loss.

Business interruption: When a recall situation arises, the business suffers an interruption in its ability to operate and produce income. Business interruption coverage covers the income that the company would have made during the period during which the recall process is taking place. This amount will be determined by looking into the company's past accounts.

Brand rehabilitation: After a large-scale recall of products a company must rebuild consumer confidence and loyalty. Such efforts generally involve substantial expenses to cover additional advertising, special promotions, and extra expenses to bring new products to market. These costs can be insured under product recall insurance which covers the additional costs necessarily and reasonably incurred by the insured to re-establish brand name or reputation of the insured products affected by the insured event to the projected level of sales or market share prior to the defect or contamination.

Third-party recall liability: Businesses should cover financial loss incurred by third parties caused by the recall, for which the insured is liable. Some examples might be transport costs or salaries of extra workers to perform the recall. This may also cover third party losses, where a third party's product quality has been affected because it incorporated the insured product as a part or component.

Defence costs: Insurance must cover legal costs, fees and expenses incurred by the insured or the underwriter in the investigation, defence or settlement of a third party recall liability claim.

(c) *Exclusions*

Product recall policies also contain a number of exclusions. The most common are the following:

- a product defect which has arisen solely due to exposure to weather or the deterioration or decomposition of a product (eg, fresh food items);
- improper or abusive use of the product;
- faulty electrical connections;
- use of replacement/repair parts that do not accord with the manufacturer's instructions;
- mechanical or electrical breakdown damaging the product;
- repair by a non-authorised service provider or the insurer during the warranty period;
- earthquake, seaquake, hurricane, flood or natural disaster;
- prototypical or experimental products which, by their very nature, are expected to experience problems in the nascent stages of development are also generally excluded;
- product recalls which are forced upon the insured by the government or a public authority in circumstances where the insured would not have conducted the recall but for the said intervention. The rationale for this is to protect insurers against situations where a government or public authority forces compulsory recalls upon manufacturers or distributors;
- coverage will not be effective if the insured does not notify the insurer as soon as it becomes apparent that expenditure will need to be incurred in respect of a product recall; and
- expenses incurred in a product recall which are not recorded. The insured should submit proof that such costs were reasonably and properly incurred

5.2 Contaminated products

Companies involved in the commerce chain, including distributors and retailers can be affected by a product contamination. Therefore it is advisable to assume action plans in order to handle and mitigate product contamination.

It is important to note that under Argentine Insurance Law 17,418, Section 114, intentional and wrongful contamination is not covered by insurance companies. Thus if a producer or distributor intentionally contaminate a product, the coverage will not be effective.

(a) Insuring provisions

The same rules apply as with product recall insurance.

(b) Exclusions

The same rules apply as with product recall insurance.

(c) Conditions

The same rules apply as with product recall insurance.

5.3. Product liability

(a) Liability for injury or damage

We have seen that Section 40bis of the Consumer Protection Act limits the amount of damages to an equivalent of five household baskets, level 3, according to the Argentine National Institute of Statistics (INDEC), and that in the Civil Code regime the measure of damages differs and a 'full compensation' principle applies.

(b) Insuring provisions

Under a 'losses occurring' cover, a loss is covered if it occurred during the term of the insurance, no matter when the policy in question was issued. Any claim occurring after the insurance contract expiration date is not covered.

Injury: The basic indemnity provided by product liability insurance policies is for protection of the insured from legal liability in respect of bodily injury, illness or disease or physical damage to property.

Damage: This liability comprehends not only loss and injury, but also damage caused to the purchaser's property.

Generally, the 'product' will not normally be defined as a specific item (or items) and the definition will normally include any goods or products after they have ceased to be in the insured's possession or control, including packaging materials and containers.

(c) Exclusions

There are a number of exclusions under a product liability policy that varies from one insurer to another. But common features may be listed as follows.

Breach of contract

- deliberate non-compliance with any statutory provision by the insured;
- pure financial losses like loss of goodwill of the business or loss of marketshare;
- fines, penalties, etc. imposed on the insured by authorities;
- deliberate disregard of the need to take reasonable steps to prevent claims under the policy;
- injury or loss or damage occurring beyond the policy period or not claimed within the extended period or a specified period after the first of a series of claims arising out of the same fault of design, labelling, manufacture or instructions of use;
- injury to employees;
- any product used as part of an aircraft;
- efficiency risks, which are commercial risks;
- liability for damage to property belonging to the insured or held in trust by the insured or within the custody or control of the insured or of a person in the service of the insured.

Repair, replacement

- liability for claims for the costs of the recall of any product or any part thereof;
- liability arising out of any product guarantee;
- liability for costs for the repair, reconditioning, modification or replacement of any part of any product, which is or is alleged to be defective.

(d) Conditions

Claim

- Coverage will not be effective if the insured does not notify insurers as soon as it becomes apparent that expenditure will need to be incurred in respect of product liability insurance.
- The insurers may not include conditions within their policies that seek to impose any unreasonable conditions precedent to liability, or require the insured either to take reasonable precautions or to comply with current legislation and regulations.

5.4 Financial loss

Financial loss is where a product fails to perform its function causing pure economic loss – which can be seen only on the balance sheet, rather than as physical injury to the consumer.

This risk may be insured in Argentina. However, company liability must be determined in terms of quantities: amount, time and class – in order to allow insurance companies to issue this kind of insurance.

It is advisable to cover financial loss insurance with a 'loss occurring' policy, under which all claims occurring during the period of the contract, irrespective of when the underlying policies incepted, are covered.

This option seems to be better than a 'claims made' policy which covers all claims reported to an insurer within the policy period irrespective of when they occurred. Moreover, it is important to note that 'claims made' basis policies in Argentina have been voided by the courts.

(a) ***Provisions***

As product liability policies are principally directed to prevent or cover damage caused to persons and other property by a defective product supplied by the insured, it will not normally extend to liability for pure economic financial losses which are not consequential upon the damage, such as loss of income, loss of market or loss of production suffered by others.

Some policies contain financial loss extensions which cover liability for third party financial losses but such coverage tends to be limited. These extensions can be combined with product guarantee insurance which provides protection against an insured's legal liability for claims arising out of the failure of its product to fulfil its intended purpose or function.

We can define the scope of a financial loss insurance extension as liability for any pecuniary loss, cost or expense incurred by any person other than the insured.

(b) ***Exclusions***

There are a number of exclusions generally included in a financial loss insurance policy wording which can operate to exclude liability otherwise falling within the scope of the cover. The most common exclusions are:

- third-party injury or third-party damage;
- losses known prior to cover;
- incidents/claims which are known about before cover;
- financial default;
- war and radioactive contamination;
- financial failure;
- punitive and exemplary damages;
- pollution except where sudden and unforeseen;
- aviation products;
- intellectual property rights;
- losses before the retroactive date;
- liability arising overseas;
- breach of contract;
- losses under other sections of the policy;
- exclusions within other parts of the policy, insofar as they apply;
- fraud or dishonesty;
- breach of antitrust law (in Argentina, Law 25,156);
- deliberate acts; and
- previously known circumstances or incidents.

5.5 Product guarantee

(a) *Insuring provisions*

Product guarantee insurance is the most common insurance service that retailers and companies offer to consumers in Argentina, acting as proxy agents of well-known insurance companies. However, in the great majority of the cases, the policy covers the repair and replacement of a product which fails due to a manufacturing or workmanship defect beyond the obligatory six-month period of guarantee established by Section 11 of the Consumer Protection Act. Thus, it operates as an extension of the legal guarantee.

The first option offered by the insurers is to repair the item, free of charge. If the product is not repairable, or if the cost of repairing the item exceeds the cost of a new one, it will be replaced.

The legal warranty period must be free of charge.

The insurer will conduct repairs free of charge if the following defects occur:

- malfunction;
- defective components; or
- defects in workmanship.

(b) *Exclusions*

The most common exclusions and limitations which may be included in a product guarantee policy are the following:

- the warranty claim must be filed within a certain number of days of the product failure date;
- units must not be disassembled and must be in 'as removed' condition;
- only personnel authorised by the insurer can repair the product;
- no substitute part can be installed in the product without prior authorisation of the insurer;
- the product shall not have been disassembled, repaired, or altered outwith the insurer's installations unless express prior written authorisation was granted;
- the product shall not have been subject to misuse, accident or improper installation unless proof is submitted to the satisfaction of the insurer that such abuse was not a cause for the claim defect;
- use of the product other than as described in the product specification;
- incorrect parameter settings;
- incorrect positioning or installation.

Australia

Philippa Briggs
Pamela Madafiglio
Minter Ellison

Australia is a federation, consisting of several states and territories. There is federal and state legislation regulating product safety. If there is any inconsistency between federal and state/territory legislation, federal legislation prevails.

In addition to legislation, Australia has common law based on the English common law system. Australian law relating to product liability is, therefore, a mixture of federal and state/territory legislation and common law.

1. Product safety regulation

1.1 Product risks

The system adopted in Australia for product safety is a mixture of measures and procedures that rely on consumers, suppliers, regulators and government agencies working together to ensure new and existing products are safe and free of defects. Product safety initiatives in Australia consist of, among other things, legislative requirements, safety standards (voluntary and mandatory), recalls and the imposition of liability for defective products. Governments, consumers, regulators, suppliers and manufacturers play a vital role in the success of the product safety initiatives. Over time the product safety regime has developed within Australia at a Commonwealth, state and industry level. There has also been a recent move towards the harmonisation of product safety laws and regulations throughout Australia.

Australian law relating to consumer product safety has recently been revised with the introduction of the Australian Consumer Law (ACL) on January 1 2011. The Consumer Law replaces previous Commonwealth consumer protection legislation and is contained within Schedule 2 to the Competition and Consumer Act 2010 (Cth; CCA).[1] Each state and territory within Australia has enacted application legislation which adopts the Consumer Law as the law of that state or territory. As a result, there is now one uniform Australian consumer law applicable to all jurisdictions throughout Australia, which operates as a single law to protect consumers and ensure fair trading.

The Consumer Law is not, however, intended to cover the entire field nor is it intended to exclude or limit the concurrent operation of any law of a state or territory. Throughout Australia there is, in addition to the Consumer Law, specific

1 The CCA was formerly called the Trade Practices Act 1974 (Cth). The CCA is essentially the same Act, renamed and amended.

legislation relating to product liability and there are numerous regulatory bodies which oversee the implementation of that legislation.

The Consumer Law sets out general principles and provides for consumer protection, a national product safety regime and enforcement powers for regulators. The Consumer Law imposes a strict liability regime for defective products. Additional legislation in force throughout Australia generally provides for the regulation of specific products within various industries, such as the health, automotive and food industries and is aimed at ensuring that products available on the Australian market comply with certain safety standards.

1.2 Safety standards

Manufacturers and suppliers have an obligation, at common law and under the Consumer Law, to ensure that they market only safe products. All products must meet relevant safety standards, adhere to relevant information standards, be free of defects and be fit for their intended purpose.

A 'manufacturer' is defined under the Consumer Law to include a person who grows, extracts, produces, processes, assembles or imports goods. 'Supply' is defined to include the sale, exchange, lease, hire, hire-purchase of goods, or the provision, grant or conferring of product-related services.

(a) Safety standards: consumer goods and product related services

The Consumer Law[2] creates a national regime for safety standards applicable to consumer goods and product-related services. Consumer goods are defined as goods that are either intended to be used, or are of a kind likely to be used, for personal, domestic or household use or consumption.[3] A product-related service is defined as a service relating to the delivery, installation, assembly, maintenance, repair or cleaning of consumer goods.[4]

Mandatory safety standards are designed to protect consumers by specifying minimum requirements that products must meet before they are supplied, to ensure that all goods and product-related services available on the Australian market are safe.

Under the Consumer Law, a mandatory safety standard made under the Trade Practices Act 1974 (TPA), as it was then called, continues to apply. Mandatory safety standards currently in force in Australia include standards for aquatic toys, baby walkers, bicycle helmets, child restraints for use in motor vehicles, toys for children up to and including 36 months of age, treadmills, sunglasses and tobacco products' labelling. A full list of all Commonwealth mandatory standards in force are available on the internet at www.productsafety.gov.au.

The Consumer Law provides that the Commonwealth minister may declare mandatory safety standards for a consumer good or product-related service, that are reasonably necessary to prevent or reduce the risk of injury to any person. Under the

---

2 Part 3-3, Divisions 1 and 2.
3 Section 2(1) of the ACL.
4 Section 2(1) of the ACL.

Consumer Law, the supply or manufacture of consumer goods and product-related services that do not comply with the mandatory safety standards is prohibited.

Suppliers may be found guilty of a criminal offence if they fail to comply with a mandatory safety standard. The maximum fine is $220,000 for an individual or $1.1 million for a body corporate. Civil penalties for the same amounts also apply. This is an offence of strict liability, which means the courts need not consider the party's intentions before finding them guilty of the offence.

(b) *Information standards*

Under the Consumer Law, a Commonwealth minister may also stipulate information standards for goods or services of a particular kind. This information standard may prescribe the content of information and the manner or form in which such information is provided. The application of information standards, unlike safety standards, is not limited to consumer goods or product-related services.

Information standards require manufacturers or suppliers to give consumers prescribed information when they purchase specified goods: for example, ingredient labelling for cosmetics, labelling for tobacco products and care labelling for clothing and textile products.

Since January 1 2011, a prescribed consumer product information standard made under the TPA (which was still in force on January 1 2011) continues to be in force as if it were an information standard made under the Consumer Law.

(c) *Special provisions: specific industries and legislation*

Specific information and/or warning requirements are also imposed on individual products. For example, strict information and labelling requirements are associated with tobacco products, children's toys, pharmaceutical products and cosmetics. These requirements are contained within specific legislation.

(d) *Voluntary standards*

Voluntary standards are also extensively utilised within Australia. These standards are published documents setting out specifications and procedures designed to ensure products are safe, reliable and perform in accordance with their intended purpose. Voluntary standards are aimed at ensuring products meet consistent and reliable standards by establishing common criteria for quality and safety.

Voluntary standards are not legally binding and it is, therefore, not illegal to supply or manufacture products which do not meet voluntary standard requirements. Voluntary standards may, however, be used as a benchmark when considering whether a manufacturer or supplier has breached its duty of care in relation to a particular product.

Although a relatively small number of products in Australia are covered by bans or mandatory safety standards, many products are covered by voluntary standards.

(e) *Standards Australia*

Standards Australia is an independent, non-governmental standards body responsible for developing specific standards for a range of products and services within Australia. Standards Australia works with government bodies, businesses, industries, communities and consumers, to develop internationally-aligned standards and related publications. These standards are designed to help ensure the safety, reliability and performance of products within Australia.

These standards are voluntary and not legally binding within Australia, unless they are subsequently adopted into applicable legislation.

(f) ***Bans on consumer goods and product-related services***

Under the Consumer Law, there are two different types of bans: interim or permanent. Such bans make it unlawful for anyone, in trade or commerce, to supply, offer to supply, manufacture, possess or have control over particular consumer goods or product-related services.

An interim ban may be imposed by a Commonwealth or state/territory minister, on certain consumer goods or product-related services, if the minister considers that the goods or services will or could injure someone, that using or misusing the goods, or goods to which the service relates in a reasonably foreseeable way will or could injure someone, or another minister has imposed an interim ban on the goods or service which is still in force. An interim ban lasts for 60 days and can be extended by the minister by up to another 60 days.

Permanent bans can only be imposed by a Commonwealth minister and may apply throughout Australia. Permanent bans may be imposed on a consumer product or product-related service if it appears to the minister that consumer goods or services of that kind will or may cause injury to any person, or if a reasonably foreseeable use or misuse of the consumer product or consumer product to which the service relates will or may cause injury to any person.

Bans are currently in force in Australia in relation to smokeless tobacco products, combustible candle holders, baby dummies with decorations and tinted headlight covers for motor vehicles. A full list of all Commonwealth interim and permanent bans can be found at www.productsafety.gov.au.

A supplier who fails to comply with a ban may be found guilty of a criminal offence. The maximum fine is $220,000 for an individual or $1.1 million for a body corporate. Civil penalties for the same amounts also apply. This is an offence of strict liability.

1.3 Compliance: administration by sector

In addition to the above, there are a variety of organisations and regulators throughout Australia that regulate sectors, administer specific standards and ensure that safe products enter the Australian market. The regulators of specific products include the following.

(a) ***Foods***

The Food Standards Australia New Zealand Act 1991 (Cth) establishes the Food Standards Australia New Zealand (FSANZ) which administers the Australia New Zealand Food Standards Code (the Code). The Code provides for legally enforceable food standards under the Act and regulates food, beverages and packaging.

Enforcement and interpretation of the Code is the responsibility of state and territory departments and food agencies within Australia (and New Zealand).

Foods imported into Australia are subject to requirements under the Quarantine Act 1908 and the Imported Food Control Act 1992 which are implemented by the Australian Quarantine and Inspection Service.

(b) *Therapeutic goods and medicines*

The Therapeutic Goods Act 1989 (Cth) sets out the legal requirements for the import, export, manufacture and supply of therapeutic goods in Australia. The act is supported by regulations, orders and determinations which provide detail on matters covered in the act. The act is Commonwealth legislation that provides a substantially uniform national system of controls over therapeutic goods.

The Therapeutic Goods Administration (TGA) is a division of the Australian Government Department of Health and Ageing which is responsible for regulating medicines and medical devices.

(c) *Motor vehicles*

The automotive industry is regulated by the Department of Infrastructure, Transport, Regional Development and Local Government.

The Australian Design Rules are national standards for motor vehicle safety. These standards are enforceable under the Motor Vehicle Standards Act 1989. The Act requires all vehicles, whether they are manufactured in Australia or imported (new and/or second hand), to comply with the relevant design rules at the time of manufacture or supply in Australia.

The Federal Chamber of Automotive Industries works closely with the Australian government to ensure that standards for vehicle design comply with the design rules. There are also a range of groups within Australia concerned with motor vehicle safety, including the Strategic Vehicle Safety and Environment Group and the Australian Motor Vehicle Certification Board.

(d) *Electrical products and gas products*

Electrical safety, including equipment safety, in Australia is regulated by each Australian state and territory separately. For example, the regulator within NSW is the NSW Fair Trading Department of Services, Technology and Administration. The Electrical Regulatory Authority Council aims to co-ordinate the Australian states/territories and New Zealand to manage their activities in respect of regulatory strategies, policies and ongoing reforms.

Each state and territory within Australia and New Zealand has its own legislation and regulations in respect of gas appliances, products and services. The Gas Technical Regulators Committee is an association of government departments responsible for the safe use of gas. The committee includes representatives from every state/territory in Australia and New Zealand.

(e) ***Chemicals***

The National Industrial Chemicals Notification and Assessment Scheme (NICNAS) regulates industrial chemicals used in manufacturing, products, building, construction and cosmetics. NICNAS prohibits or restricts harmful use of chemicals in these products.

The NICNAS operates under the Industrial Chemicals (Notification and Assessment) Act 1989 (ICNA). The director of NICNAS reports to the minister for health and ageing.

The National Drugs and Poisons Schedule Committee also regulates and monitors poisons, household cleaners and chemicals.

(f) ***Toys***

Toys are closely monitored and highly regulated by federal and state governments within Australia. The Australian Toy Standard (AS/NZ 8124) has been established by Standards Australia. The Australian Toy Association (ATA) administers, monitors and oversees product safety in relation to toys within Australia.

State and federal regulations have been enacted within Australia to make various standards relating to toys mandatory, especially standards relating to toys for children under three years of age. For example, the mandatory standard for toys for children up to and including 36 months of age came into effect on December 17 2003 under the TPA and is based on Australian Standard AS/NZS ISO 8124.1:2002 Safety of Toys Part 1: Safety aspects related to mechanical and physical properties.

1.4 Corrective action

If a product is banned or fails to meet any requisite standards, there are several corrective actions which may be taken, including withdrawing the product from the market, recalling the product from the market (either voluntarily or compulsorily) and/or issuing a warning about a product which is under investigation. These corrective actions are discussed in further detail below.

1.5 Obligations of producers and distributors

(a) ***Sources of duties***

Australian law relating to product safety is generally focused on two areas. First, is the preventative aspect of product law which aims to regulate products placed on the market to ensure they are safe. This includes measures such as the safety and information standards described above. The second aspect of product law provides for compensation to parties who are injured or have suffered loss or damage as a result of a defective product.

In respect of the first, duties are imposed on parties involved in the supply chain to ensure that safe products are placed on the market. These duties may be imposed by way of statute, contract and/or tort law.

Statute: The main statute regulating product safety in Australia is the Consumer Law. This provides a national, unified system for product safety in relation to consumer goods and product-related services.

Part 3-2, Division 1 of the Consumer Law also provides for a number of statutory rights/guarantees in relation to the supply of goods. This includes the following guarantees:

- the goods are of an acceptable quality, being fit for the purposes for which they are supplied, acceptable in appearance, free from defects, safe and durable;[5]
- the goods are reasonably fit for any disclosed purpose;[6] and
- the manufacturer of the goods will comply with any express warranty given or made.[7]

There is also an abundance of industry-specific legislation which regulates product safety and imposes duties on manufacturers, suppliers and other parties to the supply chain to ensure products are safe, and sets out requirements for the pre-market stage (as described above).

The legislation creates a legally enforceable duty on manufacturers and suppliers to comply with mandatory safety standards, information standards, product bans and recalls, to prevent unsafe or defective products from being placed on the Australian market.

Tort (negligence): The law of negligence imposes a general duty of care on manufacturers, and in certain cases on suppliers and other parties in the supply chain, to take all reasonable steps to prevent injury or damage caused by defective or unsafe goods. A manufacturer will generally owe a duty of care to the consumer, purchaser and any other user to prevent any foreseeable risks of injury when using the product as intended.

Under this common law duty of care, a manufacturer or supplier will be required to act in the manner of a reasonable person in the position of that producer or distributor. A producer or distributor has a duty to undertake all reasonable precautions against harm where the risk is foreseeable (not far-fetched or fanciful) and not insignificant.

This common law duty of care extends to all consumers of the product and any other person who may foreseeably suffer loss, injury or damage as a result of a defect to the product. Any testing, research or other pre-market precautions will be relevant to the issue of whether the manufacturer complied with the common law duty of care.

The duty of care applicable to a supplier, retailer or distributor may be different to that of a manufacturer, as they may not have been involved with the product prior to it being packaged for sale or distribution. A supplier will not normally be expected to test products which are delivered by the manufacturer in sealed containers or packaging and which would not normally be opened until they reach the consumer. Accordingly a supplier, retailer or distributor may only have a duty, in the absence of

5 Section 54.
6 Section 55.
7 Section 59.

any special circumstances which would put them on notice of a potential risk, to take reasonable steps to prevent risks which may reasonably be known to them.

These common law duties are, however, subject to specific contractual duties.

Contract: Australian contract law is primarily regulated by common law but it is increasingly supplemented by statute, particularly in relation to consumer protection.

Parties are generally able to enter into a contract on any terms agreed between the parties. The specific terms of a contract could, therefore, impose certain duties on the parties to the contract. The Consumer Law,[8] however, states that the guarantees provided in relation to the supply of consumer goods cannot be modified or limited and any term of a contract which purports to exclude, restrict or modify the guarantees will be void.

Furthermore, under the Consumer Law, unfair terms of consumer contracts will be void if the term is unfair and where the contract is a standard form contract. A consumer contract is a contract for the supply of goods or services or a sale or grant of an interest in land, to an individual whose acquisition of the goods, services or interest is wholly or predominantly for personal, domestic or household use or consumption.

If a defective product or a product that is not fit for its intended purpose is supplied, this will often amount to a breach of contract. Where a breach of contract has occurred, the non-breaching party may be entitled to a range of remedies against the party that breached the contract including damages and equitable remedies.

As a general rule, however, a contract is only enforceable against a party to the contract. This is referred to as privity of contract. As contracts for the provision of products are generally between a purchaser and supplier, the supplier will often bear the liability for any defective product in accordance with the express and implied terms of the contract. Under contract law, consumers normally cannot sue manufacturers for a breach of contract. The Consumer Law has, however, imposed direct liability on manufacturers in some cases. This is discussed in further detail below.

1.6 Pre-market obligations

Whilst pre-market processes and systems are often not legally required, good manufacturing and supply practices assist in ensuring that only safe products are placed on the market and may ultimately assist manufacturers and suppliers avoid potential claims.

In addition to pre-market obligations to ensure that products meet mandatory information and safety standards, there are a variety of general and industry-specific pre-market practices which may be adopted by manufacturers and suppliers.

(a) Traceability

Tracing products across the supply chain can be of considerable importance in relation to product safety. The efficient removal of deficient products will be

---

8 Section 64 of the ACL.

facilitated if the products can be traced from their source to the consumer, and will also assist in locating and identifying any defects in the manufacturing or supply process at the source.

The ability to track goods across the supply chain is essentially in the hands of suppliers and requires them to maintain records on the party from whom they purchased the product and to whom they sold the product, together with maintaining batch and serial numbers. Where a supplier manufactures or assembles products, records should also be maintained with respect to the origins of components of the product.

Suppliers should, therefore, have systems in place to track the product through the supply chain and trace the product from the manufacturer through to the consumer.

(b) Record keeping

While there is no general legal requirement for suppliers in Australia to maintain tracking records for products, there are specific regulations which require record keeping for specified products. For example, the Therapeutic Goods Act 1989 prescribes information that is to be provided to the TGA in relation to the registration of therapeutic goods.

Furthermore, whilst suppliers are generally not legally required to maintain specific records, this information may assist in protecting the supplier against potential claims.

(c) Testing

All manufacturers and suppliers are under an obligation to ensure that products supplied are not banned and comply with mandatory safety and information standards. As bans and standards (mandatory and voluntary) often prescribe technical requirements and standards, suppliers may want to arrange testing by independent and specialist bodies to ensure compliance. This will test whether a product complies with technical performance specifications in any standard and will also provide evidence of such compliance.

The Australian Competition and Consumer Commission (ACCC) has developed guidelines with respect to product safety testing: *Product Safety: A guide to testing*, and *Testing to Product Standards: Principles for test organisations*. These guidelines are aimed at all businesses that deal in consumer products including retailers, wholesalers, importers, distributors and manufacturers, as well as product-testing agencies.

While suppliers are generally not under a legal obligation to undertake testing, they may be required, or it may assist, to confirm that products comply with relevant standards. To that end, it is also important that manufacturers and suppliers test products at various stages of the production, development and distribution process.

(d) Sector-specific rules

Foods: The Food Safety Practices and General Requirements (Standard 3.2.2, a mandatory standard) sets out specific food handling controls related to the receipt, storage, processing, display, packaging, transportation, disposal and recall of food. Mandatory Standard 3.2.3, Food Premises and Equipment, sets out the requirements for food premises, fixtures, fittings, equipment and food transport vehicles.

The *Policy Guidelines on Food Safety Management in Australia: Food Safety Programs*, identify those food businesses that are required to follow a food safety programme based on the food safety risk they pose.

In Australia, compliance with the Code for all foods is monitored by authorities in the states and territories. Complaints about potentially non-compliant foods are directed to the relevant agency in each state or territory.

'Novel foods' are non-traditional foods with no history of safe use. FSANZ assesses novel foods rigorously before permitting them to be sold in Australia. Any food manufacturer wanting to sell a novel food or ingredient must apply to FSANZ for the Standards to be amended to include the food or ingredient in the list. Upon receipt of any such application FSANZ conducts a pre-market safety assessment, and the food is added to the list only after it passes that assessment.

FSANZ has also established an Advisory Committee on Novel Foods (the Committee). The Committee considers whether particular foods meet the definition of 'non-traditional food' in the Standard and, if they do, whether they need to be assessed for public health and safety compliance. The Committee makes a recommendation to FSANZ.

All genetically modified foods intended for sale in Australia must undergo a safety evaluation by FSANZ. Genetically modified foods are regulated under Standard 1.5.2, Food Produced using Gene Technology, contained in the Code. The standard makes provision for mandatory pre-market approval and labelling requirements. Accordingly, only approved genetically-modified foods are supplied in Australia and it is mandatory for genetically-modified foods to be identified on food labels.

Products regulated under the New Zealand Dietary Supplements Regulations are considered in Australia as either foods or therapeutic goods. There is no separate dietary supplement category.

There are extensive food labelling and information standards, which require the display of information such as date marking, ingredients, instructions for storage and preparation, and advisory and warning statements. The requirements for food labelling are found in various standards in the Code, including Standard 1.2.8, Nutrition Information Requirements; Standard 2.7.1, Labelling of Alcoholic Beverages and Food Containing Alcohol; Standard 2.9.2, Foods for Infants; and Standard 2.9.3, Formulated Meal Replacements and Formulated Supplementary Foods.

Pharmaceutical products: The Therapeutic Goods Act 1989 details the requirements for listing, registering or including medicines, medical devices and biological products on the Australian Register of Therapeutic Goods. The act also regulates many other aspects of therapeutic products, including advertising, labelling and product appearance.

The Therapeutic Goods Act administers the Therapeutic Goods Act 1989, applying a risk management approach designed to ensure therapeutic goods supplied in Australia meet acceptable standards of quality, safety and efficacy (performance), when necessary. The risk management approach involves a pre-market assessment of products, where the potential benefits of therapeutic goods are weighted against the potential risks in determining whether the product should be made available in Australia.

Under the Therapeutic Goods Act 1989, a 'sponsor' is someone who imports therapeutic goods, manufactures therapeutic goods, has therapeutic goods imported or manufactured on their behalf, or exports therapeutic goods from Australia. The sponsor is responsible for applying to the TGA to have their medicine included in the Australian Register of Therapeutic Goods.

The TGA also regulates therapeutic goods through the licensing of Australian manufacturers and verifying compliance by overseas manufacturers with the same standards as their Australian counterparts.

Motor vehicles: The Australian Design Rules are national standards for vehicle safety, anti-theft and emissions. The current standards (3rd edition) are administered by the Australian government under the Motor Vehicle Standards Act 1989. The Act requires all road vehicles, whether they are newly manufactured in Australia or imported as new or second-hand vehicles, to comply with the relevant rules at the time of manufacture and supply to the Australian market.

Electrical equipment: Regulations and standards apply to all household equipment that is sold or offered for sale in Australia. For example, the Electrical Safety Act 2002 and the Electrical Safety Regulations 2002 regulate electrical equipment and services in the state of Queensland.

Under various state/territory legislation electrical equipment is listed as either prescribed/declared or non-prescribed/non-declared. Prescribed/declared equipment must have a certificate of approval before it can be sold in Australia. If the equipment is not listed as prescribed/declared, a certificate of approval does not need to be obtained before it is supplied for sale. Once equipment is approved it must be correctly labelled to indicate approval. For example, the NSW Electricity (Consumer Safety) Act 2004 lists the various declared products in NSW.

In order to carry out certain electrical work in Australia, it is necessary to obtain the correct electrical licence for the work. Each state and territory administers their own system of electrical licensing. A new national licensing scheme has been in operation since July 2012 for occupations in property, electrical, plumbing, gas fitting and refrigeration and air conditioning.

Gas equipment: All gas appliances in Australia and New Zealand must be tested and certified. Since 2012, the Gas Safety Certification Mark must be attached to all new gas appliances to assure consumers the product is safe. This mark replaces stickers from AGA, SAI Global, IAPMO and Global-Mark.

Extensive testing is required to establish safety for gas equipment. These tests must be carried out by laboratories with the required competence and standards. Furthermore, only licensed gas fitters (those who do gas work), who have been trained to competency standards can undertake gas-fitting work.

Toys: The Australian Toy Standard (AS/NZ 8124) has been established by Standards Australia. Toys are tested to ensure their compliance with these standards. While there is no requirement that toy manufacturers and distributors abide by the industry's voluntary standards, the ATA strongly advocates adherence by the entire toy industry to the voluntary safety standards.

Cosmetics: The NICNAS sets national standards for cosmetics imported into, or manufactured in, Australia and regulates the enforcement of those standards.

A 'cosmetic' is defined as a substance or preparation intended for placement in contact with an external part of the human body, with a view to altering the odours of the body, changing its appearance, cleansing it, maintaining it in good condition or protecting the body. These products are distinct from 'therapeutic goods' within the meaning of the Therapeutic Goods Act 1989.

ACCORD Australasia is the national industry association for the consumer, cosmetic, hygiene and speciality products industry. ACCORD has established a number of codes and guidelines which regulate the cosmetic industry.

(e) Occupational health and safety

Occupational health and safety laws aimed to protect people in the workplace and ensure safe working environments. Legislation enacted by the Commonwealth and territories in Australia impose duties on manufacturers and suppliers of products for use in the workplace. For example, the Occupational Health and Safety Act 1991 (Cth) states that a manufacturer of plant (defined as including any machinery, equipment or tool, and any component thereof) or substance that the manufacturer ought reasonably expect will be used by employees at work must take all reasonably practicable steps to:

- ensure that the plant or substance is designed and constructed to be safe for use by employees;
- carry out research, testing and examination necessary to discover, and to eliminate or minimise, any risk to the health or safety of employees, that may arise from the use of the plant or substance; and
- make available to an employer, in connection with the use of the plant or substance by employees at work, adequate information concerning the use for which it is designed and has been tested, details of its design and construction and any conditions necessary to ensure that it will be safe for employees.

A breach of these duties may be subject to civil action or a criminal prosecution under the Occupational Health and Safety Act 1991.

1.7 Post-market obligations

Once a product is placed on the market, there are various legal requirements and practical procedures that deal with reporting an unsafe product, removing an unsafe product from the market and enforcing penalties against any wrongdoers, if necessary.

(a) *Compulsory reporting*

Mandatory reporting was introduced by the Consumer Law on January 1 2011. Under this obligation, suppliers are required to report to the Commonwealth minister any death or serious injury or illness of any person they believe was caused by the use of a consumer product they supplied. A supplier must report any product that they supplied which may have caused, or may lead to a serious injury, illness or death. Therefore, an injury, illness or death does need not have occurred to invoke this requirement. This is aimed at improving the government's responsiveness to serious product-related hazards.

All participants in the supply chain of a consumer product or product related-service are required to comply with the reporting requirement. This includes retailers, dealers, hirers, distributors, installers, repairers, importers, manufacturers and exporters. Suppliers are required to report the information to the minister in writing within two days of becoming aware of the hazard.

A supplier who fails to notify the minister within two days of becoming aware of the incident may be found guilty of a criminal offence. The maximum fine is $3,330 for an individual or $16,650 for a body corporate. This is an offence of strict liability.

There are also specific reporting requirements for particular goods, including:

- sponsors of pesticides and veterinary medicines must report to the APVMA;
- sponsors of therapeutic goods must report adverse events to the TGA; and
- hazards relating to foods must be reported to the relevant health authorities.

If a consumer seeks to report an unsafe product, they can make a report to any of the product safety regulators. This can include reporting the unsafe product to the ACCC, or the state/territory-based regulator, such as the NSW Fair Trading Agency, Queensland Office of Fair Trading or South Australian Office of Consumer and Business Affairs.

(b) *Recall*

When a safety problem in a product is identified, manufacturers, suppliers or regulators may determine that the product needs to be recalled from the market. A recall may be initiated either by the supplier taking action on its own initiative (voluntary recall), or the regulator issuing a recall notice (compulsory recall).

The ACCC administers a national database for recalls of specific and general consumer products. The ACCC has issued the Consumer Product Safety Recall Guidelines, which provide information on how to conduct a product safety recall. These guidelines set out the legal requirements for suppliers conducting a recall, together with responsibilities of suppliers and agencies when conducting a recall.

There are also specific provisions in the Consumer Law setting out the requirements with respect to a recall of consumer goods. Other products are the responsibility of specialist agencies and regulators and are governed by specific laws and requirements.

Voluntary recall: Parties who undertake a voluntary recall must notify the Commonwealth minister within two days of doing so. The minister may then publish a copy of the recall notice on the internet. The Commonwealth minister will also advise state and territory agencies of any voluntary recalls within their jurisdictions.

In conducting a recall, a supplier generally has responsibility to conduct a comprehensive risk analysis of the hazard, stop distribution of the product, cease production or modify the manufacturing process, remove unsafe products from the marketplace, notify the public (and international recipients of the product), facilitate the return of products by consumers and develop a recall strategy.

Following a voluntary recall, the ACCC will assess whether the recall strategy is adequate and will intervene if the proposed action is deemed inadequate.

As manufacturers and suppliers owe a continuing duty of care at common law to prevent a product from causing foreseeable harm, there are continuing obligations after the product is sold. For example, if they are aware of a defect in a product and fail to undertake a recall where it would be considered reasonable to do so, this may amount to negligence and the manufacturer or supplier may be liable to any person who suffers injury, loss or damage as a result of the defective product.

Compulsory recall: Under the Consumer Law, a responsible minister can order a compulsory recall, if the product could cause injury to a person; or a reasonably foreseeable use (including misuse) of the product could cause injury to a person; or if the product does not comply with a safety standard in force or where there is an interim or permanent ban in force; and it appears to the minister that one or more suppliers have not taken satisfactory action to prevent those products causing injury.

Prior to conducting a compulsory recall, the minister through the ACCC, must issue a proposed recall notice. This gives notice to suppliers of the intended recall. This requirement is waived if the product may present an imminent risk of death, serious illness or serious injury.

In conducting a compulsory recall, the responsible minister must publish a recall notice on the internet. This notice may require suppliers to recall the product, disclose the nature and/or dangerous characteristic of the product or defect, repair it, replace it or refund the price. If a compulsory recall notice is issued for goods which have been exported outside Australia, the supplier must provide the overseas recipient with a written notice.

All product recalls conducted within Australia can be viewed online at www.recalls.gov.au.

(c) *Warnings*

Under the Consumer Law, a minister may publish on the internet a safety warning notice about consumer goods or product-related services:

- stating that goods or services of a particular kind are under investigation to determine whether they may/will cause injury to a person; and
- warning of possible risks involved in the use of consumer goods of the kind specified in the notice.

If an investigation is conducted in conjunction with a warning notice, and a recall notice or ban notice is not subsequently issued, the minister must announce, as soon as practicable, the results of the investigation.

(d) Sector-specific rules

Foods: Reports of food being potentially non-compliant with the code should be made to the relevant agency in each state or territory, for example the NSW Food Authority, ACT Health Protection Service or Northern Territory Department of Health. A food recall may be initiated as a result of reports referred from a variety of sources, including manufacturers, wholesalers, retailers, medical practitioners, government agencies, health authorities or consumers. A food recall is defined as 'an action taken to remove from distribution, sale and consumption, food which may pose a health and safety risk to consumers'.

Food Standards Australia New Zealand (FSANZ) coordinates and monitors food recalls within Australia. Recalls occur in consultation between state and territory authorities and a sponsor, who is usually the product's supplier. The Food Industry Recall Protocol, developed by FSANZ, is a guide. It explains what should be done when in the interest of public health and safety food products need to be removed from supply or use by consumers.

Pharmaceuticals: The TGA is largely responsible for post-market monitoring and enforcement of standards for pharmaceutical products. The public and healthcare professionals are encouraged to report problems with medicines, vaccines or medical devices, to assist the TGA identify and respond to safety concerns. Such reports may be received by manufacturers, wholesalers, retail and hospital pharmacies, pathological departments, research facilities, medical practitioners or consumers.

The TGA adopts a risk management approach to regulating therapeutic goods. This means that the TGA identifies, assesses and evaluates the risks posed by therapeutic goods, applies any measures necessary for treating the risks posed, and monitors and reviews the risks over time. Therapeutic goods are divided broadly into two classes: medicines and medical devices. Medicines must be entered as either 'registered' or 'listed' medicines and medical devices must be 'included' on the Australian Register of Therapeutic Goods before they may be supplied in or exported from Australia.

The TGA has established a pharmacovigilance system for the collection and evaluation of information relevant to the benefit/risk balance of registered medicinal products. The TGA continually monitors the safety profile of the products available in Australia and takes appropriate action where necessary. The 'Australian Guideline for Pharmacovigilance Responsibilities of Sponsors of Registered Medicines Regulated by Drug and Evaluation Branch' provides for the reporting of adverse reactions to registered medicines regulated by the Drug Safety and Evaluation Branch (DSEB) of the TGA. The guidelines state that "each sponsor of registered medicines must ensure that it has an appropriate system of pharmacovigilance in place in order to assure responsibility and liability for its products on the market and to ensure that appropriate action can be taken, when necessary".

A recall may occur as a result of a simple problem or defect, such as errors in labelling or packaging, or as a result of more serious problems posing a risk to the health of consumers. Pharmaceutical recalls are classified into three levels, depending on the varying risk they pose to safety and ranging from potentially life threatening products to those that do not pose a significant risk to health but need to be withdrawn from the market.

The TGA coordinates the recall, advising sponsors of the correct procedures and monitors the recall. The sponsor has responsibility for the recovery of goods and corrective action. Once a recall has been initiated, the TGA notifies a number of key stakeholders including state and territory health departments. A list of state and territory health department representatives and other stakeholder groups who may be notified of recalls by the TGA can be found in the Uniform Recall Procedure for Therapeutic Goods.

The TGA also maintains a current 'Rapid Alert System' to communicate urgent safety information to public and private hospitals in an emergency.

(e) Motor vehicles

Procedures for the Recall of Vehicles and Associated Products with Safety-Related Defects is a voluntary recall code of practice. This code describes procedures to be followed by suppliers for the rectification of safety-related defects in any vehicle, part, accessory or service. This code applies to all suppliers in Australia of vehicles, as well as vehicle-related parts, accessories and services. Under the code, suppliers are responsible for the investigation and rectification of safety-related defects. The code sets out the minimum requirements in relation to the product recall of an automotive vehicle, however, suppliers may adopt more stringent procedures in relation to investigating potential defects and conducting a recall.

There are also Procedures for the Recall of Vehicles and Associated Products with Safety Related Defects by Registered Automotive Workshops (RAW) which describe procedures to be followed by RAW for the rectification of safety-related defects in any vehicle, part, accessory or service.

2. Enforcement

Product safety in Australia is regulated, administered and enforced by a number of different Commonwealth, state and territory authorities.

2.1 Sector organisations

(a) General consumer products

Enforcement and administration of the Consumer Law is conducted by the ACCC, Australian Securities and Investment Commission (commonly referred to as 'ASIC') and the state/territory administrative agencies. Particular products may be subject to regulation by industry authorities and any products that fall outside the specific product categories are known as 'general consumer products' and monitored largely by the ACCC, in conjunction with state/territory consumer protection agencies.

If a regulator is notified or informed that a supplier is selling products that are banned or fail to meet mandatory safety standards, the regulator's priority will generally be to ensure that the hazardous products are removed from the market.

The ACCC assesses what compliance and enforcement action it will take against suppliers who have breached mandatory standards or bans. This will depend on a range of factors including the seriousness of the safety hazard, how many products were supplied, how blatant the breach is, the supplier's past conduct and the extent to which the supplier cooperates.

(b) ***Foods***

In Australia, compliance and enforcement of the Code for all foods is monitored by authorities in the states and territories. For example, in New South Wales, the Code is enforced and administered by the NSW Food Authority.

Although FSANZ does not have any actual enforcement powers, it has a national role in coordinating mandatory recalls. FSANZ also collaborates with the Implementation Sub-Committee (ISC) to ensure that compliance methods are developed by the jurisdictions in parallel with standards development.

(c) ***Motor vehicles***

The Department of Infrastructure, Transport, Regional Development and Local Government has a range of enforcement powers in relation to motor vehicle safety. Such powers are discussed further below.

(d) ***Pharmaceuticals***

If a problem is discovered with a medicine, device or manufacturer, the TGA is able to take action. Possible regulatory actions vary from continued monitoring to withdrawing the product from the market. The level of TGA regulatory control increases with the level of risk the medicine or device can pose. To ensure the ongoing quality of approved therapeutic goods, the TGA conducts regular inspections of sites where they are manufactured. The TGA has a range of compliance and enforcement powers to take appropriate action should any potential non-compliances with labelling and packaging requirements be detected.

The Secretary of the Department of Health and Ageing also has a range of enforcement options under the Therapeutic Goods Act 1989.

2.2 Powers of authorities

The ACCC has access to a range of compliance and enforcement options, including powers to issue an infringement notice, issue a public warning notice, pursue civil pecuniary penalties, pursue disqualification orders or issue a substantiation notice.

(a) ***Substantiation power to check standards claims***

The Consumer Law provides the ACCC with a new investigative power to issue a 'substantiation notice'. These notices require a supplier to provide information and/or produce documents to confirm that products comply with standards where a claim of compliance with a particular standard has been made by the supplier. This may ultimately lead to further action if a supplier is unable to provide the requested information or documentation.

(b) ***Administrative resolution***

Where the ACCC assesses that a risk flowing from a contravention is minimal, the ACCC may accept an administrative resolution in response to the contravention. Administrative resolutions generally involve the party entering into an agreement to stop the conduct and compensate those who have suffered a detriment and/or to take other measures necessary to ensure that the conduct does not recur.

(c) ***Infringement notices***

The ACCC has power to issue an infringement notice where it has reasonable grounds to believe a person has breached various product safety provisions. Such notices are generally issued where the ACCC considers that the contravention requires a more formal sanction than an administrative resolution but where it is of the view that the matter may be resolved without legal proceedings.

Infringement notices provide an opportunity for a person to pay a penalty and resolve the matter with the ACCC. If a party fails to pay an infringement notice penalty, the ACCC may commence proceedings in respect of the underlying alleged contravention of the Consumer Law. The ACCC must issue the notice within 12 months of the alleged contravention.

(d) ***Legal action***

The Consumer Law enables the ACCC to institute proceedings in court for recovery on behalf of the Commonwealth of a pecuniary penalty for consumer protection matters. The courts may order a person who has contravened certain product safety provisions, to pay a civil pecuniary penalty if satisfied that the person contravened or attempted to contravene a product safety-related provision of the Consumer Law.

The ACCC may also, where the conduct is considered to be particularly serious, commence legal action. Such action may result in courts undertaking one or more of the following:

- granting an injunction restraining conduct or compelling certain actions;
- requiring suppliers to publish notices about their conduct and corrective advertising and to disclose relevant information to others;
- finding that the action amounts to a breach of the law, such that affected persons could recover damages;
- imposing fines; and
- convicting businesses and/or individuals found to have breached the law.

The Compliance and Enforcement Policy sets out the principles adopted by the ACCC in respect of its enforcement powers. The ACCC's enforcement response should be proportionate to the conduct and resulting harm. The implementation of the ACCC's enforcement policy is governed by the guiding principles of transparency, confidentiality, timeliness, consistency and fairness.

2.3 International enforcement

Section 5 of the Competition and Consumer Act 2010 extends the Consumer Law to conduct outside of Australia by companies carrying on business within Australia,

Australian citizens, and/or persons ordinarily resident within Australia. If a claim for damages is made under Section 5, however, a person is not entitled to rely on conduct to which the Consumer Law has been extended by virtue of this section, unless with the written consent of the minister.

Some provisions of the Consumer Law also extend to the supply and export of products outside Australia. For example, if a compulsory recall notice is issued for products that have been supplied overseas, the supplier must give the person outside Australia written notice informing them that the goods are the subject of a recall and advising them of the nature of the defect or associated hazard.

Australia has also signed international agreements dealing with mutual enforcement assistance and coordination of enforcement activities. These agreements are listed at www.accc.gov.au. The agreements include the Australia–European Commission Arrangement on Consumer Protection, ACCC–Korea Fair Trade Commission arrangement and ACCC–PNG Consumer Affairs Council Cooperation Agreement.

2.4 Appeals

In virtually all jurisdictions of Australia, there is the right of appeal from a decision of a court. The appeal process varies depending on the jurisdiction.

In relation to decisions of specific regulators, particular appeal procedures may be prescribed. For example, the Trade Practices (Consumer Product Information Standards) (Cosmetics) Regulations 1991 provide that an application may be made to the Administrative Appeals Tribunal for a review of a decision of the minister refusing to give permission under Regulation 7 on the labelling of ingredients. There may also be other administrative law reliefs available in respect of decisions by regulators.

3. Product liability

3.1 Potential defendants

Liability for defective or faulty products will ultimately depend upon the particular facts of each case, together with the cause of action relied upon by an injured person.

Under the Consumer Law, supply includes being in the business of sale, exchange, lease, hire or hire-purchase of goods, or the provision, granting or conferring of services. 'Manufacturer' is defined under the Consumer Law to include a person who grows, extracts, produces, processes, assembles or imports goods. Product liability may ultimately rest with any party in the supply chain, subject to the individual circumstances of each case.

3.2 Sources of liability

A person who claims to have suffered injury, loss or damage as a result of a product may be entitled to commence an action for compensation under statue, contract or tort. Claims may be brought concurrently under the different areas of law available to that person.

(a) ***Statute***

Parts 3–5 of the Consumer Law contain provisions on product liability. Under these provisions, consumers can seek compensation or damages for personal injury or other loss caused by a safety defect in products supplied by a manufacturer.

Manufacturers are liable to compensate an individual if the manufacturer supplies goods in trade or commerce, the goods have a safety defect and an individual suffers injuries because of the safety defect. The definition of 'manufacturer' under the Consumer Law is broad and can potentially include anyone in the supply chain. If two or more parties are liable for the same loss or damage, they are jointly and severally liable.

If, however, other suppliers, such as retailers, cannot identify the manufacturer or importer, they may be deemed liable for the damages under the Consumer Law. In these circumstances, the consumer can write to the supplier requesting details of the manufacturer. If the consumer and supplier cannot establish the identify of the manufacturer after 30 days, then the supplier is deemed to be the manufacturer.

The Consumer Law specifically states that, where a supplier has reported information to a minister under the mandatory reporting requirement, it is not to be taken as an admission of liability, nor is it to be taken as an admission that a consumer product or product-related service fails to comply with relevant safety standards. The Consumer Law also requires that reports are to be treated confidentially unless the reporter consents to the disclosure of the information, except where disclosure is in the public interest, required by law, or reasonably necessary for the enforcement of the criminal law or a pecuniary penalty.

There is also further legislation in force in each state/territory within Australia which governs the liability of manufacturers and suppliers. For example, in New South Wales, the Sale of Goods Act 1923[9] sets out certain liabilities of manufacturers and suppliers related to the sale of goods. This legislation operates in addition to the Consumer Law.

There may be some circumstances where claims arising from or in connection with product liability are covered by this further legislation. For example, certain provisions of the Consumer Law only apply to a 'consumer', as defined in Section 3, and certain claims by 'non-consumers' may be covered by the Sale of Goods Act 1923. Furthermore, implied contractual terms under the Sale of Goods Act 1923[10] can be excluded in a contract that is not a 'consumer sale'.

Where there is any inconsistency between Commonwealth and state/territory legislation, Commonwealth legislation will prevail.

(b) ***Tort***

The law of negligence was crystallised in the English House of Lords' decision of *Donoghue v Stevenson* [1932] and adopted into Australian law in the decision of *Grant*

---

9 The equivalent legislation in other states/territories is: the Victorian Goods Act 1958, Queensland Sale of Goods Act 1896, Western Australian Sale of Goods Act 1895, South Australian Sale of Goods Act 1895, Tasmanian Sale of Goods Act 1896, ACT Sale of Goods Act 1954 and Northern Territory Sale of Goods Act.

10 Sections 18, 19 and 20.

v Australian Knitting Mills [1936]. The law of negligence has since developed within Australia and imposes a duty of care on all people to take reasonable care to avoid foreseeable injury and loss or damage to another person where there is a relationship of proximity.

The issue of proximity is more complex and problematic where the claim is for pure economic loss rather than personal injury or damage to property. In a claim for pure economic loss, the reasonable foreseeability of a real risk of such loss occurring is not of itself sufficient to give rise to a duty of care. Australian courts have indicated that the concept of vulnerability is a relevant criterion for determining whether a duty of care exists in respect of a claim for pure economic loss: the plaintiff must be in a position of vulnerability compared with the defendant.[11]

In order to bring an action against a party within the supply chain for negligence, a plaintiff must prove that a duty of care was owed by the defendant to the plaintiff, the defendant breached that duty and the plaintiff sustained injury, loss and/or damage as a result of the breach. This will be an objective consideration. The plaintiff must prove each of the elements of negligence on the balance of probabilities.

Duty of care: A duty of care is the obligation on a person to exercise reasonable care in the conduct of certain actions. Liability in tort is not dependent upon a contractual relationship: there is a duty of care on people who are in a proximate relationship, such as a relationship between a manufacturer or supplier and potential consumer of goods. Policy considerations and the concept of vulnerability are also relevant.

All parties in the supply chain have an obligation to exercise due care and diligence in respect of their actions to ensure all products they manufacture or supply into the Australian market are safe and of merchantable quality. Manufacturers and suppliers owe a duty of care to take reasonable care to prevent foreseeable injury, loss or damage being caused to consumers, users and recipients of the products. The extent of the duty of care is proportionate to the potential risks involved. It is not an absolute duty to prevent any loss, injury or damage from occurring.

Breach of duty: A person will be found to have breached their duty of care if they do not act in a way in which a reasonable person in their position would be expected to act. In assessing whether a party has breached their common law duty of care, issues such as the magnitude of the risk, the probability or likelihood that the risk would eventuate, and the question of what actions have been taken to prevent the risks occurring, will be relevant.

Parties in the supply chain may reduce their exposure to a product liability action by utilising responsible business practices. These may include conducting regular reviews of product designs and production, implementing quality assurance procedures, conducting regular testing of products, reviewing and identifying

11 *Perre v Apand Pty Ltd* (1999) 198 CLR 180.

relevant standards, conducting appropriate marketing and, where necessary, conducting a voluntary recall of products that are defective or unsafe.

Under the common law, the injured person must establish the identify of the manufacturer or supplier of the product that was responsible for the defect.

(c) *Contract*

If a contract exists governing the supply of a product, a party to the contract may be held liable if another party to the contract suffers injury, loss or damage as a result of a breach of the contract. A breach of contract will generally occur where the product is faulty or not fit for the purpose for which it was sold. The question of whether there has been a breach of contract will depend on an interpretation of the contract, including any oral, written or implied terms. The terms of the contract will form the basis of any duties owed by the parties.

Liability under contract law will generally be limited to a party to the contract and there will often be no privity of contract between a manufacturer and consumer, meaning an action under contract law will often not be available to the consumer against the manufacturer. In respect of product liability, contracts will more commonly be between a supplier and a consumer. This has, however, largely been overcome by legislation creating 'strict liability' for manufacturers. Contract law may also be relevant in circumstances where manufacturers or suppliers have given specific warranties and guarantees in relation to particular products, which may give rise to contractual rights for the purchaser or consumer.

For the breaching party to be liable under contract law, the loss claimed must be caused by the breach and must not be too remote. The injured party must also reasonably mitigate (minimise/reduce) any damage suffered by the breach of contract.

Remedies available in respect of a breach of contract include damages, restitution, specific performance and injunction. Damages for breach of contract are viewed as a 'substitute' for performance and are designed to put the plaintiff in the position they would have been in had the contract been performed. Punitive damages are not available.

3.3 Claimants and class actions

Class actions in Australia have become more common in recent times, and that includes product liability class actions.

Class actions must be commenced in the Federal Court (Federal Court of Australia Act 1976 (Cth)). That act provides that where seven or more persons have claims against the same person, and the claims are in respect of, or arise out of, the same, similar or related circumstances, and the claims give rise to a substantial common issue of law or fact, a proceeding may be commenced by one or more of those persons as representing some or all of them. The representative person must describe the class of persons represented, but need not specify the name or number of persons represented.

Each state and territory within Australia has different requirements and procedures relating to class actions. For example, Victoria has enacted similar provisions to the Federal Court Act in Part 4A of its Supreme Court Act 1986 (Vic).

The Consumer Law also provides for representative actions by the ACCC. The Consumer Law states that the ACCC may commence a defective goods action on behalf of one or more persons who have suffered loss or damage in relation to which the action is commenced. The ACCC must, however, obtain written consent from each of the parties on whose behalf the application is being made.

Class actions within Australia have included actions against:

- *Kraft Peanut Butter:* following an incident in 1997 where more than 1,000 people suffered salmonella poisoning as a result of consuming contaminated peanut butter. This action was settled with Kraft agreeing to pay the claimants varying amounts depending on the seriousness of their illness;
- *Wallis Lake Oysters:* where a number of people were contaminated with hepatitis A after consuming oysters and were ultimately awarded compensation; and
- *Sydney Water:* in 1998 in relation to businesses that suffered financial loss as a result of contaminated water in Sydney and were compensated in relation to these losses.

3.4 Causation

For a claim under contract, negligence and some statutory provisions, the plaintiff has the burden of proving that the product was defective and the defect caused the injury, loss or damage. The claimant must, therefore, establish that loss, damage or injury has been suffered, that there was either a breach of duty of care, breach of contract or a breach of the relevant statute law, and that the breach caused the loss, damage or injury. In order for the causation element to be satisfied, there must be a sufficient causal link between the relevant conduct/breach and the injury, loss or damage suffered.

The test for causation that has largely been applied by Australian courts is a 'commonsense' test. Causation is, however, determined on a case-by-case basis, and the specific test for causation may vary. Tests for causation adopted within Australia include whether the negligence or breach was a necessary condition for the occurrence of the loss, injury or damage (factual causation) and whether it is appropriate for the scope of the person's liability to extend to the loss, injury or damage caused. An intervening act, such as the deliberate misuse of a product, may break the chain of causation, so that the negligence is no longer considered to be the cause of the injury, loss or damage.

Causation may be difficult to establish where scientific or technical evidence does not clearly demonstrate a causal connection between the product and the injury, especially with respect to pharmaceutical products.

Under the 'strict liability' provisions of the Consumer Law, including provisions relating to bans, safety standards and consumer guarantees, the claimant has to establish that the product was defective or failed to comply with the relevant standards but does not need to prove any intention or fault on the part of the supplier or manufacturer. In this sense, it is a 'strict liability' regime.

3.5 Failure to warn

Even if a product is not defective, it may be held that loss, injury or damage to a person was caused by a failure to warn or properly instruct. A manufacturer or supplier will not be held liable for a failure to warn, unless the failure was the cause of the loss, damage or injury, and it was not caused by some other act or omission, such as a deliberate misuse of the product. The question is whether the injured person would have had regard to the warnings or instructions if they had been provided whereby any such loss, damage or injury would have been prevented. The injured person will, therefore, need to establish that the loss, injury or damage would not have occurred if an adequate warning had been provided. Manufacturers and suppliers may also be required to comply with specific labelling or warning requirements under any applicable statute and may be liable if such warnings or labelling are not provided, especially in relation to products such as medicines, electrical/gas appliances and cosmetics.

3.6 Remedies for injury/damage and consequential loss

Any person who suffers loss, injury or damage as a result of a defective product may seek to recover compensation. There are no formal compensation schemes in relation to product liability in Australia.

(a) *Compensation*

Compensatory damages at common law are intended to place the injured person in a position that they would have been in had the tortious act or omission not occurred. At common law, an injured person may be entitled to general damages in respect of pain and suffering caused by the injury, together with damages in respect of lost income (past and future), medical expenses and other expenses incurred as a result of the injury, loss or damage suffered.

Damages in respect of a breach of contract are designed to place the plaintiff in the same position that they would have been in had the contract been performed.

The compensation available to claimants is often limited under statutory schemes. For example, the Civil Liability Act 2002 (NSW) applies to any claim for damages resulting from negligence and provides for maximum damages available in respect of certain heads of damages.

(b) *Pure economic loss*

Claims made for pure economic loss are distinguished from claims relating to personal injury or damage. At common law, the courts have indicated that the reasonable foreseeability of a risk of purely economic loss occurring may not, of itself, be sufficient to give rise to a duty of care to avoid such economic loss. Courts may also be reluctant to impose a duty of care to avoid pure economic loss where the consequences of such loss have expressly been provided for by way of contract between the parties.

Damages in negligence for pure economic loss caused by a product are, therefore, limited to certain circumstances. As noted above, damages will only be recoverable where there is a special relationship between the defendant and the plaintiff, such as the plaintiff being in a position of vulnerability. A person will generally not be able to recover damages for lost expectation or loss of anticipated profit, unless it can be proved that, but for the defective product or breach, the person would have taken some other course of action which would have resulted in the expectation occurring.

3.7 Procedure, limitation, funding, costs

Limitation periods apply to all causes of action in respect of product liability within Australia. There are, however, considerable variations between the limitation periods throughout the various jurisdictions.

The limitation period for personal injury actions is commonly three years from the date that the cause of action is discoverable or three years from the date the cause of action accrued.

The Consumer Law provides that a person may commence a defective goods action at any time within three years after the person became aware, or ought reasonably to have been aware, of the alleged loss or damage, the defect and the identity of the person who manufactured the goods. The Consumer Law also provides that a defective goods action must be commenced within ten years of the supply by the manufacturer.

Product liability claims commenced within the relevant limitation period may either be brought in the Federal Court of Australia or the state Supreme Court. Civil proceedings are generally tried by a judge without a jury.

Following court proceedings, a judge generally has the discretion to awards costs. As a general rule, costs follow the event which means the successful party may be entitled to payment of their legal costs by the unsuccessful party. Costs are generally awarded on a limited party/party basis, but full indemnity costs may be awarded in certain circumstances.

The Federal Court in Australia has also introduced pre-litigation requirements under the Civil Dispute Resolution Act 2011, which requires that 'people take genuine steps to resolve disputes before certain civil proceedings are instituted'.

3.8 Trends

With the introduction of the Consumer Law, there is a general trend towards conformity throughout Australia in relation to product law and product liability. Whilst such conformity is aimed at creating a consistent and unified approach to product safety, Australia still has a long way to go, given that it still has a myriad of standards, regulators and product safety provisions across different industries and within different jurisdictions in the country.

The Consumer Law does, however, point to a more uniform trend towards further vigilance by regulators in monitoring and enforcing product safety regulations and standards. This is reflected in the range of new enforcement powers for the ACCC and other regulators under the Consumer Law.

In respect of the liability of defendants in Australia, there is now proportionate liability where the liability of a wrongdoer, if there is more than one, is limited to an amount reflecting that proportion of the loss or damage which is considered to be just, having regard to the extent of that defendant's responsibility. Under proportionate liability, concurrent wrongdoers are not joint and severally liable but rather are liable for the proportion of the total damages awarded for which that wrongdoer is held liable. Proportionate liability does not apply to claims for personal injury.

In respect of product liability, there is a growing trend towards class (or representative) actions. This is particularly relevant for products which are accessible to a large class of consumer or user, as any defect may result in wide-ranging consequences for those consumers or users. Australian legislation currently reflects this growing recognition of class actions. For example, NSW has recently introduced a more comprehensive class action regime under the Civil Procedure Act 2005. This trend will have significant implications for the potential liability of manufacturers and suppliers and reinforces the importance of good business practices and procedures to ensure that only safe products enter the market.

4. Products insurance

In Australia, product liability risks are commonly covered under combined public and product liability insurance (often referred to as 'broadform' although increasingly, the different insurers in the Australian market adopt their own names such as 'commercial liability' or 'combined general liability' insurance). At the risk of over simplification, the public liability part of the insurance covers exposures whilst the product is being manufactured and the product liability part covers exposures after the product has been manufactured and, usually, after it has left the insured's premises or control.

Product recall cover for an insured's own recall expenses is usually a standard exclusion to the broadform wording but cover can be purchased and added by way of an endorsement or it can be in the form of a standalone policy. It tends to be expensive, with relatively significant excesses per occurrence. Nevertheless, it should at least be considered as part of an insurance programme and a costs/benefits analysis undertaken, particularly given the increasing number of recalls in the Australian market and the increasing vigilance of the Australian regulators.

It is also possible to purchase cover for an insured's exposure to third parties, such as retailers, who incur recall expenses. This is a liability exposure and, depending on the circumstances, it could even be covered under combined public and product liability insurance. It is important, therefore, to consider the scope of cover available under that broadform insurance in the context of possible loss scenarios and consider whether further protection is required.

Contaminated products insurance is becoming more readily available in Australia. It has been referred to as the 'new D&O'. The main reason for this may be the increasing trend in Australia for suppliers to be contractually required to obtain this kind of insurance.

Financial loss insurance (to cover an insured's liability to others for financial loss where products do not perform as contracted or as required by legislation) and product guarantee insurance (to cover the insured's recall expenses where products do not perform as contracted or as required under legislation) are rare in Australia. Product guarantee insurance is more common in the extended warranty areas for consumer goods.

There are no standard or prescribed wordings as such for the different kinds of cover in Australia. All are, however, governed by the Australian Insurance Contracts Act 1984 which is consumer-oriented. The act has a significant impact on insurer/insured relationships and how a policy wording can operate. For example, the act:

- imposes a continuing duty of utmost good faith as an implied term of the insurance contract;
- has provisions relating to unusual terms and the extent to which they can be relied upon;
- contains a provision (Section 54) which has a significant impact on the operation of insurance provisions (regardless of whether they are in the insuring clause or are a condition or an exclusion) that would otherwise have the effect of limiting or restricting cover – so classifying a provision as a condition precedent will not override Section 54; and
- prescribes and limits grounds for cancellation by an insurer (Section 60).

The ASIC is the regulator responsible for administering the act.

4.1 Product recall

(a) Insuring provisions

Generally, the policies discussed below are either 'occurrence-based' (where the personal injury or property damage occurs) or 'discovery-based' (where the insured discovers the possibility of personal injury/property damage). Some of the cover, especially the cover for third party recall expenses and financial loss, is 'claims made'. This means that there will be cover only if there has been a claim by the third party first against the insured during the policy period and notified to the insurer during the policy period.[12] A product recall policy covers the insured's recall expenditure as a result of actual or likely bodily injury or property damage because of a defect in the insured's goods.

There are significant variations in wordings and so, for example, one policy might define a defect as a 'harmful condition' in the goods and another might define it as 'an unintended error in manufacturing, production, processing, packaging or distribution of the product'.

The policies cover both 'actual' and 'likely' bodily injury or property damage. Again, the exact words used in the different policies vary. In relation to 'likely', a policy might refer to 'substantial likelihood of injury' or another might refer to a product that 'would if used result in injury'.

Generally, the policy will only provide cover where it is the insured's decision to recall and it will not cover recall expenditure incurred where the recall is mandated by a regulator (unless the insured would have made the decision in any event).

The policy cover is for the reasonable and necessary expenses incurred by the insured in recalling the product. These usually include advertising, additional staff

12 Section 54 of the Insurance Contracts Act 1984 can cure lack of notification by the insured during a policy period provided the insurer has suffered no prejudice.

costs and transport, storage and disposal costs. Other reasonable and necessary expenses can include fees paid to consultants and advisers leading up to the recall and during the recall, and the costs of experts incurred prior to the recall to determine scientific issues around whether a recall is necessary.

It is possible to get broader cover which also insures an insured's consequential financial loss[13] such as business interruption, brand rehabilitation and replacing or repairing/reworking of the product.

Product recall policies can also include cover for the insured's liability to third parties for the recall expenses of those third parties. It is possible that these recall expenses may be covered under the insured's standard public/product liability insurance and so it may be necessary to consider the extent of any overlap. However, as the standard public/product cover requires actual personal injury or property damage and does not cover likely personal injury or property damage, the extent of overlap may be minimal.

It would be unusual but these policies can also cover loss of profits of the third party (third party financial loss) if they are not otherwise covered under the standard public/product liability insurance.

Increasingly, we are seeing the emergence of contaminated products insurance. The main reason for this may be the increasing trend in Australia for suppliers to be contractually required to obtain this kind of insurance.

Contaminated products insurance covers actual or alleged tampering or contamination of products so as to render them unfit for use or consumption. Contaminated products insurance provides protection against:

- *accidental contamination:* covering accidental or unintentional contamination, impairment or mislabelling which has or would result in bodily injury, sickness, disease or death of any person, possibly within a particular number of days (usually 120) after consumption or use;
- *malicious product tampering by employees and third parties:* covering actual, alleged or threatened malicious contamination of product so as to render it unfit or dangerous for use or consumption, or to give such an impression to the public;
- *product extortion:* any threat to commit malicious tampering for the purpose of extorting money; and
- *government recall* as a result of actual or suspected contamination.

There are a variety of losses covered under contaminated products policies and including business interruption/loss of gross profits, replacement costs, recall costs, third party recall costs, consultant and adviser costs, rehabilitation expenses and costs incurred as a result of litigation directly resulting from product recall.

---

13 There still needs to be actual or likely bodily injury or property damage. Product guarantee insurance is the kind of cover that would respond to an insured's financial loss absent such damage or likely damage and financial loss insurance is the equivalent cover for a third party's financial loss.

(b) ***Exclusions***

There are many exclusions restricting cover available under product recall insurance, some of which are common to all insurance policies. If the policy is a simple products recall one, then there will be exclusions for the kind of cover you can expect will be provided under other policies such as contaminated products insurance and product guarantee insurance. Other exclusions will include exclusions for:

- liability to third parties (so it remains first party insurance for the insured and does not become liability insurance for an insured's exposures to third parties);
- losses where an insured had knowledge of the relevant defect before distribution or losses that occur after an insured gains knowledge of a defect and fails to take action which would have prevented the losses;
- intentional acts or breaches of safety regulations;
- misdirection or misdelivery by an insured;
- situations where the product is still in the insured's care, custody or control (including the care, custody or control of a parent company or subsidiary);
- personal injury or property damage (which should be covered under standard public/product liability insurance);
- fraud, dishonesty or illegality of the insured;
- fines and penalties;[14]
- aggregated, exemplary, multiple or punitive damages; and
- products that have been banned.

(c) ***Conditions***

There are many conditions that apply to the cover, some of which are standard to all insurance policies. Conditions include:

- a requirement for notification to the insurer as soon as possible of any possible claim;
- an obligation to take reasonable precautions or to do everything reasonably practicable to avoid a recall situation (pre-loss) or diminish its consequences (post-loss). Sometimes this can give rise to a dispute between the insurer and the insured about what might be reasonable and so it is important to seek input from the insurer or legal advisor, as appropriate; and
- in the case of liability policies, an obligation not to make any admissions in respect of the claim or possible claim or to settle one, without the insurer's consent.

Section 54 of the Insurance Contracts Act 1984 can cure breaches of conditions such as these unless the insurer can prove prejudice. There are also other provisions in that Act which could ameliorate or eliminate the effect of a breach.

14 It is possible to get certain limited penalties cover and/or defence costs cover under D&O or management liability policies. This might include penalties under the occupational health and safety legislation in Australia which has strict liability regimes for offences. Such penalties may have arisen from a product liability exposure.

Significantly, Section 133 of the Australian Consumer Law provides that the liability of an insurer under an insurance policy that relates to recall of consumer goods or liability for possible defects in consumer goods is not affected because the insured gives information relating to the consumer goods to a responsible minister, the relevant regulator, or certain government employees and officers/authorities – that is, it cannot be construed as an admission in respect of any claim or possible claim.

4.2 Product liability

(a) Insuring provisions

A typical product liability insuring provision is as follows:

> *Subject to all the provisions of this insurance, the insurer will pay damages that the insured is legally liable to pay for bodily injury or property damage that happens during the policy period within the territorial limits as a result of an occurrence in connection with the insured's business.*

The 'damages' the policy covers are intended to be compensatory in nature. The policy will not generally respond to punitive or exemplary damages or applications for declarations and injunctions.

Subject to any particular exclusions, the policy will cover the insured's 'legal liability' under the common law (contract or tort) and statute.

The concepts of 'bodily injury' and 'property damage' are usually defined within the policy.

Definitions in the insurance industry of 'bodily injury' are broad and varied. They usually include recognised medical conditions including nervous shock but can go further to cover humiliation and mental anguish. Problems can arise as to when bodily injury occurs. A notorious example here is in the asbestos area. Policies can include provisions that attempt to deal with these issues including in the case of latent injuries, when they are deemed to have first occurred.

The concept of 'property damage' has been the subject of a considerable amount of case law. One reason for this is the variety in definitions but a fairly common one is something like:

Property damage means:

- physical injury to tangible property, including resulting loss of use of such property; or
- loss of use of tangible property that is not physically injured, provided such loss of use is caused by a physical injury to other tangible property.

Sometimes, there is a requirement for the property damage to be 'sudden' or 'sudden and unintended', or for the damage to be the result of a 'sudden, specific, identifiable event'.

The concept of 'physical damage' has been held to include 'rendering useless' or interfering with the 'integrity' of the insured products. Examples are:

- a primer coat of paint was applied in too diluted a form to a 26-storey block of units and it failed to achieve adequate cohesion within itself and to the

walls. As a result, two other coats did not adhere properly and the paintwork began to flake off in many areas. The court held that the 'rendering useless' of the second and third coats of paint and the necessary stripping from the building constituted physical loss or damage to the building: *Graham Evans & Co Pty Ltd v Vanguard Insurance Ltd* (1986);[15]
- frozen scallops, while waiting to be loaded at a wharf in Melbourne for export to Canada, were found to be at a temperature outside the range required by the Exports (Fish) Regulations. They were rejected for export but were sold on the Australian market for less than if they been sold to the Canadian importer. The court found that, even though the scallops could be used within Australia, the change in temperature that they had experienced amounted to damage because an alteration in temperature involves a physical change to a substance; this change had the effect of removing one of the primary qualities of the scallops – their export ability; and as a result, their usefulness was impaired, their value was reduced and that fell within the concept of 'physical damage': *Ranicar v Royal Insurance Pty Ltd* (1983);
- during the course of certain excavation work, there was a rock fall which imperilled an existing building and necessitated its underpinning. Unless and until that was done, the area where the excavation was taking place was susceptible to further collapse and the court held that this in itself was damage to property because there was a disturbance of the 'physical integrity' of the excavation area: *Guardian Insurance Co Ltd v Underwood Constructions Pty Ltd* (1974).

In the typical insuring provision set out above, the reference is to damages 'for' bodily injury or property damage. Traditionally, 'for' has been considered to be narrower than a phrase like 'in respect of' or 'in connection with'. Traditionally, 'in connection with' has been considered to be the broadest concept. Recently, in *Zurich Insurance Limited v Regal Pearl Pty Ltd* (2006), the New South Wales Court of Appeal gave a very extended meaning to the word 'for' in a product liability context. The insured was an importer which had supplied prawns to a wholesaler. It was liable to the wholesaler for breach of implied conditions of merchantable quality and fitness for purpose and made a claim under its insurance policy. The insurer denied the claim on the basis that the insured's liability was not one to pay compensation 'for' bodily injury. The Court of Appeal upheld the insured's claim by effectively interpreting 'for' to be the same as 'in respect of'. The Court was influenced by the fact that the insured was a wholesaler and did not supply its products directly to the public. In such a setting, if cover were restricted to a narrow reading of 'for', then as a wholesaler, the insured would not receive any cover in the most likely circumstances in which it was exposed to risk.[16]

The precise definition of 'occurrence' (where that word is used in the insuring clause) can be very important for a number of reasons. For example, it can be

15 This and other cases mentioned below are considered to be leading authorities for the principles stated.
16 This case is also relevant for the meaning of a policy exclusion relating to contractual liability.

relevant to exclusion clauses for risks which happen over a period of time such as pollution and reasonable wear and tear. It can also be used to 'aggregate' limits of liability and excesses. In product liability insurance, there is usually an aggregate, or maximum/total, overall limit of liability per occurrence and only one excess is payable per occurrence or series of occurrences attributable to the one originating source or cause. In Australia in the 1970s, the High Court looked at such a provision in the context of the thalidomide drug and the personal injury it caused to unborn children. The High Court considered that the individual incidents of personal injury were attributable to the one originating source or cause (whether it was a remote cause such as the distribution of the drug or a more proximate cause such as the affects of the drug itself) and so, while there was only one excess payable, there was also only one limit of liability available to the insured: *Distillers Co (Biochemicals) (Aust) Pty Ltd v Ajax Insurance Company* (1973).

'Territorial limits' are usually to be found in the policy schedule or certificate and can be specific named jurisdictions or worldwide. In Australian policies, there are often standard exclusion clauses for claims made in North America or subject to the jurisdiction of courts in North America.

The requirement for the occurrence to be 'in connection with the business' is a broad concept and generally only limited by how the insured describes its business to the insurer when proposing for the insurance or how 'business' is defined in the policy.

(b) Exclusions

There are many exclusions restricting cover under product liability insurance, some of which are common to all insurance policies. The following are some of the major exclusions to consider.

Contractual liability: The liability that an insured has under contract is usually excluded unless the insured would have had that liability in the absence of the contract (or words to that effect). This type of exclusion will apply to guarantees and indemnities, if the insured would not have had the liability apart from the guarantee/indemnity. It is possible, however, to obtain cover for specific contracts disclosed to the insurer covered by endorsement. Some policies actually have a standard inclusion for indemnities that are given in the normal course of the insured's business or that are disclosed to and agreed to by the insurer.

In the *Zurich v Regal Pearl* case mentioned above, there was an exclusion for contractual liability. The NSW Court of Appeal held that the exclusion did not exclude every contractual liability. The court interpreted the commercial purpose of a product liability policy to be, absent any clear intention to the contrary, insurance to cover the range of obligations generally associated with product liability in Australian law, including the implied terms of merchantable quality and fitness. The court found no intention to the contrary in the policy in question.[17]

17 This case has limited precedent implications because of its particular facts but it does show a willingness to interpret insuring clauses broadly by reading insuring clauses together with other clauses in the policy and looking at the evident commercial purpose of the policy.

Efficacy: There is usually an exclusion in a product liability policy for the failure of products to perform according to the contractual requirements. For example:

The failure of any product to correctly fulfil its intended use or function and/or meet the level of performance, quality, fitness or durability warranted or represented by the insured.

The sorts of exposures which are excluded may be covered under a product guarantee policy (which is not really available in Australia – see below) but the exclusion may not operate as broadly as you would think, depending on the circumstances.

This happened in *Selected Seeds Pty Ltd v QBEMM Pty Ltd* (2010). The High Court held that the efficacy exclusion had to be read in the context of the policy as a whole including, significantly, the insuring clause itself. The court reasoned as follows. The insuring clause gave cover for legal liability in relation to property damage. An exclusion clause is designed to reduce, or detract from, that cover. In this case, which concerned the supply of the wrong type of seeds which became weeds and damaged crops and the farming land where the crops had been planted, the efficacy exclusion operated to exclude indemnity for what the seed failed to achieve, not for what it did to the land. In reaching its decision, the High Court had regard to the English decision of *Wyeth v Cigna* (2001) which had similarly limited an efficacy exclusion to only exclude cover for claims for failing to make a claimant better or prevent some condition arising, but not claims for causing or exacerbating existing conditions.

Deliberate acts: Policies will invariably exclude cover for expected or intended injury or damage (although there may be a 'write back' of cover where it is as a result of the need for reasonable force to protect persons or tangible property). The precise wording of this type of exclusion can be important because the exclusion may relate simply to the act or omission of the insured or it may go further and require that the injury or damage itself have been intended by the insured.

It is also a basic principle in insurance that an event must be associated with a 'fortuity' so that, for example, if there is an inherent vice in a particular product that makes the result inevitable, this will probably not be covered.

Design defects: An example of this exclusion is:

Claims arising directly or indirectly out of any defect or deficiency in goods sold or supplied after such goods have passed from the physical custody of the insured or of any person in the direct service of the insured.

Such an exclusion is considered to confine the operation of the particular product liability policy to a policy that gives protection against manufacturing defects. Exclusions are not always this broad. Sometimes, they give cover for design defects but exclude the cost of any redesign work or of carrying out the redesign work.

This exclusion might be extended or there may be another exclusion in the policy to cover 'defects reasonably suspected when a product passes from the physical custody of the insured'.

Repair, replacement and recall cost: These are generally excluded and there would need to be an endorsement adding the cover or a standalone policy for product recall.

Damage to the insured's products: It is a standard exclusion to exclude liability for property damage to the insured's own product or any part of it and also to property damage to any property owned by the insured. There can be write backs of cover for the property of others which is in the physical custody or legal control of the insured.

Professional services/advice: A common exclusion is in relation to the rendering of or failure to render any professional advice, service or instruction. The exclusion may not, however, exclude first aid or advice as to how to use the product in question.

(c) ***Conditions***

The conditions discussed above for product recall insurance also appear in product liability insurance. Other conditions relevant to consider are as follows.

Alteration to the risk: Most policies contain a condition requiring the insured to notify the insurer of any material alteration to the risk insured. In the product liability context, this can be relevant if an insured may have changed status in respect of its products by becoming a manufacturer where previously it may have been a distributor or where the nature of the products manufactured or supplied materially changes.

If there is an alteration to the risk (and it needs to be material), then the insurer may be able to charge a higher premium or cancel the policy. In Australia, an insurer's rights are limited under the Insurance Contracts Act 1984 (see in particular Sections 54 and 60(2)) but it is possible that if there is a failure to notify and a loss occurs which is relevant to the change in risk, then the insurer may have no liability in respect of the loss.

Reasonable precautions: Again, and as noted above, there is usually (if not always) a condition in a product liability insurance policy that an insured must take reasonable precautions. This clause is directed towards a pre-loss situation: ie, in the day-to-day operations of the insured, it must take reasonable precautions. (Conditions requiring the insured to minimise losses usually relate to post-loss situations: ie, where a loss has occurred and what the insured must do then.) In the product liability context, if the insured suspects a defect and does nothing about it, this would be in breach of the condition and would probably lead to the insurer declining indemnity. Potentially, a failure to recall a product known to be faulty would be in breach of this condition. Section 54 of the Insurance Contracts Act 1984 would need to be considered but if the breach is causative of the loss, the insurer will be able to decline indemnity.

4.3 Financial loss

Financial loss insurance covers a third party's[18] financial loss where the product does not perform as contracted or as required under legislation. It does not require personal injury or property damage.

---

18 The third party could be the customer or consumer.

This kind of cover is not readily available in the Australian market. There are one or two insurers who can provide it. If they do, then it is usually in conjunction with a broader product recall policy which might (but will not necessarily) also cover product guarantee (see below) or as an extension to their standard product liability wording.

Financial loss insurance will primarily cover a third party's loss of profits together with rehabilitation expenses and fees paid to consultants including public relations advisers. The period of cover may be limited.

Many of the standard conditions and exclusions discussed above would apply (although not the contractual liability exclusion).

4.4 Product guarantee

In Australia there is a kind of cover known as 'product guarantee insurance' but it is not readily available to manufacturers. It provides cover to the manufacturer or supplier for recall expenses where their products do not perform as contracted or as required under legislation. It does not require actual or likely bodily injury or property damage.

There is one scheme which relates to automotive parts but it is insured with a Lloyds syndicate in the UK. There are one or two other insurers who will consider writing it but because of the breadth of cover, it is difficult to obtain.

More common is insurance of extended warranties that are provided by manufacturers and suppliers to consumers in a consumer sale. With the recent changes to our Competition and Consumer Act 2010 (previously called the Trade Practices Act 1974) and the introduction of statutory guarantees,[19] these extended warranty programmes (and the insurance that backs them) have had to be reworked to ensure that they are providing cover which is in addition to the rights the consumer has already under the statutory guarantees.

19 Implied contractual warranties have been abolished but replaced with statutory guarantees. These statutory guarantees are discussed earlier in this chapter.

Brazil

Rosângela Delgado Barreto
Lívia Miné
Veirano Advogados

1. Product safety regulation

1.1 Regulatory authorities

The Brazilian government has the power to enact laws and regulations with specific safety standards for certain products (eg, products that may pose a risk to public health).

(a) *National Agency of Sanitary Surveillance*

The National Agency of Sanitary Surveillance (ANVISA) is the governmental body responsible for establishing regulations applicable to all kinds of products that are deemed to be relevant to public health and risk control. Products regulated by ANVISA include: medicines, food, beverages, packaging and labelling, additives, pesticides, cosmetics, personal hygiene products, perfumes, disinfectants, medical equipment, cigarettes and other tobacco products, and genetically modified foods. ANVISA is also responsible for inspecting, investigating and imposing sanctions where there are violations of if its regulations. ANVISA regulations set out specific provisions on prior approval for some products. Ordinance 27/2010 lists products which are exempt from registration and those which must be mandatorily registered. Examples of products that must be registered with ANVISA are children's foods, new technology, (recycled) packaging and novel food and ingredients.

(b) *National Institute of Metrology, Standardisation, and Industrial Quality*

The National Institute of Metrology, Standardisation, and Industrial Quality (INMETRO) is the regulatory body responsible for determining the rules applicable to industrial products and establishing procedures for certification. Some examples of products that must be certified by INMETRO are fire extinguishers, baby bottles, school supplies, steel wire, plastic cups, and bicycle parts. The National Council of Traffic (CONTRAN), along with INMETRO, sets out provisions relating to the certification of vehicle parts.

Other governmental bodies are responsible for enacting regulations applicable to other products. However, we have concentrated below on food, medicines and vehicles.

1.2 Regulatory framework

In Brazil, there is no general requirement for prior approval of products placed on the market. However, this is required in some cases where registration and certification are necessary before certain products may be put on the market.

Prior certification applies to a wide variety of products. There are safety standards for foods, beverages, medicines, cosmetics, and several industrialised products (eg, baby cribs, baby bottles, baby pacifiers, plugs, some types of plastic chair, some types of mattress, bicycle components, automobile components, disposable plastic cups, steel and other types of cables, helmets, some types of packaging, fire extinguishers, microwaves, some types of rubber products, some types of tank).

All parties in the production chain must respect the regulations, rules and standards laid down by the relevant governmental body for each type of product. The ANVISA legislation expressly states that the regulations apply to all aspects of production or manufacture, including premises, equipment, technology and procedures, across all phases and manufacturing processes.

Even if they are in conformity with the relevant governmental regulations, manufacturers must still ensure that their product does not pose any risks to consumers and is adequate for the purposes for which it was designed.

All products placed on the market must be safe (not pose any risk to consumers), except products which are inherently dangerous. Some products, such as medicines, drugs and cosmetics, require prior approval by relevant regulatory bodies. For these products, failure to comply with legal standards will mean the supplier will not obtain the proper pre-market authorisation. The regulatory bodies have powers to decide whether or not to issue the product registration. Only in rare cases would a court of law intervene in such a decision. In any event, registration or certification does not necessarily exempt suppliers from liability where a product is later found to be non-compliant with safety standards or to present other risks.

(a) Medicines

Federal Law 6,360/76, applicable to medicines, drugs, pharmaceutical raw materials, cosmetics, disinfectants and similar, sets out rules relating to contents/ingredients and pre-market registration with the Ministry of Health. This law is the most significant in this sector. In terms of registration, for example, it requires this group of products not only to comply with regulations relating to their content/ingredients, but requires the products also to be recognisably safe and effective based on scientific evidence. In addition, it is important that labelling and advertising could not mislead consumers. When registering a new product, ANVISA will require the manufacturer to present full information as to its composition, use, and indicate its safety and effectiveness. A product registration in this category will be cancelled if the manufacturer makes unauthorised changes in the medicinal product's formula, dosage, manufacturing conditions or usage instructions.

(b) Foods

ANVISA regulations contain many technical guidelines and definitions applicable to various types of food. ANVISA has specific regulations on sugar, salt, water, ice, vegetables, coconut, peanuts, candy, cookies, chocolate, coffee, tea, mushrooms, tomato sauce, jelly, flour, yeast, bread, fruit, fruit juice, soup, spices, vitamins, frozen food, foods with soy, diet foods, food supplements, pregnancy supplements, etc. Regulations enacted by ANVISA on these subjects set the maximum permissible content of certain ingredients, as well as other rules on the composition of such food products, and establishes labelling and packaging requirements. For example, ANVISA sets a limit on the quantity of chemical content allowed in mineral or natural waters.

Novel foods: ANVISA Ordinance 27/2010 determines that novel foods and their packaging must be registered and Ordinance 16/99 adds detailed specific technical regulations applicable to the registry of novel foods and/or ingredients. For example, the registration of a novel product must include information regarding the product's name, purpose, recommended use, scientific description, composition/contents and scientific evidence regarding the safety of the use of such products. When a novel food is marketed in the form of capsules, pills, or other pharmaceutical form, and there are no scientifically proven functional or health properties attributed to it, the packaging must state that there is no scientifically proven evidence that the novel food prevents, treats, or cures any disease.

Genetically modified foods: Law 11,105/2005 sets out the rules on safety and inspection procedures for activities that involve genetically-modified organisms. It defines 'genetically modified organisms' and related terms. It also establishes that businesses involved in activities that involve any GM products must request authorisation from the CTNBio to do so. It also prohibits certain activities (eg, destruction or disposal of genetically-modified organisms and derived products in the environment in breach of CTNBio regulations), and establishes certain obligations, such as notifying CTNBio as well as the health and agriculture authorities whenever there is an accident that may cause the dissemination of genetically-modified organisms and derived products.

Food enhancers and supplements: ANVISA Ordinance 31/98 sets out provisions on food enhanced with essential nutrients, such as maximum levels and labelling requirements. It also determines that essential nutrients used to enhance food products must be present in a concentration that is not excessive nor insignificant, considering the needs of the final consumer with respect to the essential nutrient.

Food contact materials, labelling: Several ANVISA ordinances deal specifically with different types of food contact materials (plastic, metal, glass). For example, Ordinance 130/2002 sets maximum levels of substances in packaging that may be in contact with food, and stipulates that packaging may not transfer to food any antibacterial constituents. There are also very specific ANVISA regulations on labelling.

(c) ***Motor vehicles***

There are several CONTRAN and INMETRO ordinances applicable to certification of specific vehicle parts such as tyres (INMETRO Ordinance 342/2008), window shields

(CONTRAN Ordinance 784/94) and motor parts, such as cylinders (INMETRO Ordinance 171/2002). In addition, CONTRAN sets out regulations for registration of vehicle motors.

(d) ***Electrical equipment***

INMETRO sets out provisions on electrical equipment, such as electrical plugs, electronic reactors, and appliances in general. For example, INMETRO Ordinance 136/2001 sets out that plugs and sockets for domestic use under certain specifications must be duly certified, in conformity with the technical regulations approved by the Brazilian Association of Technical Regulations (ABNT).

(e) ***Toys***

INMETRO sets out provisions on safety of toys and for other products destined for children, such as baby bottles, pacifiers, and baby cribs. INMETRO Ordinance 326/2007 establishes that toys manufactured and sold in the Brazil must be certified according to the MERCOSUR Technical Regulation rules.

(f) ***Cosmetics***

Law 6,360/76 is the most important regulation applicable to medicines, drugs, pharmaceutical raw materials, cosmetics, disinfectants, and similar products. For example, it provides that cosmetics must be registered and any modifications made in their formula must be approved by the Ministry of Health. ANVISA Ordinance 211/2005 is specifically applicable to cosmetics packaging, determining what information must be contained in the primary and secondary packaging, eg, name of product, expiry date, content, registration number, country of origin, warnings, composition and other details.

1.3 Occupational health and safety

The Labour Ministry sets out specific technical provisions on hazardous products and materials in the workplace. These technical provisions are essentially focused on the employment relationship and not on the manufacturer of a product. Ordinance 6 of the Ministry of Health provides that products sold and used for mandatory occupational safety and health purposes must be certified and carry an approval certificate, issued by the competent authority in the Ministry of Labor and Employment for safety and health in the workplace. The manufacturer of a product or equipment used in the workplace can be held liable for product defect.

2. Obligations of producers and distributors

2.1 Pre-market obligations

The same governmental bodies also regulate pre-market obligations on manufacturers for certain products.

(a) ***Standards markings***

Products that require mandatory certification will carry a marking (usually a label) affirming that the governmental body has certified the product. For instance, INMETRO determines that some products must carry a specific label in order to be commercialised: eg, water and gas heaters, centrifugal pumps and motor pumps, air conditioning installations, domestic stoves and ovens, domestic refrigerators, some types of light bulb, washing machines, and televisions.

(b) *Traceability and record keeping*

Traceability and record keeping is not mandatory but a recall procedure via mass media must be mandatory under Ordinance No. 487/2012 even if the supplier can trace consumers.

2.2 Post-market obligations

The Consumer Protection and Defence Department (DPDC) is part of the Department of Justice and is responsible for running recall procedures together with the Consumer Protection Foundations (PROCONs) and the competent normative or regulatory authority. Recalls must occur if a supplier learns that any product it placed on the market (not just products that are regulated by the above-mentioned governmental bodies) is found to pose unexpected risks to consumers.

Even if products are in conformity with the regulations, rules, requirements and specifications of those governmental bodies, manufacturers must in any case ensure products offered to consumers do not pose any risks to consumers and are adequate for the purposes they have been designed for.

The manufacturer must communicate to the appropriate governmental authorities and to consumers whenever it learns that a product it has placed onto the market poses a possible risk and proceed with a recall.

Federal Law 6,360/76 (applicable to medicines, drugs, pharmaceutical raw materials, cosmetics, disinfectants and similar products) first introduced the concept of recall in Brazil in 1976, imposing on manufacturers a duty to immediately remove from the market products that are not in compliance with defined standards and could pose any risk to consumers. Later, the Consumer Defence Code, enacted in 1990, provided for a more general concept of recall. The Consumer Defence Code extended the obligation to recall to any product or service that offers risks to consumers beyond those provided for by Federal Law 6,360/76.

(a) *Recall*

Based on Article 10, Section 1 of the Consumer Defence Code, the manufacturer is compelled to communicate to the appropriate governmental authorities and to consumers whenever it becomes aware that a product it has already placed on the market is unsafe. The law does not define what kind of risks would trigger the obligation to recall. It simply refers to the product being found unsafe. Such communication is to be made immediately as soon as the manufacturer learns about the hazard. The Consumer Defence Code determines that such communication must be carried out via mass media channels (press, newspapers, magazines, radio, television and the internet).

At the same time as communicating the risk to the authorities the manufacturer should also engage in a recall procedure, incurring all expenses related to the recall.

The official guidance for manufacturers as to the recall procedure (which includes communication to the proper authorities and to consumers) is Ordinance 487/2012. The ordinance, enacted by the Ministry of Justice, regulates the recall procedure for all products, setting out very specific rules which must be followed, governing, for example, how the recall should be publicised and what information must be released to the appropriate authorities and to consumers. The recall should be communicated to the DPDC, to PROCONs and to the competent normative or regulatory authority.

Ordinance 487/2012 determines that when informing the authorities about the recall, the manufacturer must provide the following information:

- identification of the manufacturer of the product subject to the recall, including the names of the company's representatives, with their respective designations;
- a detailed description of the defect detected, along with the necessary technical information about the product, such as brand, model, lot, series, registration number, initial and final date of manufacturing and product image;
- a detailed description of the risks posed to consumers as a result of use of the product;
- number of products placed on the market that might be unsafe, number of consumers subject to such risks and of consumers that will be affected by the recall;
- information on where among the Brazilian states the products are distributed and all countries to which the defective product was exported;
- date when the manufacturer became aware of the risk and details of how the risk came to light;
- measures taken or proposed by the manufacturer to solve the defect and to avoid the risks deriving from its use;
- detailed description of advertising campaign planned (media plan);
- detailed description of the customer service planned (customer service plan); and
- detailed description of notification to customers about the recall.

The media plan should contain information on:

- duration (ie, initial and final dates) of the recall campaign, although the law does not impose a time-limit;
- media channels to be used to announce the recall;
- scheduled time and the frequency of public notices, considering the need to reach the greatest number of people;
- model of the customer's warning of the risk which may include, besides radio, television and press ads, information released via the internet and electronic media, including an image of the product; and
- the costs of the advertising campaign (which can be marked as confidential).

The DPDC may always ask the manufacturer to present additional information with regards to the communication made to the relevant authorities and to be included in the media plan.

The communication to the competent authorities should also contain detailed information on any consumer accidents involving the recalled product, in cases of injuries to consumers' physical integrity, and detailed information on existing lawsuits relating to those accidents.

In addition to communication to the relevant authorities, Article 5 of Ordinance 487/2012 establishes that the supplier must immediately inform consumers about the dangers posed by the product by means of a warning. Paragraph 1 of that article determines that public notices should inform consumers about the defects in the product and the risks posed by the defects, as well as preventive and corrective measures that should be taken by consumers to avoid such risks. The supplier must also include contact details to enable consumers to have the product repaired, along with necessary information to identify the product (the same information referred to in the procedure for notifying the recall to the relevant authorities) and must expressly indicate that the recall will be free of charge to consumers.

The media campaign for notification of the recall to the public must be carried out in addition to individual notification to all affected consumers or of notification on the internet.

The supplier shall provide a certificate of customer service to any consumer involved in the recall, indicating the place, date, time and duration of the replacement service and measures adopted.

While communicating a recall to consumers, the manufacturer should present to the DPDC updated reports every 60 days. Manufacturers may also be required by the appropriate authorities to submit reports within a shorter timeframe. Such reports should include information on how many consumers were affected by the recall, the states in which such consumers are domiciled, and the number of products that have been effectively repaired or replaced during the recall.

As soon as the recall is over, the manufacturer will have to present a final report:

- stating the number and percentage of consumers affected, in total and in every state;
- presenting a justification for the percentage of products not repaired or replaced and the proposed further measures to be taken; and
- identifying the means by which consumers became aware of the manufacturer's warnings regarding the risk of accident.

After receiving the final report presented by the manufacturer, the DPDC will decide whether or not the recall is complete. The DPDC may extend or enlarge the recall if it deems the results unsatisfactory. Regardless of whether the recall is considered completed or not, the manufacturer will continue to be responsible for repairing or substituting the product.

(b) Criminal liability

A manufacturer may be held criminally liable for not carrying out a recall. It will face criminal charges if it becomes aware that a certain product that it has placed on the market offers risks to consumers and fails to:

- communicate this fact to the appropriate authorities and to consumers; and
- carry out a recall.

The possible penalty is imprisonment for a minimum term of six months rising to two years.

3. Enforcement

The Consumer Defence Code is a federal law and, as such, it is applicable to all Brazilian states. In addition, ANVISA, INMENTRO and CONTRAN are all federal governmental bodies, which means that they have the authority to enact regulations that are also applicable to all Brazilian states.

3.1 Powers of authorities

The Consumer Defence Code created specific authorities focused solely on inspecting commercial establishments and practices in order to:

- ensure consumer rules are being complied with;
- allow consumers to make complaints about suppliers' practices if abusive;
- settle consumer disputes; and
- impose administrative penalties on suppliers.

In this regard, the Consumer Defence Code created the DPDC and the PROCONs. These bodies are legally authorised to request information from suppliers, start an administrative procedure and impose penalties on suppliers (which may vary from fines to suspension of their commercial activities). Also, there are fully specialised Public Attorney Offices dedicated to consumer protection. Such bodies are very active in conducting preliminary investigations, which can lead to the filing of collective lawsuits. The ability to successfully negotiate with such authorities has proven to be an effective tool to prevent litigation.

As to governmental bodies, ANVISA has powers to access documents and facilities where services that may pose health-related risks are being rendered (industrial processes, manufacturing, production, commercialisation, distribution, storage, import, export or transport). ANVISA also has powers to collect samples, run inspections searching for infractions or risks, check for compliance with rules on health conditions and hygiene, issue notices of infractions, apply fines or issue interdictions.

3.2 International enforcement

There is no specific international enforcement treaty dealing with recall. There are, however, broader consumer-related initiatives. Brazil ratified a treaty in 2004, along with other countries belonging to the MERCOSUR, with respect to enforcement of consumer rights. This treaty emphasises the protection of tourists' consumer rights. In addition, Brazil has ratified another treaty with Argentina in 2005 to facilitate the cooperation of consumer rights authorities from both countries in exchanging information about piracy and counterfeit products, as well as compiling comparative data on the two countries' consumer protection laws.

3.3 Appeals

Proceeding with a recall is the manufacturer's duty and, as such, should be voluntary. However, if the DPDC learns that products placed on the market may pose any risk to consumers or are not fulfilling the purposes they were intended for, it may order a recall through an administrative procedure. Manufacturers would be entitled to appeal the DPDC decision to mandate the recall.

3.4 Sanctions and compensation

Penalties: Breaching regulations set by different governmental authorities may result in different penalties depending on the regulation and nature of the infraction. Penalties may vary from fines to seizure of goods or closure of businesses. Failure to proceed with a recall may result in criminal charges.

Compensation: Victims will always be entitled to compensation where injury has been suffered as a result of a product defect, regardless of whether the product has been recalled. The limitation period for actions is five years counting from the date the consumer learns of the injury and the identity of the party that caused it.

4. Product liability

Brazil has developed a protective legal system through which manufacturers, distributors, and retailers ('suppliers') are required to comply with strict product liability rules and may be held liable for damages or defects related to those products.

4.1 Potential defendants

The Consumer Defence Code defines as 'suppliers' all individuals or public or private entities, national or foreign, that develop activities related to manufacturing, setting up, creating, constructing, transforming, importing, exporting, distributing or commercialising products or rendering services. Liability may extend to all parties involved in the production chain of a product.

4.2 Sources of liability

(a) Statute

The complex set of rules applicable to consumer relations and product liability is comprised of the Federal Constitution, the Consumer Defence Code, the Civil Code, and a significant number of Ordinances issued by administrative bodies.

Before the enactment of the Consumer Defence Code in 1990, liability in consumer relations was governed by the general liability rules of the 1916 Civil Code. Based on such code, subjective liability (ie, fault-based) was the standard and, as such, fault was a legal requirement for liability.

The idea of strict liability in consumer relations was introduced with the enactment of the Consumer Defence Code in 1990 (in force from 1991). Strict liability is the current standard and it therefore does not require (or even analyse) fault. The mere occurrence of damages caused to a consumer as a result of a product defect is enough to give rise to the obligation to indemnify the victim.

The Consumer Defence Code represents a great milestone in the history of consumer protection in Brazil. The Consumer Defence Code has become one of the most popular statutes ever passed in Brazil and consumers are invoking its consumer protection provisions which are being enforced by the courts. The strict liability standard is probably the most significant innovation introduced by the Consumer Defence Code but other important innovations are judicial powers to shift the burden of proof in favour of consumers and to modify and declare null and void contractual provisions that are considered harmful to the consumer or abusive.

Duty of care and to inform: Suppliers are required to provide clear and proper information about the product, with specifications related to weight, characteristics, composition, quality, and price, and about the risks these products may present. The duty to inform is an essential right provided for in the Consumer Defence Code and is the basis for the legal relation between consumers and suppliers.

The Consumer Defence Code also forbids misleading and abusive advertising. Consumers are protected against misleading or abusive advertising, and in view of that, suppliers are liable for the advertisements made available to the public. 'Misleading advertising' is defined as false advertising that can lead consumers to error with respect to any features of the product. Advertising will be considered misleading not only where the supplier provides false information, but also in a failure to provide essential information. Abusive advertising includes advertising which incites violence, exploits fear or superstition, takes advantage of children's judgment limitations, disrespects environmental values, causes consumers to behave in a manner which is detrimental to their safety or health, or is discriminatory in any way.

Suppliers may even be required to carry out counter-advertising with the purpose of correcting abusive or misleading advertising it may have engaged in.

Defective products and liability for damages: The Consumer Defence Code defines what it means by a 'defective product' and situations under which the supplier will be held liable for damages caused to consumers as a result of a product defect.

A 'defective product' is one that does not meet the consumer's legitimate expectation considering its presentation, the risks usually expected from its use, and the circumstances in which the supplier has made such products available to consumers.

Suppliers may be held liable for quantity or quality defects (*vícios*) found in products even if these do not lead to the consumer suffering any damages.

The Consumer Defence Code determines that all suppliers of durable and non-durable products are jointly liable for defects of quantity or quality, which make the product inadequate for the purposes they are intended for or which reduce its value. Suppliers are also liable for defects deriving from disparities in the presentation of the product: ie, indications in its advertising, labelling or packaging, even if no damage or injury results from those disparities.

When the supplier places a product on the market, it is required to establish that the product is adequate for the purposes it is intended for. The Consumer Defence Code provides for statutory warranties which suppliers must supply to consumers for their products.

If the product is deemed defective, the supplier will be initially required to repair it within 30 days. If the supplier fails to fulfil this obligation, consumers have three possible alternatives. The may:

- ask for the replacement of the product for another of the same kind;
- receive a refund of the amount paid for the product (without waving the possibility of claiming an indemnification for damages suffered); or
- receive a discount on the price of the product proportional to the extent of the value decrease due to the defect.

Where only a part of the product is defective, the consumer may require the replacement of the defective part.

Suppliers, regardless of the existence of fault, will be held liable for the damage or injury caused to consumers for defects deriving from the design, manufacture, construction, assemblage, formula, appearance or packaging of products, as well as for providing insufficient or inadequate information about the product's use and its potential risks.

Suppliers can be held liable for damage or injuries under the Consumer Defence Code caused in the three following stages:

- where imperfections or mistakes arise in the product's *creation phase*, ie, defects of design or formula that make the product not as safe as one should expect;
- if imperfections or mistakes arise in its *development phase* (which covers manufacturing, consumption, assembling, manipulation and packaging); or
- where there is judged to be insufficient or inadequate information through advertisement or any other means of publicity in the product's *packaging or general appearance*.

Note that it is irrelevant whether or not the supplier has intentionally or negligently contributed to the product defect. The supplier is therefore prevented from alleging that it took all measures to avoid the defect. As long as the supplier has placed a defective product on the market, and there is direct and immediate causation between the damages suffered and the product defect, the supplier will be held liable for all damages caused to consumers.

Valid defence arguments to avoid liability for damages caused in consumer relations must refer either to the non-existence of a defect or the lack of causal connection between the defect and the damage alleged by the consumer. The applicable causation standard in Brazil is direct and immediate, which means a damage must result directly from the product defect. Consequently, the supplier should prove that the product the consumer claims to have caused damages was in perfect condition and presented no defect (again, the concept of defective product is not only related to the product's safety, but also to the legitimate expectations of consumers while using such product, which is related to the supplier's duty to inform).

Additionally, suppliers may also prove that:

- it did not place the product on the market
- the damages suffered by the consumer resulted from his/her – or from a third party's – exclusive fault (other parties in the production chain are not deemed 'third parties' for the purpose of this provision) or
- the damages suffered by the consumer were the result of force majeure.

(b) Contracts

Generally, the provisions foreseen in the applicable statutes and regulations govern consumer relationships in Brazil. Contractual arrangements are less common, except for warranties. The Consumer Defence Code allows the courts to nullify contractual clauses that are considered detrimental to the consumer and abusive and to review and adjust contractual provisions imposing disproportional obligations on consumers or that have become excessively onerous to consumers.

4.3 Class actions

Collective litigation is expressly provided for in the Consumer Defence Code and is becoming more frequent in recent years, especially for consumer protection cases.

The idea of a collective lawsuit was first introduced in Brazil in 1965 with the enactment of the Popular Lawsuit Act (Law 4,717/65). Popular lawsuits were not destined to protect consumer rights, as they could only be filed by members of the public to question any action that was believed to damage public property or that was against ethical principles. It was only in 1985 that consumers were able to pursue their rights through a collective lawsuit, based on the provisions contained in the Collective Lawsuits Act (Law 7,347/85). Differently from popular lawsuits, collective lawsuits aimed at protecting a more comprehensive range of public interests and collective rights, such as consumer rights and the right to a safe environment.

Pursuant to Law 4,717/65, public prosecutors, public defenders, the government, certain public entities and associations which have consumer protection as part of their remit have standing to file collective lawsuits in consumer litigation. Anyone with standing to sue may file a collective lawsuit by declaring themselves to be a representative of a class. In relation to plaintiff associations, they must have been created at least one year before the filing of the collective lawsuit. However, the law allows the courts in Brazil some flexibility to reduce this one-year time-limit in the public interest.

In 1991 the Consumer Defence Code introduced rules applicable to collective lawsuits in consumer litigation. Based on those rules, collective litigation would be the proper route for diffuse rights (pertaining to the public at large), collective rights (pertaining to a certain class), and homogeneous individual rights (pertaining to individuals that have suffered damages based on a common cause).

4.4 Causation

The applicable causation standard in Brazil is direct and immediate, which means that any damage must have resulted directly from the product defect.

4.5 Remedies

Damages are awarded to consumers who have suffered injuries or damage and consequential loss. Compensation will be measured by the judge on a case-by-case basis. Economic damages must correspond to the damage suffered by the individual, ie, the level of injury suffered by the consumer will define how high the compensation will be. As a general rule, the Brazilian courts will not award more than 200 times the minimum wage (corresponding to approximately $60,000) as moral damages. Punitive damages are not permissible under Brazilian law.

In addition to compensation, the Consumer Defence Code offers another remedy for consumers – statutory warranties: suppliers have an obligation to grant certain minimum warranties (statutory warranties) and also to grant additional warranties (contractual warranties).

The Consumer Defence Code provides for three different types of statutory warranties, which suppliers cannot be exempted from or attempt to limit.

The first type of statutory warranty refers to the supplier's guarantee that the product offered and sold to consumers is capable of fulfilling the purposes it has been designed and created for. Suppliers must ensure that consumers who purchase a certain product will be able to get results intended for that given product, according to the information provided by the supplier. This warranty will last for the estimated lifetime of the product.

The second type of statutory warranty is related to the repair, replacement or return of a defective product. This is so because the Consumer Defence Code holds suppliers responsible for the reliability of the product against defects. Thus, whenever a product presents a quality/quantity defect, the consumer has the right to request its correction.

The third statutory warranty allows consumers to return a product when the product was bought at a distance. Pursuant to the Consumer Defence Code, when a consumer purchases a product outside of the supplier's commercial establishment, especially by phone or online, it is possible to return it, provided that the return is requested within seven days counting from the purchase date or the day the product was actually received by the consumer. This statutory warranty does not require any product defect.

The consumer can request correction or repair of the product within time-limits which differ according to whether the defect is apparent or not, and on whether the product is durable or non-durable. If the product defect is apparent, the consumer will have 30 days counting from the date of receipt of the product or from the date the product is installed (non-durable products). The timeline is extended to 90 days for durable products. If the defect is not apparent, but is detected by the consumer only while using the product, the time-period for requesting the defect's correction (i.e 30 days for non-durable products; 90 days for durable products) will start running on the day the defect becomes apparent.

The Consumer Defence Code does not impose any time-limit for consumers to have the product in their possession before a hidden defect becomes apparent or how long after acquiring a product consumers will be able to request a supplier to correct a hidden defect. If the hidden defect becomes apparent during the estimated lifetime of the product, the consumer will be able to seek correction of the defect.

The supplier has a 30-day term to fix the product counting from the date the consumer makes a complaint. The Consumer Defence Code allows parties to negotiate this term, provided that it is never shorter than seven days or longer than 180 days. If the defect is not corrected within the term established by the Consumer Defence Code or negotiated by the parties within the legal limits, consumers can choose, at their own discretion, between three options, namely:

- replacement of the defective product by a new one of the same kind;
- refund of the amount paid for the defective product, with interest, and without excluding any potential indemnification for damages suffered as a result of the defective product; or
- a discount on the price of the defective product proportional to the extent of the value decrease due to the defect.

The Consumer Defence Code allows consumers and suppliers to agree on additional contractual warranties. Contractual warranties are complementary to statutory warranties and, as such, cannot be shorter than the corresponding statutory warranties provided for in the Consumer Defence Code. However, contractual warranties that are longer than the statutory ones will be binding on the supplier.

Suppliers must grant contractual warranties to consumers in a written agreement. Additionally, the Consumer Defence Code provides that contractual warranties must be standardised and clear with respect to what kind of guarantee is being given to the consumer. Therefore, the agreement through which the contractual warranty is being granted must contain information about:

- the guarantee;
- how consumers can invoke it;
- the time limits and jurisdictions within which it may be invoked; and
- any costs that will be incurred by the consumer in invoking it.

When granting a contractual warranty, the supplier must provide a written agreement with the above information and also an instruction manual for installing and using the product, written in clear and consumer-friendly language, along with pictures to help the consumer understand the instructions.

4.6 Procedure, limitation, funding, costs

Litigation in Brazil is generally not costly and is based on the general right of access to justice. Therefore, any party who can prove that they have no means of paying judicial costs are exempt from judicial costs. In collective litigation, plaintiffs are not required to advance payment of court fees, expert fees or any other expense related to the class action (Article 18 of Law 7,347/85).

4.7 Trends

The Consumer Defence Code has brought many important innovations to liability rules in consumer relations and is still viewed as providing an effective consumer protection system. However, an amendment to the Consumer Defence Code is being considered. Among the proposed modifications are:

- the possibility of the judiciary power or the public administration being empowered to declare ex officio violations to consumer laws; and
- a provision stating that the law that is most favourable to consumer must be applied.

The amendment is expected to be enacted within the next two years.

As the Brazilian class lawsuit system is relatively new and not yet fully developed, we may see further developments there also: a Collective Lawsuits Code may possibly be enacted in the near future, as well as a bill for the amendment of the existing Code of Civil Procedure to include provisions on collective litigation and a bill on amendments to the existing collective litigation provisions in the Consumer Defence Code. This is likely to increase the number of collective consumer lawsuits taken in Brazil.

5. Product insurance

Insurance is subject to stringent regulation in Brazil. All insurance contracts must be in accordance with the regulations set by the National Council of Private Insurance (CNSP) and Brazilian Superintendence of Private Insurance (SUSEP). The former is an inter-ministerial body which establishes the main policies on private insurance and reinsurance activities whereas the latter is an executive agency which implements and further regulates CNSP policies.

A few product insurance lines are available on the Brazilian market. Except for product guarantee insurance, they are usually offered as an accessory coverage to general civil liability insurance policies for commercial or industrial establishments. Automotive, pharmaceutical, food, electronic and machinery are the main sectors seeking product insurance coverage in Brazil.

Like in many other jurisdictions, the law on insurance is very insured-friendly. Since insurance policies are largely standardised and typically drafted by the insurers, allowing no or very little room for modification by the insured, they fall within the broad category of contracts called 'adhesion contracts'. The Brazilian Civil Code expressly establishes that "when there are ambiguous or contradictory clauses in adhesion contracts, an interpretation shall be adopted more favourable to the adherent." This means that the Brazilian legal system adopts the contra proferentem doctrine as a fundamental rule of construction of insurance policies, which, in practice, may compel courts to construe exclusions narrowly and to construe insurance police clauses establishing the risks being covered broadly.

Brazilian law has always required insurers and insured parties to abide by the principle of utmost good faith not only throughout the duration of the insurance contract, but also, if not above all, prior to its execution, given that the insurer will generally rely on information unilaterally provided by the insured when assessing the specific risk involved and rating the premium to be charged.

5.1 Product liability

General product liability coverage is offered in Brazil as a subset of special conditions that may be contracted by a product manufacturer attached to a general civil liability insurance policy.

The policy is framed on an 'all-risks' basis and usually provides coverage for losses resulting from accidents caused by defects in those products specifically contemplated in the policy and either manufactured, sold and/or distributed by the policyholder. An example of such a clause would be as follows:

Covered Risks

1.1 It is considered to be a covered risk the civil liability of the insured characterised in the form of clause 1 of the general conditions, and resulting from accidents caused by defects in the products specified in this contract, and manufactured, sold and/or distributed by it [ie, the insured].

General Conditions of General Civil Liability Insurance

I – Scope of the Insurance

1. Scope of the Insurance

This insurance aims to reimburse the Insured, up to a maximum insured amount, for the quantities it comes to be liable through a court order which becomes res judicata or through a settlement duly authorised by the Insurer, in connection with compensations for unintended physical or economic damages caused to third parties, taking place during the enforcement period of this contract and which result from risks covered in the Special Conditions and Particular Conditions, which are an integral part of this policy.

Typically, product liability policies are structured on a 'per occurrence' basis. Also, such policies usually include a provision that losses resulting from products originated from a single defective manufacturing process or affected inadequate storage conditions, shall be considered one occurrence only, regardless of the number of claimants.

The most common exclusions on coverage which are specific to product liability insurance are that of:

- illegal products;
- distribution or sale beyond the product's shelf life;
- expenses related to partial or total replacement of the product, as well as its removal from the market (eg, recall);
- use of the product as an aircraft component;
- use of the product in sports tournaments;
- experimental products, including transgenic products;
- losses resulting from inadequate advertising, wrongful information, warnings or recommendations on the part of the insured, his/her/its partners, agents or employees;
- losses resulting from genetic modifications caused by the use of the product;
- the product being unfit for the use expected from it; but physical injuries and property damage resulting from the accidents caused by the defective product will be covered; and
- pollution, contaminants or leakage, unless caused by a sudden and

unexpected event commenced at a clearly defined date and with a maximum time period of 72 hours.

5.2 Product recall[1]

Although product recalls are becoming more common, product recall insurance is still not as common in Brazil as it is in other countries, especially in North America and Europe.

In order to contract product recall coverage the insured is required to have a plan for implementation of recalls, full information on the product design and list of customers, as well as complete data on past losses related to the risks to be covered under the policy, regardless of whether the insured has ever contracted to have product recall insurance or not.

Coverage extends through the product's lifespan, which will usually be between two and five years.

Product recall insurance can provide for either first party or third party cover. In the former case, the insurance covers losses and expenses suffered by the insured party, who will be the supplier of the defective product and the party responsible for instigating the recall. In the former insurance, coverage extends to third parties. This would be the case, for instance, if an automobile company determines a recall even though the insured party is actually the supplier of a defective part subcontracted by the automobile company.

Typically products recall insurance has been marketed as 'specified-risk' ('named perils') coverage. The main risk covered includes the recall of products found to pose risks to health or an economic risk to the public resulting from a defect or a negligent contamination caused by the policyholder. Among other risks covered are the costs and expenses of communicating the recall to the public in mass media channels (TV, newspapers, etc.), and may also include contacting customers in person, by letter or phone calls. Transportation/removal costs of recalled products are covered, as well as costs for storing, repairing and destroying them. Costs of disassembling and reassembling recalled products are not usually covered, but coverage for such risks may be available in specific situations. Coverage may also include hiring marketing experts to diminish the harmful effect that the recall will cause to the insured's brand reputation.

Experimental products and products which are still undergoing tests are always excluded from coverage. Another common exclusion relates to products which fall short of the technical standards expected given the state of the scientific knowledge at the time the product is marketed.

Because of the high value of expenses incurred in a product recall and covered by a product recall insurance policy, policyholders will be required to share part of the loss with the insurer.

---

1 This section has been based on the analysis of insurance policies and on the legal literature available in Brazil, especially in the articles authored by Walter Polido, *"Retirada de produtos do mercado : Products Recall"*, published in Seguros & Riscos Review, January 2000, 42–48, and by Alvaro Igrejas, *"Product recall – você conhece este seguro?"* published in *Caderno do Seguro*, 2002, 71 73.

5.3 Product guarantee

Product guarantee insurance has been widely marketed in Brazil. Such insurance is regulated by the CNSP Ordinance 122/2005 and by the SUSEP Circular 366/2008.

Product guarantee insurance extends or supplements the warranty attached to the product by operation of law. Warranty extension under such policy shall become effective upon expiration of the mandatory warranty provided for by law. Supplementary warranties, when covered by the policy, become effective much earlier, as they operate in parallel with the mandatory warranty provided for by law.

Typically, this line of insurance is purchased by the consumer (ie, the policyholder) at the point of sale of the consumer product via the supplier of the product. Under the Brazilian legal framework, coverage under a product guarantee policy can be of three types, namely:

- original – contemplating, compulsorily, the same coverage provided for by the supplier of the product under the legal warranty;
- expanded original – contemplating, compulsorily, the same coverage provided for by the supplier of the product under the legal warranty, but also including additional risks, unless such additional risks would suggest other specific lines of insurance; and
- differentiated – contemplating coverage that (i) does not match all risks covered by the supplier of the product under the legal warranty; and (ii) does not suggest other specific lines of insurance.

The specific type of coverage must be expressly indicated in the policy, as well as in the offer and advertising materials relating to the product guarantee policy.

In terms of remedies, the product guarantee policy may oblige the insurer to:

- compensate the insured with the equivalent price of the product;
- repair the defective product; or
- replace it with a similar product.

Canada

Louis P Brien
Paul A Melançon
Lapointe Rosenstein Marchand Melançon LLP
David Kyffin
Canadian Department of Foreign Affairs and International Trade
Emma Lambert
Irving Mitchell Kalichman

Occupying the northern half of the continent of North America, Canada has a unique legal and political system. Two major elements of this system have a particular impact on the fields of product recall, liability and insurance: Canada's federal nature and its cultural, linguistic and legal duality.

Canada is organised as a federation of 10 provinces united in a federal government. Provincial jurisdiction includes property and private law, which covers the areas of product liability and insurance. Canada's 10 provinces have for historical reasons been divided into two groups: a first group of nine majority English-speaking provinces with similar systems of British-inspired common law (the common law provinces) and, secondly, the province of Quebec, a majority French-speaking province making up a quarter of Canada's population with a distinct civil law tradition. Legal differences between both groups will be highlighted wherever relevant. In addition, the federal government has some general powers which have been interpreted to include public health and safety, notably in the field of product recall.

1. Product safety regulation

1.1 Product risks

Canada's product recall legislation has recently been reshaped with the adoption of the Canada Consumer Product Safety Act,[1] which came into force in June 2011 and replaced the previous Hazardous Product Act.[2] The new Act modernises the regulation of product risk by granting Health Canada, the federal ministry charged with public health, sweeping powers to issue mandatory product recalls and require product safety tests, powers similar to those already existing under the Canadian Food Inspection Agency Act[3] in the area of food. Application of the Canada Consumer Product Safety Act is restricted to products usually obtained by an individual for non-commercial purposes and applies to them the general criterion of the "danger for human health and safety", and applies to an existing or potential hazard posed by a product during its normal use and which can cause death or have an adverse effect on the individual's health in the short or long term. Specific risks

1 SC 2010, c 21.
2 RSC, 1985, c H-3.
3 SC 1997, c 6.

relating to particular classes of products, such as candles (risk of spontaneous re-ignition), children's jewellery (lead content) and especially toys, are further dealt with in regulations.

Risks associated with other types of products are covered by particular laws such as the Food and Drugs Act[4] (food, drugs, cosmetics, medical devices, etc.), the Motor Vehicle Safety Act[5] (eg, tyres and car seats) and the Criminal Code[6] (firearms and ammunition), among others.

Health Canada is the federal department charged with administering the Canada Consumer Product Safety Act and the Food and Drugs Act, among other laws, whereas Transport Canada is charged with administering the Motor Vehicle Safety Act. Both organisations have a full range of powers at their disposal to enforce compliance, including the ability to inspect, investigate and impose administrative and penal sanctions.

1.2 Safety standards

Under the Canada Consumer Product Safety Act as well as under the Hazardous Products Act which preceded it, the federal government has the power to adopt regulations which contain more specific safety standards for particular types of products. For examples, regulations regarding ice hockey helmets and face protectors as well as children's playpens each refer to standards set out by the Canadian Standards Association (the CSA).

However, unlike in some other jurisdictions, in Canadian law, conformity with a required technical standard does not give rise to any presumption of conformity with the general safety standard, although conformity with the former remains a relevant element of fact.

1.3 Prior approval

(a) Medicines, foods, vehicles

Health Canada reviews and assesses all drug products before they are authorised for sale in Canada. This includes any product intended to treat or prevent disease, including prescription and non-prescription pharmaceuticals, disinfectants and sanitizers with disinfectant claims. Manufacturers must provide scientific evidence of the safety, efficacy and quality of these products. On the other hand, food is not subject to a generalised pre-approval process, although food imports and some domestically-produced foods are subject to inspection.

As for vehicles, pursuant to the Motor Vehicle Act, conformity with technical standards is based on a "self-certification" system whereby manufacturers certify that every class of motor vehicle or vehicle part meets the Motor Vehicle Safety Regulation applicable. In addition, despite the "self-certification" system, Transport Canada's Motor Vehicle Test Center undertakes sporadic investigations to ensure

4 RSC, 1985, c F-27.
5 SC 1993, c 16.
6 RSC, 1985, c C-46.

compliance. It further possesses the power to impose administrative procedures to compel manufacturers to bring vehicles or vehicle parts into conformity with applicable Canadian standards and requirements.

(b) ***Other sectors***

There is no generalised requirement of prior approval or testing on all consumer products. However, when regulations impose specific technical standards, Health Canada does perform tests. Some consumer products are independently tested by the CSA for conformity with its own standards, which are referred to in regulations with respect of a number of products. Additionally, under the Canada Consumer Product Safety Act, Health Canada can order a manufacturer or importer to have tests performed in order to verify compliance or prevent non-compliance.[7] Health Canada inspectors have a wide range of powers to verify compliance or prevent non-compliance of products that are not yet on the market. They may, for example, enter a facility at any reasonable time, in which they have reasonable grounds to believe that a consumer product is manufactured, imported, packaged, stored, advertised, sold, labelled, tested or transported. In practice, these procedures can either be initiated as part of a periodical or random inspection process or following a complaint made by a member of the public.[8]

1.4 Safety issues

Health Canada is charged with consumer product oversight as an aspect of public health and safety. Transport Canada plays a similar role with respect to motor vehicles, while the Canadian Food Inspection Agency (the CFIA) is tasked with the specific oversight of food. Also relevant are the independent non-profit standards and testing groups, mainly the CSA and Institute for Safe Medication Practices Canada (ISMP Canada) for medication safety.

All parties in the product distribution chain are obligated to respect any technical specifications which may be required by law and more generally to produce a product which is not a danger to consumers. Additional technical and scientific requirements can exist and are particularly numerous in the area of food and drugs. Actors are furthermore required to cooperate with Health Canada for the purpose of inspections and respect any order for testing, recall or other measures. A major change under the Canada Consumer Product Safety Act is the requirement that manufacturers report to Health Canada any incident with respect to their product.

1.5 Types of corrective action

Under the Canada Consumer Product Safety Act, Health Canada has a wide variety of corrective actions at their disposal, up to and including inspection, seizure of goods, ordering tests, issuing public advisories, and ordering measures which can include stopping production, withdrawal from the market and ultimately recall. The CFIA has a similar range of powers available with respect to food, as does Transport

7 Section 12 of the Canada Consumer Product Safety Act.
8 Section 21 of the Canada Consumer Product Safety Act.

Canada with respect to motor vehicles, although in the latter case there is no power to order recalls or other proactive measures.

1.6 Criminal liability

In addition to each law's quasi-criminal provisions, which provide for fines and prison terms of up to three years, Canada's Criminal Code[9] contains the offence of criminal negligence and allows prison terms rising to 10 years when the negligence causes bodily harm to a person.

2. Obligations of producers and distributors

2.1 Sources of duties

(a) Statute

Obligations are created with respect to product safety and recall in several federal statutes, most notably the Consumer Products Safety Act, the Food and Drug Act and the Motor Vehicle Safety Act.

(b) Tort

An obligation to effect a recall can exist in either the common law provinces or Quebec; in the former, a manufacturer's liability may arise as part of the general duty to warn, and in Quebec, as a necessary step to invoke the defence of the state of knowledge at the time of manufacture.

(c) Contract

No distinct obligation with respect to product safety or recall is created in either the common law provinces or Quebec other than as it arises under the general product liability regime for contracts.

2.2 Pre-market obligations

(a) Standards markings

The 'CSA' mark is broadly equivalent to the European CE marking insofar as it indicates a certain level of pre-tested product safety. It is not required for all products – only for those few for which a CSA standard has been integrated into the regulatory framework by way of reference.

(b) Traceability and record keeping

The Canada Consumer Product Safety Act requires that manufacturers, importers, advertisers, vendors and testers of consumer products maintain records that identify the names and addresses of the persons from whom they obtained the products. They must also document to whom the consumer products were sold, although retailers only have to note where and when the product was sold. These records must

---

9 RSC, c C-46.

be kept for at least six years and Health Canada must be granted access to them on request.

(c) ***Consumer protection laws***

All Canadian provinces have adopted consumer protection legislation. However, due to Canadian federalism, these acts mostly pertain to the rights and obligations between consumers and sellers, examined in the second part of this chapter. Provincial consumer protection laws have little impact on product recall.

(d) ***Food safety***

Foods: The Food and Drugs Act and regulations made under it contain a developed system of rules governing the preparation and sale of food. This includes general sanitary requirements, such as that the food be free of poison and harmful substances, be fit for human consumption, not be rotten or adulterated by an agricultural chemical or veterinary drug and be prepared and stored in sanitary conditions. Additional requirements with respect to food labelling must be respected. Finally, the Food and Drug Regulations contain many specific technical guidelines and definitions applicable to various types of food. Additional norms exist in several other federal laws, such as the Canada Agricultural Products Act, the Feeds Act, the Fertilizers Act, the Fish Inspection Act, the Health of Animals Act and the Meat Inspection Act.

Novel foods and genetically modified foods: Under Sections B.28.001 to B.28.003 of the Food and Drug Regulations, novel foods, including genetically modified foods, must go through a Health Canada approvals process.

Food enhancers and supplements: Under Sections B.24.200 to B.24.306 of the Food and Drug Regulations, meal replacements, dietary supplements and other such types of foods are subject to requirements as to their nutritional content as well as labelling requirements. Separate Natural Health Products Regulations also exist.

Food contact materials, labelling: Under Sections B.01.401 to B.01.467 of the Food and Drug Regulations, most food is subject to defined nutritional labelling requirements. Food contact materials are not dealt with in any specific way.

(e) ***Medicines***

Part C of the Food and Drug Regulations contains many technical standards and definitions applicable to different drugs, which must of course be respected. The regulations also cover new drugs, experimental studies and clinical trials. It should be noted that a licence is required to manufacture, package, distribute, import or wholesale a drug.

(f) ***Motor vehicles***

Motor vehicles are subject to a complete safety regime, expressed mainly as exhaustive technical standards laid out in Schedule IV to the Motor Vehicle Safety Regulations and verified by Transport Canada's Motor Vehicle Test Centre.

(g) *Electrical equipment*

A broad range of technical standards have been developed by the CSA with respect to many types of consumer, commercial and industrial electrical products. However, these have not generally been adopted at the federal level, as is the case for other products such as hockey helmets and children's toys. Certain of these electrical standards may be integrated into provincial legislation in building codes and the like.

(h) *Toys*

The Toys Regulations adopted under the Canada Consumer Product Safety Act contain many technical requirements applicable to all toys, notably with respect to packaging and electrical, auditory and toxicological hazards, as well as some more specific requirements for different varieties of toys such as plush toys and rattles.

(i) *Cosmetics*

The Cosmetic Regulations of the Food and Drugs Act lay out the various safety, labelling and technical requirements applicable to cosmetics.

(j) *Occupational health and safety*

Labour is a shared jurisdiction under the Canadian federal structure. In general, provincial and federal occupational safety and health laws address the dangers of hazardous products and materials in the workplace to ensure that employees can work safely. However, these are essentially focused on the relationship between employer and employee and not manufacturer and seller.

2.3 Post-market obligations

Unlike the former Hazardous Products Act regime, the Canada Consumer Product Safety Act commands that manufacturers, importers and vendors report 'incidents' involving a consumer product to Health Canada within two days and provide all the information in their control regarding the incident.[10] Such incidents include occurrences which caused or could have caused death or injury; situations where a dangerous defect is noticed; situations where an incorrect, insufficient or nonexistent label creates a risk of death or injury; and situations where another domestic or foreign public body initiates a recall.[11] When the reporting party is a manufacturer or an importer who imports goods manufactured outside Canada, it must submit a detailed written report within 10 days, unless otherwise specified by Health Canada.[12] The report must state general information about the incident, the nature of the product involved, any other product that may be manufactured or

---

10 Section 14(2) of the Canada Consumer Product Safety Act.
11 Section 14(1) of the Canada Consumer Product Safety Act.
12 Section 14(3) of the Canada Consumer Product Safety Act.

imported into Canada that to their knowledge could be involved in a similar incident and any measures that they propose be taken with respect to the products.[13] Health Canada provides a form to that effect on their website.[14] A similar form also exists for consumers who have been victims of an incident.

Other post-market obligations include cooperating with Health Canada inspections of locations where a consumer product is manufactured or stored, including giving access to locations, documents and computer systems; on order from Health Canada, conducting tests or studies, compiling information or providing documents which will allow Health Canada to verify compliance; and complying with any recall or other orders.[15]

(a) *Food*

Under the Food and Drugs Act and its regulations, after a food product is brought to market, the manufacturer and seller have a number of obligations including fully cooperating with Health Canada inspections,[16] providing information on demand[17] and respecting a recall order should one be issued.[18] The Canadian Food Inspection Agency also requires that producers notify it when it is suspected that products which pose a serious risk to consumers have been sold, distributed or imported.

(b) *Pharmaceuticals*

The Food and Drug Regulations set up a mandatory reporting regime under which serious adverse drug reactions and unusual failures in the efficacy of new drugs must be reported to Health Canada within 15 days.[19] An annual report covering the same topics and summarising the incidents over the course of the year must also be produced. Prescribed information must be submitted to Health Canada in the event of a manufacturer recall, including the various scientific, common and brand names, quantities sold, distributed and produced and the reason for the recall.[20] In addition, manufacturers must on an annual basis confirm the same information regarding their drug and cooperate with inspections and document requests from Health Canada.[21]

(c) *Motor vehicles*

In addition to the record-keeping requirements already mentioned, manufacturers, sellers and importers of vehicles are required to notify Transport Canada, the other parties in the chain of distribution, and the current owner of the vehicle when a defect is identified.[22] A report must be produced thereafter within 60 days regarding

13 Section 14(3) of the Canada Consumer Product Safety Act.
14 www.hc-sc gc ca/cps-spc/advisories-avis/incident/cpir-ricpc-i-eng.php
15 Section 21of the Canada Consumer Product Safety Act.
16 Section 23 of the Food and Drugs Act.
17 Section 23(3) of the Food and Drug Regulations.
18 Section 19 of the Canadian Food Inspection Agency Act.
19 Section C.01A.013 of the Food and Drug Regulations.
20 Section C.01.018 of the Food and Drug Regulations.
21 Section C.01.014.5 of the Food and Drug Regulations.
22 Section 10 of the Motor Vehicle Safety Act.

the defect and how it is to be remedied.[23] Full cooperation with Transport Canada inspectors is also an obligation under the Motor Vehicle Safety Act.[24]

3. Enforcement

3.1 Sector organisations

(a) General consumer products

Under the Canada Consumer Product Safety Act, Health Canada is the federal department responsible for regulating consumer product safety.

(b) Food

The Canadian Food Inspection Agency is responsible under the Food Inspection Agency Act,[25] for the administration and enforcement of a number of food-related federal statutes, including among many others the Feeds Act, the Fertilizers Act, the Fish Inspection Act and the Health of Animals Act, as well as the Food and Drugs Act as it relates to food.

(c) Motor vehicles

Under the Motor Vehicle Safety Act, Transport Canada is the federal department responsible for regulating motor vehicle safety.

(d) Medicines

As with general consumer products, Health Canada enforces all regulations and standards with respect to medicines.

3.2 Powers of authorities

(a) General consumer products

The Canada Consumer Product Safety Act affords Health Canada a spectrum of powers in order to ensure compliance with the legislation. At the lower end of the scale, Health Canada can name inspectors who can enter private property, test anything that is found, collect samples, seize articles, search computers and gather information.[26] Health Canada can additionally order a manufacturer or importer to conduct tests or studies, compile information or provide access to documents.[27]

If necessary to address a serious danger to human health or safety, Health Canada may disclose personal information, confidential business information or any other information to the public or foreign governments, all without the interested party's consent.[28]

---

23 Section 15 of the Motor Vehicle Safety Regulation.
24 Section 16 of the Motor Vehicle Safety Act.
25 SC 1997, c 6.
26 Section 21 of the Canada Consumer Product Safety Act .
27 Section 12 of the Canada Consumer Product Safety Act.
28 Section 15 of the Canada Consumer Product Safety Act.

Further up the scale, if Health Canada believes a consumer product poses a danger to human health or safety, it has broad powers to order measures to address the issue and restore compliance.[29] These include ordering the parties in the chain of distribution to halt production and sale, and ultimately ordering a mandatory recall of the product.[30] Full scientific certainty with respect to the danger is not a requirement for action under the Canada Consumer Product Safety Act.

Finally, should a manufacturer, importer or vendor refuse to comply with an order for a recall or other corrective measure, Health Canada may proceed to carry out the order at the expense of the recalcitrant party.[31] Injunctions may also be taken to prevent a person from doing something which constitutes an offence under the Canada Consumer Product Safety Act.[32]

(b) ***Food***

The Food and Drugs Act provides for the naming of inspectors with the same wide-ranging powers detailed above with respect to consumer products.[33] In addition, under section 19 of the Canadian Food Inspection Agency Act, where the Canadian Food Inspection Agency believes on reasonable grounds that a regulated product poses a risk to public, animal or plant health, it may order that the product be recalled.

(c) ***Motor vehicles***

Transport Canada can name automotive inspectors with the usual wide-ranging powers to ensure that the prescribed standards are being respected.[34] However, although Transport Canada monitors manufacturer-initiated recalls, it does not have the ability under current legislation to force a recall of motor vehicles.

(d) ***Drugs***

The Food and Drugs Act provides for the naming of inspectors with the usual wide-ranging powers to ensure compliance with the act.[35] Although current legislation does not provide for government-initiated recall of drugs, Health Canada does have the power to suspend and eventually cancel a drug identification number[36] or the establishment licence[37] of a party who does not respect prescribed standard or requirements. Other powers include the ability to issue warning letters and public advisories, to order a halt to the sale of a drug and to seize products or inspect facilities which do not respect the law. Penal sanctions are also available.[38]

---

29 Paragraph 32(1)(2) of the Canada Consumer Product Safety Act.
30 Section 31 of the Canada Consumer Product Safety Act.
31 Section 40 of the Canada Consumer Product Safety Act.
32 Section 36 of the Canada Consumer Product Safety Act.
33 Sections 22 and 23 of the Food and Drugs Act.
34 Section 14 and 15 of the Motor Vehicle Safety Act.
35 Sections 22 of the Food and Drugs Act.
36 Section C.01.014.6 of the Food and Drug Regulations.
37 Sections C.01A.016. to C.01A.018.1 of the Food and Drug Regulations.
38 Sections 31 and 31.1 of the Food and Drugs Act.

3.3 International enforcement

Although a member of the International Consumer Product Safety Caucus, Canada does not belong to any kind of international enforcement system similar to the Rapid Alert System for Food and Feed or Rapid Exchange of Information System in the European Union. However, as covered at 3.6, it is open to taking cues from developments in other countries with respect to product safety.

3.4 Appeals

The Canada Consumer Product Safety Act provides a procedure for the review of recall orders and orders for measures.[39] A written request for review must be submitted to Health Canada stating the grounds for review and setting out the supporting evidence and the desired decision.[40] This request must be made within seven days after the issuance of the order, or within a shorter period specified in the order if there exists a serious and imminent danger to human health or safety.[41] Frivolous, vexatious or bad faith requests may be summarily rejected.[42] Also, Health Canada may itself initiate a review.[43]

Once requested, the review must be carried out within the 30 days; however, this time period may be extended.[44] The review process can lead to confirmation, amendment, termination or cancellation of the order.[45] The party affected by the order is immediately notified in writing of the decision.[46]

Judicial review is available to persons that wish to contest administrative decisions in the court system, but a relatively non-interventionist criterion of 'reasonableness' will be applied to the government's decision.

3.5 Sanctions and compensation

(a) Penalties

General consumer products: The Canada Consumer Product Safety Act divides breaches of its product safety regime into two categories: offences and violations. Offences are breaches of the provisions of the Canada Consumer Product Safety Act itself and may lead to fines of up to C$5,000,000 or a prison term of up to two years, but only after penal proceedings in court.[47] Offenders may invoke the defence of due diligence, unless they acted knowingly or recklessly.[48] In sentencing, courts may consider the harm or risk of harm caused by the offence and the vulnerability of the affected consumer product users.[49] Moreover, directors, officers, agents and

---

39 Sections 34 and 35 of the Canada Consumer Product Safety Act.
40 Section 35(2) of the Canada Consumer Product Safety Act.
41 Section 35(2) of the Canada Consumer Product Safety Act.
42 Section 35(3) of the Canada Consumer Product Safety Act.
43 Section 35(5) of the Canada Consumer Product Safety Act.
44 Sections 35(6) and (7) of the Canada Consumer Product Safety Act.
45 Section 35(10) of the Canada Consumer Product Safety Act.
46 Section 35(11) of the Canada Consumer Product Safety Act.
47 Section 41(1) of the Canada Consumer Product Safety Act.
48 Section 41(2) of the Canada Consumer Product Safety Act.
49 Section 41(4) of the Canada Consumer Product Safety Act.

mandataries may be prosecuted for contravening the act if they participated in some way in the commission of the offence, even when the company itself was not.[50]

A 'violation' is defined as a breach of a recall order or other order for measures.[51] The penalty associated with such violation is an administrative monetary penalty, which does not require court proceedings. The amount of these penalties is meant to be set in regulations, an operation which has not yet been carried out, although the law caps them at C$25,000.[52] A defendant may not invoke against an administrative monetary penalty the defence that they exercised due diligence to prevent the violation or that they reasonably and honestly believed in the existence of facts that, if true, would exonerate them. Health Canada will take a view, based on the balance of probabilities, whether the defendant committed a violation.

Food and drugs: Offences under the Food and Drugs Act are punishable by fines of up to C$5,000 and prison terms of up to three years, although the fine rises to C$250,000 if the offence relates to food.[53] Contravening a food recall order under the Canadian Food Inspection Agency Act is punishable by a fine of up to C$50,000 and up to six months' imprisonment.[54]

Motor vehicles: Offences under the Motor Vehicle Safety Act are punishable by fines of up to C$10,000 for individuals and C$1,000,000 for corporations, with individuals being additionally liable to a prison term of up to two years.[55]

(b) Compensation

Canadian product safety law does not provide for statutory compensation of victims except in very specific instances, such as for some health products (vaccines and HIV or Hepatitis C-adulterated blood). Some provinces also provide for compensation for bodily injury resulting from motor vehicle accidents.[56]

3.6 Multiple jurisdictions

Broadly speaking, Canada constitutes a single jurisdiction for the purposes of product recall legislation, although in some very specific areas provincial regulators may have some concurrent powers. Canadian law is generally open to influence from the global community in this area. Under the Canada Consumer Product Safety Act, recalls and similar measures taken by foreign governments are considered incidents which must be reported to Health Canada. Likewise, under the Motor Vehicle Safety Act, vehicles certified by foreign regulators under equivalent standards are deemed in compliance with Canadian standards.

---

50 Section 42 of the Canada Consumer Product Safety Act.
51 Section 49 of the Canada Consumer Product Safety Act.
52 Section 50(2) of the Canada Consumer Product Safety Act.
53 Section 31(1) of the Canada Consumer Product Safety Act.
54 Section 19(2) of the Canadian Food Inspection Agency Act.
55 Section 17 of the Motor Vehicle Safety Act.
56 See eg, Erik S Knutsen, "Auto Insurance as Social Contract: Solving Automobile Insurance Coverage Disputes Through a Public Regulatory Framework" [2011] 18 Alta L Rev 715.

4. Product liability

4.1 Potential defendants

In general, liability may extend to all parties involved in the chain of distribution of a product. Thus, defendants in a product liability case in Canada may include manufacturers, sub-manufacturers, suppliers, designers, retailers and packagers. The same rule applies in Quebec under Articles 1468 and 1730 of the Civil Code of Quebec[57] (the Civil Code or CCQ), applicable to extra-contractual and contractual liability respectively, which specifically cite manufacturers, sellers, wholesalers, retailers and importers.

4.2 Sources of liability

(a) Statute

Common law provinces: Every common law province in Canada has enacted sale of goods legislation that codifies the implied warranties of reasonable fitness and merchantability developed by the common law. Also, in some provinces the warranty of durability for a reasonable time is also included. Moreover, in most of the provinces, implied warranties cannot be excluded in a consumer sale. A typical example is the Sale of Goods Act[58] of Ontario, Canada's most populous province.

Quebec: In addition to the rules laid out in its Civil Code, Quebec legislation included a Consumer Protection Act[59] which applies to relationships involving natural persons contracting for non-commercial purposes. This Act reproduces in large part the substantive rights already afforded by the Civil Code and examined more closely below, with certain additions, such as the obligation that replacement parts and a repair service be made available for a reasonable time after the contract. Its major innovation is to allow consumers to seek a number of remedies concurrently with a claim for damages, including among others specific performance, authorisation to perform at the merchant's expense and reduction of the consumer's obligations. Consumers are in addition allowed to claim punitive damages, which in Quebec are not usually available to litigants. Another relevant statute is the Quebec Charter of the French Language,[60] a cultural, French-language protection act which requires among other things that directions and warranty certificates be drafted in French.

(b) Tort

Common law provinces: The product liability law of the common law provinces has its roots in both British and American law. Since the seminal British House of Lords case of *Donoghue v Stevenson*,[61] it is accepted that all persons should take

---

57 RSQ 1991, c 64.
58 RSQ 1990, c S.1.
59 RSQ, c P-40.1.
60 RSQ, c C-11.

reasonable care to avoid acts or omissions where one could reasonably foresee one would be likely to injure another person. Thus, the House of Lords broadened the scope of the duty of care from immediate purchasers to include foreseeable third parties. In doing so, the court outlined the importance of reasonableness and foreseeability, which constitute key considerations in modern negligence law, as laid out below. In Canadian law, a defective product will give rise to the following three chief causes of action in tort: negligent design of a product, negligent manufacture of a product and negligent failure to warn. In practice, product liability claims often invoke more than one of these causes of action.

There is no regime of strict liability in tort in Canadian product liability law. An individual's or company's liability is predicated on fault. Thus, based on a balance of probabilities, a plaintiff has the evidentiary burden to establish that:

- the defendant owed a duty of care to the plaintiff;
- the defendant breached the applicable standard of care;
- the plaintiff suffered damages as a result;
- that there was a causal link between the plaintiff's damages and the defendant's breach; and
- the damages in question were not too remote.

Duty of care: Based on the Donoghue decision, the existence of a duty of care is predicated on a sufficient proximity between plaintiff and defendant: was the harm that occurred a reasonably foreseeable consequence of the defendant's act? Case law has determined that with regard to product liability, a duty of care amounts to a duty to take all reasonable steps necessary in the design, manufacture, distribution, advertising and sale of products in order to protect the public from health and safety risks.

Breach of duty: Since the case of *Bolton v Stone,*[62] the applicable standard of care has been recognised as being that of a reasonable person under like circumstances. Among the relevant circumstances are the risk involved and the likelihood of harm that could result. In the context of product liability, in determining whether a product was sufficiently safe, producers have a duty to turn their mind to the inherent and foreseeable risk of injury created by the nature of the product and to exert due diligence in trying to minimise the risk associated with such product before making it available to consumers for its intended use. A defendant will have been deemed to have breached the standard of care if he knew or ought to have known about the nature and extent of the danger associated with the use or foreseeable misuses of the product by the public. In the specific context of product liability, failure to abide by regulatory standards may inform the analysis of this standard. The standard of care in question has been adopted by Canadian case law, particularly with regard to negligent manufacturing, design and warning.

First, liability for negligent manufacturing of a product occurs when a product designed to be free of defects leaves the manufacturing plant with a defect,

61 [1932] A.C 562 (HL).
62 [1951] AC 850, [1951] 1 All ER 1078.

unbeknown to the manufacturer. Though such cases are rare because of the obvious challenges to leading evidence to that effect, the early case of *Donoghue v Stevenson*[63] remains a clear example of a claim based on such grounds. *Daishowa-Marubeni International Ltd v Toshiba International*[64] is another recent example. There, the plaintiff was an operator of a pulp mill whose generator stopped working.[65] The court was asked to consider whether Siemens' negligent manufacture of the switchgear caused the fingers on the secondary disconnect device of the generator to become bent, which in turn caused an electric failure in the plant.[66] The plaintiffs were able to show, based on the balance of probabilities, that Siemens had been negligent in manufacturing its switchgear because the placement of the secondary disconnect device did not meet its own design standards.[67]

Second, negligent design of a product is a well-established principle in Canadian case law. This type of action involves an analysis different from that used to determine negligent manufacturing because the plaintiff has to demonstrate that the design was not reasonably safe as the risk of harm was foreseeable and it was feasible to design the product in a safer manner.[68] This duty has been applied to a wide range of manufactured products. For example, the case *Gallant v Beitz*[69] touched upon the issue of adequate design required to minimise the harm caused when vehicles are engaged in accidents.[70] It was found that a manufacturer could be found liable under Canadian tort law where the design of a vehicle resulted in a vehicle not being "reasonably crashworthy".[71] In this regard, Justice Linden held:

> *Since motor vehicle manufacturers know, or should know, that many of their vehicles will be involved in collisions and that many people will be injured in those crashes, they must turn their minds to this matter during the process of planning the designs of their vehicles and they must employ reasonable efforts to reduce any risk to life and limb that may be inherent in the design of their products.*[72]

Similarly, Justice Granger, in *Rentway Canada Ltd v Laidlaw Transport Ltd*, applied criteria such as these to determine that a headline electrical circuit in a transport truck had a design defect:

> *(1) the utility of the product to the public as a whole and to the individual user;*
> *(2) the nature of the product – that is, the likelihood that it will cause injury;*
> *(3) the availability of a safer design that would have prevented the injury;*
> *(4) the potential for designing and manufacturing the product so that it is safer but remains functional and reasonably priced; and*
> *(5) the manufacturer's ability to spread any costs related to improving the safety of design.*[73]

---

63 *Donoghue*, n. 61.
64 [2010] AJ 1128 (ABQB).
65 *Ibid.*, at 57–61.
66 *Ibid.*
67 *Ibid.*
68 *Rentway Canada Ltd v Laidlaw Transport Ltd* (1989) 49 CCLT 150 (Ont. HC), *affd* [1994] OJ 50 (QL.), *per* Granger J.
69 [1983], 42 OR (2d) 86 (HC).
70 *Ibid.*
71 *Ibid.*
72 *Ibid.*
73 *Rentway*, above note 69.

This analysis was further applied in *Mayburry v Ontario (Liquor Control Board)*.[74] In that case, the plaintiff bought a bottle of Bacardi from the Ontario Liquor Control Board, who sustains a monopoly on the sale of alcohol in the province of Ontario. The bottle slipped off a table and shattered, causing a serious eye injury to the plaintiff. The court found Bacardi liable on the basis that "the risks to the consumer far outweighed the efforts made by the manufacturer to reduce that risk".[75] Indeed, evidence showed that the risk of serious injury from flying glass fragments was foreseeable. This was a "risk factor" no matter what caused a bottle to break and consumers should not assume total responsibility for injuries resulting from it. According to the court, Bacardi knew that a safer system was reasonable and necessary and was both affordable and available. The court ruled that Ontario Liquor Control Board could not be held liable since it had nothing to do with the defective design. However, the court found that the plaintiff's negligence in handling the bottle had contributed to the fault, and, thus, held the manufacturer liable for only 40% of the damages.

Third, in situations where the manufacturing of a product may be safe for its intended use, inadequate labelling of the product may result in extra-contractual liability. Members of the chain of distribution have a positive duty to warn consumers of the inherent and non-obvious dangers associated with the product's foreseeable use, whether learned before or after sale,[76] through adequate labelling, packaging, and other forms of communication.[77] This principle was enunciated by Justice Laskin (as he then was), for a majority of the Supreme Court of Canada, in *Lambert v Lastoplex Chemicals Co.*[78] In finding Lastoplex liable for putting a dangerous product onto the market without providing a sufficient warning with regards to the level of danger entailed by the ordinary use of the product, he stated:

> *Manufacturers owe a duty to consumers of their products to see that there are no defects in manufacture which are likely to give rise to injury in the ordinary course of use. Their duty does not, however, end if the product, although suitable for the purpose for which it is manufactured and marketed, is at the same time dangerous to use; and if they are aware of its dangerous character they cannot, without more, pass the risk of injury to the consumer.*[79]

Furthermore, Laskin stated that such warnings had to be clear and specific in proportion with the level of danger involved. In that case, the plaintiff purchased the defendant's fast-drying lacquer. Before commencing its use, he read the manufacture's three warnings and, to comply with them, turned down the thermostat to prevent the furnace from turning on. Nevertheless, a fire and explosion occurred apparently because the pilot light had been left on. The

74 [2001] OJ 1494 (Ont. HC), *aff'd* [2002] 163 OAC 192 (Ont CA), [*Mayburry*]; see also *Tabrizi v Whallon Machine Inc*, [1996] BCJ 1212.

75 *Ibid.*, at ¶169.

76 See *Rivtow Marine Ltd v Washington Iron Works*, [1974] SCR 1189, at 1200, per Ritchie J.

77 See *Setrakov Construction Ltd v Winder's Storage & Distributors Ltd* (1981), 11 Sask R 286 (CA); *Meilleur v UNI-Crete Canada Ltd* (1985), 32 CCLT 126 (Ont HC); *McCain Foods Ltd v Grand Falls Industries Ltd* (1991), 116 NBR (2d) 22 (CA).

78 [1972] SCR 569, at 574.

79 *Ibid.*

manufacturer had provided no warning in that regard. Commenting upon this omission, Justice Laskin said:

Where manufactured products are put on the market for ultimate purchase and use by the general public and carry danger (in this case, by reason of high inflammability), although put to the use for which they are intended, the manufacturer, knowing of their hazardous nature, has a duty to specify the attendant dangers, which it must be taken to appreciate in a detail not known to the ordinary consumer or user. A general warning, as for example, that the product is inflammable, will not suffice where the likelihood of fire may be increased according to the surroundings in which it may reasonably be expected that the product will be used. The required explicitness of the warning will, of course, vary with the danger likely to be encountered in the ordinary use of the product.[80]

More recently, the Supreme Court of Canada applied this reasoning to the duty to warn with regards to medical products. Indeed, in *Hollis v Dow Corning Corp*,[81] the court was asked to consider whether a manufacturer of silicone breast implants could be held liable in tort to a patient who suffered injuries from an unexplained rupture in the implants when the manufacturer had failed to give adequate warning to the patient or the surgeon concerning the risks of rupture. Justice La Forest, for a majority of the court, reiterated Laskin's reasoning in Lambert and further stated:

Given the intimate relationship between medical products and the consumer's body, and the resulting risk created to the consumer, there will almost always be a heavy onus on manufacturers of medical products to provide clear, complete and current information concerning the dangers inherent in the ordinary use of their product.

In sum, manufacturers have a duty to take reasonable care in the manufacture of their products, they must choose a design that is reasonable in the circumstances and, even when held to meet the standard of care in the manufacture and design of a product, they have a separate duty to give clear and specific warnings in proportion to the level of danger involved in the use of their products. Failing to do so would result in a breach of the duty of care.

Defences: In demonstrating diligence, one can raise traditional common law defences to either demonstrate that there was no duty of care, and if there was a duty, that there was no breach, or if there was a breach, that there was no (or only partial) causation between the breach and the injury sustained. In the specific context of product liability cases, a "no breach of duty defence" may take the particularised form of alleging that:

- alternatives were not available or acceptable;
- there was compliance with regulatory standards (while this has not traditionally been a defence, it may nevertheless serve as evidence of what is a reasonable standard of care);
- the product was 'state of the art' and the defendant met the reasonable limits of science and technology when it manufactured its product; or
- the product was unavoidably unsafe, but the societal benefits it offered outweighed the risks.

---

80 *Ibid*, at p 575.
81 [1995] 4 SCR 634.

With regards to the 'no or partial causation' defence, a defendant may plead:

- the plaintiff's voluntary assumption of risk, where the defendant contends that the defect did not cause the injury since the plaintiff was aware of the danger and chose to accept the risk (however, courts are not likely to apply this defence unless it is clear that the plaintiff did appreciate the nature and severity of the risk);
- misuse or alteration of product;
- obvious and apparent danger to the plaintiff; or
- that a learned intermediary intervened, where a manufacturer proves that it directed a warning about the product's risk to a skilled person or learned intermediary who would normally relay this information to the consumer.

Finally, where applicable, it will always be open to a defendant to plead that a particular claim is bared by the statute of limitations.

Injury and damage: Once a breach of duty has been established, it is incumbent upon the plaintiff to establish that he has suffered injuries and that the injury was caused by the breach in question. The general test used to show a causal connection is the common law 'but for' test, which characterises as causal all events without which a particular injury would not have resulted. However, in a recent case by the Supreme Court of Canada, the law of causation was extended so that in some exceptional circumstances, where the 'but for' test could not or did not apply, a plaintiff could use a different test in order to prove causation. This test is referred to as the 'material contribution' test.

The 'but for' test has generally been applied to cases of product liability.[82] For example, in *More v Bauer Nike Hockey Inc*,[83] the plaintiff sued Bauer Nike and the CSA for damages arising after suffering a hockey injury.[84] He claimed that Bauer Nike breached its duty to warn him of the dangers that may be incurred when playing hockey wearing their helmets.[85] He further claimed that the CSA was negligent in failing to set the safety requirements for helmets to more rigorous standards.[86] In his reasoning, the trial judge first stated that Bauer Nike did not have to use the safest design available so long as the design was reasonable in the circumstances.[87] He then considered that the helmet in question was successfully tested to a more rigorous standard than those established by the CSA.[88] Thus, the plaintiff failed to established that 'but for' the alleged breach, the injury and alleged losses would not have happened.[89]

Another example is *Daishowa-Marubeni International Ltd v Toshiba International, HA Simons Ltd, and Siemens Electric Limited Corp*.[90] After concluding that the

82 [1990] 2 SCR 311.
83 [2010] BCJ 1954, *aff'd* [2011] 2011 BCCA 419.
84 *Ibid.*
85 *Ibid.*
86 *Ibid.*
87 *Ibid.*
88 *Ibid.*
89 *Ibid.*
90 [2010] AJ No 1128.

defendant Siemens had been negligent in the manufacturing of a switchgear, the trial judge concluded that 'but for' Siemens negligence, the damage to the plaintiff's generator which in turn resulted in irreparable damage to the plaintiff's mill would not have occurred.[91]

However, when factors outside the plaintiff's control make it impossible for the 'but for' test to be met and when the injury falls within the risk created by the defendant's breach of his duty of care, the Supreme Court of Canada accepted the application of the 'material contribution' test. In *Resurfice Corp v Hanke*,[92] the plaintiff, the operator of an ice-resurfacing machine, was badly burned after hot water overfilled the gasoline tank of the ice-resurfacing machine, releasing vapourised gasoline which was then ignited by an overhead heater, causing an explosion and fire. The plaintiff sued alleging negligent design of the machine. The Supreme Court of Canada held that in exceptional circumstances, causation may be established where the defendant's conduct 'materially contributed' to the occurrence of the injury.[93] It stated two requirements to be able to apply this alternative test:

> *First, it must be impossible for the plaintiff to prove that the defendant's negligence caused the plaintiff's injury using the 'but for' test. The impossibility must be due to factors that are outside of the plaintiff's control; for example, current limits of scientific knowledge. Second, it must be clear that the defendant breached a duty of care owed to the plaintiff, thereby exposing the plaintiff to an unreasonable risk of injury, and the plaintiff must have suffered that form of injury. In other words, the plaintiff's injury must fall within the ambit of the risk created by the defendant's breach. In those exceptional cases where these two requirements are satisfied, liability may be imposed, even though the 'but for' test is not satisfied, because it would offend basic notions of fairness and justice to deny liability by applying a 'but for' approach.*[94]

Note that the Supreme Court of Canada was unable to apply the test to the facts of that case because they did not meet the second requirement. A unanimous Court confirmed the trial judge's conclusion in finding that the plaintiff's carelessness was the cause for his injuries rather than the alleged design defects.[95]

Though the test was officially established in 2007 by the Supreme Court of Canada, we can nevertheless trace its application to product liability cases as far back as two decades. For example, in *Buchan v Ortho Pharmaceutical (Canada) Ltd*,[96] the Court was asked to consider whether the defendant had been negligent in failing to warn the plaintiff of the risks of oral contraceptive use and whether the failure materially contributed to the plaintiff's stroke.[97] In doing so, it was unable to conclude that 'but for' taking the pill, the plaintiff's would not have suffered a stroke. However, in finding the defendant liable, it stated that, at the very least, taking the pill "materially contributed" to her stroke.[98] It further stated that had the defendant

91 *Ibid.*
92 [2007] 1 SCR 333.
93 *Ibid*, at ¶24–25.
94 *Ibid*, at ¶25.
95 *Ibid*, at ¶17.
96 [1984] OJ 3181.
97 *Ibid.*
98 *Ibid.*

warned the plaintiff of the dangers associated with taking the drug, "there was a reasonable likelihood that she or a reasonable person in her situation would not have taken the drug".[99]

The concept of 'remoteness' also factors into causation: a fault too far removed from the injury will not give rise to liability. However, an exact sequential relationship between fault and injury is not required, nor even a reasonable probably. In *R v Côté*,[100] it was determined that the general foreseeability of the class or character of injury which occurred is sufficient.

Quebec: Due to its distinct history, Quebec's fundamental private law exists not in the common law but in codified form in the Civil Code of Quebec. Contractual and extra-contractual (ie, tort) obligations are dealt with in the Code's *Book Five – Obligations*. Fault, injury and causality remain the three constituent parts of extra-contractual liability and the causes of action are broadly speaking similar to those which exist in the common law provinces, although presented slightly differently. It is worth noting that these rules apply to manufacturers but also to all other parties in the chain of distribution, including importers, wholesalers and retailers.

Articles 1468 and 1469 of the Civil Code of Quebec set up a presumption under which a plaintiff need not directly prove the manufacturer's fault: proof of the existence of the product's safety defect will effect a transfer of the onus of proof to the manufacturer. Safety defects are defined as the absence of "the safety which a person is normally entitled to expect". Mirroring the common law causes of action, potential safety defects include faulty design, manufacture, preservation or presentation of the product as well as the lack of sufficient instructions regarding the risks and dangers of the product.

The Civil Code provides manufacturers with two specific causes of defence under Article 1473. The first is the victim's knowledge or presumed knowledge of the defect, or the foreseeableness of the injury, either in the form of a specific warning on the label, packaging or otherwise or as a part of "common knowledge" regarding the inherent risks of some activities, such as smoking.[101] The second is the state of knowledge at the time of manufacture. Liability will not be incurred for safety defects which were undetectable given the knowledge then available, but only if the manufacturer provided sufficient information to the public once the defect was discovered. Knowledge in this context refers to the general body of scientific and technical knowledge which existed at the time and not the manufacturer's subjective knowledge. Parallels to some other common law defences, such as limitation periods, also exist in Quebec law.

(c) *Contract*

Common law provinces: In the context of a contract, a defective product may also give rise to an addition cause of action: a breach of warranty. This warranty may be

99 *Ibid.*
100 *Ibid.*
101 *Létourneau v Imperial Tobacco ltée*, REJB 1998-07025 (QCCQ).

established in a formal contract or in documentation accompanying the product, it may be implied, or it may be created by statute under provincial sale of goods legislation. The plaintiff is only required to prove the defect in the product and the breach of a warranty to engage the defendant's strict liability. Proof of the defendant's negligence is not required.

Under current case law, statutory warranties can only be excluded or limited when clear and direct language is used and where the parties are commercial entities of similar size. As for other defences, manufacturers can invoke essentially the same set of defences available as in tort liability.

Quebec: The contract of sale is a nominate contract in the Civil Code of Quebec and is subject to specific rules. Article 1726 requires that the seller guarantee to the buyer that the sold goods are free of defects which:

- are serious enough that they render the property unfit for its intended use or sufficiently less useful such that the buyer would not have bought it or only would have bought it at a lesser price;
- are not apparent to a prudent and diligent buyer without expert assistance; and
- existed at the time of sale.

This obligation is amplified for 'professional sellers' who habitually sell identical or similar products. As confirmed in the Supreme Court's 2007 *ABB Inc v Domtar Inc*[102] decision, manufacturers are considered professional sellers, as they are the ultimate experts with respect to the goods they produce. The existence of the defect at the time of sale is presumed against professional sellers, who are additionally liable for damages beyond the simple reimbursement of the sale price and who are prevented from contractually excluding or limiting their liability.

Though not provided for in the Civil Code, the category of "professional buyer", a counterpart to the professional seller who habitually buys similar or identical products, was examined by the Supreme Court in the *ABB Inc v Domtar Inc* decision. Although such experienced buyers might exist, their "professional" status does not have the effect of negating the specific rules relating to professional sellers. Rather, professional buyer status simply heightens the buyer's obligation to inspect the product before buying, as a greater proportion of defects may be considered apparent to him whereas they may be considered latent to a less experienced buyer.

4.3 Claimants, class actions

Every province except the smallest, Prince Edward Island, has adopted specific legislation to permit class proceedings. Though their individual characteristics vary ('opt-in' versus 'opt-out', possibility of subclasses or defendant classes, allowance of otherwise-barred statistical evidence, financial assistance to plaintiffs, reduction in costs, extension of limitation periods, possibility of including extra-provincial claimants in the class), they all aim to strike a new balance between plaintiffs and

102 [2007] 3 SCR 461.

defendants in situations of centralised fault and diffuse damages. In Prince Edward Island, a common-law version of class actions is allowed under a local rule of court.[103]

Certification of a class remains the first step in the class action process and generally requires the following elements: an alleged cause of action; an identifiable class of persons; commonality of issues raised by class members; the class proceeding shall be the most efficient method of resolving the claims; and the plaintiffs shall be sufficiently representative and without conflict of interest.

4.4 Remedies for injury/damage, and consequential loss (measures of compensation)

Compensatory damages are the favoured remedy for injury. Provincial sale of goods statutes may lay out guidelines for estimating damages in actions in warranty; as an example, the Ontario Sale of Goods Act takes as a yardstick the estimated loss directly and naturally resulting in the ordinary course of events from the breach of warranty. Awards in negligence claims aim more broadly to compensate victims for their physical, financial or psychological injury, and at times to prevent the unjust enrichment of the defendant. Compensatory damages for pecuniary damages such as cost of future care, lost earning capacity and so on are not capped.

Punitive damages are also available in the common law provinces when the defendant's conduct was so egregious as to offend the court's sense of decency, but are rarely awarded in product liability cases. Such damages are available under similar circumstance in Quebec under the Consumer Protection Act and for breaches of the Quebec Charter of Human Rights and Freedoms,[104] but are likewise not frequently awarded.

As for non-pecuniary damages for pain and suffering and loss of enjoyment of life following physical damages, these were capped by the Supreme Court in 1978 to C$100,000 in 1978 Canadian dollars. As of 2011, this represents over C$300,000 and the limit is strictly enforced.

Aside from compensatory and punitive damages, courts may also order injunctions or compel defendants to attempt to remedy injuries that have already occurred.

4.5 Procedure, limitation, funding, costs

Court procedure is specific to each province, although they are generally similar to each other and clear parallels can be drawn with American civil procedure. Product liability in particular is not subject to any special procedure except with respect to class actions, which go through the prior step of class certification. Trials are almost exclusively before a judge sitting alone without jury.

In the common law provinces, generally speaking, successful claimants are entitled to recover some portion of their legal fees and disbursements, although in practise this is at the judge's discretion and rarely surpasses half of the actual costs paid out. In Quebec, there is no discretionary recovery of legal fees and

103 *Western Canada Shopping Centres v Dutton* [2001] 2 SCR 534.
104 LRQ, c C-12.

disbursements; rather, costs are paid to the successful plaintiff according to a regulatory tariff which has not been substantively updated in decades and which generally provides only a small fraction of actual costs paid out.

Aside from class actions, where funding assistance may be available depending on the province, legal aid programs available in Canada are not geared towards litigating civil claims, are generally considered underfunded, and are in practice unavailable to most potential claimants due to low revenue thresholds for access to those programmes.

As for limitation periods, these vary between two and six years, depending on the province and the type of action, counting from the time the claimant knew or ought to have known about the cause of action. In the common law jurisdictions, limitation periods are mostly set out in a Limitations Act or similar statute, whereas in the province of Quebec, they are fixed in the Civil Code of Quebec. Some jurisdictions additionally impose an ultimate deadline after a set number of years from the act or omission, notwithstanding the state of the claimant's knowledge, after which no claim can be made. For example, in Ontario, this period is 15 years, while in Alberta it is 10 years.

4.6 Trends

Many Canadian analysts believe that the new Canada Consumer Product Safety Act regime for product recalls, with its mandatory reporting and increased powers for Health Canada to initiate recalls and other measures, will likely give rise to increased class action litigation following a predicted rise in the overall number of product recalls.

5. Product insurance

In the Canadian federal system, insurance falls under provincial jurisdiction and so each of the 10 provinces has its own specific legal framework. However, due to substantial legal similarities, the existence of many national insurers as well as the influence of the Insurance Bureau of Canada (IBC), a pan-national industry association representing the great majority of the property and casualty market, the field of insurance can in most respects be analyzed as a generally uniform body of law.

Canadian product liability insurance is most often included as part of a widely-used standard policy known as the Commercial General Liability (CGL) policy, developed, published and periodically reviewed by the IBC. However, variations exist with respect to specific industries or insurers and endorsements can be added to fill some of the gaps and exclusions in the standard CGL coverage. The following sections use the CGL policy as a starting point to discussing various types of product liability insurance.

5.1 Coverage

(a) Product recall

Product recall insurance in Canada will generally cover the expenses and loss of profit resulting from malicious product tampering, accidental product contamination or other risks described in the policy. It must be taken out separately from the basic CGL policy, which excludes coverage for the costs of recalls.

(b) *Contaminated products*

In Canada, contaminated products insurance is very generally integrated into product recall insurance, which covers both accidental and malicious product tampering.

(c) *Product liability*

Product liability insurance in Canada is generally standardised along the Insurance Bureau of Canada's Commercial General Liability policy, though some variation exists between insurers. Bodily injury and property damage are both covered, but the cost of product recalls and the cost of repairing or replacing a damaged product are excluded.

(d) *Financial loss*

Financial losses caused by product failure of a nature to engage the manufacturer's liability are excluded from coverage under the Insurance Bureau of Canada's Commercial General Liability policy but supplementary insurance products are available.

(e) *Product guarantee*

There are still debates in Canada as to whether extended warranty programs should be considered a form of insurance product. Legislation varies between provinces, although warranty liabilities contracted by manufacturers can be covered through a customised insurance product.

5.2 Product recall

The cost of product recalls is generally excluded from coverage under the most commonly-used product liability insurance policies. That being the case, such insurance must be obtained separately from general liability coverage or standard property coverage, but distinct product recall insurance remains a niche product in Canada, despite a number of major, highly-publicised recalls in the past years. Premiums remain high, encouraging organizations large and small to bear alone the risk of an eventual recall or similar occurrence. In addition, recall coverage is not standardised across insurers, as is the case with the CGL policy, and many insurers offer specialised recall insurance products tailored to different industries, so it is difficult to make generalisations.

(a) *Insuring provisions*

Most policies will be triggered by the first discovery of circumstances justifying a recall, such as an occurrence of an actual case of bodily injury or property damage or the discovery of some kind of defect or contamination of the product likely to give rise to such a case. Policies vary in their treatment of recalls of products due to adulterated constituent ingredients.

(b) ***Insured losses***

Pre-recall expenses, testing etc: Coverage for these types of expenses, which include a number of important steps such as pre-recall identification of potential problems, planning and testing recall and public relations strategies and testing potential faulty products to determine the necessity of a recall, is available but varies from policy to policy.

Consultant costs: Coverage for these types of expenses is available, but varies from policy to policy. They can include pre-incident consultants, who give advice on preparing and implementing recall procedures, or consultants who help manage the actual recall once it gets underway.

First-party recall expenses: These costs are generally covered in product recall insurance and include notification of customers, shipping, warehousing, disposal, and extra staff to manage it all.

Business interruption: Business interruption coverage to cover losses incurred during the public relations and sales downturn can be obtained in a variety of contexts, including as a part of product recall insurance.

Repair, replacement, refunds: Coverage for the repair and replacement of recalled products or for the refunding of customers for whom the product is not replaced is available but varies from policy to policy.

Brand rehabilitation: Coverage for publicity efforts necessary to restore prior brand image, including radio, television, print and digital advertising, is available but varies from policy to policy.

Third-party recall liability: Coverage for the manufacturer's liability towards third parties for the damages they may incur as a result of the recall is available but varies from policy to policy. As further explained below, distinct financial loss insurance is also available to cover liability in the case of product failure as opposed to product recall.

Defence costs: Coverage for defence costs relating to litigation following third party damages is available but varies from policy to policy. It tends to be linked with the abovementioned third party recall liability insurance.

Impairment: Impaired property coverage is available to component manufacturers to protect against liability to third parties whose product incorporated the component and may be made less useful due to actual or potential component deficiency if it can be corrected by recall and repair or replacement. It is important to note the distinct trigger of coverage as well as the conceptual difference with coverage of products which go directly to end users.

(c) ***Exclusions***

Common exclusions include recalls for defects caused by exposure to weather or by the inherent deterioration or decomposition of a product, experimental products and prototypes, and recalls initiated by government in situations which do not fulfil the criteria of the coverage trigger. Also excluded are fraudulent acts by a trustee, director or officer of the named insured and the intentional failure of the insured to comply with regulations.

(d) ***Conditions***

Non-disclosure of the existence of the insurance is a common characteristic of Canadian product recall insurance policies.

Although many insurance companies offer emergency hotlines and recall consultants as part of their service, use of these services has not generally been elevated to a condition of the policy, although refusal to use them may at some point run foul of the requirements that the insured immediately notify the insurer of an occurrence and that the insured offer full cooperation to the insurer.

5.3 Contaminated products

Contaminated products insurance, which concerns itself with intentional forms of contamination such as malice and extortion, is almost exclusively found as an element of a broader product recall insurance scheme. As such its provisions, exclusions and conditions are generally the same as for product recall insurance.

(a) ***Insuring provisions***

A typical insurance clause providing for the indemnification of accidental product contamination can be read as follows:

Scope of coverage

Underwriters agree to indemnify the named insurer for loss resulting directly from an accidental product contamination first discovered by the named insured during the certificate period …

Definitions

Product(s): All goods or products (fished or in process), including all ingredients or components thereof, manufactured, distributed, handled by the named insured (or manufactured by a contract manufacturer for the named insured) and which are (or will be) available for sale by the named insured.

Accidental product contamination shall mean:

(1) any accidental or unintentional contamination, impairment or mislabeling (including mislabeling of instructions for use) during the manufacture, blending, mixing, compounding, packaging, labeling, preparation, production or processing of the named insured's products (including their ingredients or components), or

(2) fault in design specifications or performance of the named insured's product(s)

provided always in the consumption or use of the named insured's contaminated product(s) has, within 120 days of such consumption or use, either resulted, or may likely result in: (1) physical symptoms of bodily injury, sickness or disease or death of any person(s) and/or (2) physical damage to (or destruction of) tangible property, including animals and/or livestock.

Contaminated product(s): the named insured's product(s) which have been the subject of an accidental product contamination.

This very same clause was interpreted in the British Columbia case of *Premium Brands Operating Limited Partnership v Lloyd's Underwriters.*[105] In that case,[106] Premium Brands Operating Limited Partnership (the insured), a processor and marketer of food products insured under a policy issued by Lloyd's Underwriters (the insurer), brought an application to determine whether its 'accidental product contamination' insurance covered for a loss arising out of the recall and destruction of sandwich products. The insurer, on the one hand, contended that the insured's products were not contaminated; the decision to recall the products was rather due to the fact that the machinery had been contaminated. The insured, on the other hand, contended that it decided to recall its products after the CFIA had concluded that certain of the insured's products may be contaminated with Listeria monocytogenes and that those products might cause sickness or disease.[107] In interpreting the accidental product contamination clause (see above), Justice Willcock held that proof of actual contamination was not a prerequisite to trigger the application of the accidental product indemnification clause at issue. Rather, what was required by the judge, to justify the recall and to entitle it to coverage, was proof of a likelihood of some injury to the purchaser of the product within 120 days, as provided for in the policy.

(b) *Exclusions*

See product recall insurance above.

(c) *Conditions*

See product recall insurance above.

5.4 Product liability insurance

Policies closely modelled on the IBC's standard CGL policy dominate the field of product liability insurance.

(a) *Insuring provisions*

Under the CGL policy's 'Coverage A' section, both bodily injury and property damage are covered. This bodily injury or property damage must flow from an "occurrence", a concept defined as an "accident, including continuous or repeated exposure to substantially the same general harmful conditions". Expected or foreseen events are therefore excluded, although negligent acts by the insured remain covered to the extent that the eventual damaging consequences of such acts

105 2011 BCSC 1470.

106 The court held that proof of actual contamination was not a prerequisite to trigger the application of the accidental product indemnification clause. Rather, what was required by the judge was proof of a likelihood of injury to the purchaser of the product within 120 days, as provided for in the policy.

107 *Ibid.*

108 *Progressive Homes Ltd v Lombard General Insurance Co of Canada*, 2010 CSC 33.

were not actually expected or intended.[108] Only compensatory damages deriving from liability imposed by law are covered; punitive damages are not considered compensatory and therefore are not covered. There is no requirement that liability be recognised in court or otherwise be judicially determined, nor that the insured pay the claim before being reimbursed by the insurer. These conditions are usually included into a clause that resembles the following:

> *a. We will pay those sums that the insured becomes legally obligated to pay as compensatory damages because of "bodily injury" or "property damage" to which this insurance applies. No other obligation or liability to pay sums or perform acts or services is covered [...]. This insurance applies only to "bodily injury" and "property damage" which occurs during the policy period. The "bodily injury" or "property damage" must be caused by an "occurrence". The "occurrence" must take place in the "coverage territory"[...]*
>
> *b. Compensatory damages because of "bodily injury" include compensatory damages claimed by any person or organisation for care, loss of services, or death resulting at any time from the "bodily injury".*
>
> *c. "Property damage" that is loss of use of tangible property that is not physically injured shall be deemed to have occurred at the time of the "occurrence" that caused it.*[109]

The basis for coverage can vary from one policy to another. Hybrid policies combining 'claims-made' and 'occurrence-based' elements are becoming more common in the Canadian marketplace.

Injury: Bodily injury is defined in the CGL policy as "bodily injury, sickness or disease sustained by a person, including death resulting from any of these at any time". Case law has determined that the terms 'sickness' and 'disease' can include psychological traumas such as stress, depression and emotional impairment.

Damage: The definition of 'property damage' is "physical injury to tangible property, including all resulting loss of use of that property; or loss of use of tangible property that is not physically injured". However, it must be noted that loss of use caused by the product's own failure is later excluded.

(b) Exclusions

Breach of contract (with exceptions): Although a debate once existed as to the inclusion of contractual obligations under the CGL policy, due to the limitation of coverage to compensatory damages for "liability imposed by law", damages which occur in a contractual relationship are considered to be covered by the CGL policy. However, these damages must still result from an "occurrence", being an accident. Breaches of contract not related to an occurrence are not covered. Also, under the standard CGL policy, if the insured contractually assumes liability for compensatory damages which it would not otherwise be liable for, liability is excluded from coverage. This latter clause reads as follows:[110]

---

109 Marcus B Snowden and Mark G Lichty, *Annotated Commercial General Liability Policy*, vol 2, Canada Law Book, Toronto, at Appendix A, p 2 [annotated].

110 *Ibid.*

This insurance does not apply to:

a. [...]

b. 'Bodily injury' or 'property damage' for which the insured is obliged to pay compensatory damages by reason of the assumption of liability in a contract or agreement. This exclusion does not apply to liability for compensatory damages:

1) Assumed in a contract or agreement that is an 'insured contract'; or

2) The insured would have anyway in the absence of the contract or agreement.

Repair, replacement, recall: Under the standard CGL policy, the cost of a recall, withdrawal, inspection, repair, replacement, adjustment, removal or disposal of the insured's own product, or of any product into which it had been incorporated, is not covered. This type of exclusion is often referred to as the 'sistership' exclusion. It applies when such methods are used preventatively, and not when the same faulty product causes several instances of actual damage. Damage to the insured's own product is excluded. This CGL exclusion clause reads as follows:[111]

This insurance does not apply to:

1. *Any loss, cost or expense incurred by you or others for the loss of use, withdrawal, recall, inspection, repair, replacement, adjustment, removal or disposal of:*

1. "Your product"

2. "Your work"

3. "Impaired property"

if such product, work or property is withdrawn or recalled from the market or use by any person or organisation because of a known or suspected defect, deficiency, inadequacy or dangerous condition inherent in it.

There are some circumstances where "pure economic loss" to the insured and "property damage" to a third party are intermingled in the same event. In those types of cases, Canadian courts have had to separate compensable losses from those that were not. As a general matter, courts have interpreted the events purposively in order for damages to third parties to be fully compensated.

In *Carwald Concrete and Gravel Co Ltd v General Security Insurance Company of Canada,*[112] the insured party provided defective concrete which was used to create foundations covering a variety of elements, including steel girders, electrical lines, cables and bolts. Once the defect was discovered, the concrete had to be removed, replaced and re-poured. The Alberta Court of Appeal determined that under the CGL policy and its 'own product' exclusion, the insurer did not have to pay for the replacement concrete, but that it did have to pay for the damage caused to the underlying structure during the removal of the defective concrete. A similar result was reached in the case of *Bulldog Bag Ltd v Axa Pacific Insurance Company,*[113] in regard to a claim for losses incurred to a third party's product as a result of defects in the bags it had bought from the insured.[114] The Court in that case held that the insurer had to indemnify the third party for the cost incurred in removing its product from

111 *Ibid,* at 24-1.
112 (1985) 17 CCLI 241 (Alta CA).
113 2010 BCSC 419.
114 *Ibid.*

the defective packaging, disposing of that packaging, and subsequently re-packaging it, as well as for the portion of the product that had been lost in the process. The Court refused, on the other hand, to indemnify the insured party for the cost of replacing the defective bags themselves.

In *Ocean Construction Supplies Limited v Continental Insurance Company,*[115] a light cement platform was built to float on seawater and house an aquarium. The aquarium sank and the owners took action against the insured and insurer. The British Columbia Supreme Court determined that the 'own product' exclusion did not apply, since the platform itself was not damaged, only the aquarium.

In *Himont Canada Inc v Correpro-Fap Québec ltée,*[116] Correpro sold to Himont a set of stainless steel tubes to be built into a production line. It came to light shortly thereafter that steel particles were being stripped from the tubes and mixed into the product. The Quebec Superior Court, applying the exclusion, determined that the replacement of the steel tubes was excluded but that the value of the damaged product and its replacement cost were covered as damages to a third party.

It should also be noted that the insured's 'own product' is taken to include any constituent parts of that product. For example, in *Timberline Equipment Company Inc v St Paul F & M Insurance Co,*[117] a set of ropes manufactured by another company were included in the insured's product, a collapsible tower. The tower was sold to a client and the ropes gave way on first use. The ropes, though made by a third party, were considered a part of the insured's own product and the exclusion was applied to the entire tower.

A similar exclusion applies in relation to work performed by the insured party, putting the cost of repairing faulty workmanship on the insured rather than the insurer.

Efficacy: A standard exclusion in CGL policies limits coverage so that the efficacy of the insured's own product is not included. Indeed, the CGL policy is not meant to guarantee the performance or adequacy of the product itself, only guard against the potentially destructive effects of product failure.

Aircraft: Several exclusions apply to bodily injury and property damage arising from the use of aircraft, hovercraft and watercraft.

(c) *Conditions*

Claims: All occurrences (ie, accidents which may give rise to a claim) must be notified promptly to the insurer along with appropriate details. The insured must additionally provide prompt written notice of claims made and actions brought against the insured to the insurer. Full cooperation at all times between insurer and insured is required.

---

115 [1978] 5 WWR 181 (BCSC).
116 AZ-96021905.
117 576 P 2d 1244 (Supreme Court of Oregon, 1978).

Other: The standard CGL policy includes a number of other conditions covering insured's bankruptcy (does not affect insurer's obligations under the policy), use of Canadian currency, cancellation of policy, changes to policy and insurer's right to carry out inspections, among others.

5.5 Financial loss

(a) Insuring provisions

Liability for pure economic loss: As stated in the previous section on product liability insurance, the definition of 'property damage' in the widely used CGL policy includes "loss of use of tangible property which is not physically injured". However, loss of use caused by product failure, insofar as it does not cause bodily injury or property damage to other property, is subsequently excluded from the CGL policy. Supplementary insurance must therefore be obtained to cover this gap.

Financial loss insurance policies, often called 'errors and omissions' insurance or E&O, provides coverage for the financial loss of a third party arising from failure of the insured's product to perform as intended or expected. It is usually available as an endorsement to an organisation's main CGL policy.

(b) Exclusions

Breach of contract (with exceptions): The breach of contract exclusion explained above with respect to product liability insurance usually applies to financial loss insurance, insofar as the financial loss insurance is most often contained in an endorsement to the CGL policy.

Advice: Financial loss insurance is available to persons who provide advice as a part of their business, such as professionals. However, in most product-focused financial loss insurance, any damages suffered by third parties based on financial advice given by the insured will be excluded.

Repair, replacement, recall: Coverage varies between policies but repair, replacement and recall expenses are not typically a part of financial loss insurance, although they can be covered under product recall insurance as laid out in an earlier section.

(c) Conditions

See above.

5.6 Product guarantee

The aim of the CGL policy is to cover damages to third parties; it is not meant to be a warranty for the insured's product. Indeed, property damage to the insured's product itself is expressly excluded from the standard CGL policy, so that manufacturers, sellers and distributors must themselves bear the cost of replacing the product. This exclusion serves as a powerful incentive to create and sell a reliable product, with beneficial effects for both parties as well as the end user. For the exclusion to apply, the damage must be caused by the product, to the product. The insured's 'own product' is taken to include any constituent parts of that product.

The nature of warranty programmes has been the subject of debate in the insurance field. This type of insurance is not often seen in Canada, as such risks are widely considered a part of the business risk associated with any consumer product enterprise. Yet specialised insurance products do exist, although their individual provisions vary widely.

5.7 General principles

(a) *Attachment*

Reinsurance is not a foreign concept to Canada and excess insurance policies can be attached to principal policies to ensure coverage beyond the latter's limits.

(b) *Aggregation*

The standard CGL policy and many other types of insurance policies in Canada include aggregate limits to coverage over the period of the insurance contract.

(c) *General conditions*

General conditions to product liability contracts vary but are likely to include: continued coverage in the case of insured's bankruptcy; both parties' right to cancel policy; procedure for amendments to the policy, insured's duty to promptly notify insurer in the case of occurrence or action, insurer's right to examine insured's books and records; insurer's right to proceed with inspections and surveys; a method for determining how to distribute costs and obligations when multiple insurers are covering the risk; premium audits; named insured's responsibility for payment of premiums; and transfer of rights to insurer upon payment of indemnity.

(d) *General exclusions*

General exclusions to product liability contracts vary but are likely to include: any bodily injury, property damage and clean-up costs relating to pollution, the operation of a nuclear energy hazard and war risks.

Injury and damage expected or intended by the insured is generally explicitly excluded from insurance policies. The insured's subjective point of view is the accepted frame of reference here, with its knowledge and expertise and personal motives being considered alongside the timing of the injury or damage, the availability of information and any deviations from standard practice. Negligent behaviour will not normally be excluded unless the damaging consequences were known or expected, a rule fleshed out by the Supreme Court of Canada in *Canadian Indemnity Co v Walkem Machinery & Equipment Ltd.*[118]

118 [1976] 1 SCR 309.

(e) *Interpretation*

Insurance contracts in Canada have historically been interpreted according to the ordinary rules of contractual interpretation, with some modifications.

The Supreme Court of Canada set out some general principles in *Consolidated-Bathurst Export Ltd v Mutual Boiler & Machinery Insc Co,*[119] mainly to the effect that ambiguous insurance provisions must be read in the context of the entire contract and interpreted in line with the protection that was reasonably sought when the contract was made. Fairness, reasonableness and the parties' intent should rule. In its later *Reid Crowther & Partners Ltd v Simcoe & Erie General Insurance Co*[120] decision, the Supreme Court added that if doubt persists, a very technical reading of the wording used was to be avoided, as the results would tend to deprive the insured of its reasonably expected coverage.

As a last resort, courts have traditionally been inclined to interpret an unclear provision in favour of the insured party, a rule justified by the 'utmost good faith' required by insurance contracts as well as the fact that most are contracts of adhesion in which the insured has little negotiating power. Other general principles, such as the broad interpretation of coverage and narrow reading of exclusions, also exist to help courts and parties find their way.

(f) *Effect of breaches*

Breaches of the insurance contract (eg, prolonged delay for notification to the insurer of the occurrence), can prevent an insurer from conducting a thorough investigation and, depending on their severity, justify denial of coverage.

5.8 Extra-contractual defences (misrepresentation, non-disclosure)

Misrepresentation and non-disclosure by the insured party as to the risk being underwritten can serve as justification for the insurance contract being retroactively cancelled from the beginning, with the insurer returning already-paid premiums to the insured and concurrently being held to no further obligations to defend or indemnify.

---

119 [1980] 1 SCR 888.
120 [1993] 1 SCR 252.

China

Alex YG An
David JD Dai
MWE China Law Offices

1. Overview

The Chinese regulatory framework governing product safety control is mainly based on the Product Quality Law (first published in 1993 and amended in 2000), which governs quality control of commodities and services; and the Law on the Protection of the Rights and Interests of Consumers 1993, which governs the sale of commodities and services. In relation to motor vehicles, the Administration of the Recall of Defective Auto Products 2004 (Auto Recall Rules) have supplemented Chinese consumers' existing rights under general contract or tort-based legal remedies.

In 2007 three recall regulations were enacted respectively for food, children's toys and drugs and in the same year the State Council published Special Rules of the State Council on Strengthening the Supervision and Management of the Safety of Food and Other Products (Special Rules). Article 9 of the Special Rules imposes recall obligations on manufacturers and sellers of products with hidden safety risks. These cover all products with possible implications for the health and safety of people, such as food, edible agricultural products, cosmetics, medical devices and medicines, household appliances, children's toys, automobile products, dangerous chemicals and their packaging and containers, etc.

The Tort Liability Law 2009 (also extended the coverage of product recall to all products manufactured or sold in China, providing that if any defect is found after the product is put into circulation, the manufacturer or seller must take timely remedial measures such as warning and recall; if the manufacturer or seller fails to do so; or where the remedial measures are insufficient or ineffective and damage is caused, it will be liable for the tort (Article 6 of the Tort law).

To implement the general recall system under the Special Rules and the Tort Law, the Chinese government has drafted a universal defective product recall regulation to govern recall of all products (excluding pharmaceutical and military products). The draft Administrative Regulations on the Recall of Defective Products (Draft Recall Rules) are undergoing legislative scrutiny but are not yet finalised and not in force.

The Chinese government also recently promulgated Administrative Measures for the Recall of Medical Devices (Interim) (Medical Devices Recall Rules) to regulate the recall of medical devices sold in China, which came into effect on July 1 2011.

On confirming the existence of a defect in the product which relates to personal health and safety, manufacturers must effectively prevent, control and eliminate any harm which may be caused by the defective products by taking various recall measures, including issuing public warnings, supplementing or revising the instructions or enabling the withdrawal, return, exchange, repair or destruction of the defective products. Where a manufacturer fails to execute the recall or tries to hide the defects, the Chinese product quality supervisory authorities may intervene to order the recall and the manufacturer may face administrative sanctions.

2. Product safety regulation

The Product Quality Law establishes a general mechanism for controlling product quality to ensure the production and sale of safe products in China. It requires that products must not have any 'unreasonable dangers'[1] that could threaten the personal health and the safety of people or property (Article 26 of the Product Quality Law). It also authorises product quality supervisory authorities to carry out onsite random sampling and inspections and, when the products are found defective, to impose various administrative sanctions, such as revocation of the production licence, confiscation of the defective products and imposition of penalties (Articles 15, 17 and 19 of the Product Quality Law).

The Consumer Law protects the rights of consumers and imposes certain obligations upon manufacturers and sellers in respect of the circulation of their products. According to this law, business operators (including manufacturers and sellers) must guarantee that the commodities and services they supply meet the requirements to ensure personal or property safety. As to commodities and services which may harm personal or property safety, business operators must provide consumers with clear and transparent explanatory information and adequate specific warnings of any risks, and must explain or indicate the correct way to use the commodities or to receive services as well as means to minimise any risk of injury (Article 18(1) of the Consumer Law).

The Chinese government has also enacted various specific laws and regulations to govern the safety of specific products or industries, including: the Law on the Administration of Drugs (first enacted in 1984 and amended in 2001); Regulations on Supervision over Hygiene of Cosmetics (1990), Administrative Regulations on Hazardous Chemical Products (first enacted in 2002 and amended in 2011); Agricultural Product Quality Safety Law (2006); and the Food Safety Law (2009); etc.

2.1 Product risks

According to Article 46 of the Product Quality Law, a 'defective product' is:

- a product that has unreasonable dangers that threaten the safety of a person or property; or
- a product that does not conform to the standards set by the state or the specific industry such that the health and safety of people and safety of the property is ensured.

---

1 There is no specific guidance or rules on how Chinese courts should interpret 'unreasonable dangers' (and Chinese courts need not follow precedent under China's civil law tradition), but the consensus among Chinese academic scholars is that both subjective factors (producers' and consumers' reasonable expectations of the safety of the products) and objective factors (ie, technical limitations at the time when the products are made) will be taken into account.

To trigger a recall, the defects must be found to widely exist in a batch, type or class of products. For example, under the Auto Recall Rules, the 'defects' refer to unreasonable dangers inherent in a certain batch, type or class of vehicle, due to design or manufacture faults, such that the vehicle may endanger the safety of persons or property; or otherwise, the vehicle does not conform to relevant state standards for auto safety (Article 5 of the Auto Recall Rules).

Manufacturers and sellers must maintain internal quality inspection systems to ensure the quality of their products prior to release on the market (Article 3 of the Product Quality Law). They must also conduct relevant investigations and risk assessments where a potential product defect is suspected. The product quality supervisory authorities may also initiate their own independent investigation and risk assessment. On the discovery of product defects, business operators must take remedial actions according to the recall regulations or other product quality laws and regulations.

2.2 Safety standards

According to Article 26 of the Product Quality Law, industrial products which may be hazardous must conform to state and industry standards to ensure the health and safety of persons and property. In the absence of state or industry standards, products must conform to the general minimum requirements to ensure health and the safety of life and property.

Under the Standardisation Law of China 1988, the state administrative authority in charge of standardisation is responsible for the administration of industrial standards. Standards to ensure the health and safety of persons and properties are mandatory (Article 7 of the Standardisation Law). Products failing to conform to the mandatory standards must not be produced, sold or imported (Article 14 of the Standardisation Law).

Products supplied under a contract may be deemed to meet state and industry standards (including the mandatory and recommendatory standards) as implied terms of the contract in the absence of express contractual clauses on quality requirements (Articles 61 and 154 of the Contract Law of China 1999). Where quality requirements agreed between parties are lower than mandatory safety standards imposed by Chinese laws and regulations, those agreed lower requirements may be deemed invalid (Article 52(5) of the Contract Law) and the mandatory safety standards will be deemed as default terms of the contract.

2.3 Compliance

In addition to complying with all of the above mandatory product safety standards, business operators need special licences and permits to engage in the manufacturing and sale of certain products. The Chinese government encourages manufacturers to obtain accreditation with various quality conformity verification systems, and imposes a compulsory certification system for certain products listed by the Chinese government which it considers potentially affect the safety and health of persons. Relevant listed products must pass the Chinese Compulsory Certification (CCC) and bear a CCC mark, or else may not leave the factory, be sold on the market or used by consumers in China (Article 28, of the Regulations on Certification and Accreditation 2003).

Business operators found to be violating these product safety laws and regulations will subject to various administrative and criminal sanctions as discussed below.

2.4 Safety issues

The Product Quality Law authorises the quality supervisory department of the State Council – that is, the General Administration of Quality Supervision, Inspection, and Quarantine (AQSIQ) and its local agencies as the main bodies overseeing product safety control. Other government agencies are also empowered to administer product safety in their respective sectors: (eg, the State Administration for Industry and Commerce (SAIC), State Food and Drug Administration (SFDA), Ministry of Health, Ministry of Agriculture, Ministry of Commerce (MOFCOM), General Customs Administration (GAC) and National Development and Reform Commission (NDRC)).

While the manufacturer is the primary party responsible for the safety of its products, other business operators, such as the distributor or related service providers are also responsible for various statutory duties and obligations under the product safety and recall laws and regulations. For example, according to Article 17 of the Auto Recall Rules, distributors, car-renting operators and car-repairing operators must notify the manufacturer and the relevant quality supervisory authorities of any potential defects they discover in automobile products. They must also cooperate with the quality supervisory authorities in investigations, providing all relevant information required for such an investigation, and assist the manufacturer in the recall of the defective automobile products.

2.5 Types of corrective action

Where a business operator becomes aware of the existence of a major defect in its products or services, it must promptly notify the quality supervisory authorities and consumers and take relevant measures to prevent potential harm (including repair, remanufacture, replacement and return of products; Articles 18(2) and 44, Consumer Law).

Article 9(1) of the Special Rules provides that, a manufacturer that finds any latent safety risk in its products such that it could cause harm to personal health and safety, must disclose the relevant information to the public, notify sellers and consumers that they must cease sales and use of such products, recall the products, and report the defects to the relevant quality supervisory authorities. Sellers which discover the same must immediately stop selling the products, notify the manufacturer or supplier, and report the issue to the relevant quality supervisory authorities.

The recall regulations discussed above also impose various statutory obligations on business operators in connection with product information management, safety risk investigation and assessment, public notification and recall, disposal of recalled products, and reporting and recording recall activities, etc.

Where parties fail to undertake those voluntary corrective actions, the quality supervisory authorities may order mandatory recall and impose relevant administrative penalties (Article 9(2), of the Special Rules).

2.6 Administrative liabilities

The Product Quality Law imposes various administrative liabilities on manufacturers, sellers and other related parties, including seizure and attachment of defective products and related materials and equipment, confiscation of defective products and illegal income or profits, administrative fines and cancellation of business licences.

Further laws and regulations also set out similar administrative liabilities for specific product types. For example, Article 85 of the Food Safety Law provides that if a manufacturer or seller, among others, produces or engages in the business operation of staple or supplementary foods exclusively for infants or for other targeted groups of people, and where the ingredients do not meet the relevant food safety standards, all illegal gains, illegally produced or operated food, utensils, equipment, raw materials and other articles used for the illegal production or business operation will be confiscated by the quality supervisory authorities. If the monetary value of the illegally produced or operated food is less than Rmb10,000, the manufacturer will be fined not less than Rmb2,000 but not more than Rmb50,000 concurrently. If the monetary value of the food is Rmb10,000 or more, the manufacturer will be fined not less than five times but not more than 10 times the monetary value concurrently. In serious cases, the manufacturer's operating licence will be revoked.

2.7 Criminal liability

In addition to the various administrative sanctions discussed above, if the circumstances are serious enough, criminal sanctions may also apply (Article 49 of the Product Quality Law).

The Criminal Law sets out various criminal offences and related sanctions for manufacturing and selling defective products. For example, any person who produces, or knowingly sells, products that do not conform with State or industry safety standards, with serious consequences, will be sentenced to up to life imprisonment with a fine of up to 200% of the sale value (Article 146, Criminal Law). Companies committing such criminal offences will be subject to a fine, and their officers directly in charge and other directly responsible personnel will be personally subject to punishment by both fine and imprisonment (Article 150, Criminal Law).

3. Obligations of manufacturers and distributors

3.1 Sources of duties

(a) *Statutory obligations*

The Product Quality Law and Consumer Law, as well as various laws and regulations governing product safety control for specific products or industries, impose a variety of statutory obligations and duties on business operators regarding safety of products and corrective actions required to eliminate risks of defective products, including repair, replacement and return of defective products.

The Chinese recall regulations also impose various statutory obligations on business operators in connection with product recall, including defect investigation, risk assessment, warning, notification, recall and reporting requirements.

(b) *Tort*

Manufacturers will be held liable for damages if a product defect causes damage to other persons and that liability is strict (Article 41 of the Product Quality Law; and the Tort Law). In other words, claimants need not prove the default on the part of the manufacturer; the manufacturer will be held liable unless its can make out a valid defence. Its available defences are any of the following:

- the product has not yet been released onto the market;
- the defect causing the damage did not exist when the product was put onto the market; or
- at the time when the product was made available to the public, the level of science and technology was such that it was not possible to detect the defect (Article 41 of the Product Quality Law).

Sellers and other third parties such as transportation and warehouse service providers may become liable if products become defective due to their default and cause damage to other persons or properties (Article 42 of the Product Quality Law and Articles 42 and 44 of the Tort Law). For this type of fault-based tort liability claim, the claimant will have to prove that the damage was caused by the wilful act or negligence of the defendant.

Moreover, where a product is found to be defective after having been circulated, its manufacturer and seller must promptly take such remedial measures as warning and/or recall to prevent any harm being caused by that defect (Article 46 of the Tort Law). Failure to warn and/or recall will render the manufacturer and/or seller liable for indemnifying any losses arising. The Tort Law also confirms product recall as a general legal remedy against defective products.

(c) *Contract*

Under a sale contract, a provider of products is considered to give an implied warranty to its customers that the product it provides is safe. If the product does not conform to the higher of either the implied safety warranty or agreed quality requirement, the provider may be found liable for breach of contract and may have to repair, remanufacture, replace or return the defective products (Article 111 of the Contract Law).

The Contract Law does not allow parties to exclude or limit liability arising from personal injury or death or caused by a wilful act or gross negligence. Any contractual provisions to that effect will be deemed invalid (Article 53 of the Contract Law). Moreover, the Contract Law grants injured or affected parties the option to take claims based on tort liability, if the products provided under a contract caused damage to personal health and property (Article 122 of the Contract Law).

3.2 Pre-market obligations

(a) *Production licensing*

Chinese law establishes a production licensing system for the manufacture of a long list of industrial products that could have health and personal or property safety implications (Article 5 of the Administrative Regulations on the Production Licence for Industrial Products 2005 (Production License Regulations), replacing the 1984 regulation). The production licence is a prerequisite before enterprises can manufacture products listed in the catalogue; and companies and individuals may not sell such products or use them in their business activities without a licence.

The list is as follows (Article 2 of the Product Licence Regulations):

- dairy products, meat products, beverages, rice, noodles, edible oil, liquor and other processed food that could directly affect people's health;
- electric blankets, pressure cookers, gas water heaters and other products that may endanger people's personal and property safety;
- safety nets, safety helmets, construction fastenings and other products for protecting the safety of workers;
- power pylons, bridge abutments, railway products, hydraulic metal structures, dangerous chemicals and their packaging and containers, and other products that may affect production safety and public safety; and
- other products required by law and administrative regulations to be subject to the production licensing system.

(b) *Compulsory certifications*

China implements a product quality compulsory certification system for manufacturers (Regulations on Certification and Accreditation 2001; Administrative Regulations on Compulsory Product Certification 2009; Compulsory Certification Regulations and related implementation rules). These apply to products which could have an impact on the health and safety of people, animals and plants, environmental protection or public security.

The catalogue of products subject to compulsory certification lists a variety of industries, including electronic products and electrical appliances, telecommunications products, vehicles and motorcycles, safety glass, fire prevention products, security products, agricultural machinery, medical devices and children's toys.[2]

Products listed in the compulsory product certification catalogue must be certified by designated certification bodies, granted the relevant certificate and affixed with a 'CCC' mark before they can leave the factory and be imported, sold or used (Article 2, Compulsory Certification Regulations).

2 A list of the products subject to compulsory certification may be found at the official website of Certification and Accreditation Administration of the People's Republic of China at www.cnca.gov.cn/cnca/rdht/qzxcprz/rzml/images/20080701/4755.htm.

(c) *Quality control*

The primary obligation of the manufacturer under the Product Quality Law is to ensure that products meet the following conditions (Article 26 of the Product Quality Law):

- They must be free from any unreasonable dangers which could threaten the safety of people and property. Where state or industry standards exist, the products must conform to such standards;
- They must be fit for normal use, except where flaws are clearly stated and explained; and
- They must conform to the technical standards noted on the product or its packaging, and conform with the standards and quality indicated on the product or the product sample.

The manufacturer must also ensure that the proper marks are placed on the products or their packaging, including the following statutory contents (Article 27 of the Product Quality Law):

- a certificate of quality inspection;
- the name of the product and the name and address of manufacturer in the Chinese language;
- where required, the specification, grades or names and contents of the major ingredients, specified clearly in Chinese. Consumers must be informed in advance and the information must be marked on the outer packaging;
- where products have a time limit for use, the date of production or the period for safe use or the date of expiry;
- warning signs or warnings written in Chinese, for products which may be damaged or could injure persons or property due to improper use; and
- for products which are fragile, flammable, explosive, toxic, erosive or radioactive, which cannot be handled upside down in the process of storage or transportation or for which other special requirements apply, warning signs or warnings written in Chinese or carry special information about handling in accordance with the relevant statutory provisions (Article 28 of the Product Quality Law).

(d) *Traceability*

A taceability system was first adopted for meat products in China in early 2004 on a pilot basis. In the past a few years, despite various difficulties in establishing such system in the food supply chain in China, China has made considerable progress in establishing the traceability system for meat and vegetable products in a few big cities such as Beijing and Shanghai. For example, in August 2008, Beijing enforced a food traceability system along the full supply chain for food supplied to the Olympic Games.

To implement the mandatory requirement about food information management under the Food Safety Law 2009, the MOFCOM issued Guiding Opinions on Establishing a Traceability System for the Circulation of Meat and Vegetables on a Pilot Basis (2010) to promote the traceability system in the circulation of food in more Chinese cities.

3.3 Post-market obligations

(a) General

Business operators are subject to various statutory post-market obligations under the relevant product safety and recall laws and regulations, which may be summarised as follows:

- The manufacturer must record and maintain information relating to the design, production and sale of products. Such records must be kept for a reasonable period of time consistent with the products' warranty period.
- The manufacturer must maintain a product defects monitoring system to collect, record and analyse information on quality problems and accidents which arise. Based on that information, the manufacturer must make assessments about product risks.
- The seller must maintain accounts for sales and receipts of products to accurately reflect types, specifications, product batch numbers, quantity and buyers.
- The manufacturer may not conceal or mis-state facts relating to any dangers associated with the defective products and must timeously report to the quality supervisory authorities relevant information regarding any defects.
- Upon discovering defective products which may cause danger to personal health or property safety, the manufacturer, seller or other related service providers must take corrective measures, such as issuing warning, notifications, and/or withdrawing or recalling products.

(b) Food

Food manufacturers must carry out food safety investigations and food safety risk assessments if they become aware of potential safety risks in their products or if they receive written food safety risk investigation notification from the local quality supervisory authority (Article 13 of the Administrative Regulations on the Recall of Food 2007 (Food Recall Rules[3])). The food manufacturer must promptly report the result of its investigation and risk assessment to the local quality supervisory authority.

In the event the food manufacturer fails to carry out the food safety risk investigation and assessment, the local quality supervisory authority may form an expert panel to investigate and assess the food safety risk. In such a case, the food manufacturer must fully cooperate and assist in the investigation (Articles 14 and 15 of the Food Recall Rules).

On confirmation that the food safety risks were caused by production-related reasons, the food manufacturer must decide on the extent of the recalls and implement the recalls based on a true approximation of the circumstances (Article 17 of the Food Recall Rules).

---

3 In July 2011 the State Food and Drug Administration issued the draft Administrative Regulations on the Recall of Health Food to solicit public opinions, which are still undergoing legislative scrutiny but not yet finalised. Once enacted, they will impose similar recall procedures for health food sold in China.

Upon identifying the defective food, the manufacturer must immediately stop its production and sale, and must notify the seller to cease sales and consumers to stop using the unsafe food. At the same time, the manufacturer must disclose recall information to the public and report it to the quality supervisory authority. The recall plan must be submitted to the quality supervisory authority with updates about progress of the recall following timeframes set out in the Food Recall Rules (Articles 19 to 24 of the Food Recall Rules).

The quality supervisory authority may order a food producer to recall its unsafe food, and take other corrective actions in any of the following events (Article 25 of the Food Recall Rules):

- the manufacturer deliberately conceals food safety hazards, or fails to recall food where it must implement a voluntary recall;
- it appears that food safety hazards have increased or have recurred due to the manufacturer's fault; or
- the quality supervisory authority discovers, during a random sampling inspection, latent safety problems that may be hazardous to human health or life.

Upon receipt of the mandatory recall notice from the quality supervisory authority, the manufacturer must make a recall according to procedures which are similar to those for voluntary recalls (Articles 26 to 27 of the Food Recall Rules).

The manufacturer must keep records of its recall activities and must promptly provide a recall report to the quality supervisory authority, which is subject to review and assessment by the expert panel formed by the quality supervisory authority. If the recall report does not pass the review of the expert panel, the manufacturer may have to continue the recall or repeat the recall (Articles 28 to 30 of the Food Recall Rules).

Food manufacturers must safely treat/dispose of any unsafe food. They must keep detailed records about any follow-up treatment of recalled food, report to the local municipal quality supervisory authority, and be prepared to be subject to the supervision of the quality supervisory authority (Article 31, Food Recall Rules).

(c) ***Medicines***

Entities trading in or using drugs must immediately cease the sale or use of the drugs if they discover any safety risks. They must also notify the manufacturer or supplier and report the risk to the drug supervisory authority, and must assist in any investigations instigated by the drugs supervisory authority (Article 6 of the Administrative Measures for Drug Recalls 2007 (Drugs Recall Rules)).

Drugs manufacturers must also investigate the potential safety risks of its drugs and must assist in any investigations instigated by the drugs supervisory authority (Article 11 of the Drug Recall Rules).

As for foods, the recall of drugs may be classified on three levels according to the perceived seriousness of the risk (Article 14 of the Drug Recall Rules). The drug manufacturer must promptly make and implement a recall plan by notifying the entities trading in or using the drugs to cease sales or use and report to the provincial drugs supervisory authority (Article 16 of the Drug Recall Rules).

After the commencement of the drug recall, the manufacturer must submit its investigation and assessment report and the recall plan to the provincial drug supervisory authority, which may set up an expert panel to review and assess the recall plan and make relevant adjustments as necessary. The manufacturer must update the provincial drugs supervisory authority about progress of the recall during the recall procedure (Articles 17 to 21 of the Drug Recall Rules).

The drug manufacturer must keep detailed records about the disposal of the recalled drugs and report on this to the provincial drug supervisory authority. Drugs which must be destroyed must be disposed of under the supervision of the above authority (Article 22 of the Drug Recall Rules).

The drug manufacturer must also evaluate the effect of the recall and submit a drug recall summary report to the drug supervisory authority for its review. The authority may then organise experts to undertake further examinations and evaluations as necessary. If the recall is deemed insufficient, the authority may ask the drug manufacturer to re-recall or extend its scope (Article 23 to 24 of the Drugs Recall Rules).

(d) *Medical devices*

The Ministry of Health recently enacted the Administrative Measures for the Recall of Medical Devices (Medical Device Recall Rules), which impose similar post-market statutory obligations on the medical device manufacturers.

Under the rules, manufacturers of medical devices must establish and refine mechanisms for product recall and proactively collect safety information to investigate or assess potential defects. They must also be prepared to do the following as necessary:

- recall defective products on the market;
- issue warnings;
- undertake inspections;
- repair;
- re-label;
- revise instructions for use;
- upgrade product software; and
- replace, retrieve or destroy the product.

Drug regulatory authorities may demand a mandatory recall of certain medical devices based on their own investigation or assessment of product safety information. Manufacturers of the medical device in question must implement the mandatory recall according to similar procedures which apply to voluntary recalls.

(e) *Automobiles*

The Auto Recall Rules constitute the first recall regulation issued by the Chinese government. Under the rules, automotive product manufacturers (or importers) are responsible for recalling defective automotive products manufactured (or imported), and bear the expenses of eliminating defects and necessary shipment costs. Distributors, lessors and repair shops of automotive products must also assist manufacturers in discharging the obligation to recall (Article 2 of the Auto Recall Rules).

The limitation period for defective automotive product recall commences when a complete vehicle is delivered to the first owner and ends when the safe period for use expressly indicated by the manufacturer expires. Where automotive manufacturers fail expressly to indicate the safe period for use, or where the safe period for use is less than 10 years, the time limit ends 10 years from the date on which the automotive product is delivered to the first owner. With regard to 'quick-wear' parts of safety components of automotive products, the service life is the recall time-limit (eg, the recall time-limit for tyres ends three years from the date when an automotive product is delivered to the first owner (Article 7 of the Auto Recall Rules)).

Chapters 5 and 6 of the Auto Recall Rules set out two procedures for the recall of defective automotive products: voluntary recall by manufacturers (Chapter 5) and compulsory recall ordered by governing authorities (Chapter 6).

Where manufacturers detect by themselves or otherwise learn of defects (through their internal information systems, reports or complaints by parties such as distributors, repair shops and owners, or through notices by governing authorities), they must submit recall plans to the governing authorities before instigating the recall of defective automotive products according to voluntary recall procedures. Where manufacturers aware of existing defects fail to make the voluntary recall, or intentionally conceal defects, or handle defects improperly, the governing authorities will instruct manufacturers to conduct the recall according to the compulsory procedure.

In the process of a compulsory recall, the competent Chinese authorities may order Chinese certification institutions to suspend or revoke mandatory verification certificates for such automotive products. For automotive products manufactured overseas, the Chinese authorities may issue public announcements about suspended imports in conjunction with the Ministry of Commerce and General Administration of Customs, and the latter may impose customs entry formalities. Where the products are en route to China or already shipped to China with customs formalities not yet completed, importers must go through return formalities according to Customs' rules. The Chinese authorities will then review the seriousness of the defect and urgency of the situation and decide whether to notify the public of the defects and order emergency measures and/or other relevant actions (Article 30).

(f) *Children's toys*

The Administrative Regulations on the Recall of Children's Toys (Toy Recall Rules) were issued in 2007. They impose similar statutory post-market obligations on toy manufacturers, including information management, defect investigation and risk assessment, notification, recall and reporting.

A manufacturer must, on being informed of any possible defect in the children's toys provided by it, immediately initiate a defect investigation to confirm whether the defect exists (Article 14). The Chinese quality supervisory authorities may also initiate a defect investigation and notify the manufacturer of risks found in association with the toys (Article 15).

If a defect is confirmed following an investigation, a risk assessment must be conducted to assess the possibility of the defect causing damage to children's health and safety and the extent and scope of any such damage. The toys must be recalled depending on the outcome of the risk assessment (Article 19).

After a toy defect is confirmed, the manufacturer must immediately stop manufacturing and distributing the defective toys, release relevant information about the defect, notify distributors that they must to stop selling the toys and consumers that they must stop purchasing them, and make a voluntary recall of the defective toys (Article 21).

The quality supervisory authority may order manufacturers to carry out a compulsory recall if:

- after a toy defect is confirmed, the manufacturer does not voluntarily recall the defective toys as required by law; or
- it is confirmed in a random inspection made by the state that the toys produced by the manufacturer have a latent danger and may pose a threat to the health and safety of children (Article 27 of the Toy Recall Rules).

Both voluntary recall and compulsory recalls will be subject to the supervision, guidance and approval of local quality supervisory authorities (Articles 25, 26, 33 and 34).

4. Enforcement

Generally speaking, the AQSIQ and its local agencies are the main bodies which oversee product safety control and products recall, while the AIC and its local agencies is the principal administrative body responsible for protecting consumer rights. Other Chinese government agencies may share the responsibility for ensuring product safety and administering product recalls in their respective areas.

4.1 Sector organisations

(a) General consumer products – AQSIQ

Pending the official enactment of the draft Defective Products Recall Regulation, there are no universal recall regulations governing all general consumer products, even though the Special Rules and the Tort Liability Law impose recall obligations on manufacturers and sellers of all products made or sold in China.

Currently, AQSIQ oversees the recall of children's toys according to the Toy Recall Rules and handles product quality related problems for general consumer products jointly with the SAIC and other related government agencies.

(b) Food

In recent years, particularly after the contaminated milk incidents of 2007, the Chinese government has taken significant steps to enhance food and product safety protection. In February 2010, the State Council established the Food Safety Commission to coordinate food safety efforts across the myriad of national, provincial and local agencies responsible for China's food and product safety.

Subsequently, the Ministry of Health established national committees on food safety standards and food safety risk assessment. To date, both the State Council and the Ministry of Health , along with the AQSIQ and other government authorities oversee food safety in China.

In accordance with the Food Recall Rules, AQSIQ and its local agencies oversee the recall of defective food, and the Food Safety Law also provides that AQSIQ, SAIC and SFDA and their local agencies may order a recall or stop the business operation if the operator fails to recall or stop producing defective food products (Article 53 of the Food Safety Law).

(c) *Motor vehicles*

The Auto Recall Rules were jointly issued by AQSIQ, MOFCOM, NDRC and GAC. While AQSIQ and its local agencies are mainly responsible for the administration of the recall of auto products, MOFCOM, NDRC and GAC and their local agencies also provide assistance and coordination within their respective areas.

Since the enforcement of this auto recall system, manufacturers (including international and domestic ones) have recalled millions of automobiles in China. The Chinese government is now poised to enact a new regulation on the recall of auto products. Once implemented, the new rule will be much more stringent than the above 2004 recall rules, as it will impose much bigger administrative penalties on violations of recall rules.

(d) *Medicines and medical devices*

The Law on Administration of Drugs was first enacted in 1984 and then amended in 2001. It set out the regulatory framework governing the production, sale and use of medicines in China. According to this law, the production and sale of medicines is licensed and quality management standards issued by the State Administration of Drugs (the predecessor of the SFDA) must be followed.

In 2007, the SFDA issued the Drug Recall Rules, which state that drugs found to be potentially hazardous should be recalled voluntarily by manufacturers. If a voluntary recall is not executed or fails, the SFDA may order a mandatory recall. In July 2011, the Ministry of Health promulgated the Medical Device Recall rules, which impose similar obligations on manufacturers of medical devices.

4.2 Powers of authorities

To administer the performance of the recall obligations by manufacturers or other related parties associated with the defective products, the quality supervisory authorities may exercise the following statutory powers:

- carry out onsite random sampling and inspection (eg, Article 18(1) of the Product Quality Law; Articles 77(1) and (2) of the Food Safety Law; Article 15(1) of the Special Rules);
- review, copy, attach, seize relevant contracts, invoices, accounts and other related documents (Article 18(3) of the Product Quality Law; Article 77(3) of the Food Safety Law; Article 15(2) of the Special Rules);
- seize or attach products which are not consistent with the statutory

requirements, illegally used raw materials, auxiliary materials, additives, and tools and equipment used for unlawful production (Article 18(4) of the Product Quality Law; Article 77(4) of the Food Safety Law; Article 15(3) of the Special Rules);

- seal off and close production or operation premises which have material hidden/latent dangers which could threaten personal health and safety (Article 77(5) of the Food Safety Law; Article 15(4) of the Special Rules);
- set up an expert panel to assess any risks posed by the defective products (Article 11 of the Auto Recall Rules; Article 20 of the Toy Recall Rules);
- notify the manufacturer and request it to make a mandatory recall of the defective products in the event product defects have been discovered but where the manufacturer refuses to make a voluntary recall (Article 9 of the Auto Recall Rules; Article 27 of the Toy Recall Rules; Article 25 of the Drug Recall Rules; Article 25 of the Food Recall Rules; Article 24 of the Medical Device Recall Rules);
- review the recall plans and make revisions if necessary (Article 33 of the Auto Recall Rules; Articles 23, 29 and 30 of the Toy Recall Rules; Articles 22 and 24 of the Food Recall Rules; Articles 17, 19 and 27 of the Drug Recall Rules; Articles 16, 18, 19 and 26 of the Medical Device Recall Rules);
- review the recall report and order a re-recall if necessary (Articles 29 and 38 of the Auto Recall Rules; Articles 25, 26 and 33 of the Toy Recall Rules; Articles 29 and 30 of the Food Recall Rules; Articles 24 and 28 of the Drug Recall Rules; Articles 22, 23 and 27 of the Medical Device Recall Rules); and
- impose relevant administrative sanctions on the manufacturer if it fails to undertake a recall and take other corrective actions (Articles 40 and 42 of the Auto Recall Rules; Article 35 to 41 of the Toy Recall Rules; Articles 35 to 39 of the Food Recall Rules; Articles 29 to 37 of the Drug Recall Rules; Articles 28 to 34 of the Medical Device Recall Rules).

4.3 Sanctions and compensation

Where manufacturers violate the obligations and duties imposed by the recall regulations, they will be subject to various administrative sanctions, including warnings, public criticism, administrative fines, cancellation of production licences and, in the case of serious violations, criminal sanctions.

For example, under the Medical Device Recall Rules, if a manufacturing enterprise fails to voluntarily recall defective medical devices in accordance with the recall rules it will be ordered to recall the devices, and will receive a concurrent fine equivalent to three times the value of the medical devices. In serious cases, the licence-issuing authority may revoke the medical device registration certificate or even the operating licence of the enterprise (Article 29 of the Medical Device Recall Rules).

A manufacturer that refuses to recall the medical devices despite a mandatory order for a compulsory recall issued by the drug regulatory authority will receive a fine equivalent to three times the value of the medical device that should have been recalled. In serious cases, the device registration certificate or the licence will be revoked (Article 30 of the Medical Device Recall Rules).

If a manufacturing enterprise is found to be in breach of the rules by virtue of having failed to do any of the following, it will receive a warning and will be ordered to rectify the situation within a specified time limit, as well as receiving a concurrent fine of no more than Rmb30,000 (Article 31 of the Medical Device Recall Rules):

- failure to inform the medical device trading enterprises, the entities using the medical devices or users of the decision to recall the medical devices within a prescribed time under the recall rules;
- failure to take rectification measures or re-recall the medical devices again as required by the drug regulatory authority that has reviewed the recall plans and results; or
- failure to keep detailed records of the medical devices recalled or failing to report such records to the drug regulatory authority.

Where a manufacturing enterprise involves any of the following situations, the relevant authority may issue a warning to it and order the enterprise to make rectification within a specified time period. If the enterprise fails to undertake necessary measures within the time limit, a fine of no more than Rmb30,000 will be imposed (Article 32 of the Medical Recall Rules):

- failure to establish a recall system in accordance with the recall rules;
- refusal to assist the drug regulatory authority in conducting an investigation;
- failure to submit a medical device recall incident report, an investigation and evaluation report, a recall plan, a report on the implementation of the medical device recall plan or a summary report on the recall plan; or
- failure to report a change to the recall plan to the drug regulatory authority.

If a medical device trading enterprise or an entity using the medical device discovers a defect but continues to use or sell the defective medical device and fails to report this to the manufacturer and relevant authorities, it may be ordered to suspend the sale or use of the defective medical device, and may receive a concurrent fine of not less than Rmb1,000 and not more than Rmb30,000. In serious cases, the original licence-issuing authority may revoke the enteprise's licence (Article 33 of the Medical Device Recall Rules).

If an enterprise or an entity using the medical device refuses to cooperate in the investigation of the defect of the relevant medical device or refuses to assist the medical device manufacturing enterprise in recalling the devices, the enterprise or the entity may be issued with a warning and ordered to make amends. An enterprise or entity refusing to rectify the situation will receive a fine of no more than Rmb30,000 (Article 34 of the Medical Device Recall Rules).

The imposition of the above administrative sanctions may not discharge or release the manufacturers from other civil liabilities to compensate customers that may have suffered harm based on general contractual or tort claims.[4]

4.4 Appeals

If the manufacturers or other parties disagree with any administrative decision or actions made by the quality supervisory authorities in the process of product recall, they may initiate an administrative review to challenge the administrative decision or action. If they are not happy with the administrative review decision, they may commence administrative litigation proceedings in the local courts.

4.5 International enforcement and cooperation

The product safety regulations and recall rules are generally applicable to products produced or sold in China, including imported products sold in China and exported products made in China.

The Law on the Import and Export Product Inspection China (first enacted in 1989 and amended in 2002; Inspection Law), provides for Chinese import and export commodities inspection authority to maintain a catalogue of import and export products which are subject to mandatory inspection rules in order to uphold the protection of the health and safety of human beings, protection of the life and health of animals or plants, protection of the environment, or prevention of fraud and the safeguarding of national security (Article 4, Inspection Law).

Import and export products listed in the catalogue must be inspected by the Chinese authorities in accordance with mandatory standards. Without passing the inspection, no products may be imported or exported (Articles 5 and 6 of the Inspection Law).

Although manufacturers of certain imported or exported products (eg, food) are subject to Chinese laws on registration and filing, it is generally the Chinese importer or agent of a foreign manufacturer of imported products that will be directly subject to the recall obligations in China under the product recall regulations. The Chinese importers may seek damages against their foreign manufacturers based on breach of contract; and Chinese consumers may file tort claims against the foreign manufacturers; but, generally speaking, the cross-border enforcement of Chinese recall regulations may not be easy for various technical and practicable reasons.

Given the above jurisdictional restrictions in the enforcement of the recall obligations, and in order to promote international cooperation to ensure product safety, the Chinese government has signed various cooperation agreements and memoranda with many foreign governments.

The most influential international product safety cooperation programme is the Consumer Product Safety Trilateral Summit, first begun in 2008, between China, the United States and the European Union. According to a joint statement by the tripartite participants at the Shanghai Summit 2010, ensuring a high level of product safety is a matter of shared concern for China, the United States, and the European Union. Coordination and cooperation between the governments to enhance product

---

4 The Medical Device Recall Rules are very typical and representative of other sectors. Similar fines and penalties are imposed in other sectors, except that, like the drug recall rules, the Medical Recall Rules impose for the first time a penalty up to three times the sale value of the defective products for certain bad-faith misconducts of the producers, eg, the producers are aware of the defects but refuse to make a voluntary recall, or the producer refuses to recall the defective products despite the fact that it has been ordered to do so by the authority. It is also notable that the draft Recall Rules as well as the Administrative Regulations on the Defective Automobile Products (discussion draft), both of which are still in the pipeline, once enacted, may considerably increase the range of the administrative penalties under the current recall rules.

safety administration are in the mutual interest of consumers and economies of these countries and regions.

5. Potential defendants

5.1 Manufacturer

Manufacturers are liable for defective products in China under a statutory strict liability regime. Article 41 of the Tort Law provides that 'where a defective product causes any harm to others, the manufacturer shall assume the tort liability' and there are similar clauses in the General Principles of the Civil Law of PRC (eg, Article 122) and the Product Quality Law (eg, Article 43).

5.2 Seller

Sellers' liability mainly arises under the system of fault-based tort liability. Article 42 of the Tort Law provides that "where a product with any defect caused by the fault of the seller causes any harm to others, the seller shall assume the tort liability". However, that liability becomes strict where a seller can identify neither the manufacturer nor the supplier of a defective product according to Article 42(2) of the Tort Law.

Sellers' product liability can also arise from contractual obligations. According to the Contract Law, the buyer is entitled to claim against the seller for product liability based on breach of contract if the quality of products provided by the seller fails to meet the agreed standards or implied warranty standards and causes damage to the buyer.

The Consumer Law also addresses the seller's product liability from the perspective of consumer protection. Article 35 of the Consumer Law provides that 'consumers whose legitimate rights and interests are infringed upon in their purchasing or using commodities may demand compensation from the sellers concerned'.

5.3 Third parties

Third parties may be held liable by the manufacturer or seller if the product defect is their fault. Article 44 of the Tort Law provides that "where any harm is caused to others by a defective product and the defect is caused by the fault of a third party such as a transporter or storekeeper, the manufacturer or seller of the product that has paid the compensation shall be entitled to be reimbursed by the third party". Article 122 of the Civil Law Principles also provide that "if a defective product causes property damage or physical injury to others, the manufacturer or seller shall bear civil liability according to law; if the transporter or storekeeper is responsible for the matter, the manufacturer or seller shall have the right to demand compensation for its losses".

6. Sources of liability

6.1 Civil liabilities

The manufacturer, the seller or related third parties may be liable for tort liability or contractual liability under different scenarios in the form of monetary compensation or other legal remedies such as repairing, reproducing, replacing, returning products or reducing the price of the products.

As to the burden of proof, claimants must prove the following:

- the product is defective;
- they used the defective product; and
- the injury or damage was caused by the defective product.

The claimant need not prove whether the defendant is at fault.

According to Article 46 of the Product Quality Law, defects refer to unreasonable risks endangering human beings or properties, or the nonconformity of products with relevant standards.

7. Claimants

For tort liability, claimant(s) could be buyers or users of the products or any third party harmed by the defective products.

For contractual liability, the claimant would be the buyer who is a party to the purchase or supply contract.

Multiple claims can be brought using the vehicle of representative action as provided for in the Civil Procedure Law. For a representative action to proceed there must be more than 10 claimants. Claimants may elect representatives to act on their behalf, and any acts of the representatives will be binding on the claimants. The court will deliver one single judgment to resolve the claims of all the claimants.

There are substantial differences between the Chinese representative action and class actions in some Western countries, the most significant being that the judgment made in a representative action can only apply to injured parties who apply to join the action or initiate a lawsuit with the same or similar claims (this is known as 'opt-in'). In practice, the effect of this is that representative actions can be much less effective than class actions. In any case, the Chinese courts are reluctant in practice to accept representative actions for various reasons.

8. Causation

Causation is an essential evidentiary step in supporting any product liability claim. The burden will be on the claimant to prove causation between the damage or injury and the defective products. Chinese law does not provide specific tests for proof of causation and in practice the claimant will have to show the defendant's product was a proximate and direct cause of the claimant's injury.

No specific guidance or case law is available here, however, the area being led by practice: causation may be determined by expert opinion or will be decided according to a judge's common sense.

With respect to injuries caused by failure to warn, Article 27 of the Product Quality Law provides that products should bear warning marks or statements to explain that improper use of the product is likely to cause damage or injury. In addition, Article 46 of the Tort Law provides statutory warning obligations on the manufacture or sellers where any product defect is found after the product is put into circulation. Failure to warn will result in tort liabilities for the manufacturer or sellers if damage or injury is caused. Hence, the claimant may hold the defendant liable if it can establish that its injury was caused by the defendant's failure to provide proper warning in advance.

To make out a defence, the manufacturer of the product may prove the following:

- the product has not been put into circulation;
- the defects did not exist when the product was put into circulation; or
- the defects could not be detected when the product was put into circulation due to scientific and technical limitations.

9. Remedies for injury/damage, and consequential loss

9.1 Compensation

Where any harm is caused by a defective product, the injured party may require compensation to be made by the manufacturer of the product or the seller of the product (Article 43 of the Tort Law).

If the defect in the product is caused by the manufacturer and the seller has paid compensation for the defect, the seller is entitled to be reimbursed by the manufacturer. Likewise, if the product defect is caused by the fault of the seller and the manufacturer has paid compensation for the defect, the manufacturer shall be entitled to be reimbursed by the seller.

Property damages and bodily injury caused by tort must be fully compensated by the tortfeasor. Compensation for bodily injury must include the reasonable costs and expenses of treatment and rehabilitation (eg, medical treatment expenses, nursing fees and travel expenses), as well as a sum to cover the cost of the injured party's lost wages (Article 16, Tort Law). If the injured party suffers any disability, the compensation must also cover costs of any disability assistance equipment needed to support the lifestyle of the injured party and the disability indemnity. If it causes the death of the injured party, the tortfeasor shall also pay the funeral expenses and fatal injury compensation. If the injured party financially supports family members, compensation shall also include maintenance fees for such family members if the injured party loses labour capacity or dies. The formula to calculate fatal injury compensation is the local disposable income per capita in the previous year, multiplied by up to 20 (for 20 years). The maintenance fee is calculated by local consumer spending per capita in the previous year, multiplied by no more than 20 (years). In calculating such compensatory sums, lost earnings are generally deemed as consequential losses.

Where a serious mental distress was suffered by the injured party, the injured party may also be entitled to compensation for inflicting of mental distress (Article 22, Tort Law).

9.2 Punitive damages

Where a manufacturer or seller with knowledge about any product defect continues to manufacture or sell the product and the defect causes fatal injury or any serious damage to the health of another person, the injured party shall be entitled to claim punitive compensation (Article 47 of the Tort Law). However, Article 47 is a general provision and newly introduced so we do not as yet have any clear or specific implementation rules. In practice the Chinese courts are reluctant to grant punitive damages unless expressly provided for in relevant laws or regulations (eg, in the Food Safety Law which provides that in certain circumstances, food consumers are entitled to claim for punitive damages equivalent to ten times the value of the product in addition to compensation for actual losses).

10. Procedure, limitation, funding, costs

According to the Civil Procedure Law, tort cases are subject to the jurisdiction of the court in the place where the tort is committed or the domicile of the defendant. Contractual disputes must be brought to the court of the defendant's domicile or of the place of performance of the contract. It is also permissible for parties of a contract to elect the court with jurisdiction by mutual agreement. Depending on the sums of money involved, any of the district court, intermediate court, high court or even the Supreme Court may be the court of first instance. The trial hearing (first instance) must be completed within six months of the date of the court's acceptance of the case, which may be extended for a further six months with good cause.

If one party is not satisfied with the judgment made by the court of first instance, it can appeal to the next higher court except in cases instigated in the Supreme Court.

The statutory limitation period for actions for damages due to product defects is two years, starting from the date when the claimant knew or should have known about the infringement (Product Quality Law). Actions also become time-barred after 10 years counting from the date when the defective products were delivered to the first consumer, unless there is a specified safe-use period which has not expired by then. For claims based on tort liabilities or contractual liabilities not covered by the Product Quality Law, the limitation of actions is also two years as of the date when the claimant knew or should have known about the infringement. However, the limitation period is one year for claims relating to bodily injury; or for the sale of substandard products without notice.

In any case, all civil claims under Chinese law become time-barred after 20 years from the date on which the claimant's rights were infringed.

The statutory limitations period may also be interrupted or suspended for various statutory reasons specified under the Civil Procedure Law.

Court fees will be borne by the losing party, but generally the courts will not order the losing party to bear the costs of the attorney fees of the prevailing party.

Free legal aid is available to claimants under certain circumstances; the court may even waive the court fees upon the claimants' application if the claimants cannot afford the courts fees.

11. Trends

As food and product safety remains a serious concern in China, with several high-profile cases in recent years, the Chinese government is under intense domestic and international pressure to beef up its management, supervision and regulation of product liability. The newly promulgated Tort Law is believed to represent a significant effort in this regard. It is expected that the Supreme Court in the near future may issue judicial interpretations to implement punitive damages, and improve the existing system for multiple claims to facilitate large group actions against companies producing defective products.

12. Products insurance

Legal entities and other organisations within the territory of China which need domestic insurance must purchase insurance from insurance companies based in China (this includes Chinese domestic insurance companies and foreign-invested insurance companies registered in China; Article 7 of the Chinese Insurance Law). However, in practice, some Chinese manufacturers of exported products, at the request of the foreign importers, also purchase product liability-related insurance from international insurers to cover product liabilities in foreign countries. We are not aware of any clear prohibition from the Chinese government on such foreign insurance coverage.

Product liability-related insurance is still relatively new and does not represent common practice yet within the Chinese insurance industry. There are various reasons for this, including low awareness of product insurance and the non-litigious nature of Chinese society. Although things are changing in the light of the increasing number of food and product safety crises in recent years, some types of product insurance (eg, contaminated products insurance and financial loss insurance) available in the international market are still not very common in China.

The following common product insurance types are currently being offered by major Chinese domestic insurance companies.

- product recall insurance, which covers the reasonable and necessary costs of a recall;
- product liability insurance, which covers statutory liabilities for injury or damage caused by defective products; and
- product guarantee insurance, which covers contractual liability for the cost of repairing or replacing a product where it fails to perform its function.

In China, generally, financial loss insurance does not cover loss resulting from product recall or product liabilities, and is thus not included in the list above.

As there are no specific laws and regulations governing the above product liability-related insurances in China, we will base our introduction of these insurance products on the prevailing practice of the leading Chinese insurance companies.

12.1 Product recall insurance

(a) Trigger

The legal burden of proof is on the insured to prove that an operating clause is probably triggered.

(b) Insured voluntarily decides to recall

The recall date is the date on which the insured issues a recall statement (ie, a statement published to let the public know about the recall); or when the insured submits a recall report to the insurer. The policy is likely to cover costs resulting from such 'recall dates' within the period of insurance. The terms of the policy are likely to cover the requirement that all recalls must be reasonable and necessary. Where there is any cause for dispute in this regard, the parties can resort to the courts.

(c) ***Government authorities order insured to recall***

The recall date shall be the date on which the government authorities issues a recall order.

(d) ***Pre-recall expenses, testing***

Generally, such preliminaries are not covered by the typical product recall insurance policy in China. Such expenses and fees are very unlikely to be covered because the insurer will indemnify only recall expenses, defined as expenses incurred during the compensation period starting from the recall date.

It may be possible to negotiate with the insurer if the insured wishes to include pre-recall expenses in the policy.

(d) ***Consultancy costs***

Generally, such costs are not covered by the typical product recall insurance policy in China. It may be possible to negotiate with the insurer if the insured wishes to include expenses in the policy.

(e) ***First party recall expenses***

According to a typical product recall insurance policy in China, recall expenses mainly cover the following:

- media fees for announcing the recall;
- transportation fees for retrieving the products;
- labour costs for additional non-employee workers;
- overtime pay for employees;
- fees for storing recalled products;
- transportation fees for replacing consumers' or distributors' products; and
- repair costs.

(f) ***Business interruption***

Losses caused by business interruption are generally not covered, being seen as indirect losses and as such often excluded by typical product recall insurance policies in China.

(g) ***Repair, replacement, refunds***

Repair and replacement costs (exclusive of the cost of new parts) are generally covered, but refunds are not covered under the typical Chinese product recall insurance policy.

(h) ***Brand rehabilitation***

This is generally not covered by a typical product recall insurance policy (indirect loss).

(i) ***Third-party recall liability***

If other products which use the recalled products as parts are recalled during the insurance period due to the defects in the recalled products, the insurer will generally indemnify the insured for the compensation of recall expenses it pays to the manufacturers, sellers and other related third parties of such other products, as required by Chinese law.

(j) ***Defence costs***

Arbitration fees and court fees, and other necessary and reasonable legal costs previously agreed by the insurer, are generally covered by a typical product recall insurance policy.

(k) ***Impairment***

Losses caused by impairment of the recalled products themselves are generally not covered.

(l) ***Exclusions***

Under a typical product recall policy in China, liabilities (first and third party) are excluded if mainly caused by the following:

- wilful misconduct or gross negligence by the insured;
- war, warlike operation, terrorism or similar;
- nuclear radiation, radioactive contamination or similar;
- earthquake, tsunami or similar;
- administrative actions or judicial actions (excluding government recall orders);
- air pollution, soil pollution, water pollution or other pollution;
- recalls instigated prior to the commencement of the insurance period; and
- the impossibility of detecting the defects due to technical or scientific limitations at the time the products were put into circulation.

In addition, in the following scenarios, the expenses, costs and losses of a recall are generally excluded:

- the recalled products had been on the market for more than five years at the commencement of the insurance period;
- the quality guarantee period had expired by the time the recall was conducted (so the insured will bear no obligations to repair the products when the guarantee period expires); or
- the recalled products are prototypes or made to order.

The following are also excluded:

- contractual or tort liabilities arising from the defective products;
- fines, penalties and punitive damages;
- compensation for non-economic losses;
- indirect losses; and
- any deductible excess.

(m) ***Conditions***

Under a typical product insurance policy in China, the following conditions must be satisfied in order to be able to claim successfully:

- the recall date is within the insurance period;
- the recall occurs in the territory of coverage;
- the expenses and costs are covered by the insured liabilities and do not fall into the above exclusions;
- the expenses, costs and losses are greater than the deductible excess;
- the expenses, costs and losses are within the insurance amount; and
- the expenses, costs and losses are generated within the agreed maximum time-period for compensation.

12.2 Product liability insurance

The legal burden of proof is on the insured to prove that an operating clause is properly triggered.

(a) ***Insuring provisions***

Injury and damages: The insurer will generally indemnify the insured in the manner and within the limit of liability specified in the policy against such sums as the insured shall become legally liable to pay, in respect of claims made against the insured arising from bodily injury to or illness or fatal injury or loss of or damage to property of one or more persons using, consuming or handling the insured products or goods, or of any other persons consequent upon an occurrence taking place in the territory of coverage within the insurance period caused by products or goods manufactured or sold by the insured.

Legal costs: In respect of any claim covered under the policy, the insurer will generally also indemnify the insured against the relevant legal costs payable by the insured and other expenses incurred with the prior written consent of the insurer, but the total liability of the insurer for the sums of compensation and the legal costs and expenses shall in no way exceed the limit of indemnity stated in the policy.

(b) ***Exclusions***

Exclusion clauses of a typical product liability insurance policy generally include the following:

- liability assumed in accordance with any agreement between the insured and other parties, unless such liability would have attached to the insured notwithstanding such agreement;
- liability assumed by the insured under any labour law or employee compensation statute;
- liability of the insured to employees based on the employment relationship;
- loss of or damage to the insured products;
- costs arising out of replacement or recall of the insured products and parts;
- loss of or damage to property belonging to or held in care, custody or control

of the insured;

- bodily injury, illness or fatal injury or damage to property sustained by any person caused by products or goods manufactured or sold by the insured in wilful violation of any law;
- liability arising out of pollution of any kind or description whatsoever caused by the insured products;
- liability for loss of or damage to aircrafts or ships caused by the insured products;
- liability for any consequence arising directly or indirectly from war, warlike operation, hostilities, armed conflicts, terrorism, conspiracy, insurrection or coups d'état;
- liability for any consequence arising directly or indirectly from strike, riot, civil commotion or malicious acts;
- liability arising directly or indirectly from nuclear fission, nuclear fusion, nuclear weapon, nuclear material, nuclear radiation and radioactive contamination;
- fines, penalties, punitive or exemplary indemnities; and
- any deductibles referred to in the policy as being borne by the insured.

(c) ***Conditions***

A typical product liability insurance policy in China generally provides for the following conditions:

- the injury and/or damage must occur during the insurance period;
- the injury and/or damage must occur in the territory of coverage;
- the first claim must be submitted in the insurance period;
- the insured must be legally liable for the loss;
- the liability must be covered by the insured's liabilities and not fall within an exclusion; and
- the indemnification must be within the insurance amount.

12.3 Product guarantee insurance

(a) ***Insuring provisions***

The insurer will generally indemnify the beneficiary for repair, replacement and refund liabilities borne by the insured and related testing fees, transportation and communication expenses due to quality problems caused by the following reasons:

- the insured product is not of the agreed or implied quality without notice;
- the insured product does not conform to the standard indicated on the product or its package; or
- the quality of the insured product does not conform to the specification or the quality of a sample.

(b) ***Exclusions***

Under a typical product guarantee policy in China, the insurer will not indemnify losses and expenses caused by the following:

- criminal or wilful conduct of the insured or its representatives;
- fraudulent actions of the insured or the beneficiary;
- war, warlike operations, terrorist event, strike, riot, theft and robbery;
- confiscation by government agencies;
- nuclear reaction, nuclear radiation, radioactive pollution or other kinds of pollution;
- acts of god and accidents such as earthquake, thunder strike, fire, explosion, rainstorm, flood and typhoon;
- the consumer's failure to operate the product in accordance with the operation instructions;
- ordinary wear and tear of products;
- recall of the product;
- transportation or storage issues; or
- non-detection of defects due to technical or scientific limitations at the time the products were manufactured.

Further, the insurer will generally not indemnify the following losses and expenses:

- bodily injury and property damages other than damages to the insured products;
- claims between affiliate companies;
- fines and punitive damages;
- indirect damages caused by insurance accidents; and
- costs of free repair services offered by the insured.

Moreover, the insurer generally will not indemnify losses and expenses of the following products:

- defective products accepted and acknowledged by the consumer;
- products that entered the market without testing or with non-certificated testing results, or whose manufacturing date or sale date cannot be confirmed;
- products sold after the expiry of their safe service life, effective life or guarantee period; and
- products sold after the termination, liquidation or bankruptcy of the insured.

(c) ***Conditions***

The following conditions should generally be satisfied to justify a claim under a typical product guarantee policy in China:

- the first claim is submitted within the insurance period;
- the insured is legally liable for the loss;
- the liability is covered by the insured liabilities and does not fall within any exclusions; and
- the indemnification is within the insurance amount.

England and Wales

Mark Kendall
Jason McNerlin
Sedgwick, Detert, Moran & Arnold LLP

1. Product safety regulation

1.1 Regulatory framework – an overview

Product safety is highly regulated, and various regulatory techniques are used to increase the probability that products reaching the market are acceptably safe. Those methods include domestic and international product safety regulations, which impose safety requirements as well as criminal penalties for failure to comply with those requirements. For certain classes of product, typically ones that could pose serious risks to great numbers of people, such as medicines and automotive vehicles, regulations also impose requirements to obtain official authority to supply new products within those classes.

There are regulations of general application, and regulations that apply only to specific categories of products. The Consumer Protection Act 1987 is important 'general' legislation. It set out a general safety requirement (now superseded) and provides for the making of safety regulations for specific types of product (see below for some examples). The general safety requirement in the act was largely superseded by the General Product Safety Regulations 1994. For almost all products, the General Product Safety Regulations 2005 now apply, except to the extent of more specific regulations.

In addition to regulations, there are many product safety standards, which are of great practical importance. Safety standards relate to the design and/or performance of products. Although compliance with applicable safety standards does not conclusively determine the issue of 'safety', the General Product Safety Regulations 2005 provide that, where a product conforms to certain types of standard, it is presumed to comply with the general safety requirement.

Before the General Product Safety Regulations 2005 came into force, certain specific products had safety regimes requiring notification and corrective actions. The 2005 regulations introduced measures of general application to almost all products, including a notification duty, and powers of enforcement authorities to order or perform corrective actions.

The Consumer Protection Act 1987 remains the key source of 'strict liability' for claims by consumers for injury and property damage caused by a product defect (see "Product liability" below).

1.2 Safety regulation – safety requirements, offences and penalties

There is a wide range of safety regulations, governing production, distribution, record keeping, and corrective actions. Unsurprisingly, products that carry significant safety risks, or are consumed or used universally or by a great proportion of the public, are subject to more detailed regulation.

Safety regulations can be broadly classified into two categories:

- 'general' provisions, which apply generally to all products, except to the extent that more specific regulations apply; and
- 'special' provisions, which apply only to specified types of product.

Provisions of general application impose a general requirement that products be 'safe'. Special regulations set out additional, more detailed, requirements concerning safety. The various regulations use different language in imposing obligations and prohibitions.

(a) General provisions – the General Product Safety Regulations 2005

The General Product Safety Regulations 2005 apply to all new and used products, except secondhand products supplied as needing repair or reconditioning before use (provided that the buyer is clearly informed of this), and except where products are subject to other specific safety requirements.

The regulations set out a 'general safety requirement'. Regulation 5 provides that "No producer shall place a product on the market unless it is a safe product". (For the meaning of 'safe,' see below.) 'Producer' is defined to include own-branders, persons who recondition products, and others whose activity may affect the safety properties of a product. For products manufactured outside the EEA, 'producer' also includes an EEA representative or party importing the product into the EEA.

Regulation 29 provides for the defence of 'due diligence'; in relation to any offence under the General Product Safety Regulations 2005, it is a defence that the relevant party took all reasonable steps and exercised all due diligence to avoid committing an offence.

Under Regulation 20, contravention of Regulation 5 is an offence, punishable when tried summarily by a term of imprisonment of up to three months, and/or by the statutory maximum fine (currently £5,000). If convicted on indictment, the maximum penalty is 12 months' imprisonment and/or a fine of £20,000.

(b) Special provisions

Section 10 of the Consumer Protection Act 1987 set out a 'general safety requirement', but this requirement has been replaced by Regulation 5 of the General Product Safety Regulations.

Section 11 of the Consumer Protection Act 1987 provides for the making of "safety regulations", except for certain specified products including food and medicines. Below, we refer to examples of such safety regulations, relating to toys, cosmetic products and electrical equipment.

The supply of goods in contravention of such safety regulations is an offence (Consumer Protection Act 1987, Section 12). Generally, a person convicted after summary trial is liable to imprisonment for a term not exceeding six months and/or to a fine not exceeding level 5 on the standard scale (currently £5,000). There are exceptions, however, some of which are noted below.

The Consumer Protection Act 1987 provides (in Section 39) for the defence of 'due diligence', which applies where a defendants shows that it "took all reasonable steps and exercised due diligence to avoid committing the offence".

Toys (Safety) Regulations 2011: These regulations replaced the Toys (Safety) Regulations 1995, and came into force on August 19 2011. Regulation 5 sets out the 'essential safety requirements' of a toy. These requirements consist of the general safety requirements (set out at Regulation 5(2) to 5(5)), and the particular safety requirements, set out at Annex II of Directive 2009/48/EC. The particular safety requirements cover physical, mechanical, chemical and electrical properties of toys, as well as their flammability, hygiene and radioactivity. The new requirements as to chemical properties of toys are subject to a transitional provision for toys placed on the market before July 20 2013.

Regulation 10 prohibits manufacturers from placing a toy on the market unless the toy complies with the essential safety requirements, and the manufacturer has complied with Regulations 11 to 13, 15, 17(1) to (3), and 19 to 21. These impose obligations regarding design and manufacture (Regulation 11), safety assessment (Regulation 12), conformity assessment procedure (Regulation 13), EC declarations of conformity (Regulations 15 and 16), CE marking (Regulations 15 and 18), technical information (Regulation 17), information identifying the manufacturer (Regulation 19), instructions, safety information and warnings (Regulation 20), and compliance procedures for series production (Regulation 21).

Under Regulation 26, importers must not place a toy on the market unless the importer has complied with Regulations 27 (identifying the importer) and 28 (storage and transport conditions), and has ensured that the manufacturer has complied with Regulations 13, and 17 to 20. Under Regulation 33, distributors must not make a toy available unless they have complied with Regulation 34 (storage and transport conditions), verified that the manufacturer has complied with regulations 18 to 20, and verified that any importer has complied with Regulation 27.

A breach of these regulations is an offence under Section 12 of the Consumer Protection Act 1987, and the penalty is as set out above.

Cosmetic Products (Safety) Regulations 2008: These regulations contain 'general' and 'particular' safety requirements. The general safety requirement is set out in Regulation 4, which requires that no person supply a cosmetic product that "may cause damage to human health when applied under normal or reasonably foreseeable conditions of use".

More particularly, the regulations prohibit the supply of certain cosmetic products that contain prohibited substances set out in Schedule 3 to the regulations. The inclusion of other specified substances, including certain colouring agents, preservatives and UV filters, is permitted, subject to conditions.

Regulation 22 sets out various penalties, applicable according to the specific regulation that has been breached.

Electrical Equipment (Safety) Regulations 1994: Electrical equipment must be safe

(Regulation 5), and bear the CE marking (Regulation 9). 'Safe' is defined to have generally the same meaning set out in Section 19(1) of the Consumer Protection Act 1987. Schedule 3 sets out the principal elements of the safety objectives, including general conditions regarding design and manufacture, as well as protection against particular hazards, including those caused by external influences on the equipment.

Regulation 14 makes it an offence to supply any electrical equipment that does not comply with Regulations 5 and 9. The penalty for contravention is as set out above. As an exception, where the supplied equipment creates a risk of property damage or injury to animals, but no risk of injury to persons, the maximum penalty on summary conviction is imprisonment for a term not exceeding three months and/or a fine not exceeding level 5 on the standard scale (currently £5,000).

Food – Regulation (EC) 178/2002: There are many regulations relating to aspects of food safety, including licensing, processing, production, labelling, packaging, distribution and marketing.

Article 14 of EC Regulation 178/2002 sets out the 'food safety requirements', including that "food shall not be placed on the market if it is unsafe". Article 14 also provides that food is deemed to be unsafe if it is injurious to health, or unfit for human consumption (see below).

By the General Food Regulations 2004 (Regulation 4(a)), contravention of Article 14 is an offence. Under Regulation 5, a person convicted on indictment is liable to imprisonment for a term not exceeding two years, and/or to an unlimited fine. On summary conviction, the maximum penalty is a term of six months and/or a fine of £20,000. Regulation 7 applies certain provisions of the Food Safety Act 1990, including the defence of due diligence.

Human Medicines Regulations 2012: The Human Medicines Regulations 2012 came into force on August 14 2012, and set out the consolidated legal framework for the control of medicinal products for human use.

The regulatory method is, for any new product, to require the following:

- authority to conduct clinical trials to test safety (and quality and efficacy); and
- authority to market the product; and
- operation of a pharmacovigilance system, involving ongoing monitoring and reporting of safety issues, eg suspected adverse reactions (Part 11 of the regulations).

The Medicines and Healthcare Products Regulatory Agency (MHRA), an agency of the Department of Health, remains the responsible regulating authority. Before a marketing authorisation is granted, it is necessary to obtain the MHRA's permission to conduct clinical trials. The MHRA assesses subsequent licensing applications and, if necessary, obtains independent expert advice from the Commission of Human Medicines. If the MHRA is satisfied that a medicine is effective, and acceptably safe, it may issue a marketing authorisation.

Under Regulation 17 of the Human Medicines Regulations 2012, a person without a licence may not manufacture any medicinal product. Regulation 18 imposes similar obligations for licences to distribute ('wholesale dealer's licences'). Under Regulation 34(1), breach of either obligation is an offence.

Under Regulation 46, a person may not sell or supply an unauthorised medicinal product, or an authorised product otherwise than in accordance with the terms of an authorisation or registration.

In the event of breach of the above duties concerning manufacture and supply, Regulations 35 and 47 state that the penalty is, on summary conviction, a fine not exceeding the statutory maximum (currently £5,000), or, on conviction on indictment, an unlimited fine and/or imprisonment for a term not exceeding two years. There are numerous other relevant duties and offences, including those relating to pharmacovigilance.

Automotive vehicles, systems and components: The General Product Safety Regulations 2005 and other safety regulations apply to automotive products. It should also be noted that vehicles, and their component systems and parts, are subject to detailed regimes of 'type approval'. For new products, this involves testing by reference to certain performance requirements. Once all systems and components have been approved, a whole vehicle is assessed. A satisfactory assessment will lead to whole vehicle type approval, and documentary evidence of approval, depending on the approval regime concerned. Generally, approval is valid until the point of any change in design, or change in the applicable standards.

As an example of legislation regarding type approvals, Directive 92/23/EEC requires member states to give type approval to tyre types that satisfy the requirements of Annex II of the directive.

In addition to the General Product Safety Regulations 2005, other safety regulations may apply. For example, the Motor Vehicle Tyres (Safety) Regulations 1994, made under Section 11 of the Consumer Protection Act 1987, prohibit the supply of tyres that do not bear a valid approval mark. In addition, Section 75 of the Road Traffic Act 1988 prohibits the sale of vehicles that are in an unroadworthy condition.

1.3 Compliance with safety requirements

The examples above show that there are different safety requirements for different products. Some products must be 'safe', while others (such as toys) have detailed particular safety requirements.

Below, we set out further detail on the general meaning of 'safe', as well as specific safety requirements for foods, medicinal products, and automotive products.

If an unsafe product has been put onto the market, in addition to possible criminal penalties, producers and distributors have obligations to notify the authorities and to conduct corrective actions.

1.4 Statutory definition of 'safe'

The Consumer Protection Act 1987, Section 19(1), defines 'safe' as:

such that there is no risk, or no risk apart from one reduced to a minimum, that any of the following [essentially use or consumption] will (whether immediately or after a definite or indefinite period) cause the death of, or any personal injury to, any person whatsoever ....

The General Product Safety Regulations 2005 define 'safe product', and provide guidance by listing the factors to be considered when assessing whether a product is safe. Regulation 2(1) provides:

'safe product' means a product which, under normal or reasonably foreseeable conditions of use including duration and, where applicable, putting into service, installation and maintenance requirements, does not present any risk or only the minimum risks compatible with the product's use, considered to be acceptable and consistent with a high level of protection for the safety and health of persons.

The Consumer Protection Act 1987 definition permits only minimum risk, and the General Product Safety Regulations' definition permits the minimum risks that are acceptable and consistent with a high level of consumer protection. These definitions are similar, each requiring a judgement as to whether a risk is acceptable.

It should also be noted that, for the purposes of the General Product Safety Regulations 2005, a producer should anticipate 'abnormal' uses of a product: it is likely this will apply particularly to products that might be misused by children.

1.5 Presumption of conformity

Regulation 6 of the General Product Safety Regulations 2005 sets out presumptions of conformity, by reference to compliance with certain national and international product safety standards. For example, Regulation 6(2) provides that:

Where a product conforms to a voluntary national standard of the United Kingdom giving effect to a European standard the reference of which has been published in the Official Journal of the European Union in accordance with Article 4 of the GPS Directive, the product shall be presumed to be a safe product so far as concerns the risks and categories of risk covered by that national standard. The Secretary of State shall publish the reference number of such national standards in such manner as he considers appropriate.

Compliance with such standards is not equivalent to the product being 'safe', so is not a bar to enforcement action. However, it is unlikely that a court would decide that a product which complies with standards is nevertheless unsafe, unless, for example, aggravating factors are present. More detailed official guidance is available to assist with risk assessment, some of which is summarised below.

2. Other obligations of producers and distributors

Regulation 7 of the General Product Safety Regulations sets out other important general obligations relating to safety issues and corrective actions:

(3) Within the limits of his activities, a producer shall adopt measures commensurate with the characteristics of the products which he supplies to enable him to—

(a) be informed of the risks which the products might pose, and

(b) take appropriate action including, where necessary to avoid such risks, withdrawal, adequately and effectively warning consumers as to the risks or, as a last resort, recall.

(4) The measures referred to in paragraph (3) include—

(a) except where it is not reasonable to do so, an indication by means of the product or its packaging of—

(i) the name and address of the producer, and

(ii) the product reference or where applicable the batch of products to which it belongs;

and

(b) where and to the extent that it is reasonable to do so—

(i) sample testing of marketed products,

(ii) investigating and if necessary keeping a register of complaints concerning the safety of the product, and

(iii) keeping distributors informed of the results of such monitoring where a product presents a risk or may present a risk.

Failure to take a measure specified in Regulation 7(4) is an offence (Regulation 20(2)), triable summarily and punishable by a term of imprisonment of up to three months and/or a level 5 fine (currently £5,000).

2.1 Compliance with safety requirements

(a) General products

ISO/IEC Guide 51 (International Standardisation Organisation) states a non-exhaustive list of factors that are to be taken into account when assessing whether a product is 'safe'. Those factors include:

(a) the characteristics of the product, including its composition, packaging, instructions for assembly and, where applicable, instructions for installation and maintenance,

(b) the effect of the product on other products, where it is reasonably foreseeable that it will be used with other products,

(c) the presentation of the product, the labelling, any warnings and instructions for its use and disposal and any other indication or information regarding the product, and

(d) the categories of consumers at risk when using the product, in particular children and the elderly.

Importantly, the guide goes on to clarify that:

The feasibility of obtaining higher levels of safety or the availability of other products presenting a lesser degree of risk shall not constitute grounds for considering a product to be a dangerous product.

Additional guidance is set out in *Notification guidance for producers and distributors*, published in September 2005 by the Department of Trade and Industry (DTI) (now the Department for Business Innovations and Skills). This guidance reinforces the requirement that a product should not give rise to unacceptable risk, and that risk should be assessed before marketing, and reassessed as new information becomes available. It is envisaged that the risk assessment will form the basis of the manufacturer's belief that its product is 'safe'.

This document also provides more detailed assistance on risk assessment, including a reference to the European Commission's guide. This guide advises that the following be taken into account:

- *The gravity of the outcome of a hazard, depending on the severity and probability of the damage to human health and safety. Combining the severity and probability gives an assessment of the gravity of the risk ...*
- *The severity of health/safety damage for a given hazard should be that for which there is reasonable evidence that the health/safety damage attributable to the product could occur under foreseeable use. This could be the worst case from health/safety damages that have occurred with similar products.*
- *The probability of damage to human health and safety resulting from an exposure corresponding to the intended or reasonably expected use of the product has also to be considered as well as the probability of the product being or becoming dangerous in normal or reasonably foreseeable use including duration.*
- *The factors which affect the level of the risk such as the type of user and, for non-vulnerable adults, whether the product has adequate warnings and safeguards and whether the hazard is sufficiently obvious.*

(b) Food

EC Regulation 178/2002, Article 14 provides that food shall be deemed to be 'unsafe' if it is considered to be injurious to health, or is unfit for human consumption.

Article 14 also sets out guidance for assessing safety, as well as providing for a presumption of conformity:

3. In determining whether any food is unsafe, regard shall be had:

(a) to the normal conditions of use of the food by the consumer and at each stage of production, processing and distribution, and

(b) to the information provided to the consumer, including information on the label, or other information generally available to the consumer concerning the avoidance of specific adverse health effects from a particular food or category of foods.

4. In determining whether any food is injurious to health, regard shall be had:

(a) not only to the probable immediate and/or short-term and/or long-term effects of that food on the health of a person consuming it, but also on subsequent generations;

(b) to the probable cumulative toxic effects;

(c) to the particular health sensitivities of a specific category of consumers where the food is intended for that category of consumers.

5. In determining whether any food is unfit for human consumption, regard shall be had to whether the food is unacceptable for human consumption according to its intended use, for reasons of contamination, whether by extraneous matter or otherwise, or through putrefaction, deterioration or decay.

6. Where any food which is unsafe is part of a batch, lot or consignment of food of the same class or description, it shall be presumed that all the food in that batch, lot or consignment is also unsafe, unless following a detailed assessment there is no evidence that the rest of the batch, lot or consignment is unsafe.

7. Food that complies with specific Community provisions governing food safety shall be deemed to be safe insofar as the aspects covered by the specific Community provisions are concerned.

8. Conformity of a food with specific provisions applicable to that food shall not bar the competent authorities from taking appropriate measures to impose restrictions on it being placed on the market or to require its withdrawal from the market where there are reasons to suspect that, despite such conformity, the food is unsafe.

9. *Where there are no specific Community provisions, food shall be deemed to be safe when it conforms to the specific provisions of national food law of the member state in whose territory the food is marketed, such provisions being drawn up and applied without prejudice to the Treaty, in particular Articles 28 and 30 thereof.*

(c) ***Medicinal products***

Prior to obtaining a marketing authorisation, each new medicinal product is officially assessed for safety, quality and efficacy. The issue of whether a medicinal product is acceptably safe is therefore resolved prior to any supply. However, after initial supply, as further information is gathered about the effects of the product, the known risks are kept under review, along with the issue of whether the known benefits outweigh those known risks.

Regulation 43 of the Human Medicines Regulations 2012 imposes various obligations upon holders of wholesale dealer's licences. These obligations include keeping documents that may facilitate recall or withdrawal of products, and maintaining an emergency plan to ensure effective implementation of any recall ordered by an authority, or carried out in cooperation with the manufacturer or holder of an authorisation or registration.

A similar obligation to keep documents needed to facilitate recall or withdrawal is placed on holders of marketing authorisations (Regulation 77), holders of certificates of registration (Regulation 117), and holders of traditional herbal registrations (Regulation 147).

For medicinal products liable to be imported from outside the EEA, under Regulation 50(4), the licensing authority may require an application for marketing authorisation to include an undertaking from the manufacturer to comply with matters set out in Schedule 9 to the Human Medicines Regulations 2012. Paragraph 11(1) sets out an undertaking to implement a system to recall promptly, and at any time, the medicinal products in the distribution network.

(d) ***Automotive vehicles, systems and components***

Prior to the granting of a vehicle type approval, new vehicle types are assessed by reference to various requirements and standards, including many relating to safety. If new requirements or standards become relevant, approval ceases to be valid, giving rise to the need to submit the product for fresh assessment and approval.

2.2 Notifying product risks

(a) ***General notification requirements – General Product Safety Regulations 2005***

Regulation 9(1) of the General Product Safety Regulations 2005 obliges producers and distributors, who know they have supplied a product that does not comply with the general safety requirement, to "forthwith notify an enforcement authority in writing". The 'enforcement authority' is generally the local authority (Regulation 10).

The requirement does not apply in specified cases, including in "conditions concerning isolated circumstances or products" (Regulation 9(2)(b)).

The notification must provide details of the action being taken to prevent risk to the consumer. In addition, where the product has been marketed or supplied outside the United Kingdom, the notification must identify the EEA member states involved.

Where the risk is 'serious', the notification must also include information to enable a precise identification of the product or batch in question, a full description of the risks, all available tracing information, and a description of the corrective actions (Regulation 9(3)).

(b) Official guidance on notification

The DTI's Notification guidance for producers and distributors (September 2005) provides the following guidance.

No duty to notify:

Producers and distributors do not need to notify under these Regulations:

- *products that are not within the scope of regulation 3 or the definition of 'product' in Regulation 2, or products that are covered by regulation 4;*
- *products that are covered by specific notification procedures under sector-specific legislation (eg medical devices and medicinal products);*
- *products for which the manufacturer has been able to take immediate corrective action for all the items concerned. The defect is limited to well identified items or batches of items and the producer has withdrawn the items in question;*
- *problems related to the functional quality of the product, not to its safety;*
- *when the producer/distributor knows that the authorities have already been informed and have all the required elements of information.*

What to notify:

Producers and distributors could give the enforcement authority preliminary information about a potential product risk as soon as they become aware of it. With this information the authorities may be able to help producers and distributors assess the risk and the appropriate response and to carry out their notification duty correctly. There is no requirement to give the enforcement authority preliminary information, but it is desirable.

The notification must provide details of the action being taken to prevent risk to the consumer. In addition, where the product has been marketed or supplied outside the United Kingdom, the notification must identify the EEA member states involved. The guidance includes a standard form, which should be sent to the enforcement authority.

When to notify: Although the General Product Safety Regulations 2005 require immediate notification, the practical guidance is to report as follows:

- within 10 calendar days of obtaining reportable information;
- for 'serious risks', within three calendar days of obtaining reportable information; and
- in 'emergency' situations, notification should be immediate, and by the 'fastest means possible'.

(c) Products with specific notification requirements

Food: Where a food business operator (FBO) has reason to believe that it has made or supplied food that does not comply with the safety requirements, Article 19 of EC Regulation 178/2002 requires it to inform the 'competent authorities'. Where the FBO has reason to believe that the food may be injurious, the requirement is for immediate notification. Under the General Food Regulations 2004 (Regulation 4(d)), contravention of Article 19 is an offence. Under Regulation 5, a person convicted on indictment is liable to imprisonment for a term not exceeding two years, and/or an unlimited fine. On summary conviction, the maximum penalty is a prison term of six months and/or a fine of £20,000.

The 'competent authorities' are the Food Standards Agency (FSA), and the local authority where the FBO is based, or, in the case of imports, the relevant Port Health Authority. Under the Food Law Code of Practice, local authorities have agreed to notify the FSA of food incidents. The Code of Practice sets out instructions and criteria to which the local and port health authorities should have regard in conducting enforcement actions.

The FSA's Principles for Preventing and Responding to Food Incidents gives the following practical advice:

> *It is advisable for a company to collate all appropriate data and undertake an initial risk assessment prior to formal notification; if in doubt an early call could be made to the relevant local food authority and/or the Agency... for advice. Collating data and having accurate information in place will greatly assist with the understanding of the incident by local authorities and/or the Agency.*

The FSA has an online form, which FBOs may use to notify recall or withdrawal incidents.

Medicinal products: It is necessary to distinguish 'defective' medicines, which are those not conforming to specification (perhaps because of contamination), from medicines that are produced to an authorised specification, but cause unexpected adverse reactions.

Medicinal products are authorised subject to reporting requirements, set out in the Medicines (Standard Provisions for Licences and Certificates) Regulations 1971. Regulation 9A(2) sets out a standard provision that requires licence holders to immediately inform the licensing authority (MHRA) of any defect that could result in a recall or abnormal restriction on supply or export.

The reporting of adverse reactions is a matter of pharmacovigilance. Regulation 182 of the Human Medicines Regulations 2012 requires holders of authorisations or registrations to operate a pharmacovigilance system. Regulation 182(4) requires the holder to use this system to, among other things, take appropriate measures as soon as is reasonably practicable to investigate potential risks, communicate the risks, and implement actions for minimising and preventing risks of a medicinal product.

Regulation 188 imposes obligations on holders to report to the EudraVigilance database suspected adverse reactions, and collect and report follow-up information. This is currently subject to a transitional arrangement, set out at Regulation 212.

For medicinal products liable to be imported from outside the EEA, under Regulation 50(4), the licensing authority may require an application for marketing authorisation to include an undertaking from the manufacturer to comply with matters set out in Schedule 9 to the Human Medicines Regulations 2012. Paragraph 11(2) sets out an undertaking immediately to inform the licensing authority of any defect that could result in a recall or abnormal restriction on supply or export.

Automotive vehicles: The General Product Safety Regulations 2005 notification obligation applies to automotive products. The Vehicle and Operator Services Agency (VOSA), agent of the secretary of state for transport, is the relevant enforcement authority for the purposes of notifying vehicle safety defects under the General Product Safety Regulations 2005. A safety defect is, in the view of the Vehicle Safety Branch of VOSA, "a feature of design or construction liable to cause significant risk of personal injury or death".

VOSA has published a Code of Practice on Vehicle Safety Defects (Issue 2, March 2008). There are separate VOSA codes for bicycles, tyres, wheels and associated parts. The Code of Practice will apply where there is evidence of a safety defect, which "appears to be common to a number of units" available in the United Kingdom.

The primary responsibility is that of the supplier to inform VOSA as soon as there is, under the terms of the code, evidence of a safety defect that requires remedial action. At that stage, the supplier is obliged to confirm:

- the nature of the defect;
- the estimated number of units involved; and
- the proposed corrective action.

Where the defect appears to be a fault in a component or part produced by another supplier, the supplier should inform that other supplier and VOSA.

The supplier should also inform VOSA of all subsequent decisions on remedial action. This includes cases in which component suppliers are involved, unless the vehicle supplier and the component supplier agree that the latter is responsible for carrying out remedial actions and keeping VOSA informed.

VOSA has also produced the Manufacturers' Guide to Recalls in the UK Automotive Sector. This includes forms for notification of intention to recall registered products, and non-registered products.

In addition, there are notification provisions in the Road Vehicles (Approval) Regulations 2009, which implement Directive 2007/46/EC. Under Regulation 23(1), if a manufacturer is obliged (under the General Product Safety Regulations 2005 or other regulation) to recall vehicles, it "shall inform the approval authority immediately". In the United Kingdom, the approval authority is the Vehicle Certification Agency). Regulation 23(2) requires the manufacturer also to propose to the approval authority a set of appropriate remedies. If the approval authority is not satisfied that remedies are being implemented effectively, it may withdraw the vehicle type approval.

Toys: The Toys (Safety) Regulations 2011 impose notification duties on a manufacturer, where it has reason to believe a toy that has been placed on the market does not comply with the Regulations and presents a risk. In such a case, Regulation 24(1)(b) requires the manufacturer immediately to provide to the relevant enforcement authority information about the risks, the non-compliance, and the corrective measures being taken.

Regulations 30(2) and 30(3)(b) impose similar notification duties on importers, and Regulations 35(2) and 35(3)(b) impose similar duties on distributors.

2.3 Corrective actions: recall obligations and procedure

(a) General products

Although there are many legal measures in force aimed at preventing unsafe products being placed on the market and setting out penalties for breaching those requirements, there is no express general statutory duty to recall unsafe products.

However, Regulation 7(3)(b) of the General Product Safety Regulations 2005 requires producers to adopt measures to enable them to take appropriate action in relation to product safety risks, including, where necessary, warning, withdrawing, or (as a last resort) recalling products. This is in essence an obligation to have in place a response plan, which should include product recall.

Moreover, although almost all recalls and withdrawals are voluntary, the enforcement authorities have powers under the General Product Safety Regulations 2005 to impose legal obligations by ordering a wide range of corrective actions, from warnings to consumer recalls.

Official guidance on best practice for corrective actions may be conveniently considered according to sector.

(b) Food

Under EC Regulation 178/2002, Article 19, FBOs are obliged to withdraw unsafe food from the market. If the unsafe food may have reached the consumer, the FBO must inform the consumers of the reason for withdrawal, and, if necessary, recall the food from consumers. Under the General Food Regulations 2004 (Regulation 4(d)), contravention of Article 19 is an offence. Under Regulation 5, a person convicted on indictment is liable to imprisonment for a term not exceeding two years, and/or to an unlimited fine. On summary conviction, the maximum penalty is a term of six months and/or a fine of £20,000.

The FSA has issued detailed guidance for FBOs, including:

- Guidance Notes for Food Business Operators on Food Safety, Traceability, Product Withdrawal and Recall (July 2007);
- Principles for Preventing and Responding to Food Incidents (April 2008); and
- Food Law Code of Practice (June 2008).

The detail that follows is quoted from the April 2008 publication.

The risk of unsafe food reaching consumers can be minimised through the development and implementation of an effective incident management plan and product withdrawal/recall procedures. An effective plan will help ensure compliance with legal requirements; provide a systematic assessment of incidents; manage and control serious

incidents; and protect company assets, which include brand reputation. The key components of an incident management plan are:
1. Product incident policy
2. Incident management team
3. Procedures and supporting documentation
4. Supporting systems
5. Resources
6. Training.

An Incident Management Plan should include detailed procedures and supporting documentation covering, as appropriate, the following:

- *objective*
- *incident investigative procedures*
- *incident management procedures*
- *list of incident management team members and deputies*
- *specified responsibilities and tasks of the members of the incident management team*
- *operational procedures for the incident management team*
- *operational procedures for specific tasks*
- *product withdrawal/recall procedures*
- *incident status register*
- *checklists for tasks*
- *internal company contact list*
- *customer contact list*
- *supplier contact list*
- *enforcement agency contact list (including police)*
- *service providers/consultants contact list*
- *key document samples or templates*
- *training procedure*
- *testing procedure*
- *plan review procedure.*

The FSA informs consumers and local authorities about any recall by issuing a product withdrawal information notice or product recall information notice. These provide details of corrective actions being taken to protect consumers.

(c) ***Medicinal products***

Article 117 of Directive 2001/83/EC requires member states to take all appropriate steps to ensure that a medicinal product is withdrawn from the market if it is (amongst other things) harmful under normal conditions of use. In the Human Medicines Regulations 2012, Regulations 68 to 70 give the licensing authority powers to revoke or suspend a marketing authorisation, or to suspend supply, if (amongst other things) it believes a medicinal product is harmful. In such cases, Regulation 71 states that the licensing authority may give written notice to the holder to comply with certain requirements, including taking all reasonably practicable steps to withdraw the product from the market in the United Kingdom within a specified timeframe.

If there is a risk to public health, the MHRA will issue a 'drug alert' letter to healthcare professionals. This alert is classified on a scale from '1' to '4', depending on the degree of risk, as follows:

- Class I is the most critical, and involves life-threatening issues, eg, where there has been serious mislabelling, microbial contamination or incorrect ingredients, requiring immediate recall.
- Class II involves a risk of harm, without threat to life, and requires action within 48 hours.
- Class III involves products that are unlikely to cause harm, and requires action within five days.
- Class IV is the least critical, and advises 'caution in use'.

(d) *Automotive vehicles, systems and components*

There is no express statutory duty to recall vehicles, although there is a duty to propose remedies to an approval authority. In addition, under the General Product Safety Regulations 2005, the enforcement authority has powers to order withdrawal and recall.

VOSA's manufacturers' guide sets out detailed requirements for corrective actions, including the following steps:

- A recall should begin within six weeks of any notification.
- Notice should be sent to the registered keepers of the vehicles. There is guidance on the structure and content of letters, which should be drafted and then reviewed by VOSA – for example, the letter should discourage keepers from themselves carrying out the repairs. It should also state that repairs are free of charge, and should include a change of ownership card. The envelope should be marked 'safety recall', and should be sent by first class mail, or registered/recorded/special delivery.
- In addition, manufacturers should consider notifying any recall by telephone, text, or email, and advertising in the media.
- If a large number of letters must be issued, it is acceptable to stagger mailings (but all letters must have been sent within eight weeks of the first).
- It may be appropriate to send early warning and/or interim letters (drafts also to be reviewed by VOSA).
- Depending on the rate of response to the letters, follow-up action may be necessary.

(e) *Toys*

The Toys (Safety) Regulations 2011 impose recall duties on manufacturers where they have reason to believe a toy that has been placed on the market does not comply with the Regulations and presents a risk. In such cases, Regulation 24(1)(a) requires manufacturers immediately to take the corrective measures necessary to ensure the toys become compliant, or to withdraw or recall the toys. If the toys present a risk, Regulation 24(1)(b) requires manufacturers to inform the enforcement authority of corrective measures taken.

Regulation 30(3)(a) imposes a similar duty on importers, and Regulation 35(3)(a) imposes a similar duty on distributors.

3. Enforcement

For products governed by safety regulations made under Section 11 of the Consumer Protection Act 1987, the relevant enforcement regime is generally as contained in the Consumer Protection Act 1987's own provisions. Products governed by specific regulations may have specific enforcement regimes. In the absence of more specific enforcement regulations, the General Product Safety Regulations 2005 regime applies. A brief summary of the key powers available to enforcement authorities under the General Product Safety Regulations 2005 follows. For other products, and for further detail on powers and procedure, the relevant regulations should be consulted.

Part 3 of the General Product Safety Regulations 2005 contains enforcement provisions detailing the powers of the enforcement authority (the local authority) in relation to enforcement of regulations, safety notices, and prosecutions for breach of regulations. Regulation 10(5) sets out criteria, including proportionality, to be used in enforcement:

> *An enforcement authority shall in enforcing these regulations act in a manner proportionate to the seriousness of the risk and shall take due account of the precautionary principle. In this context, it shall encourage and promote voluntary action by producers and distributors. Notwithstanding the foregoing, an enforcement authority may take any action under these Regulations urgently and without first encouraging and promoting voluntary action if a product poses a serious risk.*

The enforcement authority has powers to serve the following safety notices:

- Suspension notices (Regulation 11) – if there may have been a breach of the General Product Safety Regulations 2005, this notice temporarily prohibits the placing on the market of, or the supply of a product, while tests are undertaken and results evaluated.
- Requirement to mark (Regulation 12) or requirement to warn (Regulation 13) – these regulations permit enforcement authorities to order the marking of a product with suitable warnings, or require that specific warnings be given to certain persons considered to be at particular risk (eg, young children).
- Withdrawal notices (Regulation 14) – these notices permanently prevent a person from placing a product on the market, or from further supplying a product that is already on the market. For products already on the market, authorities have power to serve withdrawal notices only if the measures being taken by the producer or distributor are insufficient.
- Recall notices (Regulation 15) – where an unsafe product has already been made available to consumers, and voluntary action is insufficient to remove the risk, there is a last-resort power to serve a recall notice. The authority must give at least seven days' notice of the intention to serve a recall notice. The notice requires the addressee to take such steps as are specified in the notice to arrange the recall of the product from consumers, or the disposal by consumers of the product concerned.

In the event of disagreement between the authority and the producer or distributor as to whether recall is necessary, the latter may require the authority to seek a reasoned advice under a scheme operated by the Chartered Institute of Arbitrators. The cost of an opinion will be met by the producer or distributor. Enforcement authorities are expected to have regard to the advice when reaching a final decision on whether or not to serve a recall notice. Detailed guidance on this scheme is available.

Regulation 15(9) allows an enforcement authority, where a recall notice has not fully been complied with, to undertake the recall itself. Associated costs can be recovered as a debt (Regulation 15(10)).

Regulation 16 sets out supplementary provisions regarding safety notices, providing, eg, that, where feasible, the authority should give an opportunity to make submissions before or after service of a notice. In addition, there are provisions imposing liability on the authority to compensate producers (eg, where a notice is served erroneously in respect of a safe product, causing loss to the producer or distributor).

Regulation 17 sets out appeal provisions in respect of each type of safety notice. In addition, the General Product Safety Regulations 2005 set out powers of forfeiture of products, entry and search of premises, and seizure of records and products from premises. In the event of conviction or forfeiture, a court may order the reimbursement of an enforcement authority's expenses (Regulation 27).

4. Product liability

4.1 Sources of civil liability

Product liability can be established on several different bases (statutory and common law), according to whether the relevant injury or property damage results from:

- breach of contract;
- negligence, which is based on fault, ie, breach of an objective duty of care; or
- product safety defect, regardless of breach of contract or fault (ie, 'strict liability').

In each case, the claimant has the burden of proof (on the balance of probabilities), in relation to the following:

- product safety defect, breach of contract or negligence;
- causation; and
- recoverable damage.

(a) Consumer Protection Act 1987

EC Directive 85/374/EEC was implemented in the UK by the Consumer Protection Act 1987. Section 2(1) of the Consumer Protection Act 1987 provides for liability that is 'strict', in that it does not depend on breach of a duty of care, and cannot be defended on the ground that the defendant took all reasonable care. It provides that, regardless of whether the defendant was negligent, if a defective product causes recoverable damage, there will be liability:

> *Subject to the following provisions of this Part, where any damage is caused wholly or partly by a defect in a product, every person to whom subsection (2) below applies shall be liable for the damage.*

Parties: Any person suffering personal injury or certain property damage may make a claim. In addition, as in tort, in the event of a fatal injury, the estate of the deceased may pursue the deceased person's claim under the Law Reform (Miscellaneous Provisions) Act 1934, and dependants may also claim specific limited damages under the Fatal Accidents Act 1976.

Section 2(2) identifies those potentially liable, as follows:

- producer;
- brander; or
- importer into the European Union.

In addition, a distributor may be liable, if, following a request by the claimant to identify one of the above, the distributor fails to do so within a reasonable period of time. A consumer will probably have purchased from a retailer, but, as most products identify the manufacturer, there may be few instances where it is necessary for a claimant to make such a request.

Defect: For the purposes of the Consumer Protection Act 1987, there is a defect in a product if its safety is "not such as persons generally are entitled to expect" (Section 3(1)).

Two main questions must be resolved:

- the safety of the product at the time of supply – there may be a dispute as to whether an alleged defect existed at the time of supply, or arose after supply; and
- the level of safety that consumers are generally entitled to expect. There is a non-exhaustive list of factors to be taken into account when assessing what persons are entitled to expect. This list includes the following:
  - *the manner in which, and purposes for which, the product has been marketed, its get-up, the use of any mark in relation to the product and any instructions for, or warnings with respect to, doing or refraining from doing anything with or in relation to the product;*
  - *"what might reasonably be expected to be done with or in relation to the product"; and*
  - *"the time when the product was supplied", which effectively provides a 'state of the art' defence, so that improvements (and corresponding increased consumer safety expectations) since supply do not make the supplied product defective.*

It is likely that the court will require expert opinion evidence on one or both of these issues. The following cases illustrate the approach of the English courts when assessing 'defect' for the purposes of the Consumer Protection Act 1987.

Generally, if the public is entitled to expect that a product, when used normally, will not cause any loss, claimants may succeed if they prove simply that the product probably did cause the loss because of its condition at the time of supply.

However, if the legitimate expectation is that there will be some failures, claimants must prove the existence of a particular design or manufacturing defect, and the fact that this defect (rather than the inherent risk) caused the injury or damage.

Manufacturing defect cases will include products that have not been produced as intended, because, for example, of contamination or another physical flaw.

The case of *A v National Blood Authority* (2001) concerned 114 claims for damages arising from blood transfusions, involving blood infected with the Hepatitis C virus. The case clarified that, even if the public actually expects some incidence of defect, if the court decides that the public is entitled to expect a safer product, there is a 'defect' for the purposes of the Consumer Protection Act 1987.

A consumer could find it very difficult to identify precisely an alleged manufacturing defect. Therefore, although the claimant has the burden of proof, the courts are prepared to infer the existence of a 'defect'. In *Ide v ATB* (2007), a claimant alleged that his bicycle's left handlebar fractured during use, causing injury. The claimant could not prove the mechanism by which the alleged fracture occurred, and the defendant alleged that the claimant had fallen from his bicycle, breaking the handlebar as he fell. The Court dismissed the defendant's version of events. In the absence of another plausible explanation, the High Court inferred defectiveness. The Court of Appeal upheld this decision.

Design defect cases involve products that have been manufactured as intended, but which allegedly are insufficiently safe because of a design defect, or inadequate instructions or warnings. This often involves consideration of design standards.

In *Tesco v Pollard* (2006), Tesco supplied dishwasher powder in a container with a screw-top. A British Standard required the screw top to have a minimum torque. In this case, the cap did not meet the British Standard, and a young child opened the container, swallowing powder. The Court held that, although the Standard was breached, the container satisfied the general legitimate public safety expectation (ie, that the cap would be harder to open than a normal cap), so was not 'defective'.

Factors to be considered when assessing 'defect' include the instructions and warnings provided with a product. In *B v McDonald's* (2002), there were claims for personal injury (scalding) to young children, caused by spilled hot drinks. The Court said that, even though there were no warnings, the drinks were supplied with lids, to adults, in insulated cups. Consumers expected to be able to remove the lid, and were already aware of the risk of spillage. The drinks were not therefore 'defective'.

Damage: Section 5 of the Consumer Protection Act 1987 contains provisions defining the 'damage' in respect of which liability may be established.

Generally, 'damage' means "death or personal injury or any loss of or damage to property (including land)" (Section 5(1)). 'Personal injury' is defined in Section 45(1) to include disease and "any impairment of a person's physical or mental condition". This will include:

- 'general damages', for "pain, suffering and loss of amenity", which will increase according to the severity of injuries; and
- 'special damages', which are quantified financial losses, including loss of earnings and costs of care, which are caused by injuries.

For property damage, the Consumer Protection Act 1987 generally applies only to property for private use or consumption, ie, consumer goods, not commercial property. This appears to exclude the possibility of recovering loss consequential upon property damage.

Pure economic losses (where there is no bodily injury or property damage) are probably not recoverable under the Consumer Protection Act 1987, although there may be scope for argument regarding property, because damage to property is defined to include loss of property.

Where a component product harms only itself, or the other parts of the relevant end-product with which it was originally supplied, this is not 'damage' (Section 5(2)). The word 'originally' suggests that, where a component is defective and harms another part of the end-product, there is potential liability only if the component was a replacement. It is unlikely that the costs of recall, repair or replacement would be 'damage'.

There is no limit to the amount of recoverable damages. However, 'small claims' – for property damage of value £275 or less (not including interest) – are excluded (Section 5(4)).

Causation: The claimant has the burden of proving, on the balance of probabilities, defect, causation and damage. In practice, the difficulty of proving causation may deter many would-be claimants from pursuing a claim.

Proof is especially challenging in pharmaceutical cases, because very many physical and environmental factors may contribute to a condition. In the case of *XYZ v Schering* (2002), the claimants agreed that their claim would fail if they could not show 'epidemiological causation', ie, that statistically, it is measurably more than twice as likely that a user of the relevant product would suffer the relevant injury, compared with persons not using the product.

In cases of failure to warn, the claimant must prove that, had the warning been given, the injury or damage would have been avoided.

Defences: The Consumer Protection Act 1987 specifies several defences, as follows. In each case, the defendant has the burden of proving that, on the balance of probabilities, the defence applies:

- The defect was caused by compliance with applicable regulations (Section 4(1)(a)).
- The defendant did not supply the product (Section 4(1)(b)).
- The defendant did not supply the product in the course of its business (Section 4(1)(c)).
- The defect did not exist at the relevant time (ie, the date of last supply by the producer, brander or importer; Section 4(1)(d)). *Piper v JRI* (2006) concerned a hip replacement that failed, necessitating a further replacement. The claimant alleged a manufacturing defect, while the producer alleged that the defect did not exist when it supplied the prosthesis to the hospital, but occurred during implantation. The Court was impressed by the producer's inspection system, to the extent that it decided that the defect was probably

not present at the time of supply.

- The state of scientific and technical knowledge at the relevant time was not such that a producer of products of the same description as the product in question might be expected to have discovered the defect if it had existed in his products while they were under his control (Section 4(1)(e)). This is the 'development risks' defence, which is intended to protect a producer in relation to risk that was not discoverable. This involves an objective assessment of industry knowledge at the time of supply. In *Abouzaid v Mothercare* (2000), there was a claim for injury caused by an elastic strap, which had a metal buckle. The producer sought to rely on Section 4(1)(e), arguing that it was unaware of the risk of injury, because there were no recorded accidents. The Court of Appeal doubted whether accident records were 'scientific and technical knowledge'. Even if they were, and although there were no recorded accidents, the risk and defect were nevertheless discoverable.
- The defect is a defect in an end-product, and is wholly attributable to the design of the end-product (Section 4(1)(f)). Such a defence may be relied upon by the supplier of a safe component or ingredient.

In addition, Section 6(4) provides for a defence of 'contributory negligence', where damage is caused partly by a defect and partly by the fault of the person suffering damage. It is likely to be relevant where although the defective product causes loss, the claimant is at least partly blameworthy, for example in misusing a product, failing to obey a warning, or failing to notice an obvious defect.

Section 7 of the Consumer Protection Act 1987 prevents exclusion of liability, by contract term, notice or other provision.

Limitation periods: The Consumer Protection Act 1987 applies to products supplied after March 1 1988. The relevant limitation periods are found in the Limitation Act 1980, as follows:

- personal injury – three years from the date when the injury occurred, or from the date the claimant first knew, or should have known, of the injury;
- property damage – three years from the date the claimant knew, or should have known, of the damage.

Both of these are subject to a longstop of 10 years from the date of supply.

(b) ***Tort (negligence)***

Claims in negligence may be brought regardless of whether a claim is made under the Consumer Protection Act 1987. Negligence claims generally allege fault by reference to the same functions of a producer, namely design defect, manufacturing defect, and failure to warn. Unlike the Consumer Protection Act 1987, tort imposes a duty that continues after the time of supply. Whereas the Consumer Protection Act 1987 focuses on the issue of defectiveness with regard to consumer expectations of safety, a claim in negligence will seek to resolve the reasonableness of the conduct of the producer.

Parties: In *Donoghue v Stevenson* (1932), the House of Lords decided that a manufacturer owes a duty to all persons (not only purchasers) that it can reasonably foresee might be injured by its product.

Breach of duty: Manufacturing defects essentially attract strict liability, as the producer will usually be liable for inadequate processes, or, where the manufacturing process is adequate, will be vicariously liable for operator error. A manufacturing defect can be inferred from evidence, so it is not necessary for a claimant to identify exactly what went wrong during the defendant's production (*Carroll v Fearon* (1998)).

In contrast, issues of alleged design defect, and duty to warn, require consideration of the inherent risks of a product that is manufactured as intended. In these cases, the producer's negligence will be determined according to the relevant industry standards. A design may be negligent in not complying with a standard, because it inadequately provides for known risks, or causes unknown unacceptable risks.

Where there is a known risk, and an allegation of failure to warn, the producer may rely on the defence of 'the learned intermediary'. For example, in *Holmes v Ashford* (1950), a hair dye carried a risk of dermatitis. The producer printed a warning on the bottles of dye, but the hairdresser did not relay the warning to the consumer. It was held that the producer was not negligent. This principle is of great significance in the field of pharmaceutical liability, where producers rely on doctors to assess risk, and to prescribe accordingly.

Damage: Generally, a claimant may recover only physical loss caused by the negligence, as well as the loss that is consequent on that injury or damage, for example loss of earnings or business interruption.

As with the Consumer Protection Act 1987, where a defective product causes injury, negligence allows the recovery of general damages, as well as special damages, including consequential losses such as loss of earnings and costs of care that are incurred by reason of the injury.

Unlike the Consumer Protection Act 1987, negligence allows recovery for damage to commercial property, together with loss of profits (business interruption) consequent on property damage.

Recoverable damages are subject to rules on remoteness; loss of a type that is not reasonably foreseeable is not recoverable. Also, subject to limited exceptions, there is no liability for 'pure economic loss', ie, loss that is not consequent on personal injury, or on damage to the claimant's property. Generally, such loss is recoverable only in contract. The main exception will be where there is a 'special relationship' between the injured party and the defendant, so that, even in the absence of a formal contract, it will be fair, just and reasonable to impose a duty not to cause economic loss.

When considering whether there is property damage, or whether a product has caused it, there are several possible issues.

Where the defective product is an ingredient or component of an end-product, in relation to harm to the end-product itself, liability will depend on whether the end-product is an 'integrated' product, or "one thing for the purposes of tort";[1] if it is, there can be no 'damage', so no tortious liability.

In *Bacardi-Martini v Thomas Hardy Packaging* (2001), one party supplied carbon dioxide to a beverage manufacturer for use in making sparkling drinks. It was discovered that some carbon dioxide was contaminated, and this caused the loss of end-product drinks. A contract limited liability in respect of property damage. The Court decided that the carbon dioxide had not caused property damage; instead it was mixed with other ingredients, creating a new end-product, which was defective from the beginning. The limitation clause did not apply.

Causation: The claimant has the burden of proving, on the balance of probability, that the producer's negligence caused or materially contributed to the loss complained of, ie, 'but for the negligence, the loss would not have occurred'. Generally, the courts will assess whether there is factual causation, and, if there is, whether the damage is too remote to be recoverable.

Where there are multiple possible causes of the injury or damage, the claimant must prove that the defendant's breach of duty was, on balance of probabilities, the operative cause. In practice, particularly in pharmaceutical cases, this can be a difficult obstacle for claimants.

In the absence of substantial direct evidence, where circumstances justify it, the court may rely on indirect evidence to infer negligence and causation.

A producer may avoid liability if a claimant's use of a defective product has been so grossly careless that it should be regarded as the sole cause of the injury or damage.

Defences: In addition to causation defences, the partial defence of contributory negligence is available. There are several other established defences to a claim in negligence, summarised below:

- the defect was not present at time of supply;
- it was probable that an intermediate party would examine the product; and
- the claimant knew about the defect before use or consumption.

Limitation periods: The relevant limitation periods are found in the Limitation Act 1980, as follows:

- personal injury – three years from the date when the injury occurred, or from the date the claimant first knew, or should have known, of the injury; and
- property damage – six years from the date the claimant knew, or should have known, of the damage.

Both of these are subject to a longstop of 15 years from the date of supply.

(c) *Breach of contract*

A claim in contract can be attractive, as there is no need to prove fault on the part

1 *Linklaters v McAlpine* (2010).

of the producer, only a breach of contract. In addition to damages, there may also be a claim for economic loss, such as the cost of repairing the unsafe product (subject to rules on recoverability, or remoteness).

However, there are significant restrictions to a claim in contract. Generally, a claim is available only to the purchaser, and can be brought against only the seller. Contract claims are not available to patients who obtained their medicines or medical devices via an NHS prescription.

5. Products insurance

5.1 Types of coverage

In the United Kingdom, there are several categories of insurance policy relevant to products, covering various risks, as follows:

- product recall, or contaminated products;
- product liability;
- financial loss; and
- product guarantee.

Each of these policies can stand alone, but more often, a single policy will cover product recall, product guarantee and financial loss, or all of the above. None of these policies is compulsory, although they might be required under contract terms with customers including retailers.

An insured may obtain some product coverage from one insurer, and other coverage from a different insurer. This increases the risk of differing interpretations, and an unexpected gap in coverage.

Product liability cover is relatively common, and is often included in a public liability policy. The product recall market is significant, particularly for food and automotive products. Financial loss and product guarantee policies are relatively expensive because of the nature of the risk involved, and are less common as a result.

5.2 Product recall

There are around 12 insurers in the London market offering product recall cover. Some specialise in, or avoid, certain types of products; for example, some insurers currently consider safety-critical automotive components to carry too great a risk.

A typical policy is issued to a single insured, or a number of related companies. Occasionally, a policy may identify a customer, who will have the benefit of the cover.

The insured products will usually be one or more specified products that the insured manufactures and/or distributes. The policy usually defines the product as including all packaging.

The period of insurance will usually be a period of 365 days, and cover may be for insured events that are first discovered by the insured during the period, and reported to the insurer during the period (or within a specified number of days after the period ends).

Insured products may be defined as those supplied during the period, or also within a specified time before the period, and insurers limit their liability under the policy by applying a limit for the period.

(a) Insuring provisions

The policy typically provides first party cover for defined loss that is caused by one or more insured events. Each insured event may have its own limit of insurance, and its own 'deductible'. All policies provide cover for an accidental product safety issue, often defining the insured event as the discovery of a 'defect' or 'manufacturing error', or the insured's decision to recall its affected products.

In any case, to be an insured event, the insured must also show that use or consumption of its product has caused, or would cause, personal injury or damage to third party property. The policy will usually require the insured to prove that any injury would be caused within a specific period of time after use of or consumption of the product. This manifestation period typically ranges from 120 days to 365 days.

Coverage usually includes the following, as a minimum:

- expenses of a 'crisis consultant': the policy may identify specific consultants, and make it a condition that the insured notifies one of these consultants, as well as insurers, immediately. Such expenses are often unlimited;
- other pre-recall expenses, which are essentially intended to cover the costs of deciding whether there is a safety issue, or defining the scope of the recall. These costs typically include scientific tests; and
- reasonable recall costs, including:
- advertising the recall;
- additional costs of staff, including their overtime, and transport and accommodation costs; and
- costs of the recalled products, including transport, storage and disposal, and possibly the transport costs of redistributing products.

Some policies provide substantially greater coverage, most notably the following heads of loss:

- business interruption (lost profits) for a specified period of time, typically 12 months from the date of recall;
- the cost of rehabilitating the brand, so that the pre-recall level of anticipated sales is restored;
- the costs of repairing or replacing the recalled products (but excluding the products themselves); and
- liability for the costs incurred by third parties, including customers, in recalling end-products that incorporate the insured's products.

In addition to cover for accidental safety issues, it is possible to obtain insurance for malicious product tampering, and product extortion. This coverage can be found in some product recall policies, as well as contaminated product insurance policies.

In some circumstances, recall costs may be incurred by a party other than the insured, so that the insured will face a third party claim for the recall costs. Examples include where it sells only through retailers. In such a case, an Insured might consider requesting that the policy wording be amended to reflect this. However, this potentially provides a form of liability insurance, and may not be acceptable to insurers, unless, for example, costs are limited to the costs that the insured would reasonably and necessarily have incurred, had it carried out the recall.

Where the insured's products are ingredients or components, product recall cover that does not extend to cover the costs of recalling end-products because of the insured's products may not be suitable. This can be a particular issue in the food and auto sectors. However, increasingly, policies are extending cover to apply to these costs.

(b) *Exclusions*

Most product recall policies contain numerous exclusions. Insurers have the legal burden of proving that, on the balance of probabilities, an exclusion operates. Typical exclusions include the following:

- liability to third parties;
- products that have not been the subject of unqualified acceptance by a third party (usually a customer). This exclusion may apply where, eg, a customer is contractually entitled to inspect delivered insured products before accepting them. In such cases, the exclusion reinforces the insured's duty to deliver only safe products;
- end-products incorporating insured products. If the products are used only as components, the recall of the end-products may be the insured's main risk, and this exclusion may be unacceptable to the insured;
- business interruption;
- costs of repair or replacement;
- breach of safety regulations, including the use of prohibited substances such as asbestos, lead or carcinogens;
- fines, penalties and punitive damages;
- losses arising from circumstances, which, at the time of inception, the insured knew of, and could reasonably foresee might result in a claim; and
- dishonesty.

The exclusion relating to prohibited substances and carcinogens has reportedly excluded coverage in recent high-profile food recalls, including the Sudan I recall in 2005, and the pork dioxin recall originating in Ireland in 2008.

5.3 Product liability

Product liability insurance is not compulsory, but is widespread, and is often stand-alone, or included in public and product liability policies, or in product recall, liability and financial loss cover.

(a) *Insuring provisions*

A typical product liability insuring provision is as follows:

> *The insurers will indemnify the Insured against all sums that the Insured shall become legally liable to pay as damages and costs and expenses of claimants in respect of accidental*

(a) injury to any person

(b) loss of or damage to material property

occurring anywhere in the world during the period of insurance and caused by any insured product.

As this is insurance for liability to third parties, there is also cover for liability to pay claimant's costs. The limit of indemnity will usually be inclusive of claimants' costs and expenses. Defence costs are usually covered in addition to the limit of indemnity.

The words 'legally liable' will cover, subject to exclusions (see below), a strict liability under the Consumer Protection Act 1987, as well as liability in tort, and liability in contract.

The above example provides coverage on a 'loss occurring' basis. However, there is an increasing prevalence of what are known as 'claims made' policies (where the policy is triggered by claims made during the period of insurance). These are desired by insurers who wish to avoid long-tail claims, essentially claims that are made after the expiry of their policy period. In pharmaceutical liability insurance, policies are typically claims made.

Loss occurring policies can give rise to dispute about the date of injury or damage, including where there are multiple policy periods and different insurers. In determining the date when injury occurred, it is likely that the courts would decide this is the date when an injury in fact occurs, rather than the date when a claimant knew he had suffered the injury. The limit of indemnity will relate to all occurrences within the policy period.

'Injury' is defined, usually in terms such as "bodily injury, death, disease, illness or nervous shock". There may be an issue as to whether an alleged psychological condition is a recognised illness. 'Damage' may be defined, usually in order to limit coverage to tangible or material property.

Where a defective component causes damage to other parts of the relevant end-product, it is likely the component producer cannot be liable in tort for this loss. Any liability will be contractual, and the policy may cover or exclude such liability (see Exclusions, below). The following decisions illustrate the courts' approach.

In *Pilkington v CGU* (2004), the insured installed glass ceiling panels in a building. There was a risk that the glass would fall, causing injury and/or damage. A net was installed as a safety measure, and the insured claimed the costs from its liability insurer. It was held that the insured's product had not caused any damage to other property, and the costs of the safety measures were not covered.

In *Horbury v Hampden* (2004), the insured supplied suspended ceilings to a cinema complex. The ceiling in one auditorium collapsed, and the other screens were closed for inspection works. Investigations showed the insured's defective washers were responsible. The Court found that the closed auditoria had not been damaged, so any liability on the part of the insured for lost income from the other auditoria was not covered.

In *Tioxide Europe v CGU* (2004), a pigment was supplied for use in uPVC doors and window frames. In certain circumstances, a defect caused the end-products to turn pink. This gave rise to claims for breach of contract by the consumers, and the liability was claimed along the contract chain to the pigment supplier, which was (for the purpose of coverage proceedings) assumed to be liable. The Court considered the question of whether the liability was "on account of property damage", as stipulated in the policy. The Court decided that pinked end-products had suffered 'damage', and this wording was wide enough to apply to liability for repair or replacement costs (in contrast, see 'In respect of', below).

Some doubt exists about whether a defective ingredient or component can cause 'damage', to other ingredients or components, and/or to the relevant end-product. In the case of *Bacardi-Martini v Thomas Hardy Packaging* (2001), carbon dioxide contaminated with benzene was used to make fizzy drinks. The claim was for the finished drinks, and the Court had to consider a contractual limitation clause, which purported to limit liability for property damage. The Court said that, logically, the carbon dioxide could not be said to have caused damage to the drinks, because the drinks did not exist until the carbon dioxide became a part of them. Instead, the contaminated carbon dioxide had caused the new finished product to be defective from the beginning.

Some policies expressly provide that there is cover, or no cover, for such losses. If not, there is scope for argument.

The policy will typically cover only those liabilities for damages that are 'in respect of' injury or damage. In this way, insurers restrict coverage to the physical loss itself, ie, the injury or damage, as well as the direct consequences, such as loss of earnings caused by personal injury. Liability for other loss, which is not directly caused by injury or damage, is not liability for 'damages in respect of injury or damage', so is not covered. This requirement has been applied in several recent cases, including the following:

- In *AS Screenprint v BRI* (1995), the insured defectively printed its customer's food packaging. The customer sold the packaging to Mars, which successfully sued the customer, and cancelled future contracts. The customer sued the insured for the settlement sum, in addition to the profits it lost from the cancelled contracts. The Court of Appeal decided the lost profits were not 'in respect of' the damage to the packaging, but were instead caused by Mars' decision to cancel contracts.
- In *Rexodan v Commercial Union* (1997), the insured supplied large bags of soap powder, which were packaged and later caused spoiling of the end-product. The customer cancelled future purchases from the insured, and decided to establish a new replacement brand. The insured was liable in contract for the associated losses. However, the Court of Appeal held that none of these liabilities was in respect of the actual physical damage caused by the defective powder.
- In *James Budgett Sugars v Norwich Union* (2002), the insured supplied contaminated sugar to a customer, who used it to produce mincemeat. The customer alleged that this caused it to lose business, and claimed the losses from the insured. The insured and insurers asked the Court to decide whether, if the insured was liable for the lost orders, this liability would be covered. The Court of Appeal decided such liability would not be 'in respect of' damage.

(b) Exclusions

A product liability policy will usually contain various exclusions, depending on the function of the insured products.

Purely contractual liability: This exclusion applies to liability assumed under an agreement, except liability that would have arisen in the absence of agreement. This has the same effect as the insuring clause, which limits cover to liability for injury or damage. Such liability will not be exclusively contractual, because it arises in tort as well.

The High Court recently considered this type of exclusion in *Omega Proteins v Aspen* (2010). The insured supplied some unusable animal by-products to Omega, which unwittingly mixed them with good material, and sold onwards in its supply chain. Omega's customer sued Omega in breach of contract, and established liability on this basis alone, with no consideration of tortious liability.

As the insured was in liquidation, Omega sued its insurers directly. The insurers denied liability on several grounds, and the High Court decided as follows:

- The test is to apply the facts as they are, except that there is no contract between the insured and its customer.
- Even though the underlying judgment did not consider non-contractual liability, the court considering the insurance exclusion can assess the issue of liability in tort.
- In this case, the insured would have been liable in negligence, in supplying a product that could not be used without unacceptable risks to human health and damage to other products with which it was mixed.
- The insurers had the burden of proving that, had there not been a contract, the insured would not have been liable.

Efficacy: Generally, liability insurers intend to cover the risk of a functioning product causing injury or damage, but do not intend to 'guarantee' the product itself, or the risk of its non-performance. Efficacy exclusions apply to exclude liability for injury or damage caused by a product's failure to perform its intended function. For example, if a fire extinguisher performs its function, but causes injury to a user, an efficacy exclusion may not exclude liability to the injured user. However, if the extinguisher failed to perform, giving rise to liability for resulting fire damage, the efficacy exclusion may operate in respect of that liability.

The case of *Wyeth v Cigna* (2001) concerned allegations of unsafe pharmaceuticals. The High Court considered, among other things, the meaning of an efficacy exclusion. The Court said, in comments later endorsed by the Court of Appeal, that the exclusion was clearly intended to exclude cover for claims "for failing to make the Claimant better or failing to prevent some condition arising (eg contraception or vaccines)". As the claims were instead for causing or exacerbating conditions, the exclusion was not relevant.

Deliberate acts: This is intended to exclude injury or damage that is 'accidental' from the perspective of an injured party, but which is caused by the insured's recklessness, for example where the insured supplies a product despite knowing it to be defective.

Miscellaneous exclusions: Typically, a policy will also exclude cover for the following:

- injury or damage that is 'expected or intended' – this is common in certain pharmaceutical liability policies, where a certain level of claims is expected;
- injury to employees of the insured;
- products supplied before a specified date ('retroactive date');
- aviation products and components;
- US and Canada liabilities;
- pollution and contamination (except sudden and accidental); and
- the costs of recalling, repairing or replacing insured products.

(c) *Conditions*

As is typical in liability insurance, there will be conditions relating to third party claims, including requirements to notify insurers, and the right to control the defence and settlement of claims. If a condition is a 'condition precedent', breach will entitle the insurers to reject the claim entirely, whether or not breach has caused prejudice to insurers.

5.4 Financial loss

This liability cover may be available as an extension to product liability insurance, or as a stand-alone policy, or with product recall and/or product guarantee policies.

Where the insured product fails to perform its intended function, resulting in financial loss for which the insured is liable, this insurance covers the insured's liability.

A typical insuring clause is as follows:

The Insured is indemnified by this section in accordance with the operative clause for damages and claimants' costs and expenses arising as a result of any financial loss which is incurred by customers or third parties as a result of any product (or part thereof) which fails to perform the function for which it was manufactured, designed, sold, supplied, installed, repaired, altered, treated, dispatched or delivered by or on behalf of the Insured.

In some policies, the phrase 'financial loss' is not defined; this may create scope for argument about its meaning. In some policies, 'financial loss' is effectively defined as loss that is not consequent on injury or damage. Such liabilities may include business interruption liabilities.

Usually, financial loss cover will be subject to exclusions. Common examples are for design liability, and purely contractual liability. In this way it may be possible to restrict cover to tort liability for pure economic loss caused by manufacturing error.

5.5 Product guarantee

Typically, where the insured's product fails to perform its intended function, the insured will have a legal liability for the costs of repair or replacement. This liability, which is excluded from most product liability policies, can be covered under product guarantee insurance. As this is guarantee insurance, it is relatively expensive and uncommon.

A typical insuring clause is as follows:

The insured is indemnified by this section in accordance with the operative clause for their legal liability for the costs of removal, recovery, repair, alteration, treatment or replacement of any product (or part thereof) which fails to perform the function for which it was manufactured designed, sold, supplied, installed, repaired, altered, treated, dispatched or delivered by or on behalf of the insured.

In many cases, a claimant will require the insured to repair or replace the defective insured product. If so, the insured will be making a first party claim for its own costs. In contrast, where the claimant incurs the costs, then seeks to recover these from the insured, this is effectively a third party liability cover. The policy may restrict cover to the costs that the insured would reasonably and necessarily have incurred, had it carried out the repair or replacement.

Many product guarantee policies contain a number of exclusions, most of which may also be found in product recall and financial loss policies.

France

Florian Endrös
Endrös-Baum Associés

Producers and distributors of products in France must comply with stringent French product liability laws.

The French product liability system essentially grew from a system based on the contractual liability of distributors, extending to capture producers and manufacturers even where the claimant has no direct contractual relationship with the producer.

The system is one of strict liability: claimants need only prove lack of safety, not gross negligence or any intentional act.

Therefore it would be strongly in the interests of any producer or distributor on becoming aware of a safety risk relating to a product on the market, to implement a recall campaign or to withdraw it from the market.

However, even if a product recall campaign is executed, the producer or distributor will not escape liability if a consumer is injured by the product (despite the recall operation).

Directive 2001/95/EC[1] defines 'recall' as "any measure aimed at achieving the return of a dangerous product that has already been supplied or made available to consumers by the producer or distributor" (Article 2(g)).

This European definition applies directly in French law despite the French Consumer Act, which refers to 'recall' as one of the appropriate measures possible when handling risks due to unsafe products. Under that act, producers or distributors must:

- alert the public or issue appropriate and efficient warnings;
- withdraw the product from the market, and
- recall the product directly from the consumer (Article 221(1)2 II b of the Consumer Code).

1. Product safety regulation

1.1 Regulatory framework

Articles L212(1) and L221(1) of the Consumer Code refer to:

- a duty to verify if products comply with statutory safety requirements prior to their release on the market; and
- a duty to ensure levels of safety that can legitimately be expected.

1 Of the European Parliament and of the Council of December 3 2001.

These are 'self-regulatory' duties: the company must create its own safety standards including collection of statutory information and safety control procedures at all stages in production. Those procedures must be regularly tested and updated.[2]

Failures in the self-regulatory system will lead to penal liability of the firm.[3]

1.2 Safety standards

In general, and for most products, the safety rules in France are based on European standards, such as those contained in the European directives for machinery, toys, medical devices, pharmaceutical products, food and genetically modified products.

The conformity of a product with industrial standards and norms constitutes a simple presumption – that is, the product can conform to the standards and still be unsafe in fact; or it might not conform and be safe nevertheless. This will be a question of proof in practice.

Where a producer, manufacturer or other party that is subject to the product liability regime considers that a safety standard is not relevant to a product, a request for derogation can be made to the French Association for Standardisation (AFNOR), which will assess the safety of the relevant product for consumers (Article 18 of Decree 84-74 of January 26 1984).

A product cannot be considered as defective just because a more advanced product has subsequently been placed on the market (Article 1386(4), Civil Code; law of May 21 1998 (98-389)[4]).

In applying that law, AFNOR must consider all criteria relevant to the legitimate expectation of the public concerning the safety of the product, such as:

- any intrinsic risk or danger in the product;
- degree of care taken by the producer to inform the public about how to properly use the product; and
- measures taken by the producer to ensure that the product is safe.

2. Obligations of producers and distributors

2.1 Sources of duties

(a) Statute

In France, the product safety requirements are in particular regulated by Statute 83-660 of July 21 1983[5] and Decrees 2004-670 and 2008-810, passed on July 9 2004 and August 22 2008 respectively,[6] implementing the General Product Safety Directive (2001/95/EC). These pieces of legislation are also incorporated into the Consumer Code (Book II, Title II).

---

2 Sylvie PUGNET, *La réglementation de la sécurité des produits, Contrats concurrence consommation* October 10 2009, study 10.
3 (*Cass Crim* October 30 1990, 89 (83.827).
4 Transposing EU Directive 85/374/EEC.
5 *Official Journal of the French Republic* (JORF), July 22 1983, p 2262.
6 JORF 0196, p 13238 and JORF 159, p 12520.

More specific provisions applicable to particular safety issues, such as certain specific provisions of the French Code on Public Health pertaining to drug safety.

(b) *Tort*

The fact that a product is considered dangerous cannot by itself trigger a manufacturer/producer's liability. Producers have several obligations in relation to safety. They must:

- bring to the market only products which are safe for their normal use and their foreseeable (not abnormal) misuse;
- provide consumers with adequate information about products;[7]
- comply with advertising rules (for tobacco or alcoholic beverages); and
- in general, take adequate precautions at all times in relation to safety.[8]

Failure to observe any of these obligations could lead to action by the administrative authority Article L 221(7), Consumer Code), eg, serving a caution on the producer.

(c) *Contract*

Where there is a contract, the victim or injured party can claim indemnification on the basis of the contractual legal guarantee against hidden defects (Article 1641, French Civil Code) or on the basis of contractual non–fulfilment (Article 1147, French Civil Code).

2.2 Pre-market obligations

According to Decree 2004(670 of July 9 2004 and Ruling 2008-810 of August 22 2008, a product will be considered to satisfy the general duty of safety (as defined by Article L221(1)) when it complies with any specific regulation which has as its purpose the protection of health or consumer security (Article L222(1), Consumer Code).

(a) *CE marking*

It is always the producer/manufacturer who should mark a product with the CE sign, if appropriate. The CE mark is the producer's guarantee that the product conforms to European standards, having been evaluated for this purpose. The European directives determine whether this evaluation must be made by a specific body or by the producer itself.

(b) *Traceability, record keeping*

The Consumer Code provides for product traceability requirements to facilitate recalls.

Producers are obliged to take measures to ensure traceability of their products as a means to control and monitor potential risks, including adding – either on the

---

7 Article L 221-1-2, Consumer Code; and *Cass 2e civ*, December 9 1975: JCP G 1977, II, 18588 – *Cass 1re civ*, June 10 1980: Gaz Pal 1980, 2, somm 569.)

8 Article L221(1)1 of the Consumer Code

product itself or on its packaging – information about the identity and address of the producer, as well as a product reference number and batch number (Article L221(1)2 II of the Consumer Code).

French case law has established a 'precautionary principle', which applies to product traceability cases (French Supreme Administrative Court decision of December 29 1999).

(c) Sector-specific obligations

Foods and novel foods: The Decree of April 15 1912 sets food safety requirements, such as a prohibition on the use of chemicals products.

Safe temperatures for the storage and transportation of products with animal origins or food containing products with animal origins are set by a ministerial decree of September 21 2009 (annexes). For example, fresh milk cannot be transported over 4°C.

'Novel foods' are defined as including "foods and food ingredients with a new or intentionally modified primary molecular structure" or "foods and food ingredients containing or consisting of genetically modified organisms" (Article R1323(1) of the Public Health Code and Article 1 of EU Resolution 58/97). Producers may neither produce novel foods that present risks to consumers nor produce novel foods that differ from the foods they are intended to replace in such a way that their consumption would be nutritionally detrimental or hazardous to the consumer; and producers may not attempt to mislead consumers (Article 3 of EU Regulation 258/97). In addition, the Consumer Code (Article 1323(2)) establishes a food safety enforcement agency, to which manufacturers and regulatory authorities must declare any problems or risks.

The placing on the market of genetically modified foods must be pre-approved by a competent administrative authority, depending on whether the product is a genetically modified organism for use in medicinal products, foods, or other uses (Article L533(5) of the Environment Code).

In cases of breach of this provision, the Ministry for the Environment can impose penalties on a sliding scale: first giving the company notice that it must meet the requirements in a set time period (Article L535(5) of the Environment Code). Where there is continued breach beyond that time limit, the authority can enforce compliance or suspend the approval (Article L535(5) of the Environment Code). If those remedies also fail, the company will face a penalty of up to two years' imprisonment and a fine of up to €150,000 (Article L536(5) of the Environment Code).

Food contact materials: According to Article 3 of EU Regulation 1935/2004:

> *Materials and articles, including active and intelligent materials and articles, shall be manufactured in compliance with good manufacturing practice so that, under normal or foreseeable conditions of use, they do not transfer their constituents to food in quantities which could endanger human health or bring about an unacceptable change in the composition of the food or bring about a deterioration in the organoleptic characteristics thereof ....*

'Active materials and articles' is defined in an EU guidance note[9] as:

... materials and articles that are intended to extend the shelf life or to maintain or improve the condition of packaged food; they are designed to deliberately incorporate components that would release or absorb substances into or from the packaged food or the environment surrounding the food ...

'Intelligent materials and articles' is defined in the same note as:

... materials and articles which monitor the condition of packaged food or the environment surrounding the food....

Medicines Regulations 1971: The preparation, import, export and distribution of medicines must meet good practice rules set by the *Agence Nationale de sécurité du medicament et des produits de santé* (ANSM – the National Agency for Security of Medicaments and Health Products (former AFSSAPS) (Article L 5121(5) of the Public Health Code). Non-compliance is punishable by a fine of €3,750 (Article L 5421(1) of the Public Health Code).

An industrially produced medicine must be approved by the ANSM before being put on the market (Article L5121(8) of the Public Health Code). If the medicine is put on the market without such approval, the company will incur a penalty of up to two years' imprisonment and/or a fine of up to €30,000 (Article L5421(2) of the Public Health Code).

Motor vehicles (Decree 2011-368 of April 4 2011): Motor vehicles must not produce smoke, toxic, corrosive or odorous gas in volumes that may disturb the population or compromise public health or security. Vehicle manufacturers can be punished by a fine of the fourth class (maximum €750; Article R318(1) of the Road Code). Motor vehicles must be produced and marketed in such a way that they ensure the safety of all road users (Article L311(1) of the Road Code). Vehicles can be taken off the road if it is shown that these requirements have not been fulfilled (Article R311(3) of the Road Code).

Electrical equipment ((Safety) Decree 2009-1139 of September 22 2009): Electrical equipment must not contain lead, mercury, cadmium, chromium hexavalent, prolybromobiphenyl or polybromodiphenylether (Article R543(175) of the Environment Code). Companies which fail to observe these restrictions may incur a fine of the fifth class (€1,500 maximum; Article R543(206) of the Environment Code).

Standard EN 60204 establishes safety requirements for electrical equipment, such as making sure users are guarded against direct contact, protection against overload and earthing. All electrical equipment must be designed so that any batteries inserted can be easily extracted (Article R543(176) of the Environment Code). All electrical equipment placed on the market must be accompanied by instructions that indicate to users which type of battery is integrated and how to extract the batteries without any risk. Any item of electrical equipment placed on the market after August 13 2005

9 http://ec.europa.eu/food/food/chemicalsafety/foodcontact/docs/guidance_active_and_intelligent_scfcah_231111_en.pdf.

must be marked with information identifying its producer and confirming that it was put on the market after August 13 2005.

Toys (Decree 2010-166 of February 2010 on Toy Safety): Manufacturers must respect all security requirements set out in Annex 1 of Decree 2010-166. For example, toys must present no risk of asphyxia and must be physically robust enough to be able to resist the pressures to which they are likely to be exposed, without causing injury because of breakages or damage (Annex I of the decree). Before placing a toy on the market, the manufacturer must analyse any threats or potential exposure to dangers of a chemical, physical, mechanical or electrical nature, and any risks concerning flammability, radioactivity or hygiene presented by the toy (Article 7 of the decree). Manufacturers must also mark their toys with the CE safety compliance marking to indicate that the essential security requirements of Article 3 of the decree are satisfied (eg, to declare that the toy will not expose a child to strangulation risks and is not flammable (Article 7 of the decree)).

Cosmetics (Law 2011-12 of January 5 2011): Any enterprise engaged in manufacturing, preparing or importing cosmetics must be pre-approved by the AFSSAPS (Article L5131(2) of the Public Health Code); breach of this requirement may incur a fine of €30,000 and up to two years' imprisonment (Article L5431(2) of the Public Health Code). Cosmetics may be placed on the market only if the packaging bears the name and address of the manufacturer or distributor (Article L5131(6) of the Public Health Code). Article L5131(7) of the code requires manufacturers to convey information about the constituent ingredients used in the cosmetic to the relevant authority. EU Directive 76/769/EEC lists banned substances (eg, zoxazolamine, procainamide, its salts and derivatives, and benzidine).

Occupational health and safety: The EU Machinery Directive (2006/42/EC) aims to ensure the free movement of machines and their accessories, while imposing essential requirements regarding the health and safety of consumers. Before placing machinery on the market and/or putting it into service, manufacturers must ensure that it meets relevant essential health and safety requirements (set out in Annex I) and must provide essential information such as instructions. Manufacturers must also draw up the EC declaration of conformity and affix the CE mark, which creates a presumption of conformity with harmonised standards.

Liability attaches to manufacturers both when:

- the machine is used under conditions intended by the manufacturer; and
- it is used in foreseeable abnormal situations.

The French Supreme Court has held that an accident resulting from inadequate training of personnel in the use of the machine is a foreseeable abnormal situation (*Cass Crim*, December 6 2005). In another example, an employee using machinery in a manner that contradicted its instructions, and in spite of pictograms illustrating these instructions, was also considered to be a foreseeable abnormal situation (*Cass Crim* April 12 2005). The interpretation is very broad and onerous on the manufacturer.

To verify the safety of machinery and conformity with the directive, the relevant work inspection authority has the power to:

- enter company premises without notice;
- inspect machinery; and
- engage experts to evaluate the machinery.

Their report could lead to:

- written observations;
- formal notice to comply with the directive;
- fines; and
- a reference to the courts to deal with urgent matters to stop any high-risk activity.

Employers are responsible for appraising any risks presented to the health and security of workers (Article R4412(5) of the Labour Code).

2.3 Post-market safety obligations

(a) Corrective action

Parties responsible for marketing a product must immediately notify the competent administrative authorities if they notice that a product does not comply with the general product safety requirements provided by Article L221(1) of the Consumer Code.

Producers and manufacturers must take any necessary actions including withdrawal of the product from the market; giving adequate warnings to consumers; and recall of products already on the market (Article L 221(1)2 II of the Consumer Code).

Where products do not comply with statutory safety requirements, either permanent or temporary/urgent measures can be taken. See section 2.3.

2.4 Criminal liability

Article 223(1) of the Penal Code creates the offence of endangerment. The elements of this offence are satisfied when:

- a person owes a particular duty to ensure the safety of a product;
- violation of this duty creates the risk of death, serious injury or permanent disablement;
- the risk that this poses to third parties is immediate; and
- the breach of the duty to ensure safety was intentional.

Criminal prosecution may result from the following circumstances:

- negligent homicide – Article 221(6) of the Penal Code;
- negligent bodily injury – Article 222(19) of the Penal Code;
- threat to life of a third party – Article 223(2) of the Penal Code; and
- fraud (in relation to substantial properties of the product) – Article L213(1)[10] of the Consumer Code.

10 This article is not solely applicable to consumers.

A case involving Volvo is relevant here. It involved the death of two children in a car accident. Volvo Sweden, in its capacity as manufacturer of the vehicle, was held responsible for the deaths and prosecuted jointly with the driver of the vehicle (Appeal Court of Colmar, December 28 2008).

According to the courts both at first instance and on appeal, Volvo had been grossly negligent, since it had been aware of faults in the braking system for several years but had not implemented a product recall campaign at any point.

Volvo France – the distributor of Volvo cars in France – was acquitted on technical grounds (not because it was only a distributor, and not the producer/ manufacturer, but because it had been taken over by a third company and had thus ceased legally to exist). This illustrates the point that criminal liability is personal and does not transfer to an acquirer. It is a pity, however, that the criminal liability of the French Volvo distributor was not addressed in the case.

The car dealer that had sold the vehicle and carried out repairs and maintenance was acquitted. It may be relevant, in this regard, the dealer was a small company which had merely followed the partially inadequate instructions of the manufacturer.

(a) Notification duties

Distributors or marketers must inform the relevant authorities immediately if a product does not comply with the safety requirements of Article L221(1)3 of the Consumer Code.

The European Commission's Guidelines 2004/90 define the criteria to be used when determining when a defect must be notified as follows:

- The product is likely to be used by consumers (Article 2a of the General Product Safety Directive);
- Article 5 of the directive applies;
- The product is on the market;
  There is evidence that the product is dangerous according to the directive or that the product does not satisfy the safety requirements of the relevant EU sector-specific legislation; and
- The risks are such that the product may not remain on the market.

If the manufacturer, acting in a professional capacity, considers that the decision of the competent authority is not justified, it can lodge an appeal before the administrative jurisdictions.

Timeframe: The manufacturer must immediately notify the competent administrative authorities of the incident (Article L221(1)3 of the Consumer Code). The term 'immediately' is not precisely defined.

The European Commission's decision of December 14 2004 stipulates that the company must inform the competent authorities as soon as the relevant information has come to light and in any event within 10 days, or no later than three days after obtaining the information when there is a serious risk.

Addressee: The notifications should be sent to one of the following authorities (Ministerial Order of September 9 2004 on the application of Article L221(1)3 of the Consumer Code):

- the Directorate General for Road Safety and Traffic, for car manufacturers and their distribution networks whenever vehicles and equipment sold under the manufacturer's brand are involved;
- the Directorate General for Food, for foods and animal feed. Notifications concerning food products not included in these categories (eg, additives, flavourings) must be submitted to the Directorate General for Competition Policy, Consumer Affairs and Fraud Control;
- the ASNM, for medicines; and
- the Directorate General for Competition Policy, Consumer Affairs and Fraud Control, for all other products.

Product information and other data required: The following information should be provided in the notification to the authority (Article 2 of the Ministerial Order of September 9 2004):

- the date of the notification;
- the name and address of the manufacturer or company providing the notification, as well as of its suppliers and the businesses which have been supplied with the product;
- a product description (name, brand, batch number, volumes);
- a description of the danger and any measures taken by the manufacturer; and
- any other information that could be useful to the authorities.

The forms required are available on the Directorate General for Competition Policy, Consumer Affairs and Fraud Control (DGCCRF) website at www.dgccrf.bercy.gouv.fr/ securite/alertes/documents/formulaire_prof.pdf.

(b) ***No obligation to provide updated information***

Under French law, there is no explicit obligation to inform authorities about risks unless they affect consumers (Article L221(1)2 of the Consumer Code).

The authorities do have investigatory powers in relation to consumer products however, and can for example require producers to convey all information concerning the product to enable the authorities to determine whether the product is dangerous or not (Articles L215(1) and L218(1) of the Consumer Code).

The Sanitary Surveillance Institute can also request that a party communicates necessary information concerning serious threats to human health (Article L1413(5) of the Public Health Code).

3. Enforcement

3.1 Sector organisations

If products do not comply with the general safety obligations of Article L221(1) of the Consumer Code, which applies to all products, recalls can be ordered by decree of the French Administrative Supreme Court (Article L221(3) of the Consumer Code), or, in cases of grave or immediate danger, by ministerial order (Article L221(5) of the Consumer Code).

General consumer products: The Consumer Safety Commission is the regulator for safety and the prevention of risks in products or services (Article L534(5) of the Consumer Code).

Food: The National Agency for food, environmental and occupational health and safety (www.anses.fr) conducts research and scientific surveys and is in charge of evaluating food-related risks and reporting its findings to the relevant authorities (Article L1313(1) of the Public Health Code). It promotes public health and proposes measures to be taken where there are perceived serious threats (Article L1313(1) of the Public Health Code).

Motor vehicles: Before being placed on the market, new, modified, reconstructed, or imported vehicles must be approved by the regional arm of the Industry, Research and Environment Agency, which ensures that vehicles comply with technical regulatory requirements concerning safety.

Medicines: The ANSM is in charge of evaluating and monitoring all matters concerning medicines and health products for human use. Its main roles are research, laboratory testing, conducting on-the-spot inspections and providing information for health professionals and the public (Law 98-535 of July 1 1998; and Articles L5311(1) and following of the Public Health Code). The ANSM can restrain or suspend the manufacture, preparation, import, export or supply of any product, which may present a risk to human health (Article L5312(1) of the Public Health Code).

3.2 Penalties

If the producer fails to comply with any decree or ministerial order requiring corrective action or recalls, the Consumer Code provides various penalties as follows:

- a fine, as established in the decree, for failure to comply with a decree taken under Article L221(3) of the Consumer Code by the French Administrative Supreme Court
- fine of €1,500 for an individual or of €7,500 for a corporate entity if the producer or manufacturer fails to comply with a ministerial order taken under Article L221(5) of the Consumer Code
- forfeiture of the dangerous product (Article R.223(1) Consumer Code)
- fine of €750 for an individual or €3,750 for a corporate entity if the producer/manufacturer fails to comply with measures ordered by the government authority at 'department' level (Article L221(6) Consumer Code and Article R. 223(2).

In addition, the Public Health Code (CSP) provides criminal consequences for products relating to health (Article L5451(1) and following):

A producer who continues trading a product despite a banning order; who does not comply with a sales restriction; who does not pass on warnings or provide instructions for use; or who fails to withdraw the product from the market, can face:

- a criminal fine of €30,000 for individuals or €150,000 for corporate entities
- a sentence of two years' imprisonment.

Several additional provisions apply to food-related products.

A criminal fine of €37,500 and a sentence of two years' imprisonment applies to any producer who tries to create the false impression that a product on the market complies with standard, when it does not (Articles L213(1) and L213(3) Consumer Code).

A failure to withdraw from the market a product considered as unsafe or a failure to warn consumers about the risks of a product could also potentially result in criminal offences such as:

- involuntary manslaughter;
- negligent bodily harm; and
- endangerment.

Endangerment arises when:

- the producer owes a duty to ensure the safety of the product;
- violation of this duty creates an immediate risk of death, serious injury or permanent disablement;
- another person is exposed to this risk,
- the breach of the duty to ensure the safety of the product was intentional (Article 223(1) of the Penal Code).

3.3 International enforcement (RASFF, RAPEX)

The authorities and especially the DGCCRF will act to enforce RAPEX or RASFF international measures.

The Rapid Alert System for non–food dangerous products (RAPEX) is an alert system that facilitates in the European Union the rapid exchange of information between the member states and the European Commission concerning measures taken to restrict the placing on the market of all products (except food and feed) that may represent a serious risk to the health and the safety of consumers.

The DGCCRF informs the European Commission about products which appear to pose a serious risk and about measures taken by the producers and distributors and by the DGCCRF itself.

The European Commission then passes on this information to the national contacts points of the other member states.

The Rapid Alert System for Food and Feed (RASFF) applies for food and feed control.

The DGCCRF must notify the European Commission if it takes corrective measures such as withdrawing or recalling food or feed products from the market to protect consumers' health. The Commission immediately relays this information to all members of the network.

3.4 Appeals

Measures taken by the regulatory authorities constitute administrative acts, so, where producers or distributors consider that a measure taken by one of the above agencies is not justified or illegal, they can refer the matter to the competent administrative court to make a claim against the authority for an appropriate indemnity for any illegal measure.

However, the administrative courts in France are in practice unlikely to reverse the findings of the administrative authorities. The courts might consider, looking at a proposed ban on the sale of a product, that the company's alleged future loss is neither proven nor justified and reject the company's claim (and support the regulatory ban).

In practice, the French Authorities tend to avoid positive measures, preferring instead to persuade distributors to implement 'voluntary suspension or withdrawal' of products. This forces producers to direct claims against the distributor who had unduly – albeit under pressure from the authority – suspended or withdrawn the product (there being no possibility of suing the administration). However, such an action against a distributor is unlikely to be commercially advantageous.

4. Product liability

In France the main legal source of product liability is the jurisprudence contractual liability.

According to the French jurisprudence the special hidden defect guarantee and the special guarantee of compliance with the contractual specifications in a sales contract is an accessory to the sold product. In consequence the right to bring an action on the grounds of the contract is transferred to the end user. He can also act against every participant in the distribution chain.

This situation is highly protective of the end user because he is not under the obligation to prove a fault in order to initiate an action, the presence of a hidden defect being sufficient for this purpose.

Due to this contractual liability, the buyer and the consumer is in practice always entitled to claim indemnification for the consequences of safety problems of a product based on this contractual obligation as well as on the special law/Sections 1386(1) of the French Civil Code, which is the French transposition of the EC directive on product liability.

4.1 Potential defendants

(a) General law (Sections 1384 and 1641 and following of the Civil Code)

French jurisprudence treats all parties (in the Directive described as 'professionals') involved at any stage from conception to distribution of a product as potentially liable for defects. Thus, 'professionals' include manufacturers, producers, suppliers, importers, distributors and retailers.

(b) Special law (Sections 1386 of the Civil Code)

Section 1386(6) of the Civil Code essentially defines the producer as the manufacturer. However, any party affixing its name or trademark on a product will also be considered 'producer', which therefore captures the following parties:

- manufacturers of industrial products;
- companies providing power supplies;
- farmers; and
- subcontractors.

French jurisprudence treats the right to bring an action on a contractual basis as transferring cumulatively with the product to its different buyers.

Therefore end users are entitled to act against their direct sellers but also against each member in the contractual chain as well as directly against the producer (*Cass ass plén*, February 7 1986).

4.2 Sources of liability

(a) Statute

Product liability is governed by the statute of May 19 1998, passed in implementation of EU Directive 85/374/EEC and incorporated in Sections 1386(1) and following of the French Civil Code. These provisions are applicable to claims under contract or tort but claimants must first prove a defect in the product and a causal relation between the defect and the damage.

The victim can choose between tortious or contractual liability (Section 1386(18) of the Civil Code), but under the principle of non accumulation, must choose one or the other of these options, not both.

The victim can also initiate an action under criminal law via various routes:

- Endangering a third party – producers or sellers who endanger human lives can be criminally liable under Section 121(3) of the French Penal Code. For defective products, this offence occurs when a producer puts into circulation a product which it knows is defective or when the producer does not retrieve the product from the market after a defect has emerged. This offence is prosecuted as wilful or negligent and obliges all parties (manufacturers as well as distributors) to take every possible precaution.
- Criminal assault Section 221(6) of the Penal Code establishes several unintentional elements to this crime for cases of fatal injuries or harm to the person or health of a user. An example of a criminal assault would be putting toxic comestible goods into circulation. The defendant could be a person or corporate entity.
- Fraud – Section L213(1) of the Consumer Protection Statute provides for liability when the producer or seller delivers a product which does not match the product description.
- Misleading advertising – Section L121(1) of the Consumer Protection Statute establishes liability for deceptive trading.

(b) Tort

Duty of care: Section L221(1) of the Consumer Protection Statute requites that products and services must, under normal conditions of use or under other conditions of use which would be reasonably foreseeable, comply with the safety requirements that may be legitimately expected, and must not be hazardous to health.

Section L221(1)(2) obliges manufacturers to inform consumers about any inherent risk in the product if this risk is not clearly perceptible before the purchase. Special information (eg, warnings or instructions) may be required.

If a defect is detected after a product has been put into circulation, the manufacturer must notify the relevant authorities detailing any measures taken to avoid or minimise the risk.

Lack of safety: EU Regulation 85/374, implemented in Section 1386(4) of the Civil Code, states that "A product is defective .... where it does not provide the safety which a person is entitled to expect".

Lack of conformity: The manufacturer will be liable where a product does not have the characteristics agreed pre-sale. The onus is on the purchaser to prove lack of conformity.

Latent defects: This applies when the product is unfit for the use for which it was intended (Section 1641 of the Civil Code).

Duty to inform: The producer must inform the consumer as necessary and must be able to prove that it has correctly informed the buyer.

Safety obligation: The manufacturer must deliver a safe product (in the sense that using the product following information given with it carries no risk).

(c) Contract

Contractual liability is provided for in Sections 1641 and following of the Civil Code.

The victim can act on this ground only if he has contracted with the manufacturer. He must prove the existence of a defect, that the defect existed before the purchase, and finally that the defect caused the damage.

However, the purchaser is entitled to ground his claim on a different section (eg, Section 1384 or Section 1386(1) and following, Civil Code) as long as this respects the general principle of non-accumulation between contractual and tortious liability (see above).

It has been held that even a third party harmed by a contractual breach can initiate an action based on tort (the contractual breach is considered as the faulty action constituting the tort: *Cass ass plén* October 6 2006).

4.3 Claimants, class actions

Class actions are generally not possible under French law, although a parliamentary bill submitted to the French Senate (High Chamber of the French Parliament) on December 22 2010 did propose the introduction of a group action based on the 'opt-in' principle, intended for consumer protection. In September 2012 the French government declared that it would bring a proposal to Parliament in February 2013.

At present, some exceptions do already exist, where several claimants can form a group to act together. Section L422(1) of the Consumers Guarantees Act provides such associations representing consumer victims with the right to group individual interests in a single action under a 'joint representation'. Nevertheless, this exception cannot be defined as class action because:

- the association must be authorised and accepted as a representative at national level;
- several consumers (ie, at least two individual and identified persons) must have mandated the association in writing; victims who have not mandated the association are not represented and retain their individual right to file an action separately. However, the association is not allowed to call for a mandate, eg, via TV or radio commercials, posters, flyers or personalised letters; although publicity using print media is permitted; and
- the victims' individual injuries/damages must have had the same origin.

The aim is to obtain payment of damages for individual claims and therefore the damages are sought on behalf of the consumer victims. The jurisprudence does allow actions by associations without a power of attorney in the public interest (*Cass 2e civ*, May 27 2004).

4.4 Causation

In French law, even though the seller has warned the buyer about a risk, the seller's liability is maintained in cases of bodily injury.

(a) Lack of safety

The victim must prove that the product presented an abnormal danger (Section 1386(9) Civil Code). The manufacturer can conversely prove that the defect appeared after the putting it into circulation. Nevertheless, the judge can found his or her decision on a presumption of facts (Section 1353, Civil Code): eg, to assume an existing defect, which is obviously very pro-consumer.

(b) Latent defects

Since the defect is not visible, the victim bearing the burden of proof must prove the defect by means of inspection. In case of damages suffered due to an unknown cause, it is assumed that the product (the source of the damage is necessarily flawed (*Cass 2nd civ*, December 2 1992).

4.5 Defences

(a) 'State of the art' and development risk defence

The manufacturer can argue that, given the state of scientific knowledge at the time it put its product into circulation, it could not discover the defect or the risk (Section 1386(11)4 of the Civil Code).

Nevertheless, this argument is not available where the damage was caused by a reaction in the human body something in the human body or a product of the human body (Section 1386(12) of the Civil Code).

In the context of latent defects (general law), the possibility that a defect will develop in the course of time will exempt the seller or manufacturer from escape liability (*Cass 3rd civ*, July 17 1972).

(b) Compliance with standards or requirements

The manufacturer may be discharged if it proves that it has respected all the provisions of statutes or regulations (Sections 1386(1) and following of the Civil Code).

Nevertheless this argument might be rejected because of Section 1386(10) of the Civil Code, which stipulates that 'a producer may be liable for a defect although the product was manufactured in accordance with the rules of the trade or of existing standards or although it was the subject of an administrative authorisation'.

(c) Other defences

General law: In the case of latent defects, the manufacturer cannot argue that it has respected the regulations and thus avoid liability altogether, but it is possible that the judge may split liability if the victim has not respected the instructions for use of the product or has used the product incorrectly (*Cass 1st civ*, June 16 1992).

Tort: The producer or manufacturer may prove that the defect has been caused by an external cause '*force majeure*' (Article 1384(1) Civil Code), although that may be a very difficult exercise where the victim can demonstrate a structural defect.

The liability of a manufacturer may be displaced if another company had effective control of the product post-sale (*Cass 2nd civ*, November 14 1979). Moreover, liability is subject to a limitation period – so, for example, it was decided that a manufacturer could not be held liable 12 years after a product was sold (*Cass 2nd civ*, June 5 1971). Finally, the manufacturer can be exonerated if the victim continues to use the product after the manufacturer has advertised the risk (*Cass 2nd civ*, December 13 1989).

Special law: Section 1386(11) of the Civil Code lists other cases of exemption from liability for the manufacturer as follows:

- The manufacturer did not put the product into circulation.
- The defect which caused the damage did not exist at the time that the product was put into circulation by the manufacturer or came into being afterwards; or
- The product was not for the purpose of sale or of any other form of distribution.

Another defence exists for the producer of a component integrated in a machine. It can prove that its component is not the origin of the damage or that the damage occurred as a result of a fault in the product design independent of that component.

4.6 Remedies

(a) *Compensatory damages*

There are some differences between the general law and the special provisions stipulated in Sections 1386(2) of the Civil Code.

(b) *General law*

According to liability law (Sections 1384 and following, French Civil Code): damage suffered as a result of product defects will be compensated without any exception. This includes loss of profit, damage to reputation and loss of opportunity.

(c) *Section 1386(2) of the Civil Code*

The special provisions in Section 1386(2) of the Civil Code apply to damage resulting from personal injury or to a property other than the defective product. Under that section, all damages resulting from a personal injury can be claimed by the victim. Economic damages and business interruption may also be recompensed. There is one restriction: Section 1386(2) prescribes that the damages caused to the product itself are not compensatable but the material damage caused by the product to another product can be claimed if the amount is at least €500 (Regulation of February 11 2005).

(d) *Personal injury*

The French courts generally calculate compensation with the help of an expert and apply an indicative scale in case of personal injury. The most commonly used scale is *barème Dintilhac*, but this is indicative only and judges can adjust the sums. Insurers would like to see an official scale published by the state but this is still being debated, some observers believing that each case is different and must be evaluated individually.

(e) *Non-compensatory damages*

The French system does not provide for punitive damages since the legislator refuses to acknowledge the possibility of legal entities being subject to a 'penalty' under civil law. In practice, however, the judge can, when evaluating the harm done, consider indemnification of the company's loss of reputation or detriment to its brand. Thus, the judge can adjust the figures in favour of either side, and is free to penalise unacceptable business behaviour.

4.7 Procedure, limitation, funding, costs

(a) *Limitation periods*

In the case of latent defects, the victim must act within two years of detection of the defect (Section 1648 of the Civil Code).

In the case of the manufacturer's failure to observe the duty of care, the victim has five years to act. This period is longer (10 years) in case of personal injury (Section 2226 of the Civil Code).

In the tortious context, the victim has a period of five years to act (Section 1384 of the Civil Code). This period begins to run from the time that the purchaser discovers the defect (Section 2224 of the Civil Code).

Under Section 1386(17) of the Civil Code, the victim may act during the three years starting with the date of first becoming aware of the defect and of the producer's name. Should the defective product have been brought into circulation prior to the entry into force of the Act of May 19 1998, the period during which the victim may file an action against the seller begins to run from the date of the purchase (Com, January 24 2006).

(b) *Expert opinions*

The opinion of an expert is very important in civil liability. He or she will determine exactly the cause of the damage and the liability of each person. The expert investigates many routes to establish the origin of the damage. In practice, the recommendation of an expert weighs very heavily as proof and judges more often than not will follow expert opinion, so it is very hard to contest.

(c) *Summons*

The plaintiff must deliver a summons through a bailiff to the defendant. The summons contains a summary of the facts, the reasons for the procedure and the objective of the demand. A period of at least 15 days is set for the defendant to choose a lawyer.

(d) *Proceedings in the main action*

A first hearing will be organised by the judge to ensure that both parties are represented and fairly exchange their statements. As a next step, the judge appoints an expert and several hearings are organised after completion of the expert procedures. This process, from the request of an expert opinion until the date the president schedules a hearing on the pleadings in the main action, may take from three to seven years.

(e) *Trial*

Parties must produce documents to prove their arguments and to enable the judge to decide the case. Parties give to the judge their pleadings and all supporting documents. The judge bases his or her decision on these elements to approve or refuse the allegations. The court file contains all the documents about the procedure and eventually copies of precedents cited in the pleadings and is shared to the other side. The commercial court and the Superior Court in Paris will request the file several days before the hearing to enable the judges to examine the case before the pleadings. Before the other courts, lawyers present their file when they plead. Under French law several forms of litigation are possible depending on the nature of the proceedings. In summary procedure the President will fix a hearing date as soon as possible for pleading. If it is a complex case, the judge will propose a schedule for the exchange of submissions and documents and at the end of the procedure, set a date for a hearing to plead. Witness evidence is not very effective in proving an allegation. Judges prefer a written proof over verbal statements.

(f) *Timing*

The preliminary procedure to gather evidence for a product liability claim can take from two to six years. The first judgment of proceedings in the main action, from summons until the pronouncement of the judgment, can take two to three years. If an appeal against the decision in the first instance is filed, the average time for the Court of Appeal to render its judgment is approximately two years. Decisions of the Court of Cassation also take approximately two years.

(g) *Fees and costs*

Legal aid: French law provides a procedure to obtain legal aid when the claimant or the defendant has insufficient funds to pay for their defence. The amount of legal aid will depend on the financial status of the party. Aid is transmitted directly to the lawyer representing the party. Aid may cover all fees necessary during the trial, experts' costs, bailiffs' fees and lawyers' fees. Aid cannot be paid to a company or to a party in receipt of insurance. However, legal aid may be requested by French nationals and foreigners in certain conditions. After the judgment, in French law, the losing party must pay the fees of the other party, but not the lawyers' fees. If a party in receipt of legal aid wins the case, the state may request reimbursement of the aid. Legal aid may only be cancelled in two cases: if the beneficiary has obtained it by making a false declaration or has acquired sufficient money during the proceedings. Section 71 of the French Regulation dated December 19 1991 stipulates that this clawback may be requested *ex officio* or by any interested party, in particular by the other side or by the lawyer.

Third-party funding: Under French law, a party cannot use funds from another party. The lawyer must be sure of the origin of the funds used to pay him.

Contingency fees: Under French law, lawyers cannot operate on a no win, no fee basis.

'Loser pays' rule: This rule in general does not exist in France. Only certain defined expenses (eg, bailiff's fees, fees for an expert opinion) as defined in Section 695 of the Civil Procedure Code are advanced and finally borne by the losing party. However, legal fees are not included in this rule. The judge may order at his or her own discretion that the unsuccessful party pay a lump sum indemnity for the legal fees of the other party (Section 700 of the Civil Procedure Code), or leave the successful party totally or partially to cover its own legal fees.

4.8 Trends

The Civil Code imposes a new obligation on manufacturers of equipment or a component of equipment. The manufacturer is liable only if its product is not modified after leaving its control and is used in compliance with the manufacturer's instructions. Furthermore, manufacturers may be held liable on the grounds of the general law governing the sale (eg, if there is a guarantee regarding latent defects; where there is an additional duty to provide a caution notice). A liability is different from the manufacturer's, and can be based only on Section 1386(1) of the Civil Code.

5. Product insurance

As France is a high-risk jurisdiction for product liability, appropriate insurance coverage is particularly important for every company in the distribution chain.

Since exclusion and limitation of liability will in practice commonly not be accepted by a French commercial partner – and, even if it is accepted, is unlikely to be recognised under French law – adequate coverage for product liability is vital for companies working in France.

Even pure financial losses are normally covered in France due to the fact that liability for these kinds of damages is automatic and cannot be safely excluded by appropriate contractual wording. Special pure financial losses coverage (losses due to the sole non-functioning of the sold product) is common and important in France and referred to in practice as 'DINC coverage' (*dommages immatériels non consécutifs*: ie, immaterial damages generated by a non-insured event). This definition is based on the broader French insurance practice according to which insurance policies are drafted on an 'all risks, excepted ...' basis, which is then diluted by a list of exceptions, the first among which is generally the indemnity for (the value of) the product itself. The product is thus neither insured nor included in the coverage. Pure financial losses due to a loss of function of the product are thus, in French theory, the consequence of a non-insured event (the product). To be covered, the producer/distributor must obtain coverage in a special DINC extension. This extension is common but expensive and often granted with thresholds.

On the contrary, albeit in a way along the same lines, special product guarantees are nearly impossible to insure (see below, 'Product guarantee').

5.1 Available cover

Forms of insurance tend to be available in France under the following broad categories.

(a) Product recall

This will cover the cost of a recall (including brand damage), where necessary to prevent injury or damage but generally covers only the administrative costs of the recall.

(b) Contaminated products

As above, but also covering malicious contamination and extortion as an extension of the normal assembly and disassembly coverage.

(c) ***Product liability***

This covers the indemnification for personal injury caused by the product to the buyers or any third party as well as damages caused to any other goods or property of the buyer and/or a third party.

(d) ***Financial loss***

Where a product fails to perform its function and causes pure economic loss (not consequent on damage), this clause covers [contractual] liability for this pure economic loss.

(e) ***Product guarantee***

Where a product fails to perform its function, the contractual liability for special agreed performances and characteristics is generally not insurable in France because it falls to be considered as a form of 'entrepreneurial risk' of the producer.

(f) ***Product recall***

The product recall extension is generally an exception to normal coverage and will therefore be interpreted restrictively.

5.2 Product recall

(a) ***Insuring provisions***

The recall must be initiated:

- in response to an immediate product safety problem;
- in compliance with a legal duty to implement a recall; and
- in order to prevent bodily injury.

Trigger: The trigger for a recall in France will usually be a decision (administrative act) of the competent authority obliging the manufacturer/distributor to implement a recall.

> *This Policy is extended to reimburse the ASSURED for XX% of the Expenses incurred by or on behalf of the ASSURED for the recall of Products under a mandatory order of the Administration issued during the Policy Period because of an existing, alleged or suspected like defect, fault or condition in a Product. All such Expenses incurred by the ASSURED shall attach to the Policy Period in which the mandatory order is issued.*

The leading French text on insurance law emphasises, in relation to recalls without a mandatory order of an authority, the need for an "important and imminent danger" with significant safety motivations (*Lamy Assurances* 2012, 2546), ie, the recall must be motivated by a product safety problem and be intended to prevent imminent bodily injury (*Dictionnaire Permanent Assurances*, edition January 14 2011).

The immediacy of the measures as well as the imminence of the risk of bodily injury must not be in doubt. French legal academics tend to focus on the core problem, namely, the question of whether there is a legal duty to proceed to a recall (as opposed to taking other possible actions like normal repair work on the part of the producer in order to fulfil its normal contractual warranty duties). Those normal contractual warranty duties are by nature and by definition not insurable falling into the category of general 'entrepreneurial risk'.

In France, the conditions leading necessarily to a covered product recall initiated by the assured have not been clearly defined by the jurisprudence. It is commonly accepted that a necessary prerequisite of a recall without a mandatory order by authority is a concrete and immediate risk of bodily injury, but there is no clear precedent so manufacturers and producers must negotiate their agreement with the insurer on a case-to-case basis (*Endrös, Florian, Der Rückruf und die Rücknahme von Produkten in Frankreich*, PHI 2000, 222, and following).

If the risk of bodily injury can be efficiently prevented by the simple provision of information or warning to users to check for defects and to carry out repairs conforming to instructions provided by the producer, recall would seem to be not legally necessary (and therefore will not be covered by the insurance policy). The end user must of course have the necessary technical competencies to be expected to conduct such inspections.

In other words, the conditions for a recall upon a legal recommendation are not fulfilled in this last case and the insurer would seem to be entitled to refuse cover when there is no risk for third parties necessitating an 'immediate recall in urgency'.

In a January 21 2003 decision, the Paris Court of Appeal ordered an insurer to cover a recall operation because the insurer, having been informed about the circumstances surrounding the recall, never expressed its opposition to the recall, and immediate urgent recall was deemed necessary to prevent the risks (CA Paris, January 21, Chamber 7, section A, 2000/22503 – not published).

The courts will consider whether the recall was necessary. If the insurer opposed the recall but the measure was necessary because of emergency and risk of bodily injury, the courts will support the insured. If the recall was unjustified, however, the insurer need not reimburse the manufacturer.

The principle of estoppel does not exist in French law but this Court of Appeal case does seem to be influenced by this principle of common law: the insurer did not oppose the recall so the manufacturer believed that its insurance would cover the costs of the recall. Consequently, the insurer cannot change its position (to decide subsequently that the recall was not covered), even although an emergency was not proven.

(b) Insured costs

Costs covered by recall insurance are generally specifically listed in the policy.

Pre-recall expenses, testing, and development costs for replacement or repair: These are generally covered in the standard policies.

Consultancy costs: These costs are understood as costs for technical consultants, technical studies, and are also generally covered.

Business interruption suffered by third party: The recall coverage does generally not include any business interruption of third parties. Such interruption is, according to French insurance practice, a loss related to the excluded product itself and has therefore to be qualified as DINC, potentially covered by a special DINC extension (see above).

Repair, replacement, refunds: The standard losses covered by recall insurance generally also include repair and replacement costs, ie, costs of manpower, intervention of technicians or experts and travel expenses. Refunds of the price of the repaired or replaced product is generally not covered by the standard clauses of French recall policies.

However, recall insurance generally does cover as a common extension the extra costs of assembly and disassembly where necessary in complex products using components.

Brand rehabilitation: Brand rehabilitation costs are not normally seen in insurance policies in France and are certainly non-standard.

Third-party recall liability: Third-party recall liability generally does not require manufacturers and distributors in France to take out extra cover. Under French law damage resulting from the integration of a defective component of the producer or distributor by a third party in a different product in a value-added production chain is viewed as a material damage incurred by the next producer in the chain and a normal product liability policy will apply to that material damage.

(c) Exclusions

The general and normal exclusion of the product also applies to the recall insurance cover. The product itself is not insured; only accessory costs to carry out repair work, identify and determine the defective products, such as manpower costs for repair and replacement, travel expenses, and various other expenses which are clearly defined in the insurance policy, will be covered.

5.3 Contaminated products

Insurance for contaminated products is in practice not often seen as special cover on the French market. Cover is generally included in normal product liability policies, under preventive measures: a producer of a contaminated product obviously cannot wait for actual damage to occur and must take preventive actions including possibly implementing a recall. However, to avoid the possibility of the insurance company excluding the preventive measure, any producer exposed to contamination risks has a clear interest in subscribing to specific recall insurance cover.

5.4 Product liability

Conforming to the general insurance provisions and to French practice, policies are worded conforming to the principle 'all risks, excepted ...'.

(a) Insuring provisions

Personal injury and material damages are covered by the product liability insurance.

Damage means all material damages to property or products of a third party, with the exception of the product itself. The material damage can also be loss of function of the third party product in which the component produced by the policyholder is integrated. There is precedent from the highest French courts here: in a case where a defective transistor integrated into a small electronic card, leading to a loss of function of the whole card, constituted a material damage, on the grounds that the transistor could not easily be taken out of the card and repaired.

In this context 'easily' means removable without damage to the equipment and without incurring major expenses.

(b) Exclusions

Breach of contract: Breach of contract is not a common exclusion, due to the fact that French product liability is based on contract law, which includes a safety duty and the possibility of damages to contractual partners as well as to any third parties. The defective product itself is always excluded as a non-insurable 'entrepreneurial risk'.

Conditions: Before the conclusion of a contract of insurance the insured informs the insurer about the product and any potential risks. If the insured lies about the product or risks the contract will be null and void.

French product liability insurance can be triggered by the claim or on the occurrence of a damage event. Since the French reform of the insurance act by Law 2003-706 (August 1 2003), the two triggers are confirmed as:

- 'damage event'; and
- 'claims made'.

It is very important for the trigger to be defined in detail in the policy, the interpretation of which, in case of litigation, will of course be subject to the discretion of the judge.

The damage event is not a synonym with 'damage occurrence'. It is instead defined in detail by the French Insurance Act as the date when a technical cause for a damage was set, even if the concrete manifestation of the damage appears at a subsequent date. This definition of the damage event as the initial technical cause is indirectly foreseen by the law in the definition of a 'serial damage'.

The second trigger foreseen by the law and often seen in current French insurance practice is the 'claims made' principle. Litigation between insurer and insured may arise if both principles are combined in the policy. For example, if the 'claims made' principle is linked with the damage event in a way that both the claim and the damage event must occur during the validity of the policy. This can lead to gaps in the insurance coverage, if the insured changes insurance companies which have different trigger definitions.

5.5 Financial loss

Financial loss insurance is generally not a specific insurance but should fall under the cover of a DINC extension.

Germany

Sabine Faust
Andreas Lachmann
RWP Rechtsanwälte

The statutory arrangements for product safety and liability in Germany can be roughly divided into two groups: preventative and punitive (imposing civil and criminal law sanctions for non-compliance). The preventative provisions are mainly determined by European guidelines and directives. These stipulate qualities certain products must have in order to be safe and set out the consequences, should a product fail to meet the requirements. In Germany, the federal states are responsible for monitoring compliance with those provisions.

Then there are the civil law provisions which are triggered once a product constitutes a hazard or has caused harm. These apply in cases where a person harmed by a product has a legal claim due and, where appropriate, against whom that claim may be asserted. These provisions are to be found in particular in the Civil Code and Product Liability Act.

1. Product safety regulation

1.1 Product risks

In Germany, the regulatory regime applying to commercially sold products is outlined in the Product Safety Act, which superseded the Equipment and Product Safety Act as of December 1 2011 and implemented the European Directive on General Product Safety (2001/95/EC). However, the Product Safety Act does not apply to product groups governed by sector-specific legislation. These include for example:

- medical devices (governed by the Medical Devices Act);
- pharmaceutical products (governed by the Pharmaceuticals Act); and
- food and feeds (Food and Feed Act; Section 1(3) of the Product Safety Act).

The Product Safety Act applies in addition to sector-specific legislation, wherever the latter does not expressly exclude the application of the Product Safety Act (eg, for cars, clothing, toys and cleaning agents.

All of the product safety legislation has in common the requirement that a product may in principle only be put on the market if there is no risk that it will harm the safety or health of persons or other interests protected by specific legislation when used in accordance with its intended purpose or under conditions which can reasonably be foreseen. The regulatory regime applying to certain products is more detailed and set out in supplementary statutes and directives.

European product safety laws must also be heeded. Where there is directly applicable European legislation, this will take precedence over German legislation. Having said that, in practice the German legislature has in any case mostly implemented much of the European legislation into national law.

1.2 Safety standards

If a product conforms with a European standard published in the *Official Journal* of the European Union, its safety is presumed (Section 4(2), Product Safety Act and Principle 14, Directive 2001/95/EC). So, for example, if a product bears the European CE label, it will be presumed to be safe. The same applies if a product conforms with national standards or other technical specifications (Section 5(2), Product Safety Act), but only if passed by the Product Safety Committee and published by the Federal Institute for Occupational Safety and Health in the *Joint Ministerial Gazette*.

1.3 Market surveillance

Market surveillance (ie, monitoring compliance with product safety regulations) is the responsibility of the federal states. Each federal state has assigned this role to a certain public body, for example: in North Rhine-Westphalia the regional government or in Bavaria the Trade Supervisory Office. These bodies also receive complaints from consumers about products they would like to report. Market surveillance for special product groups can be assigned to a particular public agency.

1.4 Prior approval

There is in principle no prior approval requirement for products marketed in Germany. The producer or manufacturer is responsible for ensuring that its product conforms with the pertinent provisions. However, so-called 'novel foods' under EU Regulation 258/98 and genetically modified foods under EU Regulation 1829/2003 must be subject to prior examination.

Medical devices may in principle only be placed on the market or used in Germany if they bear a CE marking or have passed a conformity assessment procedure (Sections 6 and 10 of the Medical Devices Act).

Finished pharmaceutical products, on the other hand, require an express prior marketing authorisation (Section 21 of the Pharmaceuticals Act). Furthermore, pharmaceutical products may only be produced by companies which have been granted a corresponding manufacturing authorisation (Sections 13 and following of the Pharmaceuticals Act). Anybody wishing to import pharmaceutical products from outside the European Economic Area requires authorisation pursuant to Section 72 of the Pharmaceuticals Act.

Motor vehicles require type approval pursuant to Sections 20 and 21 of the Road Traffic Approval Order, which can be granted for either classes of individual motor vehicles.

1.5 Safety issues

In Germany, there are in principle no sector-specific product safety laws or regulators. However, there are special compliance burdens for products in the field of defence, motor vehicles and medical devices.

The Product Safety Act imposes a general duty on both the producer and its authorised representatives (importer and retailer) to supply only safe products.

Under the Pharmaceuticals Act, 'pharmaceutical entrepreneurs' are responsible for the product safety of pharmaceutical products. A 'pharmaceutical entrepreneur' is the party that holds the authorisation for certain pharmaceuticals or has introduced the pharmaceutical onto the market in its own name. If the pharmaceutical entrepreneur has its corporate headquarters outside the European Economic Area, it must authorise a representative within the EEA. In such cases, both the pharmaceutical entrepreneur and its representative are responsible for ensuring the safety of supplied products.

1.6 Corrective action

The product safety regulations apply a wide range of measures to prevent products not complying with the statutory requirements from causing harm to consumers. These measures may also be ordered by the authorities if not voluntarily undertaken by the producer. The measures vary from prohibition (ban on putting products on the market until the product's safety has been definitively determined), to an order to have the product examined by the proper authorities. If it has been established that the product does not conform with the statutory safety requirements, the following actions may be taken:

- withdrawal or recall of sold products;
- seizure or destruction of products; and
- informing the general public about the risks.

However, these measures will always be subject to the principle of proportionality: the ordered measure may not impact the affected party/parties to an unnecessary extent.

1.7 Criminal liability

Under product safety legislation and also the Criminal Code, breaching product safety legislation can also result in criminal liability of those responsible.

2. Obligations of producers and distributors

2.1 Sources of duties

(a) Statute

The duties of producers, importers and retailers in Germany are determined in particular by public law product safety provisions. These require persons responsible to ensure in particular that the products they put on the market satisfy the requirements for products of that kind.

(b) Tort

In Germany there is also a general duty to maintain safety. This requires that the person creating a source of hazards must prevent any risks which result from the hazard as far as possible. The producer of a product must prevent such risks as far as possible and also provide clear warning about those risks.

(c) ***Contract***

Concluding a contract also grounds the duty to show consideration for the legal interests of the other party and also, where appropriate, to inform that party about the risks associated with the product or its use. Furthermore, it is conceivable that a party provides a contractual guarantee which establishes a responsibility that goes beyond the duties imposed by law.

2.2 Pre-market obligations

Producers of products that are to be marketed in Germany must heed good manufacturing practice in advance.

(a) ***General safety requirements***

A product that falls within the scope of particular regulations may be marketed only if it fulfils the requirements of that regulation and, additionally, under its intended or foreseeable use, does not endanger human safety or health or other legally protected interests mentioned in the Regulation (Section 3(1), Product Safety Act).

A product that does not fall within the scope of a particular regulation may be marketed if its appropriate and foreseeable use does not endanger human safety or health (Section 3(2), Product Safety Act). For the determination of its safety, its characteristics including its composition, packaging, instructions for its assembly, its installation, its maintenance and its period of use as well as its impact on other products and accompanying warnings and instructions are taken into account.

(b) ***CE marking***

In the European market, the producer, importer or retailer may affix the CE label to a product, if CE labelling is possible for the product and the product satisfies the requirements for its CE labelling. CE certification is possible, for example, for certain machines, medical devices and lifts. For the introduction of some products, a CE labelling is mandatory (eg, medical products or toys). Sometimes the examination as to whether the product conforms with the requirements of the CE labelling may be carried out by the producer himself and sometimes the assessment bodies named in the directives or guidelines must be involved. An overview of the CE certification procedure, the pertinent directives and the assessment bodies to be involved is provided by the European Commission at http://ec.europa.eu/enterprise/policies/single-market-goods/cemarking/index_en.htm.

(c) ***Traceability, record keeping***

The need to be able to track products plays an important role in product safety. If the product is meant for the end consumer, products must bear the name of the company and the address of the producer, its representative within the European Economic Area or the importer (Section 6(1)2, Product Safety Act). This allows consumers and government bodies to trace back the product's origin. This requirement also directly results from many sector-specific regulations. Besides the obligation to label their products, producers are required to keep corresponding records.

(d) *Consumer protection laws*

Section 6 of the Product Safety Act contains a special provision for consumer products. Beside the traceability requirement, it must be ensured that consumers are informed about the risks associated with the use of the product where such risks are not immediately obvious without the warning. The producer, its authorised representative in the European Economic Area and also the importer must take precautions to avoid risks to the consumer, which may extend as far as a recall, and carry out sample testing of the products they make available. If they become aware that any of their products does not satisfy the safety requirements, they must inform the market surveillance authorities immediately.

Retailers may not sell products if they know that they do not comply with the product safety requirements. Once they become aware of safety deficiencies of products, they too have a notification duty to inform the market surveillance authorities.

(e) *Disputes*

Disputes between the producer and the regulator on whether a product is safe or unsafe falls under the competence of the administrative courts. Such disputes arise in particular in connection with an administrative prohibition of the product or an order to initiate corrective actions. In general, the administrative courts have an obligation to clarify the safety of a product ex officio. The producer also has a duty to furnish the court with all documents necessary to determine the safety of the product. However, if the production or characteristics of a product comply with harmonised standards, the product is presumed to be safe. An authority claiming that it poses a risk therefore must provide evidence of lack of safety. However, as long as it is not demonstrated that the product endangers human safety or health though being in accordance with harmonised standards, the product is considered safe within the meaning of Section 3 of the Product Safety Act.

(f) *Penalties*

Breaching product safety legislation, ordinances and directives may constitute either an administrative or criminal offence. The penalties for a breach of the Product Safety Act are set out in Sections 39 and 40 of the Product Safety Act. Marketing a product which does not comply with the requirements of Section 3 of the Product Safety Act is, however, not penalised as long as the producer immediately after receiving knowledge of the safety defect informs the authorities. The failure to inform the authorities in time or of all relevant circumstances may result in a fine of up to €10,000.

Non-compliance with orders by the authorities, issued in order to prevent harm to the consumer, may result in a fine of up to €100,000. If this conduct results in a threat to human life or health, to property of significant value or the non-compliance is repeated persistently, this may constitute a criminal offence, meaning that a custodial sentence of up to one year or a fine may also be imposed (Section 40, Product Safety Act).

(g) ***Food***

Food safety is generally governed by the Food and Feed Act and European Regulation 178/2002/EC. The Food and Feed Act repeatedly cites the European Regulation. It is forbidden to produce or process food such that its consumption is harmful to health within the meaning of Article 14(4) of Regulation 178/2002/EC. Food and feed traders must ensure traceability of the products they stock (Article 18, Regulation 178/2002/EC).

In addition, the Food and Feed Act empowers the Federal Ministry of Nutrition, Agriculture and Consumer Protection to issue restrictions and requirements affecting the production and labelling of foods. The Federal Ministry has exercised this power, for example, to issue its own ordinances for individual foods such as fruit juices, cheese, beer and honey.

Products of animal origin are subject to European Regulation 853/2004/EC. This requires a health certificate for such food to prove that it was produced in compliance with the rules of hygiene set out in the Directive.

In general, in case of any dispute, the burden of proof of the safety of a product lies with the producer. However, foods which are in accordance with the specific requirements of the EU are presumed to be safe (Article 14(7), Regulation 178/2002/EC). Only where there is reasonable suspicion that the product is unsafe would the authorities restrict its marketing. In any lawsuit, the authorities must prove that it was reasonable to assume the product to be harmful.

Sections 58 to 60 of the Food and Feed Act list offences according to whether they are criminal or administrative. The production or handling of a product with the result that its consumption carries a health risk is a criminal offence (Section 58(1)1), punishable by a custodial sentence of up to three years or a fine. The custodial sentence can be up to five years, if an 'especially serious case' is involved, ie, the illegal act jeopardised the health of a large number of people, exposed a person to the risk of fatal or serious injury or impairment of health, or the offender gained a significant pecuniary advantage through gross self-interest for himself or another. Any attempt to market a product that does not conform with the requirements will also be penalised.

Novel foods: In 1997, 'novel foods' – which include in particular genetically modified foods – were subjected to particular monitoring by EU Regulation 258/97. If a food has not hitherto been used for human consumption to a significant degree and falls under one of the categories named in Article 1(2) of the Regulation, placing that food on the market requires a marketing authorisation. The Regulation is in particular relevant for genetically-modified foods, which however in 2003 became subject to a separate Regulation. Since then, the Novel Food Regulation has had only limited application.

Foods and food ingredients falling within the scope of the novel food regulation may neither present a danger for the consumer nor mislead the consumer or differ from foods or food ingredients which they are intended to replace to such an extent that their normal consumption would be nutritionally disadvantageous for the consumer (Article 3, Regulation 258/97/EC). These restrictions correspond to the restrictions contained in Section 11 of the Food and Feed Act.

The regulation also provides for specific labelling requirements for novel foods and food ingredients: Their packaging must provide for information on their ingredients, nutritional value and their intended use (where not equivalent to an existing food or food ingredient).

In the event of any dispute, the producer bears the burden of proving the safety of its product.

The European regulations do not provide for punitive measures as the effective enforcement of European regulations is within the competence of the member states of the European Union. With regard to breaches of food safety provisions, the Foods and Feeds Act applies and the sanctions generally equate to those imposed where there is a breach of a corresponding German provision (Sections 58(3), 59(3) and 60(4), Food and Feed Act).

Genetically modified foods: Genetically modified food is now governed by EU Regulations 1829/2003 and 1830/2003, which place increased demands on the safety of genetically modified food, its labelling and information for the general public. Such foods are subject to an authorisation procedure. They will only be granted authorisation if:

- they are not associated with any adverse effects to humans;
- their consumption is not nutritionally disadvantageous compared with the corresponding conventional food; and
- they do not mislead the consumer.

Authorised products should be safe and in accordance with the regulation. Anybody who disputes this must therefore provide evidence in support of this and, if applicable, explain why he or she thinks the product deviates from the authorised version.

Article 45 of EU Regulation 1829/2003 explicitly grants competence to the member state for providing for sanctions to enforce compliance with the regulation. In Germany, penalties for the breach of EU Regulation 1829/2003 are included in the German Act to Implement the European Regulations on Genetic Engineering. A custodial sentence of up to three years or a fine may be imposed for the introduction of a product which does not conform to the safety requirements of Regulation 1829/2003 (Section 6(1) of that act). A custodial sentence of up to five years or a fine may be imposed only if the product posed a hazard to the physical integrity or life of human beings, to property of significant value or to elements of the natural environment of significant economic importance.

Food enhancers and supplements: The authorisation of food additives is governed by the national Ordinance on admission of additives in foodstuffs for technological purposes. The appendix to the Ordinance contains lists of authorised additives, restricted additives and additives authorised only for certain purposes. The list corresponds to the list of additives authorised at EU level.

In case of a dispute, where the facts are in doubt, the producer must furnish the authorities or the court with all documents to show that food enhancers or supplements have not been used beyond admissible proportions.

The Ordinance on Admission of Additives in Foodstuffs for Technological Purposes (in Section 10) explicitly adopts the provisions of the Foods and Feeds Act. Accordingly, breaches of the ordinance may be sanctioned by a custodial sentence of up to three or five years respectively, or a fine.

Food contact materials, labelling: The requirements for materials that come into contact with food are uniformly governed at the European level by EU Regulations 1935/2004 and 450/2009. EU Regulation 1935/2004 covers all types of packaging, bottles (plastic and glass), cutlery and also adhesives and printing ink for labels. These products may not release substances to the food in quantities that would pose a risk to human health or unjustifiably change the composition of the food. Regulation 450/2009 deals with so-called 'active and intelligent materials' which are meant to extend the storage life of packed foods or to preserve or better their condition (active materials) or to monitor the condition of packed foods or their environment (intelligent materials), such materials are consumer goods which fall within the scope of the Foods and Feeds Act (Section 2(6) of the 1 Food and Feed Act).

The labelling of food is still currently governed by the Food Labelling Ordinance, which will however be largely replaced in 2014 by a new European regulation (1169/2011/EU). Nutrition or health claims for food are governed by EU Regulation 1924/2006/EC.

In case of a dispute, producers must furnish the authorities or the court, respectively, with evidence that their food contact materials fulfil the safety requirements of the Regulation.

It is up to the member states to ensure compliance with the Regulation by providing for adequate penalties (Article 25 of EU Regulation 1935/2004). In Section 2(6)1 of the Food and Feed Act, the German legislature pointed out that food contact materials as defined by EU Regulation 1935/2004 are 'consumer goods' as defined by the Foods and Feeds Act. A custodial sentence of up to one year or a fine may be imposed for the marketing of food contact materials that do not comply with the requirements of EU Regulation 1935/2004 (Section 59, 15 in connection with Section 31(1) of the Foods and Feeds Act).

(h) Medicines

There are special safety precautions for medical and pharmaceutical products. The sale and supply of medical devices is governed by the Medical Devices Act (MPG) and sale and supply of pharmaceutical products by the German Pharmaceutical Act. The production of pharmaceutical products requires a marketing authorisation, whilst medical devices may be marketed only with a CE mark. Finished pharmaceutical products require an individual marketing authorisation.

It is forbidden to market, manufacture, put into operation or use medicinal products when it is reasonable to assume that these products are or could be hazardous to the health and safety of human beings where used and stored correctly and where that risk exceeds tolerable levels (Section 4, MPG, 1). The same applies to products whose expiry date has passed.

Finally, it is forbidden to market medicinal products which might mislead the consumer because of their appearance or by the information provided with them. If there is any doubt as to whether there has been deception, the law leans in favour the consumer and presumes that the product is not performing as it impliedly says it should.

The German Pharmaceutical Act deals with the marketing and use of pharmaceutical products. It prohibits the marketing and use of pharmaceutical products which might, according to scientific knowledge, have deleterious effects beyond a tolerable degree (Section 5, Pharmaceuticals Act). Moreover, pharmaceutical products may not be produced or marketed when they are labelled wrongly or might mislead the consumer. For the production of those pharmaceuticals mentioned in Section 13(1) of the German Pharmaceuticals Act, a production manufacturing authorisation is required. For example, an authorisation is required for the production of pharmaceuticals produced by genetic engineering. And drugs require formal approval (Section 21, Pharmaceuticals Act).

In the production and quality control stages, medical and pharmaceutical products must also comply with the GMP guidelines of the European Union for medical and pharmaceutical products.

In case of a dispute, generally, the manufacturer or producer must furnish the authorities and courts with all documents relevant for the determination of their product to be in conformance with the applicable product safety regulations. However, where a medicinal or pharmaceutical product has received formal approval, the person claiming that it poses a hazard must first raise reasonable doubts as to the safety of the product. In particular, where a medicinal product is in conformity with harmonised standards or other standards, it is presumed that the product also complies with the safety requirements of the Medical Devices Act. This presumption leads to a shift of the burden of proof, in that a person claiming the hazardousness of a product must provide that the safety standards have in fact not been met.

If a producer sells a product which does not fulfil the safety requirements of Section 4(1)1 of the Medical Devices Act, a custodial sentence of up to five years or a fine may be imposed. If it is not an 'especially serious case', the custodial sentence will be up to three years. Where products are marketed with misleading information, a custodial sentence of up to one year or a fine may be imposed (Section 41(1) of the Medical Devices Act).

The sale of a product after its expiry date is an administrative offence punishable by a fine of up to €25,000 (Section 42(2)1 of the Medical Devices Act). The act lists which breaches constitute administrative offences and which criminal offences.

For breach of the ban on marketing potentially hazardous pharmaceuticals, a custodial sentence of up to three years or a fine may be imposed (Section 95,

Pharmaceuticals Act). This is a strict liability offence and therefore it is not necessary to prove that the producer acted in a negligent or culpable manner. In especially serious cases, breaches of the German Pharmaceutical Act can incur a custodial sentence of up to ten years or a fine. The marketing of a pharmaceutical product after its expiry date is an administrative offence punishable by a fine of up to €25,000 (Section 97, Pharmaceuticals Act).

(i) *Motor vehicles*

Motor vehicles in Germany are governed by the provisions of the Product Safety Act. In addition, they also require approval under the Road Traffic Approval Ordinance.

Motor vehicles in Germany must be manufactured and equipped in such a way that their operation with due care does not harm or endanger anybody and does not interfere with anybody's interest (Section 30, Road Traffic Approval Ordinance). They must conform to safety requirements such that in the eventuality of involvement in accidents, the driver and passengers will stay as safe as possible and the consequences of any personal injury will be minimised by preventative design safety measures. In addition, several European regulations impose particular requirements for certain types of vehicles, eg, Regulation 2003/37 for tractors.

In the case of a dispute, where the facts are in doubt, the onus is on the manufacturer to furnish the court with evidence of the fact that its product is in accordance with all applicable safety provisions.

With regard to penalties, the provisions of the Product Safety Act apply. The marketing of a product with a safety defect will not by itself attract a fine; but failure to notify the authorities upon becoming aware of a safety defect will. A criminal offence has been committed in particular, if the producer does not obey an official order intentionally and persistently or when the non-obeyance jeopardises the life or health of another person or property of significant value. Criminal offences under the Product Safety Act are punished with custodial sentences of up to one year or a fine reflecting the severity of the offence and income of the offender.

(j) *Electrical equipment*

Electronic products are governed by the Product Safety Act and its First Enactment. In addition, the producers of electronic equipment also must meet the statutory requirements for the placing on the market, withdrawal and the environmentally sound disposal of electrical and electronic equipment (Electrical and Electronic Equipment Act). That act focuses more on waste management than safety issues.

Electronic products may only be marketed if they conform to the present state of the art in the European Union and do not pose any risk to the safety of human beings, farm animals or property (Section 2, First Enactment to the Product Safety Act). The essential characteristics of the product must be printed on the product or its packaging. The same applies to the producer's name or sign. Article 3 of the First Enactment makes clear that electronic devices always require a CE-certification before they can be supplied.

In case of a dispute, where the facts are in doubt, the onus is on the manufacturer to furnish the courts with evidence that its product is in conformity with all relevant regulations and does not pose any danger to the legally-protected interests mentioned in the First Enactment to the Product Safety Act.

Where there has been a breach of the First Enactment to the Product Safety Act, the general provisions of the Product Safety Act apply.

(k) *Toys*

Toys are consumer products as defined by the Food and Feed Act. The Product Safety Act also applies to toys as does European Directive 2009/48/EC as implemented in German law by the second Enactment to the Product Safety Act.

Toys (including their chemical ingredients) may not endanger safety and health of users or third parties, as long as the toy is used in accordance with its intended or any foreseeable use. The likely and foreseeable behaviour of children is to be taken into account. Specific requirements with regard to their physical, mechanical, chemical and electrical characteristics and hygienic requirements result from Attachment II of Directive 2009/48/EC. Article 15 of the Directive requires a conformity assessment and according to Article 13, toys that are to be sold in the European Economic Area require a CE certification.

In general, the onus is on the manufacturer to provide for documents to prove that its product is safe. However, a toy which complies with certain harmonised rules or parts of it is presumed to be in conformity with the safety requirements of Article 10 of the Directive as well as Attachment II to the Directive (Article 13, Directive). Any person who wants the authorities to interfere with the distribution of the product therefore must prove the contrary – that the product is not in conformity with the provisions of the Directive or hazardous in spite of compliance with the provisions of the Directive. Therefore, as long as the product complies with the provisions of the Directive and no one is able to provide evidence of any hazard it presents, the product will be considered to be safe.

Whenever a producer has breached its obligations under any of the Directives, Food and Feed Act or Product Safety Act respectively, the sanctions as outlined above apply. Repeat offences attract more severe sanctions.

(l) *Cosmetic products*

The authorisation of cosmetic products is governed by the Food and Feed Act and the Product Safety Act and by the (national) Cosmetics Ordinance. It is prohibited to produce or handle cosmetic products in a way that might cause harm to human health and to introduce compounds which could have the same effect (Section 26, Food and Feed Act). Cosmetic products must not be accompanied by misleading information and their advertising must not be deceptive. The Cosmetics Ordinance contains in particular lists of prohibited and restricted substances. It also imposes strict labelling requirements. The EU Cosmetics Directive comes into force in July 2013 and will replace large parts of the Food and Feed Act and Cosmetics Ordinance.

In case of a dispute, the onus is on the manufacturer to provide evidence of the fact that its product does not pose a danger to legally protected interests.

The production, handling or sale of products contrary to the ban of Section 26 Food and Feed Act may incur a custodial sentence of up to three, in particularly serious cases up to five years, or a fine (Section 58(1)11, Food and Feed Act). The introduction of cosmetic products accompanied with misleading information may incur a custodial sentence of up to one year or a fine, Section 39(1)13. Section 6 of the Cosmetics Ordinance ('criminal and administrative offences') adopts the sanctions as provided in the Food and Feed Act. The use of forbidden or excessive use of restricted materials is qualified as a criminal offence leading to the above-mentioned sanctions, whereas breaches of labelling or testing provisions are administrative offences punishable by fines of up to €50,000.

(m) Occupational health and safety

There is no separate legislation peculiar to health and safety at work and the general rules prevail. However, where there is an employer-employee relationship, the employer will be responsible for the protection of employees.

(n) State compensation

German product safety legislation does not provide for state compensation for product safety violations. A claim for compensation against the state may be possible, however, if the state was contributorily negligent in allowing the product to be put on the market: eg, if the state authorised a product which it should not have authorised.

2.3 Post-market obligations

(a) Notification

The Product Safety Act requires producers to inform their local market surveillance authorities without delay if any of their consumer products pose a risk to the safety or health of the public (Section 6(4)). Details of this are to be found in Attachment I to the EU General Product Safety Regulation (2001/95/). The information to be provided must in particular allow for:

- the exact identification of the product;
- include a comprehensive description of the risks associated with the product;
- all information in order to trace back the product; and
- measures taken, or planned, by the producer to prevent the risk.

Failure to notify the authorities, to notify them in time or to notify them fully is an administrative offence which may incur a fine of up to €10,000. Producers are obliged to cooperate with the market surveillance authorities after notification also (Section 28(4), Product Safety Act).

(b) Corrective action

The producer, its representative and importer must apply all measures necessary in order to prevent a risk which might be associated with their having placed a product on the market (Section 6(2) of the Product Safety Act). These measures may involve withdrawal of products from sale, a warning or recall ('recall' in this context covers all measures necessary to prevent a product being placed on the market or inviting consumers to return the product).

The market surveillance authorities are entitled to order compliance with any recommended measures. These measures may range from examining or testing the products to recall (as listed in Section 26(2) of the Product Safety Act). Costs are to be borne by the addressee of the order, ie, the producer, its representative or the importer of the product.

If the authorities do not consider that initial measure to be sufficient, they may order further or different measures, and in particular may order recall, withdrawal from the market or issuing warnings to the public. The addressee (producer, representative or importer) may appeal this to the regulator and, afterwards, to the courts. The order will be voided if it does not comply with the principle of proportionality (ie, the measure must be necessary and the same result not achievable via alternative measures less burdensome on the addressee). The regulator has no choice, however, but to order a recall and to prohibit further selling if the product constitutes a serious risk in particular for the safety and health of the public (Section 26(4) of the Product Safety Act).

If a producer or any other party responsible for initiating corrective actions does not fulfil those obligations, the market surveillance authorities may set a deadline for compliance. If compliance still does not happen within that deadline, the authorities may order the measures as they deem appropriate and necessary (Section 20(3) of the Second Enactment to the Product Safety Act in connection with Section 26 of the Product Safety Act). This decision may be challenged by the producer or any other party liable under the Product Safety Act in the administrative court (where an objection to the authority fails). The administrative court will balance the risk against the corrective action ordered with a view to judging whether the order is proportionate, and whether the objective could have been achieved by means less burdensome on the producer.

Non-compliance with an official order by the producer or any other party responsible for the marketing of toys that are safe may lead to a fine of up to €100,000 (Section 39 of the Product Safety Act). The amount of the fine will depend on the nature and the extent of the risk. In severe cases requiring recall for example, the fine may be the maximum €100,000; in cases where only examination of the product is ordered, the maximum fine is €10,000.

(c) *Foods*

Food business operators are responsible for fulfilling legal obligations relating to foods (Article 19 of EU Regulation 178/2002). If a food business operator realises that a food which it has imported, produced, processed, manufactured or distributed fails to comply with a mandatory regulation, it must immediately initiate procedures to withdraw, and where appropriate recall, from the market the food in question and inform the relevant authorities and, where appropriate, consumers. The regulation also stipulates cooperation with the regulators. In Germany, information about unsafe food is collected and distributed by the Federal Office of Consumer Protection and Food Safety.

If the producer itself does not initiate proceedings to prevent or eliminate a hazard, the authority may order the necessary steps (Section 39, Food and Feed Act).

The authority may in particular order warnings to be issued to the public, a ban on production, stopping the product being placed on the market, withdrawal of the product from the market, or recall. The producer must comply with such instructions. Non-obeyance constitutes a criminal offence which may be penalised under Section 58(1)17 with a custodial sentence of up to three years or a fine. The order may be appealed to the authority and further to the administrative court. Any appeal instigated would not, however, have any impact on the obligation of the producer to start implementing the mandated measure. Costs of any corrective actions are to be borne by the producer.

(d) Motor vehicles

No specific provisions govern vehicle safety, so the laws for general products apply also to vehicles in Germany.

(e) Pharmaceuticals

The holder of an authorisation for a proprietary pharmaceutical must keep records relating to side effects, including assumptions of causality. It must further inform the authorities of any assumption of the product to have severe side effects, where this assumption is made known to it by a healthcare professional.

This information should be sent to the Federal Institute of Drugs and Medical Devices and, if applicable, to the European Medicines Agency, within 15 days of becoming aware of the side effect. Additionally, the authorisation holder must ensure that the relevant authorities of any member where the drug received authorisation, is informed. This notification must be accompanied by all documents examining the suspected case, including the results of scientific analysis. The drug authorisation holder must also present reports at regular intervals to the German authority about the safety status of the drug and the risks it may be posing. Where there has been non-compliance with the duty to notify the relevant authorities of potential side effects, a fine of up to €25,000 may be imposed (Section 97(2) of the Pharmaceuticals Act).

The relevant authorities can order any procedure necessary to stop detected infringements of the safety provisions or prevent further infringement (Section 69(1) of the Pharmaceuticals Act). In particular, they may order withdrawal of a drug from the market or recall of a drug, where it is reasonable to assume that it has or could have deleterious effects which exceed justifiable levels of risk and where recall is required to prevent risks to human or animal health.

The Pharmaceutical Act does not, however, stipulate any specific obligation on producers or authorisation holders to initiate corrective actions by themselves.

(f) Toys

A producer must initiate necessary measures in order to conform with the European provisions as soon as it suspects non-compliance with the EU regulation (Section 3(5) of the Second Enactment to the Product Safety Act). This might mean withdrawal of toys from the market or their recall.

If a toy is dangerous, the producer also must notify the market surveillance authorities in every member state in which the toy is marketed. That notice should contain information as to the non-conformity of the product and any procedures initiated in order to prevent any (further) risks.

The same applies to the producer's authorised representative, importers and, with regard to the notification, also retailers. An 'authorised representative' is any person that has assumed the obligation to perform the duties of the producer. The producer's liabilities will be assumed by the importer/retailer in particular where a toy is marketed under its own name or carries its trademark.

3. Enforcement

3.1 Sector organisations

The monitoring of product safety and the initiation of required corrective actions in the event of breaches is the responsibility of the individual federal states (regional governments or trade supervisory offices). The Federal Institute for Occupational Safety and Health must also be informed of all actions instigated. This ensures that the market surveillance authorities of the other federal states and international authorities are alerted as necessary. Information about product safety deficiencies discovered abroad is likewise reported to the Federal Institute for Occupational Safety and Health so it can be diffused from that central point.

The regulators for medical devices, however, are the state offices for environmental protection and occupational safety. Market information is disseminated by the Ministry of Health and Consumer Protection.

3.2 Powers of authorities

If necessary, the authorities responsible for market surveillance can enter offices and business premises where products are manufactured, first used, stored or exhibited during normal business hours. They can inspect or examine the products (or have them examined). If they so request, they must be provided with samples and specimens as well as pertinent documents and information (without charge). The affected party will be given an opportunity to comment prior to any such action being taken.

An order of the market surveillance authorities or any other competent authority may be enforced under the Administrative Enforcement Act. This act can ultimately impose fines or imprisonment on defaulting parties.

3.3 International enforcement

The RAPEX (Rapid Alert System for non-food dangerous products) central information system ensures information concerning hazardous consumer products is available throughout the EU. However, RAPEX does not cover foods, medical and pharmaceutical products. Information about dangerous food is collected and distributed throughout the EU via RASFF (Rapid Alert System for Food and Feed). Risks arising from medicines and drugs are collected at the national level by the German Institute of Medical Documentation and Information which then conveys the information to European databases.

3.4 Appeals

Affected parties can oppose actions ordered by the market surveillance authorities under general administrative laws. Accordingly, they can first file an appeal against the action, before having the legality of the action reviewed by the administrative courts.

3.5 Multiple jurisdictions

Product safety laws and the powers of regulators in the event of breach are becoming ever more harmonised within the EU. Cooperation among the market surveillance authorities within the EU represents an important component of the harmonisation legislation. This enables risks to be identified and joint actions adopted more quickly to manage the risk.

4. Product liability

4.1 Potential defendants

Under the Product Liability Act, if a marketed product has caused harm, the 'manufacturer' is liable for the harm caused to the aggrieved party. The manufacturer is not only the actual producer of the end-product or a part or raw material of it, but also any party that presents itself as its producer (eg, by putting its trademark on the product). Importers also come within this definition of manufacturer for these purposes if the product is for sale in Germany. If a manufacturer cannot be identified, the supplier will be liable as producer. So for Product Liability Act claims, potential defendants include:

- the producer;
- any party presenting itself as producer (eg, putting its trademark on the product); and
- importers.

The law of torts, however, imposes product liability on importers, suppliers and distributors only if they were tasked with informing customers in Germany about the product and thus assumed a duty of information; and also only where they had cause to doubt the safety of the product but refrained from having further tests carried out.

Under the German Pharmaceutical Act, the 'pharmaceutical entrepreneur' and, if applicable, its representative (importing the drug into Germany) are jointly liable for any harm caused by the imported product.

4.2 Sources of liability

(a) Statute

The civil law liability of the producer, ie, liability towards the aggrieved party, is determined principally by the Product Liability Act. The German Pharmaceutical Act contains special provisions for pharmaceutical products. Liability is defined as strict, ie, the producer or pharmaceutical entrepreneur need not have known about the risk presented by the product. Thus, the producer is also liable for harm caused by so-called 'outliers', ie, individual defective products, which could not have been prevented despite all reasonable precautions.

The Product Liability Act distinguishes between design defects, manufacturing defects and informational defects. A product is 'defective' when it does not provide for the safety that can be expected from it, taking its presentation, its intended use and the point of time of its introduction onto the market into account (Section 3, Product Liability Act). Defects, however, only result in liability under the Product Liability Act if they have [actually in fact] caused a hazard or injury/harm.

Design defects render the entire product series unfit, whilst manufacturing defects arise during production and only in individual products (eg, as the result of screws working loose during production). Informational defects arise from unfit operating instructions or giving no or insufficient warnings about the risks posed by or potentially inherent in the product.

(b) *Tort*

If the producer or pharmaceutical entrepreneur was aware that the product does not satisfy the requirements of relevant provisions, it will also be liable in tort. The law of torts in Germany is found in Sections 823 and following of the Civil Code.

Duty of care: The producer's liability under tort in Germany is expressed in the so-called 'duty to maintain safety'. This duty is the responsibility of everyone putting a product into circulation in Germany.

Breach of duty: Under tort law, whoever culpably breaches the duty to maintain safety (intentionally or negligently), will be liable. The duty to maintain safety is breached if producers do not follow the apparent and ascertainable scientific and technical state of art in terms of design, production and information. In addition, the duty to maintain safety encompasses a producer's general organisational duty to establish its business such that design, manufacturing and informational defects are excluded as far as possible or can be discovered before a product is placed on the market. In addition, after a product has been placed on the market, producers have a duty to continue monitoring their product. Lastly, the duty to maintain safety also encompasses the producer's duty to warn the general public about risks associated with the product and, where appropriate, the duty to recall a product that jeopardises the health, lives or property of the public. If a producer breaches any of these duties, it will be liable for the harm caused.

(c) *Contract*

Liability for injury/damage caused by the defectiveness of products can also arise under contract. A product is 'defective' under contract law, when its actual state deviates from its target state to the disadvantage of the purchaser. German law provides for warranty liability on the seller for a product's defects that impair its usability or functioning or reduce its value. In such cases, the purchaser can rescind the contract, reduce the purchase price and also demand subsequent performance or damages including damages for injury or other damage or may have the purchase price discounted, depending on the gravity of the defect.

In addition, the seller is liable for any guarantee of characteristics or durability of the product that it has given.

However, if the purchase is commercial, the purchaser has a duty to inspect the product without undue delay on delivery and submit a complaint to the seller about any defects found (otherwise the purchaser cannot assert that there were (apparent) defects).

4.3 Claimants, class actions

German civil procedural law does not permit class actions. Each individual injured party must plead and prove their loss in court. However, if the damage of several persons is due to the same legal and factual reason, the affected parties can sue in joinder of parties, ie, file a claim jointly and thus reduce costs, in particular attorney fees.

4.4. Causation

The producer's breach of duty must have caused the damage.

The onus is on the injured parties to produce proof that the breach of the product safety regulations caused their loss. In that regard, the equivalence principle, which largely corresponds to the 'but for' test in common law countries, applies. It will be decisive, therefore, whether, 'but for' the producer's relevant act, the damage would not have been caused. The equivalence principle is subject to limits, however: there is no liability for exceptional or atypical harm.

In practice, the courts will verify first, whether a certain product is inherently capable of causing such damage. Frequently, an expert's opinion will be required to adequately answer this question. If that first question is affirmed, the courts will identify, as a second step, whether that damage was a consequence of the use of the product. This has been declined where a damage might have resulted from an excessive use of a product, eg, the excessive consumption of sweets (see eg, district court of Munchengladbach, decision of April 24 2002, 3 O 217/01 where a judge claimed his daily consumption of chocolate bars caused his diabetes and therefore sued the chocolate bar producer). Likewise, the district court in Bonn dismissed a product liability claim for cardiac problems, where a woman had consumed 400 grams of liquorice per day for a period of several months. It further held that such an excessive consumption was not foreseeable and therefore, a warning was not required (LG Bonn, decision of April 19 2004, 9 O 603/09).

However, there are some cases in which the burden of proof for consumers is shifted. It is, for example, assumed that damage has been caused by a pharmaceutical product, provided that the pharmaceutical is generally capable of causing such harm (Section 84(2) of the Pharmaceutical Act). This assumption leads to a shifting of the burden of proof with the result that the producer must provide evidence of the fact that the damage has not been caused by its product. Furthermore, the burden of proof shift is affirmed where the consumer provides evidence of the fact that the producer has not properly fulfilled its specific obligation to examine a dangerous product (see German Federal Court of Justice, decision of December 8 1992, VI ZR 24/92 with regard to glass bottles). Finally, the *prima facie* evidence plays an important role within product liability proceedings. According to this principle, injured parties will have fulfilled their obligation to demonstrate causation by the producer where the harm is a typical result of a specific course of events. The Federal Court of Justice, for example, held that a person who was infected with HIV after having obtained a blood infusion need not prove the contamination of the blood if that person does not belong to a particular risk group (BGH, decision of 14 June 2005 – VI ZR 179/04). In such a case, the hospital must demonstrate that the blood could not have been contaminated.

Also causal is such harm caused by a functionally distinguishable product to another product in which it has been installed or inserted. Under the law of tort, the producer of the product that causes the damage (even if it is a component or part) will in principle be liable for the total loss, not the producer of the product as a whole. However, in relation to the injured party, the producer of the complete product is generally also liable for the fault of parties whose products it incorporates if it cannot prove that it selected and supervised those parties adequately. The producer of the complete product may, however, separately seek to hold the producer of the component or ingredient liable for any damages it suffers from the defect.

4.5 Defences

Some defences are potentially available to the producer to contractual claims, tort claims and claims under the Product Liability Act.

(a) *Limitation periods*

Irrespective of whether a claim under product liability is based on the Product Liability Act, tort or contract law, the claim is time-barred after three years of the injured party becoming aware of the damage, the product defect and the identity of the defendant. The time-bar always becomes effective at the year-end. Thus, if the injured party becomes aware of all the required facts in February 2012, the compensation claim becomes time-barred at midnight December 31 2015. The time-bar is a defence which the courts heed only if the defendant asserts it. The filing of the action suspends the time-bar.

Claims under the Product Liability Act are subject to a much longer limitation period: claims may be taken within 10 years from the moment the product is been placed on the market.

(b) *'Development risks' defence*

The so-called 'development risks' defence may also be invoked. This defence is outlined in Section 1(2) of the Product Liability Act. According to the defence, a producer will not be liable if able to prove that at the time of a product's manufacture, no other similar manufacturer would have been able to reasonably spot the contested defect in a product were they producing it at the relevant time.

(c) *Further exclusions under the Product Liability Act*

Against a claim under the Product Liability Act, producers may further argue that:

- the damage/risk was not present in the product when it was brought to market;

- it was neither produced for sale nor produced or sold within the scope of the producer's professional activities; or
- the defect was the result of compliance with mandatory provisions.

Liability is further excluded by the Product Liability Act with regard to the producer of a component when the defect has been caused by a product in which the component has been inserted.

(d) *Contributory negligence*

Any contributory negligence of the injured party will be taken into consideration when determining the amount of the claim. The injured party has a duty to mitigate losses. That party must do everything necessary and reasonable to contain the damages.

(e) *Contractual exclusion or limitation*

Liability may be excluded or limited by contract. However, it may generally not be excluded where there have been intentional breaches of duty and personal injury.

4.6 Remedies for injury/damage and consequential loss

Under German law, only the harm actually suffered can be compensated. A claim for damages seeks primarily to restore the state that would have existed if the breach of duty had not occurred. Since the producer is rarely in a position to achieve this by undoing an injury or harm suffered, the injured party's claim is generally for a sum of money.

The product safety legislation stipulates in part which harms should be compensated. For example, the Product Liability Act requires that in the case of injury or impairment of health the plaintiff's medical costs are to be borne and compensation paid for financial loss because of the plaintiff's reduction in earning capacity.

In addition, in the event of personal injuries, reasonable damages for pain and suffering are to be paid depending on their severity, and at the discretion of the court. An official table of compensation levels provides guidance on the sums of compensation previously awarded for pain and suffering.

Some examples of awards for pain and suffering include the following:

- The highest sum awarded for pain and suffering was a lump-sum payment of €250,000 and a lifelong pension of €25,000 per month (Higher Regional Court of Frankfurt am Main) in favour of a three year-old boy who lost one eye and the eyesight in the other eye caused by a bursting lemonade bottle.
- A woman won compensation of €50,000 for an injury to her eye by a bursting sparkling wine bottle (Higher Regional Court of Munich).
- A man who nearly lost all the sight in one eye when a spade broke and split on its first use due to a manufacturing defect was awarded €45,000 ('outlier' case; Regional Court of Dortmund).
- A man was awarded €4,000 for injury to his left hand (partially severed tendon and nerves) because the manufacturer did not check whether its product accorded with the state of the art.

Compensation claims under the Product Liability Act are capped at €85 million in total (€120 million for pharmaceutical producers), taking into account the element of strict liability. For liability under tort there is no maximum liability limit.

German law does not permit punitive damages, however.

4.7 Procedure, funding, costs

Claims under product liability should be taken before the civil courts. This requires the submission of a statement of claim by the injured party or by an attorney if the regional court is the competent court. The regional court is the competent court if the claim exceeds €5,000; otherwise the action should be heard by the local courts. Alternative Dispute Resolution is possible (eg, mediation or arbitration) but requires agreement of the parties involved.

The injured party must assert, demonstrate and provide evidence of:

- the defect in the product (for a claim under the Product Liability Act);
- infringement of a contractual duty or duty to maintain safety (for a claim under tort law);
- the damage; and
- causality (ie, that the defect/breach of duty caused the damage).

Thus, expert opinion plays an important role in product liability proceedings. As a rule, a judge sitting alone hears the action (there being no jury in Germany). The court's decision may be appealed to the superior authority which is the regional court to a decision of the district court and to the Higher Regional Court to a decision of the regional court.

The costs of the proceedings are defined by law and are based on the value of the litigation. Legal aid may be granted if the injured party does not have the funds necessary to pay for the proceedings in advance. In such cases, the court considers whether the suit has sufficient prospects of success and does not appear vexatious (Section 114, Code of Civil Procedure). The costs of both parties and court costs are generally borne by the losing party. If only a part of the claim is awarded, costs will be divided proportionally.

4.8 Criminal liability for personal injury or property damage

An intentionally or negligently caused harm may also lead to criminal liability of the persons responsible under the German Penal Code. In particular, personal injury may lead to a custodial sentence of up to five years or a fine (Section 223). Custodial sentences can be up to ten years where injury has been caused by substances which are harmful to health or when human life has been endangered (Section 224). The same applies to cases of severe injury (eg, losing eyesight in one eye or both; losing limbs; or being permanently disfigured). For intentional or negligent property damage a custodial sentence of up to two years or a fine may be imposed. Criminal liability is excluded when the damage could not have been foreseen or was unpreventable.

4.9 Trends

The product safety legislation is becoming ever more uniform across Europe. Many national laws will largely be replaced in the coming years by European directives which will be directly applicable in the member states, in accordance with the European Union's continued drive to create a single market.

5. Product insurance

5.1 Coverage

(a) *Product recall*

In 1998 the German Insurance Association (GDV) presented and recommended to its members a concept for insuring recall costs. Its model terms and conditions are not binding, however. Policies can be negotiated on an individual basis.

It is in effect a form of third-party liability insurance, so that not only any particular terms but also the General Insurance Terms and Conditions for Third Party Liability Insurance apply. The company's own loss, apart from the direct costs of a product recall, are therefore not insured.

Special model terms and conditions apply for suppliers of motor vehicle parts. This insurance grants cover for the costs of the producer's own recall on the basis of a legal obligation (1.3 of the model terms and conditions) as well as for recall by a third party when the producer is held liable (1.1 of the model terms and conditions).

(b) *Contaminated products*

So far, separate insurance for recall of or injury/damage caused by contaminated products has not been available in Germany. However, producers can insure against the risks associated with contamination of products largely via product recall insurance and product liability insurance.

(c) *Product liability*

As a rule, product liability insurance covers the insured's liability for personal injury and property damage caused by its product, and can be concluded as additional cover under general employer's liability insurance. The wording of the insurance is largely up to the individual insurance company. Here too, the GDV has drawn up model terms and conditions. There are special terms and conditions for insuring pharmaceutical entrepreneurs. The General Insurance Terms and Conditions for Third Party Liability Insurance also apply for product liability insurance.

(d) *Financial loss*

Third party liability insurance can be extended by special agreement to financial losses not due to personal injury or damage to property (Clause 2.1, General Insurance Terms and Conditions for Third Party Liability Insurance). Liability for the loss of sales by third parties for example is not covered by product liability insurance (Clause 6.1.2, model terms and conditions). An exception is made if the loss of sales is due to combination, blending or processing and the product as a whole cannot be sold or only at a lower price (Clause 4.2.2.4, model terms and conditions).

(e) *Product guarantee*

Insurance against the risk of a producer having to rectify a defect or to deliver a repaired product is generally not available. The lack of such insurance may be intended on policy grounds to ensure that production and control of final products are conducted as accurately as possible. In any case the cover provided by product recall insurance tends to overlap with product guarantee insurance cover for products with a safety defect.

5.2 Product recall

(a) *Insuring provisions*

Trigger: By making a contract of insurance, the insurer undertakes to cover a certain risk of the policyholder by paying a benefit (Section 1, Insurance Contract Act). The benefit is payable on the occurrence of the agreed insured event. In general, the 'insured event' where there has been a product recall is the realisation of a recall arising from a legal obligation (Clause 2, GDV model terms and conditions). A recall is realised with a warning or call on end consumers, traders supplying end consumers, or authorised or other workshops to have the product tested and, if applicable, rectified by authorised persons or to take other measures explicitly mentioned.

Where there has been a third party recall, the insured event requires the producer additionally to be held liable for the recall.

Covered expenses: As a rule, cover is granted only for costs spent on the measures explicitly mentioned in the insurance terms and conditions. Those measures encompass:

- informing end consumers, traders which supply end consumers, and authorised or other workshops, including calls made via the media;
- a pre-sorting of those products affected by the recall;
- transport of affected products to the policyholder or authorised persons; and
- testing of the products affected by the recall to identify those items which are indeed defective and therefore require further measures to prevent harm. Costs for testing are, however, not covered where the costs for testing and additional measures to prevent harm will from an *ex ante* point of view probably exceed the costs which must be incurred if all items are defective (Clause 3, model terms and conditions).

With regard to the defective goods or, when testing would be unreasonable, all products, the following costs will be covered:

- costs for any interim storage up to three months;
- exchange of defective products or defective parts of products;
- rectification of defective products; and
- disposal and destruction of defective products.

Accordingly, this kind of insurance is effectively a guarantee insurance for products with a safety defect.

Exclusions: The model terms and conditions explicitly exclude insurance for the following claims:

- the costs of motor vehicle and aircraft recalls;
- costs arising for products which had not yet reached the end consumer or retailer supplying the end consumer at the time of the recall;
- costs incurred where products were released onto the market in a condition which did not meet the state of the art in that product field or were not sufficiently tested. This exclusion forces producers to adopt careful sample testing procedures. The German Federal Court of Justice has made clear that the state of the art is not identical with what is customary within a sector of industry. State of the art arguments must show that the possibility of preventing harm existed where, according to expert knowledge, there would be an operational (and economically reasonable) solution (decision of June 16 2009, VI ZR 107/08);
- where the policyholder or any co-insured party caused the insured event through intentional deviation from statutory or public authority provisions, instructions or warnings or from the insured's written instructions or conditions;
- costs deriving from recalls due to alleged, threatened or actual wilful or malicious manipulation of the products;
- where the liability is covered elsewhere by guarantees or other contractual agreements; or
- costs other than those named in Clause 3, in particular:
- for the subsequent or delivery of replacement fault-free products (also individual replacement parts) including freight costs from the address of the policyholder to place of fulfilment;
- for consequential loss, such as business interruption, loss of production and lost profits;
- fines or penalties and costs for criminal or administrative law proceedings (excluding costs of administrative law proceedings conducted at the insurer's behest);
- punitive damages;
- recalls related to the use of asbestos;
- recalls directly or indirectly connected with high-energy ionising radiation (eg, radiation from radioactive substances or x-rays);
- recalls due to genetic engineering operations; and
- genetically modified organisms, or products which contain ingredients from or are manufactured using genetically modified organisms.

Not explicitly excluded, but nevertheless not included are also costs which arise even before the actual insured event occurs, for example for examining the product. Costs incurred in seeking advice on the conduct of the recall (from attorneys and/or a PR companies) are also not covered. Finally, the costs of rehabilitating the producer's reputation (eg, via media campaigns) are likewise not generally covered by recall insurance.

Impairment: Suppliers of individual parts can take out insurance for their liability for recall of an item in which a defective part was installed. Separate recall insurance terms and conditions apply for suppliers of motor vehicle parts.

(b) Conditions

In Germany, there is no duty of confidentiality in relation to the existence of insurance cover. The use or provision of emergency hotlines or the costs associated with hiring a recall consultant are not generally covered.

Recall insurance will only apply if the recall is carried out to prevent personal injury. It does therefore not apply to measures intending to prevent property damage only. The liability is further limited by the model terms and conditions to three years from delivery of the product by the policyholder, ie, insurance coverage only applies for products being recalled within the first three years of being delivered.

5.3 Contaminated products

Separate insurance for contaminated products is not available in Germany. Risks associated with selling contaminated products are generally covered by product liability insurance and/or recall cost insurance.

5.4 Product liability

(a) Insuring provisions

Product liability insurance covers liability for both personal injury and damage to property which has occurred during the policy period. In principle, it is only required that the damage has occurred within the policy period (the moment in time of causation or assertion of the claim are irrelevant). However, where a damage results from a composition, mixture, integration, use or processing of a defective item, the moment of composing, mixing, integrating, applying or processing it is decisive. Coverage is explicitly excluded for claims made later than three years after termination of the insurance contract (Clause 7, model terms and conditions).

Injury: 'Personal injury' is defined to include fatalities, injury and impairment of health. Unborn and not-yet-conceived children are in principle covered, if they are subsequently born ill or sick because of a product defect. In principle, psychological impairments are also covered within personal injury.

Financial losses as a consequence of personal injury will be borne by the insurer. These include, for example, medical costs and loss of earnings. The payment of reasonable damages for pain and suffering is also permitted.

Damage: Damage arises if items, whether personal or real property (eg, buildings), are damaged or destroyed. Product liability insurance covers losses arising from the connection, blending or processing of the defective product into another thing, and covers consequential losses, eg loss of profit.

Since third party liability insurance in principle only covers third party claims against the policyholder, the policyholder's expenses incurred in producing its own product are not covered.

(b) *Exclusions*

Breach of contract: insurance cover is excluded if the damage was caused by the policyholder's intentional deviation from the manufacturer's written instructions or conditions (Clause 6.2.4, model terms and conditions). Any guarantee provided by the policyholder that goes beyond the scope of statutory third party liability is excluded from insurance cover, (Clause 7.3 model terms and conditions).

Repair, replacement: Costs for repair or delivery of replacement defective parts are not covered by product liability insurance. But costs for replacement, ie, in particular for dismantling defective products and installing a fault-free product, are covered (Clause 4.4.2.1 model terms and conditions).

Efficacy: A product which fails to perform its function is deemed to be legally equal to a product which is defective (German Federal Court of Justice, decision of March 17 1981, VI ZR 191/79). If such a product causes a damage, eg, because the injured person did not use another product, trusting in the functionality of the product, this damage will also covered by the product liability insurance.

Aircraft: the insurance does not cover risks arising after conclusion of a contract for the keeping or use of motor vehicles, aircraft or watercraft that are subject to separate compulsory insurance (Clause 4.3, General Insurance Terms and Conditions for Third Party Liability Insurance). There is also an exclusion of claims relating to the design, construction, production or delivery of 'aircraft and spacecraft' (Clause 6.2.6, model terms and conditions).

(c) *Conditions*

Claims: The policyholder has a duty to notify the insurer about the occurrence of the insured event, which is, in general, the occurrence of injury or damage, within one week (Clause 25.1, General Insurance Terms and Conditions for Third Party Liability Insurance). The policyholder must strive to avert and minimise the damage (Clause 25.2, General Insurance Terms and Conditions for Third Party Liability Insurance). If the policyholder fails to meet these duties intentionally or through gross negligence, this can void the insurance cover or reduce the benefit paid out under the insurance in proportion to the policyholder's fault.

Other: The General Insurance Terms and Conditions for Third Party Liability Insurance and the GDV model terms and conditions contain a large number of other conditions such as termination rights, the possibility to agree an excess, effects of changes in the insured risk and maximum liability limits. Claims under product liability insurance are time-barred after three years of the policyholder becoming aware of his liability, unless the parties have agreed otherwise (Clause 30.1, General Insurance Terms and Conditions for Third Party Liability Insurance 2010). This time-bar always becomes effective at the year-end.

5.5 General principles

(a) *Attachment*

In the event of a damage occurring, the policyholder must identify the insurance terms covering the damage (from the terms and conditions attached to the insurance policy).

The damage could potentially be covered by more than one policy, but insurance brokers tend to try to individually tailor their insurance offerings so as to avoid a multiple insurance of the same risk. Where multiple insurance does arise, a policyholder can choose to claim benefits from any one of the insurers; but cannot claim twice.

(b) *Aggregation*

Usually, the insurer's maximum indemnity limit is defined in the insurance conditions. As a rule, this is defined for both the individual insured event and also for each insurance year (see, eg, Clause 9, model terms and conditions for product liability insurance).

(c) *General conditions*

The conditions for product liability policies differ from insurance company to insurance company. In general, the policyholder is required to pay the premiums and the insurer to cover the insured risk (Section 1, Insurance Contract Act). In the event of the policyholder's insolvency, a rightful claimant acquires a right to prior satisfaction against the policyholder (Section 110, VVG). In addition, all insurance contracts determine the termination rights for both parties, the consequences of an increased risk, the duty to immediately inform the insurer about the occurrence of the insured event and the policyholder's duty to cooperate with the insurer (Section 31, Insurance Contract Act). Furthermore, the insurance conditions contain clauses on the parties' rights and duties if there is multiple insurance of an identical risk (eg, where there are several insurers). And lastly, any claims the policyholder has against a third party pass to the insurer if the latter compensates for the loss (Section 86(1), Insurance Contract Act).

(d) *General exclusions*

Excluded from the insurance cover are in principle claims because of damage due to asbestos and substances or products containing asbestos, damage directly connected with high-energy ionising radiation and harm due to genetic engineering operations or genetically-modified organisms (Clauses 7.11–7.13, General Insurance Terms and Conditions for Third Party Liability Insurance 2010).

Additionally, if the policyholder does not comply with its obligation to inform the insurer in time or of all relevant circumstances, the insurer is freed from its obligation under the insurance contract. However, in practice, many insurance companies provide for questionnaires which must be completed by the policyholder in order to obtain coverage.

(e) ***Interpretation***

The general rules of the Civil Code apply to interpreting insurance contracts. This requires contracts to be interpreted as required by good faith, taking customary practice into consideration (Section 157 of the Civil Code). When a declaration of intent is interpreted, it is necessary to ascertain the true intention rather than adhering to the literal meaning of the declaration (Section 133 of the Civil Code).

Since insurance contracts tend to be pro forma and provided by the insurer, the insurance conditions constitute the insurance company's General Terms and Conditions and are therefore subject to a content check pursuant to Sections 305 and following of the Civil Code. Any doubts in the interpretation of standard business terms will be resolved against the insurer under the *contra proferentem* principle.

(f) ***Effect of breach***

If the policyholder culpably does not comply with its duties under the insurance contract, for example by reporting the insured event too late, does not comply with co-operation duties, or does not pay premiums, the insurer can refuse or reduce the payment under the insurance contract (Section 38(2), Insurance Contract Act: insured event occurring while the policyholder is in default on payment of premiums; Section 28(2), Insurance Contract Act: no obligation to render payment in cases of intentional breach of notification or cooperation duties/reduction of the payment in the cases of grossly negligent breach of the notification or cooperation duty).

(g) ***Extra-contractual defences***

If the policyholder provided false details when concluding the insurance contract or did not declare facts relevant to an accurate evaluation of the risk, the insurer can avoid the contract on the grounds of fraudulent misrepresentation (Section 22, Insurance Contract Act in conjunction with Sections 119 and following, Civil Code). This annulment has retroactive effect so that already-rendered performances must be restituted so that any benefits already paid out to the insured can be re-claimed by the insurer. If anything that could be constituted as an aggravation of the risk was intentionally not notified to the insurer after the contract was concluded, the insurer can terminate the contract without notice (Section 24(1) in conjunction with Section 23(1), Insurance Contract Act). In the case of negligence, the notice period for the insurer is one month (Section 24(2) in conjunction with Section 23(2) and (3) of the Insurance Contract Act).

India

Dev Ashish Mishra
Siddharth Misra
Fox Mandal & Co

1. Product safety regulation

Product safety, if ignored, can have devastating effects on a company's image as well as earnings. Product safety refers to the physical health and safety of citizens with regard to products such as toys, household appliances, cars, cosmetics, food, medicines and other general consumer products.

In India, there is neither a comprehensive product liability law nor an independent consumer product safety commission to monitor the safety of consumer goods in the market. In India the potential liability of the manufacturer/supplier for supplying unsafe products arises under the Indian Contract Act 1872, as well as under the Consumer Protection Act 1986 for civil liability, whereas criminal liability arises under the Indian Penal Code. Civil liability arises under the Contract Act due to breach of contract for supplying unsafe products,whereas liability under the Consumer Protection Act 1986 arises due to supply of unsafe products.

In countries which give the highest priority to consumer product safety, product recalls are quite common. In India a product recall is a request to return to the maker a batch or an entire production run of a product usually arising because of safety concerns or design defects or labelling errors and affects diverse companies and product categories.

Ideally, companies recall products when defects have the potential to raise safety concerns for customers and could affect a large number of consumers. However, unlike many other countries, product recall practice is at a nascent stage in India where there is a low awareness level among consumers of the rules and regulations. More often than not normal warranty procedures offered by manufacturers govern the standard marketing practice of product recall. Thus, recalls are mostly preventive and voluntary in India, undertaken to pre-empt costly litigation as well as financial and goodwill losses.

And since there are no specific rules and/or statutes pertaining to safety-related product recalls, the government cannot force any company to recall any faulty product without the intervention of the courts. The exception is for food and nutrition products where the government can ask producers to take its products off the shelves due to health concerns. Otherwise, product recall will normally be a voluntary act in India.

2. Obligations of producers and distributors

The procedure followed in India in relation to defective products is that aggrieved consumers unhappy with a product or its performance are first expected to approach the company concerned for relief. If the company does not own up to its responsibility or fails to provide relief to the consumer's satisfaction, then consumers can approach the designated consumer courts. This could entail a long-drawn legal battle. Sometimes, consumers may not have access to complete information relating to the faulty product which could weaken their case and work in favour of the manufacturer. The route to relief is generally via individual actions rather mass lawsuits, as is the practice in many developed countries. Individual claimants find it difficult to stand up to the financial and legal might of large manufacturers for a sustained period of time leading to a predominance of pro-manufacturer court rulings.

Perhaps this explains why in the past there have been instances where companies have recalled a product in international markets but not in India. For example, the Toyota Motor Corporation, Japan recalled its four-wheeler vehicle, the Toyota Corolla Altis, in the United States and many European markets due to a faulty part, but did not do so in India. No statement was issued by the Indian arm of Toyota Motor Corporation as to the reasoning behind the non-recall of the car and its continuing sale in India. Toyota Motor Corporation and its Indian arm may also have been emboldened in not recalling the car in India due to the fact that it is not mandatory under Indian law to secure product safety certification in the case of big name global brands and therefore most consumer products are sold without any appropriate safety certification by manufacturers.

2.1 Sources of duties

(a) Statutes

Consumer Protection Act 1986: This act provides protection to consumers against unsafe, faulty or defective products. The Act enshrines the rights of consumers such as the right to safety, right to be informed, right to be heard, and right to choose, right to seek redress and right to consumer education. Under the Consumer Protection Act 1986, a complaint can be filed against a manufacturer/supplier for supply of goods which are hazardous to life and safety when used or being offered for sale to the public in contravention of any standards relating to the safety of such goods as required under any law currently in force; or deficiency in services which are hazardous or likely to be hazardous to life or safety of the public when used, being offered by a service provider which should have known with due care and diligence could be injurious to life or safety.

Under the Consumer Protection Act 1986, the word 'consumer' is defined separately for the purpose of goods and services.

For goods, a 'consumer' means:

- anyone who buys any goods for consideration; and
- any user of the goods other than the person who actually buys them, provided such use is made with the approval of the buyer.

(The expression 'consumer' does not include a person who obtains goods for resale or for any commercial purpose).

For services, a consumer means:

- anyone who hires any service or services for consideration; and
- any beneficiary of such service(s) provided the service is supplied with the approval of such person.

Under the Consumer Protection Act 1986, a three-tier, simple, quasi-judicial machinery has been established at national, state, and district levels for hearing cases raised by consumers. These designated consumer courts are popularly known as the District Consumer Forum, State Commission and National Commission respectively. The Consumer Protection Act 1986 was amended in 1991, 1993 and 2002. The amended Act provides for the seizure and subsequent sale of the property of any person who does not comply with an order. Where a trader or a person against whom a complaint is made or the complainant fails or omits to comply with any order made by the district forum, State Commission or National Commission, as the case may be, they will be punishable by imprisonment for a term of up to three years, or fined (Rs10,000), or both. If consumers are not satisfied by a decision of a district forum, they can appeal to the State Commission, and from there to the National Commission. Producers can avoid liability under the Consumer Protection Act 1986 by proving that the defect could not be known with ordinary due diligence or that the goods so offered are unsafe to the public.

In all cases complaints must be filed within two years from the date on which the cause of action has arisen. And the burden of proof is always on complainants to prove their case (the consumer must produce proof of the defect etc). Consumers must also prove that they purchased the goods at the price claimed and that the goods are defective; and they must report the problem promptly.

Depending on the nature of the complaint, the relief sought by the consumer and the facts of the case, the consumer court may order one or more of the following reliefs:

- removal of defects from the goods or deficiencies in services;
- replacement of the defective goods;
- refund of the price paid;
- award of compensation for loss or injury;
- discontinuance or order not to repeat unfair trade practices or restrictive trade practices;
- withdrawal from sale of hazardous or dangerous goods; and
- award of adequate costs to aggrieved parties.

However, the Consumer Protection Act 1986 does not contain any provisions for product recall as such. Additionally, while the law obligates sellers to address each aggrieved consumer on a case-by-case basis there is no provision to mandate recall of an entire range of products that may be defective, faulty or unsafe. The provision contained in Section 14 of the Consumer Protection Act 1986 grants consumers the right only to receive the value of the products purchased, plus costs to cover any damages suffered as a consequence of use of the defective products.

Food product recall and regulations: The Food Safety and Standards Authority of India has issued draft Food Recall Procedures Regulations 2009 (the regulations) with the aim of:

- guiding food business operators on how to carry out a food recall by facilitating the efficient, rapid identification and removal of unsafe foods from the distribution chain and by informing consumers (where necessary) of the presence on the market of potentially hazardous foods and ensuring that unsafe foods are contained and destroyed or rendered safe;
- guiding food business operators on how to establish a written recall plan for carrying out food recall in order to ensure the hygiene, safety and quality of food and to protect the health of consumers; and
- establishing a follow-up action/post recall report in order to ensure the effectiveness of the recall and prevent any repetition.

According to the regulations, recalls may be carried out voluntarily by manufacturers and distributors to remove unsafe food items from the market to prevent injury to consumers. Seizure or other court actions may be taken where a company refuses to undertake a recall directed by the Commissioner of the State Food Authority (LCA), or where the LCA has sufficient reasons to believe that a recall would not be effective, or determines that a recall is ineffective, or discovers that a violation is continuing. The cost incurred by the LCA for carrying this out would be recovered from the entity responsible. In addition to recovery of costs, the company would also be liable for penalties or punishments in terms of Chapter IX of the Food and Safety Standards Act 2006. This could be a fine or imprisonment, or both depending on the nature of the offence.

The implementation of the regulations is a step in the right direction and could be instrumental in boosting both domestic and international consumer confidence and help bring India in line with global standards. However, its effective implementation is fraught with numerous challenges such as:

- poor general awareness of the hazards associated with unsafe food issues and the best practices to be followed;
- lack of basic supporting infrastructure such as testing labs;
- insufficient technical expertise and skilled manpower for implementation of legislation at grass roots level;
- exclusion of primary producers from the scope of the law, putting the onus of responsibility for preventing food hazards on manufacturers/processors; and
- problems in traceability of products, especially at the stages of the upstream processors in the food chain – from the farm gate to the processing unit.

Toys: There are no mandatory toy safety standards in India. In 2008 a committee was convened by the government to examine the problem and issue a notification of mandatory standards for toys. However, no such notification has been issued to date. The Bureau of Indian Standards does have certain standards for children's toys — those dealing with safety aspects relating to mechanical and physical properties, and flammability requirements. It also lays down maximum permissible limits for some chemical ingredients in children's toys: eg, migratory lead, cadmium and chromium. But consumer groups would assert that not a single manufacturer in India follows these standards.

Consumers can take action against manufacturers or traders dealing in toys containing hazardous materials under the Environment Protection Act. That act authorises the central government to protect and improve environmental quality, control and reduce pollution from all sources, and prohibit or restrict the setting and/or operation of any industrial facility on environmental grounds. Moreover, consumers can approach bodies such as the Pollution Control Board to complain about hazardous toys.

In a positive move the Directorate General of Foreign Trade has made it mandatory to attach a certificate of conformance from the importing manufacturers attesting to the fact that a representative sample of the toys being imported has been tested by an independent laboratory (like the International Laboratory Accreditation Cooperation: ILAC). Therefore, the import of toys that fail to meet international safety standards is not permitted in India.

Motor vehicles: The Central Motor Vehicle Rules have been in force since 1989 and Chapter V of the Central Motor Vehicle Rules 1989 deals with construction, equipment and maintenance of vehicles in addition emission limits. Several of the rules impose safety requirements on motor vehicle manufacturers.

Vehicles manufactured in India must to comply with relevant Indian Standards (IS) and Automotive Industry standards (AIS).

The states also have their own state Motor Vehicle Rules. Since 2000 the United Nations Economic Commission for Europe (UNECE) Regulations have been used as basis for Indian regulations and since 2003, increased efforts are being made to technically align with the UNECE.

(b) *Contract*

Some, but not all, consumer products in India are sold with a guarantee or warranty which makes the seller liable to replace a product with a new one or remove defects in the product at no additional cost to the consumer. However, any such replacement or removal of defects will be subject to fulfilment of various conditions specified in the contract for sale, which effectively dilutes manufacturer's/seller's liability.

(c) *Tort*

In spite of inadequacies in the legal framework for product recall in India there have been instances where companies in India have undertaken partial or complete product recalls. Conversely, even when there has been public outrage over defective products, companies have made no moves towards the recall of its products. Some such instances are as follows:

Maruti 800 cars: In 1994 Maruti Udyog Limited (MIL) recalled its Maruti 800 cars due to a problem with a front axle component which endangered customer safety on the roads (for axle replacement only). MIL is India's leading car manufacturer now a subsidiary of Suzuki Motor Corporation of Japan. The Indian partners sold their shareholding in MIL to Suzuki Motor Corporation, Japan and MIL re-incorporated as Maruti Suzuki India Limited. The recall by MIL may have been influenced by the global policies followed by Suzuki Motor Corporation. Maruti Suzuki India Limited faced a similar situation in 2010 when it recalled 100,000 A-Star cars in India and overseas for faulty parts.

MDH spices: Mahashian Di Hatti Limited (MDH) manufactures, sells and exports spices (eg, chilli, coriander and turmeric) as well as blended spice mixtures, etc. under the brand name 'MDH' and is a famous brand throughout India. Recently, the UK Food Standards Agency announced the withdrawal of MDH Sambar Masala due to its contamination with Sudan I (a diazo-conjugate dye with chemical formula of '1-phenylazo-2-naphthol'). Sudan I is a powdered substance with an orange-red appearance. The additive is mainly used to colour waxes, oils, petrol, solvents and polishes. Sudan I has also been adopted for colouring various foodstuffs, including particular brands of curry powder and chilli powder, although the use of Sudan I in foods is now banned in many countries due to inconclusive reports on possible health risks. No withdrawal has been announced in India.

Cola drinks and pesticides: A few years ago, controversy was generated in India when a Delhi-based research lab reported that all Indian produced soft drinks had pesticide content far higher than internationally accepted standards. The basic cause was contaminated water in India due to indiscriminate use of pesticides in farmlands. This led to widespread protests by the general public, press and politicians causing a massive drop in sales of all cola products, ultimately resulting in recall of all cola drinks from the market. The cola manufacturers thereafter issued apologies through the media and went to great lengths to reassure the public that the new batch of drinks were clean and free from pesticides. Again it may be noted that under Indian law the producers were not compulsorily required to recall the drinks, but did so voluntarily due to tremendous public and political pressure, intense media scrutiny and the fact that sales had reduced considerably.

Cadbury chocolate: At almost same time as the cola controversy, a report about worms being found in Cadbury chocolate in Mumbai emerged. It is not known finally what steps the company took to amend the situation but the storm settled down soon after it had emerged.

Bajaj scooters: In the 1970s, Bajaj Auto Limited was India's leading two-wheeler manufacturer and as part of its product range used to sell scooters under the brand name 'Bajaj'. Bajaj scooters developed a problem where the handlebar steering lock would auto-lock causing several accidents. The scooter also had an unbalanced engine which was mounted to one side, and a poor carburettor design which forced users to tilt the scooter to be able to kickstart it successfully. Nonetheless, the company kept selling the scooters with those faults for many years without recalling them or stopping sales. Later, the company attempted to introduce a centrally-mounted engine after Lohia Machines Ltd launched a new competitor scooter in India in collaboration with a company in Italy.

3. Enforcement

3.1 General consumer products

As there are no particular statutes or regulations which govern product recall in India, where defective products are found it is for aggrieved consumers to first approach the company concerned for relief. If the company does not accept responsibility or fails to respond to the consumer's satisfaction, then the consumer can approach the designated consumer courts and enter into potentially lengthy litigation procedures.

3.2 Foods

Under the draft Food Recall Procedures Regulations 2009 (the regulations), issued by the Food Safety and Standards Authority of India, recalls may be carried out voluntarily by manufacturers and distributors to remove unsafe food items from the market to prevent injury to consumers. Seizure or other court actions may be instigated when a company refuses to undertake a recall directed by the Commissioner of the State Food Authority (LCA), or where the LCA has sufficient reason to believe that a recall would not be effective or determines that a recall has been ineffective or discovers that a violation is continuing.

3.3 Motor vehicles

Each state has a road transport authority with its own rules for providing an efficient public transportation system, controlling vehicular pollution, registration of vehicles in the state, issuance of driving licences, issuance of various permits and collection of road taxes. The department is also entrusted with policymaking, coordination, implementation, monitoring and regulatory functions for all transport-related state issues.

3.4 International enforcement

India is not a direct beneficiary or a notifying member nation of RAPEX or the Rapid Alert System for Food and Feed; however, it is closely connected to the activities of the Organisation for Economic Cooperation and Development (OECD) as an observer. India has played host to many OECD conferences and reports but continues to be a non-member.

So, India is not a notifying state under either RASFF or RAPEX but is, unfortunately, often the source of defective products. In 2007, 27 RASFF notifications were recorded in relation to fishery products originating in India. The European Commission did however find that follow-up corrective procedures were adequately followed.

3.5 Limitation of liability

A reasonable limitation of liability clause will generally be valid and enforceable under Indian law, except that exclusions of liability for death or personal injury, or for fraud or gross negligence will not be enforceable.

Contractual liability has a role to play in product liability claims under the Consumer Protection Act 1986. Courts in India have upheld limitation of liability clauses, which parties have specifically agreed to in the contract including the Supreme Court in *Bharathi Knitting Company v DHL Worldwide Express Courier* (1996) 4 SCC 704. However, such clauses may be struck out if found to be unconscionable. In *Maruti Udyog v Susheel Kumar Gabgotra* (2006) 4 SCC 644, the manufacturer of the vehicle had stipulated a warranty clause limiting its liability to merely repair any defects found. The Supreme Court upheld the warranty clause: reversing the findings of the National Commission (which was that the manufacturer must go further and replace the defective product) to hold that the liability of the manufacturer was confined to repairing the defect.

4. Product liability

4.1 Potential defendants

In India, product liability law governs the liability of manufacturers, wholesalers, distributors, and vendors for injury to a person or property caused by dangerous or defective products. The goal of product liability laws is to help protect consumers from dangerous or defective products, while holding manufacturers, distributors, and retailers responsible for putting into the marketplace products that they knew or should have known were dangerous or defective.

4.2 Sources of liability

(a) Statute

Product liability in India is essentially governed by contracts and the following statutes:

- the Consumer Protection Act 1986;
- the Sale of Goods Act 1930;
- the Drug and Cosmetics Act 1940;
- the Prevention of Foods Adulteration Act 1954;
- the Food Safety and Standards Act 2006;
- the Penal Code 1860;
- the Standards of Weights and Measures Act 1956;
- the Agricultural Produce (Grading and Marking) Act 1937 for marking and grading of commodities such vegetables, butter;
- the Bureau of Indian Standards Act 1986; and
- sector-specific statutes.

Each of those acts provides for the imposition of fines and/or imprisonment in the case of supply of defective products or adulterated consumables.

Sales of Goods Act 1930: The purchaser is protected by the Sales of Goods Act 1930 in various ways. Under the SGA if the seller knows the purpose for which the purchaser buys the goods, the law presumes that the purchaser relies on the skill and judgment of the seller that the goods are reasonably fit for the purpose for which they are bought. In other words even where purchasers have inspected a product before purchasing it, they will be protected against any defect which was not discernable by reasonable inspection carried out by the purchaser at the time of the purchase. Therefore, it cannot be automatically implied that a defect ought to have been revealed to the purchaser at the time of examining the product. The responsibility lies on the seller to provide the purchaser with a product fit for the needs of the customer. This is an exception to the rule of *caveat emptor* which provides that the purchaser of a product must be cautious, as the risk is the purchaser's and not the seller's. However, cases involving registered intellectual property are different: in such cases the risk shifts back to the seller if the purchaser relied on a trademark or patent in which it was entitled to have confidence.

Under the Sales of Goods Act, in addition to repudiation of the goods, the purchaser can sue the seller for damages in cases of breach of a condition or warranty of the sale of the defective goods.

Product liability law in India, apart from the civil liability, also imposes criminal liability in cases of non-compliance with the provisions of the relevant statutes and regulations mentioned above. Those statutes and regulations are in addition to and not instead of any other laws in force, so an action requesting penal remedies could be simultaneously initiated along with a claim under the civil law. Some of the statutes and regulations are sector-specific, pertaining to the sale of specific goods such as food, drugs, cosmetics, etc. The provisions of these enactments are intended to be preventive, though the relief envisaged is an action for breach in the civil or criminal courts.

Nonetheless, there is no elaborate or even legally enforceable general regulation in India to ensure quality and safety of products as we find, for example in the United States and other countries. However, the government does have certain powers under specific statutes to govern the quality of specified products.

Prevention of Foods Adulteration Act 1954: Parliament enacted the Prevention of Food Adulteration Act in 1954, and the Prevention of Food Adulteration Rules made under it, in 1955 with the objective of ensuring the supply of pure and wholesome foods to consumers and to protect them from fraudulent and deceptive trade practices. While water is excluded from the definition of 'food', mineral water is included, as it is considered a beverage. Any food that does not conform to the minimum standards laid down in the act is said to be adulterated. The act provides for deterrent punishment of offenders.

Under the PFAA selling, manufacturing or distributing adulterated or misbranded food and giving a false warranty is punishable by imprisonment of a period of between six months and three years and a fine of not less than Rs1,000. The penalty for selling, manufacturing or distributing adulterated food or using adulterant ingredients injurious to health is imprisonment for not less than one year (and up to six years) and a fine of not less than Rs 2,000. If the adulterant is likely to cause death or causes to grievous injury, the penalty is imprisonment of not less than three years but which may be extended to a life term.

Food Safety and Standards Act 2006: This legislation was enacted to update the law to changing needs, consolidate food-related laws and establish the Food Safety and Standards Authority of India, bringing with it a new single statutory body for the enforcement of food laws and standards-setting.

The Food Safety and Standards Authority of India in association with state food authorities are responsible for the implementation and enforcement of the act. The national food authority sets science-based standards for foods and regulates their manufacture, storage, distribution, sale and importation.

Penalties under the Food Safety and Standards Act are more comprehensive and wider in scope.

The new act refers to 'unsafe' food, not 'adulterated' food and also a sub-category of 'sub-standard' food which it defines as not meeting the specified standard. 'Sub-standard' food falls short of being as bad as 'unsafe' food.

The punishments under the act as follows:

- for the sale and supply of unsafe foods:
  - where the failure or contravention does not result in injury, imprisonment for a term which may extend to six months and also a fine up to Rs100,000;
  - where the failure or contravention results in a non-grievous injury, imprisonment for a term of up to one year and also a fine up to Rs300,000;
  - where the failure or contravention results in a grievous injury, imprisonment for a term of up to six years and also a fine up to Rs500,000;
  - where the failure or contravention results in death, with imprisonment for a term of not less than seven years but which may extend to imprisonment for life and also a fine of not less than Rs1 million;
  - for selling food not of the nature or substance or quality demanded – penalty not exceeding Rs500,000;
  - for sub-standard food – penalty of up to Rs500,000;
  - for selling misbranded food – penalty of up to Rs300,000;
  - for misleading advertisement – penalty of up to Rs1 million;
  - for selling food containing extraneous matter – a penalty up to Rs100,000;
- for possessing adulterants:
  - where the adulterant is not injurious to health, a penalty not exceeding Rs200,000; and
  - where the adulterant is injurious to health, to a penalty not exceeding Rs1 million rupees.

Industries (Development and Regulation) Act 1951: This act and the rules framed under it bring under central control the regulation of a number of industries affecting India. Section 15 empowers the government to investigate any of the listed industries if there has been, or is likely to be, a marked deterioration in the quality of any article or class of articles relating to that industry or manufactured or produced in the industrial undertaking, which could have been or can be avoided. If the central government is satisfied that action is necessary it may issue directions to the industrial undertaking to adjust the standards of production (Section 16).

Agricultural Produce (Grading and Marking) Act 1937: This act governs quality of agricultural produce which includes all produce of agriculture or horticulture and all articles of food or drink wholly or partly manufactured from any such produce, as well as fleeces and the skins of animals. The act empowers the central government to:

- grade products to indicate quality; scheduled articles under the APA include fruit, vegetables, coffee, spices, pulses and raw meat (chilled/frozen);
- define the quality level indicated by the grade designation;
- specify grade marks representing the different grade designations; and
- confiscate and dispose of produce marked incorrectly.

The act also prescribes fines and other penalties applicable where there is contravention of its provisions. However, only the products which are scheduled in the act must be graded compulsorily. The grading of products not included in the schedule to the act is purely voluntary.

Bureau of the Standards Act 1986: This act established and incorporated a Bureau of Indian Standards (BIS) to establish, publish and promote standards relating to articles covered by the act. Articles covered include 'any substance, artificial or natural, or partly artificial or partly natural, whether raw or partly or wholly processed or manufactured'. The BIS has powers of inspection and seizure of samples to check whether the Standard Mark has been improperly used in relation to any article or process, with or without a licence. However, not all products are required to be of the prescribed Indian standards and most BIS licences are obtained voluntarily by manufacturers to increase brand value.

The Food Safety and Standards Act 2006 comprehensively deals with food and the safety standards which manufacturers and producers must comply with. The penalty for non-compliance is a fine of up to Rs1 million and/or imprisonment.

Penal Code: Product liability-related provisions apply where fraud arises in the creation of the defect in a product, or in relation to false weights and measures, adulteration of goods, food or drugs (punishable by six months imprisonment and/or a fine of Rs1,000) and false property marks (punishable by one year's imprisonment, fines or both).

Standards of Weights and Measures Act 1976: This act applies to packaging, weights and measures. If any mandatory declaration is found to be missing on a package a fine of up to Rs2,000 can be levied (Rule 39).

Drugs and Cosmetics Act 1940: This act imposes criminal liability on manufacturers and producers of medicinal products or cosmetics which do not adhere to the prescribed standards.

Contracts: The laws relating to product liability in India have evolved via the process of judicial interpretation. The trend in recent times is for Indian courts to adopt a more pro-consumer approach than before, reflected in the levels of compensation and damages we now see, which have become more punitive than compensatory.

Product liability is mainly governed by the law of contracts, in general, and by the Sale of Goods Act 1930 in particular. The contract between manufacturer and purchaser governs the liability of the manufacturer and also warranties offered by the manufacturers.

4.3 Claimants, class actions

Class actions are permitted under Section 12(c) of the Consumer Protection Act 1986. A complaint in relation to any goods sold or delivered or agreed to be sold or delivered or any service provided or agreed to be provided may be filed with a district forum by one or more consumers, where there are a number of consumers with the same interest, with the permission of the District Forum, on behalf of, or for the benefit of, all interested consumers. The Consumer Protection Act 1986 provides for representative action with the prior permission of the consumer court.

4.4 Future trends

In spite of those laws mentioned above attaching a degree of product liability to manufacturers, an active and total quality assurance system for the protection of the public from harm is still required. India still needs a comprehensive system to cover the product from design to raw material to finished product, to labelling and actual use. There should be an option for manufacturers post-marketing to register consumer complaints and carry out investigations. Further, a legal obligation on users of products to report any death or serious injury resulting from its use is lacking in the system and should be legislated for. Such a law would entail the results of such investigations being reported back to the manufacturer so that recurrences might be avoided. In general consistent product vigilance should be enshrined by the law.

5. Insurance

Product liability insurance protects a business from claims related to the manufacture or sale to the public of products, food, medicines or other goods. It covers the manufacturer's or seller's liability for losses or injuries to a purchaser, user or bystander caused by a defect or malfunction of the product, and, in some instances, a defective design or a failure to warn. When it is part of a commercial general liability policy, the coverage is sometimes called 'products completed' operations insurance.

In India, there are no laws which compulsorily require a manufacturer, distributor, seller or a purchaser to take product insurance on their products. However, various insurance companies in India do offer product insurance policies which are taken by sellers and consumers voluntarily to cover for losses which might be incurred due to defects or loss of the products.

Companies in India in practice take out product insurance to cover three types of potential products 'claims':

- Manufacturing or production flaws – a claim that some part of the production process created an unreasonably unsafe defect in the resulting product.
- Design defect – a claim that the design of the product is inherently unsafe.
- Defective warnings or instructions – a claim that the product was not properly labelled or had insufficient warnings for the consumer to understand the risk.

Damages awarded in these claims include medical costs, compensatory damages, economic damages, and, in some instances, costs and punitive damages. If a company provides any products to the consuming public, then the company needs product liability or 'completed operations' coverage. In most cases, some form of cover will be present in the standard commercial general liability or business owners' policy.

Various insurers offer product liability insurance in India and each has its own policy terms, as there is no specific law stipulating the precise language of any particular insurance policy. The Insurance Regulatory and Development Authority (Protection of Policyholders' Interests) Regulations 2002 provides a general overview only of the information which a general insurance policy should state:

- the name(s) and address(es) of the insured and of any bank(s) or any other person with a financial interest in the subject matter of the insurance policy;
- a complete description of the subject matter being insured;
- the location(s) of the property or the interest insured under the policy and the insurance value;
- the period of insurance;
- the sums insured;
- the risks covered and excluded;
- the amounts deductible;
- the premium payable and, where the premium is provisional subject to adjustment, the basis for adjustment of premium;
- the terms, conditions and warranties of the policy;
- a description of action to be taken and the obligations of the insured on the occurrence of the contingency insured under the policy;
- any special conditions attached to the policy;
- the provision for cancellation of the policy on grounds of mis-representation, fraud, non-disclosure of material facts or non-cooperation of the insured;
- all relevant details of the insurer, including its address to which all communications in respect of the policy should be sent;
- the details of riders attaching to the main policy; and
- any pro formas the insurer may wish policyholders to use in maintaining the policy.

5.1 Product recall

Some insurers in India offer product recall liability insurances which cover the insured against those expenses that the insured becomes legally obliged to pay as compensatory damages arising out of recall, removal, recovery of possession or control, or disposal of a product that is manufactured, sold, marketed, handled, or distributed by the insured. Product recall insurance is typically provided as an add-on to a product liability insurance policy.

Product recall expenses covered under the policy are limited to:

- costs associated with communications to notify others of a recall, removal, recovery or disposal of a product, including but not limited to radio and television announcements and printed advertisements;
- the cost of shipping the product from any purchaser, distributor or user to the place of the insured;
- the actual cost of disposal of the products, but only to the extent that specific methods of disposal other than those usually employed for trash discarding or disposal are required to avoid bodily injury or property damage as a result of such disposal;
- the extra expense of renting additional warehouse or storage space;
- the costs of hiring additional persons other than your regular employees to assist in the process of communication, shipping; and
- other ancillary responsibilities arising out of a recall, removal, recovery or disposal of a product.

Product recall expenses can be extended to include the following (at the discretion of the insurer):

- the total amount of refunds given to purchasers, not exceeding the cost of goods sold;
- the cost of repairing the product, including cost of returning it to the purchaser, and cost of repairing unsold finished stock;
- if the product is replaced, the cost of producing or acquiring a like replacement product, including the cost of returning the product to the purchaser, not exceeding the cost of goods sold; and
- if the product cannot be repaired, reconditioned, decontaminated or otherwise treated so as to render it marketable, the cost of unsold finished stock.

Generally, this insurance applies only when physical possession of the product has passed from the insured to customers/end-users.

The policy generally does not cover:

- a drop in product sales subsequent to the announcement of a recall due to loss of customer confidence;
- any costs incurred to attempt to boost product sales or regain customer confidence;
- expenses incurred because the product is similar to, or has the same trade or brand name but is of a different batch from, the product which has been recalled;
- costs or expense of repairing, reconditioning, decontaminating or otherwise treating the recalled products so as to render them marketable;

- natural deterioration, decomposition or transformation of chemical structure, except as a result of error or omission in the manufacture of the products;
- failure of the product to accomplish its intended purpose;
- breach of warranties of fitness, quality, efficacy or efficiency;
- an intentional act or omission that was known or should have been known to lead to a recall; and
- sale of a product that had been banned or declared unsafe by any governmental authority.

Generally, manufacturers choose product liability insurance against third party claims and tend to overlook product recall cover that would protect them against recall costs, consultancy fees, lab expenses and replacement costs.

5.2 Product liability insurance

Generally, insurers in India offer product liability insurance policies to manufacturers/sellers covering sales of a faulty product for which they could be held liable for damages, exposing themselves to the risk of financial loss. Such insurance policies are not off-the-shelf and will be designed specifically in accordance with the requirements of the insured. The policies broadly cover the insured against damages which might be claimed by third parties as a result of the manufacture/sale of faulty products by the insured and would cover:

- accidental death;
- bodily injury or disease;
- loss or damage to property; and
- legal costs and expenses incurred with the prior consent of the insurer and within the limit of the indemnity.

The policy generally would not cover liability arising out of or in connection with:

- product efficacy;
- product recall;
- product guarantee;
- pure financial loss;
- terrorism, war and acts of god;
- any professional services deficiency;
- personal injuries such as libel and slander; and
- fines, penalties and punitive or exemplary damages.

5.3 Product guarantee insurance

Product guarantee insurance can be either a first party cover in respect of the cost of repair, removal, replacement and/or treatment of products failing to perform their intended function or third party cover where the other party suffers financial losses as a result of non-performance of a product.

Depending on whether the risk is first or third party, the policy might include costs of rectifying the product defect, costs to repay a third party's financial losses, and/or other costs and expenses suffered by either party to the claim.

5.4 Product contamination or tampering insurance

This is effectively a first party product recall cover for the specific risks of accidental contamination or product extortion and standard cover includes adverse publicity, consequential losses, third party recall costs and crisis management.

5.5 Conclusion

Product insurance is at a very nascent stage in India. Manufacturers and sellers may voluntarily take out a product insurance policy to cover for losses which may be incurred by them due to a defect in their product, or they may have been obligated to take out such insurance under a private contract. However, there is no legal requirement to have such insurance in place.

Consumers very rarely take out insurance to cover the products they own. Apart from the requirement under law of compulsorily insuring motor vehicles (owned by individuals or companies), the law does not otherwise require any further insurance cover be taken. The insurance sector in India is highly regulated and not influenced as yet by the practice or range of insurance products of foreign insurance companies. It remains to be seen in future whether those international insurance companies bring pressure to bear to open up the market and change the nature of India's products insurance scene.

Ireland

Caoimhe Clarkin
Michaela Herron
Liam Kennedy
Lucy Neligan
A&L Goodbody

Since the mid-1980s product safety in Ireland has been regulated through EU harmonisation legislation. Such legislation initiated the adoption of sector-specific EU directives which set out essential safety requirements for categories of products. Prior to placing any product on the market, producers and distributors should consult the national and EU legislation which is relevant to their product, in addition to any applicable compulsory or voluntary standards.

1. Product safety regulation

1.1 Product risks and safety

The European Communities (General Product Safety) Regulations 2004 (European Communities (General Product Safety) Regulations) transpose Directive 2001/95 EC[1] on General Product Safety and prohibit the placing of unsafe goods on the Irish market. The European Communities (General Product Safety) Regulations[2] state that the following should be considered in determining the safety of a product:

- the characteristics of the product;
- the effect on other products where it is reasonably foreseeable that it will be used with such other products;
- the presentation of the product (ie, labelling, any warnings and instructions for its use or disposal, and information regarding the product); and
- the categories of consumers at risk when using the product, in particular children and the elderly.

The feasibility of achieving higher levels of safety or the availability of other products presenting a lesser degree of risk does not constitute grounds for categorising a product as dangerous.[3] Generally, a 'safe product' is defined as one which poses no threat or only a reduced threat, according to what might reasonably be expected given the nature of its use, and which is acceptable in view of maintaining a high level of protection for the health and safety of persons.[4]

A key factor in determining the safety of a product is its conformity with specific standards.

1 A public consultation on the revision of EU Directive 2001/95/EC was launched in 2010.
2 Regulation 4(2) of the European Communities (General Product Safety) Regulations.
3 Regulation 4(2) of the European Communities (General Product Safety) Regulations.
4 Regulation 2 of the European Communities (General Product Safety) Regulations.

The European Communities (General Product Safety) Regulations state that a product must be deemed to be safe if it conforms with any specific national rules, drawn up in conformity with EU law setting out the health and safety requirements which the product must satisfy in order to be marketed. A product is also deemed safe if it conforms to voluntary Irish standards which transpose European standards. When no specific voluntary Irish standards exist, the conformity of a product to the general safety requirements will be assessed by taking into account additional elements, where applicable, including, for example:

- other Irish standard specifications;
- European Commission recommendations setting guidelines on product safety assessment; and
- product safety codes of good practice in force in the sector.[5]

The National Standards Authority of Ireland (NSAI) is Ireland's national standards body.[6] Its role is to develop standards governing, among other things, safety, quality, design and performance of specific products for sale in Ireland. The standards are developed to protect consumers from buying dangerous or substandard goods. Any product for sale in Ireland subject to a standard prescribed by the NSAI must reach the minimum requirements set out in that standard. For a full list of compulsory national safety standards please visit the NSAI's website at www.nsai.ie.

Notwithstanding conformity of a product with the general safety requirements, the National Consumer Agency (NCA), Ireland's product safety surveillance body, may take appropriate measures to impose restrictions on the product being placed on the market, or to require its withdrawal from the market or its recall where there is evidence that despite such conformity, the product is in fact dangerous.[7]

1.2 Compliance and safety issues

Depending on the type of product involved, a manufacturer may have to comply with the rules and procedures of a regulation or oversight body in Ireland. For example:

- prior to placing human medicines, veterinary medicines and medical devices on the market, prior approval must be sought from the Irish Medicines Board (IMB);
- depending on the food product, prior approval must be sought from the relevant competent authority (the Health Service Executive (HSE), the Department of Agriculture, Fisheries & Food (DAFF) and the Sea Fisheries Protection Authority (SFPA));
- the Food Safety Authority (FSAI) is the surveillance authority in respect of food products in Ireland;
- the NSAI and the Road Safety Authority (RSA) are the surveillance authorities in respect of motor vehicles.

---

5 Regulation 5 of the European Communities (General Product Safety) Regulations.
6 Established by the National Standards Authority of Ireland Act 1996.
7 Regulation 9 of the European Communities (General Product Safety) Regulations.

- the NCA is the market surveillance authority in Ireland for safety of non-food products covered by certain EU directives. As part of its market surveillance function, the NCA has responsibility for the monitoring and processing of non-food product recalls in Ireland. It is also the Irish contact point for the European Commission's – internet-based Rapid Alert System for Non-Food Dangerous Products (RAPEX).

1.3 Obligations of producers and distributors

(a) *Producers*

The European Communities (General Product Safety) Regulations prohibit producers from placing or attempting to place dangerous products on the EU market.[8] Producers are also obliged to provide consumers with all relevant information relating to the product, to enable the consumer to assess the risks inherent in the product where such risks are not immediately obvious without adequate warnings, and to take precautions against those risks.[9] A 'producer' includes:

- the manufacturer of a product;
- the manufacturer's representative, when the manufacturer is not established in the European Union;
- in certain circumstances, the importer; or
- other designated persons in the supply chain, insofar as their activities may affect the safety properties of a product placed on the market. These include processors and those that hold themselves out to be producers.[10]

(b) *Distributors*

The European Communities (General Product Safety) Regulations oblige distributors to ensure that any product they supply is a safe product.[11] See section 2 for further details.

1.4 Corrective action

In the event that an unsafe product has been placed on the market, the following corrective action may be taken, depending on the circumstances:

- changing the design of the product;
- temporarily stopping supplies of the product to consumers;
- recalling products from consumers;
- discontinuing the product;
- changing suppliers;
- withdrawing the product from the distribution chain; and
- sending information/warnings about the correct use of the product to consumers.

---

8 Regulation 4(1) of the European Communities (General Product Safety) Regulations.
9 Regulation 6(1) of the European Communities (General Product Safety) Regulations.
10 Regulation 2(1) of the European Communities (General Product Safety) Regulations.
11 Regulation 7(1), European Communities (General Product Safety) Regulations.

1.5 Criminal liability

The European Communities (General Product Safety) Regulations impose criminal sanctions on producers and distributors.[12] It is an offence to place unsafe products on the market in Ireland under the regulations.[13] The regulations place an affirmative duty on producers and distributors to inform the NCA where they know, or ought to know, that a product that has been placed on the market by them is incompatible with safety requirements.[14] Both producers and distributors may be criminally liable. The prosecutor under the regulations is the NCA.[15] The penalty for breach is a fine, imprisonment or both.[16]

The regulations provide for summary prosecution only, which means it is not open for the accused to elect trial by jury.

In criminal prosecutions under the regulations, the NCA will recover the costs of a successful prosecution from the convicted party, unless the court is satisfied that there are "special and substantial reasons" for not ordering the recovery of these costs.[17]

The regulations do not provide for a period within which criminal prosecutions must be brought. However, the general period applicable to summary offences is six months from commission of the alleged offence.[18]

2. Obligations of producers and distributors

2.1 Sources of duties

(a) *Statute*

Obligations are created with respect to product safety in several Irish regulations, depending on the product, but most notably under the European Communities (General Product Safety) Regulations.[19]

(b) *Tort*

General principles of negligence apply in determining liability under tort. A duty of care is owed by designers, assemblers, installers, repairers and suppliers of the products or component parts in relation to the placement of defective products on the market. Their duty includes an affirmative duty to examine the product for safety defects. The manufacturer's duty may be an ongoing one; it may include an obligation to provide information on risks discovered after the product has been put into circulation, as well as an obligation to recall dangerous products.

---

12 For example, see Regulations 4 to 10 of the European Communities (General Product Safety) Regulations.
13 Regulation 4(3) of the European Communities (General Product Safety) Regulations.
14 Regulation 8(3) of the European Communities (General Product Safety) Regulations.
15 Regulation 20 of the European Communities (General Product Safety) Regulations. The prosecutor under the European Communities (General Product Safety) Regulations was the Director of Consumer Affairs however the functions of the Office of the Director of Consumer Affairs have since been taken over by the NCA.
16 Regulations 20 and 22 of the European Communities (General Product Safety) Regulations.
17 Section 21 of the European Communities (General Product Safety) Regulations.
18 Section10(4) of the Petty Sessions (Ireland) Act 1851, as amended by Section 177 of the Criminal Justice Act 2006.
19 Regulation 4(1), European Communities (General Product Safety) Regulations.

(c) ***Contract***

A producer must comply with the Sale of Goods Act 1893 and the later Sale of Goods and Supply of Services Act 1980 – namely, the goods must be "Fit for the purpose for which goods of that kind are commonly bought and [as] durable as it is reasonable to expect".[20]

There is also an implied condition in contracts for the sale of goods that the goods supplied are of merchantable quality.[21] However, there is no implied condition as to the following:[22]

- as regards defects specifically drawn to the buyer's attention before the contract is made; or
- if the buyer examines the goods before the contract is made as regards defects which such an examination ought to have revealed.

However, this condition may be excluded where the parties to the transaction are businesses and the exclusion of this condition is fair and reasonable.

2.2 Pre-market obligations

Different pre-market obligations apply depending on the product.

(a) ***CE marking***

A CE mark certifies that the product has met the relevant EU legislative requirements in relation to safety. When assessing whether a product requires CE marking, the directive relevant to that product must be identified and the product's conformity with the assessment procedure set out in that directive followed. Products which must hold a CE mark include:

- personal protective equipment;[23]
- appliances burning gaseous fuels;[24]
- medical devices;[25] and
- toys and electrical equipment.[26]

The CE mark should appear on the product, in the instruction manual or on the packaging.

(b) ***Traceability***

Consumer products should be supplied with details of the product's name, address and relevant product reference or batch marking. This ensures product traceability.

20 Section 14(3) of the Sale of Goods Acts 1893 and 1980.
21 Section 14(2) of the Sale of Goods Acts 1893 and 1980.
22 Section 14(2) of the Sale of Goods Acts 1893 and 1980.
23 The EC (Personal Protective Equipment) Regulations 1993 state that 'personal protective equipment', defined as any device or appliance designed to be worn or held by an individual for safety requirements, must carry a CE mark.
24 The EC European Communities (Appliances Burning Gaseous Fuels) (Amendment) Regulations 1995.
25 The European Communities (Active Implantable Medical Devices) Regulations 1994, the European Communities (Medical Devices) Regulations 1994 and the European Communities (In-vitro Diagnostic Medical Devices) Regulations 2001 all require the relevant medical devices covered to carry a CE mark.
26 See below at Section 7.

Some sector-specific legislation contains more detailed requirements , such as the EC General Food Law Regulations 2007 and the EC Medicinal Products (Control of Placing on the Market) Regulations 2007. For example, Regulation 8 of the Food Law Regulations makes it an offence not to have systems and procedures (including documentation) showing the provenance and destination of food, and identifying those that have supplied food to the food business operator or those that have been supplied with food by the food business operator. Food business operators must also be able to show traceability of suppliers of food and packaging.

(c) ***General consumer products***

Prior to placing a product on the market, producers and distributors must ensure that the product is safe and does not violate any obligations prescribed by the European Communities (General Product Safety) Regulations. Producers and distributors must ensure any product they place on the marketplace complies with relevant safety standards.[27] The European Communities (General Product Safety) Regulations do not provide defences to the offences laid out in the Regulations. A person guilty of an offence is liable on summary conviction to a fine not exceeding €3,000 or to imprisonment for a term not exceeding three months or both, plus potentially the cost of the prosecution and investigation.[28] In addition, certain offences will result in forfeiture of the products.[29]

(d) ***Food***

The principal European legislation governing food products is EU Regulation 178/2002, which has been implemented in Ireland by the General Food Law Regulations 2007, the European Communities (Food and Hygiene)(Amendment) Regulations 2006 and the European Communities (Hygiene of Fishery Products and Fish Feed) Regulations 2006. The FSAI is the responsible body in relation to the monitoring of food on the Irish market.[30] Under the Food Law Regulations,[31] it is an offence to place unsafe food on the market. A food product must be deemed unsafe if it is considered to be injurious to health or unfit for human consumption.[32] In determining whether a food product is unsafe, regard must be had to the normal conditions of use of the food by the consumer and the conditions at each stage of production, processing and distribution, and to the information provided to the consumer. The penalties for breach of an offence under the Food Law Regulations are:

- on summary conviction, a fine not exceeding €5,000 or imprisonment for a term not exceeding three months or both; or
- on indictment, a fine not exceeding €500,000 or imprisonment for a term not exceeding three years or both.[33]

---

27 Regulation 5 of the European Communities (General Product Safety) Regulations.
28 Regulation 21 of the European Communities (General Product Safety) Regulations.
29 Regulation 23 of the European Communities (General Product Safety) Regulations.
30 Section 11 of the Food Safety Authority of Ireland Act 1998.
31 Regulation 5.
32 Article 14 of EU Regulation 178/2002.
33 Regulation 25, 2007 Food Law Regulations.

Prior to placing food products on the market, an application for a feed or food business approval must be obtained from the relevant competent authority.[34]

Obligations are also imposed by the Food Law Regulations in relation to the presentation, labelling, advertising and traceability of food (at all stages of production), which are issues to be considered prior to the placement of food products on the market.

The FSAI has issued legally enforceable standards, Irish Standards (IS), which relate to food hygiene, traceability, labelling and recall, and which must be considered prior to placing a food product on the market.

Novel foods: The primary EU regulation in relation to novel foods is EU Regulation 258/97. While there is no Irish implementing statutory instrument, this regulation is directly applicable and binding on all member states.

GM foods: EU Regulation 1829/2003 is the primary EU regulation in relation to genetically modified foods. While there is no Irish implementing statutory instrument, this regulation is directly applicable and binding on all member states.

Enhancers and supplements: The primary EU legislation in relation to food supplements is EU Directive 2002/46/EC, which was implemented into Irish law by the European Communities (Food Supplements) Regulations 2007 as amended by the European Communities (Food Supplements) (Amendment) Regulations 2010.

Food contact materials: The Food Law Regulations and the European Communities (Labelling, Presentation and Advertising of Foodstuffs) Regulations 2002 (as amended) set out requirements in respect of labelling and presentation of food. In addition, the European Communities (Plastic and Other Materials) (Contact with Food) Regulations 2007 set out the general principles in relation to food contact materials – for example, food contact materials must not cause unacceptable changes in the composition of food or deterioration in its organoleptic properties.

(e) Motor vehicles

The European Communities (Road Vehicles: Type-approval) Regulations 2009 transpose the EU Framework Directive (2007/46/EC) into Irish law. Prior to placement on the market, manufacturers of new vehicles must ensure that they are manufactured to prescribed safety and environmental standards. Currently, companies or individuals involved in the manufacture or registration of all new passenger cars are required to have type approval in the form of either EC whole vehicle type approval, national small series type approval or individual vehicle approval in order to be registered in Ireland.

Manufacturers are responsible to the approval authority (in Ireland, these are the

34 The relevant competent authority will vary depending on the food type; approval authorities include the Health Service Executive, the Sea Fisheries Protection Authority and the Department of Agriculture, Fisheries and Food. The approval processes and obligations are detailed in the European Communities (Food & Feed Hygiene) Regulations 2009.

NSAI and the RSA) for all aspects of the approval process and for ensuring conformity of production, whether or not the manufacturer is directly involved in all stages of a construction of a vehicle, system, component or separate technical unit.[35] A manufacturer established outside the European Union must appoint a representative established in an EU state to represent it before the approval authority.[36]

In the case of multi-stage type approval,[37] each manufacturer is responsible for the approval and conformity of production of the systems, components or separate technical units added at the stage of each vehicle completion handled by it. A manufacturer which modifies components or systems already approved at earlier stages is responsible for the approval and conformity of production of those components and systems.[38]

A large number of offences are set out in Regulation 25 of the European Communities (Motor Vehicles Type Approval) Regulations 2009. A person guilty of any offence is liable:

- on summary conviction, to a fine not exceeding €5,000 or to imprisonment for a term not exceeding six months or both; or
- on conviction on indictment, to a fine not exceeding €100,000 or imprisonment for a term not exceeding 12 months or both.

The NSAI is the Irish-appointed approval authority[39] and is responsible for issuing national small series type approval and individual vehicle approval for vehicles in Ireland. The NSAI has established a network of appointed test centres to physically examine and issue test reports for some or all of the technical requirements. These test reports are then used by the NSAI to grant a vehicle or trailer approval.

(f) *Electrical equipment*

Electrical products for sale and in use throughout the European Union are subject to safety standards. The EU Low Voltage Electrical Equipment Directive (2006/95/EC) is transposed into Irish law by the European Communities (Low Voltage Electrical Equipment) Regulations 1992, as amended by the 1994 Amendment Regulations. The Low Voltage Electrical Equipment Regulations prohibit the placing on the market of any electrical equipment unless, having been constructed in accordance with the principles of good engineering practice in safety matters, it does not endanger the safety of persons, domestic animals or property.[40] A person in breach of these regulations is guilty of an offence and is liable on summary conviction to a fine not exceeding €1,250 or imprisonment for a period not exceeding 12 months or both.[41]

---

35 Regulation 6 of the European Communities (Road Vehicles Type Approval) Regulations.
36 Regulation 6(3) of the European Communities (Road Vehicles Type Approval) Regulations.
37 Regulation 6(2)(a) of the European Communities (Road Vehicles Type Approval) Regulations – this is where one or more member state certifies that, depending on the state of completion, an incomplete or completed type of vehicle satisfies the relevant administrative technical requirements of the Framework Directive.
38 Regulation 6(2)(b) of the European Communities (Road Vehicles Type Approval) Regulations 2009.
39 Regulation 4 of the EC (Road Vehicles Type Approval) Regulations 2009.
40 Regulation 4(1) of the EC Low Voltage Equipment Regulations 1992.
41 Regulation 13 of the EC Low Voltage Equipment Regulations 1992.

In deciding whether electrical equipment complies with these requirements, regard should be had to:[42]

- safety objectives;
- the method of installation and maintenance intended for equipment as indicated on the equipment or separate notice accompanying the equipment; and
- the usage for which this equipment is stated to be suitable, as indicated on the equipment or on a separate notice accompanying the equipment.

Electrical equipment which complies with the provisions of harmonised standards must be deemed to comply with required safety provisions. Where there are no harmonised standards, electrical equipment which complies with the safety provision of standards which have been published by the International Commission on the Rules for the Approval of Electrical Equipment or the International Electro-Technical Commission and which have been published in the *Official Journal of the European Communities*, must be regarded as complying with Regulation 4.[43]

All electrical products and gas appliances must have a CE mark. The obligation to obtain CE marking of electrical equipment was introduced by the 1994 Amendment Regulations.[44]

As plugs, sockets and leads in Ireland are different from those in the rest of Europe, the NSAI has developed standards to ensure that safety standards are met. The specific standards are SI 222/1969, Electrical Appliances and SI 173/1987 Safety Requirements for Rewirable 13A Fuse Plugs.

(g) *Toys*

All toys for sale (or free as part of a promotion) in the European Union must carry a CE mark.[45] A 'toy' means a product or material designed or clearly intended for use in play by children younger than 14 years of age.[46] The placing of toys on the market is prohibited in Ireland unless the toy is safe, carries a CE mark and complies with essential safety requirements.[47] Where a toy has affixed to it any CE mark, the toy must be presumed, until the contrary is proved, to comply with the essential safety requirements.[48] The European Communities (Safety of Toys) Regulations 2011 have effect from July 20 2011, and apply to toys placed on the market since that date. These regulations set out updated safety requirements for placing toys on the market, conformity assessment and CE marking, and also set out a requirement to ensure risk assessment is carried out for toys. Offences are set out in Regulation 21 of the European Communities (Safety of Toys) Regulations 1990, and a person guilty of an

42 Regulation 4(2) of the EC Low Voltage Equipment Regulations 1992.
43 Regulation 6 of the EC (Low Voltage Electrical Equipment) (Amendment) Regulations 1992.
44 Regulation 4 of the European Communities (Low Voltage Electrical Equipment) (Amendment) Regulations 1994, which replaces Regulation 7 of the European Communities (Low Voltage Electrical Equipment) Regulations 1992.
45 Regulation 3 of the European Communities (Safety of Toys) (Amendment) Regulations 1994.
46 Regulation 8 of the European Communities (Safety of Toys) Regulations 1990.
47 Regulation 6 of the European Communities (Safety of Toys) Regulations 1990.
48 Regulation 5 of the European Communities (Safety of Toys) (Amendment) Regulations 1994.

offence will be liable on summary conviction to imprisonment of a period not exceeding six months or a fine not exceeding €1,250 or both.[49]

(h) *Medicine*

The marketing and manufacturing of medicinal products in the European Union is heavily regulated and therefore the appropriate legislation may vary depending on the nature of the medicinal product and the circumstances of its use (eg, clinical trials, herbal medicines). This section is intended as a broad overview of the obligations of manufacturers. Medicinal devices are separately regulated and are not discussed below.

The IMB is the regulatory body responsible for the manufacture and placing of medicinal products on the market.[50] The primary legislation is the IMB Act which, together with its associated regulations, governs the licensing, manufacturing, sale and supply of medicinal products in Ireland.[51]

Three main types of authorisation are required in relation to medicinal products: manufacturing authorisation, marketing authorisation and wholesaler's authorisation.

The Medicinal Products (Control of Manufacture) Regulations 2007 state that a manufacturing authorisation is required for the manufacture, batching, packaging, labelling, presentation and importation of medicinal products from outside the European Economic Area.[52] Applications for a manufacturing authorisation are made directly to the IMB. A 'qualified person'[53] must be appointed by the manufacturer to ensure batch compliance with the law, the manufacturer's authorisation and the marketing authorisation.

The Medicinal Products (Control of Placing on the Market) Regulations 2007 state that a person must not place a medicinal product on the market unless authorised to do so.[54] Authorisation can be obtained through either the National Procedure,[55] the Mutual Recognition and Decentralised Procedure[56] or the Centralised Procedure.[57]

---

49 Regulation 22 of the European Communities (Safety of Toys) Regulations 1990.

50 Irish Medicines Board Act 1995.

51 All medicinal products for human use derived from biotechnology and other high-technology processes must be approved by the European Medicines Agency (EMA). The Environmental Protection Agency is responsible for implementing regulations relating to the contained use or deliberate release of genetically modified organisms in Ireland.

52 Regulation 4 of the Medicinal Products (Control of Manufacture) Regulations 2007.

53 As defined in Section 3 of the Medicinal Products (Control of Manufacture) Regulations 2007.

54 Regulation 6 of the Medicinal Products (Control of Placing on the Market) Regulations 2007.

55 Medicinal products marketed in Ireland must be authorised by the IMB. The national procedure involves an application made directly to the IMB. This procedure should be used only to market the product in Ireland and not in any other member state or as the basis for a future mutual recognition application to other member states.

56 The mutual recognition and decentralised procedure is another means of obtaining authorisation to place a product on a single market by relying on the principal of mutual recognition. Thus, with the exception of medicinal products which are subject to the centralised procedure, a marketing authorisation or the assessment in one member state is recognised by the competent authorities of another member state unless there are grounds for supposing that the authorisation of the medicinal product concerned may present a serious risk to public health.

57 The EMA is responsible for the evaluation of applications via the centralised procedure. The centralised procedure allows companies to submit one single marketing authorisation application to the EMA. In the event that authorisation is approved, the medicinal product may be put on the market in all member states and the authorisation is valid for the entire community market.

Finally, the Medicinal Products (Control of Wholesale Distribution) Regulations 2007 state that a person must not sell wholesale unless they hold a wholesaler's authorisation,[58] which is also issued by the IMB.

(i) ***Cosmetics***

The EU Cosmetics Directive (76/768/EEC was transposed into Irish law by the European Communities (Cosmetic Products) Regulations 2004 (as amended), which govern the placing of cosmetic products on the market. The IMB is the relevant regulatory body.[59] A person must not place on the market any cosmetic product which is liable to cause damage when applied under normal conditions of use or conditions of use which are reasonably foreseeable.[60] A person guilty of an offence under these regulations will be liable on summary conviction to a fine not exceeding €3,000 or imprisonment for a term not exceeding six months or both.[61] Additional obligations are imposed in relation to animal testing, labelling, retention of information by manufacturers, notification of place of manufacture or first importation into the European Union.[62]

A responsible person[63] (a manufacturer, EU agent or importer) must notify the IMB if it:

- manufactures cosmetic products and places them on the market under its own name or trading name, or places cosmetic products on the market under its own name from a third party (the manufacturer);
- imports cosmetic products from third countries onto the Irish market ('the importer'); or
- is the 'designated responsible person' or EU agent or a cosmetic manufacturer outside of the European Union.

2.3 Post-market obligations

A producer that places a product on the market must adopt measures commensurate with the characteristics of the product to enable the producer to:

- be informed of the risks that the product might pose; or
- choose to take appropriate action, including, if necessary, withdrawing/recalling the product from the market and effectively warning customers.[64]

Recall is a last resort where other measures do not suffice to prevent the risks involved.[65]

Distributors are also subject to certain obligations in relation to products that they supply to the market. A distributor must, in relation to any product placed on

58 Medicinal Products (Control of Wholesale Distribution) Regulations 2007.
59 Since October 1 2010.
60 Regulation 7 of the European Communities (Cosmetic Products) Regulations 2004.
61 Regulation 18 of the European Communities (Cosmetic Products) Regulations 2004.
62 See Regulations 7 to 10, 12 and 13 of the European Communities (Cosmetic Products) Regulations.
63 Regulation 4 of the European Communities (Cosmetic Products) Regulations 2004.
64 Recital 19 of the European Communities (General Product Safety) Regulations.
65 Regulation 6(3) of the European Communities (General Product Safety) Regulations.

the market which it supplies, monitor the product with regard to safety and for this purpose must inform the producer of the product, the NCA and consumers as to any defects in it or risks it may pose that he becomes aware of. A distributor must keep and provide the NCA with documentation necessary to trace the origin of the product and cooperate in any action taken by the NCA.[66]

Where a producer or distributor knows – or, on the basis of information within its possession, ought to know – that a product they have placed on the market poses a risk to the consumer that is incompatible with the safety requirements of the European Communities (General Product Safety) Regulations, the producer is obliged immediately to inform the NCA of the risk and give details of remedial actions taken.[67] In the event of serious risks, the information must include at least the following:

- information enabling a precise identification of the product or batch of products in question;
- a full description of the risk that the products in question present;
- all available information relevant for tracing the product; and
- a description of the action undertaken to prevent risks to consumers.[68]

The producer of a product or a distributor must, upon request by the NCA, provide every reasonable assistance to the NCA to avoid the risks posed by any product which the producer or distributor supplies or has supplied. Failure to comply with these obligations is an offence.[69] Producers and distributors must assist and cooperate with the NCA in their investigation in relation to the unsafe product.

Once a product is found to be unsafe, the producer or distributor should trace and identify the product and its owners. It should first estimate the number of products affected and subsequently identify the products in a recognisable manner. Ideally, producers or distributors should identify the product by serial number, but identification by batch number or batch code could be acceptable identification methods as well. After identifying the product, the producer or distributor should then identify the people who have purchased the product. It may be necessary to rely on other companies in the supply chain for this information.

The producer or distributor should next establish a centralised communications programme such as a central communication centre with a free telephone hotline number. A list of audiences to be reached and the media to be used should be compiled.

In communicating a recall to consumers, the producer or distributor should consider the channel and syntax of the communication. It might consider using newspapers, personal letters, phone calls, emails, media releases, leaflets, radio and television advertising or websites. It should also pay particular attention to the language and presentation of the recall announcement. It might consider including the heading "Important Safety Warning", the product identification details, a

---

66 Regulation 7 of the European Communities (General Product Safety) Regulations.
67 Regulation 8 of the European Communities (General Product Safety) Regulations.
68 Regulation 8 of the European Communities (General Product Safety) Regulations.
69 Regulation 8 of the European Communities (General Product Safety) Regulations.

description of what is wrong with the product and the risks it presents, clear instructions on how to claim a replacement or refund, and how to deal with the current product.

Once a recall has been successfully communicated, the producer or distributor should arrange for collection of the recalled product and appropriately dispose of the product. Collection includes arranging collection from distributors and requesting that consumers take the product to the nearest retailer or arranging for collection from consumers. Disposal should subsequently be carried out, taking into account any environmental risks that may arise.

(a) Food

A food business operator (as defined in the Food Law Regulations) must immediately inform the FSAI of any grounds for believing that a food which has been placed on the market may be injurious to human health and failure to do so is an offence.[70] A food business operator must assist and collaborate with the FSAI to avoid or reduce risks posed by a food.[71] If the food business operator believes that food placed on the market is unsafe, there is an obligation on the food business operator to initiate procedures:

- to withdraw the food;
- inform the FSAI of the initiation of proceedings to withdraw a food;
- effectively and accurately inform consumers of the reasons for withdrawal/recall; and
- ensure the food is withdrawn.

As set out above, a food business operator must be able to identify a person that has supplied it with food[72] and to identify any other business to which it has supplied food.[73]

Obligations are also imposed on food business operators responsible for retail or distribution activities (not relating to the packaging, labelling, safety or integrity of a food) to initiate procedures to withdraw a food.[74] The food business operator must initiate procedures to withdraw food, ensure that a food is withdrawn, pass on relevant information to trace a food or cooperate in actions taken by the producers, processors, manufacturers and/or the authority of the official agency, in accordance with Article 19(2) of the Food Law Regulations.

Failure to comply with any of these obligations is an offence under the Food Law Regulations.

The FSAI has a role in coordinating national and international food recalls/withdrawals. Official agencies coordinate local food recalls. According to the FSAI's Product Recall and Traceability Guidance Note, food business operators must take two steps to comply with their legal obligations: planning and management.

70 Regulation 9(3) of the General Food Law Regulations 2007.
71 Regulation 9(4) of the General Food Law Regulations 2007.
72 Regulation 8 of the General Food Law Regulations 2007.
73 Regulation 8 of the General Food Law Regulations 2007.
74 Regulation 9(2) of the General Food Law Regulations 2007.

To comply with their legal obligation to plan for a recall/withdrawal, producers and distributors must[75] develop and document a recall/withdrawal policy, develop and document a recall/withdrawal plan, and review and test the recall/withdrawal plan. The recall policy should clearly state the objective of the recall and the senior management's endorsement of the policy and commitment to providing the necessary resources to effect the policy. The policy should be in place prior to the development of a recall plan. For details of what the recall plan should include, please see the FSAI's Product Recall and Traceability Guidance Note.

The management of a food recall should include the following:

- Initial information management – information should be verified at the source if possible.
- Application of the decision tree and identification of unsafe or non-compliant food – the food business operator should ask five questions:
- Does the food pose a public health risk?
- Is the food unacceptable for human consumption for reasons of contamination?
- Is the risk to public health or unacceptability eliminated by normal conditions of use?
- Is the food unsafe as defined in the general food law?
- Is the food in compliance with all EU and national provisions of food law?
- Compilation of information on distribution – data such as the food name, food description, batch codes involved, quantity of food implicated, distribution details and whether the food may have reached consumers should be collected.
- Removal of food from the market and associated communication – the incident team should execute the procedures described in the recall/withdrawal plan. Companies should note that in all circumstances, notification to the competent authority should be made before removing food from the market. Companies should notify trade contacts and, if food has reached the consumer, notify the consumer. Food companies may work with retail food business operators to notify the consumer. It may be appropriate to set up a dedicated phone line that provides information and advice on the recall or withdrawal. The recall/withdrawal incident team should also attempt to reconcile the amount of food removed from the market with the amount of food known to be distributed. Recovered food should be returned to one central site and subsequently kept separate from any unaffected food.
- Closure of the recall/withdrawal – this includes notification of the competent authorities.
- Disposal of unsafe food – producers and distributors should consult with the competent authority to determine the proper method of disposal.
- Review of the recall/withdrawal – this includes producing a final report of the recall/withdrawal.

---

75 Regulation 9 of the Food Law Regulations 2007.

(b) ***Medicines***

Post-marketing obligations of holders of a marketing authorisation include the following:

- Ensure that an appropriately qualified person is responsible for pharmacology.
- Provide updated information to the IMB in relation to an application to vary an authorisation.
- Maintain a record of reports of adverse reactions which can be made available for inspection by the IMB and supplied to the IMB.
- Maintain documents which will facilitate the withdrawal of recall from sale or supply of any medicinal product to which the authorisation or certificate relates.
- Provide the IMB with any information or documents it requires.
- Inform the IMB of the date of actual placement on the market.
- Notify the IMB if a product ceases to be placed on the market either temporarily or permanently.

Take steps necessary to take account of scientific and technical progress for the purposes of making any changes or amendments as required.[76]

Medicinal product manufacturers are obliged, under the conditions of their marketing authorisation, to submit details of adverse reactions associated with use of their products to the IMB.[77] They are also obliged to report to the IMB any defect in a medicinal product manufactured in Ireland and any defect in a medicinal product that could result in a product recall or abnormal restriction of supply.[78] The 'qualified person' responsible for batch release of the product in question is usually expected to report the quality defect to the IMB.

The IMB has three classes of product recall:

- Class 1 recalls result from quality defects of medicinal products which are potentially life threatening or could cause serious risk to health;
- Class 2 recalls are due to quality defects which could cause illness or mistreatment, but are not Class 1 recalls; and
- Class 3 recalls are due to quality defects which are not likely to pose a significant hazard to health, but have been initiated for other reasons.

Where the nature of the product quality defect is such that product recall may not be considered necessary or appropriate, consideration will be given to the need to alert healthcare professionals who may be prescribing use of or distributing, dispensing or administering the product, bringing to their attention details of the product defect. The issuing of a caution in use notification may be appropriate in such cases.

In relation to products distributed on the Irish market, it is the overall

76 See Article 23 of EU Directive 2001/83/EC.
77 Regulation 17c of the Medicinal Products (Control of Placing on the Market) Regulations 2007
78 Regulation 15(6) of the Medicinal Products (Control of Placing on the Market) Regulations 2007.

responsibility of the holder of the marketing authorisation for the product concerned to ensure that any recall required by the IMB is implemented fully and completed expeditiously. It is the IMB's preference that the holder of the Community marketing authorisation, Irish marketing authorisation or parallel product authorisation – or its Irish affiliate/subsidiary, if appropriate, takes responsibility for coordinating the recall and for issuing the recall notifications. Responsibility for these tasks may be delegated to the manufacturer or primary wholesaler which is not the marketing authorisation holder; but in any event, the recall should be closely monitored by a designated person at the marketing authorisation holder company. A decision to recall a medicinal product must be made in consultation with the market compliance section of the IMB. In general, most recalls are initiated by means of a recall letter.

According to the IMB Guidance on Recall of Medicinal Products for Human and Veterinary Use, each class has its own recall requirements, which are summarised in the table below:

	Notification period	**Method of notification**	**Extent of notification**	**Method of retrieval of recalled stock**
Class I	24 hours	Phone and fax, radio/television, press announcements followed by a letter	Wholesalers and other retailers, pharmacies, other medical practitioners and professionals, patients	Direct uplift of stock
Class II	72 hours	Phone followed by fax/letter	Wholesalers and possibly other retailers, pharmacies, hospitals, possibly doctor/dentist or veterinarian	Return of product via wholesaler

(c) ***Motor vehicles***

Where a manufacturer which has been granted an EC whole vehicle type approval is obliged, in application of the EU Framework Directive (2007/46/EC), to recall vehicles already sold, registered or put into service because one or more systems, components or separate technical units fitted to the vehicle – whether or not duly approved in accordance with this directive – present a serious risk to road safety, public health or environmental protection, it must immediately inform the approval authority that granted the vehicle approval the recall.[79] The manufacturer must propose to the approval authority (the NSAI of RSA) a set of appropriate remedies to neutralise the risk identified.

If the approval authority is not satisfied with the measures taken by the manufacturer, it must take all protective measures required, including withdrawal of the EC whole vehicle type approval, where the manufacturer does not propose and implement effective corrective measures.

In case of withdrawal of the EC whole vehicle type approval, the NSAI or RSA must notify the manufacturer, the approval authorities of the other member states and the European Commission by registered letter or equivalent electronic means within 20 working days. In Ireland, when a recall campaign is deemed necessary, the Department of Transport – which manages the National Vehicle and Driver File (a register of all vehicle owners) – must send the manufacturer the relevant names and addresses of the current owners. Those owners will then be contacted and informed of the remedial action required.

3. Enforcement

3.1 Sector organisation

(a) *General consumer products*

As discussed, the NCA is the investigatory and enforcement agency in respect of breaches both under the European Communities (General Product Safety) Regulations and the Consumer Protection Act 2007. If a complaint is made to the NCA in respect of a product, the NCA will be entitled to consider potential breaches of both the European Communities (General Product Safety) Regulations and the Consumer Protection Act. If a complaint is made, the NCA is not obliged to investigate, but may choose to do so. The policy of the NCA is to investigate cases where there is the greatest potential for consumer loss or detriment. The NCA, upon receiving a complaint about product safety, may refer the complaint to its Commercial Practices Division for investigation.

In commencing an investigation, the NCA will contact the trader involved and advise it of the allegations made. The NCA will also point out the trader's obligations under the relevant law and give it an opportunity to put measures in place to rectify any identified problems. This gives the trader an opportunity to demonstrate the safety of the product and/or flag up any remedial action it has taken since it became aware of the complaint. The focus of the NCA is to ensure that the product is in fact safe. This is known as the cooperative stage of an investigation.

If the NCA progresses the investigation beyond the cooperative stage, then the following actions can be taken:

---

79 Regulations 16 to 18 of the EC (Road Vehicle Type Approval) Regulations 2009.

- Where a product could "pose risks in certain conditions" the NCA can issue a direction requiring the producer to warn those at risk in good time.
- Where a product "could be dangerous" the NCA will issue a direction prohibiting the supply of the product pending safety checks.
- Where a product is "dangerous" the NCA can issue a direction prohibiting the placing of the product on the market and, where a dangerous product is already on the market, can take appropriate measures including immediate withdrawal and recall.

The NCA is obliged by the European Communities (General Product Safety) Regulations to take measures in a manner proportionate to the risk involved.

Where a producer has failed to comply with a direction of the NCA, the NCA may (in lieu of summary proceedings) institute High Court proceedings for an order requiring the producer to comply with the terms of the NCA's directions.[80]

The NCA has a general power to apply to the district court for an order for the forfeiture of any product on the grounds that the product is a "dangerous product" (ie, not a safe product). The court may then order that the product be destroyed.[81]

The NCA may make information available to the public relating to risks to consumer health and safety posed by the product.[82]

(b) *Food*

The Food Safety Authority of Ireland Act 1998 contains enforcement provisions designed to provide an improved means for reacting to and dealing with situations posing a risk to public health. The relevant legislative provisions are enforced by authorised officers appointed by the FSAI or its official agents under Section 49 of the FSAI Act. The powers granted to these officers are detailed in Sections 50 and 51 of the FSAI Act.

Enforcement provisions in the FSAI Act include the issuing of an improvement order, a prohibition order and a closure order.

In general, the HSE enforces food law under the General Food Law Regulations 2007 via the environmental health officers in all retail food business and food businesses processing foods of non-animal origin. It conducts official control activities under the European Communities (Official Control of Foodstuffs) Regulations 2010. The SFPA enforces food law in food businesses handling and processing fish and fishery products. DAFF and local authority veterinary services enforce food law in food businesses engaged in the handling and processing of meat and meat products.

(c) *Motor vehicles*

Manufacturers of motor vehicles must obtain type approval prior to placement of their product on the market. Once approval has been obtained, a certificate of

---

80 Regulation 6 of the European Communities (General Product Safety) Regulations.
81 Regulation 16 of the European Communities (General Product Safety) Regulations.
82 Regulation 18 of the European Communities (General Product Safety) Regulations.

authorisation is issued. If the NSAI or RSA believes that a part or equipment no longer complies with the conditions under which the certificate was given, it may withdraw the certificate of authorisation or require the manufacturer to bring the part or equipment back into conformity with those conditions.

The European Communities (Road Vehicles: Entry into Service) Regulations 2009 state that where the NSAI considers that vehicles with respect to which an EC whole vehicle type approval has been granted pose a serious risk to road safety or could seriously harm the environment or public health, the NSAI may direct that, for a specified period not exceeding six months, all certificates of conformity issued under that EC whole vehicle type approval are invalid for the purposes of Part 2 of those regulations. Under the European Communities (Motor Vehicle Type Approval) Regulations 2009 the NSAI can issue a notice of non-conformity and can cancel and amend a type approval certificate. Obligations are imposed in relation to notifying member states about such decisions. There is a general obligation on holders of an EC whole vehicle type approval to cooperate with the NSAI and those acting on its behalf[83] (eg, the Road Safety Authority).

(d) *Medicine*

All quality defects in medicines are investigated by the IMB on a case-by-case basis. Persons are obliged to provide the IMB with any data or information it requires.[84] Quality defects may result in product recalls, the issuance of a caution in use notification to pharmacists and medicinal professionals, or other actions.[85] Other authorities may be informed by the IMB of the quality defect issue.

- The IMB can investigate whether:
- a manufacturer or importer has obtained an authorisation and is complying with it; or
- a manufacturer or importer has properly appointed a qualified person approved by the IMB that meets the requirements and is fulfilling its obligations, and the manufacturer or importer is complying with its own obligations.

The IMB can put urgent safety restrictions in place and can also vary an authorisation at any time.[86] The IMB can also suspend or revoke the authorisation in total or in relation to certain medicinal products, on notice in writing to the authorisation holder, on the grounds that the authorisation holder:

- must stop carrying out the operations to which the authorisation relates;
- has specified matters in the application which were materially false or incomplete, or a material change in circumstances has occurred in relation to any of those matters;
- has failed to any material extent to comply with its obligations;
- has manufactured or imported medicinal products otherwise than in accordance with the terms of the authorisation;

83 Regulation 12 of the European Communities (Motor Vehicle Type Approval) Regulations.
84 Regulation 15 of the Medicinal Products (Control of Placing on the Market) Regulations 2007.
85 Regulation 14 of the Medicinal Products (Control of Placing on the Market) Regulations 2007.
86 Regulations 13 and 14 of the Medicinal Products (Control of Placing on the Market) Regulations 2007.

- does not have the staff, premises, equipment or facilities necessary for carrying out properly the handling, storage or distribution activities to which the authorisation relates; or
- has failed to carry out an obligation imposed by the IMB.

In addition to a potential monetary fine and/or imprisonment for offences committed under the act, the court may also order that any relevant item be destroyed or forfeited and may order the person convicted to pay any costs of such a destruction.

3.2 Powers of authorities

(a) *National Consumer Agency*

The NCA can, for the purposes of ensuring product safety and to ensure that producers and distributors are complying with their obligations, carry out safety checks on products and request necessary information in relation to a product. The NCA's authorised officers may also copy documents relevant to a product, search premises, take samples of products, seize products for the purposes of carrying out further tests and dismantle products for the purposes of carrying out further tests.[87] Where an authorised officer is prevented from entering premises, a warrant may be obtained from the district court. It is an offence to obstruct or interfere with authorised officers in the exercise of their powers under the European Communities (General Product Safety) Regulations.[88]

(b) *Food Safety Authority of Ireland*

Under the FSAI Act 1998, authorised officers can require specified people to produce records and/or give them any information the officer reasonably requires. In addition, officers can enter all premises, except private dwelling places, where a specific district court warrant is required, where there are reasonable grounds to believe that food-related activities or businesses are being or have been conducted or that relevant records are kept. Officers therefore have powers of search and seizure in relation to any records and information which may be relevant to the products which may be unsafe.

Authorised officers may, for the purposes of the Food Law Regulations and enforcing relevant provisions of EU Regulation 178/2002, at any reasonable time and subject to Section 50 of the 1998 act, enter any premises in which they have reasonable grounds for believing that any food is being produced, manufactured, imported, processed, stored, transported, distributed and traded and do any of the following:

- take readings and values recorded by measuring instruments;
- carry out examinations, tests and inspections;
- interview the food business operator and other staff;
- require the food business operator or any relevant staff to produce documents and provide any assistance necessary;

---

87 Regulation 14 of the European Communities (General Product Safety) Regulations.
88 Regulation 14(11) of the European Communities (General Product Safety) Regulations.

- inspect and take copies or extracts from records;
- take a sample of food;
- inspect and take copies or samples of labels, packaging and any other materials used in packaging and any other materials used in the advertising of presentation of food; and
- seize, remove, detain, or direct withdrawal from the market, any food they suspect fails to comply with the EU regulations.

An authorised officer may apply for an order of a district court judge directing the destruction of the unsafe food.[89] A person is guilty of an offence if it obstructs or interferes with an authorised officer in the exercise of the officer's powers under those regulations and fails to cooperate with a request or notice under the regulations.[90]

(c) ***Irish Medicines Board***

Under the IMB Act, the IMB may appoint authorised officers to carry out some of the powers conferred on the IMB. Functions of an authorised officer under Section 17 of the Irish Medicines Board (Miscellaneous Provisions) Act 2006 include the following:

- entering and inspecting sites;
- inspecting and copying records and removing any records found;
- carrying out such tests, examinations and inspections of premises or any equipment, machinery or plant at the premises;
- requiring any person on the premises to provide him with information or assistance;
- taking samples of any relevant thing found at the premises;
- directing that such relevant thing found at the premises not be sold or distributed; and
- taking possession or removing any relevant thing from the premises.

(d) ***Road Safety Authority***

Authorised officers, appointed by the RSA, have powers under Regulation 9 of the Road Vehicle Type Regulations 2009 to enter any premises owned by a manufacturer or a distributor and search and inspect the premises and any certificates, books, documents or records relating to the registration of vehicles. They may also require any person in charge of the premises to produce books, documents relating to the registration of vehicles which are in the person's control and to provide such information as is reasonably required. An authorised officer also has the power to inspect and take extracts from such books and documents and to remove them from the premises.[91] If the officer is prevented from entering a premises or place, a warrant can be obtained from a district court judge.[92]

---

89 Section 19(4) of the Food Law Regulations.
90 Section 22(3) of the General Food Law Regulations.
91 Section 26 of the European Communities (Motor Vehicle Type Approval) Regulations permits all of the preceding powers.
92 Section 26(6) of the European Communities (Motor Vehicle Type Approval) Regulations.

3.3 International enforcement

(a) *Rapid Alert System for Non-Food Dangerous Products*

If a business is conducting a recall, it is obliged to notify the NCA of the actions it proposes taking. The business is also obliged, under the European Communities (General Product Safety) Regulations, to inform consumers of hazardous products on the Irish market. If the recall involves a product which has been placed on more than one market, the NCA is required to notify the European Commission via RAPEX. The information is transmitted to all EU member states.

Once a RAPEX notification is received by the NCA, the information is reviewed and further information is sought if necessary. Notification is submitted to the European Commission via the online RAPEX system. Once validated by the commission, a notification is sent to all member state RAPEX contact points. Information is also sent to Irish contacts/businesses and customs authorities. Feedback is then received from such contacts/businesses and this information is then submitted to RAPEX. The NCA places a notification on its website and issues a press release where this is deemed appropriate.

(b) *Rapid Alert System for Food and Feed*

EU Regulation178/2002 gives effect to the Rapid Alert System for Food and Feed (RASFF). RASFF deals with the obligatory notification of any direct or indirect risk to human health, animal health or the environment within a network consisting of national competent authorities, the European Food Safety Authority and the European Commission. The regulation also confers special powers on the European Commission for taking emergency measures where it is evident that feed or food originating in the European Union and imported from a third country is likely to constitute a serious risk to human health, animal health or the environment, and that such a risk cannot be contained satisfactorily by means of measures taken by the member states. The FSAI is the responsible body in Ireland in respect of notifications to RASFF.

3.4 Appeals

The European Communities (General Product Safety) Regulations permits anyone aggrieved by a direction of the director of consumer affairs to appeal the direction under Regulation 12.

The European Communities (Motor Vehicle Type Approval) Regulations allow for a review process for any person aggrieved by a decision of the NSAI.[93] Persons aggrieved by a decision of the NSAI may seek a review of the decision under Section 29.

Generally, appeals of decisions of the court may be appealed to a higher court if certain criteria are met.

3.5 Sanctions and compensation

An offence under the European Communities (General Product Safety) Regulations may be prosecuted summarily. A person guilty of any offence under the regulations is

93 Section 29 of the European Communities (Motor Vehicle Type Approval) Regulations.

liable on summary conviction to be a fine not exceeding €3,000 or to imprisonment for a term not exceeding three months or both. In certain circumstances, a court may order that the costs of the proceedings and investigation be met by the offender. In addition, upon conviction of an offence under the regulations, the court may order that the products be forfeited, destroyed or otherwise disposed of.[94] The regulations also impose liability on officers of a company where a company commits an offence. A person convicted of an offence under the regulations must, unless there are substantial reasons for not doing so, be ordered to pay the NCA's costs and expenses.[95]

(a) ***Food***

A person guilty of any offence under the Food Law Regulations is liable:

- on summary conviction, to a fine not exceeding €5,000 or imprisonment for a term not exceeding three months or both; or
- on conviction or indictment, to a fine not exceeding €500,000 or imprisonment for a term not exceeding three years or both.[96] Provision is also made for offences committed by a body corporate.[97] Every contravention of any provision must be considered a separate contravention.[98]

(b) ***Motor vehicles***

Any offence under the European Communities (Motor Vehicle Type Approval) Regulations may be prosecuted summarily or on an indictment. A person guilty of an offence is liable:

- on summary conviction, to a fine not exceeding €5,000 or to imprisonment for a term not exceeding six months or both; and
- on conviction on indictment, to a fine not exceeding €100,000 or imprisonment for a term not exceeding 12 months or both.[99]

Provision is also made for offences by bodies corporate.[100]

(c) ***Medicines***

Breach of the manufacturing, marketing and wholesale regulations is an offence under the IMB Act, resulting:

- on summary conviction, in a fine up to €2,000 or imprisonment up to one year or both; and
- on conviction or indictment for a first offence, in a fine up to €120,000 or imprisonment for up to 10 years or both, and for a subsequent offence in a fine up to €300,000 or imprisonment for up to 10 years or both.

Provision is also made for offences by bodies corporate.

94 Regulations 15 and 16 of the European Communities (General Product Safety) Regulations
95 Regulation 21 of the European Communities (General Product Safety) Regulations.
96 Section 25(3) of the Food Law Regulations.
97 Section 23, 2007 General Food Law Regulations.
98 Section 25(1) and (2), 2007 General Food Law Regulations.
99 Section 25(4), EC Road Vehicle Type Approval Regulations 2009.
100 Section 25(5), EC Road Vehicle Type Approval Regulations 2009.

3.6 Multiple jurisdictions

Where a recall of vehicles has been commenced, the NSAI must communicate the proposed measures to the authority and the other member states without delay. The competent authorities must ensure that the measures are effectively implemented in their respective territories.[101] In addition, the NSAI must inform all member states of any measures they have taken under Regulation 14.[102]

(a) ***General products***

See RAPEX.

(b) ***Food.***

See RAFFS.

(c) ***Medicine***

The IMB may inform other competent authorities of any quality defect issues.

4. Product liability

The following is a summary of the main issues to be considered (before a recall or otherwise) when a product causes injury or damage. It is not a comprehensive guide to the law on product liability.

4.1 Sources of liability

(a) ***Statute***

Until 1991, liability for defective products was governed by common law and most actions for liability were grounded in negligence. A statutory strict liability regime was introduced by the Liability for Defective Products Act 1991.

The act implements the EU Product Liability Directive (85/374/EEC). The act supplements, rather than replaces, the pre-existing remedies in tort and contract, described below. The basic principle of liability under the act is that the producer will be liable in tort for damage caused wholly or partly by a defect in its product.[103] Although there are various potential defences, liability is otherwise strict, based not on wrongful conduct by the producer, but on proof that a defect in the product caused damage to the injured party. The act covers dangerous defective products only; products which are safe, but of poor quality are not covered.

A product is defective if it fails to provide the safety which a person is entitled to expect, taking all circumstances into account,[104] including:

- the presentation of the product;
- the use to which it may be expected that the product would be put; and
- the time when the product was put into circulation.

---

101 Regulation 18, EC Road Vehicle Type Approval Regulations 2009.
102 Regulation 14(11)(a), EC Road Vehicle Type Approval Regulations 2009.
103 Section 2(1) of the Liability for Defective Products Act.
104 Section 5 of the Liability for Defective Products Act.

In addition, sellers of products have contractual obligations to buyers under the Sale of Goods Acts 1893 and 1980. Strict liability applies in respect of these acts where goods are not of merchantable quality and liability is not dependent on injury/damage being caused to the consumer. In particular, the 1980 act operates to add an implied condition into contracts for the sale of goods – that they are of merchantable quality where a seller sells them in the course of its business. Goods are of merchantable quality if they are fit for the purpose or purposes for which goods of that kind are commonly bought and as durable as could reasonably be expected, having regard to any description applied to them.[105]

In the case of a contract for the sale of goods, any term exempting all or any of the provisions of Section 10 of the 1980 act is void where the buyer deals as a consumer[106] and in any other case will not be enforceable unless it can be shown that it is fair and reasonable. Criminal sanctions are also imposed by the 1893 act and the 1980 act.[107]

(b) *Tort*

In addition to statutory obligations, a general common law duty of care applies in Ireland and a manufacturer of a product owes a duty of care to all of those who may be foreseeably injured or damaged by the product. The injured party must prove, among other things, that there was a breach of that duty of care, and that a causal relationship exists between the breach of duty and the damage caused. Unlike liability under the Liability for Defective Products Act, liability in tort is fault based. Tortious liability can be limited using a limitation or exclusion clause. If there is an intention to limit or exclude liability for negligence, this should be expressly referred to in the clause as the courts may be reluctant to limit liability for negligence unless there are express words confirming that that was the parties' intention.

4.2 Potential defendants

(a) *Statute*

Under the Liability for Defective Products Act, the 'producer' is generally the manufacturer, but may include a person that has imported the product into the member state from a place outside the European Union, or a person that has held itself out to be the producer of the product.[108] Further, Section 2(3) of the act states that when a producer cannot be identified, then any person that supplied the product (whether to the person who suffered the damage, to the producer of any product in which the product is comprised or to any other person) will be liable as the producer. A producer can rely on statutory defences under the act.[109]

---

105 Section 10 of the 1980 act inserting new Section 14 into the 1893 act.

106 For a definition of 'dealing as a consumer' see Section 3 of the Sale of Goods Act 1980.

107 For example, Section 47(3) of the Sale of Goods Act 1980 states that a person who, not having reasonable cause to believe there is a right to payment, in the course of any business makes a demand for payment or asserts a present or prospective right to payment for what he knows are unsolicited goods sent to another person with a view to his acquiring them, must be guilty of an offence. See also Sections 6 and 7 of the act for penalties and prosecution of offences.

108 Section 2(2) of the Liability for Defective Products Act

109 Section 6 of the Liability for Defective Products Act.

Under the European Communities (General Product Safety) Regulations, both producers and distributors (generally suppliers and retailers) may be criminally liable. A 'producer' includes:[110]

- the manufacturer of a product;
- the manufacturer's representative, when the manufacturer is not established in the European Union;
- in certain circumstances, the importer; or
- other designated persons in the supply chain, insofar as their activities may affect the safety properties of a product placed on the market. These include producers and those that hold themselves out to be producers in certain circumstances.

A distributor can be any professional in the supply chain, whose activity does not affect the safety properties of the product.[111]

(b) Tort

In practice, very remote parties are often joined to actions in tort as, according to tort law, anyone that owes a duty of care towards the injured individual – such as a manufacturer, shop owner or other retailer, supplier, installer or importer.

(c) Contract

Under Irish contract law, the seller has a contractual responsibility to a buyer that goods are not defective under the Sale of Goods Acts 1893 and 1980. A 'seller' is a person that sells or agrees to sell goods. However, the principle of privity of contract applies, which makes it difficult for an injured party to sue the manufacturer of a product in contract, since the injured party's contract will probably be with the retailer of the product.

4.3 Class actions

There is no mechanism for class actions in Ireland. Irish law provides for representative actions, which can arise when numerous persons have the same interest.[112] In practice, multi-party litigation in Ireland is generally run not by representative action procedure, but by test cases (although subsequent plaintiffs and defendants would not necessarily be bound by the 'test' case).

A plaintiff may apply to court to unite in the same action several causes of action if they can be conveniently disposed of together by the court and if they meet certain limited criteria.[113] In addition, causes or matters pending in the High Court may be consolidated by order of the court on the application of any party.[114]

---

110 Section 2(1) of the European Communities (General Product Safety) Regulations.

111 Section 2(1) of the European Communities (General Product Safety) Regulations.

112 Order 15, Rule 9 of the Rules of the Superior Courts states: "Where there are numerous persons having the same interest in one cause or matter, one or more of such persons may sue or be sued, or may be authorised by the Court to defend, in such cause or matter, on behalf, or for the benefit, of all persons so interested."

113 Order 18, Rule 1 of the Rules of the Superior Court.

114 Order 49, Rule 6 of the Rules of the Superior Court.

The Irish Law Reform Commission's report on multi-party litigation[115] recommended the adoption of an opt-in class action procedure referred to as 'multi-party action' (MPA). This envisaged the nomination of a single legal representative on behalf of the MPA member, but the state has yet to amend the existing law.

It is the responsibility of a manufacturer to provide goods that are not defective or inherently dangerous in respect of their ordinary, non-negligent use. Manufacturers are obliged to take precautions against providing defective products to consumers which may cause injury. Products can be dangerous for a variety of reasons, but the dangers can be grouped into three general categories – design defects, quality of workmanship and inherent dangers.

If there is a breach of duty by the manufacturer or supplier, a consumer can choose to bring a claim under statute (if there is applicable legislation) or under common law. Statutory provisions usually give rise to strict liability. Under common law, however, a breach of duty can be quite broadly interpreted and liability does not automatically attach to a particular party. The causal connection must be sufficiently proximate to be legally recognised as grounding liability and the damage suffered must be of a type for which recovery is permitted. Failure to conform to the required standard of duty does not of itself give rise to a cause of compensatory action.

4.4 Causation

Under both common law and statute law, the plaintiff must prove a causal connection between the defendant's conduct and the plaintiff's injury or damage.[116] However, the plaintiff must show the existence of the link as a matter of probability only. In criminal matters, the prosecutor must prove its case "beyond a reasonable doubt" to establish an offence.

Proof of causation under common law is two-tiered. First, the plaintiff must establish cause in fact – that is, that as a matter of physical fact, the defendant can be said to have caused the plaintiff's damage. Second, the plaintiff must establish cause in law – that is, that as a matter of law, the court ought to hold the defendant responsible and liable to the plaintiff. The test of factual causation conventionally favoured by the common law courts is the 'but for' test – that is, but for the defendant's negligence, the plaintiff would not have suffered injury or loss.

Failure to warn cases raise a separate issue, however, in that a court is concerned with looking at the hypothetical impact that a non-existent event would have had, rather than the examination of actual events and their probable effects. The approach taken in these situations is generally objective or subjective. The objective approach entails consideration of what a reasonable person in the plaintiff's position would do if given the necessary warning; while the subjective approach entails consideration of what the particular party would probably have done. Sometimes the hypothetical inquiry may be disregarded altogether and a presumption that failure to warn was a cause may be assumed.

---

115 September 2005.

116 Except under the Liability for Defective Products Act, if the manufacturer relies on the state of the art defence, then the burden of proof rests with the manufacturer.

The courts have shown no preference with regard to the approach taken. In the UK case of *Hills v Potter*, it was held that there was uncertainty as to whether the test should be objective or subjective, and that in either case the plaintiff would fail. In the Irish case of *Walsh v Family Planning Services*, Judge Egan stated that he did not "consider it necessary that there should be proof by the plaintiff that had a proper warning been given to him, he would not have submitted to the original operation". This could be construed as support for the approach of disregarding the hypothetical inquiry.

4.5 Defences

At common law, the defences of contributory negligence and voluntary assumption of risk, if established, provide the defendant with complete protection. Contributory negligence arises where the plaintiff fails to exercise reasonable care and is considered to have partly caused his own injury. Voluntary assumption of risk is a defence based on consent, arising where the plaintiff is deemed to have accepted the legal responsibility for the risk which led to the injury, and such acceptance could be inferred from his words or conduct immediately prior to the injury.

Similarly, for a breach of contract, it is necessary to establish knowledge and intention on the part of the defendant regarding the existence and breach of the contract, respectively. Irish courts have held in *James McMahon Ltd v Dunne* that either actual or constructive knowledge of the existence of the contract will be sufficient – it is not necessary to know all the terms in detail. Insofar as intention is concerned, intention or recklessness will suffice to ground liability.

In actions for breach of statutory duty, careful consideration must be given to the statute in order to determine whether any such special provisions affect the liability of parties that breach their obligation. Courts are more reluctant to admit the defence of contributory negligence in respect of breach of statutory duties; it has been suggested that the reason for this is because full application of the defence would diminish the effectiveness of the underlying protective policies in the relevant legislation.

Under the Civil Liability Act 1961, damages are reduced if there is contributory negligence. If two or more persons are liable under the act for the same damage, they are jointly and severally liable to the injured person as concurrent wrongdoers.[117] Such claims should be asserted without delay.

4.6 Exclusion clauses

In Ireland, the European Communities (Unfair Terms in Consumer Contracts) Regulations 1995 restrict what may be validly inserted into a contract. For example, contract clauses excluding liability for death and injury are never permissible. Clauses excluding liability for negligence, defective or poor-quality goods are permitted only if reasonable. There is nothing to stop businesses from purporting to exclude liability, which may deter some claimants, but such clauses or notices would not survive challenge in court.

---

117 Sections 11 and 12 of the Civil Liability Act.

In interpreting exclusion clauses, the courts apply the principle of good faith in order to protect the insured from onerous or unusual contractual provisions. Where there is doubt about the meaning of a term, the interpretation most favourable to the consumer must prevail. This applies whether the policyholder is a consumer or not. If a term in the contract is found to be unfair, the remainder of the contract may still be legally binding on the consumer and the supplier of goods or services.

4.7 Remedies

The key heads of damages can be categorised as follows.

(a) *Compensatory damages*

The aim of compensatory damages is to compensate plaintiffs for the loss they have suffered, and to put them in the same position as if the act causing damage had not been committed. Compensatory damages can be sub-divided into:

- general damages, which cannot easily be quantified in monetary terms and are presumed to flow from the wrongdoing. Examples include injury, pain and suffering (including psychological damage); and
- special damages, which are the specifically quantifiable expenses that the claimant has incurred as a result of the defendant's act. Examples include loss of past and future income and medical fees.

(b) *Aggravated damages*

Aggravated damages are awarded where the claimant suffers further injury due to the manner in which the wrong was committed, the conduct of the defendant after commission of the wrong, or the defendant's conduct in the defence of its action, up to and including the trial.

(c) *Exemplary damages (punitive damages)*

Exemplary damages are punitive, not compulsory in nature. They do exist in Ireland, but are awarded only in exceptional circumstances. They are based on public policy and are awarded to make an example of the defendant based on the nature of the wrong, and to deter the public at large.[118]

(d) *Fatal injuries*

Dependants of the victim of a fatal accident have a limited right to compensation under Part IV of the Civil Liability Act. This is a separate right from the right to sue for injuries suffered. The dependants can pursue compensation for the loss,[119] injury, mental distress[120] and expenses arising out of the fatal injury to the relative.

---

118 The Irish Supreme Court reviewed the principles applicable when awarding punitive damages in *Shortt v Commissioner of an Garda Siochana* [2007] IESC 9 and affirmed that they are an appropriate punishment as a "deterrent generally to the arrogant use or abuse of power".

119 'Injury' is interpreted as financial loss, but not loss of society and other personal aspects of family relations.

120 The cap on compensation for mental distress is €25,394.

(e) Contributory negligence/concurrent wrongdoers

Under the Civil Liability Act, damages are reduced if there is contributory negligence. If two or more persons are liable under the act for the same damage, they are jointly and severally liable to the injured person as concurrent wrongdoers.[121] Such claims should be asserted without delay.

4.8 Procedure

Civil cases for product liability are heard by a judge, sitting without a jury.

In most cases, personal injury claims must first go through the Personal Injuries Assessment Board (PIAB), an independent body set up under the PIAB Act 2003, to assess the level of compensation payable to those who have suffered personal injuries. If the defendant notifies the PIAB that they will defend the claim on a legal basis, then the PIAB will issue the plaintiff with a release, which enables the plaintiff to issue legal proceedings.

Discovery of documents is exchanged after the pleadings have closed (ie, after the defendant delivers its defence). Discovery will be sought first on a voluntary basis;[122] if refused, either party can make an application to the court, or an application for further and better discovery if it is not happy with the discovery provided. Each side must disclose all documents relevant to the categories sought/ordered that are or have been in its power, possession or procurement, including those which may prejudice its own case. The term 'documents' is broadly interpreted, and includes all electronic documents such as emails or BlackBerry data.

Each party may appoint its own expert to assist in the preparation of the case and to prepare expert reports[123] and/or provide evidence at trial. Experts may be cross-examined and also questioned by the judge.

It is not unusual for product liability cases to last a number of years in Ireland, depending on factors such as the complexity of the issues, the volume of discovery and the number of interlocutory applications. The Irish Commercial Court can hear larger product liability cases if certain criteria are met (eg, if the issue arises out of a commercial dispute or the claim is over €1 million); however, the Commercial Court cannot hear personal injury claims. Cases in the Commercial Court are case managed, which normally results in expedited hearings.

First instance rulings in all civil cases may be appealed to a higher court, but appeals from the High Court to the Supreme Court can be made only on a point of law.

Under the European Communities (General Product Safety) Regulations, directions made by the NCA (regarding product recall or other matters) can be appealed to the circuit court within 21 days of receipt. In this regard, appeals regarding a decision of the circuit court to the High Court can be made only on questions of law.

---

121 Sections 11 and 12 of the Civil Liability Act.

122 Agreement to provide documents on a voluntary basis equates to a court order and discovery must be still be made in accordance with the Rules of the Superior Court.

123 In High Court personal injury cases there is an obligation on parties to exchange all written expert reports before trial. In all other cases, the parties can decide whether to exchange expert reports voluntarily.

4.9 Funding

Legal aid is given to a litigant in Ireland only in limited circumstances and in practice is generally available only for family law or criminal matters.

Some forms of third-party litigation funding would violate the Irish common law rule against champerty.[124] It is impermissible to charge contingency fees in Ireland, with the exception of some debt collection matters. However, it is permissible to take on a case on a 'no win, no fee' basis.

Depending on the value of the case, an agreement may be put in place which provides for a success fee whereby an additional amount is payable for the legal services, over and above the amount which would normally be payable if there were no agreement, in specified circumstances (usually if the client wins the case). A success fee must be expressed as a percentage uplift on the amount which would be payable if there was no agreement, and the maximum uplift is 100%.

4.10 Costs

The costs of and incidental to proceedings are at the discretion of the judge and generally follow the event, unless the court orders otherwise. A successful party can generally recover most, but not all of its legal fees and expenses from the unsuccessful party, including solicitor fees, court fees and incidental expenses necessarily incurred in the prosecution or defence of the action. In reality, a successful party never recovers 100% of its costs, as these are generally awarded on a 'party and party' basis.[125]

4.11 Limitation periods

(a) *Tortious liability*

Under Irish law, a plaintiff generally has six years from the date on which the cause of action accrued to institute proceedings.[126] However, the time limit is two years for actions for personal injury, although this period runs only from the later of:

- the date of accrual of the action; or
- the date on which the injured party became aware of the existence of the cause of action.

The limitation periods are extended where the claimant was a child at the time the cause of action arose.[127]

Different limitation periods apply to contribution claims as between concurrent wrongdoers, and it is important that any such claims be asserted promptly by one defendant against another potential party.[128]

---

124 That is to say aiding a claimant to litigate without good cause and taking a share of the profits. An exemption relates to recovery of a debt or a liquidated demand. The rule was upheld in the 1991 High Court case of *McElroy v Flynn*.

125 As opposed to on a solicitor and client basis, which are generally on a more generous scale.

126 Generally the date the period runs from is the date on which the cause of action is complete, which may be later than the date of the wrongful act if the initial loss only arose later.

127 Minors are allowed three years from the date of their majority (ie, 18 years).

(b) ***Breach of contract***

Under Irish law, a time limit of six years applies from the date of the accrual of the cause of action (ie, the date on which the breach of contract occurred). Any proceedings must be issued within this period.

(c) ***Liability for Defect of Products Act***

Under Section 7(1) of the Liability for Defective Products Act, a limitation period of three years applies to proceedings for the recovery of damages under the act. This period runs from the date on which the plaintiff became aware, or should reasonably have become aware, of the damage, the defect and the identity of the producer. Section 7(2)(a) provides for a 'longstop' provision, which extinguishes the rights conferred on the injured party pursuant to the act on the expiry of 10 years from the date on which the producer put into circulation the actual product which caused the damage, unless the injured person has instituted proceedings against the producer in the meantime.

The courts do not have discretion to disapply statutorily imposed time limits.

Section 71(1) of the Statute of Limitations 1957 extends the limitation period where there has been concealment or fraud – the limitation period does not begin to run until the plaintiff has discovered the fraud or could, with reasonable diligence, have discovered it.

The courts have general discretion to strike out proceedings where there has been an inordinate or inexcusable delay by the plaintiff and the defendant has suffered prejudice.

4.12 Trends

(a) ***Pro-consumerism***

In recent years there appears to be greater awareness among consumers of their rights, perhaps due in part to the current economic climate. The Consumer Protection Act 2007 provided for the transposition of the EU Unfair Commercial Practices Directive (2005/29/EC) into Irish law. It also established the National Consumer Agency and defines its functions and enforcement options. The NCA 'polices' consumer rights. The aim of the act is to protect consumers against unfair, misleading or aggressive commercial practices, and it outlaws over 30 different practices, including pyramid selling and making false claims about products or services.

The act provides for civil[129] and criminal[130] proceedings. It allows a consumer who is aggrieved by a prohibited act or practice to have a right of action for relief by way of damages, including exemplary damages, against any trader that commits or engages in the prohibited act or practice or, if the trader is a body corporate, any director, manager,

---

128 Section 31 of the Civil Liability Act effectively allows a claim for contribution to be brought either within the limitation period for the main action or within two years of determination of liability in the main action (or payment of damages to the injured party), whichever is the greater. There is also an obligation created by Section 27 to bring a claim for contribution as soon as is reasonably possible, and therefore any such claims must be asserted promptly against another potential party.

129 Chapter 2, 2007 Act.

130 Chapter 4, 2007 Act.

secretary or other officer of the trader, or a person who purported to act in that capacity who authorised or consented to the doing of the prohibited act or practice.[131]

Some of the main features of the act are as follows:

- Section 55 prohibits a trader from representing that a product can cure an illness, dysfunction or malformation that it cannot.
- Section 68 states that if the truth of a factual claim in a representation is in issue, then the representation must be presumed to be untrue unless the trader that made the representation establishes that it is true on the balance of probabilities. This provision reverses the usual burden of proof and requires a trader to substantiate representations.
- Section 86 requires the National Consumer Agency (NCA) to maintain a Consumer Protection List with details of traders against which enforcement actions have been taken. The NCA publishes this list periodically on the website www.consumerconnect.ie. The list details enforcement actions taken against businesses for breaches of consumer legislation.

From August 2010 to January 2011, the NCA took 58 enforcement actions against businesses for breaches relating to misleading pricing or failure to display prices.

The NCA's approach can further be seen in its consumer-focused websites, such as www.itsyourmoney.ie and www.consumerproperty.ie.

5 Product insurance

In Ireland, product liability insurance is often included as an extension of public liability insurance and accordingly, the policies are generally known as 'public and product liability' policies. The nature and extent of those policies varies depending on the insurance provider and the nature of the insured's business.

Irish law does not provide a statutory definition of an 'insurance contract'; nor does it define the elements required for the formation of such a contract. Instead, the general principles of contract law apply, coupled with the duty of good faith, which obliges both parties to disclose all facts which are material to the formation of the contract.

In Ireland, due in part to a keen desire on the part of insurers to avoid adverse publicity, arbitration clauses are commonly included in insurance policies and arbitration is availed of in preference to litigation when disputes arise. If an insurer initiates legal proceedings, it is often with the aim of reaching a settlement. Both of these factors have led to a lack of development of Irish precedent in the area of product insurance law and indeed insurance law generally.

Product insurance can be offered:

- on a 'claims made' basis, whereby claims must be notified to the insurer during the life of the policy or during a specified timeframe thereafter; or
- on an 'occurrence' basis, whereby the insured event occurs while the policy is in force but the claim itself is maintained after the period of insurance has expired.

131 Section 74(2), 2007 Act.

The latter wording can cause difficulties for insurers, as claims can be made many years after the occurrence of an insured event. However, the former wording is less satisfactory for the insured and means that the insured will need to implement continuous and comprehensive cover so that insurers in subsequent years will provide indemnity in respect of claims arising from goods put into circulation in past years.

An insured will be required to disclose, at the time of policy inception or renewal, all issues which have given rise to a claim or which may give rise to a claim. Disclosing potential claims can be difficult for an insured and an inadvertent misrepresentation or non-disclosure in this regard could result in the policy being avoided. Furthermore, the insurer will generally include a 'basis of contract' clause within a proposal form, which acts as a declaration on the part of the insured warranting the truth and accuracy of statements made. These clauses provide a method by which an insurer can convert representations into warranties which then become the basis of the contract between the parties. The duty of disclosure is therefore made a contractual obligation, which, if breached, means that the contract can be avoided by the insurer.

Finally, in relation to product liability insurance, an insured should be aware of any condition in a policy for subcontractors engaged by them to maintain a certain level of liability insurance themselves.

5.1 Coverage

Manufacturers, distributors and retailers are increasingly aware of the risk of liabilities and costs associated with defective products. A company may require some form of products insurance in various situations, including for a product recall or a product failing to carry out its intended function on a large scale.

(a) Product recall

The implementation of a product recall can have catastrophic effects on a business, in terms of both financial cost and reputational damage. Product recall insurance can be of significant financial benefit. Depending on the nature of the business, careful consideration must be given to whether product recall insurance is likely to be necessary and the nature and level of cover required.

A product recall may be effected on a compulsory[132] or a voluntary basis. Increasing regulation has led to a rise in the number of recalls, as companies are obliged to comply with stricter legislative requirements. In the event of a product safety issue arising, the proportionality of a voluntary recall should be assessed on the basis of a full technical risk assessment.

(b) Contaminated products

Some companies use contaminated products insurance to mitigate against the risks and costs associated with the potential contamination of their product. Such insurance can cover accidental and/or deliberate contamination. Obviously, certain

---

132 Section 9(1)(f) of the European Communities (General Product Safety) Regulations.

products are more susceptible to contamination than others – notably, products in the food, beverage and pharmaceutical industries. Any product recall, but particularly one based on contamination, can be damaging to a company's brand. Considerable costs can be incurred in recalling, disposing of and replacing the contaminated product, not to mention the cost of rebuilding brand confidence.

(c) ***Product liability***

Product liability can arise under statute, both Irish and European, and in tort and in contract. This is dealt with in more detail below. In practice, product liability claims will often be pleaded under each of these heads. Manufacturers of products, distributors and retailers carry the risk of product liability and accordingly may wish to take out product liability insurance as a means of attempting to eliminate or manage this risk.

(d) ***Financial loss***

In the main, product liability policies focus on damage caused to persons or property as a result of an insured's defective product and do not generally indemnify against pure economic loss which is not consequential upon that damage. It may be possible, however, to extend a product liability insurance policy to provide cover in respect of financial loss sustained by third parties. Financial loss insurance is intended to provide cover in respect of legal liability for pecuniary loss sustained by a third party where there has been no bodily injury to that third party or loss or damage to their property.

(e) ***Product guarantee***

Product guarantee insurance, referred to in greater detail below, is intended to indemnify against an insured's legal liability arising from a product failing to carry out its intended purpose. Sellers of products have contractual obligations to purchasers under the Sale of Goods Acts 1893 and 1980, discussed above. Furthermore, the European Communities (Certain Aspects of the Sale of Consumer Goods and Associated Guarantees) Regulations 2003, which implemented EU Directive 1999/44/EC in Ireland, state that consumer goods delivered under a contract of sale to the consumer must conform with that contract.[133] A number of options are available in the event that the goods are not in conformity with the contract such as, in certain circumstances, having the product replaced or repaired, having the price reduced or having the contract rescinded.[134] This means that a seller of goods is liable to a consumer for any lack of conformity. The cost of removing, repairing and replacing products can be significant, especially if it needs to take place on a large scale, and some companies opt to take out product guarantee insurance.

---

133 Section 5(1) of the European Communities (Certain Aspects of the Sale of Consumer Goods and Associated Guarantees) Regulations.

134 Section 7(2) of the European Communities (Certain Aspects of the Sale of Consumer Goods and Associated Guarantees) Regulations.

5.2 Product recall insurance

As set out below, the level of product recall insurance available, if any, tends to be industry and product specific. Standard product liability insurance policies do not generally cover the costs of a product recall. If product recall insurance is required, a company should, before purchasing such insurance, undertake a careful analysis of the nature of its business and any potential risk exposures in order to customise its product recall insurance policy as appropriate.

(a) Insuring provisions

Trigger: Coverage under a product recall insurance policy will depend on the policy wording, but might typically be triggered upon the recall of a product caused by a defect in the product, or upon malicious product tampering or product extortion (threatening to damage, destroy or to contaminate a product with a view to eliciting a ransom from an insured). The wording of the triggers in the policy should be examined so that an insured is satisfied that the scope of the policy is adequate to protect against risks which the company faces. One limitation in product recall policies is a clause which states that cover is operative only in respect of actual or imminent danger of injury or damage as a result of the use of the product. This type of clause could preclude recovery by an insured in respect of a precautionary recall undertaken where such actual or imminent danger has not yet been demonstrated.

Insured losses: First-party expenses of a product recall are those direct expenses which an insured faces as a result of a product recall. The cost of a product recall will depend upon the circumstances, such as the type and number of products to be recalled.

Expenses attributable to a product recall can further include:

- business interruption costs;
- costs associated with notifying customers of the recall;
- warehousing and transportation costs;
- disposal costs;
- costs associated with repair, replacement and refunds;
- consultancy and advisory costs; and
- costs of additional personnel required to manage the recall.

An insured may also incur costs in respect of brand rehabilitation – that is, the cost of rebuilding consumer confidence in the brand after a product recall has taken place. Standard recall policies may not cover all of these costs; an insured should thus determine which costs ought to be covered under a product recall insurance policy, taking into consideration the nature of its business, and tailor that policy according to its specific needs if possible

Even before product liability issues arise, many companies will have taken the time and incurred the expense of designing an early warning and a product recall system. Advance planning and periodic reviews can be cost effective for a company. If a product safety issue does arise, a company may incur the expense of assembling a crisis management team, conducting a detailed investigation of the facts, securing relevant evidence, dealing with public and media queries and dealing with insurers and/or legal advisers. A risk assessment will generally be conducted in order to determine the appropriate corrective action in the circumstances. Depending on the wording of the product recall policy, many of these expenses can be covered as pre-recall expenses.

If a product recall could cause loss of income or damage to the reputation of third parties, a company may also need to consider whether specific third-party liability coverage is required. This type of cover may, for instance, be of particular interest to manufacturers of component parts or ingredients. Third-party recall insurance can cover damages to third parties sustained as a result of the recall of the insured's product and may relate to:

- the expense of recalling products which incorporate the insured's product;
- the cost of repairing or replacing such products;
- business interruption costs suffered by third parties; and
- the cost of sourcing substitute products.

Some insurance companies also offer an endorsement to their product recall policies to provide coverage in respect of impaired property. Such cover is intended to indemnify the insured in the event that the insured's property is incorporated into another company's product and causes that product to malfunction or become less useful. This can be useful for companies involved in the supply of ingredients or component parts.

Defence costs: Another issue to consider in relation to product recall insurance is cover in respect of the cost of defending proceedings which may be brought against an insured as a result of the defective product, or in respect of the legal costs which may be recoverable at law by any claimant. As mentioned above, in Ireland, product liability insurance is often included as an extension of public liability insurance. Public liability insurance policies may include cover for any legal costs associated with defending claims against the business. Although an insured is often covered for reasonable and necessary fees and expenses incurred, with the prior written consent of the insurer, an insured should be mindful of whether there are any exceptions to the type of costs recoverable, such as fines imposed by a court or the jurisdictions covered.

Related to this issue is the extent to which an insured will be able to control any ensuing litigation. Many policies which indemnify against defence costs associated with proceedings provide that the insurer will take over the defence of those proceedings. This can be particularly important where the insured and the insurer's interests are not fully aligned. In light of the above, an insured may wish to consider the possibility of having named lawyers written into the policy to handle claims.

(b) ***Exclusions***

The exclusions in product recall insurance vary, but examples of typical exclusions include the following:

- property belonging to, or in the custody of, the insured;

- property outside the jurisdictional scope of the policy;
- liability assumed by the insured by way of contact or agreement, which would not necessarily attach to the insured;
- circumstances where the insurer can show (on the balance of probabilities) that the insured had knowledge of a defect or likely defect in the product, and failed to take corrective action (proving a state of knowledge can be a difficult task, however);
- recalls due to copyright, trademark or other IP infringements;
- civil or criminal fines or aggravated, punitive or exemplary damages;
- intentional violation by the insured of governmental or regulatory requirements; and
- liability arising from an error or inadequacy in instruction advice accompanying a product, or in respect of design of the product.

If the insurer seeks to rely on an exclusion clause, it is for the insurer to show that the clause was incorporated into the insurance contract. In interpreting exclusion clauses, the courts apply the principle of good faith in order to protect the insured from onerous or unusual contractual provisions. This applies whether the policyholder is a consumer or not. Further, the construction of exclusion clauses by the courts can be influenced by the nature of the insurance policy, and in particular, the purpose of the policyholder in taking out the policy, as was noted by the High Court of England and Wales in *Amey Properties v Cornhill Insurance plc*.

In construing insurance policies, the courts strictly apply the *contra proferentem* rule (ie, an ambiguous term will be construed against the party that included it). This rule received consideration in the insurance context in the Irish case of *Rohan Construction Ltd v Insurance Corporation of Ireland Ltd*, in which the High Court stated, in the context of construing an insurance policy, that an ambiguous term will be construed in favour of the party that did not draft it – which in most cases is the insured. The strict application of the *contra proferentem* rule in insurance cases was also emphasised in *Fitton v Accidental Insurance Co*, where the court held that it is extremely important, with reference to insurance, that the insured be protected where any ambiguity arises on the face of the policy.

(c) *Conditions*

Insurers in the Irish market tend to have standard policy conditions for each product which accord to industry practice. An insured must take care that any notifications to the insurer under a policy are made in strict adherence with the terms of that policy and are carried out in a timely fashion. The insurance policy may also contain conditions stating that the insured will:

- assist and cooperate with the insurer in all matters relating to the policy;
- keep the existence of the policy confidential;
- exercise due care to avoid any insured events occurring;
- mitigate any loss arising; and
- not conceal, misrepresent or fail to disclose any material fact which could have a bearing on the policy.

Furthermore, and specifically in relation to product recall matters, an insured may be required to contact a hotline operated by the insurer, to explain the nature of the issue which has arisen and to seek advice from particular consultants to determine the initial steps to be taken on the occurrence of an insured event. This may or may not be a condition of the insurance policy.

5.3 Contaminated products insurance

Product contamination insurance, which is often linked to product recall insurance, is typically taken out by food, beverage or pharmaceutical companies. Product contamination can be either accidental or deliberate (sometimes known as malicious product tampering), but either way such contamination can have a disastrous effect on a company's brand and its finances.

(a) *Insuring provisions*

Coverage will generally be available on a product recall consequent upon the accidental contamination of a product, the deliberate contamination of a product, or depending on the policy, product extortion. Product contamination insurance may cover pre-recall costs and recall costs such as business interruption costs, replacement costs, rehabilitation costs, disposal costs and consultants' costs.

(b) *Exclusions*

Please refer to the exclusions mentioned in relation to product recall insurance above. Particular exclusions in a product contamination insurance policy might also include contamination occurring:

- subsequent to an insured being made aware of a defect in the manufacture of a product, or of circumstances likely to cause such a defect, where it fails to take corrective action;
- due to natural deterioration, decomposition or transformation of a product; or
- due to failure by a party to comply with instructions regarding the appropriate storage, consumption or use of a product.

(c) *Conditions*

Please refer to the conditions mentioned in relation to product recall insurance above. A condition requiring an insured to exercise due care or to undertake reasonable precautions with a view to guarding against potential insured events is likely to be important in a product contamination insurance policy.

5.4 Product liability insurance

(a) *Insuring provisions*

Product liability insurance in Ireland is generally treated as an extension of public liability insurance. The scope of product liability insurance will vary depending on factors such as the nature of the relevant industry and jurisdiction, but these policies generally indemnify against "all sums which the insured must become legally liable to pay as compensation for accidental bodily injury or illness to any person or accidental damage to property, occurring during the period of the policy and caused by any defect in goods sold, supplied or repaired by the insured". Depending on the role of the insured within a product supply chain, the wording of a policy may need to be tailored appropriately. Furthermore, many policies will indemnify the insured only in respect of compensation which it is obliged to pay for accidental bodily injury or accidental damage to property, and can exclude liability for deliberate or intentional acts on the part of the insured.

(b) Exclusions

A purchaser of product liability insurance should be mindful of some of the typical exclusions under such a policy, although the number and extent of exclusions will vary depending on the policy. First and foremost, an insured should be aware that a standard product liability insurance policy will generally not cover the cost of repairing, replacing or recalling defective goods. There may also be a product efficacy exclusion, whereby the insurer will not indemnify against liabilities which arise due to the failure of a product to carry out its intended purpose. Furthermore, a product liability insurance policy will generally not indemnify the insured for liability arising due to any error or inadequacy in instruction advice, for professional services, or for design, plans or specifications which accompany a product. These losses may or may not be covered by an insured's professional indemnity insurance policy. Damage to the defective product itself may not be covered and many policies will not cover liability in respect of aviation products. Please also refer to the exclusions discussed above in relation to product recall insurance.

5.5 Financial loss insurance

(a) Insuring provisions

Traditionally, insurers have been reluctant to provide cover for pure financial loss – that is, loss which does not result from injury or damage – and many product liability insurance policies do not afford cover in respect of liability for pure economic loss. However, some insurers are now willing to offer extensions to their product liability insurance policies to cover certain pure financial losses sustained by third parties that do not flow from injury or damage caused by a defective product – albeit that coverage of this nature is generally limited in scope.

(b) Exclusions

Please refer to the exclusions referred to above in the context of product recall and product liability insurance. Some potential exclusions in the context of financial loss insurance might include:

- liability arising out of advice, design or specifications relating to a product;
- liability arising as a result of breach of contract or breach of IP rights on the part of the insured; and
- the cost of removing, rectifying and replacing defective products.

(c) ***Conditions***

Please refer to the conditions referred to above in the context of product recall and product liability insurance. In relation to financial loss insurance, an insured should be mindful of gathering and retaining the relevant supporting documents to evidence the financial losses suffered by a third party for which it is legally liable. Such supporting documentation can minimise the potential for challenge from an insurer. The claims cooperation condition is likely to be particularly important in a financial loss insurance policy, as is any obligation on the insured to minimise the loss suffered.

5.6 Product guarantee insurance

(a) ***Insuring provisions***

Product guarantee insurance provides cover in respect of the insured's legal liability arising from a product's failure to perform according to its intended purpose. Product liability policies generally exclude this kind of liability and accordingly a company may require that specific product guarantee insurance be indemnified. Such insurance may cover the costs incurred due to the transportation, repair, alteration, treatment or replacement of products which do not carry out the function for which they were manufactured, designed, supplied, sold, installed, repaired or delivered. It is not a prerequisite of cover that injury or damage have actually occurred due to the defective product, or that there be a risk of such injury or damage.

(b) ***Exclusions***

Particular exclusions in product guarantee insurance policies might include:

- liability arising due to deliberate acts or omissions by the insured which could reasonably be expected to cause the damage that is the subject of the claim;
- liability in respect of experimental products or prototypes; or
- liability arising from an error or inadequacy in instructions accompanying a product.

(c) ***Conditions***

Many insurance policies will contain a reasonable precautions condition obliging an insured to take all reasonable measures to guard against insured losses or damage occurring. Such a condition is important in the context of product guarantee insurance, and the insured should conduct adequate checks on a product before it is released.

5.7 General principles

An insured should be mindful of the general principles of insurance when considering its product liability insurance policies, or any extensions to those policies. For example, an insured may wish to consider:

- how and when premiums are to be paid;
- whether premiums can be adjusted;

- the extent to which it can treat separate losses as a single loss for the purpose of a deductible required under the policy;
- what constitutes notice of a claim to the insurer;
- the timeframes for such notification;
- the claims procedure;
- its duty to cooperate with the insurer;
- the existence of any rules on contribution;
- the circumstances under which the policy can be cancelled or avoided; and
- the jurisdiction governing the policy and applicable choice of law.

The exclusions contained within any insurance policy should be carefully considered by both the insurer and the insured. For example, fraud and dishonesty will not be covered and insurance policies will generally contain a reasonable precautions or due care condition clause as referred to above. Furthermore, the interpretation of the policy document can become contentious and accordingly all interested parties should be comfortable with how the wording of the policy document is to be determined, including what documents are to be considered for the purpose of interpreting the policy.

All parties should be aware of the effect of a breach of the policy – whether it is a breach of a warranty or a condition. Warranties necessitate strict compliance and, subject to any express provision in the policy, breach of a warranty will enable an insurer to avoid liability as from the date of breach (but without prejudice to any liability incurred prior to the breach). Insurers generally require applicants to warrant that statements made on their proposal form are true and form part of the basis of the insurance contract.

The effect of the breach of a condition will depend on the nature of the condition breached. If it goes to the root of the contract, the insurer may be in a position to terminate the policy; whereas if the breach is trivial in nature, an insurer will generally be required to pay the claim, but may be able to cross-claim for damages where it can prove loss.

In practice, an insurer may seek to defeat a claim under a contract of insurance based on non-disclosure, misrepresentation, fraud or illegality of any act on the part of the insured. Conversely, an insured should ensure strict compliance with the policy conditions and collate the necessary supporting documentation in support of its claim to minimise the prospect of a challenge by the insurer and to make sure that a claim can be processed as promptly and efficiently as possible.

Japan

Kazuhiro Kobayashi
Yugo Komori
Kagenori Sako
Oh-Ebashi LPC & Partners

1. Product recall

1.1 What is a product recall?

There is no single meaning of a 'product recall' in Japan. In a narrow sense, a product recall is the calling in of products from consumers to replace components or to refund the purchase price. On the other hand, in a broader sense, a product recall could refer to all actions which aim to reduce the risk of accidents and prevent any spread of potential dangers. The most common use in Japan is the latter.

For instance, the recall of consumer products under the Consumer Product Safety Act[1] means:[2]

- stopping the manufacturing, distribution and sales of products, or recalling them from the market;
- informing consumers about the risks relating to the products;
- supplying consumers with or reminding them about information on operating precautions, etc., to avoid similar accidents; and
- replacing, repairing or picking up the products from consumers.

It is also important to note that there are two kinds of product recalls in this broader sense. One refers to measures ordered by regulatory authorities, and the other one to voluntary actions by companies. In Japan, product recalls are usually voluntary. It is rare for regulatory authorities to order companies to recall products.

(a) *Legislative background*

Regulating product accidents is a fairly old problem. The Consumer Product Safety Act was enacted in 1973. It has a general consumer protection function: to regulate the manufacture and sale of specified products and to foster voluntary activities by private businesses to ensure the safety of consumer products in order to prevent any

---

1 Act 31/1973.
2 The *Recall Handbook for Consumer Products 2010* issued by the Ministry of Economy, Trade and Industry. This handbook was first published in 2002, and was revised in 2007 and 2010.
3 The Consumer Product Safety Act has been amended, so the purpose of the act is "to regulate the manufacture and sale of specified products, to promote proper maintenance of specified maintenance products and to take measures, such as collecting and providing information regarding product accidents, thereby protecting the interests of general consumers, in order to prevent any danger caused by consumer products to the lives or person of general consumers".
4 Act 85/1994.

danger caused by the products to the lives or person of general consumers.[3] The Product Liability Act[4] described under 'product liability' below was enacted in 1994. This act protects any victim of an injury to life, body, or property, which was caused by a defect in a product by placing liability on the manufacturer for damages where incidents occur.

Despite such regulations, some incidents have occurred recently in Japan, for example, accidents involving instantaneous water heaters, BSE problems, and a scam involving disguising imported beef as domestic beef, etc. This has heightened awareness of the importance of consumer safety. In 2004, the Consumer Basic Act[5] was enacted and in 2005, the Consumer Basic Plan formulated under that act. The plan sets out to expand the recall system.

In response, the Consumer Product Safety Act was revised in 2006 and regulations concerning the recall system strengthened. *The Recall Handbook for Consumer Products 2007* was published in 2007 and revised in 2010 (footnote 2). The Consumer Commission also proposed revising the recall system for cars. On July 1 2011, notices for the system of recalling cars, namely, *Points for Handling Written Reports, etc, of a Recall* and *Guidelines for a Recall* were revised.

Despite these regulations the definitions of 'product risk' and 'product safety' remain unclear in Japan. For example, under the Product Liability Act, a 'defect' is defined as "a lack of safety that the product ordinarily should provide, taking into account the nature of the product, the ordinarily foreseeable manner of use of the product, the time when the manufacturer, etc., delivered the product, and other circumstances concerning the product", but the meaning of "the safety that the product ordinarily should provide" is left open to interpretation.

Similarly, there are no unified standards concerning quality of products, although individual laws and various organisations have formulated some standards and guidelines (eg, JIS by the Japan Industry Standards Committee) which should be referred to if considering a product recall.

2. Obligations of producers and distributors

2.1 Source of duties

The basic sources of the duty to conduct a product recall in Japan are the statutes. There is no specific obligation to conduct a product recall under tort or contract laws except where the parties have specifically agreed to do so.

The legislation can be divided into two groups: the Consumer Product Safety Act, and 'other'. The Consumer Product Safety Act applies widely to general consumer products including toys. Under this act, a 'consumer product' means any product to be supplied mainly for use by general consumers for their routine everyday activities, with the exception of those products listed in an appended table in the law (Article 2(1)). Products excluded from 'consumer products' under the Consumer Product

---

5 Act 70/2004. The act is the partial amendment to the Consumer Protection Basic Act (Act 78/1968).
6 Act 185/1951.
7 Act 145/1960.
8 Act 233/1947.

Safety Act, such as cars, medicines and food, are regulated by individual laws, such as the Road Trucking Vehicle Act,[6] the Pharmaceutical Affairs Act[7] and the Food Sanitation Act[8] (this act also regulates toys that are likely to harm the health of infants who come into contact with them).

In addition, there are some other sector-specific laws, such as the Electrical Appliances and Materials Safety Act[9] (includes electric toys) and the Gas Business Act[10] for gas equipment, etc. In such cases both the Consumer Product Safety Act and the specified law will apply to consumer products.

2.2 Pre-market obligations

There are many and various pre-market obligations, but the main ones are licences to be obtained or notifications to be given by businesses and the duty to conform to technical standards and labelling requirements. There are also some traceability obligations.

(a) Consumer Product Safety Act[11]

Under this act, products are classified into four groups:

- 'consumer products' – that is, products supplied mainly for the use of general consumers for their routine everyday activities,
- 'specified products' – that is, consumer products that are deemed highly likely to cause danger particularly to the lives or person of general consumers due to their structure, material, usage or similar as provided for by a Cabinet order (eg, pressure cookers for home use, motorcycle helmets, laser pointer/use as a toy);[12]
- 'special specified products' – that is, those specified products for which the manufacturers or importers must achieve levels of safety and quality in order to prevent dangers to the lives or person of general consumers as provided for by a Cabinet Order; (eg, beds for infants, lighters, etc.); and
- 'specified maintenance products' – that is, consumer products that are deemed highly likely to cause serious danger particularly to the lives or person of general consumers because of their lack of reliable safety due to deterioration caused by long-term use as identified by a Cabinet order; and which are likely to need to be maintained during their usage (eg, gas combi boilers, indoor gas-heated baths, iron pots).

No person engaging in the manufacture, import or sale of specified products (including special specified products) may sell or display them for sale without

9 Act 234/1961.
10 Act 51/1954
11 See footnote 1.
12 Under the Consumer Product Safety Act, toys as well as general consumer products are not regulated before they are marketed except for specified products, but electric toys and similar are regulated by the Electrical Appliances and Materials Safety Act before they are marketed. Toys that are likely to harm the health of infants when they touch them are also regulated by the Food Sanitation Act – before they are marketed. Thus toys that do not conform with the standards are prohibited from being produced, imported, sold, etc (Article 11).

labelling them (Article 4(1)) with the Product Safety of Consumer (PSC) mark: Figure 1).

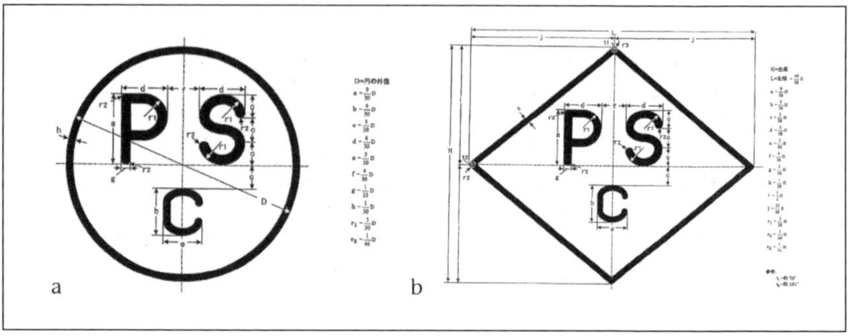

Figure 1. The design of a PSC mark. (a) A PSC mark for specified products. (b) A PSC mark for special specified products.[13]

A manufacturer or importer of specified products may notify the relevant minister of the "notified business operator's" name and address, the name and address of the premises manufacturing the products, etc., as provided for by the Ordinance (Article 6). The notified business operator must place the PSC mark on the products (Article 13), but no person may place the PSC mark or a label confusingly similar to it other than the person who made the notification (Article 5).

When a notified business operator manufactures or imports specified products of the type subject to notification, the operator must ensure that the products conform to the technical requirements (Article 11). Where the specified products manufactured or imported by the operator fall under the category of special specified products, the operator must have certain items inspected by a person registered with the competent minister, and obtain and preserve the certification prior to the sale of the products (Article 12).

A manufacturer or importer of specified maintenance products must notify the relevant minister of its name and address, the name and address of the factory or workplace manufacturing the products, etc., within 30 days of the starting date of the business (Article 32-2). Manufacturers, etc., must also indicate the following matters concerning the specified maintenance products that they manufacture or import prior to sale: name and address of manufacturer, year and month of manufacture, design standard use period, time of commencement and expiration of inspection period, contact information for inquiries for inspection and other maintenance, etc. (Article 32-4).

(b) *Electrical Appliances and Materials Safety Act*[14]

The purpose of this act is to regulate the manufacture and sale of electrical appliances and to encourage the supply of safe electrical appliances (Article 1).

13 www.meti.go.jp/policy/consumer/seian/shouan/contents/pscmark.pdf.
14 See footnote 9.

There is a duty to notify regulatory authorities of the name and location of the premises of the manufacturer (Article 3), and to conform to technical standards (Article 8), and to label products with PSE marks (Product Safety of Electrical Appliances and Materials marks; Articles 10 and 12).

(c) ***Gas Business Act***[15]

This act protects the interests of gas users and to ensure public safety and prevent pollution by regulating the construction, maintenance and operation of gas facilities as well as the manufacture and sale of gas equipment such as gas combi boilers, gas heaters and gas bath burners (Article 1).

Manufacturers have a duty to notify regulatory authorities of the name and location of the factory (Article 39-5), to conform to technical standards (Article 39-10), and to label using marks PSTG marks (Product Safety of Town Gas equipment and appliances marks; Article 39-12).

(d) ***Road Trucking Vehicle Act***[16]

Car manufacturers or importers must offer to consumers appropriate information to ensure proper maintenance and servicing of cars produced and operated in Japan, or imported into Japan (Article 57-2).

A car model attestation system operates in Japan, whereby the car manufacturer must report to the regulator the models of cars they produce and any changes made to those models.

The act also sets out the car registration system (Article 4), a duty to display the car registration number plate (Article 19), technological standards on safety, pollution control and other environmental protection issues (Article 40, etc.), and regulations on servicing and maintenance (Article 47, etc.).

(e) ***Pharmaceutical Affairs Act***[17]

No person may engage in the marketing, manufacturing or retailing of drugs, quasi-drugs, cosmetics or medical devices without first obtaining a licence based on the classification of drugs, quasi-drugs, cosmetics or medical devices (Articles 12, 13, 24, etc.).

Manufacturers must conform to the Ordinances of the Ministry of Health, Labour and Welfare (eg, *Good Manufacturing Practices*), when they produce drugs, quasi-drugs, cosmetics or medical devices, and obtain the prior approval of the minister of health, labour and welfare to market them (Article 14).

The name and address of the marketing authorisation holder, the name of the drug, the manufacturing number or code and the ingredients must be indicated on the immediate container or packaging of a drug (Article 50). Necessary precautions for use and handling, including dosage and administration must be indicated on the insert leaflet or on its container or packaging (Article 52).

---

15 See footnote 10.
16 See footnote 6.
17 See footnote 7.

(f) ***Food Sanitation Act***[18]

This act regulates all food, additives, meat, bones, milk, organs and blood of livestock, equipment or containers and packaging that may be sold, collected, produced, imported, processed, used, cooked, stored, or displayed for marketing purposes (Articles 6, 9, 10, 11, etc.). A 'positive list' system applies whereby food containing substances that are ingredients of agricultural chemicals of a quantity in excess of levels which the minister of health, labour and welfare deems safe must not be marketed. However, this restriction does not apply to cases where standards have been established with regard to the residual limit of such substances in specified foods (Article 11(3)).

The minister may establish standards for methods of producing, processing, using, cooking or preserving food or additives or for the ingredients of food or additives. Anyone who intends to produce or process such food must first obtain approval from the minister (Article 11(1) and Article 13). Foods or additives which comply with such standards must carry a label certifying that they have been inspected and passed the inspection (Article 11(2) and Article 25).

Food business operators must take responsibility to ensure the safety of foodstuffs and must equip themselves with the knowledge and technology necessary to ensure this, conduct voluntary inspections of their food and take other necessary measures (Article 3(1)).

They must also keep a record of necessary information including the name of the original supplier of the food or raw materials (Article 3(2)). Such traceability systems are important to help deal with difficulties promptly if they occur (eg, BSE, deceptive labelling by manufacturers).[19]

Food, additives, equipment or containers and packaging must not be sold, displayed for marketing purposes, or used in the business without necessary labelling (Article 19, etc.). False or misleading labelling or advertising, which may harm public health must not be used (Article 20).

A licence system also applies to restaurants (Article 52) and further regulations on food labelling based on the Japanese Agricultural Standard (JAS) and the Health Promotion Act.[20] Toys that are likely to harm the health of infants when they come into contact with them are also regulated by the Food Sanitation Act (Article 62(1)).

2.3 Post-market obligations

There are also many and various post-market obligations, the main ones applying to collecting and reporting information, and preventing the occurrence or spread of any danger.

Penalties for the breach of these safety requirements and the appeals process is discussed in Sections 1.3.3 and 1.3.4.

---

18 See footnote 8.

19 There are some regulations on traceability systems besides the Food Sanitation Act, such as the Act on Special Measures concerning Measures against Bovine Spongiform Encephalopathy (Act 70/2002) and the Pharmaceutical Affairs Act Enforcement Regulations. The importance of traceability systems is also pointed out in the recall handbook (footnote 2).

20 Act 103/2002.

(a) ***Consumer Product Safety Act***

Any manufacturer, importer or retailer of consumer products must collect information on product accidents, and endeavour to provide that information to general consumers. 'Product accidents' mean those accidents resulting from the use of consumer products as follows (assuming the accident was caused by a defect in the consumer product):

- accidents where a danger to the lives or to the person of a consumer has occurred; or
- accidents in which the consumer products that were damaged are deemed likely to cause danger to the lives or person of general consumers.

Although there is no concrete rule in the Consumer Product Safety Act about the content of such information, according to the recall handbook (footnote 2), business operators must record, among other things:

- details of the accident (eg, source of the information, background to the occurrence of the accident, information regarding similar accidents, degree of injury); and
- manufacturing information (eg, dates of manufacture or import, time of marketing, amount manufactured).

Any manufacturer or importer of consumer products who comes to know of a serious product accident originating from consumer products that they manufactured or imported, must report the matter to the prime minister in the prescribed form (name and type of consumer product; detailed account of the accident; quantity of consumer products manufactured or imported; quantity sold: Article 35(1)). This report must be made within 10 days of becoming aware of the serious product accident. 'Serious product accidents' are product accidents as so defined by Cabinet Order. Any person who comes to know of a product accident other than a serious product accident must report it in the prescribed form to the National Institute of Technology and Evaluation (NITE).[21] The name and type of the product, details of the accidents and any other matter that may contribute to avoiding risks associated with its use will be published by the prime minister or NITE on their official websites (Article 36).

Any manufacturer or importer of consumer products should, in cases where product accidents (even if not serious) have originated from the consumer products that they manufactured or imported, investigate the cause of such product accidents, and where necessary recall the product or otherwise take measures to prevent the occurrence or spread of the danger (Article 38(1)).

Conversely, under the Consumer Product Safety Act, in the absence of any accident, a manufacturer or importer of a consumer product is under no obligation to notify anyone about safety concerns or to recall the subject consumer product. However, in practice, they should endeavour to take all necessary measures to avoid health risks.[22]

---

21 www.nite.go.jp.

22 In the recall handbook (footnote 2), it is pointed out that a manufacturer should positively take necessary preventative measures to prevent an accident.

(b) ***Road Trucking Vehicle Act***

The Ministry of Land, Infrastructure and Transport has powers to impose restrictions on the sale of defective vehicles and parts, and to order preparations to be made for necessary remedial measures, including recall by the car manufacturer (Article 63-2), but does not impose any obligation on the manufacturer actually to take necessary remedial measures. The act imposes an obligation on the manufacturer only to report the contents of problems and remedial measures and so on to the minister of land, infrastructure and transport in the prescribed form prior to taking any action (Article 63-3).

Details of how to recall are provided in the notices issued by the regulatory authorities, for example, in *Points for Handling Written Reports, etc., of a Recall*. There a 'recall' is defined as a remedial measure to make cars and devices in conformity with the standards. A manufacturer must specify the cause of the problem, details of remedial measures necessary and the scope of the recall, reporting these facts within five days of the day following the day when the recall is deemed necessary. A manufacturer must conduct a recall not only to resolve an identified problem where some parts do not conform to the standards, but also to make all other parts conform to the standards and be free of any problem affecting safety and/or pollution issues. A manufacturer must also conduct a recall for all cars and devices that do not conform to standards, excluding those that are no longer in circulation or have been dismantled and can no longer be used.

In the notice, after reporting the recall to the minister of land, infrastructure and transport, manufacturers must give notice of the details of the recall by post and must publicise the matter in the official newsletter of the Japan Automobile Service Promotion Association. They must then endeavour to conduct the recall immediately, and after that report on the stage of the implementation of the recall to the minister on the 20th day of the months of January, April, July and October every year until:

- the time when they can report the completion of the recall of all affected cars;
- three years from the day on which they can report execution of a recall of 90% or more of the affected cars; or
- the time when the head of the Road Transport Bureau of the Ministry of Land, Infrastructure and Transport accepts that such reporting is no longer necessary.

Additionally, manufacturers must take remedial measures for cars or devices even where they do conform to the standards, but where they are assessed to have problems relating to safety, pollution or similar. 'Remedial measures' are different from a recall, but are a form of recall.

Where manufacturers take other measures (not a recall or remedial measure), they must report those details too to the head of the Examination of Parts Safety Office of the Road Transport Bureau of the Ministry of Land, Infrastructure and Transport. Such measures are referred to as a 'service campaign'.

(c) ***Pharmaceutical Affairs Act***

Certain entities must collect and review necessary information for the proper use of drugs and medical devices, covering matters affecting their efficacy and safety, and endeavour to provide that information to physicians, proprietors of hospitals or other health professionals (Article 77-3). Entities who have such obligations are marketing authorisation holders for drugs or medical devices, a person who has obtained a licence for wholesaling drugs or medical devices, a retailer or rental dealer of a medical device or a foreign restricted approval holder.

When marketing authorisation holders learn of the occurrence or spread of a hazard to the public health suspected to be associated with the use of a drug, they must take necessary measures to prevent the hazard, including disposal or recall of the drug, suspension of consumer sales, and must supply appropriate information (Article 77-4). Three principal considerations will inform any decision to instigate a recall:

- efficacy and safety;
- the extent of the defect; and
- the kind of foreign matter involved, the nature of the drug and so on.

Marketing authorisation holders must classify the known risks on a scale of Level I, II or III based on the level of danger to health brought about by the recalled product. This information must be publicised by an independent administrative agency, the Pharmaceuticals and Medical Devices Agency.

The marketing authorisation holder must report to the minister of health, labour and welfare in the prescribed form, both when it starts the recall and when it completes the recall (Article 77-4-3).

Additionally, the act provides for a system of reporting adverse reactions (Article 77-42). Marketing authorisation holders must report the fact of an adverse reaction to a drug to the minister of health, labour and welfare in the prescribed form within 15 or 30 days of learning about it, depending on the circumstances.

(d) ***Food Sanitation Act***

In order to prevent food health hazards resulting from the sale of food, food business operators must endeavour to take any necessary measure appropriately and immediately, such as the provision of the record described above (Article 3(3)).

The minister or a prefectural governor may request a business person or other relevant person to submit necessary reports (Article 28). Non-compliance with such a request will be punished by a fine of up to Y500,000.

Recall regulations are also implemented via ordinances of the administrative division. For example, in Tokyo, the Food Safety Ordinance provides for a voluntary recall report system where business operators must report the fact of a recall to the governor in the prescribed form both when they start the recall and when they complete it.

Toys that are likely to harm the health of infants when they come into contact with them are also regulated by this act (Article 62(1)).

3. Enforcement

3.1 Sector organisations

(a) Consumer products

The prime minister and relevant minister must endeavour to collect information on serious product accidents (Article 33). The prime minister can decide to make such information public where necessary (name and type of consumer product involved, details of accidents and any other matter that may help mitigate dangers associated with the use of the said consumer products; Article 36).

The relevant minister may order a notified business operator to take necessary measures to improve methods of manufacturing, import or inspection of products or any other business methods, or to improve measures taken to prepare for the compensation of victims where the lives or persons of general consumers have been damaged due to a product defect (Article 14).

Where a person engaged in the manufacture or import of consumer products fails to make a report or has made a false report concerning a serious product accident, the prime minister may decide to order that person to develop a system for the collection of information on serious product accidents that have occurred in relation to consumer products manufactured or imported by that person, and for the proper management or communication of the information (Article 37).

Where the relevant minister believes that a risk of danger to the lives or persons of general consumers exists due to any event, if the minister finds it particularly pressing to prevent the occurrence and spread of such a risk, the minister may order the person engaging in the manufacture, import or sale of the products to recall those that have been sold and to otherwise take all necessary measures to prevent the occurrence and spread of the danger or risk (Article 32).

In cases where serious product accidents have occurred due to a product defect (even in non-specified products) or where a serious danger has occurred affecting the lives or persons of general consumers, or where such a danger is considered imminent, the minister may choose to order the person engaging in the manufacture or import of the consumer products to recall them or otherwise to take necessary measures to prevent the occurrence and spread of any serious risk due to the consumer products (Article 39).

For example, in a case involving the recall of gas combi boilers, pursuant to Article 39, the minister ordered the manufacturer:

- to recheck the product and submit the results with concrete evidence (eg, onsite records);
- to publicise the matter widely in the media to warn consumers to have their products checked immediately;
- to establish a testing team, radically strengthen organisational controls and invite a third party to inspect testing procedures; and
- to report the Ministry of Economy, Trade and Industry every week until the checking activities were completed.

(b) Motor vehicles

If the defect has been found to have been created in the process of the design or production of a car or where the performance of a 'specific fixed device' may not conform to the safety standards, the minister of land, infrastructure and transport may recommend the manufacturer take remedial action including a recall in reference to the notice on *Points for Handling Written Reports, etc., of a Recall*, to ensure conformity with safety standards. In such cases, the minister may have an independent administrative agency or a traffic safety environmental laboratory conduct a technical verification. If the car manufacturer does not follow the recommendation, the minister may make that fact public, and if the manufacturer still does not take the recommended action, the minister may order the manufacturer's compliance (Article 63-2).

The minister may also order the manufacturer to supply details of its business, such as operational information, and inspect it on the spot on receipt of any report implying the manufacture of a car that is not in conformity with the standards (Article 63-4).

According to the notice on *Points for Handling Written Reports, etc., of a Recall* the minister must publish the manufacturer's written report.

(c) Medicines

The minister of health, labour and welfare or a prefectural governor may order a marketing authorisation holder of a drug to permit an inspection (Article 71). The minister may also order the authorisation holder to make improvements in its quality control methods or medical marketing safety management, or to suspend all or part of its business until such improvements are made (Article 72).

When the minister confirms the need to prevent the occurrence or spread of a hazard to the public health due to a drug, the minister may order a marketing authorisation holder to suspend the sale or supply of the drug and to take any emergency measure including a recall to prevent the occurrence and spread of any hazard to the public (Article 69-3).

The minister or a prefectural governor may also order a person handling drugs at work to dispose of or recall the products or take adequate measures to prevent the occurrence of any hazard to the public (Article 70, etc.). For example, if deaths frequently result due to side effects of a drug, the minister may order the person handling the drug to recall it.

Additionally, the act provides for a procedure for cancelling approvals and licences (Articles 74-2, 75, etc.).

(d) Food

Where the minister of health, labour and welfare or a prefectural governor finds food that does not conform to certain standards the minister may order the person to permit an inspection by a registered conformity assessment body (Article 26). The minister or a prefectural governor may also request a business or other relevant person to submit reports, or have their officials visit the business premises and inspect the food, business facilities, books and documents and other articles (Article 28).

In cases of violation of the Food Sanitation Act, the minister or a prefectural governor may order the business to dispose of the food or to take any other necessary measure including a recall to eliminate any food sanitation hazard (Article 54).

The minister and a prefectural governor must publicise a food sanitation hazard on their official websites and other materials identifying the person in violation of the act or rule or regulation made under it (Article 63).

Additionally, the act provides for a procedure for cancelling approvals and licenses, prohibiting the business in whole or in part or suspension of the business for a specified period (Article 13(5), Article 55, etc.). Toys that are likely to harm the health of infants when they touch them are also regulated by this act (Article 62(1)).

3.2 International enforcement

Japan does not belong to the Rapid Alert System for Food and Feed (RASFF) or Rapid Alert System for non-food dangerous products (RAPEX) in Europe, but the European Commission and Japanese Government signed Statements of Intent on July 30 2009, which gave authorities in Japan access to the RASFF electronically and the ability to acquire real-time information on warnings and notifications concerning food and feed that are exchanged between EU and Japan.

3.3 Appeals

When a disposition, such as a decision refusing a pre-market authorisation (see Section 1.2.2), or giving the business operator various instructions is made by the minister, a person may occasionally request the review of that decision or object under the Administrative Appeal Act,[23] except for certain dispositions (eg, a disposition decided by the Diet).

Under the Administrative Appeal Act, a review request or objection must be made within 60 days of the day following the day when the person became aware of the disposition.

Moreover, the person objecting to an administrative disposition may file an action pursuant to the Administrative Case Litigation Act[24] for its revocation.

When a decision denying an authorisation is set aside via this procedure, the original decision loses its validity and the new decision will be complied with by the relevant minister, ignoring the litigation. When an instruction is set aside, it just loses its validity.

3.4 Sanctions and compensation

(a) Penalties

A person who violates the acts or regulations detailed above is punishable by imprisonment with labour or a fine or both. When a representative, agent, employee or other worker of a corporation or other legal entity commits a violation with

23 Act 160/1962.
24 Act 139/1962.
25 Act 131/1948.

respect to the business of the said legal entity, both the offender and the legal entity will be punished under the Criminal Procedure Act.[25]

Some examples follow.

Consumer Product Safety Act: A person who violates a recall order or sells a specified product without a PSC mark will be punished by imprisonment with work for not more than one year or a fine of not more than Y1 million, or both. A person who makes a false notification as required by the provisions of Article 6 will be punished by a fine of up to Y300,000. Persons who fail to report product accidents shall not be punished under this act.

When the representative, agent, employee or other worker of a corporation or other legal entity commits a violation with respect to the business of said legal entity, both the offender and the legal entity will be punished. The legal entity shall face a fine of up to Y100 million.

Road Trucking Vehicle Act: A person who violates a recall order, fails to make a prior report of a recall or submits a false report, will be punished by imprisonment with work for up to one year or a fine of not more than Y3 million, or both. A person who fails to make a report after a recall faces a fine of up to Y300,000.

When the representative of a corporation or other legal entity commits the violation both the offender and the legal entity will be punished. The legal entity will be punished by a fine of up to Y200 million.

Pharmaceutical Affairs Act: A person who violates the regulations concerning licences and prior approvals to market drugs or a recall order, will be punished by imprisonment with work for up to three years or a fine of up to Y3 million, or both. A person who violates an order to make improvements, etc., will be punished by imprisonment with work for up to one year or a fine of up to Y1 million. A person who fails to report product accidents is not punishable under this act.

When the representative of a corporation or other legal entity commits a violation with respect to the business of the legal entity, both the offender and legal entity will be punished. The legal entity will be punished by a fine of up to Y100 million.

Food Sanitation Act: A person who violates a recall order or regulations on sales provided by Article 6 of the act will be punished by imprisonment with work for up to three years or a fine of up to Y3 million, or both. A person who fails to make an Article 28 report will be punished by a fine of up to Y500,000.

When the representative of a corporation or other legal entity commits a violation with respect to the business of said legal entity, both the offender and legal entity will be punished. The legal entity will be punished by a fine of up to Y100 million.

(b) Compensation

There is basically no statutory compensation for victims except in specific instances, and such instances are covered by special laws such as the Act on Special Measures concerning Hepatitis C Relief.[26]

3.5 Multiple jurisdictions

Japan generally constitutes a single jurisdiction for the purpose of product recall legislation, although some of the powers of the Ministries are delegated to the prefectures.

4. Product liability

4.1 Potential defendants

The sources of liability are the Product Liability Act,[27] tort and contract.

Under Article 2(3) of the Product Liability Act, the term 'manufacturer, etc.', means:

(i) any person who manufactured, processed, or imported the product in the course of trade (hereinafter referred to as 'manufacturer'),

(ii) any person who provides his/her name, trade name, trademark or other indication (hereinafter referred to as 'representation of name, etc.') on the product as the manufacturer of such product, or any person who provides the representation of name, etc. on the product which misleads the others into believing that he/she is the manufacturer, and

(iii) any person who provides any representation of name, etc. on the product which, in light of the manner concerning the manufacturing, processing, importation or sales of the product, and other circumstances, holds himself/herself out as its substantial manufacturer.

Under tort law, product liability may theoretically extend to all the parties involved in the chain of distribution of a product, such as producers and distributors. However, because it is difficult to prove the negligence of any party other than the manufacturer, the defendants in a product liability case based on tort in Japan are usually the manufacturers or producers, importers and the regulatory agencies which approved the marketing of the product.[28]

Under contract law, the defendant will be the other party to the contract because privity is required. We do therefore see a few product liability cases claiming damages against manufacturers based on contract.

4.2 Sources of liability

(a) Statute

Japan is a civil law country. Therefore, all sources of liability are statutes, and tort and contract laws are also basically codified in the Civil Code.[29]

The Product Liability Act is a special law of tort concerning product liability. The "manufacturer, etc." will be basically "liable for damages arising from the infringement of life, body or property of others which is caused by the defect in the

---

26 Act on Special Measures concerning the Payment of Benefits to Relieve the Victims of Hepatitis C Infected through Specified Fibrinogen Concentrates and Specified Coagulation Factor XI Concentrates (Act 2/2008).

27 Act 85/1994.

28 State Redress Act (125/1947).

29 Act 89/1896.

delivered product which was manufactured, processed, imported, or provided with the representation of name, etc." (Article 3). Therefore, the elements of a cause of action under the Product Liability Act are as follows:

- The defendant is the "manufacturer, etc";
- There is a defect in the delivered product, which was manufactured, processed, imported or provided with the representation of name, and so on; The defect caused damage to the plaintiff's life, body or property; and
- There is a causal link between the infringement and the damage.

The plaintiff does not need to prove negligence. In sum, the liability is strict. However, although product liability is often called no-fault liability since negligence is not required, such liability is not absolute liability because it is necessary to prove the defect and because there is a 'development risk defence' (see below).

The plaintiff under the Product Liability Act could be an individual consumer or a private corporation.

The 'defect' "shall mean a lack of safety that the product ordinarily should provide, taking into account the nature of the product, the ordinarily foreseeable manner of use of the product, the time when the manufacturer, etc. delivered the product, and other circumstances concerning the product" (Article 2). Defects are classified into types, as in the United States, as follows:

- manufacturing defects;
- design defects; and
- inadequate warnings.

Ultimately, the court decides whether or not a defect exists taking into account the factors set out in the act, past cases and the product itself.

The 'nature of the product', as provided in the act, is an important factor. It includes the indication of the product, its utility or efficacy, its cost effectiveness, the probability and degree of damage, and the ordinary period of use/life of the product. The indication would encompass whether a warning would be required to avoid an improper use of the product, or whether a warning is adequate. For example, in a case where a medicine develops a side effect, if its efficacy outweighs the side effect and there are no substitutes for the medicine, then a claim for a design defect would be denied.

The ordinarily foreseeable manner of use of the product is also an important factor. In a case where the plaintiff suffered a thermal burn by using a cellular phone, one high court ruled that proof of the occurrence of an abnormality harming the body or property, notwithstanding the ordinary manner of use, constituted sufficient evidence of the defect and that the plaintiff did not have an obligation to prove the cause of the defect or the scientific mechanism of the defect by identifying the specific defect.[30]

"The manufacturer, etc. shall not be liable when the damages occur only with respect to such product" (the proviso to Article 3 of the act). In such a case, the plaintiff has to claim damages under tort or contract law.

30 *Panasonic Mobile Communications* 2086 HANREI JIHO 42 (Sendai High Ct, April 22 2010), aff'd 2011 WLJPCA 10276001 (Supreme Ct, October 27 2011).

One of the statutory defences is that "the defect in such product could not have been discovered given the state of scientific or technical knowledge at the time when the manufacturer, etc. delivered the product" (Article 4(i)). This is called the 'development risk defence'. But the state of scientific or technical knowledge is interpreted as the best available in the world, so the defence is rarely accepted.

The other statutory defence is used where "the product is used as a component or raw material of another product". The requirements for this defence are:

- "the defect occurred primarily because of the compliance with the instructions concerning the design given by the manufacturer of such another product"; and
- "the manufacturer, etc. is not negligent with respect to the occurrence of such defect" (Article 4(ii)).

Other defences include that:

- the infringement was caused by a clear danger; and
- there was adequate warning about the danger that caused the infringement.

(b) *Tort*

Tort is codified in the Civil Code. The Japanese Civil Code was enacted in 1896 and influenced by the French and German Civil Codes. Its interpretation has also been influenced by the interpretation of the German Civil Code.

Article 709 of the Civil Code stipulates that "A person who has intentionally or negligently infringed any right of others, or legally protected interest of others, shall be liable to compensate any damages resulting in consequence". Thus, it has been held that the elements of a cause of action for tort are:

- any right or legally protected interest of the plaintiff;
- the defendant's infringement of such right or interest;
- the defendant's intent or negligence;
- the amount of the damages arising from the infringement; and
- causation between infringement and damages.

Duty of care: In order to prove the defendant's negligence, the plaintiff needs to prove a duty of care and breach of that duty. Generally, all the parties involved in the chain of distribution of a product owe a duty of care not to disregard the safety of the plaintiff's life, body or property.

Breach of duty: Although all of the parties involved in the chain of distribution of a product owe a duty of care, the standards of care vary. The standard of negligence is that of a reasonable average person.[31] Generally speaking, however, manufacturers owe a much higher duty than distributors. The Osaka District Court has even held that negligence will be presumed from the presence of a defect (in a case involving the explosion of a television).[32]

Injury and damage: The plaintiff must prove that the defendant infringed any right or legally protected interest of the plaintiff and that there is causation between the defendant's infringement and the damage. If the plaintiff's life, body or property is injured, the former requirement is satisfied.

(c) *Contract*

In the subject matter of a sale is not a specified thing, if a seller "fails to perform consistently with the purpose of its obligation", including failure to deliver defective products, a purchaser "shall be entitled to demand damages arising from such failure" (Article 415, Civil Code) unless the purchaser accepts the delivery as 'performance'. If the purchaser "demands performance of the obligations, specifying a reasonable period and no performance is tendered during that period", the purchaser "may cancel the contract" (Article 541, Civil Code). Such liability is called a "default" and the defence thereto is no fault.

If the subject matter of a sale is a specified thing, which has a latent defect, [or where the purchaser accepts the delivery of defective unspecified things as performance, "if the buyer cannot achieve the purpose of the contract on account thereof, the buyer may cancel the contract", or "if the contract cannot be cancelled, the buyer may only demand compensation for damages" (Articles 570 and 566, Civil Code). Such damages, however, are generally interpreted to be limited to damages for "reliable interest", which means damages that the purchaser should not have incurred if the purchaser had known about the defect, and usually excludes lost profits. Such liability of a purchaser is called a "warranty against defects" and is a no fault liability.

As mentioned above, however, because privity is required, a plaintiff cannot usually sue the manufacturer.

4.3 Claimants, class actions

The plaintiff in a product liability case is not limited to consumers even under the Product Liability Act as mentioned above.

In 2006 a new right was introduced enabling qualified consumer organisations to request an injunction against certain actions of business operators, such as certain violations of the Consumer Contract Act[33] (Article 12 of the act) as a kind of class action. There are, however, no other kinds of class action in Japan. Thus, no class actions are available for product liability suits.

4.4 Causation: including failure to warn

Causation is not interpreted as scientific causation but legally sufficient causation as influenced by German legal theory. Although it is a condition that scientific causation is found under the 'but for' test, it is not sufficient. Causation for "damages which would ordinarily arise" and "damages which arise from any special circumstances if the party did foresee, or should have foreseen, such circumstances" may be upheld (Article 416, Civil Code). Even under the Product Liability Act, the

---

31 *Fukuyama v Nakamura* 17 TAIHAN MINROKU 617 (Great Court of Judicature, November 1 1911).

32 *Taishi Kensetsu Kogyo v Matsushita Denki Sangyou* 1493 HANREI JIHO 29 (Osaka District Court, March 29 1994).

33 Act 61/2000.

plaintiff must prove causation. A finding of causation will also depend on the court, past cases and the product itself.

First, the plaintiff needs to prove that the product has caused personal injury or damage to property. Then, the defect in the product will need to be proven. The issue of whether or not there was a failure to warn will also be considered.[34] If a failure to warn is established, then causation between the failure to warn and the damage will usually be found. However, where a plaintiff him/herself could have foreseen that their manner of use could have caused the damage notwithstanding the manufacturer's failure to warn, or if the plaintiff had used the product in such manner notwithstanding the warning, then no causation will be found between the failure to warn and the damage.

4.5 Remedies

The remedy for injury/damage in a product liability case is limited to compensation for damages, although the purchaser might cancel the contract and "the amount of the damages shall be determined with reference to monetary value" (Article 722(1) and Article 417, Civil Code).

Damages to be compensated will be "damages which would ordinarily arise" and "damages which arise from any special circumstances if the party did foresee, or should have foreseen, such circumstances" (Article 416 of the code). There is no limit to damages. Future losses such as future costs of care/treatment and loss of earnings are recoverable. But in cases involving a 'warranty against defects' under contract law, damages are generally interpreted to be limited to damages for 'reliable interest'. Punitive damages are not allowed.

Japan adopts a kind of comparative negligence doctrine. "If a victim is negligent, the court may determine the amount of compensation by taking that factor into consideration" in cases under the Product Liability Act or tort (Article 6, Product Liability Act and Article 722(2) of the code). And for contracts, "If the obligee is negligent regarding the failure of performance of the obligation, the court shall determine the liability for damages and the amount thereof by taking such elements into consideration" (Article 418 of the code). In sum, it is mandatory in case of contracts, but not in tort cases including the Product Liability Act, for the court to take into consideration the negligence of the plaintiff.

4.6 Procedure, limitation, funding, costs

There are some alternative dispute centres for product liability, such as the Association for Electric Home Appliances. No specific legal procedure for product liability suits is provided. Judges, not juries, determine the facts in civil cases. Broad discovery procedures are not provided. There is no deposition procedure. The defendant, however, may not refuse to submit documents (with some exceptions, eg, documents concerning technical or professional secrets and documents prepared exclusively for use by the holder; Article 220, Code of Civil Procedure).[35] Therefore, the plaintiff may file a petition for an order to force the submission of documents by

34 See Section 4.2 on "Sources of liability".

the defendant (Article 221 of the code). If the court finds that such a petition is well-grounded it will make the order (Article 223 of the code). If the defendant does not comply with the order, the court may go ahead and presume that the plaintiff's allegations concerning the statements in the documents are true (Article 224 of the code). In principle, any evidence, including liability insurance or subsequent remedial measures, is admissible.

A plaintiff must file a complaint under the Product Liability Act within a period of either three years from the time when the plaintiff becomes aware of the damages and the party liable for the damages; or 10 years from the time when the manufacturer delivered the product, whichever comes soonest (Article 5(1)), provided, however, that the latter period "shall be calculated from the time of the occurrence of the damages where such damages are caused by substances which become harmful to human health when they accumulate in the body, or where the symptoms which represent such damages appear after a certain latent period" (Article 5(2)).

In tort cases, the complaint will be filed within the earlier of three years from the time when the plaintiff comes to know of the damages and the identity of the perpetrator or 20 years from the time of the tortious act (Article 724). The time from when the latter period "shall be calculated has been interpreted as the time of the occurrence of the damages where such damages are caused by substances which become harmful to human health when they accumulate in the body, or where the symptoms which represent such damages appear after a certain latent period".[36]

Where plaintiffs wish to claim damages based on default under a contract, they must do so within 10 years (Article 167, Civil Code). If plaintiffs wish to claim damages based on a warranty against defect, they must do so within one year from the time when the purchaser learns about the latent defect (Article 570 and 566, Civil Code). Furthermore, in the case of a sale between merchants, the purchaser must claim damages within six months of taking delivery (based on either default of performance or warranty against defects; Article 526, Commercial Code).

In 2006, the Japan Legal Support Center (JLSC) was established to render prompt and proper comprehensive legal support under Article 14 of the Comprehensive Legal Support Act,[37] although there is no specific fund for product liability cases. The JLSC provides civil legal aid to people with financial difficulties (Article 30(1)(ii) of the act).

In principle, the "defeated party shall bear court costs" (Article 61, Code of Civil Procedure). 'Court costs' are defined by the Act on Costs of Civil Procedure,[38] and include the fee for filing an action but exclude attorneys' fees. The court, at its discretion, may admit a certain proportion of attorneys' fees as damages under tort law (including the Product Liability Act) but not under contract law.

35 Act 109/1996.
36 Japan 58 MINSHU 4 1032 (Supreme Ct April 27 2004).
37 Act 74/2004.
38 Act 40/1971.

4.7 Trends

The Product Liability Act has been the most significant source of law since its enactment because a plaintiff does not have to prove the negligence of the defendant except the defect of the products, although the scope of the application of the act is limited and its limitation period shorter.

5. Products insurance

In general, and very broadly, insurance policies vary from insurer to insurer.

On July 1 2011 there were 50 general insurance companies operating in Japan, 28 of which were licenced as domestic insurers, including five foreign capital domestic insurers, and 22 licensed as foreign insurers.[39] On April 1 2012, there were 26 insurance companies in the General Insurance Association of Japan.[40]

According to the website of the Japan Chamber of Commerce and Industry (JCCI),[41] product liability insurance is available for Small and Medium Enterprises (PL Insurance for SMEs), to provide product liability insurance for members of the JCCI, Central Federation of Societies of Commerce and Industry, and National Federation of Small Business Associations. Based on a brochure on *PL Insurance for SMEs* (the PLI brochure), an insured company has the option to take out product recall insurance (*Product Recall Insurance for SMEs*).

In addition the new Insurance Law of Japan,[42] which covers insurance contracts, was enacted in 2008 and fully implemented in 2010. The new law stipulates the rights and obligations of policyholder, the insured, beneficiary and insurer. For example, it provides for the duty of disclosure, delivery of documents upon execution of an insurance contract, notice of the occurrence of any damage, cancellation of an insurance contract, subrogation of claims, etc. It also introduces mandatory provisions that might render certain provisions of an insurance contract invalid.

5.1 Coverage

(a) Product recall

Generally in Japan, product liability insurance does not cover the cost of recalls (including brand damage) when necessary to prevent injury or damage. However, additional or supplemental insurance to cover the cost of recalls is available.

(b) Product liability

Product liability insurance in Japan generally covers bodily injury and property damages caused by the product specified in the insurance policy.

(c) Financial loss

Pure economic losses (not consequential damage) caused by a product that has failed

---

39 *General Insurance in Japan Fact Book 2010–2011* at www.sonpo.or.jp/en/publication/fact_2011.html
40 www.sonpo.or.jp/en
41 www.jcci.or.jp/member/pl/index.html
42 Act 56/2008.

to perform its function are generally excluded from product liability insurance and supplemental insurance will be necessary.

(d) ***Product guarantee***

Product liability insurance generally does not cover the cost of repairing or replacing a product that has failed to perform its function. However, supplemental insurance for that cost is available.

5.2 Product recall insurance

Under product recall insurance, the insurer is typically required to pay insurance benefits to the insured for the costs associated with a product recall in the event that:

- a bodily injury or property damage arises or is objectively likely to arise from the product that was produced or sold by the insured; and
- the insured recalls the products.

Generally, product liability insurance does not cover product recall insurance; however, product recall insurance can be obtained. The scope of product recall insurance varies from policy to policy so it is difficult to make generalisations. However, more than 10,000 companies have taken out 'product recall insurance for small and medium-sized enterprises (SMEs)' policies in the past four years. The following is based on that brochure.

(a) ***Insurance provisions***

Requirements: Under a product recall insurance for SMEs policy, the conditions for the payment of insurance benefits are as follows:

- the insured must give notice of the recall to the insurance company;
- the recalled products must be located within Japan; and
- the insured must have reported the occurrence of the insured event to the administrative authorities under to relevant laws and regulations, or has been forced to recall by the administrative authorities.

Conditions, however, vary from policy to policy. For instance, some policies will not require the recalled products to be located within Japan. If there is a dispute between the insured and the insurer regarding the reasonableness/necessity of a recall, or the scope of a recall, then the dispute can be resolved by the courts or through the Sonpo ADR centre.

Coverage: The following costs and expenses are covered in a product recall insurance for SMEs:

- expenses for company announcements in newspapers, magazines, televisions, radios or other similar media;
- expenses for communication such as telephone calls, faxes, mail (including fees for the preparation of documents);
- costs of confirming whether a product must be recalled or is defective;

- shipping costs for recalled products or replacements;
- costs of leasing a warehouse or facility for the purpose of temporary storage of the recalled products;
- extra personnel costs arising from the recall (excluding personnel costs for the repair of the recalled products or manufacturing/purchase of replacements);
- travel expenses and accommodation expenses arising from the recall (excluding expenses for the repair of the recalled products or manufacturing/purchase of replacements); and
- costs of disposal of the recalled products.

This insurance does not cover costs of repairing the recalled products or manufacturing/purchasing replacements, or refunds.

However, some insurers offer product recall insurance to cover those costs, so the insured may choose such additional insurance.

(b) ***Exclusions***

The PLI brochure sets out cases where the insured will not be paid the insurance benefits. For example, if an insured caused the insured event intentionally or by gross negligence, the insured will not receive payment. Also, the insurance benefits will not be paid if the accident occurred as a result of events like normal wear and tear, mould, decomposition, discolouration of a product, etc.

Generally, the burden of proof regarding exclusions is on the insurer. For example, the insurer has the burden to prove the fact that the insured caused the insured event intentionally. The Code of Civil Procedure[43] does not mention any standard of proof however. Some scholars consider that a decision based on a preponderance of evidence will be sufficient. However, the prevailing view is that the standard is 'high probability', which is higher than a mere preponderance of evidence.

(c) ***Conditions***

Under the new Insurance Law of Japan, if the insured becomes aware of the occurrence of any loss arising from the insured event, the insured shall notify the insurer thereof without delay.

The new Insurance Law also requires the insured to exert efforts to prevent the occurrence or aggravation of any loss arising from the insured event after the insured becomes aware of the occurrence of the insured event. Generally, if the insured intentionally fails to exert such efforts, the insured would receive the insurance benefits minus the amount of the loss that it could have prevented or mitigated.

Non-disclosure of existence of insurance: Insurance provisions vary from policy to policy, but some insurance policies require the insured not to disclose the fact that it has product recall insurance.

---

43 Act 109/1996.

Provision of hotline/consultant: In Japan, generally, using a hotline or contacting a consultant is not a condition of the policy and it appears that insurers do not encourage their use.

5.3 Product liability insurance

Under a product liability insurance in Japan, it is common for the insurer to pay insurance benefits to the insured for losses suffered by the insured in the event that the insured becomes legally liable for bodily injury or property damage arising from the product that was produced or sold by the insured. For example, in the event that a toaster produced by the insured ignites due to a defect and the fire that spreads burns the house down, and the insured becomes legally liable for the losses due to the fire, then the product liability insurance will cover those losses.

Product liability insurance has become common since the enactment of the Product Liability Act in 1995. Based on the PLI brochure, insurance benefits have been paid under *PL Insurance for SMEs* policies in about 13,000 cases since 1995.

(a) Insurance provisions

Generally, product liability insurance covers both bodily injury and damages.

(b) Exclusions

Breach of contract (with exceptions): If the damage arose because of the intentional conduct of the insured, that damage will be excluded from the cover. Likewise, if an insured contractually assumes liability for something he or she would not otherwise be liable for, liability is not covered. For example, if the insured paid a penalty under a special clause in a contract, that penalty would not be covered.

Repair and replacement: Product liability insurance in Japan generally does not cover the cost of repair or replacement.

Efficacy: Generally, loss of the use of tangible property (which has not been physically damaged or destroyed) resulting from failure to meet performance levels, quality, fitness or durability is not covered. For example, if a rust inhibitor fails to prevent rust, the loss of the use of the inhibitor is not covered.

(c) Conditions

Claims: When a third party makes a claim relating to a damage against the insured, or the insured becomes aware of the occurrence of an accident which could be the cause of a third party making a damage claim against the insured, the insured must promptly notify the insurance company of the details of the incident. Generally, if the insured intentionally fails to promptly notify the insurance company, the insured would be liable for the damages suffered by the insurance company due to the breach. In such a case, the insurance company may deduct the amount of damages from the insurance benefits.

Mitigating loss: The product liability insurance policy provides a number of conditions. For example, when the accident occurs or the insured becomes aware that an accident is likely to occur, the insured should promptly take appropriate measures (eg, examination, repair, recall) in order to avoid the occurrence or aggravation of that accident.

5.4 Financial loss insurance

(a) Insurance provisions

The insurance company may provide customised financial loss insurance. The insurance provisions vary from policy to policy. For example, under one financial loss insurance the following damage/loss was covered: a machine tool produced by the insured failed to work in a factory; that failure halted the production line of the manufacturer using that machine tool; the insured became legally liable for the losses due to the stoppage of the production line.

(b) Exclusions

Breach of contract (with exceptions): Generally, if under the contract the insured assumes liability that it would not otherwise assume under contract or tort, liability is excluded.

Repair, replacement and recall: In general, repair, replacement and recall expenses are not covered under financial loss insurance.

(c) Conditions

General conditions are likely to apply, but will vary from policy to policy.

5.5 Product guarantee insurance

(a) Insurance provisions

Generally, product liability insurance does not include product guarantee insurance. The standard provision of general product liability insurance clearly excludes damage to the product itself. However, supplemental insurance for the cost of repairs or replacements is available. The insurance provisions vary from policy to policy.

(b) Exclusions

General exclusions are likely to apply but will vary from policy to policy.

(c) Conditions

General conditions are likely to apply but will vary from policy to policy.

5.6 General principles

Supplemental insurance can be attached to the principal insurance.

The PLI brochure sets out aggregate limits to the coverage.

(a) General conditions

General conditions of product liability insurance include: the cover, term, insured's duty to notify the insurer of material facts regarding the likelihood of a claim, exclusions, the insurer's right of inspection, procedure for amendments to the policy, the insured's duty to notify the insurer of the accident along with detailed information, the method for cancellation of the policy, method for claiming payment of insurance benefits, dispute resolution mechanism, and governing law.

(b) General exclusions

Product liability insurance contracts generally exclude: damages arising from the intentional conduct of the insured, war, riot, labour dispute, earthquake, volcanic eruption, flood and tsunami.

(c) Interpretation

The new Insurance Law of Japan includes mandatory provisions. It states that any provision in the insurance contract which is inconsistent with those mandatory provisions and is disadvantageous to the insured will be invalid.

(d) Effect of breach

Breach of certain provisions in an insurance contract may result in its cancellation or denial of cover for certain damages. For example, if the insured has committed or attempted to commit a fraud in claiming an insurance benefit, the insurer may cancel the insurance contract. When the insured fails to promptly take appropriate measures in order to avoid aggravation of an accident after its occurrence, cover for additional costs resulting from that failure will be denied.

(e) Extra-contractual defences (misrepresentation, non-disclosure)

When the insured has made a false disclosure or has failed to disclose material facts regarding the likelihood of a claim by wilful misconduct or gross negligence, the insurer may cancel the contract. Although the cancellation will become effective prospectively under the new Insurance Law, in such cases the insurer will not be liable to cover any damage (except for damages that did not arise from the undisclosed facts).

Netherlands

Pieter van Regteren Altena
Lorijn van der Valk
Van Doorne NV

1. Product safety regulation

1.1 Legislative framework

The basis of Dutch product safety and recall legislation can be found in the EU General Product Safety Directive (2001/95/EC). This general directive covers all products for which no sector-specific legislation exists and fills any gaps in sector-specific legislation. The objective of the General Product Safety Directive and the sector-specific directives is to ensure that only safe consumer products are placed on the market. 'Safe' means that a product does not endanger the safety and health of consumers when used in accordance with its purpose. The General Product Safety Directive has been implemented in the Netherlands in:

- the Commodities Act (Articles 18 and 21), which provides general rules on public health and product safety; and
- the Commodities Act Decree on General Product Safety.

1.2 Safety standards

Regulations regarding safety standards for specific foods and consumer products are set out in a large number of decrees linked to the Commodities Act. A product marketed in the Netherlands will be presumed safe insofar as the risks and risk categories covered by relevant Dutch standards are concerned when – in the absence of specific EU provisions governing the safety of the product in question – the product conforms to the specific Dutch rules. For example, electrical appliances bearing the Dutch quality control mark 'KEMA-KEUR' are presumed safe. However, when a product is designed and constructed to meet the specifications of Dutch standards, this will not guarantee that the product is in fact safe. Nor will compliance with such standards bar liability.

1.3 Regulation

The Food and Consumer Product Safety Authority (NVWA) monitors food and consumer products to safeguard public health and welfare in the Netherlands. The Centre for Vehicle Technology and Information (RDW) is responsible for the safety and environmental regulation of motor vehicles whereas the Dutch Medicines Evaluation Board (CBG) assesses and monitors risks and quality of medicinal products in the Netherlands.

1.4 Prior approval

(a) Medicines

Before a pharmaceutical company is allowed to market a drug in the Netherlands, the product must be reviewed and assessed by the CBG. On approval by the CBG, the product will be included in the Dutch Drug Register.

(b) Motor vehicles

Manufacturers of vehicles or components for the automotive industry must have an EC type approval, a United Nations Economic Commission for Europe type approval, or national type approval to register and sell their products throughout the European Union. In order to receive such approvals, the RDW, the regulator for the Netherlands, may conduct certain tests.

(c) Food

Except for novel foods for human consumption, which are subject to assessment by the CBG, and genetically modified (GM) foods, which are subject to assessment by the European Food Safety Authority (EFSA), foods in principle are not subject to the prior approval of any authority. Producers are responsible for ensuring that the products they put on the market are safe.

(d) Other

Most consumer products will not normally be subject to prior approval by the NVWA or other authority. However, pursuant to the General Product Safety Directive, producers and distributors have a duty to observe the general safety requirements, as a consequence of which a producer should be able to prove compliance with safety standards. Whether a product does indeed comply with the applicable requirements may be checked when the product has been put into circulation.

1.5 Safety issues

The main obligations for producers and distributors under Dutch law in respect of unsafe products are to:

- notify the relevant authorities of a dangerous product;
- warn consumers of the risks posed by dangerous products already supplied to them;
- trace and withdraw those products from the market; and
- recall them when necessary.

In order to ensure that producers and distributors comply with their obligations under the relevant legislation, authorities have a wide range of powers to order corrective actions and impose administrative fines. The NVWA, for example, can prohibit a company from putting a dangerous product on the market, order the recall of dangerous products or even instigate a recall itself.

1.6 Types of corrective action

Possible corrective actions may include:[1]

- modifying the design or production method of products;
- preventing the distribution of the products;
- improving the instructions supplied with a product;
- providing additional information to consumers about the correct use of products;
- recalling products from consumers and offering consumers replacements or refunds for recalled products;[2] and
- instructing consumers to dispose of products.

1.7 Criminal liability

In the Netherlands, an offence under the Commodities Act or a Commodities Act decree will result in sanctions as follows:

Standard fines imposed under the Commodities Act Decree on Administrative Fines can range from €525 to €2,100, depending on the seriousness of the incident, the potential risk to public health and the size of the company. For repeat offences committed within 24 months or where the circumstances demand, the fine may be increased to up to €4,500.

- In case of repeat and/or more severe offences (see the Guidelines for the Prosecution of Offences under the Commodities Act), penalties may alternatively be imposed under the Economic Offences Act. Depending on the offence, this could attract a fine of the fourth category (€19,500), a community punishment or a custodial sentence of up to six months (Article 6(2) of the Economic Offences Act). Other sanctions under this act include confiscation of goods and a ban on trading for a maximum period of one year (Article 7).

2. Obligations of producers and distributors

2.1 Sources of duties

(a) Statute

The definition of a 'defective product' is laid down in Book 6, Article 186 of the Civil Code. According to this provision, a product is defective when it does not provide the safety which a person is entitled to expect, taking all circumstances into account, especially:

- the presentation of the product;
- the use that could reasonably be expected to be made of the product; and
- the time when the product was put into circulation on the market.

---

1 See http://ec.europa.eu/consumers/cons_safe/action_guide_en.pdf

2 Before the enactment of the General Product Safety Directive, which replaced the former Directive 92/59/EEC, producers and distributors were not obliged to recall unsafe products (Article 21(2) of the Commodities Act).

A product will not be considered to be defective for the sole reason that a better product was subsequently put into circulation on the market.

According to Article 2(1) of the Commodities Act Decree on General Product Safety: "Producers shall provide consumers with relevant information to enable them to assess the risks inherent in a product throughout the normal or reasonably foreseeable period of its use, where such risks are not immediately obvious without adequate warnings, and to take precautions against those risks."

Furthermore, producers must take appropriate measures that enable them to:

- be informed of risks which these products might pose; and
- choose to take appropriate action including, if necessary to avoid these risks, withdrawing the product from the market, adequately and effectively warning consumers, or recalling the product from consumers (Articles 2(1) and (2) of the Commodities Act Decree on General Product Safety).

Distributors in turn must participate in monitoring the safety of products placed on the market, in particular by passing on information on product risks and keeping and providing the documentation necessary for tracing the origin of products (Article 2(3) of the Commodities Act Decree on General Product Safety).

(b) Tort

According to a consistent line of Dutch case law, it is unlawful to put a product on the market that does not offer the levels of safety that a user is entitled to expect, taking all circumstances into account (HR December 6 1996, NJ 1997, 219 (*Du Pont/Hermans*)). In the *Koolhaas/Rockwool* case (HR October 22 1999, NJ 2000, 159), the Supreme Court ruled that this also applies to semi-finished products. The party responsible for the wrongful act will be liable under Book 6, Article 162 of the Civil Code.

(c) Contract

Under Dutch contract law, a buyer may claim damages if the delivered product is unsafe and therefore does not possess the quality that the buyer was entitled to expect. Generally speaking, liability of the seller can be excluded or limited except in cases of wilful misconduct or gross negligence.

2.2 Supply obligations

(a) Standards markings

CE marking on a product (CE stands for '*Conformité Européenne*') indicates that a product conforms with the applicable regulations and has been subject to all relevant conformity assessment procedures. CE marking is obligatory for all products to be put on the EU market within the scope of the directives (eg, electrical appliances, machines, toys and personal protection gear). Breach of the CE-marking obligations will result in sanctions under either:

- the Commodities Act Decree on Administrative Fines; or
- the Economic Offences Act.

(b) *Traceability and record keeping*

Although the Commodities Act Decree on General Product Safety does not contain explicit and detailed obligations to trace products put into circulation, traceability is covered by the more general duty of Articles 2(1) and (2) of the Commodities Act Decree on General Product Safety, which requires producers to take appropriate measures to avoid risks which the products they supply might pose. A similar duty for distributors is laid down in the paragraph 3 of that article, and requires them to participate in monitoring the safety of products placed on the market by, among other things, retaining the documentation necessary for tracing the origin of products.

An offence under Articles 2(1) and (2) will result in a fine under the Commodities Act Decree on Administrative Fines ranging from €795 to €1,590.

Repeat and/or more severe offences under this article may result in sanctions under the Economic Offences Act.

Some sector-specific legislation contains more specific traceability and/or record-keeping duties for certain products (eg, Article 3 of the Commodities Act Decree on Toys 2011; Article 6 of the Commodities Act Decree on Cosmetic Products; Article 18 of EU Food Regulation (178/2002) and Articles 33 and 38 of the Medicines Act).

(c) *Consumer protection laws*

The EU Sale of Consumer Goods Directive (1999/44/EC) has been implemented in the Netherlands in the Civil Code.

The Netherlands Consumer Authority, which was established under the Consumer Protection Enforcement Act, has been charged with enforcing several consumer protection provisions, covering the following areas, among others:[3]

- unfair commercial practices;
- misleading advertising;
- e-commerce;
- consumer purchases;
- general contract terms;
- distance selling;
- timesharing;
- canvassing (doorstep selling); and
- pricing (price visibility).

(d) *Food safety*

Safety of products in the food and beverage industry in the Netherlands is governed by the directly effective EU Food Regulation, which sets out the general principles and requirements of food (and feed) law. It is also the legal basis for the powers of the EFSA to carry out independent risk assessments and lays down other procedures in matters of food safety.

The EU Food Regulation aims to ensure a high level of protection for human life

3 See www.consumerauthority.nl

and health, also taking into account the protection of animal health and welfare, plant health and the environment (Article 5). Pursuant to Article 14, "food shall not be placed on the market if it is unsafe". Acting contrary to Article 14 is unlawful (Article 2(10) of the Commodities Act Decree on Preparation and Treatment of Food). Member states determine measures and penalties applicable to infringements of food and feed law (Article 17). In the Netherlands, as for offences under the Commodities Act and/or Commodities Act decrees, an Article 14 offence will result in sanctions under either the Commodities Act Decree on Administrative Fines, imposed by the NVWA, or, in case of repeat and/or more severe offences, under the Economic Offences Act.

Food is deemed to be unsafe under the EU Food Regulation if it is considered to be:

- injurious to health; and/or
- unfit for human consumption (Article 14(2)).

Pursuant to Article 18 of the EU Food Regulation, producers are obliged to trace and follow their products through all stages of production, processing and distribution. Under the same article, importers are also required to identify the exporter.

Novel foods: Both the EU Novel Foods Regulation (258/97) and the Commodities Act Decree on Novel Foods contain legislation applicable in the Netherlands to the placing on the market of novel foods and novel food ingredients (ie, foods and food ingredients that have not been used for human consumption to a significant degree in the European Union before May 15 1997).

The premise of the law is that novel foods and novel food ingredients must be safe for consumers and should be adequately labelled so as to not mislead them.

Before a company is allowed to market a novel food or novel food ingredient, it must apply for authorisation and present the scientific information and safety assessment report to an EU country authority. The Dutch novel foods assessment body is the Novel Foods Unit of the CBG.

Genetically modified foods: The EU GM Food and Feed Regulation (1829/2003) contains general requirements for GM food and feed in the European Union. Dutch legislation on GM food is provided for in the Commodities Act Decree on Novel Foods.

According to Article 3(1) of the regulation (and Article 2(2) of the Commodities Act Decree on Novel Foods), GM food must not:

- have adverse effects on human health, animal health or the environment;
- mislead the consumer; or
- differ from the food which it is intended to replace to such an extent that its normal consumption would be nutritionally disadvantageous for the consumer.

Before being placed on the EU market, GM food and feed should undergo a safety assessment through the EFSA (Article 5(2) of the regulation).

The regulation is supplemented by EU Regulation 1830/2003, which ensures traceability and labelling of GM organisms (GMOs) placed on the market. Specifically, the fact that the product consists of or contains GMOs must be stated clearly on the labelling of GM food and feed. As regards traceability, everyone in the supply chain of the GM food or feed must be able to identify the supplier as well as the parties which it has supplied.

Food supplements: The EU Food Supplement Directive (2002/46, as modified by Regulation 1170/2009) contains rules for the labelling of food supplements and introduces specific rules on vitamins and minerals in food supplements. It has been implemented in the Netherlands in the Commodities Act Decree on Supplements and the Commodities Act Regulations on Supplements.

Annex II to the Food Supplement Directive contains a list of permitted vitamin or mineral preparations that may be added for specific nutritional purposes to food supplements.

Food supplements may be marketed without prior approval if they contain vitamin or mineral preparations which are listed in Annex II to the Food Supplement Directive.

Food contact materials, labelling: EU Framework Regulation 1935/2004 contains general requirements for food contact materials (ie, materials and articles intended to come into contact with foods, such as packaging materials and cutlery). In addition to these general requirements, there is separate legislation on specific materials such as plastics and ceramics and certain other substances.

Dutch legislation on food contact materials can be found in the Commodities Act Decree on Packaging Materials and Consumer Items. Food contact materials may be used in the Netherlands only after examination and approval of their components.

The central requirements are that food contact materials be safe and not transfer their components into food in unacceptable quantities, change food composition in an unacceptable way or cause deterioration in taste or odour.

An offence under the Commodities Act Decree on Packaging Materials and Consumer Items will result in a fine under the Commodities Act Decree on Administrative Fines ranging from €525 to €1,050. Repeat and/or more severe offences may result in sanctions under the Economic Offences Act.

The labelling of pre-packed foods is subject to the Food Labelling Commodities Act Decree. Under Article 5, all pre-packed food should be labelled, among other things, with:

- the product name;
- the net quantity;
- a list of ingredients;
- instructions for use;
- any special storage conditions;
- the minimum 'best before' date or latest consumption date; and
- information on the manufacturer, packager or seller.

Some products must be labelled with additional information (Food Labelling Commodities Act Decree).

(e) ***Pharmaceutical products***

The marketing of any pharmaceutical product in the Netherlands which does not have a marketing authorisation for the Netherlands is prohibited (Article 18 of the Medicines Act, which entered into force on July 1 2007).

Under that act, the Healthcare Inspectorate is entitled to impose an administrative fine for violations, with a maximum fine of €450,000 per violation (Article 101(1)). Repeat and/or more severe offences under Article 18 will result in a penalty under the Economic Offences Act: namely, either a penalty of the fourth category (€19,500), a community punishment or a custodial sentence of up to one year.

The CBG assesses and monitors the risks and quality of pharmaceutical products in the Netherlands.

(f) ***Motor vehicles***

The RDW is the national authority responsible for the safety and environmental regulation of motor vehicles in the Netherlands, and may perform certain tests before granting manufacturers of vehicles or components for the automotive industry the approvals required to register and sell their products throughout the European Union (Articles 22, 25a and 26 of the Road Traffic Act). The production, importation or sale of vehicles or components for the automotive industry in the Netherlands without approval from the RDW is prohibited (Article 34 of the Road Traffic Act). An offence under Article 34 will result in a penalty of the fourth category (€19,500), a community punishment or a custodial sentence of up to six months under the Economic Offences Act.

(g) ***Electrical equipment***

The EU Low Voltage Directive (2006/95/EC) contains requirements regarding electrical equipment to ensure that electrical equipment within its scope (ie, all electrical equipment designed for use with a voltage rating of between 50 and 1,000 volts (V) for alternating currents and between 75 and 1,500 V for direct currents) is safe for its intended use. The Commodities Act Decree on Electrical Equipment implements the Low Voltage Directive.

Electrical equipment may be placed on the market only if it does not endanger the safety of persons, domestic animals or property when properly installed and maintained and used in applications for which it was made (Article 2 of the directive).

Offences under the decree will attract a fine under the Commodities Act Decree on Administrative Fines ranging from €525 to €1,050.

Repeat and/or more severe offences of the Commodities Act Decree on Electrical Equipment may result in sanctions under the Economic Offences Act.

Annex 1 to the Low Voltage Directive contains the mandatory safety provisions with which electrical equipment must comply in order to be allowed onto the EU market.

(h) ***Toys***

The EU Toys Directive (2009/48/EC), which substantially amends Directive 88/378/EC, has been implemented in the Netherlands by the Commodities Act Decree on Toys 2011. Pursuant to the decree, the design, manufacture, sale and import of toys should accord with specific requirements set out in the Toys Directive. If a toy is found to be unsafe, a fine under the Commodities Act Decree on Administrative Fines ranging from €525 to €1,050 may be imposed on the manufacturer, distributor or first importer into the European Union of the product in question. Repeat and/or more severe offences of the Toys Decree may result in sanctions under the Economic Offences Act.

(i) ***Cosmetic products***

The EU Cosmetics Directive (76/768/EEC) ensures that only cosmetic products which conform to this directive are put into circulation in the European Union. The Cosmetics Directive will be replaced by EU Regulation 1223/2009 from July 11 2013. The Commodities Act Decree on Cosmetic Products, which implemented the Cosmetics Directive, will be repealed from that date, the EU regulation being directly effective.

The decree contains, among other things, requirements on product information, product safety, composition/ingredients, product labelling, notification to the relevant authority and animal testing.

The main safety requirement is set out in Article 3 of the decree, which states that cosmetic products may not cause damage to human health when they are applied under normal conditions of use. The marketing of cosmetic products that do not meet the safety requirements – for example, because they contain certain forbidden substances – is prohibited (Article 2 of the decree). An offence under Articles 2 and 3 of the decree will result in a fine under the Commodities Act Decree on Administrative Fines ranging from €525 to €1,050. Repeat and/or more severe offences may result in sanctions under the Economic Offences Act.

2.3 Post-market obligations

(a) ***Notification***

Producers and distributors that know or ought to know that a consumer product which they have placed on the market does not comply with the general safety requirements must inform the NVWA or the sector-specific authorities (eg, the Healthcare Inspectorate, the RDW or the Telecommunications Agency) (Article 21b(1) of the Commodities Act).

The notification should be sent to the relevant authorities as soon as information about the dangerous product has become available, and in any event:

- in the case of serious risk, within three days; and
- in other cases, within 10 days.

Until recently, where a defective product had been marketed in more than one member state, notifications had to be sent to each member state separately. Now the

General Product Safety Directive Business Application – a new online notification system which has been operational since May 2009 – makes it possible for businesses to alert all concerned member states at the same time.

This online notification form can be accessed via the European Commission's website at https://webgate.ec.europa.eu/gpsd-ba/index.do. The notification should contain the following information:

- the member states and companies to receive the notification;
- details of the producer/distributor submitting the notification;
- details of the product;
- details of the hazard;
- details of corrective actions already taken or planned;
- details of other companies in the supply chain which hold defective products; and
- relationship to any other notifications.

Once completed, the notification will be made available to the authorities of the selected member states.

An offence under Article 21b(1) of the Commodities Act will result in a fine under the Commodities Act Decree on Administrative Fines ranging from €795 to €1,590. Repeat and/or more severe offences may result in sanctions under the Economic Offences Act.

(b) Food

Food business operators must withdraw foods from the market if they consider or have reason to believe that a food product that they put on the market does not comply with applicable food safety requirements and where the food has left the immediate control of the initial food business (Articles 19(1) and (3) of the EU Food Regulation). The operator should also notify the relevant authorities. Food business operators must also inform the relevant authorities immediately if food they have placed on the market might be injurious to human health.

Member states set the rules on measures and penalties applicable to infringements of food and feed law (Article 17 of the EU Food Regulation). In the Netherlands, as for an offence under the Commodities Act and/or Commodities Act decrees, an offence under Article 19of the EU Food Regulation will result in sanctions under either the Commodities Act Decree on Administrative Fines or the Economic Offences Act.

(c) Pharmaceutical products

Any company which markets a pharmaceutical product in the Netherlands (eg, manufacturers, importers, distributors, pharmacies) is obliged to notify the Healthcare Inspectorate and the CBG if it becomes aware of a defect in a drug product, including its packaging (Article 77(5) of the Medicines Act). Depending on an assessment of the level of risk, a decision will be taken as to whether to recall the product and at what level (consumer/patient level or pharmacist/distributor), and whether the relevant authorities in other countries must be informed.

The Healthcare Inspectorate can impose an administrative fine for violation of Article 77 of the Medicines Act, up to a maximum amount of €450,000 per violation (Article 101(1) of the Medicines Act). Repeat and/or more severe offences under Article 77 will result in either a penalty of the third category (€7,800), a community punishment or a custodial sentence of up to six months (Articles 101(2) and (3) of the Medicines Act).

(d) *Motor vehicles*

A notification of any dangerous motor vehicles or automotive parts in the Netherlands should be filed with the RDW, which will organise and supervise possible recall procedures.

2.4 Powers of authorities

The relevant authorities have the power to order a wide range of (corrective) actions, as appropriate. For example, they can:

- order a manufacturer to recall (potentially) dangerous products from the market or to start a media campaign to inform the public to refrain from using the product;
- make information regarding the health and safety risks of the product available to the general public;
- supervise measures taken by the manufacturer and/or distributor; and
- order a company to re-label its products in order to eliminate the safety risk.

Where a company disagrees with a corrective action ordered by an administrative authority, it can start administrative pre-proceedings by addressing a notice of objection to the authority that issued the order (Articles 6(4) and following of the General Administrative Law Act). The authority will review its order and may change or revoke the order or issue a new order replacing the original order (Articles 6(18) and following of the General Administrative Law Act). If the company disagrees with the decision obtained in the objection proceedings, it may appeal before the administrative division of the competent district court. Depending on the type of the order, a judgment of this administrative division of the district court can be further appealed to one of five types of appellate court, and in the final instance to the Supreme Court.

If a company does not comply with a corrective action ordered by an administrative authority, the authority may rectify the situation by means of administrative coercion (Articles 5(21) and following of the General Administrative Law Act) and perform the corrective action itself – for example, if the situation is unchanged and poses a direct threat to human health. The costs reasonably incurred to enforce an administrative order are payable by the offending company (Article 5(25) of the General Administrative Law Act).

3. International enforcement

The General Product Safety Directive establishes the Community Rapid Information System (RAPEX). The objective of RAPEX is to facilitate the rapid exchange information between member states and the European Commission on measures and actions in relation to consumer products that pose a serious risk to the health and safety of consumers (Article 2(a) of the directive). Examples of products covered by RAPEX are toys, cars and household appliances. The RAPEX system does not cover all consumer products (ie, not pharmaceuticals, active implantable medical devices and food and feed), because certain products are covered by specific and similar systems for the rapid exchange of information (eg, the Rapid Alert System for Food and Feed).

The aim of RAPEX is to prevent the supply to consumers of products which pose a serious risk to their health and safety, and where necessary, to withdraw or recall them from consumers. According to Article 2(d) of the General Product Safety Directive, a 'serious risk' is any risk which requires intervention by public authorities, including risks where the effects are not immediate. The guideline of RAPEX provides further information and criteria for identifying serious risks.

Where a product poses a serious risk the national RAPEX contact point must submit to the European Commission (Directorate-General for Health and Consumer Protection) all relevant details about the product, the risks it poses to consumers and measures taken to prevent risks and accidents. This information will then be rapidly circulated to the other national contact points of other countries participating in RAPEX.

In the Netherlands the primary contact point for RAPEX is the NVWA. For cars and tyres, the contact point is the RDW.

4. Product liability

4.1 Sources of liability

In the Netherlands, claimants can base a product liability claim on one or all of the following three grounds:

- contractual liability;
- tort-based liability; and/or
- the Product Liability Act (which implements the EU Product Liability Directive (85/374/EC)).[4]

(a) Statute

The Product Liability Act has been incorporated in Book 6, Articles 185 to 193 of the Civil Code.

Article 185 imposes strict liability (regardless of fault) on producers and manufacturers that put defective products into circulation on the market, if the defective product causes personal injury or damage to property.

According to Book 6, Article 187(2), a 'producer' is not only the manufacturer of the finished product, raw material or of other component parts, but also anyone that represents itself as the producer of the product by affixing to the product its name,

4 The Product Liability Act applies only to products put into circulation since July 30 1988, which is the date on which the directive should have been implemented in the Netherlands.

trademark or any other distinguishing feature. Importers into the European Economic Area will also be deemed to be 'producers' and may therefore be held liable in respect of defective products too. In addition, suppliers may be liable if the producer or person that supplied them with the product cannot be identified.

The overriding principle is that any product put into circulation by a producer must be safe. A product will be considered unsafe or defective if it does not provide the levels of safety that users are entitled to expect, taking into account all circumstances of the case, such as how the product is presented, the reasonably expected use of the product and the time when the product was put into circulation on the market (Book 6, Article 186).

A producer must take into consideration that a product may not be used in conformity with its purpose and that warnings might not be (fully) heeded. The producer therefore should anticipate any wrongful use of a product that could reasonably be expected.

The Product Liability Act applies only where:

- there is damage in the form of fatal injury or personal injury (Book 6, Article 190), or damage to property other than the product itself;[5]
- the product is intended for private use or consumption; and
- the value of the damage exceeds €500 (Book 6, Article 190).

The Product Liability Act imposes strict liability on producers. The injured person thus need not prove fault of the part of the producer, but must only prove the defect, the damage, and the causal relationship between the two (Book 6, Article 188).

If the injured person successfully proves all elements of the claim, the producer is liable for damage caused by the safety defect in its product, unless it proves one of the following defences outlined in Book 6, Article 185:

- it did not put the product into circulation;
- it is probable that the product did not have the defect which caused the damage at the time when the producer put it into circulation; or
- it did not manufacture the product for sale or for any other form of distribution for economic purposes, or did not manufacture or distribute the product in the course of its professional practice or business;
- the defect has occurred as a result of compliance of the product with mandatory regulations of public authorities;[6]
- in the case of the manufacturer of a component, the defect is attributable to the design of the end-product or to the instructions given by the manufacturer of the end-product; or
- the state of scientific knowledge at the time when the product was put on the market was not such as to enable the defect to be discovered. This so-called 'development risk' defence plays a major role in the Netherlands, as the

5 Damage to the defective product itself is excluded from Book 6, Article 185.

6 However, the mere fact that the product has been put into circulation 'with the permission' of the government in this way will not necessarily relieve the producer from liability. The producer must prove that the design or composition of the product has been described as mandatory by the government, and that the defect directly results from that obligation to comply with mandatory regulations.

country did not choose – as was an option under the Product Liability Directive – to exclude it. The burden of proof regarding the state of scientific and technical knowledge at the time of supply rests with the producer.

Producers may not limit or exclude liability under the Product Liability Act in relation to injured persons by a contractual term or provision (Book 6, Article 192).

Contributory fault: The liability of the producer is reduced or extinguished, having regard to all of the circumstances, if the damage has been caused both by a defect in the product and by the fault of the injured person or of a person for whom the injured person is liable (Book 6, Articles 185 and 101). For example, if a motorist knows that his car's braking system is defective, but nevertheless keeps on driving the car, the obligation of the manufacturer of this braking system to pay compensation may be reduced or extinguished if the damage can also be attributed to the motorist's behaviour.

Limitation period: A right to claim damages by the injured person against the producer pursuant to Book 6, Article 185(1) :

- becomes prescribed three years after the day on which the injured person became aware or should reasonably have become aware of the damage, the defect and the identity of the producer; or
- shall be extinguished10 years from the day on which the producer put the product which caused the damage into circulation. The same time period applies to the rights of a third party against the producer.

(b) ***Tort (negligence)***

Any injured person may also use other rights and actions and therefore – in addition to a product liability claim based on the Product Liability Act – can also base its claim on tort (Book 6, Article 193).

Since only damage to property belonging to a private person can be claimed under the Product Liability Act, a product liability claim for commercial property damage to companies should at all times be based on the tort of the producer or distributor (Book 6, Article 162), or – if a contractual relation exists – on contract law. Additionally, any other claim (of either a consumer or company) for compensation of damages not recognised under Book 6, Article 190 may be based on tort, as under tort law no limitation exists on the kind of damages that can be reimbursed. Product liability losses which can be compensated for under tort law include physical, economical and non-material losses and damage to property, including the defective product (Book 6, Articles 95 to 110).

Also, liability claims that can no longer be based on the Product Liability Act because of limitation periods under that law will mostly be based on tort, since the limitation period for a claim based on tort is longer than that in case of a claim under the Product Liability Act (in general, five years from the day following that on which the injured person has become aware of both the damage and the identity of the person liable for this damage, and in any event 20 years from the day on which the event that caused the damage occurred: see Book 3, Article 310).

Unlawful acts: A person who commits an unlawful act against another person that can be attributed to him is liable to pay compensation (Book 6, Article 162).

An 'unlawful act' includes:

- violation of a right;
- an act or omission breaching a statutory duty; and
- an act or omission breaching a rule of unwritten law relating to proper social conduct (Book 6, Article 162).

In the *Dupont/Hermans* case (HR December 6 1996, NJ 1997, 219) and later in the *Koolhaas/Rockwool* case on semi-finished products (HR October 22 1999, NJ 2000, 159), the Supreme Court ruled that it is unlawful to put a product on the market that does not offer the degree of safety that a user is entitled to expect taking all circumstances into account.

Burden of proof: Contrary to liability under the Product Liability Act, which imposes strict liability on the party that puts the product into circulation, tort liability is considered negligence based and requires fault on the part of the producer.

Under Dutch law, the burden of proof in principle rests with the claimant (Article 150 of the Code of Civil Procedure). The claimant in a product liability case must therefore provide *prima facie* evidence that:

- there was a fault/defect;
- damage occurred; and
- there is a causal relationship between the fault and the damage.

However, under certain circumstances the burden of proof may be mitigated or shifted to the defendant. For example, if the producer fails (adequately) to warn consumers of risks posed by dangerous products supplied to them, the court may decide to shift the burden of proof to the producer. The producer must then prove that it provided consumers with adequate warnings about the unsafe product.

Contributory fault: Where circumstances which can be attributed to the claimant suffering the loss have contributed to the damage, the obligation of the producer to pay compensation is reduced by apportioning the damage between the claimant and producer, *pro rata* according to their contribution to the damage, provided that a different apportionment can be made or the obligation to repair the damage can be extinguished in its entirety depending on the seriousness of the faults or other circumstances of the case (Book 6, Article 101).

(c) ***Contract***

Where there is a contractual relationship between the claimant and producer/supplier, the claimant may also base a product liability claim on contractual liability. Purchasers can claim damages from sellers where a product does not possess the qualities that the purchaser is entitled to expect from the contract, taking into account the nature of the product and any statements made by the seller (Book 7, Article 17).

If the product does not conform to the contract, according to Book 7, Articles 21 and 22 of the Civil Code, the purchaser may demand:

- delivery of anything missing;
- repair of the product, provided that the seller can reasonably comply with this;
- replacement of the product;
- dissolution of the contract, unless the divergence from what was agreed would not justify dissolution because it is so insignificant; an
- a reduction in the price in proportion to the divergence from what was agreed.

The purchaser may exercise the rights and powers mentioned above in addition to any rights under general contract law such as compensation for damages (eg, consequential injury or property damage) and dissolution of the agreement on the basis of Book 7, Article 265 of the Civil Code (Book 7, Article 22).

However, if in the case of a sales agreement between a consumer and a seller, the product sold is defective in the sense of the Product Liability Act, only the producer (not the seller) is liable for damages as referred to in the Product Liability Act (Book 6, Article 190 DCC), unless:

- the seller was (or should have been) aware of the defect;
- the seller promised that the product would be free from defects; or
- the damage does not fall under the Product Liability Act because its value is less than the prescribed minimum limit of €500 (Book 7, Article 24).

The right to claim performance of a contractual obligation to give or to do something expires five years from the day following that on which the obligatory claim has become due and payable.

4.2 Class actions

Certain qualifying foundations or associations can institute a collective action, under Book 3, Article 305 of the Civil Code, provided that that collective action protects the interest of other persons. The foundation or association will be unable to claim collective damages (eg, as a result of a defective product), but can only apply for a declaratory ruling that the defendant is liable. In order to obtain compensation, the individual parties can then go on to start negotiations as regards compensation or start legal proceedings, in which the actual damages sustained have to be established.

Furthermore, on the basis of the Act on Collective Settlement of Mass Damages 2005, an organisation representing several claimants may reach a collective settlement which may be declared binding by the Amsterdam Court of Appeal on behalf of all individuals that suffered damage. Any individual who does not want to be bound by the settlement can opt out within a certain timeframe (Book 7, Articles 907 and following of the Civil Code).

5. Products insurance

5.1 Coverage

(a) ***General liability***

General liability insurance covers the insured's loss caused by third-party claims for personal injury and loss of property damages. The insurance offers broad cover for both contractual and legal liability of the insured.

(b) ***Product recall***

A first-party product recall insurance will generally, up to certain limits and limitations, cover the financial consequences of a recall caused by criminal tampering with the insured products or unintentional error creating a threat to health. Whether such a threat to health exists and whether the measures taken by the insured have thus been necessary are often the subject of negotiation between the insurer and the insured.

(c) ***Contaminated products***

As stated above, product recall insurance usually covers both accidental and malicious product tampering, as a consequence of which recall expenses caused by contaminated products are generally covered under the product recall insurance policy.

(d) ***Product liability***

Generally Dutch companies will have taken out liability insurance which will also apply to product liability.

(e) ***Financial loss***

Financial loss insurance to cover liability for pure economic losses is rare in the Netherlands, as liability for the financial losses incurred by the insured arising from a defective product (eg, loss of turnover or market share) is deemed to be 'entrepreneurial risk'.

(f) ***Product guarantee***

Product guarantee insurance for consumers and/or industrial products that cover contractual liability to repair or replace or improve a product that fails to perform its function or does not meet the agreed specifications is rare and comparatively expensive in the Netherlands.

5.2 General liability insurance

(a) ***Insuring provisions***

General liability insurance covers liability, including product liability, for property damage and bodily injury, and direct financial loss resulting therefrom.

In 1996 a new model policy was introduced, which resulted in a change from 'loss occurring' coverage to 'claims made' coverage. This means that coverage is triggered if, during the period of insurance, a company first becomes aware of the possibility of a claim and/or a claim is actually made against it.

Injury: In the model policy, 'injury' is generally defined as bodily injury, whether or not resulting in death, and direct financial loss resulting therefrom. This generally includes compensation for non-pecuniary losses (eg, psychiatric illness) to which a person that sustained physical harm is entitled pursuant to Book 6, Article 106 of the Civil Code.

Damage: Most general liability policies define 'property damage' as damage, destruction or loss of property other than property of the insured, and direct financial loss resulting therefrom. Property damage generally also includes the pollution or contamination of the product. Unlike loss of use as a consequence of non-conformity, loss of use caused by a material damage of the product is covered under general liability policies.

(b) Exclusions

The burden of proving facts and circumstances that entitle the insurer to rely on an exclusion rests with the insurer.

Liability for loss other than property damage or bodily injury, like pure economic loss, is not covered under a general liability policy. Nor is damage to/repair of products delivered by the insured and damage related to replacement of the product.

In addition, general liability policies will typically contain the following exclusions of coverage:

- Breach of contract – liability for damages caused by the insured's non-compliance with the undertakings under a contract is generally excluded, as this is considered 'entrepreneurial risk'.
- Efficacy – general liability insurance only covers property damage and bodily injury caused by a defective product, but does not guarantee the intended function of the product itself.

War, terrorism, asbestos – bodily injury and property damage arising from war, terrorism, asbestos, electromagnetic fields, fines and punitive damages or from the use of motor vehicles or aircrafts are excluded in most general liability policies.

(c) Conditions

One of the most important insurance conditions is that the insured promptly notify the insurer once it becomes aware of the possibility of a claim and/or that a claim has actually been made. Furthermore, the insured must provide the insurer with all relevant details and documents and must fully cooperate with the insurer in the investigation, settlement or defence of a claim. If the insured does not comply with the duty to notify or to inform, it will be liable for the damage caused to the insurer. The burden of proving that the breach of the condition did not cause damages usually rests with the insured.

5.3 Product recall insurance

Part of the recall costs, like the warning of consumers, can under some circumstances be claimed under general liability insurance as 'costs of mitigation' as mentioned in Book 7, Article 759 of the Civil Code. The insured is obliged by that article to take, within a reasonable period, all measures that could lead to the prevention or reduction of damage as soon as it becomes aware or ought to be aware of the materialisation of the risk, or of a serious threat of such a materialisation.

The mitigation measures should be objectively reasonable and should be performed in order to avert an immediate threat (*Forbo/Centraal Beheer*, HR May 2 1997, NJ 1998, 281). The cover is strictly limited to the costs involved in avoiding the immediate threat – for instance, the costs of a media campaign to inform the public to refrain from using the product. In turn, the insurer will reimburse the expenses connected with these mitigation measures and compensate damage to objects used in this process (Book 7, Article 759(2)).

If the insured has not complied with its mitigation obligation, the insurer is entitled to deduct the value of the damage it has suffered as a result of this non-compliance from the insurance benefit to be paid.

Although the aim of a product recall is to reduce possible damages, not all costs related to a product recall can be claimed as mitigation costs where there is no immediate threat (eg, when the product is still in the distribution chain, but will be harmful only when used), or because these recall costs are considered pure economic loss. For example, the following may be excluded:

- advertising costs to remedy any loss of reputation;
- the costs of destroying/replacing the defective products;
- the value of destroyed products;
- business interruption; and
- loss of turnover.

To cover those costs, and depending on what the insurer is willing to contract, companies might choose either to have a specific product recall clause added to their general liability insurance or to take out a standalone product recall insurance with greater coverage.

Standalone product recall insurance is primarily intended for producers and traders of products in the food, beverage, pharmaceutical, cosmetic and tobacco industries.

(a) *Insuring provisions*

Product recall insurance is triggered on discovery of the following:

- Accidental product contamination – an unintended production error that creates a risk to health or property damage when used; or
- Malicious product tampering – an intentional, criminal alteration or contamination of products (or a threat to do so), by any person (including an employee of the insured), which renders those products unfit or dangerous to use

Companies can choose to have coverage extended to cover official recalls ordered by governmental or regulatory bodies. Recently, for example, such governmental recalls were imposed during the E.Coli scare in the first half of 2011. Since these types of recall take place where the government considers that there is an immediate threat to the health of consumers, it could be argued that (part of) the costs related to such governmental recalls are covered by general liability insurance.

Although coverage will vary from policy to policy, the following costs are generally covered by product recall insurance:

- operational recall costs, including transportation, market communications, storage, scientific tests and destruction of defective products, additional costs of staff, and the value of the recalled products. Usually, the insurer and experts are involved from the beginning of the recall. The actual costs are covered, up to a maximum specified in the policy conditions, calculated in agreement with the insurer/experts;
- loss of gross profit caused by a recall for a period specified in the policy;
- rehabilitation costs – that is, the costs of re-establishing reputation or market share after a recall (eg, advertising expenses, special offers), as well as of restoring the affected product so that it is safe to be sold again (eg, repackaging); and
- the costs of crisis consulting – most policies identify specific crisis consultants that may be consulted in case of a recall.

(b) ***Exclusions***

Common exclusions include the following:

- liability to third parties;
- incidents, claims or losses that were known prior to cover;
- civil or criminal fines, penalties or punitive awards;
- intentional violation by the insured of any governmental or regulatory requirements;
- damage related to asbestos; and
- radioactive contamination.

(c) ***Conditions***

The insured must promptly notify the insurer once it has discovered the need to recall and to provide the insurer with all relevant details.

A clause on non-disclosure of the existence of the insurance policy is rare under Dutch law.

Some insurers make available a specially trained crisis team to provide assistance to insureds in emergencies. The costs of this assistance are generally covered by the insurance policy.

5.4 Financial losses insurance

In the Netherlands, it is not common to take out an insurance policy for liability for financial losses incurred by third parties arising from the defective product and for which the insured is legally liable. This type of loss is normally considered 'entrepreneurial risk' and is not insurable. Since these losses are considered to be the result of poor quality management by, or products of, the insured, the general opinion of Dutch insurers is to not cover such losses.

5.5 Product guarantee insurance

While the insured may be legally liable for the costs of repairing or replacing a product that fails to perform its intended function, these costs are generally excluded from coverage under the general liability policy, as this type of damage is again generally considered 'entrepreneurial risk' of the insured. Although it is possible to cover this guarantee through a standalone product guarantee insurance, such tailor-made insurance (eg, relating to the specific functioning of a machine) is comparatively expensive and rare.

5.6 General principles of Dutch insurance law

(a) *Disclosure obligation*

One of the basic principles of Dutch insurance law is that the insured must disclose to the insurer all facts that are important to the insurer's decision as to whether to agree to the insurance. Unless there was intent to mislead the insurer, the insured is not obliged to provide information if the insured has not raised the question.

If a non-disclosure is discovered, the insurer may terminate the contract within two months of the date of discovery. If the facts which are not (or are incorrectly) disclosed are immaterial to assessment of the risk, the insured will still be entitled to full compensation. If, in the case of non-fulfilment of the disclosure obligation, the insurer would have stipulated a higher premium had it been properly informed, or would have concluded the insurance for a lower insured sum, compensation will be reduced in proportion to the premium or insured sum. If the insurer would have stipulated other terms had it been aware of the true state of affairs, then the insured is entitled to compensation only as if those less favourable terms were included in the contract.

(b) *Indemnity principle*

The insured will not receive compensation under the insurance policy if this would place it in a clearly more advantageous position than it was beforehand, unless the value of the insured subject is assessed beforehand either.

(c) *Duty to prevent or minimise loss*

Another basic principle under Dutch insurance law is that as soon as an insured is or ought to be aware of the materialisation of the risk, it must take all possible measures and necessary steps to prevent or minimise the loss or damage. The insurer will reimburse the reasonable costs of measures taken to do so.

(d) *Policy interpretation*

Under Dutch law, contracts are to be interpreted not just literally, but by applying principles of reasonableness and fairness. Consequently, the parties' intention and reasonable understanding as to the meaning of contractual provisions play a central role (the 'Haviltex criteria'). Depending on the type of contract, other relevant factors may come into play.

As regards insurance contracts in particular, objective elements such as the wording of policy conditions are important factors for interpretation (given that parties generally do not negotiate those conditions); but the intention of the parties (ie, what they intended should be covered and what they have reasonably understood to be covered) is also important.

Finally, under Dutch law, due to the *contra proferentem* principle, where there is ambiguity on the interpretation of a contractual term or provision, that term or provision should be interpreted to the detriment of the party that drafted the contract (ie, in favour of the party that did not draft the document).

Poland

Tomasz Jaworski
Salans Warsaw

1. Product safety regulation

1.1 Product risks

The contemporary legal framework for product safety and product liability in Poland is a mix of rules established in jurisprudence based on traditional notions of tort and contract liability on the one hand, and new law adopted in the process of proximation to EU law before Poland's accession to the European Union in 2004.

The main framework of the system is based on:

- the Civil Code of April 23 1964;
- the Act of March 2 2000 on Protection of Certain Rights of Consumers and Liability for Damage Caused by a Hazardous Product (Journal of Laws 2000, 22, 271 of March 31 2000), which is a transposition into Polish law of the EU Product Liability Directive (85/374/EEC); and
- the Act of December 12 2003 on General Safety of Products (Journal of Laws 2003, 229, 2275 of December 31 2003, which is the transposition into Polish law of EU Directive 2001/95/EC and the General Product Safety Directive.

A general regime of product safety is supplemented by sector-specific regulations.

Protection of consumers and other end users from threats to their health and safety is also stipulated in the Polish Constitution of April 2 1997 (Article 76).

1.2 Safety standards

The General Product Safety Act defines a 'safe product' as a product which does not create any risks for consumers, or creates risks which are negligible and compatible with the normal use of the product and with a high standard of health and protection of life. This assessment must take into account the normal or reasonably foreseeable conditions of use, as well as the time of using the product, type of product, method of use, requirements for installation and maintenance, interaction with other products, markings and instructions, and finally the category of consumers exposed to product-related risks, especially infants and seniors.

An example of how these rules are applied in practice was given in a judgment of February 21 2008 (Case VI SA/Wa 1902/07) where the regional administrative court in Warsaw held that marking an electrical appliance as fit to be used under an intensity of up to 16A makes the manufacturer liable for the safety of the product working up to the extreme current intensity of 16A, regardless of normal use of the product by consumers.

'Products which are not safe' are defined as any products which fall outside the scope of definition of 'safe product'. A product cannot be regarded as not safe merely due to the fact that a higher safety standard is achievable or that safer products are available.

The General Product Safety Act does not apply to products covered by specific safety requirements; however the general rules on obligations, supervision and enforcement apply where these issues are not regulated specifically in sector regulations. Potential overlap of general and specific regulations sometimes causes interpretation problems, especially regarding the competence of supervisory bodies in specific sectors.

'Products' are defined as movables, new or used, intended for consumers or likely to be used by consumers even if not intended for that purpose. It is irrelevant whether a product is sold or made available gratuitously.

Specific rules pertain to 'imitations', ie, products whose appearance suggests a purpose other than their real purpose and which accordingly pose a risk to consumers. It is prohibited to suggest (through shape, scent, colour, composition, markings etc.) that the imitation is a nutritional product, if consumption of the product may cause danger to life or health. There is a requirement (among other things) that the real purpose of the imitation be disclosed on the packaging, and that information is included as to cautionary measures.

For products covered by specific safety requirements, Polish law gives precedence to EU norms. In the absence of any EU law governing the safety of a specific type of product, the product is deemed safe if it meets the provisions of Polish law pertaining to specific types of products.

Another presumption of conformity with safety standards is provided where a product meets the national safety norms of another EU member state, if such norms transpose safety norms accepted by the European Commission and published in the *Offical Journal*.

If the above provisions of law or safety norms for specific products are not in place, product safety is assessed taking into account all types of voluntary norms, Commission guidelines, good practice, legitimate expectations of consumers, state of the art, and, last but not least, so-called Polish Norms (PN) – a set of technical standards elaborated and regularly published by the Polish Standards Committee, once legally binding but now only voluntary.

Conformity with applicable norms creates a presumption of safety but does not preclude the supervisory authority from taking action if a product is found not safe despite compliance with the norms.

1.3 Sector-specific compliance

In certain sectors placing products on the market requires prior regulatory approval, or other forms of safety checks. Examples are shown below.

(a) Medicines

Medicinal products may be placed on the market only with prior marketing authorisation issued by a national authority, the Office for Registration of Medicinal

Products, Medical Devices and Biocidal Products, or by the European Commission. Likewise, the manufacturing of medicinal products requires a prior administrative licence.

The safety of a medicinal product is a major priority in the procedure for marketing authorisation, next to quality and efficacy.

The marketing authorisation or licence does not release the marketing authorisation holder or the manufacturer from liability for injury caused by the product.

(b) *Medical devices*

Placing a medical device on the market does not require administrative approval, but it does involve notifiying the regulatory authority 14 days prior to its being placed on the market for the first time.

The manufacturer (or any other entity which is responsible for placing the device on the market) is also obliged to perform a prior assessment of compliance with essential requirements and obtain a CE marking. Implants must also undergo a prior clinical assessment to assess adverse effects and a risk–benefit ratio. The procedure and scope of the assessment (depending on the category of a device), as well as a list of entities authorised to run the assessment procedure, are set out in a set of regulations from the Minister of Health. It is forbidden to market a product which does not hold a valid CE certificate.

The Act of May 20 2010 on medical devices defines the safety duties of entities involved in placing the product on the market in a manner which complies with the general safety requirements set out in the General Product Safety Act. By way of example, a general safety requirement for a medical device is defined as a prohibition to market in any way a product which poses a threat to the safety, life or health of patients, users or other persons, to the extent that it exceeds an acceptable risk determined on the basis of the state of the art, if properly supplied, installed, maintained or used in line with foreseen purposes. Importers and distributors are under a duty to act with due care in order to ensure the safety of products, including the duty to verify whether the manufacturer complied with its obligations pertaining to CE marking and whether its instructions for use are adequate.

There are also specific requirements for handling information on potential safety issues concerning medical devices (so-called 'medical incidents').

(c) *Food*

Food safety is regulated by a separate act of August 25 2006 on the Safety of Food and Nutrition.

Most safety norms pertaining to food are either transposed from EU law, or the respective EU law applies directly in Poland.

Placing food on the market does not require any regulatory approval. With respect to certain types of food (baby food, special nutritional products, food supplements, and products containing vitamins or minerals) it is a requirement that the chief health inspector be notified prior to the product being placed on the market for the first time. The Inspector may decide to launch explanatory proceedings (lasting up to 60 days) before placing the product on the market to verify whether the product meets prescribed requirements and whether it should instead be classed as a cosmetic, medical device or a medicine.

Administrative measures regarding the safety of food, including decisions to stop its sale, may be taken by the central and local health inspection authorities.

(d) *Cosmetics*

The Act of March 30 2001 on cosmetics sets a general requirement that cosmetics used in usual or foreseeable conditions must not pose a threat to human health. Certain substances cannot be used in cosmetics.

Placing cosmetics on the market does not require any special administrative permit; nor does the manufacture of cosmetics. The manufacturer is only obliged to report basic data regarding a cosmetic before first placing it on the market, which is recorded in a National System for Information on Cosmetics placed on the Market.

The Chief Sanitary Inspector may temporarily prohibit or restrict the sale of a cosmetic if it is reported that the cosmetic poses a threat to human health.

(e) *Toys, machinery, electrical equipment*

Toys, machinery and electrical equipment are examples of products which, in order to be legally marketed, must undergo a procedure of assessment of compliance with essential requirements and obtain a CE marking.

Essential requirements for toys, machinery, electrical equipment and many other types of products are regulated in regulations of the Minister of Economy which transpose relevant EU directives.

1.4 Safety issues

(a) *Sector organisation*

The competent authority regarding general product safety issues is the Chairman of the Office for Protection of Competition and Consumers (UOKiK). Other authorities supervise safety in specific sectors, eg, the Chief Pharmaceutical Inspector and regional pharmaceutical inspectors (medicinal products); the Chairman of the Office for Registration of Medicinal Products, Medical Devices and Biocidal Products (medicinal products, medical devices); or the Chief Sanitary Inspector and regional sanitary inspectors (food, cosmetics).

(b) *Obligations of producers and distributors*

The general obligations of producers and distributors are set out in the General Product Safety Act. Specific obligations may apply with respect to specific types of products, either on a supplementary basis (eg, toys, where producers are under a specific obligation to investigate reported safety incidents) or under an entirely separate regime of safety control (eg, medicinal products).

(c) *Types of corrective action*

Under the general product safety regime certain corrective actions may or should be taken by producers and distributors themselves (eg, public information on a safety issue), while others may be imposed by administrative authorities (eg, a decision to order recall). Details are presented in section 2 below.

Specific corrective actions may result from sector regulations for particular types of products (eg, the obligation to inform physicians of safety issues related to a medicinal product).

(d) ***Criminal liability***

The General Product Safety Act does not set out criminal liability for failure to comply with safety requirements. Instead monetary fines may be imposed, up to PLN100,000 (€23,000).

Manufacture or placing on the market of a product which is dangerous to human life or health may be subject to criminal liability based on general provisions of the Criminal Code, eg, for exposing another person to a direct danger of loss of life or a severe impairment to health (up to three years imprisonment) or bringing about a danger to the life or health of many people or to property of a very significant value by producing or placing on the market a substance detrimental to health, food products or other articles of common use, or medicinal products which do not meet the quality requirements (punishable by six months to eight years' imprisonment).

Criminal sanctions are also stipulated in some sector-based acts, eg, manufacturing or placing on the market of food harmful to human health or life, punishable by a fine, restriction of liberty or up to two years' imprisonment.

2. Obligations of producers and distributors

2.1 Pre-market obligations

(a) ***Statute***

The main statutory pre-market obligations of producers and distributors with regard to product safety are set out in the General Product Safety Act.

The definition of a producer under the General Product Safety Act includes:

- entities based in the EU/EEA who manufacture (or repair) the product, as well as those who act like a producer by branding the product;
- for products manufactured outside EU/EEA (importers into EU/EEA or entities appointed by the actual manufacturer as its representatives); and
- entities participating in the process of supply of the product, if their activity may impact on the safety features of the product.

Distributors are entities that participate in the process of supply of the product, whose activity does not impact on its safety.

Pre-market obligations of the producer under the General Product Safety Act include the following:

- to place only safe products on the market; and
- when placing the product on the Polish market, to provide consumers with the relevant safety information and precautions in Polish.

Polish law respects the obligation to assess compliance of products with essential requirements (where applicable) prior to placing on the market and to mark products with CE marking.

(b) Tort

Failure to comply with the pre-marketing safety duties set out in the General Product Safety Act and sector-based acts constitutes unlawful behaviour and may lead to the liability of the manufacturer or distributor for damage and injury, provided that there is an adequate causal link between the manufacturer's or distributor's behaviour and the damage/injury.

If claims are pursued based on a strict liability regime (implementing the Product Liability Directive), demonstration of fault on the part of the defendant is not required.

For cases falling outside the scope of strict liability, it must be demonstrated that the defendant's act or omission was culpable (ie, at least negligent). However courts tend to apply rules favourable to claimants, do not require proof of the fault of individual employees of the defendant and are open to accept presumptions regarding negligence on the part of the manufacturer.

(c) Contract

Producers (eg, subcontractors or suppliers of raw materials) and distributors may incur further obligations pertaining to pre-marketing product safety requirements than those stipulated by the law. Breach of such contractual obligations may give rise to liability in damages only between the parties to the contract.

The parties may not contract out of their statutory duties. Contractual arrangements which release the producer or the distributor from their statutory duties would likely be null and void. The producer or distributor may contract out performance of certain duties, eg, reporting obligations but will remain liable for failure to comply, including administrative fines and criminal liability, if the subcontractor fails to perform.

2.2 Post-market obligations

(a) Statute

Post-market obligations of the producer under the General Product Safety Act include the duty to act with due diligence and to take actions relevant to the features of the product which allow the gathering of information on potential risks and the avoidance of risks, including recall from the market, recall from consumers or issuing effective warnings to consumers.

'Due diligence' is not defined for the purpose of the General Product Safety Act, nor has it been defined by the courts.

Recalls may be initiated by the producer itself, or ordered by the supervisory authority. In theory, the recall may be actually performed by the supervisory authority (including collection of items gathered by distributors and utilisation by way of so-called 'substitute performance'. If the producer fails to comply with the order, the authority may appoint another entity to perform the necessary actions (collection from distributors, utilisation) and shall order the producer to bear the costs of using another entity to perform the duty. There is no publicly available information on using the procedure of substitute performance for recall of products.

In one case the state authorities performed a *de facto* recall using (or, as some say, misusing) a procedure of securing evidence for the purpose of criminal proceedings. The recall pertained to medicines suspected of contamination and was performed by the police and public prosecutors. As a result the majority of medicines under a suspect brand which were then present on the market were seized and stored for the purpose of laboratory tests.

In the years from 2005 to 2010 more than 500 voluntary notifications were made under the General Product Safety Act, mainly involving the automotive industry. A notable number of notifications concerned electrical equipment and infant products.

Post-market obligations of the distributor include the duty to:

- act with due diligence in order to ensure the safety of products, including an obligation not to supply products which it knows or should know are not safe;
- participate in safety monitoring, including gathering information on risks from consumers and conveying this to the producer and supervisory authorities; and
- retain documentation required to track products.

Both producers and distributors are required to:

- cooperate with the supervisory authorities to avoid or eliminate risks created by their products; and
- notify the supervisory authority without delay after obtaining information that the product is not safe.

Notification of a product which is not safe should be made in an official form prescribed by the law (see Regulation of the Council of Ministers of April 26 2005 concerning the form of notification of a product which is not safe, *Official Journal*, May 10 2005, 80, 694, available at www.uokik.gov.pl/download.php?plik=10259)

The notification should specify information about the notifying party, the product (category, brand, type, Combined Nomenclature code, country of origin), the risk (including possible risk to life or safety, conclusions from risk assessment), corrective actions already undertaken by the notifying party (type, extent, time period, party responsible for particular corrective actions), as well as other entities in the supply chain who are in possession of unsafe products, including contact data and the quantity of possessed products and batch numbers. The latter category of information may be provided separately, if not available at the date of the original notification.

The law does not prescribe a defined timeframe for notification: it should be done "without delay", immediately after the product is discovered to be unsafe.

Certain categories of products are exempt from this notification duty, for example, when:

- specific provisions regarding notification are in place (eg, for medicinal products, medical devices);
- the producer has already taken all reparatory actions, and in particular recalled all unsafe items or batches, provided that the producer can demonstrate the actions undertaken;
- the problem concerns quality but not safety of the product;
- the product does not meet safety norms but the producer is able to demonstrate that it nevertheless does not create a risk to consumers;
- it has been confirmed that the UOKiK has already been notified by another party and has all necessary information; and
- the producer is able to demonstrate that the risk was caused by a single item or the risk occurred in isolated cases which is unlikely to be repeated.

Producers are under a general requirement to take steps which enable a recall or effective warning of consumers. The duty may be fulfilled by marking the contact data of the producer or a batch number on the packaging. These obligations are neither absolute nor exclusive: the producer may act otherwise, if justified in given circumstances. In any case, the decision of a producer must be taken with due care and must take into account the features of the product.

The producer may also be ordered to ensure traceability of a product in a manner prescribed by UOKiK.

The producer should consider, to the extent required by due care and diligence and the features of a product, whether to test samples, analyse consumer complaints and/or register those complaints.

The distributor is under a duty to keep and make available at the request of the authorities any documentation required to track back the product.

(b) Tort

Failure to comply with the post-market safety duties set out in the General Product Safety Act and sector-based acts constitutes unlawful behaviour and may lead to the liability of the manufacturer or distributor for damage and injury on the same terms as for pre-market duties.

(c) Contract

As with pre-market obligations, producers (eg, subcontractors or suppliers of raw materials) and distributors may incur further obligations pertaining to product safety than those stipulated by the law. Breach of such contractual obligations may give rise to liability in damages only between the parties to the contract.

3. Enforcement

3.1 Sectors

The supervisory authority competent in general product safety matters is UOKiK, which is also the competent authority for anti-monopoly issues.

UOKiK is assisted by Regional Trade Inspectors who carry out controls to ensure compliance with general product safety requirements and who may issue decisions regarding the defective marking of products.

For certain types of products, the regulator may be a specialised body with its own sector-specific set of powers, such as pharmaceutical inspection (for medicinal products), Office for Registration of Medicinal Products, Medical Devices and Biocidal Products (medicinal products, medical devices, biocidal products) or health inspection (food, cosmetics).

(a) *Powers*

If there are grounds to question the safety of a product, UOKiK instigates explanatory proceedings. UOKiK acts *ex officio* but its actions are usually based on information from the market, from trade inspectors or its counterparts from other EU countries.

Normally the only other party to the proceedings is the producer or distributor; however, consumer NGOs and business organisations may also have standing.

Explanatory proceedings must not last longer than four months.

Before issuing a final decision, UOKiK may take certain interim measures by which it may:

- issue an interim ruling to take prescribed actions to eliminate risks created by the product;
- temporarily ban the supply, offer or presentation of the product for a maximum period of 30 days (in exceptional cases this may be extended to a maximum total of 90 days) in order to conduct tests; and
- inform the public about the issuing of the interim decision.

Proceedings should be discontinued if the producer or distributor has eliminated the risk, or if the product is found to be safe. Otherwise, UOKiK issues a final decision or decisions in which it may:

- order appropriate marking of the product in order to warn of risks;
- order that prescribed safety requirements are met before the product is placed on the market;
- order the producer or distributor to warn a specified category of consumers or to notify the general public of risks, in a specified form and within a specified deadline;
- decide to publish a warning *ex officio*;
- order the elimination of risks;
- prohibit the placing of the product on the market and order actions necessary to ensure that the prohibition is observed;
- order immediate recall from the market; and
- order recall from consumers and destruction of the product (the ultimate measure, applicable only if other measures would be insufficient to prevent serious risks caused by the product).

Any of the above decisions is a basis for entry of a product on the public register of hazardous products held by UOKiK. An entry may be deleted only at the request of an interested party who demonstrates that the product was recalled from the market (not sooner than six months following the completion of recall) or that irregularities were eliminated (not sooner than 12 months after elimination of irregularities). The register is available on the Internet. As an additional measure, UOKiK may decide to announce publicly that a specific entry has been made.

In 2010 UOKiK handled almost 300 cases of potentially hazardous products and issued 84 decisions.

'Recall from the market' is defined as collection of all items by the producer from the distributors as well as a prohibition on distributors from presenting or offering the product to consumers.

'Recall from consumers' is defined as collection of all items returned by consumers and reimbursement of the full purchase price. Consumers are entitled to require that the product is bought back for the full purchase price by the distributor (based on proof of purchase) or by the producer (if no proof of purchase is available).

3.2 International enforcement

Polish product safety authorities participate in European rapid alert systems. The national contact point for RAPEX is the Office for Protection of Competition and Consumers (UOKiK) and for RASFF the chief health inspector.

3.3 Appeals

As a rule the supervisory measures taken by the competent authorities take the form of administrative decisions.

Decisions are always appealable. Appeals are heard either by the higher instance authority (for decisions taken by regional structures) or by the authority which issued the decision (decisions issued by central authorities such as UOKiK or the Chief Sanitary Inspector). If the appeal is dismissed, a party may seek review of the decision by the administrative court.

Interim decisions (such as temporary prohibitions on selling the product until doubts regarding safety are eliminated in explanatory proceedings) are usually immediately enforceable and appeals do not have suspensive effect. Other decisions are not enforceable until the second instance hears the case or unless they are not granted immediate enforceability for safety reasons. Court appeals do not suspend the enforceability of the decision, unless the court itself decides to do so.

3.4 Sanctions and compensation

(a) Penalties

Failure to comply with General Product Safety Act requirements may lead to financial penalties. Penalties are imposed by the chairman of UOKiK, by way of separate administrative decisions.

The maximum financial penalty is PLN100,000 (€23,000). A penalty may be imposed for the following acts or omissions.

Producer or distributor:

- failure to notify of a hazardous product;
- refusal to provide information necessary to verify the safety of the product,

or provision of untrue or misleading information;
- failure to comply with UOKiK decisions; and
- placement on the market of a product entered in the registry of hazardous products.

Producer:
- failure to provide consumers relevant information in Polish on product safety;
- placement on the market of a product which is unsafe.

Distributor:
- intentional or negligent supply of unsafe products;
- failure to pass on to producers and supervisory authorities information from consumers about risks caused by products; and
- failure to disclose documents required to track the origination of the product.

(b) Compensation

Failure to comply with safety requirements may result in compensation due to persons or entities harmed. Compensation cannot be awarded in administrative proceedings. It requires a civil lawsuit or the filing of an appropriate request in criminal proceedings.

3.5 Multiple jurisdictions

The obligations of producers/distributors under the General Product Safety Act and the respective competence of authorities pertain only to events taking place in the territory of Poland. In cross-border matters Polish authorities cooperate with their counterparts in other states, especially through the RAPEX and RASFF systems.

4. Product liability

4.1 Potential defendants

The group of potential defendants depends on the source of liability.

4.2 Strict liability

In claims pursued based on the strict liability principle (Articles 449(1)-(11) of the Civil Code, implementing Directive 85/374/EEC), potential defendants include:
- manufacturers of the product;
- manufacturers of materials, raw materials or components (unless the damage resulted exclusively from the construction of a product or manufacturer's instructions);
- entities presented as manufacturers because the products bear their brands, trademarks or other distinctive marks (brander); and
- entities which import products in Poland (importer).

The liability of all entities listed above is joint and several.

Moreover the law provides for subsidiary liability of distributors. If none of the entities listed above are known, liability rests with the entity which sold the product to the injured person. The distributor may avoid liability by disclosing details of the manufacturer, quasi-manufacturer, importer, or another distributor who supplied the product. The shift of liability is effective only if the distributor disclosed the relevant data within a month of notification of damage.

(a) ***General tort liability***

In claims based on the general tort liability principle, the list of potential defendants should be assessed on a case-by-case basis, in particular taking into account the stage of manufacture or distribution where the cause of damage occurred. Depending on the circumstances of the case, the liability may be attributed to:

- end manufacturers;
- suppliers of materials or components;
- holders of administrative permits for the sale of the product (if not the manufacturer);
- entities responsible for safety instructions (if not the manufacturer); and
- importers or distributors.

Branders will not typically be held liable based on general tort rules.

If liability may be attributed to more than one defendant, they will typically be held liable jointly and severally, however other arrangements can also be taken into consideration in specific cases (eg, several defendants liable but with no right of recourse among them).

(b) ***Contractual liability***

As a rule, liability for a breach of contract may be attributed only to a party to the contract (eg, a supplier of a component towards the manufacturer; a retail distributor towards the consumer).

Where claims are pursued based on a contract, the defendant would typically be a vendor of the defective product, or, in specific cases where a defect appeared after sale, the entity which installed the product or which delivered it to the client.

For products covered by an additional quality warranty, claims may be pursued directly against a guarantor, typically a manufacturer, importer or one of the distributors.

Polish procedure allows for pursuing claims based on alternative legal bases, including suing multiple defendants based on different legal grounds (provided that one court is competent for all claims, with certain further restrictions regarding types of claims available under respective liability regimes). For example, it is possible to name as defendants in one-and-the-same case a manufacturer based on strict liability and a vendor based on contract.

4.3 Sources of liability

(a) ***Statute***

The duty to compensate for injury or damage caused by a product is based either on tort (strict liability or general tort liability), or contract.

Principles for both tort and contract liability are stipulated in the statutes:

- Strict liability is regulated in Articles 449(1)–(11) of the Civil Code;
- General tort liability is regulated in Articles 415–440 of the Civil Code, and the source of duties pertaining to legal safety may be found in numerous legal acts, starting from the General Product Safety Act; and
- Contractual liability is regulated in numerous articles of the Civil Code and, for consumer claims, also in the Act of July 27 2002 on specific terms of consumer sale.

(b) ***Strict liability***

A regulation implementing the Product Liability Directive which set strict liability for a product was introduced to Polish law in 2000. Strict liability for a hazardous product is treated by most commentators as a specific type of tort liability.

The source of strict liability arises with the manufacture of a hazardous product in the scope of its economic activity. It is no-fault liability. It is presumed that a hazardous product was manufactured and placed on the market by the manufacturer in the course of its economic activity. The claimant must prove the damage, the fact that the product was hazardous, and the causal link between the effect of the hazardous product and the damage.

A very limited range of exemptions from liability is available and the burden of proof lies with the defendant. Available defences include:

- non-placement of a product on the market, or placement on the market beyond the defendant's control;
- hazardous features appearing after its placement on the market; and
- 'state of the art' defence.

Force majeure does not exempt from liability, neither does the claimant's exclusive fault (which may however reduce the amount of compensation).

(c) ***General tort liability***

The general principle of tort liability comes under Article 415 of the Civil Code pursuant to which one who caused damage to another person due to his fault is obliged to redress it.

Prerequisites for tort liability which must be demonstrated by the claimant are:

- damage (which may include personal injury as well as actual damage to one's assets and lost profits);
- breach of law or duty (which means breach of any provision of statutory law, including but not limited to manufacturer's duties under the General Product Safety Act or under the specific sector regulations, as well as a violation of norms of behaviour which are not statutory law but may be defined as 'good custom');
- fault; and
- adequate causal link between the damage and the breach of law or duty.

Normally, where the tort liability of a corporation is pursued, fault of a specified natural person(s) acting on behalf of the corporation should be demonstrated. However, prior to the introduction of the strict liability regime based on the directive, the courts adopted the notion of 'anonymous fault' to be applied in product liability cases which discharged claimants from the obligation to demonstrate fault on the part of specific natural persons. The Supreme Court also determined that placing an unsafe product on the market constituted a tort before the new provisions on strict liability came into force.

Currently claimants may choose to base claims for damages caused by a hazardous product on strict liability and/or general tort liability. Bearing in mind the claimant-friendly provisions regarding strict liability, in certain cases it may be recommended to combine it with general tort claims, eg, where significant damage to estates is pursued.

(d) *Contract*

Contractual liability for a defective product pertains first and foremost to the obligations of a vendor to repair, replace or decrease the price of, a defective product. In consumer cases more stringent rules apply, stipulated in the Act of July 27 2000 on specific terms of consumer sale (implementing Directive 99/44/EC), with a number of presumptions and facilitations which benefit the consumer. Non-consumers may take advantage of provisions on implied warranty in sale contracts (or, as appropriate, in lease contracts, specific task contracts, or construction contracts), which, unlike a consumer warranty, may be modified at the parties' will.

Additional rights may be vested in the purchaser of the product by way of an additional quality guarantee granted either by the manufacturer, distributor or direct seller.

Liability under implied warranty or under additional quality guarantee is not dependent on a vendor's fault.

Apart from claims for replacement, repair or price reduction, purchasers may also pursue compensation if they incurred actual damage or lost profits as a result of purchasing a defective product. In this case claimants should demonstrate:

- damage;
- breach of contract; and
- an adequate causal link between the damage and the breach.

The fault is presumed, and the defendant may counter by proving that it performed the contract with due care.

(e) *Contributory negligence defence*

Contribution of the claimant to the infliction of damage or to the amount of damage results in proportionate reduction (but not entire denial) of due compensation. The scale of reduction is subject to the court's decision and should be made according to the circumstances, and particularly to the extent of both parties' fault.

4.4 Claimants; class actions

Claims under strict liability and the general tort liability regime may be pursued by persons injured or who incurred damage as a result of the dangerous features of a product, irrespective of whether they purchased the product or were only exposed to it.

Claims for compensation for personal injury may be pursued also by heirs of the injured person after the person's death. Relatives may also claim compensation for moral damages caused by the death of a family member.

Contractual claims may be pursued only by a party to a contract. The purchaser of a product acquires rights under implied warranty only towards the direct supplier, and not towards previous distributors.

Certain product liability claims may be pursued in a class (group) action. The Polish Act on Pursuing Claims in Group Proceedings was introduced in 2010. It provides for an opt-in system, with at least 10 claimants forming the initial group. Claims fit for aggregation in a group action must meet the requirement of similarity. Where monetary claims are pursued, claimants must also aggregate the amount of individual awards sought. Or they may choose to restrict the claims to the establishment of the defendant's liability, and leave actual payments to be pursued in individual proceedings to follow the group action.

Claims arising from defects of products may fall into each category of cases admitted to group proceedings – that is:

- cases for the protection of consumer rights;
- product liability cases; and
- tort cases.

An important category of claims which cannot be pursued as group actions are 'claims for protection of personal interests', which category has been traditionally understood in Polish law as including, among others, all types of claims available to a person who suffered personal injury. There is a dispute among Polish commentators and practitioners as to how broadly this exemption should be construed and whether it applies only to tort cases, or all types of cases fit for group actions. If the latter, this would appear to nearly extinguish the possibility of a group action in product liability cases.

4.5 Causation

Establishing a causal link between the defendant's act or omission, or the effect of a product, and the suffered damage is a requirement for all types of product liability discussed here. It is always the claimant's obligation to demonstrate that a causal link exists. In practice the proof of causation appears to be the most difficult element of the dispute from the claimant's perspective, especially in medicinal products cases.

The defendant will be liable only for the normal consequences of an act or omission which resulted in the damage (principle of 'adequate causality'). For strict liability this rule is applied to a link between the effect of a product and the damage. Whether the damage is a typical or atypical result of an action, omission or product's effect, must be assessed on a case-by-case basis.

In cases where damage resulted from an omission (failure to act), the causal link is usually controversial. According to the most popular view, a casual link between the omission and the damage exists if it is demonstrated that:

- the defendant was under a duty to act in a specified manner;

- the defendant could in fact act as required; and
- had the defendant acted as required, the damage would normally not have arisen.

4.6 Remedies

Compensation for personal injury may be pursued on the basis of strict liability and general tort liability. Available claims include compensation for negative mental experience associated with the injury, as well as the economic consequences of an injury, eg, loss of ability to earn a living, expenses for medical treatment.

Awarded compensation may, depending on the type of damage or injury to be redressed, take either or both the form of one-off payment and annuity (periodical) payments.

In case of death of the injured, closest relatives may pursue compensation for the loss of family ties. Costs of medical treatment and funeral are recoverable. The Polish law allows the family relatives, and in justified cases also other close persons, to claim annuity payments for loss of dependency and support. Close family relatives may also claim one-off compensation for serious deterioration of their life situation.

The average amount of compensation for personal injury, is in the region of €5,000–€10,000. In cases of serious personal injury amounts awarded by the courts reach a level of approximately €50,000–€150,000, and even more in isolated cases. In case of death of the injured, relatives are awarded amounts in the region of €10,000–€20,000, however in isolated cases compensation may amount to €50,000 and more. Compensation for economic damage covers both actual damage and lost profits. Pursuing claims for (economic) damages is available under the general tort regime with no restrictions, while it is restricted under the strict liability regime (no liability for damage to items not for personal use, no liability for damage to the product itself, for profits lost due to damage of a product, no liability for damage not higher than €500).

Contractual liability covers both actual damage and lost profits, however contractual liability for personal injury is excluded.

4.7 Limitation

Claims under the strict liability regime and under the general tort regime are time-barred after three years following the date when the injured party learned (or should have learned – under the strict liability regime) of the damage and of the identity of the liable person. The timebar shall in no case be longer than 10 years – following the placing of the product on the market (for strict liability) or following the damage causing a harmful incident (for general tort liability).

Further rules for general tort liability include:

- extension of the limitation period to 20 years for damages caused as a result of crime;
- no expiry of the limitation period for personal injury claims sooner than three years following the date when the injured party learned of the damage of the identity of the person obliged to redress it; and
- no expiry of the limitation period earlier than two years after the claimant comes of age.

Time limitation periods for contractual claims differ depending on the type of contract (from one to 10 years). Claims under warranty may expire if not notified to the other party within a stipulated deadline (typically two months for consumers, one month for non-consumers).

4.8 Procedure, funding, costs

Claims for liability for defective products are heard by common courts in civil proceedings. Claims under consumer warranty are also subject to voluntary arbitration, if chosen by the consumer. Special adjudication bodies have also been constituted recently to hear claims of patients with respect to medical errors, but they are not likely to cover pure product liability cases.

Cases involving implied warranty (consumer and non-consumer) may be handled in simplified proceedings. All other cases related to product liability are typically handled in regular civil proceedings, with the possibility to use all kinds of evidence and with a full right of appeal, which makes the proceedings lengthy (usually lasting at least one year at first instance).

In order to determine whether a product is unsafe, the court would typically appoint an independent expert. Parties are at liberty to submit their own expert opinions. However, such private opinions have only secondary bearing for the court and cannot substitute the independent opinion given by the court appointed expert.

It is also possible to pursue claims by way of a class (group) action, however the usefulness of this new procedure in product liability cases has not yet been proven.

Filing a lawsuit, or an appeal, carries a court fee (5% of the amount in dispute, 2% for group actions). Exemption from costs may be granted by the court at the request of a party with insufficient financial means (but not in group actions).

Polish procedure is governed by the 'loser pays' rule, which applies equally to claimants who were granted an exemption from the costs of proceedings. However the court may choose not to apply the rule at its discretion.

4.9 Trends

Product liability litigation is a growing phenomenon in Poland, although cases are still rare compared with other personal injury claims, especially for medical malpractice or car accidents.

There are no statistics available regarding the most common types of court disputes in the field of product liability, and in fact it is difficult to make such generalisations due to the relatively limited number of product liability disputes in Poland. It appears that cases involving adverse drug (medicinal product) reactions and incidents with medical equipment are more common.

A traditional feature of the Polish personal injury redress system has been the relatively low sums of damages awarded. This has been changing rapidly in recent years. One can note a clear trend in the increasing amount of compensation awarded in personal injury cases, for example, with awards reaching €200,000–€400,000.

A brand new element in the landscape of product liability litigation is the new law on class (group) actions. The utility of this new tool in personal injury cases, including product liability, is still to be seen. Courts have already refused to certify two class actions due to the fact that the claims pursued referred to personal injuries. However that conservative approach has not yet been verified by the Supreme Court.

5. Insurance

Product liability insurance has a relatively short history in Poland. The first product liability insurance policies offered by Polish insurers in the 1970s and 1980s were rare and designed only for products for the export market.

Product liability insurance designed for the domestic market was offered by insurers from the 1990s, although real interest in product liability insurance started to appear only around 2000, when the new product liability and product safety regime was adopted to meet EU law standards. Another important change for the domestic liability insurance market took place in 2007 when the legislation expressly accepted the introduction of new triggers in insurance contracts, other than 'act committed' which was the previous binding standard. At the same time, the legislator extended the timebar for personal injury claims by introducing the rule that claims do not expire earlier than three years following the date when the victim learned of the injury and of the identity of the liable person.

As a rule, product liability insurance is voluntary, with the notable exception of insurance for investigators and sponsors of clinical trials. This type of liability insurance is mandatory, with the sum of insurance dependant on the number of persons taking part in the trial (from €500,000 to €5 million).

Typically, product liability insurance covers tort and strict liability of the insured towards third parties due to placing a defective product on the market. Product liability insurance seldom operates as a standalone policy in Poland. It is usually joined with liability insurance for corporate clients, either as an integrated part of the liability insurance or as an extension to it.

Certain basic issues which pertain to insurance contracts are regulated in the Polish Civil Code (Articles 805–828) and compliance with these is mandatory. This includes eg, basic rules governing third party insurance, forms of agreement, statutory rights to terminate, basic rules for calculating and paying premiums, starting date and expiry of the insurance protection, basic disclosure and reporting duties, compensation payment deadlines, timebars on claims, recourse claims and a schedule of acceptable triggers.

Notwithstanding the mandatory contents of insurance contracts, in practice there are significant differences in the offered terms of insurance between particular marketplayers, from the definition of triggers, through the types of costs and damages covered by the insurance, to exclusions from liability. There are no binding industry guidelines or standards or model general terms of insurance.

As a *de facto* market standard, costs of product recall are not covered by the scope of product liability insurance. Also, pure economic loss and costs associated with product guarantee will lie outside the scope of product liability insurance.

5.1 Product recall

Costs of product recall are typically excluded from the insurance coverage.

A standard exclusion in general terms of product liability insurance would state that "the insurer is not liable for damages caused by recall from the market of a defective batch of a product".

Coverage for product recall costs may be individually negotiated, however. Some insurers also offer product recall insurance as an extension of product liability insurance, subject to an additional premium. There are standalone insurance products which pertain specifically to recall but they are not typical.

The scope of recall insurance may differ significantly among various insurers but it is typically a first party insurance which should allow recovery of the following costs associated with the recall procedure:

- costs of expert examination/testing/analysis;
- costs of public announcements;
- costs of collecting information on end users (if the product is to be recalled from end users); and
- costs of storage, transport and disposal of the recalled product.

Covering additional labour costs is not standard.

Depending on the insurer, the trigger may include only the administrative order to recall the product, or also the insured's own decision to recall.

It is not common to cover brand rehabilitation expenses. Coverage of business interruption costs is usually available only through additional insurance.

The following examples of exclusions met in recall policies are as follows:

- damage caused by placing on the market of products after their expiry date;
- damage caused by using materials or components prohibited by the law;
- damage caused by failure to comply with orders of a supervisory authority;
- penalties and fines; and
- malicious tampering with a product.

5.2 Contaminated products

Contaminated product insurance is not common as a separate type of insurance. The results of contamination of a product, either in the field of liability towards third parties or in the field of product recall, are normally covered by broader product liability insurance or product recall insurance.

The general terms of insurance exclude the insurer's liability where the insured breached statutory rules on quality control, which may be relevant in the situations of cross-contamination of products.

Some insurers offer contaminated products insurance as separately. The scope of the insurance is usually individually negotiated. It may cover malicious tampering of a product, as an extension of the basic scope of the insurance.

5.3 Product liability

Product liability insurance is offered as a stand-alone product, or, more often, as a side product accompanying liability insurance for corporate clients, either as an extension of liability insurance or integral to it.

Typically, product liability insurance is based on the 'act committed' or 'loss occurring' trigger ('placing the product on the market'; 'occurrence of the incident resulting in damage or injury'). It is also possible to use the 'claims-made' or 'loss manifestation' triggers, although these are not common.

Product liability insurance covers liability of the insured towards third parties for material damage and personal injury caused by a defective product.

A 'serial damage' clause is a standard, with insurance covering all damages resulting from the same defect present within a product batch, if the first damage occurred within the term of the insurance.

Personal injury recoverable under the insurance would include consequences of death, bodily injury or illness. The scope of due compensation for personal injury is governed by the general provisions of the Civil Code (see 4.6 above). The results of infringement of other personal interests such as dignity or reputation will not usually be covered by insurance.

As a standard, material damage is defined as a result of loss, damage or destruction of an item. Material damage typically covers both actual damage and lost profits. Due to standard exclusions applied by insurers, damage to the product itself is not covered. Neither is pure economic (financial) loss, defined as damage other than material damage and personal injury.

Some insurers offer an extension of liability to pure economic (financial) loss against payment of additional premiums. Other available extensions include, depending on the insurer: insurance of liability towards the final product manufacturer (offered to suppliers of components); liability for environmental damage; liability of a supplier of machinery for damage caused to a manufacturer using that machinery; liability for using explosives; and liability for damage caused by supplied energy.

Normally, product liability insurance does not cover liability for losses arising from interruptions to business operations which may be associated with the discovery of defects in products. Business interruption insurance is offered as a separate type of insurance, however, and the scope of protection is usually limited, eg, it may not cover costs and damages resulting from the decisions of authorities, which often arises with product defects.

Apart from the liability of the insured towards third parties, product liability insurance also covers the following costs associated with the event:

- costs of necessary actions aimed at prevention of or limitation of damage, provided that the actions taken were appropriate even if not effective;
- costs of experts, appointed by the insured or with his consent, to investigate the circumstances of the event and/or the amount of damage; and
- costs of defence in litigation (typically insurers will reserve the right to appoint the defence lawyers, or otherwise control the defence).

Other recoverable costs are included in the terms of insurance depending on the insurer. For example, some insurers cover costs of pre-litigation negotiations, or defence costs in criminal proceedings.

Insurance does not cover administrative or criminal fines. Punitive damages (which are not recognised by Polish law but which may be awarded abroad) are expressly excluded.

Costs are usually covered up to the sum of insurance, or, if above, will be capped (eg, at 10% of the insurance sum), or reduced proportionately to the amount of claims in proportion to the sum of insurance.

Product liability insurance is usually executed for one year. It is possible, at an additional premium, to extend the coverage to damages incurred by products placed on the market before the starting date of the insurance, with the statutory restriction (Article 806(2), Civil Code) that retroactive insurance cannot cover incidents of which any party knows or should have known, had they acted with due care.

A standard territorial restriction of coverage is defined by reference to damages and injuries occurring in Poland. An extension of coverage, typically to worldwide coverage or coverage in EU and EEA countries may be available for an additional premium. Coverage in the USA, Canada, and sometimes also Australia and New Zealand, is usually treated as a separate extension.

Standard exclusions in the general terms of insurance include:

- damage caused by intentional acts of the insured (some insurers also exclude liability for gross negligence);
- costs of recall (most insurers offer extension subject to an additional premium);
- damage to the product itself;
- liability for defects based on an implied warranty or additional quality guarantee;
- damage caused by specific products: eg, genetically-modified products, agricultural products, products containing blood or plasma, tobacco, explosives, nanotechnology, asbestos, contraceptives, radioactive products, silicon implants, medical devices, pesticides. These product-specific exclusions materially differ from insurer to insurer;
- injury caused by Creutzfeldt-Jakob disease or HIV;
- damage caused as a result of misrepresentation in advertising (some insurers also exclude liability for defective user instructions, which is obviously disadvantageous for the insured);
- liability for products placed on the market without a valid administrative authorisation; and
- pure economic loss (depending on the insurer, extension of liability may be available at an additional premium).

To the extent the application of the exclusion depends on proving certain facts (eg, that the damage resulted from intentional conduct of the insured), the burden rests with the insurer.

5.4 Financial loss

Liability for financial loss (pure economic loss) is typically excluded from product liability insurance. Insurers usually offer extensions of insurance coverage for liability for financial loss at an additional premium.

5.5 Product guarantee

Insurance covering first party or third party costs of product guarantee claims are not common in Poland.

Costs associated with the exchange or repair of products, or any other claims based on a quality guarantee or implied warranty regime, are typically excluded from product liability insurance.

5.6 General principles

(a) Aggregation

As a standard for product liability insurance, the sum insured is applicable for one-and-for-all events in the term of the insurance policy. Insurers offer an option to introduce sub-limits within the global sum for one event, and/or for selected risks.

(b) General condition

Product liability insurance is usually an extension of general liability insurance, or an integral part of it. As such, the general conditions applicable to general liability insurance apply.

General conditions of insurance differ among the insurers, with the exception of certain basic rules stipulated by the Civil Code, compliance with which is mandatory. These statutory conditions include the following:

- Insurance coverage may only cover events taking place within the insurance period. Retroactive extension is available only to the extent that neither party knew or could have learned when acting with due care that an event had already taken place.
- The sum insured is a maximum limit of liability of the insurer, unless the parties agree otherwise (which is not uncommon eg, for litigation costs).
- The insured has a duty to disclose facts enquired about by the insurer before signing the insurance agreement and to notify any change of circumstances regarding those facts, if required by the insurer.
- Each party has a right to demand recalculation of the premium, if circumstances changed resulting in a significant change of probability of the insured event, while the other party has a right to terminate the agreement within 14 days following delivery of such a demand.
- The insurer is legally obliged to pay out the benefit within 30 days following the notification of damage where a case is indisputable, or for disputable cases within 14 days following the date when the insurer acting with due care would be able to clarify the relevant facts; failure to comply may result in the insurer's liability for damage resulting from delay.
- The insured has a duty to use all available means to prevent damage or mitigate the damage, and the insurer is obliged to reimburse the costs for this, even if the steps taken do not produce the desired effects.
- The insurer is not liable for damage caused intentionally by the insured; the insurer is also not liable where damage was due to the insured's gross negligence, unless the parties agreed otherwise, or unless payment of compensation is justified in the circumstances.
- unless the parties agree otherwise, in first-party insurance the insurer who compensated damage to the insured acquires, by virtue of law, a recourse

claim towards the actual perpetrator of damage (subrogation). The amount of the recourse claim is equal to the amount actually paid out to the insured; the insured retains the right to claim damages directly from the perpetrator for uninsured losses.

(c) ***General exclusions***

Save for the exclusions described above, other exclusions typical of liability insurance include eg, acts of war, strikes, riots, terrorism, infringement of personal interests (other than life and health) or intellectual property rights and liability contractually extended beyond the standard of law.

Damage caused by recklessness (negligence) of the insured is not excluded from the scope of insurance. Gross negligence excludes the insurer's liability, unless the parties agreed otherwise, or unless the payment of compensation is justified in the circumstances.

(d) ***Interpretation***

Interpretation of corporate insurance contracts is governed by general rules applicable to all contracts where both parties are professionals.

The insured is bound by any unilateral amendment of general conditions, unless it/she/he terminates the contract. Individually agreed conditions of insurance prevail over general conditions in cases of conflict.

A broad set of special protective rules apply where the insured is a consumer or another natural person, even if the insurance contract is associated with that person's economic or professional activity.

The *contra proferentem* rule applies with respect to consumer insurance. The rule's extension to professional insurance contracts is sometimes theoretically debated but has not been accepted as a principle in practice.

(e) ***Effects of breaches of the insured's duties***

The general rule for insurance liability is that the injured party retains all rights to claim from the insurer even if the insured neglected his duties under the insurance agreement, provided that the negligence took place after the act occurred. In practice this means that eg, the failure to report a claim to the insurer within a prescribed period will not exempt the insurer from liability toward the injured party. At the same time, neglecting the insured's duties may give rise to a claim by the insurer against the insured, either based on the provisions of the insurance agreement (so-called 'contractual' or 'untypical recourse'), or based on the general provisions of the civil law governing performance of obligations or unjust enrichment (a point of debate in academic circles).

This general rule does not apply fully to the insured's duty to use all possible means to prevent or decrease damage. If such a failure was intentional or resulted from gross negligence, the insurer is free from liability to the extent that the damage was caused by the insured's omission.

(f) ***Extra-contractual defences***

Should the insured fail to disclose facts/circumstances which were the subject of enquiry by the insurer before signing the contract, or misrepresent such facts/circumstances, the insured shall not bear liability for events resulting from the circumstance which were hidden or misrepresented. If the non-disclosure or misrepresentation was intentional, it is will be presumed that an event covered by insurance and the results of that event were due to the hidden or misrepresented circumstances.

On the other hand, if the insurer entered into a contract even though the insured did not respond to any enquiries, the circumstances covered by the unanswered enquiries shall be treated as irrelevant.

Russia

Charles De Jager
Salans LLP

1. Product safety regulation

Russian law does not specifically legislate for product recall. However, it is covered by the Federal Law on Technical Regulation 184-FZ of December 27 2002 (as amended December 6 2011). While that statute does not define the term 'recall', it does cover procedures for recall of products and establishes when it is necessary to apply them.

The Federal Law on Technical Regulation generally sets mandatory requirements for products designed to protect the health and lives of Russian citizens. It covers not only goods and services, but also equipment, buildings, and large structures. The main principles of the statute are established in Article 3. Characteristics of technical regulation are covered in Article 5(2). The Federal Agency on Technical Regulation and Metrology (Rosstandard) is responsible for ensuring compliance with technical regulations and standards.

The initial version of the Federal Law on Technical Regulation in 2002 was heavily criticised as being inadequate and was revised in great detail by amendments in 2009 under Federal law 385-FZ. These amendments were welcomed as they potentially allow business to choose either Russian technical regulations or technical rules and standards based on 'approved' foreign standards and norms. The amendments also gave the Government of Russia authority to introduce, on a temporary basis, technical regulations of the Customs Union (Russia-Belarus-Kazakhstan), and norms and rules of the European Union in spheres where Russian technical regulations have not yet been adopted.

However, this has now been changed due to the Customs Union's Technical Regulations (the technical regulations) which are gradually superseding most existing technical regulations of Russia, Belarus and Kazakhstan. As this development is recent and ongoing, emphasis is still placed throughout this chapter on the relevant Russian provisions to the extent they may guide, influence and complete the technical regulations.

Accordingly, Chapter II of the Federal Law on Technical Regulation describes the objectives, applications and limitations of the contents of any technical regulations issued. Further, the technical regulations prescribe the process of creation, issuance and adoption of any technical regulations, as well as their possible modification or revokation. For all technical regulations, a special chapter in the law is dedicated to certificates of conformity.

The definition of 'product safety' is covered by Article 2 of the Federal Law on Technical Regulation, which is "a condition, ruling out the possibility of unacceptable risk associated with causing harm to the life or health of citizens".

Product safety is also covered within the main terms as well as Article 7 of the Law 2300-I of the Russian Federation on the Protection of the Consumers' Rights, of February 7 1992 (as amended June 25 2012).

Chapter III of the Federal Law on Technical Regulation covers standardisation: its aims (Article 11); principles (Article 12); and standardisation documents (Article 13).

Russian standards are different but usually very similar to European and International standards. CE self-declaration is not accepted in Russia and cannot replace a Russian certification of conformity.

The Russian certification of conformity, also known as GOST R, is required for any products falling within the technical regulations. GOST R is a document confirming that products are in accordance with the requirements of technical regulations.

Product compliance can be compulsory or voluntary (Article 20 of the technical regulations).

The mandatory certification of products is governed by a number of further regulations:

- Decision of Russian Federation Government of December 1 2009, 982: this provides a list of products subject to mandatory certification and a list of products for which confirmation of conformity must be carried out via a declaration of conformity; and
- Decision of Customs Union Commission, May 28 2010, 299: this sets out a list of goods which are subject to state registration.

Voluntary confirmation of compliance is covered by Article 21 of the technical regulations; mandatory confirmation of compliance by Article 23; and compliance declarations by Article 24.

1.1 Obligations

Obligations of producers and distributors are covered in the following articles of the technical regulations:

Article 37(1)

The manufacturer (performer, seller, etc.) must inform the state control body within 10 days of learning of non-compliance of the product with requirements of the technical regulations. A seller who received this information must pass it on to the producer within 10 days. A person who is not a manufacturer (seller, authorised organisation, etc.) can direct the information to the state control body.

Article 38

Article 38 covers obligations of the manufacturer in case of receipt of information of the product's non-compliance with the requirements of the technical regulations. The manufacturer must:

(1) *Verify credibility of information within 10 days and on the demand of state control body present materials of verification to state control body.*

(2) *The manufacturer must take necessary measures to prevent increase of possible harm associated with circulation of products before the verification process is complete.*

(3) *Upon confirmation of the credibility of the information, the manufacturer (seller, etc.) within 10 days of such confirmation, should elaborate a program of measures to prevent harm and agree it with the state control body.*

(4) *The program should include measures to inform purchasers, including consumers, of the presence of harm and methods for its elimination.*

Article 39(2)
Upon recognition of the credibility of the information about a product's non-compliance with the requirements of technical regulations, the state control body in accordance with its jurisdiction, within 10 days, shall give an order for a manufacturer (seller, etc.) to elaborate a program of measures to prevent the presence of harm and to assist in and exercise control over its implementation.

1.2 Types of corrective action

The manufacture and sale of affected products should be suspended, the products should be recalled, and purchasers' (including consumers') losses resulting from the products' recall should be compensated (Article 38 of the technical regulations).

Mandatory product recall must commence via a court claim filed by a state control body if Article 39(2) is not respected (Article 40; see 'Obligations' above).

If that claim is upheld, the court shall compel the defendant to perform certain actions associated with product recall within the time-limit fixed by the court (Article 40(2) of the technical regulations). The defendant must bring the court's decision to the attention of purchasers, including consumers, via mass media or other methods no later than one month from its entry into force.

Where a defendant fails to comply with the court's decision in due time, the court order will be executed in accordance with procedures established by Russian Federal legislation. In such a case, the claimant has the right to inform purchasers, including consumers via mass media about the mandatory product recall.

1.3 Criminal liability

Criminal and administrative measures may be applied in accordance with Russian Federal legislation for violations of requirements of the law relating to product recall (Article 40(3) of the technical regulations).

Article 171.1(1) of the Criminal Code of the Russian Federation covers liability for the production, purchase, storage, transportation or sale of unmarked goods and products. Such acts are punishable by fines ranging from 200 up to 500 times the minimum wage, or equal to the amount of the salary or any other income of the convicted person earned over a two- to five-month period, or by imprisonment for a term of up to three years. Those same unlawful acts are punishable by imprisonment from two to six years either with or without the confiscation of property where the following conditions apply:

- The defendant is an organised group; or
- The unlawful act is committed repeatedly or on a specially large scale.

Article 238(1) of the Criminal Code states that:

Production, storage, carriage or sale of goods and products, fulfilment of works or rendering of services which do not meet safety standards shall be punishable by a fine in the amount of 500 to 700 minimum wages, or in the amount of the wage or salary, or any other income of the convicted person for a period of five to seven months, or by restraint of liberty for a term of up to two years, or by deprivation of liberty for a term of up to two years.

(2) The same acts, if they are:

(a) perpetrated by a group of individuals under a preliminary conspiracy or by an organised group;

(b) perpetrated repeatedly;

(c) have been committed in respect of goods, works, or services intended for children under six years of age;

(d) have entailed by negligence serious damage to health or the death of a human;

shall be punishable by a fine in the amount of 700 to 1,000 minimum wages, or in the amount of the wage or salary, or any other income of the convicted person for a period of seven to 12 months, or by restraint of liberty for a term of up to three years, or by deprivation of liberty for a term of up to six years with or without the confiscation of property.

(3) Deeds provided for in the first or second part of the present Article, which have entailed by negligence the death of two or more persons, shall be punishable by the deprivation of liberty for a term of four to 10 years.

1.4 Administrative liability

Administrative liability is covered by the Code of Administrative Offences of the Russian Federation, 195-FZ of December 30 2001 (as amended June 2012).

The release or sale without marking of commodities and products which ought to be marked is subject to an administrative fine of between 30 and 50 times the minimum wage as well as confiscation of the offending products (Article 15.12(1) of the Code). The administrative fine for legal entities is 300 to 500 times the minimum wage plus confiscation of the products.

The sale of commodities and products without marking, where such marking is obligatory, as well as storage, transportation or acquisition of such commodities and products for the purpose of selling them is subject to an administrative fine of from 20 to 25 times the minimum wage of private citizens, along with confiscation of the products. For public officials, the fine is from 40 to 50 times the minimum wage accompanied by confiscation of the products. For legal entities, the fine is from 400 to 500 times the minimum wage, plus confiscation of the products.

Failure to meet obligatory requirements on state standards, obligatory certification and documentation requirements (to ensure uniformity of measurements), is punishable by administrative fines on the following scale, depending on the severity of the offence:

- on officials from five to 10 times the minimum wage plus confiscation of the products, and on legal entities from 50 to 100 times the minimum wage plus confiscation of the products;
- on officials from 10 to 20 times the minimum wage plus confiscation of the products, and on legal entities from 200 to 300 times the minimum wage; and
- on officials from five to ten times the minimum wage, and on legal entities to 100 times the minimum wage (Article 19(19), Code of Administrative Offences).

The source of product safety requirements and obligations of producers and distributors are found in the Federal Law on Technical Regulation and the Protection of Consumers' Rights Law of the Russian Federation, 2300-I of February 7 1992 (as amended June 25 2012).

These federal technical regulations are gradually superseding most existing technical regulations of Russia, Belarus and Kazakhstan. However, as the law is in a transitional state, emphasis is still placed where relevant on any Russian provisions to the extent that they may guide, influence and complete the Federal technical regulations.

2. Obligations of producers and distributors

2.1 Pre-market obligations

General and sector-specific legislation in force in Russia mainly consists of separate technical regulations for each type of product and a number of federal laws, as follows:

- compliance marking for the Russia-Belarus-Kazakhstan Customs Union – 'GOST R' is being replaced by the Eurasian EAC mark as the marking system that confirms compliance with technical regulations (this has applied since July 7 2011 across the whole of the Customs Union territory);
- the Law of the Russian Federation on the Protection of Consumers' Rights;
- 2300-I of February 7 1992 (as amended June 25 2012);
- Law 29-FZ of the Russian Federation on the Quality and Safety of Food Products of January 2 2000 (as amended July 19 2011). Article 4 ensures quality and safety of foods, materials and products. Article 5 ensures that individual entrepreneurs or legal persons producing food, etc must provide purchasers and consumers as well as state control bodies accurate information about quality and safety of foods, materials and products. Article 26(1) sets out the administrative, criminal and civil liabilities of legal persons or individual entrepreneurs violating this federal law;
- Technical Regulation 720 of the Russian Federation on Safety of Wheeled Vehicles; and
- Technical Regulation 753 of the Russian Federation on Machinery and Equipment Safety.

All national regulations are gradually being phased out as relevant technical regulations of the Customs Union enter into force, which include the following sector-specific regulations (all in force since July 1 2012):

- food labelling – Federal Law on Technical Regulation 005/2011;
- toy safety – Federal Law on Technical Regulation 008/2011; and
- cosmetic product safety – Federal Law on Technical Regulation 009/2011.

Many more technical regulations are due to come into effect from July 1 2013.

3. Product liability

3.1 Potential defendants

Manufacturers face potential liabilities for products. This includes distributors, sellers, authorised organisations or individual entrepreneurs and importers.

3.2 Sources of liability

The statutory basis is the Protection of the Consumers' Rights Law of the Russian Federation, 2300-I of February 7 1992 (as amended June 25 2012).

Article 13 establishes the liability of manufacturers for breach of consumer rights as follows:

- the manufacturer will be liable for a penalty in an amount as fixed by law or contract;
- where no law or contract applies, consumer losses will be reimbursed in full (ie, full reimbursement of the consumer's losses in addition to any penalty) (Article 13(2));
- any penalty payment or reimbursement of losses will not exempt the manufacturer from performing non-monetary obligations to the consumer; and
- any consumer claims for penalty payment (as provided for by law or contract) should be met by the manufacturer on a voluntary basis.

3.3 Claimants

Consumers benefit from the protection of product liability laws in Russia.

3.4 Defences

Manufacturers are exempt from liability for not carrying out their obligations or for improperly carrying out obligations if they can prove that such failure is the result of *force majeure*, or other grounds provided for by law (Article 13(4)).

3.5 Remedies for injury and consequential loss

Article 13(2)) provides for full reimbursement of losses and recovery of any penalty mandated by law or contract.

Where the courts find in favour of the claimant, they can recover from manufacturers a fine of approximately 50% of the sum awarded to the consumer (Article 13(6)).

Article 14(1) provides that harm caused to the life, health or property of the consumer as a result of the design, manufacture, or other defects in a product, or its inappropriate prescription, should be refunded in full.

Moral damage caused to the consumer as a result of violation by the manufacturer should be compensated by the tortfeasor if guilty. The amount of compensation will be determined by the court and does not depend on any amount of reimbursement awarded for property and/or pecuniary damage and/or harm.

4. Product insurance

Russian law distinguishes between three types of insurance:

- personal;
- property; and
- liability.

Liability insurance may be compulsory where a duty to insure is imposed by law.

Insurance is covered by Chapter 48 of the Civil Code of the Russian Federation. Article 927 deals with voluntary and mandatory insurance. In terms of mandatory insurance, where persons are required by separate federal laws to insure the lives, health or property of others, or their own civil liability towards other persons at their own expense, such insurance must be obtained by concluding contracts in compliance with the rules of Chapter 48.

Insurance is also regulated by Federal Law of the Russian Federation 4015-1 on Insurance in the Russian Federation (November 27 1992, amended April 22 2010), which lists the following specific types of civil liability insurance for injury:

- for damage resulting from defects of goods, works and services;
- for damage to third parties; and
- for any failure to perform contractual obligations.

Conditions and procedures of compulsory insurance are determined by federal laws relating to specific types of compulsory insurance and are executed according to the rules offered by insurance companies in the insurance market. The six types of compulsory liability insurance determined by federal laws in the Russian Federation cover the following areas:

- motor vehicles;
- health;
- passengers on transport;
- operation of hazardous production facilities;
- military; and
- carriers.

In general, there is a current trend of introducing more mandatory insurance cover for areas such as liability insurance of carriers and liability insurance for the operation of hazardous production facilities. The latter is a recent development in Russian law giving rise to much concern among Russian industrial companies now suddenly faced with the prospect of litigation or claims surrounding accidents: from persons, including workers, who have suffered damage to life, health or property as a result of an accident at their facility, and also from legal persons whose property may be damaged as a result of an accident.

There appears to be no legal obligation to obtain product liability insurance in Russia, although there many insurance companies seem willing to offer many types of product liability insurance for manufacturers and enterprises in Russia.

In practice, while large corporations operating under international standards of risk management are more likely to obtain product liability insurance in Russia to cover themselves against the risk of any losses, small and medium-sized companies appear less attuned to these risks and are less likely to obtain such insurance.

Insurance requirements may also be agreed contractually.

4.1 Types of coverage

(a) *Contaminated products*

Insurance against product spoilage is most relevant. This will usually be provided wrapped up with product recall insurance.

(b) *Product liability*

Product liability insurance may be extended to third-party liability and legal costs.

(c) *Product recall*

The sort of product recall insurance that is available in Russia may cover all possible causes of product recalls, including defects in the insured products, recalls at the initiative of state authorities and malicious product spoilage. Such insurance may also cover the following:

- the costs of making media announcements as well as mailing costs to publicise the recall;
- employee overtime costs for work directly related to the recall;
- the costs of hiring temporary employees solely for the purpose of assisting a recall;
- the cost of renting additional warehouse space to store recalled products for a period not exceeding 12 months;
- the cost of having the insured products returned from any buyer, distributor or consumer to the place or places specified by the insured;
- necessary travel and living expenses for company personnel directly related to the recall of the insured product;
- the cost of properly disposing of unused packaging materials and marketing materials at the point of sale in respect of recalled goods where such packaging or materials may not be used in the future; and
- the actual costs of destroying the insured product.

Insuring provisions: The following are typically covered:

- accidental contamination;
- malicious product tampering;

- government recall; and
- product extortion.

(d) ***Insurance of general civil liability for goods produced, work performed and services rendered***

Such insurance is available in Russia and covers the quality of works or services rendered or supplied.

Two types of insurance are available:

- for specified goods (specific type of works or services); and
- annual insurance for all products, works and services.

Insured event: The insured event is a liability occurrence of the insured for injury to life and health or property of consumers as a result of product defect or works or services.

(e) ***Financial loss***

Financial loss insurance is available in Russia and may cover loss of profits.

(f) ***Product guarantee***

The concept of product guarantee insurance exists in Russia, but due to a lack of awareness of enterprises about the mechanisms and purposes of insurance coverage, in practice Russian companies simply do not consider it necessary.

South Africa

Donald Dinnie
Norton Rose South Africa

---

1. Product safety regulation

Historically, product recall was dealt with under the common law. The Consumer Protection Act 2008 (as amended) changes that and provides a statutory basis for product recall and for product recall regulations. The Standards Act 2008 provides for the continued existence of the South African Bureau of Standards as a national institution for the development, promotion and maintenance of standardisation and quality control in connection with commodities but does not contain any provisions specifically on product recall.

Prior to the introduction of the Consumer Protection Act, there was no statutory obligation to recall a defective product.

Consumers who are individuals, or legal persons with an annual turnover or asset value at the time of the transaction less than the promulgated threshold (currently R2 million), have the right to receive goods that are:

- reasonably suitable for the purpose for which they are generally intended;
- of good quality and in good working order and free of any defects;
- usable and durable for a reasonable period of time, having regard to the use to which they will normally be put and to all the surrounding circumstances of the supply; and
- compliant with any applicable standards under the Standards Act 2008 (as amended) or any other public regulation (Section 55 of the Consumer Protection Act).

The first two of these requirements do not apply if the customer is expressly informed that particular goods are offered in a specific condition and the consumer expressly agrees to accept the goods in that condition or knowingly acts in a manner consistent with accepting the goods in that condition.

If a consumer specifically informs a supplier of a particular purpose for which the consumer wishes to acquire or use the goods, and the supplier ordinarily offers to supply those goods or acts in a manner consistent with being knowledgeable about the use of those goods, then the consumer also has the right to expect that those goods are reasonably suited for that specific purpose.

Any transaction for the supply of goods which falls under the scope of the Consumer Protection Act 2008 (namely with an individual or small juristic entity) contains an implied warranty (Section 56) that the goods comply with those standards, except to the extent that the goods have been altered contrary to instructions after leaving the supplier's control.

If the goods do not satisfy the safe quality goods requirements, then the consumer may within six months after delivery of the goods to the consumer, return them to the supplier or any other member of the supply chain and the supplier must, at the direction of the consumer, either:

- repair or replace the failed, unsafe or defective goods; or
- refund the consumer the price paid.

If the supplier repairs the goods and within three months after that repair, the failure, defect or the unsafe feature has not in fact been remedied or a further defect or unsafe feature is discovered, then the supplier must, at the consumer's direction, either:

- replace the goods; or
- refund the consumer the price paid for the goods.

The implied warranty and the right to return unsafe or defective goods and obtain a refund are in addition to any other warranty or condition imposed in the Consumer Protection Act, the common law, any other regulation or any other express warranty which the producer or importer, distributor or retailer provides.

A service provider also warrants every new or reconditioned part installed during any repair or maintenance work and the labour required to install it for a period of three months after the date of installation or a longer period if a supplier has specified this in writing.

That warranty:

- is concurrent with any other deemed, implied or express warranty;
- is void if the consumer has subjected the part or the goods or property in which it was installed to misuse or abuse; and
- does not apply to ordinary wear and tear, having regard to the circumstances in which the goods are intended ordinarily to be used.

The implied warranty in Section 56 attaching to all transactions for the supply of goods under the Consumer Protection Act provides a statutory remedy to consumers who are party to a covered transaction. Section 55 (the right to good quality products) does, however, also apply to consumers who are users of goods irrespective of whether they were a party to a transaction concerning the supply of those goods. Such a consumer will be bound by any specified condition that goods were sold to the original consumer. If, for example, goods were purchased on credit (taking the transaction out of the ambit of the Consumer Protection Act) then the consumer still has a right to goods complying with the quality requirements even if denied an automatic statutory remedy. Consequently there is scope for consumers to have a claim under Section 55 of the Consumer Protection Act regarding unsafe, poor quality or defective goods even if they are not entitled to the statutory warranty in Section 56.

At common law, recourse lies in the law of contract, or perhaps delict (tort).

In terms of Section 60, the National Consumer Commission (NCC) under the

Consumer Protection Act must develop, adopt and apply industry-wide codes of practice providing for efficient systems to, among other things, conduct investigations into the nature, course, extent and degree of any risk presented to the public by any failure, defect or hazard in goods; and if the goods are unsafe, recall of those goods for repair, replacement or refund.

If the NCC has reasonable grounds to believe that any goods may be generally unsafe, or that there is a potential risk to the public from the continued use of or exposure to the goods, and the producer or importer of the goods has not taken any steps required by an applicable Code (including those in respect of recall), then the NCC may, by written notice, require the producer to:

- conduct an investigation; and/or
- carry out a recall programme on any terms required by the commissioner.

A producer or importer affected by such a notice may apply to the Tribunal to set aside the notice in whole or in part.

Currently no guidance exists on what constitutes 'reasonable grounds' as contemplated by Section 60.

In May 2012, the NCC published the Consumer Product Safety Recall Guidelines. The guidelines set out the responsibilities of suppliers in relation to a recall, including: conducting a comprehensive risk analysis, stopping distribution and ceasing production of a product identified for recall, notifying and submitting a recall strategy to all regulators, retrieving the affected product from consumers and from within the supply chain, and notifying the public and international product recipients.

The guidelines also place a responsibility on the supplier to store and dispose of the recalled products safely and to provide progress reports regarding the recall to the NCC and relevant regulators. Where a supplier becomes aware of a possible safety hazard in a product, the supplier must immediately conduct an assessment to identify how the problem occurred and all possible ways to address the safety-related hazard and decide whether the product can be repaired or modified. The supplier must notify the NCC when conducting the assessment to enable the NCC to work with the supplier in determining what action can be taken to mitigate the safety-related hazard.

The guidelines also set out what actions can be taken to mitigate a safety-related hazard depending on the outcome of the risk analysis and what information must be included in a recall notice and the mandatory progress report.

There are no time periods stipulated under the 'supplier recall responsibilities' in the product recall guidelines except that the NCC must be notified in writing within two days of the supplier initiating any voluntary recall:

In terms of the guidelines, the supplier has the following general responsibilities in relation to a recall:

- to conduct a comprehensive risk analysis of the safety hazard;
- to stop distribution of a product that has been identified for recall;
- to cease production or modify the manufacturing process for a product that has been identified for recall;

- to remove an unsafe product from the marketplace;
- to notify the relevant regulator;
- to notify the public;
- to notify international product recipients;
- to notify others in the domestic supply chain;
- to facilitate the return of recalled products from consumers;
- to store and dispose of recalled products safely;
- to create and perform a written recall strategy/plan;
- to maintain records and establish procedures that will facilitate a recall; and
- to provide progress reports on the conduct of the recall to the NCC and relevant regulators.

There are no express provisions dealing with traceability of products although the elements of a recall strategy must include the number of units supplied to consumers and others in the supply chain, information about the lifecycle of the product, information about proposed communications with consumers, about the way in which the supplier will manage contact from consumers, information about the manner in which the recalled product will be collected, and an overall communication plan. Those would all impact on steps to be taken to trace the product.

1.1 Voluntary recall

In the context of voluntary recall the NCC requires notification in writing within two days of the supplier initiating the recall. That notice must state the fact that the product is subject to a recall and detail the nature of the defect(s) or dangerous characteristic(s) of the goods.

A supplier who fails to notify the NCC may be guilty of an offence under Section 110(2) of the Consumer Protection Act.

The Section 60 requirements and guidelines and codes administered by the NCC under it, create significant potential exposure for producers and importers who are likely to experience an increase in product recall claims made against them.

Damages for pure economic loss suffered as a result of a product recall need to be dealt with by the common law as discussed in relation to the *Chickenland* judgment (see below).

2. Obligations of producers and distributors

2.1 Sources of duty

(a) Statute

See the discussion above on Sections 55 and 60 of the Consumer Protection Act 2008. A non-exhaustive list of other legislation which affects products safety follows.

Medicines and Related Substances Control Act (101/1965): Strict guidelines apply to advertising, product labelling and registration of medicines. The sector's specific legislation must be read in conjunction with the Consumer Protection Act since there is currently no industry code for the pharmaceutical sector. The product liability and product recall sections of the Consumer Protection Act in particular impact significantly on pharmaceuticals.

Motor vehicles: The product liability recall provisions of the Consumer Protection Act will be applicable to the motor industry. Certain requirements of the Consumer Protection Act regarding the motor trade are covered in the ISO14001 and ISO900 standards. Codes of practice are not yet finalised. There is a motor industry ombudsman in South Africa.

Foodstuffs, Cosmetics and Disinfectants Act (54/1972): This act regulates the sale, manufacture and production, import and export of foods, cosmetics and disinfectants.

Agricultural Product Standards Act (119/1990): This act controls the sale and export of certain agricultural products, the sale of certain imported agricultural products and other related products.

Meat Safety Act (40/2000): This act sets standards of hygiene for the slaughtering of animals for the purpose of obtaining meat for human and animal consumption, and regulates the handling and keeping of meat and animal products within abattoirs, as well as transportation of such products. The act prohibits the slaughtering of animals at any place other than an abattoir which is approved and in compliance with the act's provisions regulating the design of the facility and its fixed equipment, such that meat and animal products must be handled or kept at or removed from abattoirs in accordance with the act. It is not permissible to import meat into South Africa without a permit issued by the director-general.

Tobacco Products and Control Act (83/1993): This act prohibits or restricts smoking in public places and regulates the conditions for the sale, advertising and packaging/labelling of tobacco products.

Liquor Products Act (60/1989): This act controls the production and sale of certain alcoholic products, the ingredients and properties of such products and the conditions of their sale. It also provides for the establishment of licensing schemes and for the control of the import and export of certain alcoholic products.

Atmospheric Pollution Prevention Act (45/1965): This act provides for prevention of pollution of the atmosphere and for the establishment of a National Air Pollution Advisory Committee.

Hazardous Substances Act (15/1973): This act regulates substances which may cause injury, ill health to or death of human beings by reason of their toxic, corrosive, irritant, strongly sensitising or flammable nature and for the control of certain electronic products. The act sets a scale system whereby products are ranked according to their degree of risk. It also prohibits and controls the importation, manufacture, sale, use, operation, application, modification, disposal or dumping of such substances.

Standards Act (8/2008): This act provides for the development, promotion and maintenance of quality standards in connection with commodities and the provision of conformity assessment services.

(b) Tort (negligence)

At common law, a product recall must be exercised once a manufacturer or distributor has knowledge of all these points:

- there is a defect in a product;
- the defect would not, to its knowledge as a probability, be restricted to a single item of the product, but a particular batch of a product manufactured or the stock in its entirety; and
- the defect creates a risk to the safety of end users.

The necessity for a product recall only arises in circumstances of negligent manufacture or design.

It may be that through no fault of the manufacturer, the product is nevertheless defective and constitutes a safety threat to the consumer. In those circumstances, a recall would still be required once the knowledge and the danger is brought to the attention of the manufacturer or distributor.

In the circumstances where a third party intentionally creates a defect of a product, for example, by way of contamination, and that safety risk comes to the knowledge of the manufacturer or distributor, a recall will once again be necessary.

Precisely what steps need to be taken as regards the recall depends on a combination of factors, such as the perceived extent of the safety risk posed, the likelihood of the harm eventuating and the cost of remedial measures.

A high degree of risk, coupled with grave consequences, calls for extensive precautions or total abstention, while the remote chance of trivial harm may require no precautions at all.

Even where there are negligible safety concerns, the manufacturer may institute a recall for the purposes of protecting its reputation.

Where a retailer is aware that a defect is widespread throughout a product batch and poses a risk of injury, there is a duty on the retailer, in particular where the retailer acts as an expert, to attend to a recall in appropriate circumstances to prevent injury.

(c) Contract

At common law, the terms of the seller's contract with its client may require a recall where the circumstances described in the contract eventuate.

With insurance contracts, an insurer who provides product liability or product recall cover may in appropriate circumstances insist that the insured embarks on the recall programme. The insurer's ability to insist on a recall would depend on the terms of the policy. Where there are obvious grounds for a recall campaign, and the insured declines to proceed accordingly, the insured may forfeit its rights to indemnity under the policy if the product causes injury or damage. Rejection of such a claim could be on the basis that:

- the loss and damage was inevitable;
- the danger to consumers was known and anticipated;
- the event was therefore non-fortuitous; or
- a 'reasonable precautions' clause was breached.

An insurer would have to establish that the insured's conduct constituted recklessness in order to rely on breach of the reasonable precautions clause to reject a claim. The insured must have recognised the danger to which it was exposed and then deliberately courted it by taking measures which it knew were inadequate to avert the danger or because it simply did not care about the adequacy of those measures.

Where there is a contractual nexus between the seller and purchaser, in defective product cases South African contract law allows for:

- rescission of the contract and return of the purchase price at the purchaser's election;
- reduction of the purchase price; or
- damages for breach of contract, usually limited to damages directly caused by the breach.

There are also a number of situations where a seller would be liable for not only direct, but also indirect but foreseeable damages arising from a defective product.

2.2 Pre-market obligations

Persons packaging hazardous or unsafe goods for supply to consumers must display on or within that packaging a notice that meets the plain language requirements of the Consumer Protection Act such that the consumer receives adequate instructions for the safe handling and use of those goods (Section 58 of the act).

Section 58 does not apply where a substantially similar label or notice has been applied in order to comply with another regulation. There are also extensive sector-specific labelling regulations, many of which are currently under review to align them with the requirements of the Consumer Protection Act.

A person installing any potentially hazardous or unsafe goods or supplying them to consumers while supplying services must give the consumer an original copy of any instructions for the safe handling and use of the goods or attach a similar document to the goods.

See also Sections 55 and 60 of the Consumer Protection Act above.

3. Enforcement

The NCC is responsible for enforcement of all consumer rights flowing from the Consumer Protection Act (see also the discussion above on Section 60 of that act). The NCC has the dual role of monitoring the consumer market to ensure prohibited conduct and offences are prevented, detected and prosecuted, and monitoring the enforcement of monitoring. This involves keeping watch over the effectiveness of accredited consumer groups, industry codes, alternative dispute resolution schemes, services to consumers by organs of state and the actions of any regulatory authority exercising jurisdiction over consumer matters within specific sectors. That also includes product recall, including business to business transactions.

Ultimately, the National Consumer Tribunal (NCT) is the highest enforcement body in terms of the Consumer Protection Act and is empowered to issue administrative fines.

The NCC can issue compliance notices. Where a person fails to comply with a notice the NCC can either:

- apply to the NCT for the imposition of an administrative fine or refer the matter to the national prosecuting authority for prosecution as an offence; or
- seek criminal conviction under the Consumer Protection Act with resulting penalties of fines or imprisonment not exceeding 10 years (or both a fine and imprisonment), or a fine or imprisonment not exceeding 12 months (or both fine and imprisonment), depending on which provisions of the Consumer Protection Act have been contravened.

3.1 Appeals

A producer or importer that is affected by a notice from the NCC requiring product recall may apply to the tribunal established by the National Credit Act 2005 to have the notice set aside in whole or in part.

Section 115(4) of that act states that an appeal or application for review against an order made by the tribunal suspends any right to commence an action in a civil court on the same matter, unless the court orders otherwise.

3.2 Sanctions and compensation

See the discussion on administrative and criminal sanctions under the Consumer Protection Act at product liability below.

4. Product liability

4.1. Potential defendants

Producers, importers, distributors, and retailers may be subject to product liability claims. This is not a closed list (see further Section 61 of the Consumer Protection Act, below).

4.2 Sources of liability

(a) Statute

As late as 1972, a South African court was reluctant to allow a delictual (tort) claim for product liability in a case of pure financial loss because of concerns that allowing such a claim would expose the manufacturer of the product to duplicate claims for the same defects (one claim in contract by the purchaser and another in delict (tort) by an injured third party) and that allowing claims for pure economic loss might open the floodgates of liability. (See *Combrinck Chiropraktiese Kliniek (Edms) Bpk v*

Datsun Motor Vehicle Distribution (Pty) Ltd 1972 (4) SA 185.) That is no longer the law.

A significant development came with the judgment in *A Gibb & Son (Pty) Ltd v Taylor & Mitchell Timber Supply Co (Pty) Ltd* 1975 (2) SA 457, which is the first South African case involving a claim that a merchant seller was delictually liable for damage caused to a third person by a defect in merchandise. The court determined there is no reason in South African law why such liability should not arise in accordance with common law principles.

However, there are very few reported decisions dealing with product liability in delict. There are a few more decisions (but not many) dealing with product liability in contract, particularly in the context of strict liability of the expert seller or manufacturer. Of interest here are a series of judgments dealing with strict liability for breach of implied warranty in sales of seed for agricultural use. (See, for example, the Supreme Court of Appeal in *Ciba-Geigy (Pty) Ltd v Lushof Farms (Pty) Ltd and Another* 2002 (2) SA 447.)

In the context of product liability, the Consumer Protection Act protects all natural persons suffering injury, illness or death or damage to property. Corporations are protected against damage to property. The protection covers not only buyers but also users of goods.

Section 61 of the Consumer Protection Act dispenses with the common law requirement for a claimant to establish fault, usually in the form of negligence, on the part of the producer and importer or distributor and retailer where a defective product causes harm.

All a claimant now needs to do is prove harm, as defined in this section (see below), caused wholly or partly as a consequence of:

- supplying any unsafe goods;
- a product failure, defect or hazard of any goods; or
- inadequate instructions or warnings provided to the consumer about any hazard or potential hazard arising from or associated with the use of any goods.

Suppliers cannot contract out of Section 61 liability. Section 61 applies irrespective of any exemption under the act. It is therefore available to all users of goods supplied irrespective of any prescribed monetary threshold or any other exemption under the act.

Section 61 has been in force since April 1 2011, however, it applies to goods that were first supplied to consumers on or after April 24 2010.

While Section 61 provides for no-fault liability, it does not provide for absolute liability. There are limited exclusions to liability which benefit distributors or retailers but not producers or importers, as follows.

Any supplier will escape liability if:

- the unsafe product characteristic, failure, defect or hazard that results in harm is wholly attributable to compliance with any public regulations;
- the unsafe product characteristic, failure, defect or hazard:
- did not exist in the goods at the time it was supplied by that person to another person alleged to be liable; or
- was wholly attributable to compliance by that person with instructions

provided by the person who supplied the goods to that person, which precludes the manufacturer.

A distributor or retailer will only escape liability where it is unreasonable to expect the distributor or retailer to have discovered the unsafe characteristics, failure, defect or hazard, having regard to its role in marketing the goods.

A general three-year time bar prescription period (in various forms) is applied to claims.

In terms of Section 61, the supplier of services who, in conjunction with the performance of those services applies, supplies, installs or provides access to any goods is also regarded as a supplier of those goods for the purposes of the section.

(b) *Tort/delict (negligence)*

Common law principles: South African law adopts the approach that, as a general principle, a delict can arise from the breach of a contractual obligation.

The common law action, which derives from Roman law, is a general remedy for civil wrongs to patrimonial interests. The action requires proof of both wrongful conduct and fault on the part of the defendant.

Wrongful conduct usually consists of the production of a defective article that causes physical or purely economic damage to any person or property. Fault is satisfied by showing that the claimant's damage was reasonably foreseeable; that a reasonable person could have guarded against it; that the defendant failed to do so; and that the failure to guard against it caused damages, ie, that the defendant's negligence caused the loss.

The manufacturer or seller of a defective product would be liable to the purchaser or any other person who suffers harm if the injured person can prove that:

- the product was made by the manufacturer or purchased from the seller;
- the product was defective;
- a reasonable person in the position of the manufacturer or seller ought to have foreseen the likelihood of the product being defective and causing harm to that person;
- a reasonable person in the position of the manufacturer or seller would have taken steps to prevent the harm from occurring;
- the seller did not take the steps that a reasonable person in that position would have taken to prevent the harm; and
- the failure by the manufacturer or seller to take these reasonable steps to prevent the harm caused the damage to the injured party.

In most cases, manufacturers are corporate entities and are vicariously liable for the negligence of an employee who causes a product to be defective while acting in the course and scope of that employee's employment with the manufacturer.

The liability referred to above arises from the negligence of the manufacturer, the seller or their employees. A claim will also lie for intentional conduct which causes damage.

There is no reported South African decision which finds product liability for breach of statute, although such a cause of action is technically recognised. Breach of a statutory duty usually constitutes evidence of negligence rather than an independent cause of action.

The common law principles referred to above apply equally in situations where:

- the product is unfinished and must be assembled by an intermediary;
- the product consists of separate components;
- the product is negligently serviced by an intermediary or the intermediary negligently fails to discover a defect;
- the product is inherently dangerous;
- the product is harmless unless used abnormally;
- the product suffers from an undetected patent defect; or
- the product is incorrectly labelled.

The seller or manufacturer will also be delictually liable for a negligent misrepresentation made to the purchaser or third-party user concerning a product where it can be proved that:

- the person in the position of the seller/manufacturer ought to have foreseen that the purchaser or third-party user would have relied on the statement and would have suffered harm as a result; and
- the purchaser or third-party user was entitled to rely, and did rely, on the statement and suffered patrimonial loss as a result.

The law allows for apportionment of liability between the negligent seller, manufacturer or intermediary and the negligent injured party.

Where there is a contractual nexus between the seller and purchaser, South African contract law allows, in defective product cases, for:

- rescission of the contract and return of the purchase price at the purchaser's choice;
- reduction of the purchase price; or
- damages for breach of contract, usually limited to the damages directly caused by the breach.

There are a number of situations where a seller would be liable for not only direct, but also indirect but foreseeable damages arising from a defective product.

Fraud on the part of the seller: The purchaser suing the seller for fraud arising from a concealment of a defect in a product would have to prove that:

- the defective product was purchased from the seller;
- the purchaser did not know of the defect;
- the seller knew of the defect in the product and intentionally concealed it;
- the purchaser would not have purchased the product if the purchaser knew of the defect; and
- the concealment of the defect resulted in the purchaser suffering harm.

(c) *Contract*

Breach of express warranty: The purchaser may sue for breach of contract where the seller breaches a specific term or warranty in the contract. The warranty usually relates to a particular characteristic of the product sold.

The breach would entitle the purchaser to cancel the contract and recover any direct or consequential damages that ought to have been contemplated by the parties.

Breach of implied warranty: In circumstances where the seller publicly professes skill and expert knowledge in respect of the product sold, or where the seller is the manufacturer, the purchaser may claim consequential damages for an injury caused by a product with a latent defect, without proving fault on the part of the seller or the basis of an implied warranty or in delict.

Negligent seller: In the case of an ordinary seller who does not profess to have skill and expert knowledge, or is not the manufacturer, the purchaser will be able to recover foreseeable consequential damages only if it can be shown that the breach of the implied warranty against the latent defects occurred intentionally or as a result of negligence, including a negligent misrepresentation. This is a delictual claim.

To succeed in an action for damages based on negligence, the purchaser will have to prove the various elements of liability of sellers (see above on delictual liability).

A manufacturer or seller may at common law contract out of liability for the defective products and, in such circumstances, the injured party could not seek to avoid the exemption by suing in delict, where the exemption is appropriately worded. The exemption is not binding on a third person injured by a defect in the product where there is no contractual nexus between the manufacturer/seller and that party.

4.3 Claimants, class actions

Anyone who suffers harm may make a claim (Section 61 of the Consumer Protection Act).

The Constitution allows for class actions, but only in respect of claims based on alleged breaches of constitutional rights and duties. Both the new Companies Act and the Consumer Protection Act allow for class actions. Class actions may also be pursued by accredited consumer bodies. However, in practice it has to be said that the law on class actions is undeveloped.

There is currently legislation allowing for contingency fee arrangements, for example, in personal injury cases, but a contingency fee arrangement will not protect an unsuccessful litigant from an adverse costs order.

The significant cost implications to any unsuccessful litigant reduce frivolous litigation, but can also deter legitimate but impecunious claimants.

The Constitutional Court will usually not make an adverse costs order against a losing litigant that is pursuing a human rights issue in good faith.

The combination of class actions and contingency fees increase exposure to manufacturers or suppliers of defective products to liability for injury caused by defective products in circumstances where previously injured individuals could not have afforded the costs and risks of litigation.

4.4 Causation – including failure to warn

At common law, a causal link between a defendant's fault and the harm claimed for must be established and proved on a balance of probabilities.

Under the Consumer Protection Act, the claimant will need to establish on a balance of probabilities a causal link between harm suffered, as defined, and the defective product, as defined. The liability under Section 61 can arise from inadequate instructions for safe use too. The claimant need not establish fault.

4.5 Remedies for injury/damage, and consequential loss (measures of compensation)

Damages awarded by courts at common law are:

- for breach of contract, a monetary award to place the claimant in the patrimonial position it would have occupied if proper performance of the contract had taken place; and
- in the case of delictual actions, a monetary award to place the claimant in the position it would have been in but for the wrongful conduct.

At common law damages are compensatory, not punitive.

An indemnity is provided for actual loss. The Constitutional Court has considered the position of what is termed 'constitutional damages' in the case of human rights' violations, although no such award has been made to date.

In contractual claims it is not possible to sue for general damages, namely, damages for pain and suffering, disability, discomfort, loss of amenities or disfigurement.

In delictual actions where there has been personal injury, general damages are awarded. South African courts adopt a conservative approach in awarding of damages. The quantum of such awards is generally lower than what is awarded by courts in the United Kingdom.

Special damages are those that are quantifiable either by reference to incurred expenses or with the assistance of expert opinion as to costs that will be incurred in future in treating the injury and its consequences. Those damages would include loss of past and future income.

In general, the test for damages is foreseeability, which allows awards for bodily or psychological injury in certain circumstances, as well as damage to material property plus foreseeable consequential loss reasonably contemplated.

A limiting feature of Section 61 of the Consumer Protection Act is the definition of 'harm' as:

- death of or injury to a natural person;
- illness of any natural person;
- any loss of or physical damage to any property, whether movable or immovable; or
- economic loss resulting from any of those forms of harm.

No mention is made of pure economic loss – that is, economic loss without injury or physical damage. In our view, the context in which 'harm' is used in this section does not allow for such an extension.

Pure economic loss is economic loss that does not arise directly from damage to property or person, but in consequence of the conduct complained, such as a loss of profit, being put to extra expenses or diminution in the value of property (*Telematrix (Pty) Limited t/a Matrix Vehicle Tracking v Advertising Standards Authority* 2006 (1) SA 461 (SCA)).

Because pure economic loss falls outside the ambit of the product liability provisions of Section 61, a claimant who suffers pure economic loss due to a defective product will have to consider whether the common law described above provides any remedy in the circumstances.

Of course where the claimant is able, and has the foresight of regulating its contractual relationship with a product manufacturer, supplier or distributor to provide for a remedy, this question is easily answered. The Supreme Court of Appeal in a judgment of March 31 2011 held that where the claimant suffers pure economic loss and was in the position to, or was capable of avoiding the loss contractually, there were no grounds to extend the remedy to another legal basis: ie, there was no delictual claim (*AB Ventures Limited v Siemens Limited*).

If the activities engaged in are themselves the product of a contractual arrangement, then generally the very contract that brought about the engagement will be capable of regulating exposure to loss.

The situation is different where it is not possible in any practical sense for a consumer to protect itself against pure economic loss caused by the negligence of the manufacturer.

In *Freddy Hirsch Group (Pty) Limited v Chickenland (Pty) Limited*, a Supreme Court of Appeal judgment of March 17 2011, international distributors of Nando's chicken suffered pure economic loss when products in which the spice packs containing Sudan I (a substance not fit for human consumption) were recalled. Those distributors stood in no contractual relationship with the supplier of the spice packs and were accordingly not in the position to protect themselves by contractual or other means in respect of those losses. The question was whether South African common law allowed the claim for pure economic loss in the circumstances.

South African courts are reluctant to allow pure economic loss claims. Liability is not simply imposed once there is proof of fault, usually in the form of negligence by the manufacturer. The courts also require policy factors to point in favour of imposing such a liability.

To decide whether the conduct is wrongful and therefore actionable, the courts take into account factors such as whether there are a limited number of possible claimants, whether there will be a multiplicity of actions and whether the damage suffered by the claimants was foreseeable by the manufacturer.

On the *Chickenland* facts, the court found that the nature of the distributor relationships was such that:

- the spice manufacturer was aware of the role played by the distributors in its client's business;

- liability would not bring a multiplicity of actions;
- the imposition of liability imposed no burden on the manufacturer additional to that already imposed by law or good practice internationally; and
- the manufacturer's client and the distributors were innocent victims of the manufacturer's illegal conduct and had a duty to withdraw the contaminated product from the market to mitigate their losses.

Consequently, the court determined that fault on the part of the manufacturer had been established.

So, in the case of a claim for pure economic loss arising from a defective product, the default position is to pursue recovery at common law because such claims fall outside the benefits afforded by Section 61 of the Consumer Protection Act.

At common law, recourse lies in the law of contract, or perhaps delict.

Subject to the proviso below, Section 61 of the Consumer Protection Act is unlikely to change, in the normal course of events, the nature of damages awarded by the South African courts.

The Consumer Protection Act provides that a court is required to make appropriate orders to give practical effect to consumers' rights of access to redress, including any innovative order that better advances, protects, promotes and insures a realisation by consumers of their rights under the act. The courts are empowered to award damages against a supplier for collective injury to all or a class of consumers generally and on terms considered suitable to achieve the purposes of the act. An activist court might interpret this as giving it leeway to introduce punitive damages in appropriate cases.

Under the Consumer Protection Act, suppliers are also exposed to an administrative penalty for breach of the act – a fine which may not exceed the greater of 10% of the supplier's annual turnover during the preceding financial year or R1 million. In determining the appropriate administrative fine, factors such as the nature, duration, gravity and extent of the contravention and loss or damage suffered as a result of the contravention are considered.

Criminal sanctions are also possible, including imprisonment for breaches of certain sections of the act.

A failure to notify the NCC within the specified time period (two days in the draft guidelines) that a voluntary product recall is being or has been carried out by the supplier constitutes an offence under the Consumer Protection Act potentially attracting a monetary administrative penalty or referral to the national prosecuting authority for criminal prosecution.

The courts retain the authority under Section 61 of the Consumer Protection Act to:

- assess whether any harm has been proven and adequately mitigated;
- determine the extent and monetary value of any damages including economic loss; and
- apportion liability among persons other than the claimant who are found to be jointly and severally liable.

4.6 Procedure and limitation periods

Product liability claims, whether at common law or under the Consumer Protection Act, will proceed before the South African civil courts, usually the high court. The Supreme Court of Appeal functions exclusively as a court of appeal and sits in Bloemfontein in the central province of the Free State. It is the highest court of appeal. Cases are heard by a bench of between three and five judges.

There are provincial divisions of the high court in the provinces and three local divisions in the commercial centres of Durban, Johannesburg and Port Elizabeth. Each high court has unlimited monetary civil jurisdiction and territorial jurisdiction over its defined geographic area.

Civil trials are heard by a single judge and there is no automatic right of appeal. If permission to appeal is granted by a court, then the appeal is heard either by a full bench of three judges in the relevant provincial division or, with the permission of the court, by direct referral to the Supreme Court of Appeal. If leave to appeal is refused, the unsuccessful applicant may petition the Supreme Court of Appeal for permission to appeal. Rarely, direct appeal access to the Constitutional Court may be granted on constitutional issues.

Magistrates courts are the lowest courts of the land with civil jurisdiction to entertain claims of up to R300,000 in regional courts (approximately $42,000). Each magistrates court has jurisdiction over a designated geographic area and these courts are situated in urban and rural areas throughout the entire country. There is no automatic right of appeal.

Application for leave to appeal must be made to the court. The appeal lies to the high court in whose jurisdiction the magistrates court lies. If leave to appeal is refused, application can be made directly to the relevant high court. Both the high courts and the magistrates courts have jurisdiction over persons (including corporate entities) who are resident or carry on business or are domiciled within the geographic jurisdiction of the court. A court will also entertain proceedings if the cause of action arose exclusively within its jurisdiction.

With some minor differences, the basic pleadings in both high court and magistrates court cases are as follows:

- First, a summons commencing action must set out all the necessary allegations to found the cause of action relied on by the claimant and, second, a plea by the defendant in response to the summons setting out the defence.
- Either party may call for such further particulars as are necessary to enable it to prepare for trial.
- In theory, a high court trial date may be allocated in as short a period as six months after the date of issue of the summons. In practice, a period of one year to 18 months will lapse between the issue of process and the trial date. In some divisions of the high court that delay may be extended. In complex high court product liability litigation, the period between issue of process and the commencement of the trial is frequently two to three years, depending on the extent of the discovery of documents and complexity of issues requiring evidence from expert witnesses.

- Trials are conducted before the judge or magistrate, and follow the common law adversarial system. There are no juries and the initial hearing will proceed before a single judicial officer. The party bearing the onus of proof on the issue in dispute will generally begin. Witnesses are led and cross-examined in turn.
- At a trial there is no pre-trial deposition process. Hearsay evidence is usually excluded, but may be admissible in exceptional circumstances.
- The parties are entitled to present expert evidence. The rules of the trial courts require the parties who intend to lead expert evidence to provide the opposing party with a summary of each expert witness's opinions and reasons, prior to trial. As a matter of practice, there is a meeting of opposing experts prior to trial and compilation of the minutes of the experts' meeting. The purpose of that meeting is to determine whether issues between the experts can be narrowed and points in dispute clarified. The court may, but rarely does, use experts in an advisory role.
- In both courts the judge or magistrate is generally allocated on the hearing date. The rules of court make provision for pre-trial conferences between the parties with a view to limiting the issues in dispute and encouraging settlement discussions. Different divisions of the high court have different practice rules designed to facilitate the limitation of issues and to curtail the duration of trials. At the close of the hearing judgment may be, and frequently is, reserved by the presiding officer and is delivered at a later date.
- The duration of the trial will depend on the complexity of the issues, the number of witnesses called and the length of the legal argument. The duration of trials is anything between a few days to a number of weeks or, occasionally, months.
- The Promotion of Access to Information Act 2000 allows for pre-summons access to records in certain circumstances. There is no pre-trial deposition procedure. In certain circumstances documentary evidence may be preserved by way of a court order where there is a real threat of evidence being destroyed.
- The rules of court empower a party in any civil action to call for discovery of documents and electronic records relevant to any matter in question in the proceedings which are or have at any time been in the possession or control of the other party or its agent. Discovery may only be called for after the close of pleadings in the action. In exceptional circumstances a court may, on substantive application made before it, authorise early discovery. The rules of court also provide for the giving of notice in respect of the use of, for example, photographs, videos, plans, diagrams and drawings, and an inspection of these prior to trial.
- The procedural rules relating to discovery of documents were adopted from English law and are broadly similar to discovery rules applying in England and Wales. A party to whom a discovery request is served must respond within the stipulated time period (20 court days in the high court) by service of a discovery affidavit, listing and identifying the documents in its

possession that are relevant to the issues and documents in respect of which it claims privilege. The concept of legal professional privilege conforms broadly with the law on that topic applied in common law jurisdictions and is protected.

4.7 Funding and costs

South Africa has a system of providing legal aid to impecunious claimants.

The Legal Aid Act 1969 establishes a Legal Aid Board, the object of which is to make legal aid available to indigent persons. The Board has laid down a 'means test' to determine the financial situation of an applicant for aid. In civil matters the income and assets of the applicant and the applicant's spouse are both taken into account, with certain exceptions. Assistance is provided by way of a number of legal aid clinics and justice centres.

Legal aid will cover the claimant's legal fees of litigation, subject to a specified tariff. Legal aid does not cover the costs that an unsuccessful litigant is ordered to pay to the opposing party. In the high court of South Africa, a litigant who is assisted by legal aid is exempted from providing security for the opposing party's costs of the litigation, unless ordered to do so by the court.

An agreement by which a person provides a litigant with funds to litigate in return for a share of the proceeds of the litigation is neither contrary to public policy nor void. Third-party funding rarely occurs and generally occurs on an *ad hoc* basis. There has been at least one instance of a foreign funder entering this market. Insurance for legal expenses is available (but limited).

Litigants who do not qualify for legal aid must fund their own expenses, which may later be recoverable as part of a costs order depending on the outcome of the litigation.

The general principle in civil litigation is that the unsuccessful party pays the successful party's costs according to a prescribed tariff for the court in which the litigation is conducted. Whilst the tariff does not necessarily allow the successful party to recover all attorney and client costs from their opponent, the costs recoverable would usually mean that the unsuccessful party bears the risk of having to make a significant costs payment to the successful party if the case is lost.

4.8 Trends

The Supreme Court of Appeal in *Wagener v Pharmacare Limited/Cuttings v Pharmacare* 2003 (4) SA 285 dealt with the issue of whether a manufacturer was strictly liable in delict for harm caused by defective manufacture. The court declined to develop the common law so as to impose strict delictual liability for defective products.

It was contended that South African law had reached a stage of development where strict liability should be imposed, and that imposition of such liability was appropriate in circumstances where the Constitution placed an obligation on the courts to develop the common law so as to give effect to constitutional rights and values. It was further contended that physical injuries caused by the manufacture of defective products constituted an unlawful contravention of the right to bodily integrity in the Bill of Rights.

The court held that the constitutional right to bodily integrity provided sufficient protection in product liability cases by way of the delictual action described above. To the extent that there were calls for the imposition of strict liability in delictual cases for product liability, such law reform was held to be primarily the task of legislation and a socio-economic question which had to be answered by the legislature.

Under the common law, and in the case of contractual liability, there were prospects of the court jettisoning the common law restriction on strict liability for damages arising from latent defects to sellers who profess skill and expert knowledge in relation to the particular goods (see *Langeberg Voedsel Bpk v Sarculum Boerdery Bpk* 1996 (2) SA 565 (A)). Given the opportunity and the appropriate facts, the courts may have accepted an invitation to impose liability for damages arising from latent defects in contract on the ordinary seller without proof of negligence.

It has been suggested that in a delictual action the doctrine of *res ipsa loquitur* (ie, the facts speak for themselves) could be used to alleviate the difficulty an injured party has in proving fault of the manufacturer or seller, by putting the onus on the defendant to refute the inference of blame. While the appeal court indicated that it was not, in principle, opposed to the application of that doctrine when policy considerations justified it, no South African court has applied the doctrine in a delictual product liability case.

We now, however, have the Consumer Protection Act 2008 which makes provision for no-fault product liability. The act came into full operation on April 1 2011.

The implementation of the act will probably obviate the need for a court to consider and develop South African law to apply the doctrine of *res ipsa loquitur* to infer negligence where the injured party can prove injury or loss caused by a defective product, and that the product was in the defective state when it left the control of the manufacturer, where the facts do speak for themselves.

5. Products Insurance

5.1 Types of coverage

The South African insurance industry is highly developed and sophisticated.

If disputes cannot be resolved between the insured and insurer, the following methods can be used to deal with complaints or disputes:

- in disputes concerning policy or claim rejections, the dispute can be referred to the short-term ombudsman;
- where the Financial Advisory and Intermediary Services Act is involved, the dispute can be referred to the Office of the Ombud for Financial Services Providers; and
- otherwise, disputes can be litigated in a court or arbitrated.

It is standard to exclude product liability in general public liability wording, so parties to an insurance contract need to be careful where there is a requirement for product liability cover, to ensure that exclusion is removed or specific product liability insurance is obtained.

South African and overseas insurers provide a variety of cover in respect of product liability. With the advent of the Consumer Protection Act, insured parties should ensure that the operative clauses of their product liability policies would respond to the entire range of exposure to no fault liability, and also where appropriate and if desired, provide an indemnity for claims for pure economic loss. The latter is also often excluded from cover.

Normally, product liability insurance also excludes cover in respect of product recall, and loss of use or efficacy, although broad form policies do cover these.

Insurance in respect of product recall, contaminated products, financial loss, product guarantee and business interruption are all obtainable, although at a cost. Insured parties who seek such cover would need to make appropriate arrangements with their insurer.

Having regard to the increased exposure under Sections 60 and 61 of the Consumer Protection Act, product recall and no fault product liability provisions and the operative clauses of both product recall and product liability insurance should be revisited.

5.2 Product liability

The standard policy extension in respect of product liability reads along the lines of:

Products liability [if stated in the schedule to be included]

Notwithstanding anything to the contrary contained in a specific exception .... the company will indemnify the insured in respect of defined events happening anywhere in the territory stated in the schedule elsewhere than a premises occupied by the insured, caused by goods or products (including containers and labels), sold or supplied (including wrongful delivery and delivery of incorrect goods) via the insured in connection with the business.

The amount payable under this extension, inclusive of any legal costs recoverable from the insured by a claimant or any number of claimants, and all other costs and expenses incurred with the company's consent, for any one event or series of events with one original cause or source or during any one (annual) period of insurance, shall not exceed the aggregate of the limit of indemnity for this extension stated in the schedule.

Where there is a product liability extension, there may be additional specific exceptions for, among other things, cost of repair, cost of demolition, liability arising from defect of a faulty design, and inefficacy or failure to perform.

Policies are usually on a 'claims made' basis but have provisions which allow for coverage where circumstances which may give rise to a claim change during the period of insurance, even though the claim may be instituted after termination of the period of insurance.

The product liability of the insured is the trigger for coverage. At common law, fault was required for liability, but under the strict liability provisions of the Consumer Protection Act that is no longer necessary.

5.3 Product recall

The standard operative clause provides for an indemnity in respect of expenses incurred during the period of insurance with the insurer's prior consent to recall products likely to cause injury or damage for which the insured may be legally liable.

Having regard to the expanded Section 60 of the Consumer Protection Act, exposure to the compulsory product recall, the operative clause wording would need to be revisited.

Expenses normally covered would include, if required, the reasonable and necessary costs of:

- media communication and correspondence;
- transportation in connection with the return of the products or parts to the manufacturer or the agents;
- destruction costs where those costs are higher than transportation expenses;
- expenses incurred for rental of additional warehousing space for a specified period in which the recalled products are to be stored;
- compensation paid to the insured's regular employees;
- employee compensation paid on travel and accommodation costs incurred for temporary employees to assist with a recall;
- expenses incurred to properly dispose of unused packaging and point of sale marketing materials which cannot be used or reused; and
- cancellation fees in respect of advertising or promotion programmes which were scheduled but were unable to be executed due to the need for the recall.

(a) Exclusions

Exclusions may include:

- liability arising out of any product or part;
- costs incurred in the repair, reconditioning, modification and replacement of any product or its part;
- actual or alleged intentional alteration, adulteration or contamination of the products;
- recall of products mandated by any government or public authority, where the insured would not have made a recall but for intervention of government or public policy. The insured party would need to be alert to this exclusion in the context of Section 60 of the Consumer Protection Act provisions for mandatory recall;
- recall of products in the care, custody or control of the insured or its subsidiary;
- recall as a result of any misdelivery or misdescription;
- the deliberate or intentional breach of national or local regulations by the insured or failure of insured's technical or administrative management to take precautions to prevent claims; and
- liability in respect of gradual pollution or asbestos (often excluded).

5.4 Contaminated products

Policies may provide for:

- accidental or unintentional contamination, impairment or mislabelling of products or any adverse publicity which occurs during or as a result of its production, preparation or manufacture, packaging or distribution, provided that use or consumption;

- contamination which has or would result in identifiable, internal and external visible and physical symptoms of bodily injury or sickness or disease or the death of a person within a specified period following the consumption of use;
- contamination which has caused or would cause physical damage to or destruction of tangible property;
- any actual, alleged or threatened, intentional, malicious and wrongful alteration or contamination of products, whether or not by an employee of the insured so as to render the product unfit for its intended use or consumption or to create such an impression to the public; and
- reasonable and necessary extortion costs paid in response to a demand made on the insured threatening to commit a malicious tampering.

The cover is often limited to:

- the reasonable and necessary expenses or costs of hiring consultants to investigate and identify the cause and extent of contamination, including performance of any necessary chemical or non-destructive testing to ascertain the harmful substances causing the contamination or tampering; and
- the reasonable and necessary costs of publicising the actual or alleged insured events as well as the investigating consultant's opinion with a view to reassuring consumers that the insured was blameless for the actual contamination or malicious tampering.

5.5 Financial loss

A typical operative clause of a financial loss policy may read:

The insured is indemnified for damages and claimants' costs and expenses arising as a result of any financial loss which is incurred by customers or third parties as a result of any product which failed to perform its intended function or to perform as specified, warranted or guaranteed.

5.6 Product guarantee

Product guarantee insurance is not widely available in South Africa, but can sometimes be obtained.

Spain

Cristina Ayo Ferrándiz
Uría Menéndez

---

1. Product safety regulation

1.1 Product risks

Royal Decree 1801/2003 concerning general product safety transposed into Spanish law the EU General Product Safety Directive (2001/95/CE).

Like the Directive, Royal Decree 1801/2003 is a general and horizontal, non-contractual regulation on general product safety, applicable to all product types put into circulation in Spain. However, where any sector-specific provision exists, that specific law will apply instead.

Royal Legislative Decree 1/2007 also contains some provisions regarding general safety of products. The royal legislative decree enacted the Consumers and Users Protection Consolidation Act and regulations made under it, and consolidated earlier statutes (mainly General Law 26/1984 for the Protection of Consumers and Users and Law 44/2006 Improving the Protection of Consumers and Users).

1.2 Safety standards

Under Royal Decree 1801/2003, the supply or manufacture of consumer goods or related services that are not safe is prohibited.

Product will be considered safe provided that, under normal and reasonable conditions of use it does not present any risk or presents only such risks that are acceptable and compatible with the intended use of the product, taking into consideration circumstances like the characteristics of the product, any information provided with it, or the consumer it is directed to.

Royal Decree 1801/2003 also makes a presumption that a product is safe when it has been produced in accordance with Spanish or European compulsory regulations on health and safety or, where no specific regulation exists, in accordance with Spanish standards (UNE standards), European Commission recommendations, or the current state of the art, for instance (that the state of scientific and technical knowledge at the time of putting into circulation was not such as to enable the existence of the defect to be discovered).

Conversely, Royal Decree 1801/2003 presumes that a product is not safe when it has been produced without CE or EC marks, or whenever a product has been produced without passing any compulsory authorisations or controls.

1.3 Compliance: sector-specific rules

As noted above, Royal Decree 1801/2003 is a general provision which will apply to all product types in the absence of any specific existing regulation. The National Consumption Institute is the regulator, with nationwide competence, and the regional authorities have competence[1] within their own territories.

There may also be additional regulations which apply to the type of product (eg, toys, vehicles, food, medicines or cosmetics) and that the regulator may likewise differ (eg, AESAN or AEMPS[2]).

Some specific products (eg food or medicines) need prior administrative approval to be put on the market. Under the General Health Act and the specific regulations, this will vary depending on the product and the consumers which it is directed to and, in the majority of the cases, will be time-limited.

1.4 Safety issues

Only safe products can be put into circulation on the Spanish market (Royal Decree 1801/2003). This means that each party in the distribution chain must take appropriate measures to ensure that all products are safe under Royal Decree 1801/2003 and/or the specific regulation applicable to the product in question and where any party knows that a product already put into circulation is not safe, must take appropriate corrective measures.

1.5 Types of corrective action

Royal Decree 1801/2003 does not contain a definitive list of measures or corrective actions that must be taken either by producers or public administrations. It states only that any measure that could restore or guarantee safety must be taken, including:

- stopping the product being sent out;
- taking the product out of circulation;
- drafting warnings in relation to use of the product;
- recalling the product from shops or directly from consumers;
- destroying stock; or
- issuing warnings to consumers via the media or any other measure that could ensure the success of such measures.

---

1 *Dirección General de Consumo*, in Andalucia; *Dirección General de Consumo*, in Aragón; *Agencia de Sanidad Ambiental y Consumo* in Asturias; *Dirección General de Consumo* in the Balearic Islands; *Dirección General de Comercio y Consumo*, in the Canary Islands; *Dirección General de Comercio y Consumo*, in Cantabria; *Agencia de Protección Civil y Consumo*, in Castilla y León; *Instituto de Consumo de Castilla-La Mancha*, in Castilla La Mancha; *Agencia Catalana de Consumo*, in Catalonia; *Consejería de Sanidad y Consumo*, in Ceuta; *Instituto de Consumo de Extremadura*, in Extremadura; *Instituto Gallego de Consumo*, in Galicia, *Dirección General de Salud Pública y Consumo*, in La Rioja; *Dirección General de Consumo*, in Madrid; *Dirección General de Sanidad y Consumo*, in Melilla; *Dirección General de Atención al Ciudadano, Drogodependencias y Consumo*, in Murcia; *Dirección General de Familia, Infancia y Consumo*, in Navarra; *Dirección de Consumo*, in the Basque Country; *Dirección General de Comercio y Consumo*, in Valencia.

2 AESAN refers to the Spanish Agency on Food Safety – *Agencia Española de Seguridad Alimentaria y Nutrición*, and AEMPS to the Spanish Agency of Medicines and Medical Devices – *Agencia Española del Medicamento y Productos Sanitoarios*.

2. Obligations of producers and distributors

2.1 Sources of duties

(a) *Statute*

Royal Decree 1801/2003 transposed EU Directive 2001/95/E into Spanish law. The purpose of the royal decree is to guarantee the 'safety of products' introduced on the market. It imposes a number of duties on producers and distributors relating to their obligation to identify and issue warnings about risks associated with the use or consumption of the product and take the corresponding corrective measures when a risk is identified. It also provides for a set of non-punitive administrative measures, namely empowering public administrations to remove from the market, as a preventive measure, any products in circulation which could pose risks to the health or safety of consumers. The National Consumption Institute is the competent authority to police product safety.

This regulation is a general provision applicable to all product types, in the absence of any specific existing regulation. In addition there are product-specific regulations (eg, for toys, vehicles, food, medicines or cosmetics) and product-specific regulators (eg, AESAN; AEMPS).

(b) *Tort*

The aim of Royal Decree 1801/2003 is to guarantee the 'safety of products' introduced in the marketplace, and to achieve this, it imposes a number of duties on producers and distributors related to their obligation to identify and issue warnings of any possible risks associated with the use or consumption of the product and to eliminate or minimise any risks identified in products already put into circulation.

However, it does not apply where an unsafe product is not in conformity with the contract and/or causes damage to people or other products. In those cases the affected party must either request repair, replacement or reimbursement for the product under the contract; or pursue compensation for damage or injury suffered.

(c) *Contract*

Both national and European regulation disregard the contractual or non-contractual nature of general product safety.

2.2 Safety standards

A product will be considered 'safe' provided that, under normal and reasonable conditions of use it does not present any risk or presents only such risks that are acceptable and compatible with the use of the product, taking into consideration circumstances such as:

- characteristics of the product, and in particular its composition and packaging;
- the effect that it may have on other products when used together with other products;
- information about the product provided with it, in particular the label,

instructions for use, warnings, instructions regarding the instalment, if applicable, and maintenance;

- presentation and advertising; and
- the type of consumer at which the product is directed (Article 2 of the Royal Decree 1801/2003).

Royal Decree 1803/2003 presumes that a product is 'safe' when it has been produced in accordance with Spanish or European compulsory health and safety regulations.

Where no such compulsory regulation exists, the following will be taken into account:

- technical national regulations transposing European regulations;
- UNE standards;
- European Commission recommendations on risk evaluation;
- product safety codes in force in the relevant sector; and
- state of the art considerations.

Conversely, Royal Decree 1801/2003 presumes that a product is not safe when the product has been produced without a CE or EC marking, or when the premises where it was produced are not licensed/authorised, or if it has not passed administrative controls designed to protect consumer health and safety, or when the product does not bear the minimum information required to identify the producer, or if it belongs to the same range or batch as a product that has been declared unsafe.

2.3 Pre-market obligations

(a) General regime

The general approach to pre-market regulation is contained in Royal Decree 1801/2003. Under this regulation, and taking into consideration the general obligation to put into circulation only safe products, producers must fulfil the following obligations:

- to provide consumers with relevant information about the product to enable them to assess any risks inherent in a product throughout the normal or reasonably foreseeable period of its use, where such risks are not immediately obvious without adequate warnings, and to take precautions against those risks; and
- to identify, on the product or its packaging, the producer and product reference or, where applicable, the batch to which it belongs, except lack of such information can be justified. Information on the production batch of any product must be kept by the producer for three years. For products with an expiration or "best by" date, this period may be reduced to one year.

Directive 2001/95 and Royal Decree 1801/2003 do differ on what constitutes necessary information to be carried on labelling. Directive 2001/95 mentions labelling information only as an example, whereas under Royal Decree 1801/2003 the inclusion of information on the labelling or packaging seems to be considered an obligation.

Royal Decree 1801/2003 does not expressly impose traceability requirements, but it is sound business practice for producers to include tracking information to help find sample products to analyse any suggested defect or to remove or recall products from the market.

Other regulations applicable to certain product types do include a traceability obligation.

The regulatory bodies charged with policing such obligations are the National Consumption Institute and regional authorities.[3]

(b) *Specific regulations*

Toys: Royal Decree 880/1990[4] (implementing the 1988 EU Toys Directive), sets out health and safety standards for toys (inclusive of any product or material designed or clearly intended for use in play by children younger than 14 years old).

This has been updated recently to reflect the EU Toy Safety Directive (2009/48/EC (as implemented by Decree 1205/2011)), which introduced a new definition of 'toy' and established more clearly the obligations of business operations and regulatory authorities. This royal decree largely revokes the former Royal Decree, except for some specific articles.

The most important modifications set out in Royal Decree 1205/2011 are as follows:

- A 'toy' is now defined as any product designed for or foreseeably to be used as a toy by children of under 14 years. The new definition is wider than its predecessor, capturing some products that might not have been intended to be used as toys (eg, a teddy bear key ring). It also expressly identifies in Annex I, 19 items that are not considered toys.
- New safety requirements have been introduced. Under Article 5, toys, including the chemicals they contain, must not jeopardise the safety or health of users or third parties when they are used as intended or in a foreseeable way, bearing in mind the behaviour of children.

  Annex II to the royal decree makes detailed provisions concerning physical and mechanical properties, flammability, chemical properties, electrical properties, hygiene, and radioactivity.

  Annex V sets out additional specific rules regarding warnings for different kinds of toy (eg, the toy must indicate an appropriate age; or state that it must be used only under the supervision of an adult, or labels or instructions of use must effectively alert consumers of any risks associated with the product and the means to avoid them).
- The new royal decree distinguishes between producers, authorised

3 For example, for food: see above.

4 As amended by EU laws including Directive 93/68/EEC; Regulation 1272/2008 and Directive 2008/112/EC.

representatives, importers and distributors and clearly sets out the obligations corresponding to each.

- One of the most important obligations set out in the royal decree obliges producers to make a safety and conformity assessment prior to the production of the toy in order to identify possible dangers and risks and apply solutions before putting them into circulation. Producers can choose one of two routes to conformity assessment:
  - Self-verification – the producer itself applies the new standards and describes the means whereby it has ensured conformity in production. After this assessment has been carried out correctly, the producer draws up technical documentation and the EC declaration of conformity, which with other information will be affixed on the toy.
  - Third-party verification or certification – the producer submits a model of the toy as well as technical documentation to specific bodies which issue an EC type examination certificate. The producer ensures conformity of all toys in production with the approved model. It draws up technical documentation and the EC declaration of conformity, which will be affixed to the toy together with other compulsory information.

    Importers and distributors must ensure that the producer has carried out the corresponding conformity assessment.
- Producers are also obliged to ensure that all their products can be traced via a number, batch, series, model or any other reference that allows for its identification (traceability) and that details about the producer are also provided. All this information, plus the EC mark, must be visible, legible and indelible on the toy. If the toy is very small, these indications are likely to be fixed on the packaging, label or a leaflet.

  Producers must provide all consumers with instructions and safety information in Spanish (at least).
- The EC mark carries with it a presumption of conformity with the royal decree.[5]

The regulatory body for toys, as for products in general, is the National Consumption Institute (by Royal Decree 1801/2003).

The European Commission has elaborated an explanatory guidance document intended to be used as a manual for all parties directly or indirectly affected by Directive 2009/48/EC.[6] It does not provide specific guidelines for specific types of toys. No Spanish guidance has yet been published.

Food and feed: EU Regulation 178/2002, laying down the general principles and requirements of food law, establishing the European Food Safety Authority (EFSA)

5 Royal Decree 1205/2011 refers to EU Regulation 765/2008, setting out the requirements for accreditation and market surveillance relating to the marketing of products, and repealing EU Regulation 339/93; and to Royal Decree 1801/2003 concerning the conformity assessment bodies (the National Consumption Institute and corresponding regional authorities).

6 http://ec.europa.eu/enterprise/sectors/toys/files/tsd-guidance/tsd_rev_1-3_explanatory_guidance_document_en.pdf (dated April 4 2011).

and laying down procedures in matters of food safety, is directly applicable in Spain. Under this regulation, only safe products can be commercialised.

Under Article 14 of the regulation, food must not be put on the market if it is unsafe. 'Unsafe' means any food that is harmful to health and/or is unfit for consumption. In determining whether any food is unsafe, the following circumstances should be taken into account: normal conditions of use, information provided to the consumer, likely immediate or delayed effect on health, cumulative toxic effects and, where appropriate, particular health sensitivities of a specific category of consumers. If food which is unsafe forms part of a batch, lot or consignment, the entire quantity will be presumed to be unsafe.

Feed must likewise not be put on the market or given to any food-producing animal if it is unsafe. Feed is deemed to be unsafe if it has an adverse effect on human or animal health. The entire quantity of a batch, lot or consignment is considered unsafe if any part of it fails to satisfy the requirements of the regulation.

The traceability of food, feed, food-producing animals, and any other substance intended to be, or expected to be, incorporated into a food or feed must be ensured at all stages of production, processing and distribution.

The regulator is the EFSA.

In Spain, an explanatory guidance note approved by the Standing Committee on the Food Chain and Animal Health on January 26 2010 has been produced to assist all parties in the food chain to better understand and to correctly apply the regulation in a uniform manner.[7]

Although the regulation is directly applicable in Spain, it has been very recently approved by Act 17/2011 of July 5 2011, concerning food safety and nutrition. The Act develops the detail of the Regulation for application within Spain, and adapts the Spanish system accordingly.

The regulatory body is AESAN, which was incorporated by Act 11/2001 (of July 5), with the collaboration of the corresponding regional authorities.

Pharmaceuticals (medicinal products for human and veterinary use): EU Regulation 726/2004, setting out EU procedures for the authorisation and supervision of medicinal products for human and veterinary use and establishing a European Medicines Agency is directly applicable in Spain.

In addition, Act 29/2006 on Medicinal Products implements EU directives[8] to ensure harmonisation of national regulation with the EU regulation. This law is further developed, among other things, by Royal Decrees 1344/2007 and 1345/2007, concerning pharmacovigilance and authorisation, registration and delivery conditions of medicinal products for human use, and Royal Decree 1246/2008,

---

7 Guidance on the implementation of Articles 11, 12, 14, 17, 18, 19 and 20 of EU Regulation 178/2002 on general food law; conclusions of the standing committee on the food chain and animal health; http://ec.europa.eu/food/food/foodlaw/guidance/guidance_rev_8_en.pdf .

8 Directive 2004/27/EC of the European Parliament and of the Council of March 31 2004 amending Directive 2001/83/EC on the EU code relating to medicinal products for human use; Directive 2004/28/EC of the European Parliament and Council, of March 31 2004, amending Directive 2001/82/EC on the EU code relating to medicinal products for veterinary use.

concerning pharmacovigilance and authorisation, registration and delivery conditions of medicinal products for veterinary use.

Act 66/1997 on Fiscal, Administrative and Social Measures established the Agency of Medicines and Medical Devices (AEMPS).

Under both European and Spanish regulation, any medicinal product for either human or veterinary use must be authorised prior to its commercialisation either by the European Medicines Agency, if the product is to be commercialised across Europe; or by the AEMPS for the Spanish national territory. Such an authorisation will be granted for a maximum of five years.

To achieve authorisation of a medicine, the product will be subject to very strict trials covering basic investigation, pre-clinical trials and clinical trials.

Cosmetics: Royal Decree 1599/1997 on the regulation of cosmetics implements Directive 93/35/EC, dated June 14 (modifying Directive 76/768/EEC, on the approximation of the laws of the member states concerning cosmetics).[9]

Any person or entity that produces cosmetics or takes part in any of its phases, such as control, conditioning, packaging, or labelling, in Spain, or any importer in the EU, must be previously duly authorised. This authorisation will be granted for a maximum period of five years and is granted by the AEMPS,[10] which is also the competent authority to control and evaluate the risks of the cosmetics put into circulation in Spain.

According to the Spanish regime, the label of the cosmetic must contain the following information:

- product name;
- name and address of the producer, or importer or its representative;
- nominal value;
- expiry date (except for cosmetics which have an expiry date of over 30 months);
- instructions for use;
- batch number;
- country of origin, if not produced in the European Union;
- function; and
- list of ingredients.

The royal decree also obliges producers to identify a responsible person for the cosmetic who will have to provide the AEMPS with information regarding the product (eg, brand and name of the product), its composition and intended use.

However, the European Parliament approved EU Regulation 1223/2009 concerning cosmetics on November 30 2009. This will be directly applicable to all European member states, and will replace the current European and Spanish system from July 11 2013.

---

9 Recently updated by Royal Decree 944/2010 by virtue of Directive 2008/112/EC, which modifies Directives 76/768/EEC, 88/378/EEC and 1999/13/EC and Directives 2000/53/EC, 2002/96/EC and 2004/42/EC in order to adapt them to EU Regulation 1272/2008 on classification, labelling, packaging of substances and mixtures.

10 Incorporated by Act 66/1997 on Fiscal, Administrative and Social Measures.

(c) ***Infringement***

Infringement of the duties and obligations will instigate non-punitive administrative proceedings involving the regulator and fines, when applicable.

2.4 Post-market obligations

(a) ***General regime***

Both producers and distributors have some post market obligations to fulfil (Royal Decree 1801/2003).

Producers: Articles 4 and 5 of Royal Decree 1801/2003 state that producers must keep distributors informed about any risks their products might pose. For this purpose, they must register and analyse any reported risks and, if appropriate, carry out sample testing on those products or take other appropriate measures.

On discovering that they may have placed products on the market which pose risks for consumers incompatible with the general safety requirement, they must take the following measures:

- adopt adequate measures to avoid the risk, including informing consumers by publishing special warnings, withdrawing products from the market, or recalling products from consumers; and
- immediately inform the competent authorities of the all regional authorities[11] where they have a corporate domicile; that regional authority must then immediately convey the information to the National Institute of Consumers (*Instituto Nacional de Consumo*), which will then forward on a warning to the remaining autonomous communities.

In sum, producers or manufacturers must notify the relevant authority of the existence of the risk and take adequate corrective measures to avoid or minimise it.

The communication providing notification to the authority must contain at least the following:

- information about the precise identification of the product or batch;
- a complete description of the risk presented by the products;
- any and all available information which might be useful in locating the product; and
- a description of corrective actions carried out to prevent risks to consumers.

A European Decision of 2004 has set out some detail on this issue.[12] These guidelines are applied at national level. A direct link to the Decision in Spanish can be found on the website of the National Consumption Institute.[13]

11 See fn 1.

12 Decision laying down guidelines for the notification of dangerous consumer products to the competent authorities of the member states by producers and distributors, in accordance with Article 5(3) of Directive 2001/95/EC of the European Parliament and of the Council, approved by the European Commission, December 14 2004: http://ec.europa.eu/consumers/safety/rapex/docs/RAPEXguidelinesOJL381.pdf

13 http://eur-lex.europa.eu/LexUriServ/LexUriServ.do?uri=OJ:L:2004:381:0063:0077:ES:PDF/.

To simplify and streamline such obligations, the European Commission has created an online notification system called 'Business Application', via which producers and distributors can send relevant information to a database which is accessible only by relevant authorities.

Information about this application and the official form of notification are available on the European Commission website.[14] A Spanish summary is also available on the website of the National Consumption Institute.[15]

Royal Decree 1801/2003 does not contain a definitive list of measures or corrective actions to be taken either by producers or public administrations. On the contrary, it states that any measure intending to restore or guarantee safety must be taken, taking into consideration the product, the people who might be affected and the risk it may pose.

Among them, the following steps might be appropriate:

- stopping deliveries of the product;
- banning the product's circulation on the market;
- attaching warnings to the product;
- recalling the product from shops or even consumers;
- destroying stock;
- issuing a press release, communications or warnings to consumers; and
- taking any additional measure that could help to ensure the success of these measures.

A practical guide that helps producers evaluate the risk, choose and instigate adequate corrective action is also available on the National Consumption Institute's website.[16]

Distributors: Distributors are obliged to participate in monitoring the safety of products placed on the market, especially by:

- passing on information on product risks to producers and competent authorities;
- retaining documentation for three years from the date when stock is exhausted and providing the necessary documentation to trace the origin of products – in particular, the identity of producers; and
- cooperating with producers and authorities in actions taken to remove the risks.

Producers and distributors: Both producers and distributors must, within the limits of their respective activities, cooperate with the competent authorities, when requested, in actions taken to avoid risks posed by products they supply or have supplied. Specifically, they must provide all pertinent information requested, including that which may be protected by commercial and industrial secrets; and

---

14 https://webgate.ec.europa.eu/gpsd-ba/.
15 http://www.consumo-inc.es/Seguridad/manual-productores.pdf.
16 http://www.consumo-inc.es/Seguridad/pdf/Guia.pdf)

must do so within five days, unless the urgency of a specific case dictates a shorter period. (The information protected by commercial and industrial secrets shall not be revealed or used for any purpose other than that the product safety issue.)

(b) Specific regulations

Toys: Under Royal Decree 1205/2011, whenever a producer, an importer or a distributor knows or has reason to think that a toy produced is not in conformity with the requirements set out in the Royal Decree, it must immediately take corrective measures, recall it, or, if it proceeds onto the market, ensure its replacement. Whenever a toy presents a risk, producers must immediately inform the regulator in accordance with Royal Decree 1801/2003 (the National Consumption Institute or any of the regional authorities).[17]

Likewise, whenever the authorities discover that a particular toy could damage the safety or health of consumers, they will request that the producer take corrective measures. But the relevant authority can also adopt necessary measures directly to recall a product from the market, or prohibit or limit its commercialisation, immediately informing the European Commission of the measures taken and the reasons for such a decision.

Food: Food and feed business operators who consider or have reason to believe that a food which it has imported, produced, processed, manufactured or distributed is not in compliance with the food safety requirements, must immediately communicate the risk to the competent authorities and initiate all and any procedure or corrective action to avoid the risk, including withdrawing the food from the market in cases where the food has left the immediate control of the initial business operator, and must inform the authorities of such actions (European Regulation 178/2002 and Spanish Act 17/2011). Where the product has reached the consumer, the operator must effectively and accurately inform consumers of the reason for its withdrawal, and if necessary, recall from consumers products already supplied to them where other measures would not be sufficient to achieve a high level of health protection.

Some guidance on the implementation of Articles 11, 12, 14, 17, 18, 19 and 20 of Regulation 178/2002 has been provided by the Standing Committee on the food chain and animal health, approved on January 26 2010.[18]

Pharmaceuticals (medicinal products for human and veterinary use): EU Regulation 726/2004 of March 31, laying down EU procedures for the authorisation and supervision of medicinal products for human and veterinary use and establishing a European Medicines Agency, was approved in Spain by Act 29/2006 of July 26, on Medicinal Products and the Spanish Act 66/1997, December 30 on Fiscal, Administrative and Social measures, which, among other things, incorporated the AEMPS in Spain.

17 See fn 1.
18 http://ec.europa.eu/food/food/foodlaw/guidance/guidance_rev_8_en.pdf

Under both European and Spanish regulation, producers and health professionals have an obligation to inform the European or Spanish Medicines Agency of any adverse effect which could be caused by medicine or health products, whenever this implies a risk to the life or health of persons.

If the agency is aware of such risk, it will contact the producer, which must cooperate with the agency, and order the producer to take corrective measures, or take measures directly.

The European and Spanish Medicines Agencies, acting in close cooperation with the corresponding national pharmacovigilance systems, must receive all relevant information concerning suspected adverse reactions to medicinal products for human use which have been licensed by the European Medicines Agency or the AEMPS. The holder of the marketing authorisation and, when applicable, the relevant authorities in the member states must ensure that all relevant information concerning suspected adverse reactions to medicinal products authorised under this regulation are brought to the attention of the corresponding Agency. To facilitate this, holders of marketing authorisations must have permanently and continuously at its disposal an appropriately qualified person who will be in charge of the authorisation, and another person with responsibilities for the pharmacovigilance. Their duties include the following:

Person responsible for the authorisation:

- register all suspicions of adverse reactions that may occur in Spain, Europe or third countries; and
- register and communicate all suspicions of serious adverse reactions to the corresponding pharmacovigilance authority.

Person responsible for the pharmacovigilance:

- establish and manage a system which ensures that information concerning all suspected adverse reactions reported to the personnel of the company and to medical representatives is collected, evaluated and collated so that it may be accessed at a single point within the European Union;
- prepare reports for the competent authorities of the member states and respective agencies;
- ensure that any request from the relevant authorities for the provision of additional information necessary for the evaluation of the risks and benefits of a medicinal product is answered fully and promptly, including providing information regarding the volume of sales or prescriptions relating to the medicinal product in question;
- provide the competent authorities with any other information relevant to an evaluation of the risks and benefits of a medicinal product, particularly information concerning post-authorisation safety studies; and
- ensure that the corrective measures that have been ordered to minimise risks are duly taken.

The authorisation may be suspended or revoked whenever the medicine product is assessed as presenting a risk, where the risk-benefit analysis is negative or if there is an infringement of any applicable regulation.

Cosmetics: Royal Decree 1599/1997,[19] entitles the AEMPS to prohibit the commercialisation, order withdrawal or impose special conditions on any cosmetic that could present a risk to consumer health or safety under normal or foreseeable conditions of use.

3. Enforcement

3.1 Sector organisations

(a) General consumer products

Apart from establishing the general product safety regulatory regime, the obligations and duties of producers and distributors, and the proceedings that must be initiated whenever a risk in a product in circulation appears, Royal Decree 1801/2003 empowers the National Consumption Institute and at regional level the regional authorities to enforce its terms.[20] Communications between the regional authorities, National Consumption Institute and European Commission and other competent authorities in other member states will be handled by the Rapid Alert System for non-food dangerous products: RAPEX.

RAPEX is the EU rapid alert system for dangerous products – with the exception of food, pharmaceutical and medical devices, which are reported via other channels. It facilitates the rapid exchange of information between member states and the Commission on measures taken to prevent or restrict the marketing or use of products posing a serious risk to the health and safety of consumers.

The authorities mentioned here have competence in relation to most products on the market, including toys, vehicles, machinery, textile and clothes. There are however, other sector-specific regulators, for example: (i) food and (ii) medicines or pharmaceuticals.

(b) Sector-specific regulations

Toys: The National Consumption Institute and the corresponding regional authorities[21] have competence to control the safety of products in Spain (Royal Decree 1205/2011). They communicate via the RAPEX system.

Food: Spanish Law 11/2001[22] of July 5 incorporated AESAN as the national competent authority concerning food safety with like powers to the National Consumption Institute, but for food. Likewise, at regional level each regional authority has a designated competent authority.

---

19 The Royal Decree 1599/1997,19 implemented Directive 93/35/CE (of June 14), which in turn had modified Directive 76/768/EEC on the approximation of the laws of the member states concerning cosmetics. It must be reminded, however, that on November 30 2009, the European Parliament approved the Regulation 1223/2009 (EC) concerning cosmetics that will supercede the current regulation as of July 11 2013.

20 See food, n. 1.

21 See food, n. 1.

22 And EU Regulation 178/2002 governing general principles and requirements of food law, establishing the European Food Safety Authority and setting out procedures in matters of food safety.

Communications between those national competent authorities are handled by a Coordinated Rapid Interchange System of Information, and between the AESAN and the EFSA or other competent authorities in other member states by the Rapid Alert System for Food and Feed (RASFF).

Medicines: The regulator with competence in the area of food and feed is the EFSA incorporated by Regulation 178/2002.

The AEMPS is the national competent authority on safety of medicinal and health products put into circulation in Spain.[23] Likewise, at regional level each regional authority has a designated competent authority.

Communications between those competent authorities, and between the National Consumption Institute and the European Commission or other competent authorities in other member states are handled by the Rapid Alert System.

Cosmetics: Royal Decree 1599/1997 of October 17 is the national regulation regulating the sale of cosmetics in Spain. It implements Directive 93/35/CE.[24]

The AEMPS is the competent authority to grant the authorisations to commercialise cosmetic products. However, the National Consumption Institute controls the safety of cosmetics.

3.2 Powers of authorities

Under Royal Decree 1801/2003, competent authorities have the following duties:

- monitor compliance with the obligations set out in Royal Decree 1801/2003;
- test products, request information or recover samples and submit them to testing;
- receive consumer complaints and take decisions on any measures needed;
- receive product safety alerts directly from producers or other competent authorities, whether regional, national, European or even international, and circulate them when necessary; and
- request producers to adopt administrative measures to avoid or minimise the risk, such as:
- stopping product delivery;
- banning circulation of the product;
- adding warnings on the product or its packaging;
- recalling the product from the shops or directly from consumers;
- destroying stock; or
- taking any other necessary measure.

3.3 International enforcement

The authorities are in charge of receiving and redistributing alerts from other competent authorities, either regional, national, European or international, managing the safety of products, taking necessary measures or requesting producers to take necessary measures.

23 Spanish Act 66/1997, December 30 on Fiscal, Administrative and Social Measures.
24 Dated June 14, in turn modifying Directive 76/768/EEC. Soon to be superceded.

RAPEX is the rapid alert system established by Directive 2001/95/EC and Royal Decree 1801/2003 for general product safety, whereas the Rapid Alert System for Food and Feed is established by EU Regulation 178/2002.

3.4 Sanctions

(a) *General regime*

Royal Decree 1801/2003 sets out no specific list of infringements and does not specify penalties for infringements of the general product safety. Instead it allows sanctions to be dealt according to Law 14/1986 (April 25) and Royal Legislative Decree 1/2007, which is a consumer protection measure.

The seriousness of infringements relating to product safety will be determined on a scale: depending on factors such as the seriousness of the assessed potential risk or the existence of previous offences.

Fines can be imposed on the following scale:

- minor infringements – up to €3,005.06;
- serious infringements – €3,005.06–€15,025.30; and
- very serious infringements – €15,025.31–€601,012.10.

These sums can be surpassed within a limit of five times the value of the product or service. In addition to the fines, in case of serious infringements the relevant authorities may order the closure of premises for a maximum of five years.

(b) *Sectors*

In addition to the general regime set out in Royal Legislative Decree 1/2007, there are sector-specific rules.

Toys: Royal Decree 1205/2011 on toys distinguishes between:

- minor infringements, such as defects in the CE marking or on the labelling, where these do not affect the conditions of a safety use of the toy;
- serious infringements, such as labelling defects that affect safety: eg, lack of or incorrect warnings, problems with the instructions for use or recommendation about the appropriate age of the child, lack of information about the producer, incorrect CE mark; and
- very serious infringements, such as infringements of the safety requirements required by the Royal Decree. The sanctions are described above for Royal Legislative Decree 1/2007.

Food and feed: Act 17/2011 also divides food and feed-related infingements into three categories depending on their seriousness. Minor infringements include failures to collaborate with the health administration or infringement of the labelling regulations (provided that consumer safety is not affected). Serious infringements include, for instance, failure to notify users about a risk on a product; or infringement of labelling rules (and which could affect consumer safety). Examples of very serious infringements would be: providing false documentation or the use of adulterated or contaminated products. Fines are as follows:

- minor infringements – up to €5,000;
- serious infringements – €5,001–€20,000; and
- very serious infringements – €20,001–€600,000.

For serious infringements, the competent authorities may also order closure of the premises for up to five years.

Pharmaceuticals: Act 29/2006 also divides pharma-related infingements into three categories depending on their seriousness. Minor infringements include failure to collaborate with the health administration or to provide relevant information about a medicine. Serious infringements might include the production of medicines without the necessary quality controls or production by an unlicensed organisation. Very serious infringements might be the production of medicines without authorisation or falsification of medicines.

Again, there are three corresponding levels of fine, subdivided as follows:

- minor infringements:
  - minimum – up to € 6,000;
  - medium – € 6,001–€18,000; and
  - maximum – €18,001–€30,000;
- serious infringements:
  - minimum – €30,001–€60,000;
  - medium – €60,001–€78,000; and
  - maximum – €78,001–€90,000; and
- very serious infringements:
  - minimum – €90,001–€300,000;
  - medium – €300,001–€600,000; and
  - maximum – €600,001–€1,000,000. This upper cap can be surpassed, but with a limit of five times the value of the product or service.

Cosmetics: Again, the sector-specific regulation divides offences into three levels of seriousness. Royal Decree 1599/1997 on cosmetics sets out that:

- minor infringements include events such as issues on control procedures; serious infringements include infringement of the labelling rules or failure to provide relevant information about the cosmetic to the AEMPS; and
- very serious infringements include the production or import of cosmetics which use unlicensed ingredients or putting into circulation cosmetics that could damage human health.

3.5 Compensation

Royal Decree 1801/2003 and the specific regulations described above set out no proceedings or regulations through which consumers can seek compensation for damages suffered due to an unsafe product or measures taken to avoid the risk of an unsafe product. Express reference is made to the regulations on product liability and product conformity, both set out in Royal Legislative Decree 1/2007.

4. Product liability

4.1 Sources of liability

(a) *Statute*

Royal Legislative Decree 1/2007 consolidated previous laws and is the applicable regulation in this area.

Its scope is limited to the liability of producers and suppliers exclusively for bodily harm sustained as a result of the use or consumption of a defective product and for damage caused to things other than the product itself, provided that the defective product itself was meant for private consumption (ie, not intended for professional use).

A product is deemed to be defective under Royal Legislative Decree 1/2007 where it does not sufficiently guarantee the levels of safety that are expected of it.

In order to establish whether a product is defective it must satisfy the 'unsafe test'. Other tests, including that of substandard quality or unfitness for purpose do not apply.

Royal Legislative Decree 1/2007 does not actually draw a distinction between the three types of defect traditionally identified by legal scholars, although they are commonly referred to in court:

- Manufacturing defects arise from flaws in the manufacturing process and often affect individual products within a batch (ie, other items in the same batch may not be defective).
- Project or design defects arise from flawed technical designs prior to manufacture (ie, at the technical creation stage of the product) and often affect all of the units manufactured in a batch.
- Information defects arise from flawed, incomplete, or insufficient information that causes consumers to use the product incorrectly or inappropriately and/or is misleading as to its degree of safety.

With information defects, it may be argued that in determining whether a product is defective, the law actually calls for an assessment of the extent to which the potential risks associated with a particular product are known. In this way a product will be regarded as defective if it falls short of providing the levels of safety that are expected of it or, to put it differently, when it does not provide the safety that consumers expect.

Conversely, no liability will arise where the risks associated with a given product are known by the injured person as, in these circumstances, the fact that a product is not safe is part and parcel of what is to be expected from the relevant product (theory of assumed risks). This may occur because:

- such risks are obvious (eg, a knife or a pair of scissors are cutting instruments);
- such risks are socially and culturally known by the public (eg, risks associated with tobacco or alcohol consumption); or
- the manufacturer, in compliance with its duty to provide the necessary

information about its product, provided the user with adequate instructions for use and information about the risks associated with such use.

Clearly, safety expectations are to be assessed from an objective standpoint and by having regard to the average individual's knowledge and to the manufacturer's lawful expectations about use. The subjective perspective of the particular injured person must be disregarded for these purposes.

According to EU Directive 85/374/EEC, Royal Legislative Decree 1/2007 provides that the product's presentation, the reasonable use of the product and the moment of its being put into circulation are criteria that must be taken into account to establish the expectations that injured persons could properly have of the relevant product.

(b) *Contract*

As noted above, Royal Legislative Decree 1/2007 regulating product liability disregards the contractual or non-contractual nature of the relationship existing between tortfeasor and victim.

There is also certain Supreme Court case law under which any and all bodily harm caused by the use or consumption of a product is non-contractual in nature, regardless of whether or not a prior contractual relationship existed between the victim and the tortfeasor.

Therefore, in the Spanish legal system contract theories of recovery would have no application in the context of product liability involving bodily harm.

4.2 Potential defendants

Under Royal Legislative Decree 1/2007, liability for defective products falls on producers. For these purposes 'producer' encompasses manufacturers and importers of a product or service into the European Union and those who present themselves as manufacturers or producers on the product container or packaging.

It should be noted that the statutory definition of 'producer' contained in Royal Legislative Decree 1/2007 comprises manufacturers of finished products, the producer of any component part, the producer of a raw material and importers of finished products, component parts, and raw materials.

Suppliers may also be considered liable but only under certain circumstances. Under Royal Legislative Decree 1/2007 suppliers are only liable where the producer cannot be identified or if the supplier has knowingly put into circulation a defective product.

4.3 Causation

In accordance with the general civil liability regime under Royal Legislative Decree 1/2007, the party claiming liability must provide evidence of the existence of a defect in the product, of the damage or injury, and of the causal relationship between the two.

In Spain, the standard of proof of that causal link is in theory high. The Supreme Court formally requires that evidence of the existence of a causal link must be clear and precise, and not based on mere deduction, conjecture or probability. Therefore, in principle, it requires absolute evidential certainty.

Consequently, in Spain, tests applied elsewhere like the 'more probable than not' rule are, in theory, not applicable. And statistics or epidemiology do not appear to be sufficient by themselves to prove a causal link.

In practice, however, judges and courts often reach decisions in a manner that comes close to applying the 'more probable than not' rule, in particular, through recourse to the judicial presumption (*praesumptio juris*, whereby the judge or court applies human logic rules to deduce a fact and deems it proven (deduced fact) on the basis of the evidence of one or more basic facts).

For example, the Provincial Court of Appeal of Santa Cruz de Tenerife, in a decision dated January 15 2000,[25] considered that causality had been proven between an alleged defect in a recently manufactured vehicle (which was not directly established) and an accident sustained by the vehicle's driver 50 metres away from her home, because the car swerved off the road.

Based on the evidence of a series of basic facts (the perfect condition of the road surface; the excellent weather conditions; the recent manufacturing of the car (ruling out insufficient maintenance); the slow speed at which the car was apparently being driven just 50 metres into its journey; the driver's having received a letter from the manufacturer recommending that she should take the vehicle to an official car dealer for inspection as a potential mechanical brake failure had been detected in some units of the same model – the court reached the conclusion that the accident could only have been due to a defect in the car's manufacture (deduced fact).

On other occasions, the courts have determined the causal relationship by reference to statistics and epidemiology – which are deemed to be insufficient by themselves to establish the causal link – in combination with other basic facts.

The ruling on the rapeseed oil case is an illustrative example of the use of epidemiological studies by the Spanish Supreme Court. Although the events took place in 1981, the Supreme Court did not issue a final judgment on this case until September 1997.[26]

In that case, the Supreme Court found that:

- a link between the consumption of rapeseed oil and the disease suffered by more than 20,000 injured parties had been epidemiologically determined,
- the pathology found in the injured parties was new (it had never before been diagnosed) and consequently no risk factors inherent to the disease had been identified by the scientific community;
- none of the parties to the proceedings proposed any alternative causal hypothesis other than the consumption of rapeseed oil; and
- once the denatured rapeseed oil was removed from the market and its consumption had been suspended, no new cases of intoxication were diagnosed.

25 Ruling of the Provincial Court of Appeal of Tenerife, January 15 2000 (AC 563).
26 Ruling of the Supreme Court, September 26 1997.

Importantly, epidemiology was not considered in itself to be sufficient proof of a causal relationship. Epidemiology was just one more link in the Supreme Court's logical reasoning chain that led to the evidential conclusion of the existence of a causal relationship.

4.4 Defences

Royal Legislative Decree 1/2007 provides that manufacturers or importers are not liable, as long as evidence of any of the following circumstances is provided:

- The product was not put into circulation by the relevant manufacturer or importer.
- Having regard to the circumstances, it was to be expected that no defect existed at the time at which the product was put into circulation.
- The product was not manufactured for sale or for any other method of distribution for an economic purpose, or was neither manufactured nor imported, supplied or distributed in the course of a professional or business activity.
- The defect was the result of manufacturing the product in accordance with mandatory rules in force.
- The state of scientific and technical knowledge at the time of putting into circulation was not such as to enable the existence of the defect to be discovered. This is known as the 'state of the art' defence.

Under this exemption of liability clause, damages caused by a defective product are not amenable to compensation where the state of scientific or technical knowledge at the time the damage was caused was not such so as to avoid such damage.

Therefore, manufacturers whose production activity adheres to the scientific and technical knowledge available at the time of putting their products into circulation will be relieved of liability provided that the state of scientific and technical knowledge was not such so as to allow the discovery of the defect.

Some scholars suggest that reliance on generally known empirical knowledge is not enough for manufacturers to successfully prove this exemption of liability cause. Manufacturers need also to ensure that they rely on state of the art scientific knowledge and/or research. This is tantamount to an implicit duty on the part of manufacturers to conduct research into the safety of their products whatever the manufacturer's turnover, market position or financial resources.

There are two product types where manufacturers will be liable despite having conducted their activity in accordance with the state of scientific and technical knowledge available at the time of putting their products into circulation: drugs and foodstuffs meant for human consumption. This means that the law imposes a more stringent and direct duty to conduct research into the safety of these products.

In addition to the grounds for exoneration listed above, Royal Legislative Decree 1/2007 also contemplates the possibility that a manufacturer's liability may be reduced due to the intervention of third parties or of the injured party, and in the latter case the manufacturer's liability may not arise at all.

Indeed, if a third party has intervened in the manufacturing of the product, the manufacturer who would have paid any applicable indemnity sum would be entitled, by means of a so-called 'recovery or repetition action', to recover from such third party that party's share of the cost of the damage.

With regard to intervention by the injured party (fault of the victim), the manufacturer must prove that the damage would not have occurred without the injured party's intervention, or that the injury or damage caused would, at least, not have been so serious.

4.5 Remedies

The scope of application of Royal Legislative Decree 1/2007 is limited to the liability of producers and suppliers exclusively for bodily harm sustained as a result of the use or consumption of a defective product and to damages caused to things other than the product itself, provided that the product in question is meant for private consumption.

Thus, in cases of damage caused to the product itself, or any other damages not covered by the Royal Legislative Decree 1/2007, such as moral damage (personal distress/stress/anxiety/mental impairment/non-economic loss), recourse must be had to general civil and commercial legislation.

No punitive damages are recoverable under Spanish law.

4.6 Procedure, limitation, funding, costs

(a) *Procedure*

In Spain, there are two basic declarative procedures for seeking payment of compensation: the verbal proceeding or the ordinary proceedings. Which stream a case falls under will depend on the amount claimed.

Seeking payment of a compensation amounting to up to €6,000 will be handled as a verbal proceeding. The main characteristic of this type of proceedings is that the plaintiff files a written lawsuit, while the defendant does not file a written response to the lawsuit: the court will summon the parties to a hearing where the defendant will present its response orally and the evidence will be submitted.

For cases where the amount being claimed is more than €6,000, the claim will be handled in ordinary proceedings: once notified of the lawsuit, the defendant will have a 20 working-day time period to file the brief of response. Subsequently, the court will call the parties to a preliminary hearing in which they propose the evidence they are going to submit. Finally, the court calls the parties to the trial where the evidence and final conclusions are presented.

Royal Legislative Decree 1/2007 establishes an accrued liability limit of €63,106,270.96 (this is a global civil liability for producers for death and personal damages caused by identical products affected by the same defect).

(b) *Claimants, class actions*

Royal Legislative Decree 1/2007 states that it applies to any person injured by a defective product, whether or not they satisfy the statutory definition of 'consumer', provided that the product in question is meant for private consumption.

Therefore, although Royal Legislative Decree 1/2007 seems to cover any injured person, whether consumer or not, the fact that the product in question must be meant for private consumption makes the injured person become a consumer.

With the approval of the Procedure Act 1/2000 of January 7, an action similar to the US class action regime came into force in Spain.

From that moment, and apart from those actions filed on behalf of their own members, Spanish consumer associations were entitled to file three different types of action:

- actions in support of the general and diffuse interests of consumers;
- actions on behalf of pre-determined groups of consumers; and
- actions on behalf of an undetermined number of consumers for damages allegedly caused to them.

This type of action appears to reflect the US class action options in Spanish law.

Any favourable decision issued by the court would benefit all the undetermined consumers that are represented by the Consumers Association, regardless of whether those consumers are affiliated to the plaintiff Association. The undetermined consumers will afterwards be entitled to seek enforcement of the decision on their own behalf.

However, the succinct legal provisions governing such actions and, above all, the lack of a preliminary procedure for the 'certification' of the action (ie, verification of the presence of the classical conditions for such actions to be brought: commonality, typicality, numerosity and adequacy of representation) – cast doubts on the practical importance of the reform.

Moreover, this kind of action is limited to those consumer associations that are 'representative enough' which means only those associations that are part of the Board of Consumers and Users can pursue a class action.

(c) ***Statute of limitations***

Royal Legislative Decree 1/2007 specifically provides for the statutory limitation of actions brought by virtue of this law within a term of three years from the time the victim sustained the injury or damages. Thus, it states that "actions seeking reparation for damages provided for in this chapter must lapse following a term of three years from the date on which the injured party sustained the injury or damage, whether due to the product defect or to the damages or injury caused by such a defect, provided that the person responsible for such damages or injuries is known".

It also provides that the rights of the victim will lapse 10 years after the date the product was put into circulation (provided that no legal action has been instigated in that period).

In relation to the start of the computation of the limitation period, Article 1969 of the Civil Code provides that "the time-limit for all sort of legal actions, when not otherwise provided for under a special provision, will start on the day that such actions may be brought". As for the time when the case is deemed to be actionable, it has been chiefly understood to be identified with the time when the injured party learned of the damage or injury sustained ("from the time the aggrieved party learned of it", as noted under Article 1968.2 of the Civil Code).

This criterion regarding the start of the time-limit is also applied within the product liability context: namely "from the date the injured party sustained the injury or damage".

In any consideration of limitation periods, the Spanish courts tend to lean generously in favour of the interests of the plaintiffs.

(d) ***Costs***

Finally, as a general rule, the costs of the proceedings are to be paid by the party whose claims have been rejected, unless the court perceives that there were serious doubts concerning the legal grounds of the particular case. If the decision is only partially favourable to one of the parties, then each party bears its own incurred costs, and common costs are split among the parties.

4.7 Trends

With the approval of the Procedure Act 1/2000 and the legal standing awarded to representative consumer associations, protection of consumer interests has increased in recent years, mainly in cases involving financial entities. However, for the moment this has not lead to an increase in product liability claims.

5. Products insurance

In Spain, except for very specific products and services there is no specific obligation to sign an insurance policy to cover either recall activity, nor product liability nor product guarantee. Each insurance company offers its own insurance product and the inclusion of the activities, accidents or risks covered will depend on the negotiations between the parties and the insurance premium. Act 50/1980 of October 8, concerning insurance policies, sets out the general and basic principles and regulation on insurance contracts, and will apply whenever no specific provision has been agreed between the parties.

Different kinds of policy are possible in Spain, including: damages, robbery, fire, transport, civil liability. The basic and most commonly offered civil liability insurance policies are the operating or activity civil liability, employer's liability, and product liability.

Bearing in mind that agreements between insurance companies and an insured may vary substantially from one insurance policy to another, what follows discusses general practice in Spain.

5.1 Product recall

(a) ***Insuring provisions***

In Spain, there is no specific kind of product recall insurance policy as such. It is usually a complementary guarantee to either operating or activity insurance or product liability insurance.

Therefore, damages covered by this guarantee are subject to any agreements between the parties as regards damages covered, conditions and terms. However, in general terms, the following could be said:

- This kind of complementary guarantee is limited to cases where a damage and risk in a product is known about or presumed, excluding cases where the product lacks efficiency or conformity.
- In order to avoid claims and discussions concerning the extent of the risk of damage to consumers, some insurance companies require as a condition to accept its application, that the recall comes from an official order (ie, has been ordered by a competent authority). Others accept decisions to recall taken by the insured, without prejudice to subsequent investigations.
- The recall guarantee usually covers expenses deriving from the notification of the risk to the parties possibly affected, expenses incurred in identifying the unsafe products, as well as transportation expenses, extra personnel fees, lease of premises to store returned products or destruction expenses, as necessary.

(b) Exclusions

Insurance companies do not usually cover expenses associated with the repair or substitution of the defective products, nor obviously any damage or expense deriving from the lack of conformity or efficiency of the product.

(c) Conditions

Taking into consideration that this kind of guarantee is usually a complementary coverage within the product liability insurance or activity insurance, the conditions applicable to the wider insurance policy will also apply to the guarantee.

The insurance company must usually be notified within a specified period of time, identifying the product, explaining the risk and the measures that the insured intends to apply to avoid or minimise the risk.

5.2 Contaminated products

This type of guarantee could be considered a specific kind of product recall guarantee for specific products. Given that no product recall insurance policy exists as such in Spain, it could be concluded that no contaminated product insurance policy exists either. This kind of guarantee would cover the expenses deriving from a recall of a contaminated product that might cause bodily damage or injuries to third parties due to the accidental contamination of products likely to be contaminated (food, cosmetics, medicines).

Again, any private agreement between the parties would be essential in this kind of guarantee. However, the damages and expenses would generally cover the following:

- costs of inspection, recall, destruction and replacement of the contaminated products;
- product rehabilitation and reconstruction expenses;
- consultancy expenses; and
- loss of profits due to the loss of sales.

5.3 Product liability

Under Royal Legislative Decree 1/2007, the Spanish government has powers to create a new compulsory system of insurance for product liability and a guarantee fund to cover, totally or partially, damages paid following products-related fatalities, intoxication or personal injuries. However it has as yet not enacted any such law.

(a) Insuring provisions

Product liability insurance covers the damage caused to third parties due to the use of a product produced or sold by the insured. This means that this kind of insurance applies only:

- after the delivery of the product;
- once the product has caused a damage; and
- provided that the damage is caused to a third party (not the insured).

This kind of insurance usually applies provided the damages derive from a deficiency in production, packaging, labelling, conditioning, warning or printing processes. The damages deriving from a defect in the design of product or from lack of control testing and trials are usually excluded.

The damages and expenses that this kind of insurance cover are:

- corporal/ physical damages, understood as those economic damages deriving from any type of bodily injuries;
- material damages to the defective product itself, including its repair or substitution, and to other products affected; and
- immaterial damages such as loss of profits by the third party, provided that they are directly linked to the defective product.

Damages covered by this type of insurance policy will be compensatory (as no punitive damages are recoverable under Spanish regulation).

(b) Exclusions

Apart from general exclusions such as infringement of contractual duties, the damages and expenses that are usually excluded in this kind of insurance of product liability are as follows:

- any damage deriving from deliberate acts (eg, the production or sale of a product in the knowledge that it is defective);
- failure of products to perform according to contractual requirements (lack of efficiency or conformity), except where there is a specific agreement between parties;
- damages deriving from a defect in the design of the product or from lack of control testing and trials;
- expenses related to the identification of the defective product, its repair or replacement; and
- expenses intending to avoid the risk of damage such as those related to the recall of the product or prevention of the risk.

(c) Conditions

Each insurance company will set out its own conditions to make the insurance policy apply. A notification of the damage within a concrete period of time is usually requested (which is around seven days from the damage), together with the formal complaint from the consumer or affected third party.

5.4 Financial loss

Act 50/1980 of October 8, concerning insurance policies contains some provisions regarding financial loss insurance. This type of insurance is intended to cover the loss of profits suffered by the insured (not by a third party) whenever the covered accident occurs.

This kind of guarantee can be an individual contract or be part of a wider insurance policy.

5.5 Product guarantee

An insurer might cover lack of conformity of a product and resulting expenses to repair or replace it, if that kind of cover were negotiated, but it has to be said that this kind of guarantee is rare. Where it is seen, it is usually within another policy (eg product liability insurance).

United States – California

Daniel W Bir
Steven D Di Saia
Mathew R Groseclose
Sedgwick LLP

---

1. Introduction

As product liability law has evolved, the courts in California have continued to recognise the plight of manufacturers, albeit rarely assisting them in defending claims. A manufacturer finding that its product has reached a consumer in a defective state is in a difficult, though not impossible, position.[1] On post-sale discovery of a dangerous defect, significant moral, ethical, legal, and financial issues influence the steps a manufacturer should take. In California, as in all states, the ultimate goal and responsibility is to ensure consumer safety.

The bulk of product regulation originates from and is channelled through federal agencies. These agencies, such as the Food and Drug Administration, Federal Aviation Administration, and Consumer Product Safety Commission, are charged with the protection of the public from unreasonably dangerous products which fall within their purview. Most federal regulations expressly or impliedly preempt competing state regulation, but, it is not unknown for California state agencies to go ahead with independent state regulation in spite of the existence of federal law on the same issue.[2] Federal and state agencies generally exercise broad regulatory powers, including the authority to mandate product labelling and even recalls.

Government agencies are not the only driving force behind product recalls. Discretionary corrective action by manufacturers is as common. Marketing a defective product is simply not good for business. Further, whilst the California courts have pioneered strict product liability law, they have also been at the forefront of developments which expand the scope of duty in tort for corrective measures following post-sale discovery of defect. While the law is constantly developing, certain guidelines for effective product warning, retrofit, and recall have emerged. Here we provide an overview of the somewhat nebulous rules and expectations of manufacturers in this area.

---

1 *Balido v Improved Machinery, Inc* (1972) 29 Cal App 3d 633, 649 (criticised on other grounds in *Regents of University of California v Hartford Acc & Indem Co* (1978) 21 Cal 3d 624, 641–642). *Balido* has been discussed in over 70 treatises and law review articles. The holding has been dissected, followed and questioned. Nonetheless, it is one of the most frequently cited cases in California for this area of the law.

2 For exaample, the Environmental Protection Agency regulates products that contain volatile organic compounds (VOCs). The California EPA and Air Resources Board, though, have adopted even more rigorous regulation of products containing VOCs. The manufacturers of such products are thus subject to regulation from a variety of state and federal agencies.

2. Product recall and the development of manufacturer duties in California

As nearly every consumer would lament, no sooner have we purchased a product, than advances in technology have rendered it out-of-date. In many instances, better technology allows companies to make each successive product model safer. Does that mean therefore that manufacturers should be held responsible for monitoring its products both for defect and the availability of safer additions or retrofits? The majority of jurisdictions have held such an imposition of liability to be too onerous, holding the view that there is no duty to retrofit or recall a product that was not defective when it was sold.[3]

Those jurisdictions have cited two main reasons militating against a duty to retrofit or recall. First, this duty is already the province of administrative agencies. Secondly, traditional principles of negligence and strict product liability provide remedies.[4] California, however, has eschewed the majority approach and applied expanded principles of negligence to create a model for corrective action.

Because the cost of locating, recalling, and replacing products can be tremendous and will invariably be passed on to consumers via increased pricing, recalls and retrofits are typically compelled by federal regulatory agencies only after careful consideration. The courts, however, apply their analysis necessarily on a case-by-case basis, and, as such, their findings and precedent on product recall are admittedly based on an attempt to apply general rules from an 'infinite variety of factual situations arising out of corrective efforts'.[5] The results can be varied and not necessarily consistent.

2.1 The 'all reasonable steps' approach

When a manufacturer discovers a dangerous design defect in its product, that manufacturer must take the action that a reasonable manufacturer would take to correct it.[6] This obligation arises in negligence. It is easily stated, but more difficult and ambiguous when it comes to interpreting the standard to be applied to show what is a 'reasonable' effort.

One of the first cases to address the issue, *Balido v Improved Machinery*, closely examined not only the corrective efforts needed, but also their legal effect where a consumer failed to take notice of those efforts. In *Balido*, the defendant manufactured and sold plastic injection moulding presses. On learning that press operators were suffering injuries and that the machine was not in compliance with certain California safety regulations, the manufacturer sent several letters to its customers, advising them that the press did not meet safety standards and recommending the purchase of an additional safety device. The claimant apparently ignored these warnings and never did purchase the device.[7]

---

3 47 ALR 5th 395.

4 *Tabieros v Clark Equipment Company* (1997) 85 Haw 336, 358.

5 *Springmeyer v Ford Motor Company* (1998) 60 Cal App 4th 1541, 1557.

6 *Springmeyer v Ford Motor Company* (1998) 60 Cal App 4th 1541, 1557; *Balido v Improved Machinery, Inc* (1972) 29 Cal App 3d 633, 649.

7 *Balido v Improved Machinery, Inc* (1972) 29 Cal App 3d 633, 649.

After an accident involving the press, the manufacturer argued that the failure to heed its warnings absolved its liability. In refusing to make this determination as a matter of law, the court recognised that it was an issue of fact whether a reasonable manufacturer should anticipate that a user may ignore such warnings or may refuse to spend additional money to correct the defect.[8] These were questions for the jury to decide.

A pertinent dissenting opinion in that case pinpointed the pivotal question that needs to be asked and answered in the assessment of a manufacturer's post-sale duty to provide for a warning, retrofit, or recall, namely: What more could the manufacturer have done?

2.2 When a warning alone might suffice

California clearly imposes on manufacturers a duty to warn consumers of dangerous product defects discovered after manufacture.[9] The warning must be issued soon after the discovery of any previously unknown or unknowable dangerous defect, including failure to warn about a previously unknown use for the product. To allow too much time to elapse not only creates predicate facts for a finding of negligence, but it also permits more time during which a consumer could be injured, thereby enabling a recovery in strict liability.[10]

Before initiating its warning, a manufacturer should first consider whether the discovery of the defect warrants a warning, and even prior to that decision, whether it should be continuously investigating the use of its product to assess the existence of dangers which were unknown or unknowable at the time of manufacture.

In California, the duty to test or inspect is subsumed within the manufacturer's obligation to design a reasonably safe product.[11] Thus, a manufacturer needs only test and inspect its product for known or knowable dangers at the time of manufacture. Certainly, a manufacturer could continue testing and evaluating its product for decades, and, as technology improves, it is probable that more and more potential dangers could be addressed by newly-created means. The Californian courts have nonetheless refused to place such a burden of incessant inspection on manufacturers.[12]

Instead, it is expected that a manufacturer will remain generally aware of how its product is being used and whether consumers are suffering injury in that use. This knowledge, as opposed to independent testing, creates the requisite foundation for post-sale discovery of risk and a possible duty to warn.

Even when a manufacturer discovers that its product has caused an injury, a warning is not necessarily required. Most regulatory agencies do not require that products be accident-free, but only that the rate of accidents applies to an acceptably small fraction of the products on the market.[13] When considering whether a warning is warranted, questions which will be considered include:

---

8 *Balido v Improved Machinery, Inc* (1972) 29 Cal App 3d 633, 647–649.
9 *Oxford v Foster Wheeler LLC* (2009) 177 Cal App 4th 700, 721.
10 *Torres v Xomox Corporation* (1996) 49 Cal App 4th 1, 17–18.
11 *Valentine v Baxter Healthcare Corp* (1999) 68 Cal App 4th 1467, 1486.
12 *Valentine v Baxter Healthcare Corp* (1999) 68 Cal App 4th 1467, 1486.
13 For example, *Torres v Xomox Corporation* (1996) 49 Cal App 4th 1, 16–17.

- normal expectations of how the product will perform;
- the simplicity or complexity of the product;
- the nature and magnitude of the danger to which the user is exposed;
- the likelihood of injury; and
- the feasibility and beneficial effect of a warning.

All of these fall within the grounds for judicial assessment as to whether a warning is warranted.[14]

Manufacturers of non-defective component products are not considered to have a duty to investigate the safety of a finished product designed and manufactured by another manufacturer.[15] In other words, a tyre manufacturer need not warn consumers that a particular automobile has defective airbags. Additionally, dangers resulting from the conditions of use of a non-defective product does not give rise to a duty to warn, unless that use was known or foreseeable.[16]

The court's analysis in *Temple v Velcro USA* provides some instruction on these points and provides a good answer to the 'what more could they do?' question raised in Balido.

In *Temple*, a manufacturer of a hook and loop polyester closure had learned that its product was being used to secure important deflation equipment on hot air balloons. Recognising that its product was unfit for such use, the manufacturer immediately requested that the Federal Aviation Administration take action. For three years, the manufacturer issued repeat requests that the FAA forbid this use and sent a warning and voluntary recall notice letter directly to all registered owners of balloons utilising the product. The manufacturer hired an independent data service to track down balloon owners to issue its warnings. The court found that the warning was "very clear, understandable and completely unambiguous". "What more [the manufacturer] could have done ... is hard to imagine."[17] Evidence was submitted that claimant had received the warning and ignored it. Shortly thereafter, a fatal accident occurred.[18]

This pattern of conduct highlights an important rule: a manufacturer cannot delegate the duty of safety owed to the consumer.[19] Had the manufacturer only warned the FAA, it probably would have been more difficult for the court to hold that the manufacturer took all reasonable steps to address the danger as a matter of law.[20]

---

14 *Jackson v Deft, Inc* (1990) 223 Cal App 3d 1305, 1320.

15 *DeLeon v Commercial Manufacturing and Supply Co* (1983) 148 Cal App 3d 336, 343–344; *Lee v Electric Motor Division* (1985) 169 Cal App 375, 387; *Springmeyer v Ford Motor Company* (1998) 60 Cal App 4th 1541, 1560. California courts have recently revisited the matter of expanding the duty of product manufacturers to warn about the hazards of replacement parts made by others that are subsequently incorporated into the manufacturer's original product by the purchaser; eg, *Taylor v Elliot Turbomachinery Co, Inc* (2009) 171 Cal App 4th 564. This issue is presently pending before the California Supreme Court. *O'Neil v Crane Co* (2009) 177 Cal App 4th 1019 (review granted, republished by *O'Neil v Crane Company*, 223 P 3d 1, 2009 Cal LEXIS 13491 (Cal , 2009)).

16 *DeLeon v Commercial Manufacturing and Supply Co* (1983) 148 Cal App 3d 336, 343–344.

17 *Temple v Velcro USA, Inc* (1983) 148 Cal App 3d 1090, 1095.

18 *Temple v Velcro USA, Inc* (1983) 148 Cal App 3d 1090, 1091–1092.

19 *Ford Motor Company v Poeschl* (1971) 21 Cal App 3d 694, 699 (disapproved on other grounds in *Angelus Associates Corp v Neonex Leisure Products, Inc* (1985) 167 Cal App 3d 532).

20 At least one court has questioned whether the *Temple* manufacturer would have any liability to the claimant in light of its status as a component manufacturer. *Springmeyer v Ford Motor Company* (1998) 60 Cal App 4th 1541, 1560. However, in light of the extensive knowledge possessed by the manufacturer with respect to how its product was being dangerously misused, the manufacturer could have easily been susceptible to negligence claims had it done nothing.

However, based on the facts and the nature of the warning (quoted in full in the opinion), the appellate court found no triable issue of fact and affirmed the trial court's grant of summary judgment in favour of the manufacturer.

2.3 When a duty to warn becomes a duty to retrofit or recall

In some instances, merely warning consumers of a discovered danger will not be sufficient. So, even without the intervention of a regulatory agency, a manufacturer might determine on its own that the danger warrants a retrofit or recall, particularly where a manufacturer discovers the absence of an important safety device.[21] When the retrofit or recall is mandated by a regulatory agency, the 'reasonableness' standard still applies and failure to conduct an adequate retrofit or recall can result in liability for negligence (and the presence of a dangerous defect will make a manufacturer susceptible to strict products liability as well).[22]

In practice of course, warning letters, even those notifying a recall, can be ignored: and the courts recognise this fact. At least one court commented on a manufacturer's general awareness that recall campaigns are often disregarded.[23] "A well-known history of disregard," that court noted, makes it difficult for any manufacturer to claim in a subsequent lawsuit that it could not foresee that consumers would continue using the product. The foreseeable nature of consumers' failure to heed warnings thus acts to preclude arguments from manufacturers that continued use of a defective product constitutes a superseding cause.[24] Instead, a manufacturer may argue, and the jury may consider, whether a claimant's comparative fault should reduce any award made.

As noted earlier, California is in a minority of jurisdictions which recognise that manufacturers have a duty to retrofit or recall products that were not defective at the time of sale.[25] The existence of this duty, much like the post-sale duty to warn, depends entirely on the facts of the case.

In *Hernandez v Badger Construction Co*, the defendant manufactured a crane which complied with all relevant safety regulations and was determined to be free of defect. The manufacturer offered to build in an anti-two-blocking safety device (ATBD) as an option in manufacture. At the time of purchase, the consumer declined the option. Seven years later, and after a change in industry safety standards, the manufacturer began including the ATBD as a standard feature, but did not retrofit earlier models.[26]

After an accident involving the crane, the manufacturer faced legal action on strict liability and negligence grounds. The court recognised that, even though the jury determined that there was no defect, it was not inconsistent for the jury to find that the manufacturer was still negligent because in California, the failure to conduct an adequate retrofit campaign may constitute negligence, apart from the issue of defective design. The manufacturer here did comply with government safety

21 *Lunghi v Clark Equipment Company, Inc* (1984) 153 Cal App 3d 485, 491–492.
22 *Lunghi v Clark Equipment Company, Inc* (1984) 153 Cal App 3d 485, 491–492.
23 *Springmeyer v Ford Motor Company* (1998) 60 Cal App 4th 1541, 1559.
24 *Springmeyer v Ford Motor Company* (1998) 60 Cal App 4th 1541, 1558.
25 *Lunghi v Clark Equipment Company, Inc* (1984) 153 Cal App 3d 485, 494; *Hernandez v Badger Construction Equipment Co* (1994) 28 Cal App 4th 1791, 1828–1829.
26 *Hernandez v Badger Construction Equipment Co* (1994) 28 Cal App 4th 1791, 1799–1800, 1827–1828.

regulations but was still found negligent: the jury was able to conclude that the manufacturer "did not do everything reasonably within its power to prevent injury".[27]

2.4 Conclusion

Given the plethora of factual scenarios possible in relation to how defects are notified and the reasonableness of manufacturers' reactions to discovering defects, Californian jurisprudence could well produce inconsistent precedent and thus uncertainty for manufacturers. For example, one California appellate court recently noted that the same industrial cotton picker has been the subject of multiple lawsuits regarding defective design and negligent failure to retrofit.[28] Four of those cases resulted in appellate court opinions, two of which were reported.[29] In all four the juries considered nearly identical facts and the identical question of whether a safety cut-off switch should have been added. Two were decided in favour of the claimant and two in favour of the manufacturer.[30]

However, there are arguments in favour of the expansion of negligence principles and duties to capture retrofit and recall, so manufacturers should expect to be subject to additional liabilities, above and beyond those imposed by the regulatory agencies. Simply put, California's robust framework for consumer protection means that manufacturers must take all reasonable steps to correct defects and remove risks.

3. Product liability

California has been at the forefront of the development of product liability law in the United States for quite some time. It was the first state to embrace strict products liability in the seminal Supreme Court's ruling *Greenman v Yuba Power Prods, Inc* (1963) 59 Cal 2d 57, which was subsequently followed in multiple jurisdictions and embodied in the Restatement (Second) of Torts.[31] Further alternative theories of liability developed, creating a state of constant legal evolution in California, which in turn had national influence.[32]

Since liability often rests on the application of both statutory and common law precedent, what follows is intended to provide an overview of the different theories under both routes, although they are not mutually exclusive.

3.1 Strict liability

California essentially pioneered this doctrine, guided by the principle that costs of injury properly attributable to a product defect be borne by its manufacturer, rather than the injured.[33] Justice Roger Traynor, writing for the Court in *Greenman*, was first to boldly suggest that a manufacturer's liability should be imposed, irrespective of fault.[34] Recognising the vast public policy implications of its decision, the Supreme

27 *Hernandez v Badger Construction Equipment Co* (1994) 28 Cal App 4th 1791, 1799–1800, 1827–1828.
28 *Perez v John Deere Construction Equipment Co*, 2005 Lexis 5843 (unpublished).
29 For example, *Bates v John Deere Co* (1983) 148 Cal App 3d, 40; *Sandoval v Superior Court* (1983) 140 Cal App 3d 932, 944.
30 *Perez v John Deere Construction Equipment Co*, 2005 Lexis 5843 (unpublished), *90.
31 *Brown v Superior Court* (1988) 44 Cal App 3d 1049, 1056.
32 63 Am Jur 2d (1997), Product Liability, §530.
33 *Ontiveros v 24 Hour Fitness USA, Inc* (2008) 169 Cal App 4th 424, 430.

Court was content that the imposition of strict liability would prevent manufacturers from being able to control the scope of their responsibilities to the public through contracts or other agreements.

However, despite this intent and goal, the doctrine of strict products liability is not technically 'strict'. In California, its application is, and always has been, more nuanced than traditional strict liability. In other words, strict products liability is not 'absolute liability'. The courts steadfastly hold that manufacturers are not insurers of their products; the claimant must still demonstrate the existence of a defect.[35]

(a) Proving a strict product liability claim

The claimant must prove that a defective product, where used as intended or in a manner that was reasonably foreseeable, proximately caused the claimant's damage or injury.[36] This approach is echoed in the Restatement (Third) of Torts: Products Liability Section 2(a)–(c). In fact, nearly every jurisdiction in the United States has followed California in this regard.

The limitation of liability to circumstances where the product was used as intended or in a reasonably foreseeable manner limits the seller's duty to the scope of proper use; a seller may appropriately be relieved of liability where damage results as a result of on unexpected and abnormal use of a product.[37] Unforeseeable alterations to, or misuse of, the product may similarly act to preclude liability.[38]

The crux of any products liability case is a demonstration that the subject product was in a defective condition, when it left the defendant. This condition may arise because of a defect in design, manufacture, or inadequate or erroneous warnings.[39] In California pleading practice, it is not uncommon for a complaint to include all three grounds as alternatives.

(b) Design

Two separate avenues have developed to establish a defect in design. Under the 'consumer expectations' test, the question is whether the product fails to perform as safely as an ordinary consumer would expect. Alternatively, under the 'risk benefits' test, once proximate cause has been shown, the question becomes whether the benefits of its design outweigh its inherent risk of danger.[40] These two tests are not inconsistent, and a claimant can allege defect under either or both grounds.[41]

---

34 *Greenman v Yuba Power Prods, Inc* (1963) 59 Cal 2d 57, 62: ("[A] manufacturer is strictly liable in tort when an article he places on the market, knowing that it is to be used without inspection for defects, proves to have a defect that causes injury to a human being.") The *Greenman* opinion, authored by Justice Roger J Traynor, followed Justice Traynor's reasoning in his concurrence in *Escola v Coca Cola Bottling Co of Fresno* (1944) 24 Cal 2d 453.

35 *Daly v General Motors Corp* (1978) 20 Cal 3d 725, 733. *Barker v Lull Engineering Co* (1978) 20 Cal 3d 413, 432.

36 *Souza v Squaw Valley Ski Corp* (2006) 138 Cal App 4th 262, 271.

37 *Romero v Red Plastic Co* (1995) 38 Cal App 4th 59, 69.

38 *Martinez v Nichols Conveyor & Engineering Co* (1966) 243 Cal App 2d 795, 799.

39 *Anderson v Owens-Corning Fiberglass Corp* (1991) 53 Cal 3d 987, 995; *Saller v Crown Cork and Seal Co, Inc* (2010) 187 Cal App 4th 1220, 1231.

40 *Barker v Lull Engineering Co* (1978) 20 Cal 3d 413, 426–427; 435.

41 *Bernal v Richard Wolf Medical Instruments Corp* (1991) 221 Cal App 3d 1326, 1334 (overruled on other grounds by *Soule v General Motors Corp* (1994) 8 Cal 4th 548, 574).

Nevertheless, the different tests exist in part due to their specific utility and applicability to different matters and types of product, and each has its own limitations. As its name implies, the consumer expectations test is most applicable to those products with which consumers have a greater degree of familiarity.[42] Expert testimony will usually be required to establish what 'reasonable expectation' a consumer would have.[43]

Unlike the consumer expectations test, the risk benefits test calls for a balance of factors. In assessing the propriety of a product's design, the trier of fact is called to consider, among other factors, the gravity of the danger posed, the likelihood that the proposed danger will occur, the mechanical feasibility of a safer alternative design, its financial cost, and the adverse consequences to the product and consumer resulting from such a design.[44]

For the consideration of the gravity of the potential danger, California did not adopt the Restatement (Second) of Torts' Section 402A requirement that the product is 'unreasonably dangerous'.[45] The California Supreme Court found that that placed undue burden on a claimant, creating a standard which "rings of negligence".[46] The court also pondered whether this requirement would unnecessarily bifurcate a claimant's case, requiring first proof of a defect and then of unreasonable danger and thus "a step backward in the area pioneered by this court".[47]

In some instances, the risk benefits test must be used instead of the consumer expectations test even where the latter seems more appropriate. This might occur where a complex product is alleged to have caused injury in a way that does not engage the consumer's reasonable assumptions about its performance.[48] For example, consumers have proper and reasonable expectations as to the performance of their vehicles, but not necessarily their crashworthiness. So a risk benefits analysis would be used. However, while it might be tempting for a manufacturer in certain cases to call for the risk benefits test to be applied as a counter-argument to a finding made under a consumer expectation analysis, the Californian courts have generally barred such arguments.[49]

(c) *Manufacturing defects*

Manufacturing defects occur where a manufacturer fails to comply with its own design specifications.[50] Over the past few decades, as manufacturing processes have been improved, automation more widely introduced with computer precision, and mass production increased, the general incidence of actual manufacturing defects has decreased. With these developments, claimants have tended to cite manufacturing defects less, with some exceptions (primarily where complex

42 *Boeken v Philip Morris Inc* (2005) 127 Cal App 4th 1640, 1668 (disagreed with on other grounds in *Bullock v Philip Morris USA, Inc* (2006) 138 Cal App 4th 1029, 1047).
43 *Rosburg v Minnesota Mining & Manufacturing Co* (1986) 181 Cal App 3d 726, 732–733.
44 *Barker v Lull Engineering Co* (1978) 20 Cal 3d 413, 431.
45 *Cronin v JBE Olson Corp* (1972) 8 Cal 3d 121, 133–135.
46 *Cronin v JBE Olson Corp* (1972) 8 Cal 3d 121, 132–133.
47 *Cronin v JBE Olson Corp* (1972) 8 Cal 3d 121, 133.
48 *Soule v General Motors Corp* (1994) 8 Cal 4th 548, 567–568.
49 *Bresnahan v Chrysler Corp* (1995) 32 Cal App 4th 1559, 1569–1570.
50 For example, *Lewis v American Hoist & Derrick Co* (1971) 20 Cal App 3d 570, 580.

manufacturing processes are involved, eg: involving precision in the use of elements, temperatures, or pressure; the curing of resins; forging, and other metallurgical aspects of formation).

For example, an automobile manufacturer's failure to properly connect a car's drive shaft constituted evidence of a defect in manufacture for which strict liability could be applied.[51] In addition, seemingly minute manufacturing errors, such as loose fastenings or use of fatigued metal can have significant consequences on a manufacturer's potential liability.[52] Thus, products requiring such highly technical manufacturing processes may provide further instances in which the possibility of defective design or defective manufacture can still be equally viable legal arguments.

(d) Failure to warn

Even a product made faultlessly can serve as a basis for liability when it is deemed that its warnings fail to address properly its risks and instructions for its safe use.[53] To recover under this head, it must be shown that the defendant knew or should have known of a danger inherent in a product and then failed to provide adequate warning to consumers of that risk.[54]

While this claim falls within the sphere of strict product liability, its elements sound strikingly similar to those enforced under traditional negligence. In fact, in the development of strict products liability, California's courts incorporated certain aspects of negligence law, such as actual or constructive knowledge, leading to the rather common observation that strict products liability is something less than 'strict'.[55] Despite this conceptual overlap, however, the courts have made great efforts to prevent the merger of the two theories.[56]

With California's refusal to adopt the 'unreasonably dangerous' standard under the Restatement, the law is left with a margin of ambiguity as to the level of danger which then requires a warning. In most cases where liability has been found, products have been recognised as 'substantially dangerous' in the absence of an adequate warning.[57] While a product that is 'substantially dangerous' is also likely to be 'unreasonably dangerous', the converse may not be necessarily true.

The courts have generally recognised that proper warnings fall under two categories: (1) those which adequately instruct the consumer as to how to use the product or (2) those which flag potential risks and may address foreseeable use of the product.[58] Such warnings and instructions must be clear, understandable, and unambiguous.[59]

However, a perceived failure to warn does not automatically equate with liability. Like a design or manufacturing defect, the failure must be the legal cause of the loss

51 *Elmore v American Motors Corp* (1969) 70 Cal 2d 578, 584–585.
52 *Elmore v American Motors Corp* (1969) 70 Cal 2d 578, 584–585.
53 *Oxford v Foster Wheeler LLC* (2009) 177 Cal App 4th 700, 717
54 *Anderson v Owens-Corning Fiberglas Corp* (1991) 53 Cal 3d 987, 1000.
55 *Carlin v Superior Court* (1996) 13 Cal 4th 1104, 1110–1111.
56 *Cronin v JBE Olson Corp* (1972) 8 Cal 3d 121, 133–135.
57 *Cavers v Cushman Motor Sales, Inc* (1979) 95 Cal App 3d 338, 349.
58 For example, *Midgley v SS Kresge Co* (1976) 55 Cal App 3d 67, 74; *Finn v G D Searle & Co* (1984) 35 Cal 3d 691, 699.
59 *Temple v Velcro USA, Inc* (1983) 148 Cal App 3d 1090, 1095–1097.

alleged. For example, there is no liability for failure to warn, if the claimant knew of the dangerous propensities of the product.[60] Similarly, no liability attaches where the facts demonstrate that other circumstances, apart from the failure to warn, were the actual and proximate cause of the loss or injury.

Note too that warnings are necessary to protect consumers not just from dangerous products, but also from safe products that can become dangerous in certain circumstances.[61] In this context, there is another competing principle which states that: there is no need to give a warning where the danger is generally known or obvious.[62] Thus, commonsense does play a role in this arena.

For some 'unavoidably unsafe products', special rules of policy have been created. For such products (most commonly, prescription drugs), the courts have recognised that strict products liability should not be applied in suits against manufacturers because of the significant risks to the consumer that could result if the product is not used at all.[63] For this reason, prescription drug manufactures do not carry a duty to issue additional warnings as long as the drug is properly prepared and contains necessary warnings.[64] The courts also recognise that doctors, as 'learned intermediaries', exercise discretion over the particular additional warnings that are given to patients (which helps patients by reducing the amount of precautionary information they might be given).[65]

(e) ***Causation***

Having proven a defect, and that the product was used in an ordinary or foreseeable manner, proximate cause of the alleged injuries or damages is next. Claimants must demonstrate that the product was a substantial factor in bringing about their injury.[66] As under negligence, proof of such proximate causation may be established through circumstantial evidence.[67]

Manufacturers cannot escape liability by delegating to retailers their duty to inspect products and prevent defective products from reaching consumers.[68] So a retailer's failure to inspect a defective product will not necessarily be a superseding or intervening cause. And a manufacturer can be liable even where the product is made following a consumer's plans.[69] This throws up an interesting proof of causation scenario: where a consumer orders a specially-manufactured, as opposed to mass-produced product, a defect attributable to the manufacturer may constitute the legal cause of a consumer's injuries, regardless of the consumer's specific request for

---

60 *Rosburg v Minnesota Mining and Manufacturing Co* (1986) 181 Cal App 3d 726, 734–735.
61 *Gonzales v Carmenita Ford Truck Sales, Inc* (1987) 192 Cal App 3d 1143, 1151.
62 *Johnson v American Standard, Inc* (2008) 43 Cal 4th 56, 67; *Bojorquez v House of Toys, Inc* (1976) 62 Cal App 3d 930, 933 (no duty to warn of potential dangers of a slingshot, as such dangers are common knowledge).
63 *Brown v Superior Court* (1988) 44 Cal 3d 1049 (adopting the approach embodied in the Restatement (Second) of Torts, §402A, Comment k.)
64 *Brown v Superior Court* (1988) 44 Cal 3d 1049.
65 *Carlin v Superior Court* (1996) 13 Cal 4th 1104, 1126.
66 *Rutherford v Owens-Illinois* (1997) 16 Cal 4th 953, 968.
67 *Elmore v American Motors* (1969) 70 Cal 2d 578, 584.
68 *Vandermark v Ford Motor Co* (1964) 61 Cal 2d 256, 261.
69 *Rawlings v D M Oliver* (1979) 97 Cal App 3d 890, 894.

a product of that type. Courts have found that strict liability is appropriate in such instances in light of the doctrine's 'paramount policy' of promoting consumer safety.[70]

(f) *Recoverable damages*

On damages, California generally follows the approach of the Restatement (Third): Products Liability Section 1430, which recognises that products liability law lies at the boundary between tort and contract. While losses that are purely economic can typically be recovered under contract remedies, harm to persons or property (other than the product itself) may be pursued under tort, including strict product liability. Remedies for such harm include the general and specific damages common in tort law.

'Economic loss' rule: Under this rule, a claimant suffering only financial losses not attributable to personal injury or property damage (ie, lost profits, diminution in property value or loss of use caused by a defective product), must rely on the contractual remedies that often exist between buyer and seller. Warranties, for example, may permit a consumer to sue a manufacturer for dissatisfaction with the performance of a product, even when that consumer has not been personally injured by the product. But if all warranties have expired, there will be no grounds for recovery under strict products liability or negligence, for such purely economic losses.[71]

3.2 Negligence

Since the court's landmark holding in *Greenman*, claimants in product-related actions have tended to rely on negligence principles less and less, for the simple reason that they enjoy a lesser burden. That said, it is common for claimants to assert both claims and the jury should receive instructions on both.[72] Depending on the facts and product involved, claimants may in practice find that the instructions under negligence resonate more with juries, as 'reasonable prudence' is easily understood and often applied (misapplied) in a claimant's favour: even although the standard should technically be higher than for strict product liability.

To show negligence, a claimant must demonstrate:

- legal duty of care;
- breach of that duty;
- proximate causation; and
- damage.[73]

The standard duty of care imposed is the traditional reasonable person standard, as owed to all persons who, by reasonable foreseeability, may be harmed in the use

70 *Rawlings v D M Oliver* (1979) 97 Cal App 3d 890, 897.
71 *Sacramento Regional Transit Dist v Grumman Flexible* (1984) 158 Cal App 3d 289.
72 For example, *Jiminez v Sears, Roebuck & Co* (1971) 4 Cal 3d 379, 387.
73 *Gonzalez v Autoliv ASP, Inc* (2007) 154 Cal App 4th 780, 793.

of the product.[74] In the realm of product liability, this means that foreseeable bystanders not using the product may bring such a claim in certain cases.[75]

The failure to make a product carefully may constitute a breach of duty in negligence, as well as give rise to a product defect.[76] As a corollary, a claim in negligence is necessary, in lieu of a strict liability claim, where there is a proposed breach of duty, but no product defect. For example, failure to inspect or test a product that was not defective when manufactured can conceivably lead to liability.[77]

For claimants seeking to make a case where a defect is questionable, a common avenue is to argue for a duty to warn of subsequent safety improvements or previously unforeseen dangers (breach of a duty to retrofit). Note also that, an inadequate product retrofit may be found as negligence, even if the product was not itself found defective.[78]

As an example, a manufacturer of a crane was found to have complied with all safety regulations in place at the time and to have offered a variety of optional safety equipment. Seven years later, and after changes in the applicable safety regulations, the manufacturer continued making that model, with the formerly optional safety equipment provided as a standard feature. In that case, the jury was permitted to consider, under negligence, that the manufacturer failed in its duty to warn or retrofit the former model with the additional safety equipment, even while finding the unit was not defective.[79]

In this regard, California law regarding post-sale duties to warn expands on the general rule offered in the Restatement.[80] All jurisdictions hold that, when a seller/manufacturer is informed post-sale of a danger concerning a product which was not defective at the time of sale, a post-sale duty to warn may arise.[81] Most jurisdictions, however, distinguish between the duty to warn of hazards discovered post-sale and the duty to inform customers of every post-sale development, including technology which could make a non-defective product safer. The former, but not the latter, creates a legal duty in most jurisdictions.[82] However, the Californian courts, as noted above, have adopted the minority approach, and tend to take the view that all post-sale developments affecting safety should be notified to consumers.

---

74 For example, *Gall v Union Ice Co* (1951) 108 Cal App 2d 303, 309.

75 *Zucker v Passetti Trucking Co* (1961) 191 Cal App 2d 260; *Benton v Sloss* (1952) 38 Cal 2d 399, 406. (A manufacturer or seller of a car owes a duty to occupants of the car, pedestrians and other travellers on the highway – not just an owner of the car.)

76 *Putensen v Clay Adams, Inc* (1970) 12 Cal App 3d 1062, 1076–1077.

77 *Hasson v Ford Motor Co* (1977) 19 Cal 3d 530, 546–547 (affirming a jury verdict holding a manufacturer and servicing dealership liable for negligence after an automobile accident involving faulty brakes. The jury found that no defect existed at the time the car was manufactured, but the servicing dealership was negligent because it did not properly inspect the car's brake fluid during an inspection).

78 *Hernandez v Badger Construction Equipment Co* (1994) 28 Cal App 4th 1791, 1829–1831.

79 For example, *Hernandez v Badger Construction Equipment Co* (1994) 28 Cal App 4th 1791, 1829–1831.

80 For example, *Hernandez v Badger Construction Equipment Co* (1994) 28 Cal App 4th 1791, 1829–1831.

81 Restatement (Third) of Torts: Products Liability, §10 (1998).

82 Stilwell, Thomas, Warning: You May Possess Continuing Duties After the Sale of Your Product! (An Evaluation of the Restatement (Third) of Torts: Products Liability's Treatment of Post-Sale Duties), 26 *Rev Litig* 1035, 1048–1049.

3.3 Breach of warranty

Prior to the advent of strict product liability, consumers in California sought protection from warranty law. But traditional limitations on warranties, such as privity considerations and restrictions imposed by the interpretation of contracts, left gaps in consumer protection which were filled when the strict product liability system was able to address such claims in tort. Warranty law in California survives however in the commercial setting, as governed by three separate statutory schemes:

- the Commercial Code (Sections 2101–2725);
- Song-Beverly Consumer Warranty Act (Civil Code, Sections 1790–1795); and
- the federal Magnuson-Moss Warranty Act (15 USC, Sections 2301–2312).

Since the Commercial Code applies to 'goods' generally, it has broader application than Song-Beverly, which expressly addresses 'consumer goods'. Where the two laws conflict, however, Song-Beverly applies.[83] All avenues provide for claims by express warranty, as contractual in nature, and implied warranties, where found to arise by operation of law.[84]

(a) *Types of warranty*

Express: Under the Commercial Code and Song-Beverly, express warranties are created by statements or affirmations of a seller to a buyer that goods will conform to a certain description and/or level of performance. To show breach, the claimant must prove that:

- the defendant made a statement of fact at the time of purchase that the product would perform in a certain way;
- the product did not perform as promised;
- the claimant took steps to notify defendant within a reasonable time of this fact;
- the claimant was harmed; and
- the product failure was a substantial factor in bringing about that harm.[85]

Under the Commercial Code, California courts have employed a three-step approach to resolve express warranty issues.

- First, the trier of fact determines whether the seller's statements amount to 'an affirmation of fact or promise'.
- The trier of fact then determines whether the affirmation was part of the basis of the bargain.
- Lastly, the trier of fact determines whether the seller breached the warranty.[86]

Under Song-Beverly, courts evaluate whether a written statement arising out of a sale to a consumer made claims relating to the performance of the product, or

83 Civil Code §1790(3).
84 *Hauter v Zogarts* (1975) 14 Cal 3d 104, 117.
85 *Hauter v Zogarts* (1975) 14 Cal 3d 104, 115–116.
86 *Keith v Buchanan* (1985) 173 Cal App 3d 13, 20.

assertions relating to compensation in the event of its failure. There is an important distinction there. While the buyer's reliance on the warranty is a necessary element under Commercial Code, Section 2313(1)(a), Song-Beverly does not impose a similar requirement in its definition of an express warranty.[87]

Implied: California's approach to implied warranties generally follows the approach of the Uniform Commercial Code, with some notable exceptions. California recognises the implied warranty of merchantability, and, in some instances, the implied warranty of fitness for a particular purpose.

Under the Commercial Code, the warranty of merchantability is implied in every contract for sale of goods, if the seller is a merchant for the goods sold. To be merchantable, the goods must conform to the description given and must be reasonably fit for the ordinary purpose for which they are sold.[88] Under Song-Beverly (Civil Code, Section 1791(1)), an implied warranty of merchantability means that the goods:

- pass without objection in the trade under the contract description;
- are fit for the ordinary purposes for which they are used;
- are adequately packaged and labelled; and
- conform to the affirmations of fact made on the container or label.

The implied warranties are coextensive in duration with the express warranty of the product, if that duration is reasonable, although it is possible extend that timeframe by for a further period of not fewer than 60 days and not longer than one year (Song-Beverly).

When a seller is buying goods for a particular purpose and is relying on the seller's skill and judgment to select or supply suitable goods, a warranty is ordinarily implied that the goods are fit for that purpose.[89] The warranty of fitness for a particular purpose applies to sales by merchants and non-merchants, unlike the implied warranty of merchantability (Commercial Code, Section 2315). In order to establish a breach of the fitness for purpose warranty, claimants must prove that the seller was informed of the intended use and that they relied on the seller in making the decision to purchase.[90] Under Song-Beverly (Civil Code Section 1791.1(b)), this requirement is less restrictive; a claimant needs only prove that a retailer, distributer, or manufacturer "had reason to know of the purpose" and that the buyer relied on the seller.

Express warranties and disclaimers can have a significant effect on implied warranties. When an express and an implied warranty are inconsistent, the intention of the parties determines which applies (Commercial Code, Section 2317). If conspicuous language is used, a seller can negate an implied warranty.[91] Under Song-Beverly, one cannot use an express warranty to limit, modify, or disclaim implied

87 Civil Code, §1791(2).
88 *Pisano v American Leasing* (1983) 146 Cal App 3d 194, 199.
89 Commercial Code §2315; Civil Code §§1791(1), 1792(1), 1792(2).
90 *Odell v Frueh* (1956) 146 Cal App 2d 504, 509.
91 Commercial Code, §2316(2).

warranties.[92] The only exception to this rule arises where the goods are sold 'as is' or 'with all faults'.[93] Any such disclaimer must be conspicuous and attached to the package.[94] It is important to note that when Song-Beverly conflicts with the Commercial Code, the general rule in California is that implied warranties cannot be disclaimed for commercial goods.

(b) *Products covered by warranties*

The warranty provisions of the Code apply to all transactions involving 'goods' (which are broadly defined), except for those intended only to operate as security transactions (Commercial Code, Section 2102). The Commercial Code's definition of 'goods' includes 'all things' that are movable at the time of a contract for sale (other than the money used to pay the price of sale).[95] 'Goods' also includes the unborn young of animals, growing crops and other identified things that may be severed from realty.[96] Under Song-Beverly (Civil Code, Section 1791), 'consumer goods' are more narrowly defined to include new products or parts; used, bought, or leased for use primarily for personal, family, or household purposes, except for clothing and consumables. Consumer goods include new and used assistive devices sold at retail.

(c) *Rules governing privity*

Traditionally, only the buyer was protected by warranty. This protection gradually expanded to include the buyer's immediate family in some instances. The basis of this rule was privity, which was defined in the context of warranty as a derivative interest founded on, or growing out of, a contract between two parties.[97] Historically, the only person in privity with the seller was the buyer, since a contract for sale usually included no other parties. For this reason, courts formerly held that the buyer was the only person for whom a contractual warranty could have been intended.[98]

California has since modified this rule. As early as the 1930s, the California courts began carving exceptions for the sale of food. At present, privity is generally not required in cases involving food and drugs.[99] In such cases, courts recognise that the ultimate consumer, and not just the first purchaser, should benefit from an implied warranty.[100] For 'dangerous' products, traditional privity rules have similarly been amended.[101] Additionally, when a warranty is included on a product's packaging, the manufacturer cannot repudiate that warranty on the ground that the consumer was not in privity.[102]

In general, 'vertical privity' is still a prerequisite for implied warranties.[103] Vertical

92 Civil Code, §1793.
93 Civil Code, §§1792(5), 1792(5).
94 Civil Code, §1793.
95 Commercial Code, §2102.
96 Commercial Code, §2102.
97 *Black's Law Dictionary* (6th edn, 1990).
98 *Binion v Sasaki* (1935) 5 Cal App 2d 15, 16.
99 *Magee v Wyeth Labs, Inc* (1963) 214 Cal App 602, 608.
100 *Rubino v Utah Canning Co* (1954) 123 Cal App 2d 18, 21.
101 *Alvarez v Felker Manufacturing Co* (1964) 230 Cal App 2d 987, 997.
102 *Fieldstone Co v Briggs Plumbing Prods, Inc* (1997) 54 Cal App 4th 357, 369.
103 *Fieldstone Co v Briggs Plumbing Prods, Inc* (1997) 54 Cal App 4th 357, 371.

privity simply means that a buyer and seller are parties to a sales contract; there is no vertical privity between an original seller and a subsequent purchaser who was in no way a party to the original sale of a product.[104] However, under Song-Beverly, a buyer can recover damages from a manufacturer or distributer, even where no privity of contract exists between them.[105] In other words, a buyer can recover against a manufacturer, even though the buyer may have only entered into a sales contract with a retailer. Thus, for consumer goods, careful consultation of the available statutory rights and remedies, rather than reliance on traditional privity rules, is advisable.

(d) *Remedies for breach of warranties*

In general, a claimant can recover damages that naturally arise from a breach, including lost profits, lost use of the goods, loss of goodwill, and expenses incurred in correcting or repairing defective goods.[106] The Commercial Code echoes this common law approach, with the exception of instances where parties enter into a contract that prescribes the specific remedy available in the event of a breach. Under Song-Beverly, the buyer is entitled to additional statutory remedies, including a civil penalty, which cannot be waived, except as provided by statute.[107]

3.4 Conclusion

California courts are proud pioneers in product liability law and have continually engaged with new and emerging issues, leading to a continually evolving consumer protection landscape. California product liability law presents a significant, and often onerous, standard of accountability for manufacturers, distributors and sellers of products.

4. Insurance

4.1 Overview

Products liability coverage can insure a manufacturer against liability for bodily injury or property damage resulting from defective products manufactured, sold, or distributed by the insured. Such coverage is generally limited to bodily injury or property damage that occurs away from the insured's premises and after the insured relinquishes physical possession of the products to others. For this reason, coverage can be an effective way for a manufacturer to protect itself against potential risks after a product leaves its hands.

Standard commercial general liability policies often contain the same basic terms and definitions. However, depending on the scope of cover purchased, coverage and

---

104 *Cardinal Health 301, Inc v Tyco Electronics Corp* (2008) 169 Cal App 4th 116, 138–139.

105 Civil Code, §§1792–1794.

106 *Grupe v Glick* (1945) 26 Cal 2d 680, 690; *Hicks v Kaufman & Broad Home Corp* (2001) 89 Cal App 4th 908, 923.

107 *Gitano Group, Inc v Kemper Group*, 26 Cal App 4th 49, 57 (1994). See also *Shannon-Vail Five, Inc v Bunch*, 270 F 3d 1207, 1210 (9th Cir 2001) (noting that, in order to determine the law governing a contract, California courts look first to the relevant statute and then to the 'governmental interest' test only if further guidance is necessary).

applicable exclusions can vary significantly and, not surprisingly, disputes on this issue are not uncommon.

When an insurer and insured dispute whether a particular incident of injury or property damage is covered by a policy, California courts apply their rules of contract interpretation to make a determination. The following Section analyses the law of California as it applies to commercial general liability (CGL) policies, including policies with 'products-completed operations hazard' coverage. It also considers, where relevant, the effect of different policies or exclusions on manufacturers.

4.2 California choice of law rules

It is common for an insured manufacturer to have sites in multiple states or to distribute its products in multiple states. As a result, it is important to determine which state's law will apply to resolve any coverage dispute.

In California, insurance policies are subject to the choice of law provisions codified in California Civil Code, Section 1646,107 which provides:

> *A contract is to be interpreted according to the law and usage of the place where it is to be performed; or, if it does not indicate a place of performance, according to the law and usage of the place where it is made.*

Where the policy is silent regarding place of performance, California courts typically construe Section 1646 to require application of the law where the contract was made.[108] A contract is 'made' in the place of acceptance, which is typically the insured's location listed on the declarations page.[109]

4.3 General rules on policy construction

Under Californian law, an insurance policy, like any contract, is interpreted based on the mutual intention of the parties.[110] 'The parties' intent is inferred from the " 'clear and explicit' meaning of [the policy's] provisions, interpreted in their 'ordinary and popular sense', unless 'used by the parties in a technical sense or a special meaning is given to them by usage' … . Thus, if the meaning a lay person would ascribe to the contract language is not ambiguous, we apply that meaning."[111]

In Hameid, the Supreme Court emphasised that, "[i]n order to determine whether National owed Hameid a duty to defend, we must examine the CGL insurance policy at issue".[112] The words in an insurance policy are to be interpreted according to their plain meaning and the reasonable expectations of the insured.[113] Further:

---

108 *Sentex Sys, Inc v Hartford Accident & Indem Co*, 882 F Supp 930, 937 (CD Cal 1995), *affd*, 93 F 3d 578 (9th Cir 1996); *Int'l Serv Insc Co v Gonzales*, 194 Cal App 3d 110, 121 (1987; Sims, J, concurring). See also *Ameron Int'l Corp v American Home Assurance Co* 2011 US Dist LEXIS 61486 at *4–5 (CD Cal June 6 2011) (applying *Frontier Oil* and concluding that "no 'intended place of performance can be gleaned from the nature of the contract and its surrounding circumstances' ", where policies provided coverage for property damage taking place anywhere in the US and did not have any other state-specific provisions indicating place of performance and holding that California law applied because the contract was made in California).

109 *ABF Capital Corp v Grove Properties Co*, 126 Cal App 4th 204, 222 (2005).

110 *AIU Insc Co v Superior Court* (1990) 51 Cal 3d 807, 821–822.

111 *Hameid v National Fire Insc of Hartford* (2003) 31 Cal 4th 16, 21.

112 *Ibid* at 21.

113 *Reserve Ins Co v Pisciotta* (1982) 30 Cal 3d 800, 807–808.

If the language to be construed is ambiguous, any ambiguity or uncertainty in an insurance policy is to be resolved against the insurer and … if semantically permissible, the contract will be given such construction as will fairly achieve its object of providing indemnity for the loss to which the insurance relates.[114]

The purpose of this canon of construction is to protect the insured's reasonable expectation of coverage in a situation in which the insurer-draftsman controls the language of the policy.[115]

4.4 Types of policy

Most product liability and CGL policies are 'occurrence' policies, which means that they have been written on an 'occurrence' basis. An occurrence is simply a product-related 'accident'. Such policies cover liability for damages imposed on the insured because of 'bodily injury' or 'property damage' that occurs as a result of the insured's defective product during the policy period.

Coverage for such liability is usually limited to accidents during the policy period, which is known as the time when an insurer is 'on risk'.[116] In cases involving multiple insurers, where one insurer was on risk when the product was manufactured and another insurer was on risk when a bodily injury occurred, only the latter insurer may be required to indemnify and defend the insured because the accident occurred during the latter insurer's policy period.[117]

Early CGL policies usually contained a 'one lot' provision as standard language. These policies often provided that multiple injuries would be considered to result from a single 'occurrence', if the injuries arose out of one lot of goods or products prepared by the insured.[118] This terminology is no longer in use.

Now, most policies typically define 'occurrence' to mean an accident, including continuous or repeated exposure to substantially the same general harmful conditions.[119] For many years, such 'occurrence' policies were the predominant form of coverage in California. Today, however, some insurers write product liability policies on a 'claims made' basis, which generally means that coverage is extended to claims made during the policy period. These policies define a 'claim' as a demand for payment from the insured.

4.5 Relevant coverage provisions

(a) 'Bodily injury' and 'property damage'

Californian courts have established that the mere failure of a product to perform is insufficient to trigger coverage for property damage: a defective product must cause physical injury to the property of another or loss of its use.[120] This approach stems directly from their interpretation of CGL policies, which generally contain specific

114 *McKee v State Farm Fire & Cas Co*, 145 Cal App 3d 772, 776 (1983).
115 *Ibid.*
116 *Ray v Alad Corp* (1977) 19 Cal 3d 22, 32.
117 *Travelers Cas & Surety Co v Employers Insc of Wausau* (2005) 130 Cal App 4th 99, 109.
118 *London Market Insurers v Superior Court* (2007) 146 Cal App 4th 648, 659.
119 *London Market Insurers v Superior Court* (2007) 146 Cal App 4th 648, 659.
120 *Maryland Ca Co v Reeder* (1990) 221 Cal App 3d 961, 969.

provisions defining 'bodily injury' and 'property damage'. A bodily injury usually includes "bodily injury, sickness or disease sustained by any person, including death at any time resulting therefrom", while property damage usually includes "physical injury to, or destruction of, tangible property ..." and "loss of use of tangible property which has not been physically injured or destroyed but which is caused by an occurrence ... ".

Components: While California has laid down clear rules regarding the type of damage that triggers coverage, a more complicated situation arises when an insured's component product has been incorporated into another product which is not owned by the insured. This scenario presents complications when determining whether damage to the component or the larger product triggers coverage. In general, when an insured's defective (component) product has been incorporated into another product (not owned by the insured) and it subsequently fails, the prevailing view in California is that the incorporation of the component does not constitute 'physical injury' to property, unless and until the defective component causes harm to some other part of the larger product.[121] In other instances, when an insured's defective product must be removed, and removal of the defective product requires removal or destruction of other property, then property damage exists.[122] As an example, if a concrete slab must be torn out to replace defective pipes, the cost of pouring a new concrete slab is covered damage. By contrast, there is no such property damage where only damage to the larger product results from attempts to repair the defective component part of the property.[123]

A special situation exists where a defective component product is deemed 'potentially injurious material', ie, something that by its very nature could cause harm or damage. The Californian courts have recognised property damage in potentially injurious material cases. For example, when an accident caused wood chips to be added to roasted almonds that were processed into 'nut clusters' for cereal, the presence of the woodchips, while not damaging to the almonds, triggered coverage.[124] Property damage was recognised, albeit absent the typical circumstances of damage to tangible property.

Other situations arise where 'property damage' will be found (and will be covered by insurance) where tangible property is not physically injured but 'loss of use' occurs.[125] For example, in a case where defective strawberry plants were supplied to growers, the court recognised coverage for the resulting loss of use of the field, when the plants failed to produce. The court recognised that, while the plants themselves caused no damage to tangible property, the growers had been deprived of use of their fields, and coverage was therefore triggered.

Most courts have held that 'loss of use' damages should be based on lost rental

121 *F & H Construction v ITT Hartford Insc Co of the Midwest* (2004) 118 Cal App 4th 364, 373; *New Hampshire Ins Co v Vieira* (9th Cir 1991) 930 F 2d 696, 698.

122 *St Paul Fire & Marine Insc Co v Sears, Roebuck & Co* (9th Cir 1979) 603 F 2d 780, 784.

123 *Seagate Technology, Inc v St Paul Fire & Marine Insc Co* (1998) 11 F Supp 2d 1150, 1155.

124 *Shade Foods, Inc v Innovative Products Sales & Marketing, Inc* (2000) 78 Cal App 4th 847, 868.

125 *Hendrickson v Zurich American Insc Co of Illinois* (1999) 72 Cal App 4th 1084, 1090–1091.

value or its equivalent.[126] Reduction in value of property, however, is not covered in California, as diminution in value is not a 'physical injury' to tangible property.[127] That said, the cost to repair or replace property physically damaged by the insured's defective component is almost always a covered loss.[128] Even though the risk of insuring a product is generally capped at the replacement cost, loss of use damages may exceed the replacement cost of the defective component, particularly where the defective component is incorporated into a large product.[129]

(b) 'Premises operations hazard' and 'products-completed operations hazard'

In most CGL policies, there are two different types of covered hazards, a 'premises operations hazard' and a 'products-completed operations hazard.' Coverage for a premises operations hazard is triggered for an injury or loss that occurs, while work or manufacturing is in progress on the insured's premises.[130] A products-completed operations hazard concerns defects in the merchandise/workmanship of a product that cause harm after the product is shipped. Since the purpose of this cover is to insure against bodily injury or damage to property stemming from a defective product after the product leaves the insured's hands, an 'additional hefty premium' is typically charged by the insurer.[131]

Because this coverage is so expensive, it is often excluded if it is not purchased initially as part of the policy.[132] Like most other risk considerations, the expense of the insurance is a factor that parties must examine in undertaking a cost-benefit analysis. If the party's product has significant potential for occurrences of bodily injury or property damage after it leaves the manufacturer's hands, then this type of hazard coverage could be a necessary cost of doing business and, ultimately, a good investment.

(c) Number of 'occurrences'

It is not uncommon for product liability claims to involve multiple 'occurrences.' California courts follow a 'cause' analysis when determining the number of 'occurrences' under a CGL policy.

In *Mead Reinsurance v Granite State Insurance Co* 873 F 2d 1185 (9th Cir 1988), the Ninth Circuit applied a 'cause' analysis to several lawsuits alleging violations of 42 USC, Section 1983. Eleven out of 12 lawsuits were premised on the City of Richmond's deliberate indifference to the use of excessive force by its police department. The City argued that the lawsuits stemmed from one 'occurrence'. The court agreed, finding that the City's liability did not arise from each separate act of police misconduct but was a result of an underlying policy of condoning similar acts.[133] The court stated that, while there may be a variance of injury, the time or class

---

126 *F & H Construction v ITT Hartford Insc Co of the Midwest* (2004) 118 Cal App 4th 364, 377.
127 *New Hampshire Insc Co v Vieira* (9th Cir 1991) 930 F 2d 696, 699.
128 *Geddes & Smith, Inc v St Paul Mercury Indemnity Co* (1965) 63 Cal 2d 602, 609.
129 *Anthem Electronics, Inc v Pacific Employers Insc Co* (9th Cir 2002) 302 F 3d 1049, 1057–1058.
130 *Travelers Cas & Sur Co v Employers Insc of Wausau* (2005) 130 Cal App 4th 99, 114.
131 *Baker v National Interstate Insc Co* (2009) 180 Cal App 4th 1319, 1337.
132 *Ibid* at 1339.
133 *Ibid* at 1188.

of claimant was not relevant in determining the number of 'occurrences.'[134] Thus the City's alleged policy of condoning police brutality was a single 'occurrence'.[135] The 12th lawsuit however dealt with police harassment, was a different policy and was a separate 'occurrence'.[136]

In the case of *Whittaker Corporation v Allianz Underwriters, Insurance* (11 Cal App 4th 1236, 1243 (1993)), which involved complaints regarding the insured's sealant becoming brittle and causing leaks, the court held that "the number of occurrences for the purposes of applying coverage limitations is determined by referring to the cause or causes of the damage and not to the number of injuries or claims".[137]

4.6 Exclusions

All CGL policies contain certain exclusions. The following are the most notable and which commonly affect cover in the vast majority of CGL policies:

- damage to 'your work' or 'your product' exclusion;
- damage to impaired property exclusion;
- product recall exclusion; and
- contractual liability exclusion.

The exclusion for damage to 'your work' or 'your product' applies to both defective components in the insured's product and non-defective components in the insured's product damaged by the defective components.[138] Basically, the courts in California have found that damage caused by the defective product to the product itself is not covered, nor is damage attributable to the work of the manufacturer in making the product. Essentially, this provision is meant to prevent manufacturers from claiming damage to their products which was created through the manufacturer's own faulty workmanship.

The exclusion for damage to impaired property generally excludes claims based on the product's failure to perform as intended.[139] This exclusion exists because insurance is meant to cover when a product causes some type of harm or damage, not to insure that products work correctly, or as intended by the manufacturer. For example, a claim that a malfunctioning Playstation 2 prevented a claimant from playing its DVDs did not trigger coverage. The claimant's claim was based on the failure of the product to perform as intended; the DVDs were not damaged by the Playstation and could have been viewed in any other DVD player.

Significantly for manufacturers in California, the product recall exclusion

---

134 *Ibid* at 1187.

135 *Ibid* at 1188

136 *Ibid* at 1187.

137 See also *Chemstar, Inc v Liberty Mutual Insc Co*, 41 F 3d 429 (9th Cir 1994; finding a single 'occurrence' where the insured supplied lime plaster and failed to warn that it was for exterior use only resulting in pitted plaster and lawsuits by 28 homeowners); *Eott Energy Corp v Storebrand Int'l Insc* 45 Cal App 4th 565, 52 Cal Rptr 2d 894 (1996; applying 'cause' standard, found 653 thefts committed as part of organised and systematic scheme to steal diesel fuel constituted one 'occurrence').

138 For example, *Western Employers Ins Co v Arciero & Sons, Inc* (1983) 146 Cal App 3d 1027, 1031.

139 *Sony Computer Entertainment America, Inc v American Home Assur Co* (9th Cir 2008) 532 F 3d 1007, 1019 (a defect in a Playstation 2 resulted in alleged 'loss of use' of DVDs that had been purchased but could not be played in the Playstation. Coverage was denied on the basis of the impaired property exclusion.).

precludes the cost or expenses of any loss of use, withdrawal, recall, inspection, repair, replacement, adjustment, removal or disposal of 'your product,' 'your work' or 'impaired property'. This exclusion limits the scope of an insurer's responsibility in California: an insurer may be liable to pay for damages caused by the failure of an insured's product when injury or property damage occurs, but not for costs of preventative or curative actions.[140]

Finally, the contractual liability exclusion makes clear that insurance is not meant to cover contractual liability incurred by the insured. But this does not apply to warranties which the insured has entered into contractually, and for which the insured assumes tort liability to another party for bodily injury or property damage resulting from use of the insured's product (ie contractual liabilities are generally excluded from insurance cover, but warranties are not excluded where the insured has had to pay under tort law for a user's bodily injury or property damage: see above). The effect of the contractual liability exclusion is therefore that it allows for coverage for tort claims arising from injury or property damage resulting from the insured's breach of warranty, but it does not provide coverage for actions seeking purely economic damages, which require contractual remedies under California law.[141]

4.7 Cover for entities other than the insured

(a) Successor liability

California permits successor liability, if certain factors are met or, alternatively, in the case of strict product liability claims. As an exception to the 'successor liability doctrine', this means that a purchaser of a manufacturing business who continues to manufacture its products assumes strict tort liability for defects in products previously manufactured.[142]

Unsurprisingly, some California courts have recognised that a predecessor's insurance coverage should also pass to the successor, although other courts have ruled in the opposite direction.[143] The courts that have not extended a predecessor's insurance coverage to a successor reason that the extension of liability in tort cannot justify extending contractual obligations of an insurer to an entity that was never a party to the insurance agreement.

The California Supreme Court has recognised but not yet resolved this conflict in the jurisprudence.[144] As a general rule in California, until this split of legal authority is resolved, insurers and insureds' need to fall back on the express terms of each

---

140 *Armstrong World Industries, Inc v Aetna Cas & Surety Co* (1996) 45 Cal App 4th, 1, 113.

141 *St Paul Fire & Marine Insc Co v Coss* (1978) 80 Cal App 3d 888, 896.

142 *Ray v Alad Corp* (1977) 19 Cal 3d 22, 34.

143 *Northern Ins Co of New York v Allied Mutual Insurance Co* (9th Cir 1992) 955 F 2d 1353, 1357; *General Access Insurance Co of America v Superior Court* (1997) 55 Cal App 4th 1444, 1455 ("The law can impose tort liability on a successor corporate entity; it cannot impose a contractual insurance relationship between an insurer and a stranger to the insurance contract").

144 *Henkel Corp v Hartford Access & Indemnity Co* (2003) 29 Cal 4th 934, 941.

145 For example, *Travelers Cas & Sur Co v Employers Insc of Wausau* (2005) 130 Cal App 4th 99, 110 (recognising the propriety of a policy exclusion that excluded coverage for products manufactured by a predecessor corporation while a different insurer was on risk).

policy. Insurers wishing to further protect themselves will often draft policies with additional exclusions precluding assignment of coverage rights to any successor.[145]

(b) *Vendors' endorsements*

An endorsement to an insurance policy is a written acknowledgement on the part of the insurer to extend coverage to a party other than the insured, usually through a contractual agreement. Product liability policies are typically purchased by manufacturers, but endorsements may be added to cover other entities within the stream of commerce, such as retailers or distributors. Strategically speaking, this allows the manufacturer and its insurer to coordinate the defence of multiple suits arising out of the same injury and spares a distributor or retailer certain defence costs.[146] These endorsements are also advisable because they can be inexpensive and become useful if and when the manufacturer, distributor and seller are all named in the same lawsuit, which is common in California.

4.8 Conclusion

According to the terms of each insurance policy, California generally recognises the importance of bargained-for coverage protecting manufacturers and, in some cases, their suppliers, distributors, and retailers, against liability for bodily injury or property due to defective products. While standard commercial general liability policies often contain the same basic terms and definitions, the scope and extent of coverage can vary significantly. Thus, manufacturers should carefully analyse their business' potential for liability and select their policy after careful consideration of what coverage best fits their product.

146 *Harford Fire Insc Co v St Paul Surplus Lines Insc Co* (7th Cir 2002) 280 F 3d 744, 747 (applying California law)

United States – New York

Christopher J Celentano
Christopher C Novak
Sedgwick LLP

1. Introduction

In the United States, recalls of defective or potentially harmful products are commonplace.[1] Although many recalls instruct consumers to discontinue their use of the product and return it to the retailer or manufacturer for a refund or a repair, the specifics of each recall vary. Some recalls are simply warnings to consumers to limit their use of products. Others supplement their warnings with recommended consumer actions, such as removing or disabling a hazardous part of the product. Recalls are usually highly publicised on television, in newspapers, and on the internet. Consumers who purchased the defective products may also receive notices directly from the manufacturer, particularly in the case of motor vehicles.

The decision to recall a product may have major financial consequences for a manufacturer. A company that recalls a product will incur significant expense in developing and implementing a recall strategy. The company must bear the expense of ensuring that the products are withdrawn from the market, including the costs of notifying consumers, and transporting and disposing of the defective products. The company may also be required to compensate all downstream purchasers, including wholesalers, distributors, retailers, and consumers. And of course, there are lost profits from the expected sale of the products.

Despite the immediate financial consequences, product recalls in the United States are almost always voluntary. Sometimes they occur because a company discovers a problem on their own, and other times a company may recall a product after a regulator raises concerns. But only in rare cases will a regulatory agency request a recall. In general, manufacturers will act peremptorily to reduce the risk of mass tort litigation brought against the company by consumers injured by the manufacturer's product. These concerns will often outweigh the costs of a recall.

In New York, as in all US states, companies that manufacture, import, distribute, or sell products have an obligation to ensure that the products they place in the stream of commerce are reasonably safe. Unlike many foreign jurisdictions, however, these companies are not subject to a singular, comprehensive code or statute defining what constitutes a 'reasonably safe' product. Instead, they are subject to a patchwork of federal and state laws.

Virtually all products sold in the US are subject to regulation by the federal government. Over the last 100 years, the federal government has enacted numerous

1 See www.recalls.gov.

statutes and regulations concerning various categories of products. Under New York law, however, a manufacturer's compliance with government standards and regulations is not dispositive of the issue of whether the product is 'reasonably safe'.[2] With very limited exceptions, a manufacturer may still be liable under New York state law if its product caused damage because the product was either determined to be defective or unfit for its intended purpose—even if the manufacturer complied with all applicable federal statutes and regulations.

Product liability lawsuits alleging bodily injury or property damage are generally covered under commercial general liability (CGL) policies. General liability policies, however, exclude coverage for purely economic loss incurred by the plaintiffs (ie, the purchase price of the product) and costs incurred by the manufacturer in both recalling the product, and either repairing, replacing, or refunding the purchase price of the product. Product recall insurance is intended to fill this gap and provide coverage for certain first party losses incurred by the manufacturer in connection with a recall, provided certain conditions are met.

2. Product recalls

This section discusses the major statutes generally governing safety requirements and recalls of food, drugs, consumer products, and motor vehicles.

It briefly outlines the major statutes and regulations administered and enforced by the following US regulators:

- the Food and Drug Administration (FDA);
- the Consumer Product Safety Commission (CPSC); and
- the National Highway Traffic Safety Administration (NHTSA).

2.1 Food and Drug Administration

The FDA is the US federal agency that regulates the production of food, food additives, medical devices, drugs (both prescription and over-the-counter), tobacco, and cosmetics.[3] The FDA describes its responsibilities as "ensuring that foods are safe, wholesome and sanitary; human and veterinary drugs, biological products, and medical devices are safe and effective; cosmetics are safe; and electronic products that emit radiation are safe".[4] In addition, the FDA "ensures that these products are honestly, accurately and informatively represented to the public".[5]

The FDA is authorised to carry out its stated responsibilities primarily through the Food, Drug and Cosmetic Act and its amendments. We outline below the statute's most important features and amendments.

(a) Food, Drug and Cosmetic Act 1938

The federal Food, Drug, and Cosmetic Act was passed in 1938, and grants the FDA broad powers to carry out its regulatory mandate. These powers include general rulemaking, investigative, and enforcement powers.[6] The Food, Drug, and Cosmetic

2 *Murphy v Nissan Motor Corp USA*, 650 F Supp 922 (EDNY 1987).
3 21 USC, Sections 301 and following.
4 'What FDA Regulates', at www.fda.gov/AboutFDA/WhatWeDo/WhatFDARegulates/default.htm.
5 'What FDA Regulates', at www.fda.gov/AboutFDA/WhatWeDo/WhatFDARegulates/default.htm.

Act 1938's primary purpose is to forbid "the movement in interstate commerce of adulterated and misbranded food, drugs, devices, and cosmetics".[7]

Food: The Food, Drug, and Cosmetic Act 1938 gives the FDA power to engage in economic regulation, to set legally enforceable food standards, and to establish affirmative labelling requirements. The FDA's jurisdiction over food is broad, and extends to almost all food and food additives except non-game meat and poultry.[8] The FDA ensures the safety of food and food additives by issuing regulations and standards for food packaging, processing, labelling, quality, transport, and sanitation.[9] Under the Food, Drug, and Cosmetic Act 1938, food is adulterated if it contains "poisonous, insanitary, or deleterious ingredients", if the food's constituents are altered, or if it is transported in an insanitary manner.[10] The FDA has promulgated numerous regulations addressing these issues, such as Good Manufacturing Practices, the "generally recognised as safe" ingredient or additive regime for foods, and nutrition labelling.[11]

Drugs: The Food, Drug, and Cosmetic Act 1938 was amended in 1962 to give the FDA power to ensure that drugs are safe and effective. The Food, Drug, and Cosmetic Act 1938 defines 'drugs' broadly. Any substance intended for use in the "diagnosis, cure, mitigation, treatment or prevention" of any disease in humans or animals, as well as any substance "intended to affect the structure or any function of the body of man or other animals" fall under the FDA's jurisdiction.[12] The FDA's primary tool for regulating drugs is requiring that drug manufacturers provide 'substantial evidence' of their drugs' safety and effectiveness before they can be marketed to the public.[13] This pre-approval process for new drugs is considered one of the world's most demanding. In addition, the amendments require the manufacturer to properly label their products and prohibit the manufacturer from misleading consumers through false statements contrary to test results.[14]

Medical devices: The Medical Device Amendments of 1976 to the Food, Drug, and Cosmetic Act 1938 were enacted in 1976, and empower the FDA to regulate the marketing of medical devices.[15] Manufacturers and initial distributors of medical devices must register their establishments and list their devices with the FDA.[16] The

6 21 USC, Sections 335b(b), 371–376.

7 21 USC, Sections 321–392

8 21 USC, Section 392. The US Department of Agriculture (USDA) regulates non-game meat and poultry. The US Department of Agriculture's Food Safety and Inspection Service (FSIS) is responsible for meat and poultry that is in interstate commerce. Intrastate food safety is the responsibility of state and local food inspectors. Like the FDA, the FSIS classifies hazards as Class I, II, and III, with Class I being the most hazardous.

9 21 USC, Sections 341–350 and following.

10 21 USC, Section 342.

11 *See* eg,; 21 CFR Sections 110, 111, 170.3, 170.35, 101.9, and 101.36.

12 21 USC, Section 321(g).

13 21 USC, Section 321.

14 21 USC, Sections 202.1–203.70.

15 21 USC, Sections 360c–360k.

16 21 CFR, Section 807.

1976 Amendments classify medical devices into three categories, ranging from Class I devices which are subject to only minimal regulation to Class III which present a potential unreasonable risk of illness or injury.[17] The device classification regulation defines the regulatory requirements for a general device type, and regulatory control increases from Class I to Class III.

Each manufacturer who wants to market a medical device in the US must submit either a '510(k)' or obtain pre-market approval (PMA). A 510(k) is a pre-market submission made to the FDA to demonstrate that the device to be marketed is at least as safe and effective (ie, substantially equivalent) to a legally marketed predicate device.[18] A PMA is required for Class III devices that are high risk and pose a significant risk of illness or injury, or devices found not substantially equivalent to Class I and II predicate through the 510(k) process.[19]

The FDA established the quality system regulation, which includes requirements related to the methods, facilities, and controls used in designing, purchasing, manufacturing, packaging, labelling, storing, installing and servicing medical devices.[20] Manufacturers and importers must report problems with medical devices through the FDA's Medical Device Reporting System.[21] This system allows the FDA to receive adverse events from various sources so that they may be detected and corrected quickly.

Enforcement: The Food, Drug, and Cosmetic Act 1938 makes it unlawful to engage in a range of activities that violate the Food, Drug, and Cosmetic Act or FDA regulations, including the sale of adulterated or misbranded food or drugs, obstruction of an FDA inspection or investigation, failure to register as a drug producer or supplier, or the sale of new drugs without FDA approval.[22] The FDA has expansive powers to investigate and ensure compliance with safety standards. The FDA is permitted to conduct "examinations and investigations" for any purpose under the Food, Drug, and Cosmetic Act and frequently inspects food, drug, and medical device manufacturing or processing facilities.[23] The Food, Drug, and Cosmetic Act provides three remedies for violations:

- injunctive relief;
- criminal prosecution; and
- seizure.[24]

Persons or entities that engage in these proscribed activities are subject to both civil and criminal liability.[25] The Food, Drug, and Cosmetic Act 1938 does not grant a private right of action to consumers injured by Food, Drug, and Cosmetic Act 1938

17 21 CFR, Sections 862–892.
18 21 CFR, Section 807.92(a)(3).
19 21 CFR, Section 803.
20 21 CFR, Section 820.
21 See www.fda.gov/Safety/MedWatch/default.htm,
22 21 USC, Section 331.
23 For example; 21 CFR, Section 820.
24 21 USC, Sections 332–334.
25 21 USC, Sections 333, 335(b).

violations. After giving notice to the FDA, however, individual states may initiate civil litigation to enforce or enjoin the violation of certain Food, Drug, and Cosmetic Act 1938 provisions.[26]

Recalls: One of the FDA's most significant responsibilities under the Food, Drug, and Cosmetic Act is overseeing the recall of defective products. Recalls may be conducted on a firm's own initiative, by FDA request, or by FDA order under statutory authority. It should be noted that the FDA can only order product recalls in limited circumstances, such as in the case of hazardous medical devices, tobacco products, or infant formula (but see Food Safety Modernization Act below).[27] Similarly, FDA requested recalls are usually reserved for "urgent situations".[28] In practice, companies would typically voluntarily recall potentially unsafe or defective products in cooperation with the FDA.

The FDA has published guidelines for companies to follow when recalling defective products in Title 21 of the Code of Federal Regulations, Chapter I, Subchapter A, Part 7.[29] Under these guidelines, the manufacturer takes full responsibility for product recalls. The FDA's role is to monitor company recalls and assess the adequacy of a company's action. Under the guidelines, companies must notify the FDA when beginning recalls,[30] provide the FDA with a recall strategy for agency review,[31] and periodically make progress reports to the FDA on the recalls.[32]

The FDA categorises all recalls into one of three classes according to the level of hazard involved:[33]

- Class I recall – a situation in which there is a reasonable probability that the use of or exposure to a violative product will cause serious adverse health consequences or death.
- Class II recall – a situation in which use of or exposure to a violative product may cause temporary or medically reversible adverse health consequences or where the probability of serious adverse health consequences is remote.
- Class III recall: a situation in which use of or exposure to a violative product is not likely to cause adverse health consequences.

The FDA considers a recall completed and terminated when it determines that the company has made "all reasonable efforts" to remove or correct the product and that it is reasonable to assume that the product has been removed from the market or corrected.[34] After a recall is completed, the FDA ensures that the product is destroyed or suitably reconditioned and investigates why the product was defective.

26 21 USC, Section 337(b).
27 21 USC, Section Section 360h(e), 387h(c)
28 21 CFR, Section 7.40(b).
29 21 CFR, Sections 7.40–7.59.
30 21 CFR, Sections 7.46(a); for medical devices see 21 CFR, Sections 806.10
31 21 CFR, Sections 7.42; for mandatory recall of medical devices see 21 CFR, Sections 810.14.
32 21 CFR, Sections 7.53; for mandatory recall for medical devices see 21 CFR, Sections 810.16.
33 www.fda.gov/safety/recalls/ucm165546.htm.
34 21 CFR, Sections 7.55; for mandatory recall for medical devices see 21 CFR, Sections 810.17.

(b) FDA Food Safety Modernisation Act

On 4 January 2011, the FDA Food Safety Modernisation Act was passed, which represented the most significant overhaul of the regulatory scheme for food safety in 70 years.[35] The primary focus of the statute is preventing foodborne illness. Key components are:

Preventative process controls and hazard evaluation: Section 103 of the FDA Food Safety Modernisation Act requires facilities to conduct a hazard evaluation to identify "known or reasonably foreseeable hazards", including "biological, chemical, physical, and radiological hazards, natural toxins, pesticides, drug residues, decomposition, parasites, and unapproved food or color additives". Based on this hazard analysis, facilities must first implement "preventative controls" that will "significantly minimise or prevent" such hazards and assure that food is not misbranded or adulterated. Preventative controls include sanitation procedures, training, environmental monitoring programs, food allergen control programs, recall plans, good manufacturing practices, and supplier verification activities. Second, the owner, operator, or agent in charge of each food facility must sign a substantive verification stating that the facility has implemented the required procedures and that:

- the preventive controls are in fact "adequate" and "are effectively and significantly minimizing or preventing the occurrence of identified hazards";
- the owner, operator or agent "is making appropriate decisions about corrective actions"; and
- there is "documented, periodic reanalysis of the plan … to ensure that the plan is still relevant to the raw materials, conditions and processes in the facility and new and emerging threats".

These requirements became effective in July 2012.[36]

Produce safety standards: Section 105 of the FDA Food Safety Modernisation Act directs the FDA to issue regulations establishing science-based, minimum standards for the safe production and harvesting of fruits and vegetables.[37]

Traceability: The FDA must implement pilot projects with the food industry to determine effective programs for tracking and tracing food. The FDA must also promulgate record-keeping requirements for facilities that manufacture, process, pack, or hold food the agency determines to be "high risk".[38]

Summary suspension of food registration: The FDA Food Safety Modernisation Act allows the FDA to immediately suspend a food facility's registration if the FDA

---

35 For the full text of the FSMA, see www.fda.gov/Food/FoodSafety/FSMA/ucm247548.htm.
36 *Ibid* at Section 103.
37 *Ibid* at Section 105.
38 *Ibid* at Section 204.

believes that any food associated with the facility "has a reasonable probability of causing serious adverse health consequences or death to humans or animals".[39] If the FDA issues a suspension order, it must provide the facility owner an opportunity for an informal hearing within two business days; and must vacate the order if the FDA determines that there is insufficient evidence to maintain the suspension. If the suspension is upheld, the facility must submit a corrective action plan to the FDA setting forth its plans to correct the conditions that led to the suspension.[40]

Mandatory recalls: The FDA Food Safety Modernisation Act authorises the FDA to order recalls of food.[41] The FDA may request a voluntary recall if "the use or exposure to such article will cause serious adverse health consequences or death to humans or animals". If the party refuses, the FDA may issue a "cease distribution" order requiring that the party "immediately" cease distributing the item and notify recipients of the recall. Like a summary suspension order, the FDA must provide the party with an opportunity for an informal hearing within two business days; and must vacate the order if it determines that there was insufficient evidence to support it.[42]

Prevention of intentional adulteration: The FDA Food Safety Modernisation Act requires the FDA to develop regulations and guidance in collaboration with the Department of Homeland Security (DHS) and the Department of Agriculture "to protect against the intentional adulteration of food ... for which there is a high risk of intentional contamination".[43]

Increased access to facility records: The FDA Food Safety Modernisation Act allows the FDA to inspect records of manufacturers, processors, packers, distributors, receivers, holders and importers if there is a "reasonable probability" that a food may cause "serious adverse health consequences or death to humans or animals". This expanded inspection power extends to "all records relating to the manufacture, processing, packing, distribution, receipt, holding, or importation" of a suspect food. This power applies to all entities in the supply and distribution chain, even if the FDA does not suspect the entity as the cause of the potential safety risk.

Imported foods, foreign facilities, and foreign suppliers: Importers must conduct "verification activities" to ensure that foreign suppliers are performing hazard analyses and risk-based prevention controls, that imported food is not misbranded or adulterated, and that suppliers are complying with applicable produce safety standards.[44] It is a prohibited act to import food if the importer does not have in place a foreign supplier verification programme that complies with the FDA Food Safety

39 *Ibid* at Section 102.
40 *Ibid*.
41 *Ibid* at Section 206.
42 *Ibid*.
43 *Ibid* at Sections 106, 108.
44 *Ibid* at Section 301.

Modernisation requirements. The foreign supplier verification requirements become effective in January 2013, two years after enactment. Imported food may be refused admission to the United States if the food is not accompanied by a required certification of compliance. In addition, an imported food will be refused admission if the foreign manufacturer or supplier refuses to allow FDA inspection of its facility within 24 hours of an inspection request.

Expanded authority to issue administrative detentions: The FDA Food Safety Modernisation Act allows the FDA to detain a product if it has "reason to believe" the product is adulterated or misbranded.[45]

User fees: The FDA Food Safety Modernisation Act grants the FDA authority to impose fees for re-inspections of facilities that failed a previous inspection, for facilities that fail to comply with recall orders, and for facilities participating in the voluntary qualified importer programme.[46] Where a facility did not comply with a recall order, the FDA may recoup the entire cost of implementing the recall.

Pre-emption: The FDA Food Safety Modernisation Act provides that "[n]othing in this subsection pre-empts state, local, county, or other non-federal law regarding the safe production of food. Compliance with this subsection shall not relieve any person from liability at common law or under state statutory law".[47]

2.2 Consumer Product Safety Commission

The CPSC is an independent regulatory agency created in 1973 to protect the public "against unreasonable risks of injuries associated with consumer products".[48] The CPSC is charged with collecting, investigating, analysing and disseminating information relating to illness, injury and death associated with consumer products. The CPSC also develops, implements and enforces product safety rules and regulations.

(a) Consumer Product Safety Act

The Consumer Product Safety Act grants the CPSC jurisdiction to regulate 'consumer products', defined as "any article, or component part thereof, produced or distributed (i) for sale to a consumer for use in or around a permanent or temporary household or residence, a school, in recreation, or otherwise, or (ii) for the personal use, consumption or enjoyment of a consumer in or around a permanent or temporary household or residence, a school, in recreation, or otherwise".[49]

The CPSC has broad authority to issue product safety standards, ban dangerous consumer products, issue recalls, compel manufacturers to report potentially unsafe products, investigate potential product hazards, and educate consumers about

45 *Ibid* at Section 207.
46 *Ibid* at Section 107.
47 *Ibid* at Sections 103, 105.
48 15 USC, Section 2051(b)(1).
49 15 USC, Section 2052(a)(1).

product safety. Under the Consumer Product Safety Act, manufacturers, distributors, and retailers are equally responsible and liable.[50]

Safety standards: Under the Consumer Product Safety Act, the CPSC may promulgate consumer product safety standards "reasonably necessary to prevent or reduce an unreasonable risk of injury associated with such product", including performance requirements or requirements concerning a product's warnings or instructions.[51] The CPSC has issued safety standards for products as varied as bicycles, children's toys, matchbooks, swimming pools, garage door openers, portable generators, and all-terrain vehicles.[52] The CPSC, however, must rely on industry-created voluntary standards if those standards would eliminate or adequately reduce the risk of injury addressed and there is likely to be compliance with the voluntary standards.[53] Generally, voluntary standard organisations (eg, American National Standards Institute, ASTM International, Underwriters Laboratories) develop the standards for the industry.[54]

Identifying hazards: The CPSC is responsible for identifying potentially hazardous products and working with the industry to remove those products from the marketplace. The CPSC collects data to find emerging hazards and identify products that need new standards. The Consumer Product Safety Act requires product manufacturers, distributors, and retailers to report to the CPSC immediately after obtaining information that a product:

- fails to meet a consumer product safety standard or banning regulation;
- contains a defect which could create a substantial product hazard to consumers;
- creates an unreasonable risk of serious injury or death; or
- fails to comply with a voluntary standard upon which the CPSC has relied.[55]

The CPSC also receives and investigates consumer complaints regarding product failures and injuries through the National Incident Information Center.[56] Potential product defects identified through these sources include manufacturing or production errors, defects in the design of or the materials used in the product, or defects in a product's contents, construction, finish, packaging, warnings, and/or instructions.[57] To determine whether the defects constitute a substantial product hazard, the CPSC may consider:

- the pattern of defect and the conditions under which the defect manifests;
- the number of defective products distributed in commerce;
- the severity of risk; and
- the likelihood of injury.[58]

50 15 USC, Section 2064(b). The full text of the statute is available at www.cpsc.gov/businfo/cpsa.html.
51 15 USC, Section 2056.
52 See, eg, 15 USC, Section 2058.
53 *Ibid.*
54 See www.astm.org; www.ul.com; www.ansi.org.
55 15 USC, Section 2064(b); 16 CFR, Section 1115.12.
56 See www.fs.fed.us/news/fire
57 See 16 CFR, Section 1115.4.
58 15 USC, Section 2064(b).

Recalls: The Consumer Product Safety Act gives the CPSC the authority to recall substantially hazardous products.[59] Despite this authority, the CPSC works with manufacturers to conduct voluntary recalls. When the CPSC determines that a substantial product hazard exists, it classifies the hazard using the following hazard priority system:

- Class A Hazard – a risk of death or grievous injury or illness is likely or very likely, or serious injury or illness is very likely. Class A hazards warrant the highest level of attention.
- Class B Hazard – a risk of death or grievous injury or illness is not likely to occur, but is possible, or when serious injury or illness is likely, or moderate injury or illness is very likely.
- Class C Hazard – a risk of death or grievous injury or illness is not likely to occur, but is possible, or when serious injury or illness is likely, or moderate injury or illness is very likely.[60]

The hazard priority system provides guidance for selecting the level and intensity of corrective action. The CPSC works with the reporting firm to develop a corrective action plan that quickly locates the defective products, removes them from the distribution chain and the hands of customers, and communicates information to the public about the defect and the corrective action plan. A company's corrective action plan usually includes:

- a statement of the alleged hazard and risk of injury;
- a statement of the cause of the alleged hazard;
- a public notification and communication plan;
- specification of the product description and/or model numbers;
- instructions about handling the product pending remedial action;
- instructions on the corrective action that will be taken, including repair, replacement, and/or refund information;
- statements of non-admission; and
- an agreement that the CPSC will monitor the company's corrective action and publicise the plan.[61]

The manufacturer must then repair, replace, or refund the purchase price of the defective product.[62]

The CPSC also has the power to ban 'hazardous' products, defined as products for which there are no "consumer product safety standard under [the Consumer Product Safety Act] that would adequately protect the public from the unreasonable risk of injury associated".[63]

The Consumer Product Safety Act makes it unlawful for any person to "sell, offer for sale, manufacture for sale, distribute in commerce, or import into the United States

59 15 USC, Section 2064.
60 See CPSC Recall Handbook, available at www.cpsc.gov/BUSINFO/8002.html.
61 16 CFR 1115.20.
62 15 USC, Section 2064(d)(1).
63 15 USC, Section 2057.

any consumer product … that is not in conformity with an applicable consumer product safety rule" under the Consumer Product Safety Act.[64] Persons that violate the Consumer Product Safety Act are subject to civil and criminal penalties.[65] The Consumer Product Safety Act also authorises private suits for damages against any person who engages in a "knowing (including willful) violation of a consumer product safety rule, or any other rule or order issued by the [CPSC]".[66] The CPSC and state attorney generals are also authorised to seek an injunction in federal district court.[67]

(b) *Consumer Product Safety Improvement Act 2008*

On August 14 2008, the Consumer Product Safety Improvement Act was signed into law.[68] The Consumer Product Safety Improvement Act amends the Consumer Product Safety Act and enhances the CPSC's ability to ensure the safety of consumer products. The Consumer Product Safety Improvement Act requires the CPSC to adopt the world's strictest safety standards for children's products (including mandatory pre-market testing), improved product recall procedures, strengthen CPSC's enforcement powers, and enhance the ability of consumers and state attorney generals to enforce the law.

Stricter rules for children's products: The Consumer Product Safety Improvement Act contains several provisions dealing with the safety of 'children's products'. The Consumer Product Safety Improvement Act defines a 'children's product' as "a consumer product designed or intended primarily for children 12 years of age or younger".[69] The Consumer Product Safety Improvement Act 2008 limits the amount of lead in children's products and bans the use of the plastic additive 'phthalates' in children's toys and childcare products.[70] Further, the Consumer Product Safety Improvement Act 2008 requires the CPSC to determine whether current voluntary safety standards adequately protect children and adopt mandatory standards if the CPSC finds the current standards are inadequate.[71] An independent assessment body (accredited by the CPSC) must test children's products before it enters the stream of commerce for the manufacturer to demonstrate that the product conforms to all safety standards.[72] To facilitate recalls of defective children's products, the Consumer Product Safety Improvement Act 2008 requires that children's products contain tracking labels.[73] Manufacturers must place a distinguishing mark on the product and packaging to identify the manufacturer, production date and other information such as a batch number.[74]

---

64 15 USC, Section 2068.
65 15 USC, Sections 2069–2070.
66 15 USC, Section 2072.
67 15 USC, Sections 2069, 2071, 2073.
68 Consumer Product Safety Improvement Act of 2008, Pub L 110–314, Section 101, available at www.cpsc.gov/cpsia.pdf.
69 Consumer Product Safety Improvement Act of 2008, at Section 235(a).
70 Consumer Product Safety Improvement Act of 2008, at Sections 101, 108.
71 Consumer Product Safety Improvement Act of 2008, at Section 106.
72 Consumer Product Safety Improvement Act of 2008, at Section 102.
73 Section 103.
74 Consumer Product Safety Improvement Act of 2008.

Enhanced recall authority: The Consumer Product Safety Improvement Act expands the CPSC's recall authority to products that violate any rule under the Consumer Product Safety Improvement Act or "imminently hazardous consumer products".[75] Before announcing a final determination regarding the product's safety or recall, the CPSC is authorised to immediately disseminate information about the hazardous products to the public and halt the distribution of the products.[76] If a recall is announced, the CPSC may require firms to give public notice of the product's description, the action being taken, the number of units affected, the degree of the hazard, the product's manufacturer, dates sold, the injuries or deaths, and any available remedies.[77] Once the Consumer Product Safety Improvement Act announces a recall, it prohibits the further sale or export of the dangerous product.[78]

Enforcement by state attorney generals: The Consumer Product Safety Improvement Act allows a state attorney general to bring a suit in federal court for injunctive relief on behalf of the state's residents against the parties violating the statute.[79] Under the Consumer Product Safety Improvement Act 2008, state attorneys general may sue on behalf of their states' residents to stop the sale of products that have been recalled, banned or uncertified as tested under the Consumer Product Safety Improvement Act's requirements; lack tracking labels or contain unauthorised safety markings; or otherwise violate the Consumer Product Safety Improvement Act's requirements.[80] A state attorney general may independently determine that a substantial product hazard exists, but it must notify the CPSC.[81]

Penalties: The Consumer Product Safety Improvement Act allows the CPSC to impose substantial civil and criminal penalties on firms that fail to comply with the Consumer Product Safety Improvement Act.[82] Violators of the Consumer Product Safety Act, Consumer Product Safety Improvement Act or CPSC are subject to civil penalties up to $100,000 per offence and $15 million for multiple offences.[83] Criminal penalties include asset forfeiture and imprisonment of a firm's officers and directors, even absent actual knowledge of a violation.[84]
Protections for 'whistleblowers': The Consumer Product Safety Improvement Act makes it illegal for a retailer, manufacturer, importer, or distributor to discriminate against or fire employees who report violations or testify in enforcement proceedings.[85]

---

75 Section 219.
76 Section 212.
77 Section 214.
78 Section 216.
79 Section 218.
80 Consumer Product Safety Improvement Act of 2008.
81 Consumer Product Safety Improvement Act of 2008
82 Consumer Product Safety Improvement Act of 2008, at Section 217.
83 Section 217
84 Section 217
85 Section 219.

Pre-emption: The Consumer Product Safety Improvement Act provides that the Consumer Product Safety Act does not pre-empt any cause of action under state or local common law regarding damage claims.[86]

2.3 National Highway Traffic Safety Administration

The NHTSA was established as a federal regulatory agency to carry out safety programmes for the purposes of reducing deaths, injuries, and economic losses resulting from motor vehicle crashes.[87]

(a) *National Traffic and Motor Vehicle Safety Act 1966*

The NHTSA's primary regulatory authority stems from the National Traffic and Motor Vehicle Safety Act of 1966. Under the National Traffic and Motor Vehicle Safety Act, the NHTSA must carry out its stated purpose to "reduce traffic accidents and deaths resulting from traffic accidents" by prescribing motor vehicle safety standards and conducting safety research and development.[88] The NHTSA is authorised to regulate foreign and domestic automobile manufacturers, distributors, sellers, and suppliers.[89] As set forth below, the NHTSA accomplishes this primarily by setting and enforcing safety performance standards for motor vehicles, identifying and investigating safety-related defects in motor vehicles, overseeing recalls or issuing recall orders, and imposing penalties on non-compliant manufacturers.

Setting safety standards: Under the National Traffic and Motor Vehicle Safety Act, the NHTSA is legislatively mandated to issue Federal Motor Vehicle Safety Standards (FMVSSs) that automobile manufacturers must follow.[90] The FMVSSs are the minimum safety performance requirements for automobiles.[91] Since 1967, NHTSA has issued over 500 FMVSSs, covering virtually every aspect of motor vehicle design and safety – from rearview mirrors to occupant crash protection.[92] The NHTSA has the sole authority to make final decisions on rules and safety standards for motor vehicles.[93]

Identifying defects: The NHTSA has broad authority to investigate and inspect manufacturers.[94] The NHTSA has an Office of Defect Investigation (ODI) that gathers information regarding potential defects in motor vehicles. Consumers are encouraged to notify the ODI of potential safety concerns.[95] The ODI is required to review each complaint and may, when they observe a developing safety trend, initiate a formal investigation.[96] The ODI has broad powers to "elicit [information]

86 Section 231.
87 www.nhtsa.gov/About+NHTSA/Who+We+Are+and+What+We+Do.
88 49 USC, Section 30101.
89 See generally, 49 USC, Sections 30102, 30112, 30118.
90 National Highway Traffic Safety Administration, Booklet on Federal Motor Vehicle Safety Standards, available at www.nhtsa.gov/cars/rules/import/fmvss/index.html.
91 *Ibid.*
92 *Ibid,* see also 49 CFR, Section 571, and following.
93 49 CFR, Sections 553.29 and 501.7.
94 49 USC, Section 30166.
95 See, eg, www.safercar.gov.
96 49 CFR, Section 557.8.

from every available source" and evaluate "any information suggesting the existence of a safety related defect".[97] Manufacturers are required to submit information that could assist the ODI in determining whether a safety-related defect exists in a vehicle or equipment.[98]

The National Traffic and Motor Vehicle Safety Act requires manufacturers of motor vehicles and replacement equipment to notify the NHTSA within five days of learning that a vehicle or equipment contains a defect related to motor vehicle safety, or that the vehicle or equipment does not comply with the FMVSSs.[99]

Recalls: Vehicles that do not comply with the FMVSSs are subject to mandatory recall. Vehicles in compliance with the FMVSSs, however, may still be recalled if the NHTSA determines that they contain safety-related defects.[100] Manufacturers may issue voluntarily recalls when their internal testing data evidences a potential safety defect. Manufacturers of motor vehicles have a recall responsibility for any safety-related defect or non-compliance existing in a vehicle or equipment. The manufacturer of an item of motor vehicle equipment in which a safety defect or non-compliance is determined to exist:

- is responsible for notifying the vehicle manufacturer; and
- with respect to an item of replacement equipment (including tyres), has recall responsibility for the equipment containing the safety defect or non-compliance.[101]

When a manufacturer decides that a vehicle or item of motor vehicle equipment is defective, the manufacturer is also required to notify owners, purchasers, and dealers within a "reasonable time".[102] Manufacturers typically initiate a voluntary recall by filing a "Part 573 Report" in which they notify the NHTSA of their concerns and propose a corrective action plan.[103] Federal regulations specify that the following minimal information must be included in a manufacturer's recall notices:

- a clear description of the defect;
- an evaluation of the risk to motor vehicle safety;
- a statement of the measures to be taken to obtain the remedy;
- a statement that the defect/non-compliance will be remedied without charge;
- a statement of the earliest date on which the defect/non-compliance will be remedied; and
- a description of the procedure to be followed by the recipient of the notification in informing the NHTSA whenever a manufacturer, distributor, or dealer fails to, or is unable to remedy without charge such defect or failure to comply.[104]

---

97 49 CFR, Section 554.5.
98 49 CFR, Section 579
99 49 USC, Section 30118.
100 *Ibid*; see also 49 CFR Section 554.4.
101 49 CFR, Section 579.
102 49 USC, Section 30119; 49 CFR Section 577.7.
103 49 CFR, Section 573.
104 49 CFR, Section 577.

The National Traffic and Motor Vehicle Safety Act provides that, when a vehicle is recalled, manufacturers must repair the vehicle, replace the vehicle with an identical or reasonably equivalent vehicle, or refund the purchase price less a reasonable allowance for depreciation.[105] Recalled products cannot be sold until remedied.[106]

Regardless of whether the recall is voluntary or mandatory, the NHTSA is responsible for monitoring the manufacturer's execution of the recall strategy.[107] When a defect presents a serious risk of injury to the public, the NHTSA must require the manufacturer to accelerate its recall strategy.[108]

Enforcement: Manufacturers that fail to notify the NHTSA of product defects or follow mandatory recall procedures are subject to civil penalties. The NHTSA may conduct a public hearing to investigate whether the manufacturer has reasonably met its obligations under the safety act, and may commence enforcement actions in federal court for violations.[109] Manufacturers that violate the National Traffic and Motor Vehicle Safety Act's notification and recall procedure provisions face a civil penalty of not more than $5,000 for each violation.[110] A separate violation occurs for each motor vehicle or item of motor vehicle equipment and for each failure or refusal to allow or perform an act required by any of those sections, and the maximum penalty for a related series of violations is $15,000,000.[111] If a manufacturer intentionally misleads the NHTSA about defects that cause death or serious bodily injury, the NHTSA may seek criminal penalties in the form of further fines or imprisonment.[112]

3. Liability

In New York, any individual who sustains bodily injuries from a defective product manufactured and sold within the commercial market may seek compensation for their damages. While federal statutes often set minimum safety standards for products or provide guidance as to what may constitute a 'safe' product, because federal law pre-empts state law in limited circumstances, the ultimate question as to whether a product is 'reasonably safe' is most often governed by state product liability law.[113]

New York product liability actions generally sound in tort, but some contract law theories can also apply. Generally, when a product causes injury, New York law provides that a plaintiff may pursue claims under theories of strict product liability, negligence, or breach of warranty.[114]

---

105 49 USC, Section 30120.
106 49 USC, Sections 30112, 30116, 30120.
107 49 USC, Section 30120.
108 49 CFR, Section 573.14.
109 49 USC, Section 30121.
110 49 USC, Section 30165.
111 *Ibid.*
112 49 USC, Section 30170.
113 *Riegel v Medtronic*, 552 US 312 (2008).
114 NY Jur 2d, Product liability Sections 1 and following.

3.1 Who can sue and be sued?

(a) *Plaintiffs*

Any party who has been injured by a defective product may bring a product liability action. There is no requirement that the plaintiff have some contractual relationship, or privity, with the defendants when bringing a negligence action, breach of warranty claim for injuries, or strict liability suit for personal injuries or death.[115] The plaintiff does not have to be the person who purchased the product or who used the product; injured bystanders within the vicinity of a malfunctioning product may have standing to sue.[116] So long as it is reasonable to expect a person to use, consume or be affected by a product, that individual may have a claim.[117]

(b) *Defendants*

Regardless of where it is domiciled, a corporation that is 'doing business' in New York subjects itself to personal jurisdiction in New York courts.[118] Out-of-state and unregistered corporations may also be subject to jurisdiction in New York courts if they contract to supply goods or services within New York.[119] All parties within the supply chain who had any role in placing a defective product into the stream of commerce may potentially be defendants in product liability actions. Potential defendants in product liability actions include all manufacturers of any part of the defective product, [120] retailers that sell the product in the normal course of business,[121] and used goods dealers.[122]

3.2 Strict liability

Strict liability is the most common basis for recovery in New York product liability actions, as plaintiffs are not required to prove actual negligence or an intent to harm an individual.[123] Rather, a manufacturer or seller can be held liable solely for breaching its absolute duty to produce or sell safe products, regardless of whether there was an opportunity to inspect the product before selling it.[124]

There are four threshold elements to bringing a strict liability claim. First, the defendant must be a merchant who routinely deals in goods of this type.[125] Second, there must be evidence that the product is defective.[126] New York law identifies three areas where a manufacturer's deficiency will lead to a strict liability claim:

- design defects;

---

115 *Giuffrida v Panasonic Indus Co*, 200 AD 2d 713, 715 (2d dept 1994); *Wheeler v Sears Roebuck & Co*, 37 AD 3d 710 (2d dept 2007). See also Uniform Commercial Code, Section 2–318.
116 *Ibid; Coding v Paglia*, 32 NY 2d 330 (1973).
117, *Ibid.*
118 CPLR Sections 301–302.
119 CPLR Sections 301–302.
120 *Smith v Peerless Glass Co*, 259 NY 292, 295 (1932), *reh'g denied* 259 NY 664 (1932).
121 *Denny v Ford Motor Co*, 87 NY 2d 248 (1995), *reh'g denied*, 87 NY 2d 969 (1996).
122 *Gonzalez v Rutherford Corp*, 881 F Supp 829 (EDNY 1995).
123 Michael Hoenig, *Product liability in New York* 12 (Neil A. Goldberg ed., New York State Bar Association 1997).
124 *Ibid.*
125 *Sprung v MTR Ravensburg, Inc*, 99 NY 2d 468, 473 (2003); *Coding v Paglia*, above.
126 *Coding v Paglia*, above.

- manufacturing defects; and
- failure to warn defects.

Third, the product cannot have been substantially altered when the plaintiff receives it.[127] The burden of proof lies with the manufacturer when a product has moved within the ordinary channels of distribution because the courts will presume these products have not been altered.[128] Finally, manufacturers are only liable for design defects related to a foreseeable use of the product, which may include uses unintended by the vendor.[129]

(a) *Design defects*

The New York standard for determining the existence of a design defect is whether "a reasonable person would conclude that the utility of the product did not outweigh the risk inherent in marketing a product designed in that manner" if a manufacturer would have known about the defect at the time of production.[130] Under this 'risk–utility' balancing test, New York courts weigh the following factors:

- the product's utility to the public as a whole;
- its utility to the individual user;
- the likelihood that the product will cause injury;
- the availability of a safer design;
- the possibility of designing and manufacturing the product so that it is safer but remains functional and reasonably priced;
- the degree of awareness of the product's potential danger that can reasonably be attributed to the injured user; and
- the manufacturer's ability to spread the cost of any safety-related design changes.[131]

(b) *Manufacturing defects*

Manufacturing defects can occur when a faulty product became unreasonably dangerous because at least one component emerged from the production line not in accordance with the correct specifications.[132] Manufacturing flaws can include any errors caused during the manufacturing or assembling of the product.[133] Like design defects, the plaintiff must supply expert testimony to demonstrate a manufacturing defect.[134]

(c) *Failure to warn*

A manufacturer faces liability when a dangerous product does not come with a sufficient warning label about dangers that are not obvious to consumers. Warnings

---

127 *Ibid.*
128 *Fagan v AmerisourceBergen Corp*, 356 F Supp 2d 198, 206 (EDNY 2004).
129 *Coding v Paglia*, above.
130 Michael Hoenig, *Product Liability in New York* 12 (Neil A. Goldberg ed., New York State Bar Association 1997).
131 *Denny v Ford Motor Co*, 87 NY 2d 248 (1995) (citing *Voss*, above.).
132 For example, *Opera v Hyva, Inc*, 86 AD 2d 373 (4th Dept 1982).
133 *Ibid.*
134 For example, *Riegel v Medtronic, Inc* 451 F 3d 104, 127 (2d Cir 2006).

may be defective when a reasonable person would not recognise that the object could be dangerous.[135] Open and obvious dangers within a product do not impose upon manufacturers a duty to warn.[136] Additionally, a plaintiff cannot have any knowledge of the potential risk of danger prior to the injury, and must be able to demonstrate that the lack of warning was a significant factor that caused the injury.[137] Even if a product is not inherently defective, it is prudent to include a warning label for any potential dangers that may occur during any reasonably foreseeable use of the item.[138]

After completion of the sale, a manufacturer may still be liable and have a duty to supplement the sale with a warning. New York courts apply a balancing test to determine whether a seller has any responsibility to find customers and warn them of any dangers. Such factors include the possibility of tracking post-sale items, the burden of informing customers of a warning, improvements in technology related to the product, as well as the knowledge a manufacturer has of recurring dangers.[139]

(d) *Defences*

Any misconduct on behalf of the plaintiff can reduce the percentage of damages for which the defendant is held liable.[140] There are three common defences to counter a product liability claim. First, the defendant can argue that the plaintiff did not exercise reasonable care while operating the product.[141] A second common defence is that plaintiff's conduct is not related to the alleged injuries.[142] Finally, the defendant can argue that the plaintiff misused the product.[143] New York courts define misuse as operating a product in a manner unintended by the manufacturer.[144] The misuse of a product does not automatically create a valid defence if the plaintiff's conduct was reasonably foreseeable or the manufacturer's warnings were conveyed unsuccessfully or inaccurately.[145]

(e) *Statute of limitations*

An action for strict liability must be brought within three years of the date on which the injury occurred.[146]

(f) *Punitive damages*

Punitive damages are available in strict liability actions.[147]

---

135 *Rastelli v Goodyear Tire & Rubber Co*, 79 NY 2d 289 (1992). See also *Cwiklinski v Sears, Roebuck & Co, Inc*, 70 AD 3d 1477 (4th dept 2010); *Fitzgerald v Federal Signal Corp*, 63 AD 3d 994 (2d dept 2009).
136 *Liriano v Hobart Corp*, 92 NY 2d 232, 241–242 (1998).
137 *Ibid.*
138 For example, *Ezagui v Dow Chemical Corp*, 598 F 2d 727 (2d Cir 1979). See also *Rastelli v Goodyear Tire & Rubber Co*, 79 NY 2d 289 (1992).
139 *Cover v Cohen*, 61 NY 2d 261, 275 (1984).
140 *Schumacher v Richards Shear Co, Inc*, 59 NY 2d 239, 255 (1983).
141 *Codling v Paglia*, above.
142 For example, *L.M.B. v Sevyior USA, Inv*, 43 AD 3d 1355 (4th dept 2007).
143 *Sheppard v Charles A. Smith Well Drilling and Water Systems*, 93 AD 2d 474 (3d dept 1983).
144 *Ibid.*
145 *Johnson v Johnson Chemical Co*, 183 AD 2d 64 (2d dept 1992).
146 CPLR Section 214.
147 1 NY Product liability 2d Section 14:5.

3.3 Negligence

The requisite elements of a cause of action in negligence are:

- a duty on the part of the defendant to act reasonably in designing, testing, manufacturing, selling, inspecting or marketing the product;
- a breach of that duty; and
- a reasonably close causal connection between the defendant's conduct and some resulting injury to the plaintiff.[148]

Unlike strict product liability, the duty of care owed by a defendant for negligence varies substantially based upon the defendant's role in the process of designing, manufacturing, and marketing the product. Further, the defendant's duty to warn, for negligence purposes, varies based upon the status of the particular defendant.

Under New York law, a manufacturer of a defective product is liable in negligence to persons injured by the product despite the absence of privity between plaintiff and defendant.[149] A seller or manufacturer has a duty to inspect, test, and warn of dangers in the product's use.

The test for liability in negligence to a person other than the purchaser (ie, in the absence of privity) is as follows:

- the item is a thing of 'danger,' which is defined as a product reasonably certain to place life and limb in peril if negligently made;
- the manufacturer/wholesaler/retailer has knowledge that the item will be used by persons other than the purchaser; and
- the plaintiff was using the object for the purpose for which it was intended, as well as for purposes unintended, yet which were reasonably foreseeable.[150]

(a) *Statute of limitations*

An action for negligence must be brought within three years of the date on which the injury occurred.[151]

(b) *Punitive damages*

Punitive damages are available for negligence actions.[152]

3.4 Breach of warranty

Breach of warranty claims are governed by Article II of the Uniform Commercial Code for the sale of goods. Breaches can occur when a product fails to meet performance expectations for the intended or reasonably foreseeable customary use of the item.[153] Unlike strict liability and negligence theories, a plaintiff can only recover for economic losses under a breach of warranty theory[154]

148 *Prosser and Keeton on Torts* 164–165 (West 5th ed 1984).
149 *MacPherson v Buick Motor Co*, 217 NY 382 (1916).
150 *Micallef v Miehle*, 39 NY 2d 376, 384 (1976).
151 CPLR Section214.
152 *Welch v Mr Christmas Inc*, 440 NE2d 1317 (1982).
153 *Denny v Ford Motor Co*, above; Uniform Commercial Code, Sections 2-314(2)(c) to 2-318.
154 For example, *Bristol Myers Squibb, Indus Div v Delta Star, Inc*, 206 AD 2d 177, 181 (NY App 1994).

Warranties may be either express or implied during the sale of a product. Implied warranties arise either when:

- a merchant within the industry sells a defective product; or
- a buyer, relying on the seller's expertise in goods, conveys an intent to buy an item for a particular purpose which the seller recommends, and the product does not satisfy those requirements.[155]

Both of these types of claim require the defendant to be a seller who ordinarily sells the product.[156] Express warranties occur when an overt promise made by either a manufacturer or seller becomes part of the reason for the buyer to purchase a product.[157] Plaintiffs bear the burden to show how they relied upon any such representations.[158]

(a) *Defences*

There are two key defences available for breach of warranty product liability claims. First, manufacturers may include disclaimers with their products that may negate implied warranties. A manufacturer or seller, however, may not disclaim an express warranty.[159] Additionally in New York, disclaimers for personal injury actions are invalid.[160] Second, like strict liability claims, any damages will be reduced by the percentage of which the plaintiff contributed to her or her injuries.

(b) *Statute of limitations*

An action for breach of warranty must be brought within four years of the date of the breach.[161]

3.5 Class actions

A class action is a type of civil lawsuit in which one or more individual plaintiff can sue on behalf of a class of individuals who suffered the same or similar injury. Class actions are often filed where the injury to each plaintiff is relatively small, but where the number of allegedly injured plaintiffs is large.

In order to certify a lawsuit as a class action under New York law, the court must be satisfied that questions of law or fact common to the class predominate over any question affecting only individual members, and that a class action is superior to other available methods for the fair and efficient adjudication of the dispute.[162] New York courts, however, often find that a class action is not a superior method for resolving product liability claims because individualised issues of causation and damages usually predominate over class-wide issues.[163]

---

155 Uniform Commercial Code, Section 2-315.
156 *Ibid.*
157 Uniform Commercial Code, Section 2-313.
158 *CBS Inc v Ziff-Davis Pub'g Co*, 75 NY 2d 496, 503 (1990).
159 For example, *Alaska Pacific Salmon Co v Reynolds Metals Co*, 163 F 2d 643, 660 (2d Cir 1947).
160 Uniform Commercial Code, Section 2-719.
161 Uniform Commercial Code, Section 2-725(1).
162 CPLR Section 901; *Osarczuk v Associated Universities, Inc*, 82 AD 3d 853, 854 (2d dept 2011).
163 *Osarczuk*, 82 AD 3d at 854–855; *Geiger v American Tobacco Co*, 277 AD 2d 420 (2d dept 2000).

4. Insurance

In the United States, manufacturers typically rely on their CGL insurance policies to provide coverage for bodily injury or property damage claims arising out of product liability and recall claims. These claims often give rise to a host of complex coverage issues and defences (see below). As a result, the New York courts have interpreted numerous CGL coverage issues in the context of product warranty claims, recall costs, and consequential loss caused by product defects.

As a result of gaps in CGL coverage for product recall claims, and in part due to tightening federal regulation concerning product recalls, there has been an increased demand for specific product recall and contamination coverage. These specialised policies are offered by London and Bermudian insurers, as well as a various US-based domestic carriers. In addition, business interruption and contingent business interruption policies are becoming popular forms of protection for businesses that are dependent upon supply chain manufacturers and component suppliers.

4.1 New York choice of law rules

Where an insured designs, manufactures, or distributes products in multiple states, it is important to determine which state law will apply to the interpretation of insurance policy terms. In this regard, the New York courts will generally apply the law of the state with the most significant interest in the transaction and parties at issue. In making this determination, the courts apply a 'centre of gravity' approach based upon consideration of several factors, including:

- the place of contracting;
- the place of negotiation of the contract;
- the place of performance;
- the location of the subject matter of the contract; and
- the domicile, residence, nationality, place of incorporation and place of business of the parties.[164]

With respect to coverage matters, emphasis is placed on the location of the insured risk unless another state has a more significant relationship to the transaction.[165] It is common, however, for courts applying New York choice of law rules "to disregard (or at least discount) the location of the insured risk when the risk is located in two or more states".[166] Thus, the New York courts have repeatedly held that "policies covering contracts throughout the country or the world, delivered to the insured in particular states should be covered by the laws of those states".[167]

---

164 *Empire Fire and Marine Ins Co v H Moran & Sons, Inc*, 2003 WL 22901060 (EDNY December 5 2003), citing, *Zurich Ins Co v Shearson Lehman, Hutton, Inc*, 84 NY 2d 309 (1994).

165 *Seidel v Houston Cas Co*, 375 F Supp 2d 211 (SDNY 2005); *O'Neill v Yield House Inc*, 964 F Supp 806 (SDNY 1997).

166 *Maryland Cas Co v W.R. Grace & Co*, 332 F 3d 145, 153 (2d Cir 2003); *see also*, *O'Neill*, 964 F Supp 806 (SDNY 1997) (location of the risk has less significance where policy covers group of risks that are scattered throughout two or more states).

167 *O'Neill*, 964 F Supp at 810, *quoting*, *Fireman's Fund Ins Co v Schuster Films, Inc*, 811 F Supp 978, 982 (SDNY 1993); *see also*, *Employers Ins Group of Wausau, v Duplan Corp*, 899 F Supp 1112 (SDNY 1995)(New York law applied to dispute over coverage under policies negotiated, executed and delivered in New York insured and covering risks in multiple states even where damage occurred in the Virgin Islands); *Regional Import & Export Trucking Co v North River Ins. Co*, 147 AD 2d 361 (1st dept 1989).

4.2 General rules of policy construction in New York

With respect to policy construction and interpretation, a court applying the substantive law of New York determines the parties' intent by examining the policy language and giving effect to the clear, unambiguous language of the contract.[168] The New York courts "strive to give meaning ... to every sentence, clause, and word of a contract of insurance",[169] and "a policy cannot be construed so as to render its terms meaningless or of no effect".[170] Thus, the New York courts generally enforce the plain meaning of policy provisions and will not strain the language to create ambiguities.[171] In the absence of an ambiguity, the courts are "not free to alter the contract to reflect its personal notions of fairness and equity".[172]

In New York, however, an ambiguity exists only where policy terms are "reasonably susceptible to more than one reading".[173] In the context of commercial insurance, an ambiguity may exist only where a term "could suggest more than one meaning when viewed objectively by a reasonably intelligent person who has examined the context of the entire integrated agreement and who is cognizant of the customs, practices and usages and terminology as generally understood in that particular trade or business".[174] If an ambiguity exists, New York courts may consider the "reasonable expectations" of the contracting parties.[175]

4.3 General liability coverage issues

(a) *Standard form CGL Policy*

Based on the latest ISO Form, the standard CGL policy insuring agreement provides coverage, in relevant part, as follows:

> *[Insurer] will pay those sums that the insured becomes legally obligated to pay as damages because of 'bodily injury' or 'property damage' to which this insurance applies. [Insurer] will have the right and duty to defend the insured against any 'suit' seeking those damages. However, [Insurer] will have no duty to defend the insured against any 'suit' seeking damages for 'bodily injury' or 'property damage' to which this insurance does not apply. ....*[176]

(b) *'Products completed operations hazard'*

CGL policies may include coverage for liability falling within the "products completed operations hazard", which is defined (subject to certain specified exceptions) as follows:

Includes all "bodily injury" and "property damage" occurring away from premises you own or rent and arising out of "your product" or "your work" except:

---

168 *Morgan Stanley Group Inc v New England Ins Co*, 225 F 3d 270, 275 (2d Cir 2000) (applying New York law).
169 *Northville Indus Corp v National Union Fire Ins. Co of Pittsburgh, Pa*, 89 NY 2d 621, 632–633 (1997).
170 *White v Continental Cas Co*, 9 NY 3d 264, 267 (2007).
171 *Breed v Ins. Co of N Am*, 46 NY 2d 351, 353–354 (1979), *Duane Reade Inc v St Paul Fire and Marine Ins Co*, 411 F 3d 384, 389–390 (2d Cir 2005).
172 *White*, 9 NY 3d at 267 (*citing*, *Greenfield v Philles Records*, 98 NY 2d. 562, 569–570 (2002)).
173 *Duane Reade, Inc v St Paul Fire and Marine Ins Co*, 600 F 3d 190, 201 (2d Cir 2010).
174 *Morgan Stanley Group, Inc*, 225 F 3d at 275–276.
175 *Throgs Neck Bagels v GA Ins Co*, 671 NY S 2d 66, 68 (1st dept 1998).
176 ISO CG 00 01 12 04 (2003), Section I(1).

(1) Products that are still in your physical possession; or

(2) Work that has not yet been completed or abandoned. However, "your work" will be deemed completed at the earliest of the following times:

(a) When all of the work called for in your contract has been completed.

(b) When all the work to be done at the job site has been completed if your contract calls for work at more than one job site.

(c) When that part of the work done at a job site has been put to its intended use by any person or organisation other than another contractor or subcontractor working on the same project.

Work that may need service, maintenance, correction, repair or replacement, but which is otherwise complete, will be treated as completed.[177]

Coverage may be included explicitly through a "Products/Completed Operations Coverage Form",[178] or implicitly under standard CGL provisions. Liabilities falling within the "products-completed operations hazard", however, are often subject to a separate aggregate limit of liability. Moreover, such coverage is not intended to cover damages to the insured's product, but damage to property of others for which the insured may be found liable to a third party.[179]

CGL policies also may exclude coverage for 'bodily injury' or 'property damage' included within the "products-completed operations hazard".[180] The terms of such exclusions have routinely been found to be clear and unambiguous by the New York courts.[181]

(c) ***Fortuity requirement***

CGL policies provide coverage for sums that an insured becomes legally obligated to pay as damages because of 'bodily injury' or 'property damage' caused by an 'occurrence', which is typically defined as "an accident, including continuous or repeated exposure to substantially the same general harmful conditions".[182] Accordingly, an injury that is expected or intended from the standpoint of the insured is not fortuitous or accidental, and therefore does not constitute an 'occurrence'. Indeed, the 1973 ISO CGL policy form specifically defined occurrence as "an accident ... resulting in bodily injury or property damage neither expected nor intended from the standpoint of the insured". In the current ISO form, this fortuity requirement in CGL policies is both embodied in the 'occurrence' definition (which refers to an 'accident') and further supported by a broader exclusion, which precludes coverage for bodily injury or property damage "expected or intended from the standpoint of the insured".[183]

In New York, an injury is deemed intended or expected if there was intent to cause the injury or the injury was the "direct and natural consequences" of the

---

177 ISO CG 00 01 12 04 (2003), Section V(16).
178 ISO CG 00 01 12 04 (2003), Section III(3).
179 *J.Z.G. Resources, Inc v King*, 987 F 2d 98, 102–103 (2d Cir 1993).
180 ISO CG 00 01 12 04 (2003), Section I(2)(l).
181 *Rhinebeck Bicycle Shop, Inc v Sterling Ins Co*, 151 AD 2d 122 (3d dept); *Logan's Silo Sales & Service, Inc v Nationwide Mut Fire Ins Co*, 185 AD 2d 651 (4th Dept 1992).
182 ISO CG 00 01 12 04 (2003), Section V(13).
183 ISO CG 00 01 12 04 (2003), Section I(2)(a).

intentional conduct.[184] Thus, claims based upon fraud, intentional misrepresentation, or unfair or deceptive business practices in connection with a product liability claim are not an 'occurrence' and are otherwise excludable under the 'expected or intended' exclusion.[185]

Breach of contract or warranty: The standard CGL insuring agreement provides coverage for the insured's liability that is independent of any contractual relationship between the insured and the injured party. CGL policies also specifically preclude coverage for claims based upon the insured's "assumption of liability in a contract or agreement".[186] Thus, the New York courts have acknowledged that the purpose of comprehensive general liability policies "is to provide coverage for tort liability for physical damage to others and not for contractual liability of the insured for economic loss".[187] Claims sounding in breach of contract or warranty do not allege an 'occurrence' within the purview of general liability insurance.[188] Moreover, the mere averment of negligence in a complaint does not transform the contract claim to a claim sounding in tort.[189] Similarly, the mere failure of a product to function as warranted or the failure to perform a service in a proper manner has been found to fall outside the policy's definition of a covered 'occurrence'.[190]

Determining the number of occurrences in products cases: Aggregation of claims is a significant issue with respect to product liability insurance coverage. New York has a well-developed body of law analysing the issue of determining the number of occurrences in product liability cases. The courts have traditionally inquired whether the multiple claims arise from the same "[e]vent of an unfortunate character that takes place without one's foresight or expectation".[191] Although a single occurrence may give rise to multiple claims, the "determination of the number of occurrences for insurance purposes requires a court to look to the event for which the insured is held liable, not some point further back in the causal chain".[192] The New York courts

184 *Syvertsen v Great American Ins Co*, 267 AD 2d 854, 856 (3d dept 1999).

185 *Ibid.*

186 ISO CG 00 01 12 04 (2003), Section I(2)(b).

187 *Hartford Accid & Indem Co v A.P. Reale & Sons, Inc*, 228 AD 2d 935, 936 (3d dept 1998).

188 *Jakobson Shipyard, Inc v Aetna Casualty and Surety Company*, 775 F Supp 606, 609–610 (SDNY 1991); *George A. Fuller Co v US Fid and Guar Co*, 200 AD 2d 255, 259–260 (1st dept 1994).

189 *George A Fuller Co*,200 AD 2d, at 259 (1st dept 1994).

190 *Ibid* ("the policy was never intended to provide contractual indemnification for economic loss to a contracting party because the work product contracted for is defectively produced").

191 *Michaels v Mut Marine Office, Inc*, 742 F Supp 26, 29 (SDNY 1979); (citing *Arthur A. Johnson Corp. v Indemnity Ins Co*, 7 NY 2d 222, 228 (1959)) (emphasis added).

192 *Endicott Johnson Corp v Liberty Mut Ins Co*, 928 F Supp 176, 181 (NDNY 1996) (citing *Arthur A. Johnson*, 7 NY 2d 222 (1959)) (flooding which collapsed retaining walls of two separate buildings at a construction site constituted separate occurrences).

193 *Appalachian Ins Co v General Elec Co*, 863 NE 2d 994, 1000–1001 (NY 2007) (personal injuries sustained by workers exposed to asbestos constitute multiple occurrences); *International Flavors & Fragrances, Inc v Royal Ins Co of America*, 46 AD 3d 224, 228–229 (1st dept 2007) (personal injuries sustained by workers employed at the same manufacturing plant resulting from exposure to a toxic substance found in butter flavouring constitute multiple occurrences.); *ExxonMobil Corp v Certain Underwriters at Lloyd's, London*, 50 AD 3d 434, 435 (1st dept 2008), *leave to appeal denied*, 11 NY 3d 710 (October 28, 2008) (holding that "the manufacture and sale of plaintiff's two defective products did not constitute a single occurrence.").

consider whether there is a temporal or spatial relationship between the incidents to determine if they arose from the same event or accident with no intervening agent.[193]

Temporal limitations/trigger of coverage: The insurance coverage afforded by CGL policies is limited to 'bodily injury' or 'property damage' that occurs during the policy period.[194] The New York courts have uniformly held that coverage is triggered only after the insured seeking recovery demonstrates actual property damage or bodily injury occurring during the policy period.[195] This approach is referred to as an 'injury-in-fact' trigger of coverage.

(d) *'Bodily injury' and 'property damage' requirements*

'Property damage' is defined in standard CGL policies as:

- "physical injury to tangible property, including all resulting loss of use of that property", and
- the "loss of use of tangible property that is not physically injured".[196]

Thus, the malfunctioning of defective equipment itself does not constitute 'property damage'.[197] CGL policies are intended to cover damage solely to third party property, and specifically preclude coverage for damage to property the insured owns, rents or occupies, including any cost incurred by the insured or any other entity "for repair, replacement, enhancement, restoration or maintenance of such property for any reason, including prevention of injury to another person or damage to another's property".[198]

Pure economic loss: Pure economic loss does not constitute a physical injury to tangible property. However, CGL policies may provide coverage for consequential economic damages that arise out of either direct physical injury or loss of use.[199] However, there can be no recovery for intangibles loss unless there has been actual physical damage to property other than the property of the insured.[200]

(e) *Business risk exclusions*

CGL insurance does not provide protection for risks assumed by the insured inherent to its business.[201] Thus, as noted above, CGL policies typically preclude coverage for damages the insured is obligated to pay because it agreed to assume a contractual liability that would not have existed in the absence of any such agreement.

---

194 ISO form CG 00 01 12 04 (2003), Section I(1)(b)(2).

195 *American Home Products Corp v Liberty Mutual Ins Co*, 565 F Supp 1485 (SDNY 1983), *aff'd in relevant part and modified in part*, 704 F 2d 760 (2d Cir 1984) ("[t]he most basic demand of the policy language is that to establish [coverage], the insured must prove that an 'occurrence' ... arose during the policy period")

196 ISO CG 00 01 12 04 (2003), Section V(17).

197 *J.Z.G. Resources, Inc v King*, 987 F 2d 98 (2d Cir 1993) (no 'property damage' where road surface was improperly installed).

198 ISO CG 00 01 12 04 (2003), Section I(2)(J).

199 *Aetna Casualty & Surety Co v General Time Corp*, 704 F 2d 80, 83 (2d Cir 1983).

200 *Ibid* (citations omitted).

201 *Sphere Drake Insurance Company v Tremco, Inc*, 513 NW 2d 173, 177 (Minn Ct App 1994) ("a normal, foreseeable and expected incident of doing business and should be reflected in the price of the product or service rather than as a cost of insurance to be shared by others").

Moreover, CGL policies typically contain exclusions for damage to the insured's products, professional services, product recall, and a variety of other 'commercial risks' exclusions that may apply in the context of product recall and liability claims. These business risk exclusions supplement the CGL policy's insuring agreement and defined terms as follows:

'Your product' exclusion: CGL policies typically exclude coverage for 'property damage' to 'your product' 'arising out of it or any part of it'.[202] Your product' is generally defined to include '[a]ny goods or products, other than real property, manufactured, sold, handled distributed or disposed of' by the insured, others trading in its name or an acquired business.[203] This also includes "materials, parts or equipment furnished in connection with goods or products".[204] Thus, where the claim is confined to damages for the repair or replacement of a defective product that the insured provided to the claimant, the exclusion will preclude coverage.[205]

On the other hand (and as detailed herein), where the insured's product is incorporated into a larger product and causes damage to the larger product that cannot be remedied by the repair or replacement of the insured's component product, the exclusion has been found to be inapplicable to the damage caused to the larger product.[206]

'Your work' exclusion: The 'your work' exclusion typically precludes coverage for "'property damage' to 'your work' arising out of it or any part of it and included in the 'products-completed operations hazard'".[207] Most relevant to product liability and recall claims, CGL policies typically define the "products-completed operations hazard" to include all bodily injury or property damage "occurring away from premises you own or rent and arising out of" the insured's product or work, except "products that are still in [the insured's] physical possession".[208] Thus, any damage to the insured's own work – including damages arising from either negligent design or manufacture – would be precluded from coverage.[209]

Impaired property exclusion: The impaired property exclusion precludes coverage for 'property damage' to 'impaired property' "arising out of a defect, deficiency, inadequacy

202 ISO form CG 00 01 12 04 (2003), Section I(2)(k).
203 ISO form CG 00 01 12 04 (2003), Section V(21).
204 *Ibid.*
205 *Hartford Acc & Indem Co v AP Reale & Sons, Inc*, 228 AD 2d 935 (3d dept 1996) (repair or replacement of non-performing sewage treatment facility excluded); *Lowville Producer's Dairy Cooperative, Inc v American Motorists Insurance Co*, 198 AD 2d 851 (4th dept 1993) (replacement and disposal costs of contaminated milk found excluded].
206 *Maryland Cas Co v W R Grace & Co*, above (damage for depreciation in market value of buildings due to presence of asbestos not excluded); *Apache Foam Products v Continental Ins.*, 139 AD 2d 933 (4th dept 1988) (damage to vapour barriers and roof membranes from gases escaping from urethane foam insulation not excluded); *Sturges Mfg Co v Utica Mut Ins Co*, above (where defective safety straps incorporated into ski bindings reduced the value of the bindings beyond the cost of the strap, replacements exclusion did not apply to such damage).
207 ISO form CG 00 01 12 04 (2003), Section I(2)(l).
208 ISO form CG 00 01 12 04 (2003), Section V(16).
209 *Basil Development Corp v Gen Acc Ins Co*, 229 AD 2d 640 (3d dept 1996), *aff'd* 89 NY 2d 1057 (1997); *Advanced Refrigeration & Appliance Co, Inc v Ins Co of No America*, 42 AD 2d 484 (3d dept 1973).

or dangerous condition in 'your product' or 'your work'".[210] 'Impaired property' is defined as 'tangible property, other than 'your product' or 'your work', that cannot be used or is less useful because it incorporates 'your product' or 'your work' that is known or thought to be defective, deficient, inadequate or dangerous.[211] In addition, such property will only constitute 'impaired property' if it can be restored to use by "the repair, replacement, adjustment or removal of 'your product' or 'your work'...".[212]

Product recall exclusion: CGL policies also preclude any coverage for the costs associated with the recall of a product. This product recall exclusion typically applies to "damages claimed for any loss, cost or expense incurred by you or others for the loss of use, withdrawal, recall, inspection, repair, replacement, adjustment, removal or disposal" of the insured's product, work or impaired property "if such products, work or property are withdrawn from the market or from use because of any known or suspected defect or deficiency therein".[213] It should be noted, however, that where the insured's defective product has been incorporated as a component of a product being recalled due to the work of a subsequent manufacturer (ie, not by the insured), the costs of the third party recall awarded as damages against the insured may not be barred by the product recall exclusion.[214]

(f) Product incorporation cases

Product incorporation cases have become an increasingly common source of disputes between manufacturers and general liability insurers. The New York courts have repeatedly held that the mere failure of a product to perform as warranted would not constitute an occurrence, nor would any claim which is based solely upon injury or damage to the insured's own product.[215] However, when a defective product has been integrated into a larger product, causing damage and diminishing the value of that product beyond the cost of repairing or replacing the defective component, the courts have generally found the 'property damage' and 'occurrence' requirements to be satisfied.[216]

Nevertheless, it should be stressed that the mere inclusion of a defective product into another product does not constitute 'property damage' under a CGL policy if there is no resulting harm to the other parts or surrounding product into which it has been incorporated. Moreover, it is well established that even where damage to the surrounding product may trigger third party 'property damage' coverage, there

---

210 ISO form CG 00 01 12 04 (2003), Section I(2)(n).

211 ISO form CG 00 01 12 04 (2003), Section V(8).

212 *Ibid.*

213 *Ibid.*

214 *Thomas J Lipton, Inc v Liberty Mut Ins Co*, 314 NE 2d 37, 38 (NY 1974).

215 *George A Fuller Co*, 200 AD 2d 255 (1st dept 1994) (faulty construction of a building does not constitute an 'occurrence'); *JZG Resources, Inc v King*, 987 F 2d 98 (2d Cir 1993) (faulty construction of roadways); *Jacobson Shipyard, Inc v Aetna Cas & Sur. Co*, 961 F 2d 387 (2d Cir 1992) (faulty design and manufacture of steering system for tug boat).

216 *Thomas J Lipton, Inc v Liberty Mut. Ins. Co*, above; *Chubb Ins Co*, 1999 WL 760206 (SDNY 1999) (preservative added to orange juice); *Aetna Cas & Sur Co*, 704 F 2d 80 (2d Cir 1983) (electric motors installed as internal components in radiators); *Marine Midland Ser v Samuel Kosoff, et al*, 60 AD 2d 767 (4th dept 1977) (defective roof over computer centre caused damage to building and contents); *Sturges Mfg Co v Utica Mutual Co*, 37 NY 2d 69 (1975) (defective ski straps incorporated into bindings constituted 'occurrence').

still would be no coverage for the damage to or replacement of the insured's own component product.

4.5 Product recall insurance

In response to tightening of federal regulation and the lengthening of product supply and distribution chains, there has been an increased demand in the United States for specific product recall and contamination coverage. As noted above, such coverage is now widely available from both domestic and foreign insurers. Policies are often tailored to the specific individual needs of the insured, and are intended to apply in the event a product contamination or recall. As detailed herein, product contamination and recall policies may provide first and third party coverage for various recall and rehabilitation expenses, and often provide for public relations consultants and crisis management services.

There is no established ISO form for products recall coverage. Coverage is often provided for an 'insured event', which will be specifically defined in the product recall or contamination policy. For example, an insured event may be defined to simply include the accidental contamination of covered products.[217] Coverage may also be conditioned upon whether the costs related to the withdrawal, disposal or purposeful destruction of an insured product were incurred because the contamination has or would result in bodily injury or property damage.

It should be noted that although bodily injury or property damage may be the trigger for an insured event, most recall policies are intended to provide coverage solely for costs and expenses related to the actual recall, and not for any resulting bodily injury or property damage. Again, the extent of such coverage will depend on the specific coverage purchased by the insured.

(a) Types of cover available

Accidental contamination: Product recall policies often provide coverage for accidental or unintentional contamination, impairment from use of the product, or mislabelling of an insured product during the manufacture, blending, packaging, labelling or production of the product that either results in or poses an imminent threat of bodily injury or property damage.[218] There are two recent cases which highlight certain issues that may arise under such coverage:

- In *Caudill Seed & Wharehouse Co v Houston Cas Co*, the court upheld an insurer's denial under an accidental contamination food recall policy where there was no actual contamination "during the manufacturing process" (as required by the policy).[219]
- In *Little Lady Foods Inc v Houston Cas Co*, the court upheld an insurer's denial where the insured delayed shipment of products based on possible listeria contamination where the product was later tested and found to be not contaminated.[220]

---

217 For example, *National Union Fire Ins Co v The Stroh Companies, Inc* 265 F 3d 97, 104 (2001).
218 For example, *Little Lady Foods Inc v Houston Cas Co*, 2011 WL 4473517 (ND Ill, September 22 2011).
219 2011 WL 6370366 (WD Ky, December 20 2011).

Product tampering and extortion: Product tampering policies cover actual or threatened, intentional or malicious, alteration or contamination of the insured's product such that it is rendered dangerous or unfit for use or consumption.[221] Coverage may extend to extortion of money from an insured by threatening to commit malicious product tampering on an insured product.

Coverage for 'malicious product tampering' or 'product extortion' will depend upon how those terms are defined in the particular product recall policy, and the specific timing and cause of the contaminating event. For example, in *General Mills Inc v Gold Medal Ins Co*, the Minnesota Court of Appeals, applying New York law, held that where a claim for malicious product tampering requires a subjective intent to injure the policyholder where the contamination policy at issue required "intentional, malicious and wrongful" tampering.[222]

Intentionally impaired ingredients: Policies may cover the impairment of an insured product which occurs due to an ingredient supplied to the insured where such contamination or impairment was intentional and wrongful, but not malicious.

Product recall: These policies cover any recall of the insured's product arising out of bodily injury or property damage or the threat thereof that is ordered by a state, federal or local governmental agency or judicial body. This may include a request to return to the maker a batch, or an entire production run of a product after the discovery of safety issues that present a significant risk to consumers, either because a product may be defective or violates a mandatory standard.

Product refusal: This coverage provides insurance for products that have been delivered to a customer and are subsequently refused due to the recall of a competitor's product similar to the insured's products. Covered losses, however, typically are limited to actual recall and distribution costs.

(b) Costs covered under recall policies

Products recall costs and expenses: Policies may cover all costs necessary to effectuate the recall of the insured's product, including costs to inspect, replace, withdraw, or destroy the insured's product in connection with the recall. Coverage may also be provided for certain third party recall, including costs to reimburse and/or indemnify liability to downstream parties such as wholesalers, distributors or retailers.

Consultant and adviser costs: As noted above, many product recall and contamination policies include some element of crisis management or response. Consultant costs are the fees and expenses related to retaining an approved independent security expert to advise and assist in the product recall.

---

220 2011 WL 4473517 (ND Ill, September 22 2011).
221 For example, *General Mills, Inc v Gold Medal Ins Co*, 622 NW 2d 147, 15 (Minn Ct of App 2001).
222 *Ibid*, at 155.

Rehabilitation expense: Policies may cover expenses incurred to rehabilitate the insured's reputation or re-establish the insured's product. For example, product restoration or rehabilitation costs may include advertising, promotional or repackaging expenses. The 're-establishment' of the insured's product may be based upon its projected level of sales or market share anticipated prior to the insured event.

Business interruption costs: Product recall policies often contain some type of coverage for business interruption which may include gross lost profit and extra expense as a result of an insured event. Such coverage typically is limited to the lost profits suffered as a result of the product recall, and subject to a time-limit after the recall occurs. Notably, however, recall policies may also specifically exclude coverage for any decrease in product sales realised subsequent to the announcement of the insured event.

(c) ***Recall/contamination policy exclusions***

As product recall and contamination policies are tailored to meet the needs of specific insureds, policy exclusions may vary depending on the coverage provided. Policies contain exclusions for:

- property damage or bodily injury;
- changes in population, customer tastes, economic conditions, or seasonal sales variations;
- any intentional act or omission;
- failure to adhere to any governmental agency, industry or similarly recognised body's regulation or requirements for the design and manufacture of the insured's product; or
- breach of warranty or the failure of an insured product to accomplish its intended purpose.

These policies are often heavily manuscripted. Accordingly, the specific terms and application of these policy exclusions will depend upon the terms negotiated between the insured and its insurer.

4.6 Commercial property and business interruption insurance

'All risks' policies: First party property coverage typically comes in two forms: 'named-peril' policies and 'all risks' policies. Named-peril policies, which are often manuscript, generally provide coverage for "direct physical loss of or damage to covered property" at a specific premises resulting from any 'Covered Cause of Loss'.[223] For claims under a named-peril policy, the insured bears the burden of showing that a specifically enumerated peril caused its loss. In contrast, 'all risks' policies provide coverage for all risks of "direct physical loss of or damage to the property insured from any external cause" unless specifically excluded by subsequent terms in the policy.[224]

223 ISO Form CP 00 10 04 02 (2001), Section A.

224 For example, *Album Realty Corp v American Home Assur* Co, 80 NY 2d 1008, 1009 (1992), *HoneyBaked Foods, Inc v Affiliated FM Insc Co*, 757 F Supp 2d 738, 742 (ND Ohio 2010).

Commercial property policies may contain a 'contamination exclusion', which precludes coverage for contamination unless such damage results from other physical damage. The courts have broadly interpreted the exclusion to include contamination from bacteria (eg, listeria)[225] and exposure to chemicals.[226]

Contamination exclusions, however, may also contain an exception that reinstates coverage for contamination if caused by a covered cause of loss.[227] One New York federal court has held that the only reasonable reading of this carve out "is that contamination losses resulting from perils otherwise covered by the policy are likewise covered, and contamination losses resulting from perils expressly excluded by the policy are likewise excluded".[228] Thus, contamination of an insured's product will be excluded from coverage unless the contamination directly resulted from 'other physical damage' covered under the policy.

Commercial property insurers may add contaminated products endorsements providing specific coverage for loss caused by "accidental contamination of covered products" occuring while "manufacturing, producing, processing, preparing, packaging or labelling the covered product ...".[229] Further, loss may include costs resulting from accidental contamination.

Finally, it should be noted that the insured may have the sole discretion under a commercial property policy to determine the fitness of a product for use. Nevertheless, even where the policy grants such power, the insured should proceed with caution before the disposal of any of its defective products. At least one New York court was highly critical of an insured's claiming for coverage where defective products were destroyed without approval by the insurer.

Business interruption: Business income (BI) policies (also known as 'business interruption' policies) compensate the insured for income lost during the necessary suspension of business operations while restoring the physical damage to the insured's property. The current standard form, which was introduced in the late 1980s, is the ISO Business Income and (Extra Expense) Coverage Form.[230] Thus, to recover under a BI policy, the insured must prove:

- physical loss or damage to the insured's property;
- interruption of the business due to a covered peril,
- loss of income or profits; and
- the loss occurred during the restoration period.[231]

---

225 *HoneyBaked Foods, Inc v Affiliated FM Ins. Co*, 757 F Supp 2d at 738 (although the court certified the case to the Ohio Supreme Court to determine whether Ohio law would adopt a reasonable expectations doctrine, the case was ultimately settled); *Landshire Fast Foods of Milwaukee v Employers Mut Cas Co*, 676 NW 2d 528 (2004) (exclusion applicable to destruction of prepared foods and sanitation of equipment after discovery of listeria).

226 See *Am Produce & Vegetable v Phoenix Assur. Co of New York*, 408 SW 2d 954 (Tex. Civ App 1966) (exclusion applicable to chemical exposure).

227 See *Allianz Ins Co*, 96 F Supp 2d 253 (SDNY 1999) (contamination exclusion inapplicable to cookies with off flavour and odour as result of third party cleaning of warehouse floors).

228 *Allianz Ins Co v RJR Nabisco Holdings Corp*, 96 F Supp 2d 253, 255 (SDNY 2000).

229 ISO Form CP 03 21 06 95 (1995), Section 42.

230 ISO Form CP 00 30 04 02 (2001).

231 *The Business Interruption Book*, Torpey Lentz & Barret (2004) at 12–13.

Generally, BI policies provide coverage for lost business income, including:

- net income that would have been earned or incurred; and
- continuing normal operating expenses incurred, including payroll.

For manufacturing risks, 'net income' includes the net sales value of production. BI policies may also provide coverage for 'extra expenses', which include certain necessary expenses that the insured incurs during restoration. Additionally, BI policies may provide coverage for a 'dependant property' which has sustained a direct physical loss or damage from a covered cause of loss, as well as coverage against lost business income and extra expenses where the insured's covered property is inaccessible.

In the product liability context, BI insurance may apply to supply chain disruptions which suspend an insured's operations and are caused by product liability or recall issues. Common coverage issues include whether:

- there is direct physical loss or damage to the insured's property;
- actual loss proximately caused the property damage (particularly where there are several competing factors of causation); and
- there are exclusions which may limit coverage.

Contingent business interruption: Contingent business interruption (CBI) insurance provides coverage for the insured's lost income resulting from an interruption of business at the property of a supplier or customer. To trigger CBI coverage there must be:

- physical damage to the dependent property by a covered cause of loss
- interruption or suspension to the insured's business operations;
- the proximate cause of the interruption must be physical damage; and
- actual loss during the restoration period which is caused by the interruption of business.

CBI coverage may apply in the contaminated product context where a supply chain disruption causes an interruption in the insured's ability to produce or manufacture a product.

A fundamental requirement for coverage is that the 'dependent property' is damaged. There are four categories of dependent property (which are often defined), all of which are contingent upon physical damage directly affecting the insured's business:

- 'contributing locations' where the supplier is unable to provide goods or services to the insured because of physical damage;[232]
- 'recipient locations' where the insured's customers cannot receive or use the insured's goods or services because of physical destruction or damage to the customer's real or personal property;[233]

232 *CII Carbon, LLC v National Union Fire Insurance Company of Louisiana, Inc*, 918 So 2d 1060 (La Ct App 2005).

233 *Zurich Am Ins Co v ABM Indus Inc*, 397 F 3d 158 (2d Cir 2005).

- 'manufacturing locations' where physical damage occurs to the property where products are manufactured for delivery to the insured's customers under a contract of sale; and
- 'magnet locations' where the property of a nearby business that attracts customers to the insured's business is physically damaged or destroyed.

Recent issues before the US courts have centred on the meaning of a 'supplier' within the terms of an all risks/BI policy and whether physical damage to the supplier's property proximately caused the insured's loss.[234] In the product liability context, coverage depends on whether damage to the supplier's property caused the interruption of the insured's business.

234 For example, *Pentair v American Guar & Liab Ins Co*, 400 F 3d 613 (8th Cir 2005); *Midland Co v Phoenix Assurance Co of NY*, 936 F Supp 534 (SD Ill 1996).

About the authors

Alex YG An
Senior associate, MWE China Law Offices
aan@mwechinalaw.com

Alex YG An is a senior associate of MWE China Law Offices, based in Beijing. He has extensive experience in the areas of corporate, compliance, foreign direct investment, M&A, international trade, antitrust and dispute resolution. He advises both foreign and Chinese clients on many aspects of commercial transactions. Mr An has worked with US, EU, Japanese and Korean companies on a wide range of operations in China. Industries in which he has provided advice include the retail, chemicals, food and beverage, electronics, logistics, pharmaceutical and medical device sectors. Mr An was previously in-house counsel for a large Chinese insurance company.

Cristina Ayo Ferrándiz
Lawyer, Uría Menéndez
cristina.ayo@uria.com

Cristina Ayo Ferrándiz is a member of the litigation practice area at Uria Menéndez's Barcelona office. She joined the firm in September 2000. Ms Ayo focuses her practice on advising on contentious and pre-contentious civil and commercial issues. She specialises in judicial proceedings before the Spanish courts and tribunals, and national and international arbitration proceedings relating to contractual liability, non-contractual liability and product liability – where both class and collective actions have been filed – as well as contractual, corporate, lease agreements, banking, financial and private party disputes.

Luis D Barry
Partner, Perez Alati, Grondona, Benites, Arntsen & Martínez de Hoz
ldb@pagbam.com.ar

Luis D Barry was born in La Plata, Buenos Aires in 1971. He graduated from the University of Buenos Aires Law School in 1994 and completed a masters in business law at San Andrés University in 2001.

Between December 2005 and February 2006, Mr Barry was part of the antitrust team in the Brussels office of Cuatrecasas. He headed the legal department at Unilever (Argentina) until 1997, when he joined Perez Alati, Grondona, Benites, Arntsen & Martínez de Hoz. He was made partner in 2007.

Mr Barry lectures on antitrust and consumer law at the University of Buenos Aires Law School, the Universidad Católica Argentina and the Foro de Estudios sobre Administración de Justicia. Mr Barry is a member of the Buenos Aires Bar Association.

Daniel W Bir
Special counsel, Sedgwick LLP
daniel.bir@sedgwicklaw.com

Daniel Bir's practice focuses primarily on the defence of equipment manufacturers in complex, multi-party disputes with an emphasis on product liability actions, general liability actions and catastrophic injury claims, involving heavy machinery and electrical and mechanical instruments. He also has extensive experience in the fields of commercial, business and consumer protection litigation.

As a special counsel, Mr Bir litigates matters throughout the United States and has taken hundreds of depositions from both lay and expert witnesses, has successfully argued discovery and dispositive motions, and has resolved several cases through mediations and settlement conferences. He is also an active trial lawyer who has successfully defended the firm's clients in numerous jury trials.

Louis P Brien
Partner, Lapointe Rosenstein Marchand Melançon LLP
louis.brien@lrmm.com

Louis P Brien was called to the Quebec Bar in 1989 and practices insurance law with a particular focus on civil and professional liability, product liability, as well as directors' and officers' liability. He specialises in construction matters, for which he has been called upon to represent various parties. His interests also encompass claims arising from personal injuries and municipal liability matters. Mr Brien's insurance litigation practice also includes subrogation recoveries and advising clients on coverage issues. He has extensive experience before the courts, having argued before all major courts with jurisdiction over the province of Quebec. Mr Brien is a frequent lecturer at the Quebec Bar School and an active member of a number of professional groups and committees, including the Quebec Bar's Disciplinary Committee. He is an executive member of the insurance law and civil litigation section of the Canadian Bar Association.

Philippa Briggs
Lawyer, Minter Ellison
philippa.briggs@minterellison.com

Philippa Briggs is a senior insurance lawyer in Minter Ellison's Sydney insurance and corporate disputes team. She specialises in public and product liability, professional indemnity, directors and officers, medical malpractice, general liability and commercial litigation. In addition to acting for insureds and insurers, Ms Briggs has also advised a number of corporate and commercial clients and financial institutions on a variety of matters. She has experience in managing a broad spectrum of disputes including large-scale, complex litigation across all New South Wales court jurisdictions, including the New South Wales Court of Appeal and the Supreme Court of New South Wales. Before joining Minter Ellison, Ms Briggs worked for several years in various areas of litigation, including privacy and defamation litigation.

Christopher J Celentano
Attorney and insurance claims professional
christophercelentano@hotmail.com

Christopher J Celentano has extensive experience acting on behalf of insurers in the analysis, negotiation and litigation of complex coverage disputes arising out of mass tort/product liability lawsuits, securities lawsuits, bankruptcy proceedings, professional negligence claims, construction defect claims, employment practices litigation and losses resulting from fraud and embezzlement. Mr Celentano also provides policy wording and risk assessment advice to insurers. He was previously special counsel in Sedgwick LLP's insurance practice group, and is currently an insurance claims professional at an international insurer.

Caoimhe Clarkin
Associate, A&L Goodbody
cclarkin@algoodbody.com

Caoimhe Clarkin is an associate in A&L Goodbody's litigation and dispute resolution department. She advises domestic and international clients on a wide range of commercial disputes, including product liability, EU and competition law, financial securities litigation and constitutional litigation. Ms Clarkin has experience in dealing with complex, high-profile cases in the Irish Commercial Court and specialises in advising financial institutions and professional service firms in disputes, professional indemnity matters and in regulatory matters. She also has experience in domestic and international corporate criminal/ regulatory investigations, having acted for a number of Irish and international clients in investigations by various regulatory bodies.

David JD Dai
Partner, MWE China Law Offices
ddai@mwechinalaw.com

David JD Dai is a partner and co-head of the corporate advisory group of MWE China Law Offices, based in Shanghai. With over 15 years' post-qualification experience, he has assisted hundreds of European and US clients (including many Fortune 500 companies) in their direct investments and operations in China across a wide range of sectors, including manufacturing, energy and chemical, food and beverages, commercial retails, life science and health care. Mr Dai takes a special interest in complicated compliance matters in connection with the business activities of multinationals in China. He helps multinational companies with a variety of compliance matters related to product liability, foreign exchange, state-owned assets, environmental protection and labour by proposing, negotiating and achieving solutions. He frequently writes about Chinese law and practice in the areas of M&A, corporate and compliance for numerous publications, including *China Law & Practice*, *Law360*, *EPMag.com* and *Practical China Tax and Finance Strategies*.

Charles De Jager
Counsel, Salans LLP
cdejager@salans.com

Charles De Jager assists private companies and governmental entities in regulatory and policy matters that are resolved through a combination of legal analysis and political argumentation. He has extensive experience in product safety, government affairs and international trade. In particular, Mr De Jager has advised and represented multinational manufacturers of toys, childcare articles, sports equipment, fashion items, cosmetics, furniture and motor vehicles in product safety and recall issues in various European countries and before the European Commission under the EU RAPEX system. He has also helped clients to participate actively in legislative review efforts in the field, especially with respect to EU toy safety and risk assessment guidelines. Mr De Jager is a frequent speaker and writer on these topics.

Rosângela Delgado Barreto
Partner, Veirano Advogados
rosangela.delgado@veirano.com.br

Rosângela Delgado Barreto focuses her practice in the area of complex litigation, which includes product liability, commercial, contractual, general civil and regulatory litigation. She has significant expertise in consumer products such as tobacco, automotive, cargo handling machinery, magazine publishers, marine boats and engines and hotel industries and counsels several top-tier Brazilian and international corporations.

Ms Delgado Barreto is a member of the American Chamber of Commerce, the Defence Research Institute, the International Bar Association's Consumer Litigation Committee and the World Services Group.

Steven D Di Saia
Partner, Sedgwick LLP
steven.disaia@sedgwicklaw.com

Since joining Sedgwick in 1991, Steven D Di Saia has built a litigation practice around the defence of general liability actions, mass and catastrophic injury claims and product liability actions involving medical devices, pharmaceuticals, appliances, electrical and mechanical instruments, and heavy machinery.

Mr Di Saia has served extensively as litigation and coordinating counsel in mass and complex tort litigation matters, addressing claims of environmental liability, toxic exposure and injury, unfair business practices and fraud, as well as claims based in tort and statutory compliance against health-care institutions and practitioners.

Donald Dinnie
Director, Norton Rose South Africa
donald.dinnie@deneysreitz.co.za

Donald Dinnie is a director at Norton Rose South Africa, where he heads up the national litigation and dispute resolution practice. He practises in the areas of insurance, litigation and dispute resolution, medical law and medical malpractice, personal injury litigation, professional indemnity law, and product liability and product recall law and litigation.

Mr Dinnie regularly advises major short-term insurers in South Africa and most of the major private hospital networks. He also advises Lloyd's and its syndicates as well as insurers in the United State. Mr Dinnie has published articles on a number of topics, including insurance law and medical malpractice law. He has also presented numerous lectures and discussions, including those on specific insurance and medical law topics.

Florian Endrös
Founder, Endrös-Baum Associés
florian.endros@eba-avocats.com

Registered at the Munich Bar and the Paris Bar, Dr Florian Endrös practised at an international commercial law firm for several years before helping to found a law firm specialising in industrial risk. After nearly 16 years' experience in this field, he and his team of lawyers created 5 years ago Endrös-Baum Associés. As an associate professor at the University of Cergy-Pontoise (Paris), Dr Endrös also participated for several years in a European programme to provide training in German law to French lawyers. He has in-depth experience of complex international proceedings, especially in the fields of industrial risk, plant construction, product liability and product safety, as well as general contract and commercial law. With long-standing experience in French summary expert proceedings, Dr Endrös is also the author of a number of books, essays and other publications on this subject.

Sabine Faust
Associate, RWP Rechtsanwälte GbR, Dusseldorf
s.faust@rwp.de

Sabine Faust is an associate at RWP Rechtsanwälte GbR Dusseldorf and a member of the firm's M&A, corporate and commercial law team. During her career, she has advised national and international clients on questions of product liability. Ms Faust has gained particular experience in the textile industry and the requirements of product safety as set out in European regulations. She also advises companies and directors from other sectors on questions of general corporate law, commercial law and competition law.

Mathew R Groseclose
Associate, Sedgwick LLP
mathew.groseclose@sedgwicklaw.com

Mathew Groseclose is an associate in the product liability and specialty tort practice group in Sedgwick's Los Angeles office. He has briefed and argued law and motion matters on a variety of issues, including business tort litigation, in the area of unfair competition and unfair trade practices, and construction, real estate and general liability cases.

Michaela Herron
Solicitor, A&L Goodbody
mherron@algoodbody.com

Michaela Herron is a solicitor within the healthcare and life sciences unit of the litigation and dispute resolution group at A&L Goodbody. She advises on a broad range of issues affecting predominantly healthcare and hospital clients and specialises in the area of clinical negligence. Ms Herron also advises on a wide range of legal, ethical and regulatory issues for healthcare clients, including confidentiality, consent, data protection law, freedom of information law, risk management, product liability and various other legal and ethical issues in medical practice.

Tomasz Jaworski
Counsel, Salans Warsaw
tjaworski@salans.com

Tomasz Jaworski is a member of both the litigation and the life sciences teams at Salans Warsaw. He specialises in legal advice for court and administrative proceedings, particularly with regard to regulated industry sectors. Mr Jaworski's professional experience includes advice to clients in the pharmaceutical and fast-moving consumer goods sector in disputes with consumers, competitors and regulatory bodies, advice in handling critical situations related to quality of products and advice in the process of introducing class actions into Polish law. He co-authored a commentary to the Act on Pursuing Claims in Group Proceedings (CH Beck, 2010) and is the author of numerous press publications on new Polish class action law.

Mark Kendall
Partner, Sedgwick, Detert, Moran & Arnold LLP
mark.kendall@sedgwicklaw.com

Mark Kendall is an equity partner of the international law firm Sedgwick, Detert, Moran & Arnold LLP. He has been practising in the field of product recall and liability for over 15 years, and acts for both insurer and corporate clients. He is experienced in advising on recalls in the automotive, food, consumer goods and pharmaceutical sectors. He also regularly advises insurers on their wordings (both from a coverage perspective and on the product development side). Mr Kendall routinely advises in relation to multi-jurisdictional issues arising from defective products and lectures widely on the subject.

Liam Kennedy
Partner and head of dispute resolution, A&L Goodbody
lkennedy@algoodbody.com

Liam Kennedy is the head of A&L Goodbody's dispute resolution department. Mr Kennedy specialises in international and domestic commercial disputes including product liability, M&A, securities/auditors' litigation (including international class actions), EU and competition law and constitutional litigation. He is experienced at dealing with regulators including the Financial Regulator, commissions of enquiry and the Securities Exchange Commission. Recent cases include public procurement litigation and Commercial Court litigation in major development disputes. Mr Kennedy also regularly advises auditors and other professionals on liability and regulatory issues. He is vice chairman of the International Bar Association's Litigation Committee.

Kazuhiro Kobayashi
Partner, Oh-Ebashi LPC & Partners
k-kobayashi@ohebashi.com

Kazuhiro Kobayashi has wide-ranging expertise in corporate, M&A, compliance, intellectual property, antitrust, finance, international transactions, product liability and dispute resolution. As defence attorney for pharmaceutical companies, he has handled many cases of alleged contaminated medicines. Mr Kobayashi also advises on agreements for sharing product liability in connection with distributorship and original equipment manufacturer licences.

Yugo Komori
Associate, Oh-Ebashi LPC & Partners
komori@ohebashi.com

Yugo Komori's practice focuses on corporate, M&A, reorganisation, compliance, product liability and dispute resolution, including complex business litigation. He has experience with a variety of disputes, including commercial litigation, product liability litigation and tax litigation. As attorney for pharmaceutical companies, Mr Komori has particular experience of product liability and recall issues.

David Kyffin
Foreign service officer, Canadian Department of Foreign Affairs and International Trade
david.kyf@gmail.com

David Kyffin was called to the Quebec Bar in Spring 2011. He first practised in the area of insurance law, focusing on civil liability litigation and pleading before various Quebec courts. In Autumn 2011, he moved to the Canadian Department of Foreign Affairs and International Trade, where he works as a foreign service officer and also practises law in the area of international economic sanctions.

Andreas Lachmann
Partner, RWP Rechtsanwälte GbR, Dusseldorf
a.lachmann@rwp.de

Dr Andreas Lachmann is a partner at RWP Rechtsanwälte GbR Dusseldorf and heads the firm's M&A, corporate and commercial law department. He has counselled a high number of national and international companies on questions of product liability. Dr Lachmann advises companies and directors from all sectors and has in-depth experience of the textile and the construction industry. He also advises on general corporate law, insolvency law and national as well as international transactions. In particular, Dr Lachmann has taken a leading role in several international transactions. Additionally, he is the author of several practice handbooks.

Emma Lambert
Associate, Irving Mitchell Kalichman
elambert@imk.ca

Emma Lambert was called to the Quebec Bar in 2011 and has a background in both the common law and civil law legal systems of Canada. Ms Lambert practised in the area of commercial and corporate law at Lapointe Rosenstein Marchand Melançon LLP before leaving to commence a clerkship working for the Honourable Justice Richard Boivin with the Federal Court of Canada in August 2011. In September 2012, Ms Lambert joined the Montreal firm of Irving Mitchell Kalichman, where she currently practises civil and commercial litigation as well as administrative law.

Jason McNerlin
Special counsel, Sedgwick, Detert, Moran & Arnold LLP
jason.mcnerlin@sedgwicklaw.com

Jason McNerlin's practice is focused on product recall, product liability and all types of product insurance. He advises manufacturers and insurers on regulations, compliance and crisis management, and acts on their behalf in commercial disputes relating to products. He has drafted numerous insurance policies for products insurers.

Pamela Madafiglio
Partner, Minter Ellison
pamela.madafiglio@minterellison.com

Pamela Madafiglio is one of Minter Ellison's most experienced insurance lawyers and heads the Sydney insurance and corporate disputes team. She deals with all forms of insurance, including professional indemnity, directors and officers, trustees liability and financial institutions, and has vast experience in product development including policy wordings in both retail and wholesale lines, and corporate risk. Ms Madafiglio has been involved in numerous inquiries and royal commissions, including the high-profile James Hardie matter and the Queensland Floods Commission of Inquiry. Consistently recognised in leading legal directories, Ms Madafiglio is described as "sensational" and "a first-class lawyer with enormous intellectual capacity". She is the principal author of the firm's highly regarded *Insurance Contracts Handbook*, and maintains a strong involvement with both the insurance industry and administrative law associations, having held senior positions on peak industry bodies.

Paul A Melançon
Partner, Lapointe Rosenstein Marchand Melançon LLP
paul.melancon@lrmm.com

Paul A Melançon was called to the Quebec Bar in 1972 and now specialises in insurance law and all issues pertaining to property and casualty insurance policies (property insurance and liability insurance including professional liability, directors and officers' liability and brokers' liability), whether primary, excess or complementary. His practice extends to civil liability, product liability, professional liability and personal injury liability, among others. Mr Melançon has extensive experience before all major courts with jurisdiction over the province of Quebec, including the Supreme Court of Canada. As a committed and involved member of the legal community, Mr Melançon has sat on a number of committees. He has authored and edited several articles and books pertaining to insurance law and has given lectures on the topic. He is recognised by the *Canadian Legal Lexpert Directory*, 2011 and 2012 editions, as one of the most recommended insurance lawyers.

Lívia Miné
Associate, Veirano Advogados
livia.mine@veirano.com.br

Lívia Miné works in civil law, focusing especially on torts and product liability. She has participated in several due diligences in the field of environmental law, involving the sale and purchase of companies and assets. Ms Miné has experience in public hearings for environmental licence proceedings involving relevant undertakings, and also in negotiations of consent decrees and defences of companies before federal, state and municipal bodies.

In addition, she has participated in labour due diligences, issued legal opinions and helped to develop methods to prevent disputes between workers and companies in labour litigation and in negotiations of collective bargaining agreements with unions.

Dev Ashish Mishra
Partner, Fox Mandal & Co
dev.mishra@foxmandal.com

Dev Ashish Mishra is a partner at Fox Mandal & Co and operates out of the firm's Delhi office. He joined the bar in 1999 and is enrolled with the Bar Council of Delhi; he is also qualified to practise as a solicitor in England and Wales. Mr Mishra's areas of practice include corporate advisory M&A, commercial law and dispute resolution.

Mr Mishra has considerable experience in advising and representing international and domestic clients on mergers, acquisitions and joint ventures in India. He also regularly advises foreign clients on India's foreign direct investment policy, foreign exchange laws and regulations thereunder, as well as on Reserve Bank of India regulations and guidelines. Mr Mishra started his career as a litigation lawyer and continues to represent his clients before the Supreme Court of India, and various high courts and tribunals across the country. He also represents his clients in domestic and international arbitrations.

Siddharth Misra
Senior associate, Fox Mandal & Co
siddharth.misra@foxmandal.com

Siddharth Misra is a senior associate at Fox Mandal & Co with over five years' experience in the firm's corporate practice. He handles transactions relating to acquisitions and joint ventures, and is also involved in various real estate transactions. Mr Misra's experience is primarily in acquisitions, foreign direct investment, commercial contracts, real estate, insurance and infrastructure. He has advised various domestic and overseas clients. Mr Misra has extensive knowledge of matters involving corporate law, insurance law, contractual work, real estate law and regulatory approvals, and has successfully negotiated and drafted documents for a large number of transactions.

Lucy Neligan
Solicitor, A&L Goodbody
lneligan@algoodbody.com

Lucy Neligan is a solicitor with A&L Goodbody, practising within the litigation and dispute resolution group. She advises on general commercial litigation matters, advising clients in diverse sectors such as pharmaceuticals, banking, pensions and retail. Ms Neligan advises on a broad range of issues including product liability, professional negligence and contractual disputes.

Christopher C Novak
Partner, Sedgwick LLP
christopher.novak@sedgwicklaw.com

Christopher C Novak is a partner in Sedgwick LLP's insurance practice group. His practice primarily focuses on complex insurance coverage disputes involving commercial property and casualty insurance, product liability and recall, pollution and environmental exposures, professional indemnity and financial institution bonds. Mr Novak has represented domestic and international insurance and reinsurance clients in the litigation and arbitration of property and casualty, products, toxic tort, environmental, construction defect, professional liability and bad-faith claims. In addition, he frequently provides policy wording advice to US, Bermuda and UK insurance clients. Mr Novak is a frequent presenter and author of numerous articles on a broad range of insurance-related topics.

Luis Ignacio Porthé
Associate, Perez Alati, Grondona, Benites, Arntsen & Martínez de Hoz
lip@pagbam.com.ar

Luis Ignacio Porthé was born in San Nicolas in 1984. He graduated with honours from the University of Buenos Aires Law School in 2007.

Mr Porthé has expertise in M&A approvals and has acted for antitrust authorities in various jurisdictions in Latin America. He also advises on various antitrust matters with the Argentine Antitrust Authority and handles appeals on behalf of the civil and commercial courts of appeal.

Pieter van Regteren Altena
Partner, Van Doorne NV
regterenaltena@vandoorne.com

Pieter van Regteren Altena joined Van Doorne in September 1985 and became a partner in 1988. Within Van Doorne's litigation and insurance practice group, he is particularly active in the areas of product liability, professional liability, company liability, supervisory legislation for insurers and brokers and uninsured liabilities between companies. Mr van Regteren Altena has a particular interest in product liability (foodstuffs and medicine) and the professional liability of medical professionals (liability, causality and disciplinary law).

Besides his practice, Mr van Regteren Altena is a member of the supervisory board of the Amsterdam Bar Association (acting dean and education) and regularly lectures on insurance and liability law-related topics. Mr van Regteren Altena is highly ranked by a number of independent legal directories for his litigation and insurance practice and is considered "one of the leading liability lawyers in the market with extensive experience of domestic and international cases".

Kagenori Sako
Partner, Oh-Ebashi LPC & Partners
sako@ohebashi.com

Kagenori Sako has extensive experience in dispute resolution (including litigation and arbitration), general corporate, M&A, antitrust, intellectual property, corporate reorganisation and international transactions. When dealing with these cases, he has advised on product liability matters, including product recall and insurance. Mr Sako has also been involved in international M&A cases, in which he helped negotiate how to allocate product liabilities for the target company.

Lorijn van der Valk
Associate, Van Doorne NV
valk@vandoorne.com

Lorijn van der Valk started working as a lawyer with Van Doorne in 2006, when she joined the IP group. In 2008 she switched to the litigation and insurance practice group and has since specialised in the fields of liability law and insurance law, on which she advises and litigates for her clients. Ms van der Valk is a member of Van Doorne's food and beverage team – where she focuses on product liability and product recalls – and the commercial contracting team – where she focuses on drafting and reviewing commercial contracts and general terms and conditions.

Ms van der Valk studied both Dutch law and cultural anthropology at Utrecht University. While there and afterwards she gained a wealth of international experience by studying and working abroad in Mexico and Australia.